Reflections of Hope

I was ready to end my life because I couldn't take this pain of living without my son. I had no support, so I was ready to quit. Then I read your *Reflections of Hope book*. I couldn't put it down. I just started reading and making notes. This book is going to help so many people. **Dawn K.**

I felt like a sponge reading and taking something from each and every day. I have been stuck for so many years pushing away God and people around me... I lost all faith in God and became so angry with him. I'm trying to find God again. *Reflections of Hope* has given me "Food for thought" and I'll add "Food for heart." Laura's readings opened my eyes, made me cry, made me smile and even sometimes chuckle. This book is amazing and a much needed read for any newly bereaved parent as well as anyone who has had years of tears behind them. **Michele S.**

God has given Laura Diehl a gift to help other parents climb out of this incredibly dark pit. As I read these daily writings, they have helped me to get thru my grief. There were so many that really touched my heart and spoke to me, giving me something to hold on to when everything was so dark. **Carolyn Blackall**

Reflections of Hope has helped me in so many ways. It reaffirmed that it is okay to be where I am in my grief and that I do not have to make others happy or hide it. I may need to change traditions in ways that I feel honor my son, when others don't understand. I needed the reassurance that I have to take care of me, and it is okay to say no when something does not work for me. I need to pause and reflect on how I need to stay afloat and honor my son and my living children. Thank you, Laura, for this book. **Amie Boyd**

Every month in, *Reflections of Hope* just kept getting better and better! I've shed a lot of tears, but they have been tears of HOPE and tears of release...at just the right time. There are so many powerful points in the entries that I have shared with my husband, so this has been a huge blessing to him too. You make us see things in ways we've never seen before or even considered before. Sometimes all I can say after reading the entries is..."WOW!" **Melissa Slusher**

So many of the readings hit me to my core. It's like Laura was in my heart and head, speaking directly to me. I shed so many tears, because it felt like someone TOTALLY understood how I feel. Reflections of Hope was very healing, and I thank you. **Deborah K. G.**

I love the balance of grace and truth in *Reflections of Hope*. We have this pain, and we will always miss our child, but we can move forward in life and one day thrive again. Thank you for writing this book. **Yolanda Rory**

Reflections Of Hope

Daily Readings for Bereaved Parents

Laura Diehl

Reflections of Hope

Copyright © 2022 Laura Diehl

Published by Crown of Glory Publishing
PO Box 264
Janesville, WI 53547-0264

Scripture marked MSG is taken from The Message. Copyright © 1993, 1994, 1995, 1996, 2000, 2001, 2002, 2018. Used by permission of NavPress Publishing Group.

Scripture marked NLT is taken from the Holy Bible, New Living Translation, copyright © 1996, 2004, 2015 by Tyndale House Foundation. All rights reserved. Used by permission of Tyndale House Publishers, Carol Stream, Illinois 60188. All rights reserved.

Scripture marked CJB is taken from the Complete Jewish Bible Copyright © 1998 by David H. Stern. All rights reserved. Used by permission.

Scripture marked NCB is taken from the New Catholic Bible Copyright © 2019 by Catholic Book Publishing Corp. All rights reserved. Used by permission.

Scripture marked NTE is taken from the New Testament for Everyone copyright © Nicholas Thomas Wright 2011. Used by permission.

Scripture marked PHILLIPS is taken from the J.B. Phillips New Testament, copyright © 1960, 1972 J. B. Phillips. Administered by The Archbishops' Council of the Church of England. Used by Permission.

Scripture marked AMPC is taken from the Amplified Bible, Classic Edition, Copyright © 1954, 1958, 1962, 1964, 1965, 1987 by The Lockman Foundation. Used by Permission.

Scripture marked JUB is taken from the Jubilee Bible 2000, Copyright © 2013, 2020 by Ransom Press International. Used by Permission.

Scripture marked WE is taken from the Worldwide English (New Testament), © 1969, 1971, 1996, 1998 by SOON Educational Publications. Used by Permission.

Scripture marked MEV is taken from the Modern English Version, The Holy Bible, Modern English Version. Copyright © 2014 by Military Bible

Association. Published and distributed by Charisma House. Used by Permission.

Scripture marked CEV is taken from the Contemporary English Version, Contemporary English Version. Used by permission.

Scripture marked TPT is taken from The Passion Translation ®. Copyright © 2017, 2018, 2020 by Passion & Fire Ministries, Inc. Used by permission. All rights reserved.

Scripture marked NRSV is taken from New Revised Standard Version of the Bible, copyright © 1989 Division of Christian Education of the National Council of the Churches of Christ in the USA. Used by permission.

Scripture marked NCV is taken from the New Century Version®. Copyright © 2005 by Thomas Nelson. Used by permission. All rights reserved.

Scripture marked ERV is taken from the Easy-to-Read-Version Copyright © 1987, 2004 by Bible League international.

Scripture marked ESV is taken from the English Standard Version® (ESV®), copyright © 2001 by Crossway, a publishing ministry of Good News Publishers.

Scripture marked NLV is taken from the New Life Version © Christian Literature International.

Scripture marked TLV is taken from the Tree of Life Version Copyright © 2014 - Messianic Jewish Family Bible Society.

Scripture marked NIV is taken from THE HOLY BIBLE, NEW INTERNATIONAL VERSION®, NIV® Copyright © 1973, 1978, 1984, 2011 by Biblica, Inc.® Used by permission. All rights reserved worldwide.

Scripture marked NIRV is taken from the New International Reader's Version Copyright © 1995, 1996, 1998, 2014 by Biblica, Inc.®. Used by permission. All rights reserved worldwide.

Scripture marked TLB is taken from The Living Bible copyright © 1971 by Tyndale House Foundation. Used by permission of Tyndale House Publishers Inc., Carol Stream, Illinois 60188. All rights reserved.

Scripture marked NASB is taken from the New American Standard Bible®, Copyright © 1960, 1971, 1977, 1995, 2020 by The Lockman Foundation. All rights reserved. Used by permission.

Scripture marked NKJV is taken from the New King James Version®. Copyright © 1982 by Thomas Nelson. Used by permission. All rights reserved.

Scripture marked GW is taken from GOD'S WORD®, Copyright © 1995, 2003, 2013, 2014, 2019, 2020 by God's Word to the Nations Mission Society. All rights reserved. Used by permission of Baker Publishing Group.

Scripture marked AMP is taken from the Amplified Bible, Copyright © 2015 by The Lockman Foundation, La Habra, CA 90631. All rights reserved.

Scriptures marked ICB are quoted from the International Children's Bible®, copyright ©1986, 1988, 1999, 2015 by Tommy Nelson. Used by permission.

Scripture marked VOICE is taken from The Voice™. 2012 Thomas Nelson, Inc. The Voice™ translation © 2012 Ecclesia Bible Society All rights reserved. Used by permission.

Scripture marked GNT is taken from the Good News Translation® (Today's English Version, Second Edition) Copyright © 1992 American Bible Society. All rights reserved.

All rights reserved under international copyright law. No part of this publication may be reproduced or transmitted in any form or by any means, electronic or mechanical, including photocopying, recording, or by any information storage and retrieval system – except for brief quotation in printed reviews – without the prior written permission of the publisher.

Printed in the United States of America.

ISBN: 979-8-9875820-0-8

Dedication

Reflections of Hope is dedicated to all pareavors who are seeking hope and guidance, especially those whose faith in God has been shattered.

Do you feel stuck in your grief?

Our unique personalities have a lot to do with how we grieve. However, within that uniqueness, there are a few certain traits we all seem to fall into, and those traits can make us feel like we are spinning our wheels and will never get out of this place of suffocating darkness.

Would you like to find out what that might be for yourself? Take Laura's quiz. Not only will she send you those possible traits, but you will receive some suggestions on how to get unstuck from your specific struggles.

Go to mygriefhope.com to answer a few short questions and get the help you need to start moving forward toward a greater measure of healing for your shattered heart.

mygriefhope.com

Contents

Introduction   *i*

January	1
February	53
March	103
April	157
May	213
June	269
July	323
August	379
September	437
October	493
November	551
December	603

Index of Verses	*653*
Acknowledgments	*659*
About the Author	*664*
Other Books	*665*
Connect with Laura	*667*
Free Resources	*669*
Do You Feel Stuck in Your Grief?	*670*

Introduction

My Story

I was nine months pregnant, and it was my due date, Sept. 5, 1985. I was in the hospital, but not the local one to have the baby. We were almost an hour away from home at the University of Wisconsin hospital in Madison, being told after tests and a biopsy that our three-year-old daughter, Rebecca (Becca) had bone cancer. She started chemotherapy and two months later, on November 5th, her little left leg was amputated as part of the treatment, and she continued chemo for another seven months, which saved her life.

When Becca was around twelve years old, we were told her heart needed to be tested because one of the chemo drugs used may have caused long-term heart damage. She did have moderate damage, which wasn't too much of a problem until she got married and became pregnant. At that point, Becca was given a 50/50 chance of surviving labor and delivery. Both she and the baby lived, blessing us with our first grandchild.

However, it weakened Becca's heart even more, to the point that she eventually needed a heart transplant. She was not healthy enough to be put on the transplant list and was given a pump (called a VAD) to run the left side of her heart. The next sixteen months were a huge physical and emotional roller coaster, which included at least a dozen ambulance rides and three emergency airlift medical helicopter rides. She was in the University hospital more than she was out during that time. Becca never made it to the transplant list, as her heart gave out on Oct. 12, 2011 (almost ten years to the day as I write this).

We Are All Pareavors

After Becca died, I begged the Lord to just kill me now! I was not suicidal; I just did not want to live anymore. I did not know how it was possible to live with my daughter gone. I felt blindsided, and.... Well, I don't have to explain any of that to you, do I? You totally get what I am talking about.

There is no word that can even come close to describing our pain. But there is a word that validates the fact that parents who have lost a child through death have a weight that is extremely heavy; heavier than most will experience in this life. It is not a label to give us permission to wallow in our deep sorrow, but a word that draws us together to be able to strengthen and encourage each other within our life-long club membership that none of us wanted to be in.

Maybe you have heard of this word and maybe not, but that word is *pareavor*.

- "Pa" comes from the word parent: a person who is a father or mother; a person who has a child (Merriam-Webster)
- "Reave" comes from the word bereave. The meaning of the actual word "reave" (which the word bereave comes from) is to plunder or rob, to deprive one of, to seize, to carry or tear away (Merriam-Webster)
- "Or": indicating a person who does something (Wiktionary)

This sounds like a pretty good description of what happens when our child dies, no matter the age of the child. If you want to know how to pronounce it:

- "pa" is pronounced like the u in puff
- "reav" is pronounced like it sounds in the word bereave
- "or" sound is the typical "er" sound like mother

pu reav' er = pareavor

We are pareavors: Parents who have been robbed of our children by being torn away from us through death. I will be using this term throughout the book.

What You Will Find in This *Reflections of Hope* Book

This book was written to help you receive a tiny bit of hope each day. Many days you may feel like you are going backwards. I assure you that is not the case. It is all part of the journey we are on. Getting through the day, the hour, the next breath is a victory and means you are going in the right direction.

- **You may notice the same subject coming up more than once.** That is because these are some of the things we struggle with the most, and we need to be given a reminder or a word of hope more than once in that area.

- **You may see the same sentences, or the same story more than once.** This is because even from day-to-day, we are different in how we feel and how we view our situation. What you read one day might not mean much to you, but on another day those same words can be exactly what you need. Or it may affect you more deeply because it is in a different context for that daily reading.

- **Each one of us is living out different circumstances.** Some of you aren't married (or are on the verge of divorce) and don't have a spouse to share your grief with. Some of you lost your only child. Some of you lost an infant. Some of you have grandchildren from your child who died. Some of you live outside the US and don't have the same holidays that we have here in the United States.

  I could go on, but **the point I want to make is this: There may be an occasional reading that you can't quite relate to in your specific circumstance.** I am asking you to make the decision before even starting, that if you come across something like that, you don't get angry with me for "being so insensitive." Please believe me, that is the last thing I want to be accused of! Instead, pause and ask the Holy Spirit to show you what He wants to reveal to your heart in that day's reading beyond that one thing you cannot personally relate to. And maybe even send up a prayer for the pareavors who can relate to it.

- God gave us a gift that we unwrap and use quite well as a child, but then we grow out of it. Well, in reality, most of us eventually use it in a way God did not intend. What is this gift? It is our imagination. As we grow into adulthood, we tend to imagine what can go wrong, and even play out scenarios in our minds of conversations and events that are negative. We "let our minds run wild" as the saying goes.

You will find in this book that you will be asked at times to use the God-given gift of your imagination to picture things that are good. Things that will give you peace and hope and even joy. It is not "guided imagery" as in the New Age movement. It is simply giving you permission to allow your mind to become child-like once again (not childish, as there is a difference), **to allow you to see a picture that God gives you from His viewpoint, instead of our own flesh or what the enemy tries to get us to see.**

- **Each day has a reading and ends with a reflection. Some days, this may be the only thing you have the capacity to read. That's okay.**

   When you can, I encourage you to sit with it for a while. There is a difference between reading the words and absorbing them. You will get the most from this book of reflections if you take a few minutes and actually reflect.

   There may be one or two reflections that really stand out to you and are a turning point in some area of your grief that is needed. For the most part, you won't remember exactly what you read, but you will know how it affects you.

   Any time the daily reflection does not seem to work for that day for you, do not beat yourself up! Don't feel guilty that you are doing something wrong in grieving the death of your child. There are going to be times where you are just in such deep pain or anger that nothing seems to help. You will ease out of it eventually. Just know that it usually takes longer than we want it to.

- After the reflection you will find a special message from the Word. Feel free to explore that scripture and camp out on it, including looking it up in different versions. **Allow the daily Word on the page to refresh your weary soul.**

- In the back of *Reflections of Hope,* there is an index of all the scripture verses used throughout the entire book, including those within the readings. This makes it easy to see if there might be a way to look at a specific scripture through the eyes of a pareavor.

- I highly recommend you **purchase a journal specifically for the purpose of writing your thoughts for the daily readings.** Do not pressure yourself to write in it every day, but there will be many days you will want to write down your thoughts about that day's reflection.

- **If you struggle with the fear that your child might not be in heaven, I suggest you turn to March 4th and read that entry right now.** You can also listen to a podcast that I did on this subject. Go to gpshope.org/podcast/18.

What if I miss reading a day, or two, or fifteen?

I debated and even asked a bunch of pareavors if I should only have four to five entries each week, so no one feels overwhelmed at keeping up. Some liked that idea, but most preferred to have an option to read something each day.

IMPORTANT: If you miss any days at all, don't allow yourself to feel guilty or overwhelmed, thinking you need to try and play "catch-up." Just turn to the page of today's date and read that entry. Who knows? Maybe the Holy Spirit knew the days you missed were things you just were not ready to read, so He allowed you to not pick up the book.

My Hope and Prayer for You

You and I are forever changed because of the death of our child, but that does not mean our life is over. I pray that what you read on these pages will help give you the needed strength and encouragement for learning how to take some needed steps forward, helping you be able to walk out this new life that you did not expect and do not want, with grace.

You may feel like nothing is happening day-to-day as you read, but I assure you that He is at work, deeper than you can feel through your pain. I have faith that a year from now you will be able to look back and see how far you have come, by allowing yourself to participate in doing the work of grief with the Holy Spirit as your Comforter and your Guide.

You *can* get to a place of healing that allows you to not only function again, but to live a life of meaning and purpose in a way that honors your child, not in spite of their death, but because of his or her life. I pray this book *Reflections of Hope* helps you to do that.

So, don't give up. Keep leaning in, and please remember to:

Hold **O**n **P**ain **E**ases. There is HOPE.

Offering Hope Through Him,

Laura D.

January

January 1

Dealing with Our Fears

Right now, I am sitting at my desk looking at a plaque that says, "I don't know what tomorrow holds, but I know who holds tomorrow."

When the clock turned to midnight on December 31st, and the new year kicked in, I had the thought, "I wonder what this year holds? This time next year, what will have happened in my life to bring more changes I'm not expecting?"

Maybe you had a similar thought.

This was one of the times I had to remind myself that I have a choice to either give in to fear or give in to faith. You see, they both come from the same root. They are both based on not knowing what the future holds.

I can either live in fear of the future, or I can live in faith that my future is in God's hands and He has good plans for me that I probably cannot see yet. I can choose to be tormented by what I do not know (thinking of more bad things that may never even happen) or I can allow peace to enter my soul, knowing whatever happens, God is already there to get me through it.

It all comes down to our minds and our thoughts. We make the decision of living in either fear or faith, and then we continually choose to allow our thoughts to dwell on things that support our decision.

We all let our minds wander. I have a tendency to play out the details of the things I am afraid might happen, feeding my fear of the unknown and getting myself all worked up. But when I realize my mind is wandering in that way, I have made the decision to cut that off and start dwelling on positive and even exciting things that could be in my future. Instead of imagining things that bring fear and torment, I start imagining how God will be moving in my life in His love and faithfulness to bring more healing and give my life purpose and meaning. It takes some practice, but the more I do it, the easier it gets, and the less often my mind wanders toward the fears.

Reflection: How about you? Do you want to make this a year where you move away from fear and navigate toward peace and a greater measure of healing for your shattered heart? Take some time right now and ask the Holy Spirit to help you shift away from fear and believing all the bad things and struggles you will have, to what He still wants to do in your life that is good.

> *For God gave us a spirit not of fear but*
> *of power and love and self-control.*
> *2 Timothy 1:7 (ESV)*

January 2

I Don't Want to be in a New Year!

December 31, 2012 was a rough day for me. It was only ten weeks after Becca died. I was terrified at the thought of turning the calendar, entering a new year knowing Becca was not going to be coming with me. It felt like another door slamming closed on her that I was not ready for. The phrase "Happy New Year" just did not apply at all!

It has been several years for me now, and things are better when the calendar flips to start another year without my daughter. Because of that, please allow me to pray for you.

Father,

I come to you on behalf of all of us who are now in a new year which brings so much pain and sorrow with it. I ask that You give each of us an extra measure of grace and help us to give grace to ourselves as well.

May we be overcome with peace, even within our deep pain. Help us grasp in a greater way that we are not getting further away from our

Reflections of Hope

children, but every day and every year gets us closer to seeing and being with them again.

In this coming year, may we continue to hand You the shattered pieces of our heart, and watch in amazement as you put them back together, not as if we have never been broken, but in a wholeness within the brokenness.

Cover us with your love, and let us see a hope in our future, not just our future in heaven with our child, but here on this earth as we learn to live in a way that honors You and the life of our child. Amen

Reflection: Go back to the prayer, and pray it out loud, changing the "us" to "me" and the "we" to "I", making it a personal heart cry to the Lord. Add whatever you need to say and stay in His presence for a couple of extra minutes, allowing Him to meet with you and love on you.

Lord, show your love to us as we put our hope in you.
Psalm 33:22 (NCV)

January 3

You are Not Leaving Your Child Behind

We must be honest with ourselves in whether or not we want to get past this part of our grief. As we know, there are so many reasons that deep down, cause us to be afraid to take steps toward hope, light, and living a life of purpose and fulfillment.

The two most common reasons are:

1. We feel guilty for even wanting to enjoy life again.
2. We are afraid that we are leaving our child behind by moving forward.

January

To help you with the second one right now, I would like to give a suggestion to move you in the direction of seeing things with a slightly different view.

We are not just facing a new year. It is a new month, and a new month often brings new weather. Because it is January, it means we are moving toward spring! Those of us who are in the cold northern states truly appreciate this. Yes, I understand that winter has just begun, and I know how winter makes everything look so dead (depending on where we live), and it can really affect our mood. However, winter is a season, and new life *always* returns, no matter how harsh or how long the winter has been.

You are in a season. A very long, dark and difficult season in your life. But just like the day always follows night, and spring always follows winter, hope will follow despair, light will follow the darkness, and meaning, and purpose will come into your life again. This is not in spite of your child's death, but because of his or her life.

Reflection: Allow the new month (and the new year) to remind you that it is true, God will make *all* things new. No matter how long or how deep into darkness our grief has taken us, spring IS coming at some point, with new life and new hope. Right now, you might not want a new life without your child, and that's okay. Just allow yourself to think of the possibility that maybe someday - maybe even before this year is over - you will be able to see that it is possible.

If nothing else, remind yourself that God has made everything new for your child, and you will have that same thing happen when you join him or her.

> *Be alert, be present. I'm about to do something brand*
> *new. It's bursting out! Don't you see it? There it is!*
> *I'm making a road through the desert, rivers in the badlands.*
> *Isaiah 43:19 (MSG)*

January 4
A Different Thought about the New Year

As I shared yesterday, sometimes we dread going forward, because we feel like it is taking us further away from our child who has left this earth.

I used to feel like I was on the verge of a panic attack, thinking about getting further and further away from my daughter, Becca. I could hardly breathe when thinking about being here without her for five years, ten years, twenty years... it seemed absolutely impossible.

One day when I was fighting this fear, God graciously spoke to my heart and pointed out to me that I am not getting further away from Becca, but I am getting closer to her. Each day I am here, brings me one day *closer* to being reunited with her again!

Wow! Talk about a change in perspective! It did not take away the painful thoughts of her not being with me for the rest of my time here, but it did take away the panic-type terror I kept finding myself in.

So, a new year can be a reminder that we are getting that much closer to seeing our children again. How exciting!

Reflection: *New* is a word that can mean hope. A new year *can* bring new hope, new light, new life and new possibilities. Take a few minutes and allow the words, "New Year" to take on a different meaning. Give yourself permission for the possibility that a new year means that you *can* move away from darkness and fear into peace and a greater measure of healing for your shattered heart.

Those of us who have been on this journey for a while know it can be done. You are not alone. Let's do this together!

For I, the Lord your God, hold your right hand; it is I who say to you, "Fear not, I am the one who helps you.
Isaiah 41:13 (ESV)

January 5

What is Your Word?

When a new year shows up, it brings a myriad of emotions for many of us bereaved parents, especially if this is the first time the calendar has turned since your child died. There are so many words that can describe what we think and how we feel. Numb, regret, anger, sorrow, fear, confusion... I am sure you could add quite a few of your own words to this list.

These are all valid, for sure! And as you can see, they are all negative. So, how can we start to move the needle toward the positive, especially if we don't see how that is even possible? Or maybe you are someone who doesn't know if you even want to.

I believe there is a word that is the bridge between the two.

HOPE

When we have no hope, we have no desire to live.

We know the enemy is out to steal from us and kill us. If he can't do it physically, he will do it emotionally. When our child dies, we have the biggest red target on us for the enemy to do exactly that. He steals our hope, leaving us wanting to die to go be with our child. Even if we have other children, a wonderful marriage and had a life full of purpose and passion before our child's death, it all comes crashing down and we are left in a world of darkness and hopelessness.

However, the death of our child did not blindside God like it might have done to us. That means we do not have to stay a slave, chained to our prison of darkness with no hope. Jesus came to break every chain that could ever try to keep us bound. He will carry us through this valley of death, back into a place of abounding hope.

There is a seed of hope already inside you! It may be dormant at the moment, but it is there. It just needs to be nurtured, and in time, in its season, it will begin to break through the hard ground and begin to sprout.

Reflections of Hope

Bad things happen to good people. Horrible and evil things happen to God's people. The question is: Are you going to become bitter or better? What value are you going to place on the life of your child? That is where the mind shift happens. Life or death?

I refuse to let death cause more death! I will *not* give the enemy that kind of a victory! Because Jesus lives, I can live. I have allowed my God to make good on His promises in my life, to give strength to the weary and hope to the hopeless. And I will allow that hope to continue to grow as it becomes joy that reaches beyond death, both my child's and mine.

I hope and pray in this new year, you decide to make the same choice.

Reflection: I want to encourage you to ask God to give you a specific word for this year: a word that represents what He wants to work into your life through this grief journey. This past year, my word was joy. I wanted and needed the *fullness* of His joy back in my life again, and I have begun to see that happen. As a matter of fact, someone I hadn't seen for a while told me I seem happier and more content than I have been in a long time.

Then take some time and find at least one scripture with that word that speaks to your heart about what you are asking Him to do. Write it out and put it somewhere you will see, as a reminder to keep crying out to Him to have that in your life. (Even better, make a list of verses that you can refer to when you are struggling more than you normally do.)

May the God of hope fill you with all joy and peace in believing, so that by the power of the Holy Spirit you may abound in hope.
Romans 15:13 (ESV)

January 6

Opportunities

A new year brings new opportunities. Some of you may not see that as a good thing, but it does bring new opportunities to do something different that will possibly help take some of the sting away and move you toward a needed measure of healing.

Many pareavors I know have started meaningful hobbies since the death of their child. Here are just some of them:

- Furniture restoration
- Pottery
- Photography
- Writing songs
- Writing poetry
- Jogging
- Camping
- Playing an instrument
- Making beautiful, personalized mugs

Some of these hobbies have turned into businesses. For these pareavors, knowing they are creating something others love enough to purchase, has had its own a healing element to it.

It has been many years, but I have gotten back to knitting again. I used to spend hours knitting, and one year I even knit Easter outfits for the three kids we had at the time! (I knit Becca a sweater, her brother a matching vest and sweater, and her baby sister a dress.)

Starting a new year is a great time to learn something new or pick up an old hobby you let fall by the wayside over the years.

Reflection: Starting a new year can be extremely difficult. Ask yourself what you can do differently that will help, which may include starting a new hobby.

New means change, but that doesn't just have to be a negative painful thing. It can also be a catalyst for new opportunities to move toward a healing that allows you to learn how to live in hope, light, and even move toward having meaning and purpose again.

You may think that is impossible, but those of us who thought it was impossible for us as well are here to encourage you.

Then the One sitting on the throne said, "Look! I am making everything new!" Also he said, "Write, These words are true and trustworthy!"
Revelation 21:5 (CJB)

January 7

Fighting the Darkness

It seems there are still things that can trigger me to spiral downward. It is usually from too much going on around me and I start to feel overwhelmed. I specifically remember one of the times when I was about six years into this journey when it happened again, and I went through another round of depression. I had a day and a half where I stayed in bed and just allowed myself to crash. The second day in bed I reminded myself that if He is in me, then His light is in me, and I needed to release it.

Through my tears I began to whisper and speak the name of Jesus and declare that I needed His light to come and shatter the darkness that was hanging over me and in me. Within the hour I was at least finally able to get back out of bed, come out of my room and start to somewhat function again.

In the natural world, in order to remove darkness, it just takes the smallest amount of light. Once that light is there, we can begin to see through the darkness as our eyes begin to adjust. And the closer we move toward the light, the brighter it becomes and the less the darkness affects us.

That is true in our soul as well. Jesus is light, and when we call out to Him, His light will begin to penetrate the darkness in our lives.

I will admit, our darkness is so very dark that it sometimes takes a *lot* of His light to penetrate and eventually break through the darkness we find ourselves in. But He can, and He will, when we continue to call out to Him in our darkness.

Do not give up. I know it is hard. I know you may not have the energy to fight the darkness, which is why we call on Him to do it for us. Keep calling out to Him for His light, and He will keep coming and fighting the darkness on our behalf until it breaks through.

Reflection: Another thing that helps me fight the darkness is to remember this is not the end. Our children are in a place of light and glory that we cannot even imagine, and some day, we will no longer have to fight the darkness, but will be filled with that same light and glory that our children are now living in! What a wonderful day that will be!

Take some time and try to picture His light that is shining brilliantly in heaven. Then imagine that light coming as a sword in His hands, piercing the darkness all around you. If you still feel like you are in total darkness, don't give up. In the days and weeks ahead, keep calling out to Him, to bring His light into your darkness. The light *is* on its way to you!

The light shines in the darkness, and the darkness has not overcome it.
John 1:5 (ESV)

January 8
Finding Our Way

Our life here on earth is not a destination, it is a journey. I am sure you have heard this statement before, and it may even irritate you, especially after the death of your child. Today, I want to think about this statement, specifically within the context of being a bereaved parent.

When we are going on a trip, sometimes we make plans, knowing exactly where we are going, and get there without any problems. Sometimes we know where we want to go but need a map or GPS to guide us to the right place. And sometimes the road changes and even the GPS has no idea where we are!

That is how we feel after the death of our child. We have no idea how to get anywhere here on earth and want our journey to be over, *now*!

It is easy to find ourselves feeling very lost and lonely, even when in a room full of people. Those around us are enjoying conversations, laughing and living a "normal" life, while we are still in a painful fog. We are often torn, though, because sometimes we find that while we want to be alone, at the same time, we don't want to be lonely.

Just being around other people isn't what we are longing for; it is being around people who care, and who will allow us to be whoever we need to be, at any given moment, in our grieving. People who get why we want this journey to be over and why we just don't want to be here anymore.

The good news is, no matter how lost you may feel, if you keep going one day, one hour at a time, you will eventually either:

- figure out where you are, to be able to get back on life's journey.
- find someone who knows the area who can help you navigate back to a road that will take you to a life of meaning and purpose once again.

Quite often, the second one causes the first. It is usually much easier to be able to pick up the pieces enough to figure out how to live again, with someone walking with you who has been there and done it themselves.

Reflection: You do not have to feel alone because there *are* others who have been right where you are and can help you find your way. Who can you count on to walk with you, helping you find your way back to living a meaningful life again? If you know who that is, pray for them to be the guide you need, and maybe take a few minutes to send them a thank you for being that person for you.

If you don't know of anyone, a good start is to connect with myself and others at GPS Hope, since our purpose is to be someone you can count on to get you back onto the journey of life God has for you. Let's keep going forward together!

God is my helper; the Lord is with those who support my life.
Psalm 54:4 (MEV)

January 9

Do You Have New Fears?

The death of our child can bring so many fears into our lives that we never had before. That is very understandable. Personally, the greatest fear I find myself fighting is that I will lose another one of my children from this earth.

Being fearful and feeling helpless is horrible, especially when it comes to our children. And we have faced the ultimate extreme of helplessness; we were not able to protect our child from death. Oh, the pain and guilt of being such a bad parent!

Or were we? Neither life nor death is in our hands. God is the one who gives life within the womb. And God chooses when each person takes their last heartbeat. We may cry out, "That's not fair!" May I remind you; many things are not fair in this fallen sinful world, especially from our viewpoint.

Jesus is truly the "Alpha and Omega" (Revelation 22:13). He is the beginning, and He is the end. In other words, He has the *final* word on everything, and that final Word is *life forever. Together forever.*

Fear brings torment. God does not give anyone fear. It comes from the enemy of our souls. As those who have faced the unnatural, out-of-order death of our child, we are huge targets for the enemy's fiery darts of fear.

I am determined to stay connected to God, believing that He is truly good all the time and not just when I get my own way. I believe with every fiber of my being that my daughter is with Him in the safest and most wonderful place possible, and until I join her, I will figure out how to move forward toward being happy and fulfilled in this life.

We can make the choice to fight our fears, because of our eternal future. We can fight feeling helpless by being determined to be hopeful. We can, and we must, for the sake of our sanity, for those who love us and need us, and for the sake of honoring the life of our child who is no longer here with us.

Reflection: God throws out the fearful torment of the enemy, and replaces it with peace, if we run into His arms and trust in His incredible deep love for us.

Ask yourself: Am I going to be anxious and worry, living in fear feeling helpless, or am I going to trust that even though the worst possible nightmare has happened in my life, God is still taking care of me and will continue to be the peace in my storms – no, make that hurricanes – of my life?

Look, if you sold a few sparrows, how much money would you get? A copper coin apiece, perhaps? And yet your Father in heaven knows when those small sparrows fall to the ground. You, beloved, are worth so much more than a whole flock of sparrows. God knows everything about you, even the number of hairs on your head. So do not fear.
Matthew 10:29-31 (VOICE)

January 10

He Paid the Full Price

We have so many examples in the Bible that show suffering cannot be automatically equated to punishment.

- The rich man and Lazarus - he suffered his whole life here on earth (Luke 16:19-31)
- John the Baptist - Jesus said no prophet was greater, but he was beheaded (Matthew 11:11 and Matthew 14:8-11)
- Mary, the mother of Jesus - obviously Mary wasn't being punished for some past sin
- The blind man Jesus healed - people wanted to know who sinned, his mother or father that made him be born blind, and Jesus said neither one. (John 9:1-3)
- Job - he was known for being a man of uprightness before God. (Job 1:1)

The point of Jesus dying on the cross was to take ALL of our punishment. ALL! Not most, ALL! He took your place for any punishment you deserved for anything you did in the past, and everything you have yet to do in the future!

If something like getting cancer, or the death of our child, was a punishment for something we did or did not do, then His death on the cross did not do much. His coming to earth, being brutally tortured and then being executed a horrific painful death was pointless, if God is still going to punish us anyway.

There are consequences for our actions for sure (speeding gets us a ticket, or maybe even into an accident). But poverty, sickness and suffering are part of the human condition, and it happens to both the just and the unjust. The rain falls on the good and the evil (Matthew 5:45).

I remember watching a video with Eugene Peterson (who did the Bible translation of The Message Bible and has since passed away) and Bono of the group U2. It was fascinating to me, and one of the things Bono said was, "God isn't a violent God, but the world is a violent place."

Reflection: We cannot escape the effects of this world that is decaying around us in so many ways. I am 110% positive that the death of your child was *not* God's punishment for something in your past, because Jesus already took that penalty on your behalf.

So, if you are carrying that burden of guilt, thinking the death of your child was your fault for some past sin, please drop that right now at the foot of the cross where it belongs and leave it there, once and for all! Don't just pass over this because you already know in your head the Bible says it. Right now, take care of it. Release it and thank God for taking it from you. Even see yourself handing something over to Him and watch Him reach out and receive it, turn around and nail it on the cross.

He has not punished us as our sins should be punished;
he has not repaid us for the evil we have done. As high as the sky is
above the earth so great is his love for those who respect him. He has
taken our sins away from us as far as the east is from west.
Psalm 103:10-12 (NCV)

January 11

I Don't Think I Can Ever Get Past This

In the book of Exodus, chapter three, God shares with Moses that He has seen the pain and misery of His people. He has heard them crying. He is concerned about their suffering, and He has a plan to help them out of their pain; to move them forward into the fullness of who He promised they would be, if they would allow it.

When we are in the darkness of our crushing pain, most of us do not even think it is possible to move out of the darkness into a place of light, much less have meaning and purpose in our lives ever again. I have heard so many times, "Well, maybe you have found peace and hope

January

and have a life worth living, and I am glad for you, but I just don't see that happening for me." Guess what? *I thought the same thing!*

The added horror of thinking that I was going to live out the rest of my life here on earth just waiting to die, while stuck in the shell of my earthly body, was terrifying to me. Especially when my head knew I still had things to live for, but my heart just would not allow me to believe it and want to live.

I was in such a pit of suffocating darkness but had no idea how to get out and didn't think I ever could. And I was absolutely right! I couldn't.

The only thing I knew to do, was to hang on to God with anything and everything I possibly could, no matter what. And quite often, that was not holding on to Him at all, but letting Him hold on to me as I just cried and sobbed. I am talking not just weeks, but months and on into the second and third year after my daughter's death.

Reflection: Something that helped me was when I started making myself think about what I knew about God *before* the unthinkable happened. Spend some time meditating on this list. You can probably even add to it.

- I AM with you and will *never* leave you or forsake you.
- I AM able – *nothing* is impossible for Him.
- I AM a promise keeper (which we often misunderstand or misconstrue).
- I AM love itself.
- I AM your comforter.
- I AM light in the darkness.
- I AM the Prince of Peace.
- I AM life, and resurrection power is my specialty.
- I AM the one who counts all your tears and keeps them in a bottle.
- I AM the lover of your soul.
- I AM all-knowing and all-powerful.
- I AM the giver of life, of hope, of rest.
- I AM the One who makes a way when there is no way.

- I AM the Alpha and Omega, the beginning and end of everything.
- I AM the provider of eternal life.
- I AM your rock, your anchor, and the tower you can run to for security.
- I AM everything you need.

You believed it before, and it is still true. I AM the great I AM for *you!*

> *Fear not, for I am with you; be not dismayed,*
> *for I am your God; I will strengthen you, I will help you,*
> *I will uphold you with my righteous right hand.*
> *Isaiah 41:10 (ESV)*

January 12

My Lost Identity

What I have come to know is that because of the identity of the great I AM, my identity, and therefore my life, is not over here on this earth, and I am okay with that. Even more importantly, my identity is tied to Him more than anything or anyone else, which is still slowly bringing a new measure of freedom in my life that I have never had before.

God was not blindsided by Becca's death. He did not reach His limits when she left this earth, and was suddenly unable to bring light into darkness, no matter how deep and black that darkness is. In other words, He did not stop being I AM, and all that it means, because I stopped being the me I knew as Becca's mom.

He is the exact same God I loved and trusted *before* He opened the door for Becca to go ahead of me to our eternal home. He is the same yesterday, today and forever. He was, and is, and is to come. He is not the one whose identity changed. His identity is sure and secure, proven throughout thousands of years.

January

That meant I had to find out who He really is, instead of who I thought He was. And you probably need to as well. The only way I know for us to become unscrambled in this area of our lost identity and become all that God created and intended for us to be, is to seek to understand God's identity as the I AM, within our deep pain and grief.

Go ahead, be mad at Him. It's okay. That is part of how we find out who He really is. Because no matter how we feel about Him or treat Him, He still is the same incredibly secure and great I AM. And that is something to be extremely thankful for.

Reflection: Because of God's identity being I AM, you can still have identity, purpose and meaning after the death of your child. It will take a while, but I and many other bereaved parents can tell you that it is worth pursuing and fighting for!

Who do you need God to be for you right now? Get specific. Look at yesterday's list if you need to. Ask Him to be that for you, and then don't expect it to come in a certain way. Be open to how God wants to meet you in that exact place in a way you didn't even know that He could.

I love those who love me, and those who seek me diligently find me.
Proverbs 8:17 (ESV)

January 13

Who Can I Trust?

Every step in our journey here on this earth involves trust. We either trust others, trust ourselves, or we trust God.

We know trusting others does not always work out so well. As much as we want to be in control of things that happen in our lives ourselves, we cannot be. The more we try, the more frustrated and angrier we are likely to become that we cannot even put our trust in ourselves.

That leaves trusting God. I believe this is the best choice because He is not blindsided or taken by surprise by anything that happens in our lives. That is a good thing, because it means He also knows exactly how to get us through the darkness, back to a place of light again in our lives.

However, knowing that doesn't usually change the question many of us ask: *Why, God? Why did this to happen to me and my child?*

I know of someone who had the exact opposite question: *Why **not** me? What makes me think I am better than someone else that qualifies me to be exempt from something like this happening?*

God knows the number of all our days. He knew before *you* were even conceived that you would have a child who would leave this earth before you did. He also knew the pain and darkness you would go through.

So, let me ask you this tough question. If God knew the number of days your child would be on this earth, would you rather God had given your child to someone else, so you would not have to be the one to go through this?

If you are like most pareavors I ask, they give a resounding *absolutely not!* We would rather have our child for the short time we did, than not have him or her at all.

Reflection: So now we have to circle back around. Are you going to trust God, knowing that He can see what you cannot see, and He knows what you do not know? Remember, He knew before your great-grandparents were even conceived that you would be here on earth someday without your child, and He already knew how to guide you out of the darkness of that grief and back to a place of wanting to live again.

No, that does not take away the suffocating darkness and pain we have to go through, but it does allow a seed of hope to be planted, that we *can* survive this, and at some point, even have a life worth living again until our own numbered days come to pass, and we are reunited forever with our children.

> *Trust in him at all times, O people; pour out*
> *your heart before him; God is a refuge for us.*
> *Psalm 62:8 (ESV)*

January 14

God Did Not Do this to You

Although it hurts so much that we just want to die and go to be with our child, we need to remind ourselves that our child is safe in the Father's arms. (If this is something you question or that torments you, turn ahead and read March 4th where I talk about the fear that your child is not in heaven.)

When we think of our loss, our pain can make it hard to even breathe at times. But when we think of our child's gain, it lifts some of that suffocating darkness, allowing us to see a glimmer of hope and even the possibility that maybe God isn't as cruel as we thought He was, and that it is possible to believe we can live again, even finding happiness while finishing our time on this earth.

God did not do this *to* you. Yes, for some reason (which we may never know this side of eternity) He did not stop the earthly departure of your child and my child ahead of us.

God did not do this to us, but He does have something *for* each of us.

- God has light and life that penetrates and shatters the suffocating darkness and intense pain.
- He has a peace for each of us that goes beyond anything we can understand. This peace causes us to delight in His mercy and grace in our lives within the horrible earthly loss.
- God has a plan for every single one of us. It is a plan that has blessings for you (and me) that we don't even know about yet.

Reflections of Hope

No, God did not do this to you. Once you can believe this truth, you will be well on your way to receiving the light, life, peace and blessings God has *for* you beyond the darkness and pain.

Reflection: Another thing that can help, is to remind ourselves that our child does not have to face the pain and tragedies this world puts us all through. None of us want to see our child get knocked down by the world over and over again, like we have been.

Here's another thing to think about: Your child will never have to go through the painful loss of you, their parent. Instead of them having to grieve our departure, we are taking on the greater grief of their departure instead.

If you are like me, I am willing to sacrifice myself, no matter how painful, if it means my children will not have to go through something painful and difficult. Interesting thought, isn't it? You might want to give a prayer of thanks that your child will not have to experience these dark and painful things.

> *In face of all this, what is there left to say? If God is for us, who can be against us? He that did not hesitate to spare his own Son but gave him up for us all—can we not trust such a God to give us, with him, everything else that we can need?*
> *Romans 8:31 (PHILLIPS)*

January 15

Dreaming Again for the Future

The month of January celebrates Martin Luther King Jr. Day. He was famous for his "I have a dream" speech, and I recently found myself wondering if I were to give my own "I have a dream speech," what would that be like?

January

In writing it out, I came up with six things.

1. I have a dream that no pareavor is left feeling alone, isolated and abandoned.

2. I have a dream that all grieving parents can quickly and easily connect with other pareavors for encouragement.

3. I have a dream that any pareavor who has his or her faith in God shaken has a safe place to share their hurt, their doubts and their anger without judgment or being shunned.

4. I have a dream that the family and friends of pareavors know how to give true comfort and support, both physically and emotionally, and treat the parents' grief as the long process it is, instead of an event.

5. I have a dream that even before a parent loses a child, they already know who they can contact for support and help in their pain and confusion when their own child leaves this earth.

6. I have a dream that every grieving parent who feels shattered and hopeless has the immediate opportunity to have other pareavors in their life who can be a light of hope in their place of darkness.

These six things are truly much more than a dream for me. They are my God-given calling. They are the vision and mission I am taking action on, moving forward in, one step, one day at a time.

They are now my reality.

Reflection: How about you? Do you have any dreams stirring around? It could be one that was in you before the death of your child that God is stirring in you once again, or it might be a completely new dream. Pull out a piece of paper and write the words, "I Have a Dream" and see what starts to flow out of you, no matter how small or how big it seems. Then hold it up before the Lord, allowing God to stir in you the desire to do what it takes, to see that dream come to pass.

And if you are not able to dream again, that's okay. Do not let yourself think something must be wrong with how you are grieving, because that is just not true. Keep resting in Him. Continue taking things one day at a time. I believe He will give you that dream at the right time.

> *Put it in writing, because it is not yet time for it to come true. But the time is coming quickly, and what I show you will come true. It may seem slow in coming, but wait for it; it will certainly take place, and it will not be delayed.*
> *Habakkuk 2:3 (GNT)*

January 16

With Me... Without Me...

There are not many movies I will take the time to watch more than once, but one of my favorites that we own, and I am willing to rewatch, is Knight and Day with Tom Cruise and Cameron Diaz. (Warning, there is one f-bomb if you decide to watch it.)

A woman has naively gotten wrapped up in the hero's mess of people trying to kill him and she isn't sure if he is the bad guy or the good guy. In one of my favorite scenes, he is trying to convince her that she is safer with him so he can protect her, because otherwise she will be kidnapped and killed. He gets right to the point by saying, "With me... Without me... With me... Without me..." while using a flat hand showing a higher level on the "with me" and dropping it down on "without me." (This has jokingly become one of mine and Dave's sayings to each other.)

For some reason I picture this as something God is trying to tell us sometimes. He might not be quite as dramatic, but then again, maybe sometimes He is!

We have the choice to walk on this journey either with Him, or without Him. With Him... Without Him. And just like in this movie, it can sometimes seem like life would be easier without Him, because walking with Him makes us feel like we are just a big target for the enemy.

But on the other hand, I *need* Him to be with me, because I can't fight off the enemy by myself, especially when it comes to fighting my way through something as dark as the death of my child.

Reflection: Are you confused as to whether or not you want to continue "with Him"? If you try going "without Him", at some point you will most likely find you need to be "with Him" for so many reasons. Take some time and really think through your decision, which may be to recommit yourself to being "with Him".

You know what the best part is? Even the times that we choose to go our own way without Him, He is still with us. Even though it may not feel like it, He does not abandon us, even when we abandon Him. He is now and forever "with us." And that is a wonderful thing!

*If we give up on him, he does not give up —
for there's no way he can be false to himself.*
2 Timothy 2:13 (MSG)

January 17

Getting Past the Anger

When death takes our child from us, we can be surprised and even scared at how much anger there is inside us. It can be even more shocking to realize who the cause of our anger is, as it is often not just someone who was directly involved in our child's death (like a drunk driver or an actual murderer). We can also be angry at:

- Our family and friends for telling us things like we need to "just get over it"
- Someone indirectly related to the death (like a spouse or babysitter for not keeping a closer eye on our child)
- Ourselves (if only I had... I should have...)
- God (Why didn't you stop it?)
- Our child for leaving us

Did I just say that? Yes, if you are angry at your child, let me say as awful as that sounds, you can breathe a sigh of relief because it is *normal!* Especially if the death was by his or her own doing, either directly or indirectly.

I have a friend in this "grief world", Angela Alexander, who has had to overcome the death of two brothers, the loss of a baby during pregnancy, a husband who miraculously survived a brain aneurysm (only to have to learn how to do everything again from eating, talking and walking), a brother murdering their sister who was Angela's life-long very best friend, and then the death of two of her sons in a bizarre car accident (while she was on military duty in Japan). Angela wrote a book titled *Miracles in Action* (which has also been turned into a documentary film).

Angela stands firm on Revelation 12:11, that tells us that we can overcome the enemy by the Blood of the Lamb and by the word of our testimony.

"What testimony????" you ask?

The one God is still writing in your life.

A testimony comes from being tested. We can come out the other side filled with God's love, forgiveness and mercy, which *are* miracles in action.

Losing a child from this earth is probably the greatest "test" you will face in your lifetime. You may feel like you are failing it miserably and that you will never be able to pass, especially with all the anger inside you.

Just remember others who have gone before you, like Angela. Look at those who are truly miracles in action because of what God has done on the inside of them, knowing that when you keep turning it all over to

God, your internal miracle is being worked out in you every single day, whether you feel it or not.

Reflection: How can you get past it if you are angry at those around you? Take it out on God. Yell at Him. Scream at Him at the top of your lungs. Say what you need to say. Throw something if you need to (obviously not at someone or something valuable/irreplaceable). Cry as long and as hard as you need to. In other words, let yourself get it out.

And then... then ask God to bring people into your life who will hold you, cry with you, and remember your child with you, as your testimony of overcoming the enemy is being put together in your life.

> *They won the victory over him because of the blood*
> *of the lamb and the word of their testimony.*
> *Revelation 12:11 (GW)*

January 18

Learning to Rest in God

Don't *do*, just *be*.

This was the message I kept hearing from many different places for the first two years after Becca's leaving this earth. I believe it is a message we all need at some point when working our way through the darkness and back into the light after the death of our child.

We all need that place where we can get away and rest. However, the rest we truly need to come into is not a time and a place. It is a position; a way of life. But often we must begin with the time and place in order to learn to live in that position.

This means we have to set time aside to be alone in God's presence, especially if we have a hard time believing He truly loves us after not stepping in to save our child from earthly death. We need to "just be" in the stillness of His presence, where He can speak peace to us and fill us with His extravagant love.

During that time those first couple of years, God gave me many reminders to rest in Him and His ways. It was a hard thing to do, because I could not see any light in my darkness or understand why God was allowing so much intense pain.

He would share His reminders to just "be" and rest in Him in so many different ways. He would remind me to take a breath and breathe in His love and peace. He never sugarcoated anything but would acknowledge how difficult and steep my climb was, telling me to cling tightly to His hand, reminding me to look at *Him* whenever my circumstances overwhelmed me.

He knew how weak and helpless I was, and He never tired of meeting me in my place of need. Looking back, I see now how each time He would free me from a few more of my shackles, even though most of the time I could not feel it.

Not only would He "hold" me, but He would encourage me to relax in the awareness of His presence. Some of my most precious times with the Lord were in my greatest times of weakness, just letting everything go and melting into His peace, love, and compassion. And so much peace and deep revelation came out of those times of intimacy in those first few years.

Reflection: Spend intimate time with Him. Lots of it. Let Him show you the way out by showing you the fullness of Himself. If you stick with it, I guarantee you will learn to come into that place of rest that we all so desperately need after the earthly departure of our child.

Don't be surprised if you are feeling helpless in this area, because most of us are. Lean on the Holy Spirit to be your help. He will do it because He wants you to rest in Him, allowing Him to minister to you in such a deep way that you do not even know anything is happening. Just be with

Him and let Him do the work. Feel yourself melting into His peace, love and compassion. Stay in this place as long as you need to.

I am standing in absolute stillness, silent before the one I love, waiting as long as it takes for him to rescue me. Only God is my Savior, and he will not fail me.
Psalm 62:5 (TPT)

January 19

Hanging On, or Letting Go

"Let go and grab my hand!"

"I can't!"

"You have to!"

After a final glance downward, she simultaneously releases her grip on the ledge and grabs the hand reaching down to her.

How many times have we watched a scene like this on a movie or TV show? Too many to count, right?

I was lying in bed, thinking about, and praying for the parents who are connected to GPS Hope, when that picture came to my mind.

I realized a mom who had been emailing me had just done this very thing in her grief journey. After six years, she had a light bulb moment. She had been hanging on to the sadness of her grief, thinking that is what was keeping her attached to her daughter. She finally saw that she had to release that sadness to be able to move forward with the life God was still giving her to live.

Once she chose to let go, a door that looked like had been closing in her life was swung open, giving some very needed direction she had been praying about. We were both amazed to see something happen that only God could have done!

I can say it over and over again, but the following has to become your own revelation:

You are not betraying your child by moving forward with your life!

It is not the pain of losing our child from this earth that keeps us connected to him or her. It is our *love*. It is the way we live our lives to honor them and keep their memory alive. It is knowing we still have a future with our child. You can and you should learn how to live a life of meaning and purpose again, without being cloaked in sadness.

Some of you are not at the point where this seems even remotely possible. Just like someone gripping a ledge while dangling high in the air, we only have so much strength and endurance to hold on to the pain, and it is a very scary thought to let go of it. That's okay.

Reflection: At some point, and I pray it is sooner rather than later, the same revelation will hit you as it did this mom. You will be able to let go of the ledge of sadness and grab ahold of the One who can pull you up out of that pit and give you a fulfilled life of meaning and purpose as you finish out your time here on earth.

Picture it. Picture yourself as the one afraid to let go of the ledge, because you aren't sure the hand on the other side will catch you. Then let go while you grab the hand and feel the relief of being pulled up to safety.

Now let yourself see that as a comparison to releasing the sadness that you believe connects you to your child. Start thinking about letting go of it, as you grab ahold of God's hand so that you can be pulled up to a better place within the darkness of grieving the death of your child; a place of meaning and purpose again in your life, where it is your *love* for your child that keeps you connected to him or her.

Even there your hand shall lead me, and your right hand shall hold me.
Psalm 139:10 (ESV)

January 20

A Scripture Just for Us!

Before my daughter died, there were so many verses that I could agree with, and cheer for as the truth in my life. But now, there are many verses that I need to dig into for a deeper meaning, because what I thought some of those scriptures meant, no longer made sense in my deep pain and confusion.

For instance, Ephesians 3:20 tells us that God is "able to do exceedingly abundantly beyond all that we ask or imagine, according to the power that works in us." I used to love that verse, because I could imagine a lot of good things and believed God would do even *more* than those great and wonderful things I could imagine! And that included awesome things for my kids. *Yahoo! How exciting!*

When the Holy Spirit showed me how to see that verse in a totally different way after Becca died, it became very precious to me. When we are in that place of suffocating darkness after the death of our child, we can't ever imagine coming out of the darkness. We can't imagine we can learn how to live a life of meaning and purpose without our child here. We can't imagine living out the rest of our lives in so much pain, just living in a shell wanting and waiting to die to go be with our child.

But God can! God not only imagines all of that, but He can also do way above and beyond what we thought was possible in our lives. So often we can only imagine darkness for the rest of our time here on earth. But He can do so much more than what we can imagine. He can bring light. He can bring hope. He can give us a life of meaning and purpose again, not in spite of our child's death, but because of his or her *life!*

How about you? Are you in a place of deep struggle, wondering how God could possibly tell us that He has so many good things for us? Is He lying to us? Was that just something to make us think He is good, to deceive us into believing in Jesus as our Savior? Let me answer that with a resounding no! God is good. Not only is He good, but He is perfect in all of His ways, or He would no longer be God. If I could turn Him into a magic genie to make my wishes come true, He would no longer be big enough to be God.

Reflections of Hope

It really comes down to a matter of trust. Do I trust that He can see what I cannot see? Do I trust that He can hear what I cannot hear? Do I believe that He knows the full picture, and that what I am going through fits into the plan of eternity, way beyond what my finite mind can comprehend of life here and now, on earth?

Reflection: If you cannot imagine ever having hope, light, or purpose in your life ever again, ask God to make good on this verse for you. He will. He is. Make the hard decision to *choose* to trust Him. If you are seeing the possibility of that already, then ask Him to continue working in your life in a way that is beyond what you can ask or imagine after the death of your child.

> *With God's power working in us, God can do much,*
> *much more than anything we can ask or imagine.*
> *Ephesians 3:20 (NCV)*

January 21

Going Backward

Do not be surprised if it feels like there are times you are going backward. I remember how often I would have what I considered a "good" day. Maybe I didn't cry at all. Or I was able to function with my family and not feel like I was in a total daze. Or I was able to get all my needed shopping done in one single trip out of the house.

Then from out of nowhere, I was right back at crying, feeling numb, and could barely get out of bed, much less leave the house.

Some of you may even be thinking, *I haven't even started going forward. I just keep going backward!* I know it feels that way, believe me, I know.

January

I kept feeling like I took three giant steps back for every baby step I took forward.

At the beginning, you feel like you have died yourself and you are just living in a shell. It feels like every part of you is completely out of your control. Then, ever so slowly, you will see some tiny bit of progress. It might continue, it might stop, or you may feel like you lost it.

Sometimes you may think: *Last week I could handle dealing with this specific thing, but this week I can't.* Then you convince yourself you are not getting any better and send yourself in a spiral downward. But as you keep going, one day at a time, suddenly there can be a giant leap forward.

Guess what? It might continue, it might stop, or you may feel like you lost it. Again...

That is just part of this crazy grief journey we are on. Yes, another thing that is *normal* for working through the grief that comes from the death of our child.

There is just no timeline and no rhyme or reason to any of it. I like the picture analogy of our grief being like a very tangled up ball of yarn, and each of us has our own individual mess of yarn to untangle.

If you have not felt like you have had any big leaps forward, don't allow yourself to get discouraged. You will, as you continue this unwanted journey. Give yourself *lots* of grace and don't compare where you are to *any* other pareavors. You are untangling your own ball of messy grief.

Reflection: If you have struggled, wondering if it will always be this way, ask the Holy Spirit to show you the little, tiny things that reveal you *are* working your way through it. It might be a smile you gave a stranger in the store, replacing a negative thought with a more positive one, playing a game with your kids, baking a batch of cookies (or even the fact that you are thinking about it) etc.

Just picking up this book to read it today shows that you are moving forward in some way. Keep bringing your darkness and your pain to

Reflections of Hope

God. Rest when you need to rest. Push through when that is what you feel you need to do. Those are *all* steps forward no matter how you *feel*.

> *We also pray that you will be strengthened with his glorious power so that you will have all the patience and endurance you need.*
> *Colossians 1:11 (NLT)*

January 22

How to Rest in God's Love

Here are four things that helped me be able to rest in God's love for me, even in the midst of my intense suffocating darkness, that I would like to pass on to you.

1. **Anytime you feel like you are sinking under the swirling waters, call out "Lord, save me!" just like Peter did in Matthew 14.** Whenever I did that, somehow Jesus always reached through the storm and pulled me up out of the drowning sea of emotions, into His secure arms, where I would feel like He was holding me. He knew how weak and helpless I was, and He never tired of meeting me in my place of need.

2. **Do whatever you need to do to be aware of His presence,** which might include playing some worship music, or just sitting in silence in a place of nature where there is beauty and peace. Not only would He "hold" me, but He would encourage me to relax in the awareness of His presence. Some of my most precious times with the Lord were in my greatest times of weakness, just letting everything go and melting into His peace, love, and compassion.

3. **Ask the Holy Spirit to show you some positive things that have happened because of the deep brokenness (no matter how small those things may be).** When I was only eight months into this journey, I asked God to do this for me, and I came up with a list

of eighteen things I saw Him working in me through the darkness, such as learning to become nonjudgmental (I didn't have time or energy - that kind of thing just wasn't important to me anymore), seeing the love and grace of God in a deeper way, becoming free of what man thinks of me, enjoying being in His presence (just resting and letting Him love on me), learning it's okay to be broken as a Christian and a leader, and so on.

4. **Be determined to live from a place of surrender.** This means we must learn to live from the spiritual part of our being—Christ in me and I in Him—and not out of our emotions or flesh. I always thought I did pretty good at that, but I have found a new level of living in it by tapping much more deeply into who God is in me. Here is something I wrote in my journal, eighteen months after Becca died.

4/21/13: This morning I just had to get to my prayer room, and there's been such a sweetness of just wanting to be here with Him. I finally put my finger on it: it is the contentment of surrender! I almost feel guilty for not being agitated or in some sort of emotional pain, but there is such a peace and contentment—very unnatural, and yet it should be natural, and I pray it has become a natural part of my life!

Reflection: I am guessing you were drawn to one of the four things above. Go back to it and read it again, deciding how you can act on it. You may have also felt repelled by one of them. Go back to that one as well. Ask the Holy Spirit to help you with it, knowing there may be some resistance. Fight it. Break through. You will be glad you did.

Take my yoke upon you. Let me teach you, because I am humble and gentle at heart, and you will find rest for your souls.
Matthew 11:29 (NLT)

January 23

Our Dark Feelings

Today I want us to think about a scripture that is familiar to most of us. Psalm 23:1 says "The Lord *Adonai* is my shepherd; I have everything I need. He has me lie down in grassy pastures, he leads me by quiet water, and he restores my inner person" (CJB).

God restores. He has everything we need. When we hear that, we might say, "I *need* my child back!" But we know that is not going to happen.

What many of us need is to get to the place where we stop asking God why and start asking Him how. "God, *how* are you going to get me through this? *How* are you going to be my shepherd and give me everything I need to live again, and not just live, but live a fulfilling life? *How* are you going to restore my inner person and heal these deep, deep wounds left by my child being amputated from me?"

You see, a person who has an amputation learns how to adapt; how to live with that part of them missing. I know this firsthand, because Becca, our daughter who left this earth, had her leg amputated when she was only three years old. It was horrible when it first happened, but she learned how to live with one leg missing and lived a very full life for the next twenty-six years.

Losing our child is like having an amputation. It is like a part of our very being has been cut off from us and we have to figure out how to live again with that part of us missing.

I can testify along with thousands of others that it can be done. You *can* have hope, that God is everything you need, *especially* after the death of your child. He *can* and wants to restore your soul.

Reflection: Don't try to hide from your feelings or pretend they aren't there. God wants you to bring all your feelings to Him, including the dark and negative ones. You may be wondering; *He knows these things already. Why should I have to tell Him how I am feeling?* Because you need to admit those things, so you can give them to God and let Him work with you at being set free.

If you do this persistently, those tormenting feelings of things like fear and anger will eventually lose their hold on you, and you will find yourself opening up once again to God's love and faithfulness to you through the worst trial you have ever faced, and find yourself starting to trust Him again to get you through it somehow.

Talk to God about those dark feelings and the need to change your perspective. Some of us need help even *wanting* to change it. If that's you, talk to Him about that as well.

> *The Lord Adonai is my shepherd; I have everything I need. He has me lie down in grassy pastures, he leads me by quiet water, and he restores my inner person.*
> *Psalm 23:1-3 (CJB)*

January 24

The Gift of Redemption

One day in my time with the Lord, I asked Him who He wanted to be for me right now, and the word, "Redeemer" instantly came to my thoughts. As I started meditating on that and asking God what He meant, I found myself writing His answer to me in my journal.

> *I want to take every hurt, every wound, every disappointment and bury it in Me and My Son, your redeemer. I want to redeem it all. I want to turn it into joy in your life. Yes, the theme of all death is redemption. I want to give a gift, but you need to be enlarged to receive it. Enlarged by a deeper revelation of my grace.*
>
> *Just like a store issues a coupon, it is given to the customer. And they either say "Thank you" and hold onto it, which has no value, or they turn it in to receive the benefit. I've issued the coupon, abundant life. But it is up to the receiver to cash it in. It*

> is a coupon that never expires and can also be handed in over and over and over and over again.

When we plant a seed, there is a time of waiting for it to break through the ground. Then as we continue taking care of it, we have to wait for it to start bearing fruit. This can take years, especially for fruit trees.

We have a seed inside us for everything we need in this life. That is part of the redemption process. The seed of hope is in you. The seed of peace is in you. But it is up to you to water and nourish those seeds to make those things grow. And yes, it can take a long time for it to feel like anything is happening.

Are you living from your soul or from your spirit? Living from our soul means we are living based on how we feel and what we think about the death of our child. Living from our spirit means we are choosing to live from a higher realm; from a place of being fully redeemed and the one our children are now living in.

God is in the business of redeeming. And that includes redeeming life from death. Our life. From when we felt like we died when our child died.

Reflection: Ask Him how to nourish the seeds that are already in you that may be lying dormant right now. You can start by praying the following words:

> *God, please take every hurt, every wound and every disappointment. I give them to you to be buried in Jesus, my redeemer. Help me to have a deeper understanding that in You, the theme of all death is redemption. Jesus, You died to give me life, not just in heaven, but here now, even after the death of my child. You paid a high price to redeem me, and I don't want to see that as something that has no value. You have already put in me everything I need. Show me how to nourish those seeds to help them grow. Thank you for the gift of life, both mine and my child's.* Amen.

> As you live this new life, we pray that you will be strengthened from God's boundless resources, so that you will find yourselves able to pass through any experience and endure it with courage.

You will even be able to thank God in the midst of pain and distress because you are privileged to share the lot of those who are living in the light. For we must never forget that he rescued us from the power of darkness and re-established us in the kingdom of his beloved Son, that is, in the kingdom of light. For it is by his Son alone that we have been redeemed and have had our sins forgiven.
Colossians 1:11-14 (PHILLIPS)

January 25

Compelled to Say I Am Sorry

I sometimes hear from those of you who are still quite early and fresh in your grief, that your pastor or a spiritual leader has said you should not still be in such a deep place of grief and need to be getting past the sadness.

I had a similar experience. I was a mess after Becca died. My pastor at the time accused me of having a "Jezebel spirit" because I was struggling to do everything he thought I should (or should not) be doing. At the time, I was spending hours every day in my little prayer room under the basement steps, literally crying out to God, trying my best to stay close to Him, much more than I was concerned about "obeying" a pastor.

This pastor accused my husband of not being a good enough leader in the home, saying that is why our family was such a mess. He did not seem to be allowing us to work through our grief. We were just supposed to blindly submit to his authority, because he was supposedly hearing from God on our behalf and because we were not allowing God to give us the victory in our circumstance.

One day I received a text message from his wife, telling me I was not welcome to attend services there anymore, until I was willing to submit under his leadership. It devastated our family and tore us apart. One of my children decided he was right, and she had nothing to do with us for three years as she remained "submitted" to him and his wife. (She has

Reflections of Hope

since left and is back with the family, but a *lot* of damage was done by his abuse of spiritual authority in her life for a total of six years.)

Later, at a very small conference, a righteous and compassionate spiritual leader heard about it, and did something for me that I want to do for you. He repented on behalf of the pastor who had wronged me and he and prayed over me, to break the heaviness that I was still carrying from it.

Reflection: As an ordained minister myself, I want to stand in the gap and repent on behalf of anyone's pastor or spiritual leader (or anyone else in your life) who has wronged you in such a way.

In the precious name of Jesus, the One who died to set us free, I release you from all guilt, wondering if you are wrong to grieve so deeply. I release you from any shame of not meeting the standards of a spiritual leader's thoughts of where you should be in your grief journey. I release you from the burden of not being able to "get the victory" over the darkness of your loss as quickly as someone (including yourself) thinks you should. I speak freedom over your mind, your soul, and your spirit from the heaviness of not being able to be a "good enough" Christian in your deep grief.

Holy Spirit, wash over each person reading this with peace, until they feel the overwhelming power of Your refreshing, healing touch. Restore their inner most being. Heal the wounds that were given by those who disobeyed You, by not weeping with those who weep. Saturate each one in Your love - a love that has no expectations.

Remind them that You are weeping with them, and that their tears are so precious to you that you are saving them in a bottle. And help all of us to forgive those who either abandoned us, criticized us, or judged us for how much we miss our children. Amen!

If you cannot relate to this because you have had a wonderful support system from your spiritual leadership and church family, take a minute to thank God for that huge blessing. Then write and send them a note, telling them thank you and how much you appreciate them.

> *For the Lord has comforted his people and will*
> *have compassion on them in their suffering.*
> *Isaiah 49:13 (NLT)*

January 26

This is Not Permanent

One thing I wish I had grasped sooner that has helped me, is that this is only a temporary separation. I knew that in my head, but for some reason my heart had a much harder time accepting that as a truth I could hold onto, to pull me out of my darkness. All I could see is that my daughter is not with me now, and how unfair and painful that was to me, to her dad, her siblings and grandparents. All I could think about was what she would miss, and what we would miss not having her here with us. In fact, looking back on it, I was almost consumed with the thoughts of what I had lost from this earth. There were times I could barely breathe from the pain of it.

But God in His graciousness stepped in over and over again, as I laid my pain at His feet, groaning and sobbing to Him for help.

I cannot talk about the separation from our children not being permanent without also bringing in 2 Corinthians 4:18. "We don't focus our attention on what is seen but on what is unseen. For what is seen is temporary, but the unseen realm is eternal." (TPT)

The VOICE translation says we "focus on the things we cannot see, which live on and on." That is now very exciting to me; to think that our children are already in the place where nothing harmful or hurtful can ever touch them again.

I love how the Message Bible says it.

> *So we're not giving up. How could we! Even though on the outside it often looks like things are falling apart on us, on the inside, where God is making new life, not a day goes by without his unfolding grace. These hard times are small potatoes compared to the coming good times, the lavish celebration prepared for us. There's far more here than meets the eye. The things we see now are here today, gone tomorrow. But the things we can't see now will last forever. 2 Corinthians 4:16-18 (MSG)*

Reflection: Take time to absorb the verse above, one phrase at a time, letting its light soak into your darkness. Maybe even rewrite it, making it a personal declaration. (*I am not giving up. How could I? Even though on the outside it often looks like things are falling apart on me, ...etc.*)

What we are going through now will seem like nothing, once we join our children in heaven and partake in the glory they are now part of. There really is "far more here than meets the eye."

> *Whatever was written beforehand is meant to instruct us in how to live. The Scriptures impart to us encouragement and inspiration so that we can live in hope and endure all things.*
> *Romans 15:4 (TPT)*

January 27

I Feel Like God Betrayed Me

Mary and Martha must have felt so betrayed by God. They sent for Jesus when Lazarus was sick, but their brother died because Jesus *purposely* stayed put for three days before heading to them! Both sisters questioned Jesus. "If you had come, he wouldn't have died! Why didn't you come and heal him???" (You can find this in John 11:21,32.)

They *knew* Jesus could have healed their brother because they followed him. They watched Jesus do miracles constantly. He did *so* many miracles they could not all be recorded (John 20:30), meaning there are hundreds of miracles we do not even know about!

"It's our turn! We need a miracle, now!" This time, it was not just some stranger reaching out to Jesus. Lazarus, Mary, and Martha were some of his closest friends. He often stopped at their house for a meal or to stay overnight.

January

But Jesus knew there was something greater to happen through the death of Lazarus than through a miraculous healing. Yes, I am going there... just hear me out.

One evening, while talking to a group of pareavors online, I found myself in tears as I had the realization that I am doing what I do today because Becca *did not* receive the miraculous healing that she needed for her heart.

I do not have to tell you how devastated I was and the darkness it put me in when she died. I held on to God with everything I had, like Jacob wrestling with the angel, telling Him I was not going to let go until He miraculously turned it around for me to see some kind of a blessing on the other side of this. That seemed like a crazy thing to fight for, because how is it even remotely possible to have a blessing in my life as a result of something so horrific as my daughter's death?????

But here I am. It's hard to explain how fulfilled and blessed I feel, to be a light to thousands of grieving parents who find themselves in the same darkness I was once in, through the ministry of GPS Hope. Does it make me glad Becca died so I can be doing this? ABSOLUTELY NOT! I would trade it all instantly to have her back with me here on earth, but I can't.

God did not betray me and He did not betray you! This might be impossible to believe right now, but He has something *for* you that goes *beyond* the death of your child. Just like Lazarus, just like me with Becca, and just like thousands of pareavors ahead of you, Jesus knows something greater can happen through the death of your precious child, than through a miraculous healing or His hand of protection we so desperately wanted for them.

I know what you are probably thinking. *Maybe God turned your daughter's death into something good for you, Laura, but I don't see that ever happening for me!* That is okay if you cannot see it for yourself right now. I (and other parents who have been right where you are) will be your eyes to see it and your hope to believe it, until you have your own hope to believe and your own eyes to see.

Reflection: In our darkness, we are waiting a long time because God is doing a deep work in each of us. He will even let us be angry with Him and believe He has betrayed us, as He is at work in our darkness.

Just like Lazarus, Jesus knows something greater can happen through the death of your precious child, than through a miraculous healing or His hand of protection that we so desperately wanted for each of them.

No, God did not kill your child to teach you a lesson. He just knows that at some point, the *eternal* fruit of their departure outweighs the *eternal* fruit of them staying here. The most frustrating part is that not all of us will get to see what that is, while here on this earth. But you can be sure that God has an eternal plan that was set in motion by the death of your child before he or she was even a thought to you.

Ask the Holy Spirit to help you believe that the eternal fruit of your child's death is a powerful thing that can eventually outweigh the belief that God betrayed you by not keeping your child here on earth. Even if you don't get to see that fruit until you join him or her.

His light broke through the darkness and he led us out in freedom from death's dark shadow and snapped every one of our chains.
Psalm 107:14 (TPT)

January 28

I Am Not Who I Was

As Christians, we can tend to think that we are exempt from the sorrows of the world. We treat God like He is a genie in a lamp, where we can just rub it by saying the right prayer, and He will pop out saying, "Your wish is my command." But it does not work like that. If that's how God worked (that I could just pray, and He would give me whatever I wanted) then He is not God anymore. I am God and He is restricted to doing what I tell Him to do.

January

One of the things that I have learned is that if my faith is in the answer to my prayer, I'm going to fall apart when I don't get the answer that I am wanting. But if my faith is knowing intimately and trusting the One to whom I pray, that is when I can stand. My faith will not be shattered, because it's not based on getting a certain answer. It is based on trusting God with the results of that answer.

Something Oswald Chambers says in the book *My Utmost for His Highest* is, "Whenever the insistence is on the point that God answers prayer, we are off track. The meaning of prayer is that we get ahold of God, not the answer."

We know that when our child dies, we're never the same. There is a dividing line of before and after, and we'll never go back to being who we were. I have realized it's the same thing with my relationship with God. There was a dividing line in my relationship with my Heavenly Daddy when Becca died, and our relationship will never be the same. But to be honest, I would never want it to go back. Believe it or not, I have heard that same thing from many other bereaved parents.

Some of you reading this may be thinking, "I don't see myself ever getting to that place. I mean, how can I ever trust God again? He betrayed me!"

When our child dies, we feel like everything we thought we knew about God was wrong. That means we have to reevaluate and rediscover who God *really* is. As we search, we eventually find out there is a stability in God. There is a deep love and comfort. And we discover that He is *so* much bigger than we ever knew He was. And all those things we *thought* we knew about God? Now we *know*. We personally and intimately know these things about who God is, because we are seeing it through a totally different heart and eyes.

There *is* something beyond the death of our child that God has for each one of us. And yes, I know it's really hard for you to see it or believe it when you are in that darkness of grief. But You and I have the incredible blessing to get to truly know the God of the universe *intimately* in a way that few others have the opportunity.

Reflection: Would I rather have Becca in my life? I admit that there are times I do. But since that is not going to happen, I might as well press in and continue getting to know God in new and wonderful ways.

I believe with everything in me that someday you will get to the same place. Even if you are angry right now and feel God cannot be trusted, I encourage you to take a moment and tell Him you want to know Him beyond what you are feeling. Let the dividing line of "before and after" become something you would not want to go back to either, because you have gotten ahold of God and know Him intimately in a way that you did not even know was possible.

> *But as for me, I get as close to him as I can! I have chosen him, and I will tell everyone about the wonderful ways he rescues me.*
> *Psalm 73:28 (TLB)*

January 29

A Measure of Healing

With the death of our child comes such intense darkness. Most of us lose our desire to live. We know it sounds crazy, especially those of us who have other children, spouses we love deeply, careers we enjoyed, and so on. But we just feel so lost and helpless when our child leaves this earth. There are no words to adequately describe the depth of our pain and darkness, confusion and turmoil.

We must go *through* the grieving and mourning process. We cannot go around it. And it always takes so much longer than we want it to or think it will. I remember two years into my grief saying, "I just want to stop hurting so bad!". Since that time, I have had several pareavors tell me the same thing.

When Becca died, I tried to find books and online groups to help pull me out of the suffocating darkness, but so much of what was out there was despair and hopelessness, telling me that life would never be the same and never be worth living. I knew I would never be the same, but I had a hard time with hearing that my life would never be worth living any more.

January

Something I found which helps with this process was to discover a cause.

One night I woke up in the middle of the night with a book title and ideas for chapters. I got up and wrote it down, and shortly after, started on my first book. One day at a conference, I ended up in a conversation with a New York publisher who asked me to send what I had his way, and five weeks later was offered a contract for *When Tragedy Strikes: Rebuilding Your Life with Hope and Healing After the Death of Your Child*. Once I started writing, it was like a dam inside of me burst, as I published five books in only thirteen months!

During this time, people I did not even know started reaching out to me to help them with the loss of *their* child (and a couple of friends who suffered losses shortly after us). I realized I did not want other parents to have the same struggle I had after Becca's death, only finding darkness and hopelessness. So, Grieving Parents Sharing Hope (GPS Hope) was founded.

I can't even begin to describe what all of this has done for me in the healing process! And I am convinced from the dozens of parents I have talked to directly, reaching out of your pain to help someone else will do the same for you.

Reflection: Do not let the death of your child be wasted. What was something he or she strongly believed in? Can you do something to fight their cause of death to prevent others from going through what you are going through? Did he or she have a favorite sport or activity that you can get behind, raising and donating money or starting a scholarship fund in his or her name?

If you are like I was, crying out "I just want to stop hurting so bad!", maybe it's time to find a way to honor the life of your child in a way that helps others make their life better, allowing it to ease some of the pain as you move forward to a place of hope and light again. It will also be a step toward living a life of meaning and purpose again.

Ask God what that might be, and then take the first step.

> *God-of-the-Angel-Armies speaks: Exactly as I planned, it will happen. Following my blueprints, it will take shape.*
> *Isaiah 14:24 (MSG)*

January 30
Our Scars

When I was three years old, I was riding on the handlebars of a bike my dad was peddling, and got my ankle caught in the spokes. It took out a good chunk of my ankle and I was taken to the emergency room. The injury turned into a staph infection, causing some muscle and skin to deteriorate.

I remember that summer heading to Wisconsin to visit family. My sister and cousins all got to have fun in a local swimming pool. All I got to do was dangle my good leg into the water, while keeping my injured leg up on the deck wrapped in a bread bag to keep it dry. I totally recovered, but my right ankle is weaker than the left, because of the loss of muscle. I still have a scar on that ankle and always will.

At age 48 my husband, Dave, ended up having quadruple bypass surgery. Recovery took a long time. Over thirteen years later he still has some effects from it, along with permanent scars, reminding us of what he went through.

Here is the big one. How about my daughter Becca's amputation she had at age three? Becca obviously had a scar on her stump where her leg was cut off.

Did having a staph infection in my ankle keep me from ever swimming again? No way! I love to swim and be in the water (especially in warm places with beautiful beaches).

Did Dave's heart surgery keep him in bed for the rest of his life? No. It may limit some of his activities, but he lives a very full life, keeping up with me, driving the Hope Mobile (our house on wheels) and doing much of the behind-the-scenes things for our ministry to grieving parents.

Did having an amputation keep Becca from running and playing with the other children? No, it did not. It may have slowed her down and caused her to adapt to how she ran and how she played, but it did not stop her.

When these horrible things happen, including something as terrible as the death of our child, does it mean our life is over, and we will never be able to live a full life again? No, it does not.

We need time to go through a "recovery" process (for lack of a better word) and need time to learn how to function with our child no longer here, but it does not mean we will never be able to function again.

- We will go through times when everyone around us is splashing and playing while we are unable to participate because of our wounds.
- We will go through times when we cannot function and have to wait for more healing.
- We will go through times when we have to adjust the way we do things.

We will forever bear the scar of our tragedy. We will always have things that trigger reminders. But we are not permanently injured to the point of being out of commission for the rest of our lives.

Reflection: Do you have a scar somewhere on your body? Take a look at it. That injury may have caused you to adapt the way you do things for a while, or even permanently, but it probably didn't keep you from still having a full and functioning life.

Our child has been amputated from us and we *can* learn how to live again with that part of us missing. You will never be the same, but it does not mean you will never be able to live a fulfilled life again. Our scars mean we will never forget, but they do not mean we will never be able to function again.

Ask God to wash over you with the healing balm of His love. Allow Him to bring the needed healing so you can begin to splash around in the waters of life again. Ask Him to teach you how to walk, and maybe even run once again. There will always be a scar and a limp, but it can be done. If a three-year-old child can figure it out, so can we.

> *There is hope for a tree that has been cut down;*
> *it can come back to life and sprout.*
> *Job 14:7 (GNT)*

January 31
Making Hard Choices

When our child died, it was obviously not our choice!

- Going through the darkness of grief is not our choice.
- The pain that cannot be described is not our choice.
- The way our brain is scrambled for so long and we cannot think straight, is not our choice.

I could go on, but you know exactly what I am talking about.

Unfortunately, there are no shortcuts to getting off the path of this nightmarish journey we found ourselves thrown onto. But today's reading is not about the things we cannot control and the choices we cannot make. It is about the choices we *can* make.

At the beginning, grief takes over EVERYTHING. But as the weeks and months (and years) go by, we find ourselves able to make small choices.

- We may choose to cook a small meal (instead of having fast food again or a bowl of cereal).
- We may choose to try and go out for coffee with a friend (in public).
- We may choose to pick up our Bible and try to read it (and sometimes put it right back down, for various reasons).

When you get to that point of being able to start making some choices, I want to help you move forward, so here is a key that might help you. Instead of choosing to be *against* something, choose to be *for* something.

For instance, you can either choose to be *against* facing another week because you cannot bear being away from your child for longer than you already have. OR you can be *for* going through this next week because it gets you that much closer to being reunited with your child.

January

You can choose to be *against* spending time with a friend, because you feel guilty for doing something that might be enjoyable when your child cannot have any fun with his or her friends anymore. OR you could choose to be *for* spending time with your friend because:

- You might get a chance to talk about your son or daughter with someone who will listen.
- Having an enjoyable evening might be like a needed medicine to your soul.
- You can picture your child watching you enjoy yourself, and seeing you smile (and maybe even laugh), realizing it would make them happy instead of seeing you so horribly angry and miserable.

That sounds and feels so much better to me. How about you? For or against?

Reflection: It can help to write down at least one thing you are going to ask God to help you choose to do *for* a good reason, instead of continuing to choose against something that keeps you paralyzed in your grief.

I choose to _____.

And if you can't think of something to flip around to do for a good reason, instead of being against it and remaining in the pain of it, ask the Holy Spirit to show you one.

> *I am now giving you the choice between life and death,*
> *between God's blessing and God's curse, and I call heaven*
> *and earth to witness the choice you make. Choose life.*
> *Deuteronomy 30:19 (GNT)*

February

February 1
Don't Be So Hard on Yourself

It is important to remind all of us not to be too hard on ourselves when we don't do what we thought we should do ... or needed to do ... or wanted to do.

Our energy is definitely limited, and there are going to be days when our sorrow is just too heavy to do anything else but grieve. During heavy grief, time gets away from us. It is pretty amazing how time can go so slow and so fast simultaneously, isn't it, as we sit and stare into space or cry in our beds? We also easily get distracted within our grief, especially the first couple of years as our minds wander.

And it is especially okay not to be conflicted within yourself when others are putting expectations on you that you are unable to meet right now. Then it is even *more* important to take care of yourself and be okay with where you are in your grief journey. Those of us who have lost a child will not tell you where you should be and what you should be doing (or shouldn't be doing) by a certain time. Do *not* allow others who have never experienced the death of their own child lay a guilt trip on you, for not meeting *their* unrealistic timeline.

It is also important to remind yourself that as you start to work your way out of the darkness you can fall right back into it quite easily, especially those first five years or so.

We are all going to continue to have those days (and weeks) where we struggle, even if it has been a while and it takes you by surprise because you thought you were finally past that part of the grief journey.

Do what you can and let go of what you can't.

From one bereaved parent to another, I give you permission.

Reflection: Something that can take a lot out of us are the "I should have's..." beating ourselves up with all the regrets. My friend, Glen Lord, tells other parents to stop "shoulding" on themselves. Regrets are chains that keep us bound. I am quite confident that you did the best you knew how, with the information you had at the time.

If you were talking to another grieving parent, would you be in agreement with them about the things they think they should have done? *Yes, you are right, you should have done that! You were a terrible parent, and I am sure your child up in heaven is really upset with you about that!*

Of course not! So why are you talking to yourself that way? *Let yourself off the hook*, just like you would do for another parent. Stop making excuses on why what *you* did, was not okay.

Ask God to help you stop looking back at the things you think you should (or shouldn't) have done for your child, and let Him show you what you did right, and good and even wonderful. I guarantee there are lots of these, because of the deep love you have for your child.

Since God cares for you, let Him carry all your burdens and worries.
1 Peter 5:7 (VOICE)

February 2

Giving Up

Yes, I still have days where I just want to go back to bed and ignore life! Today is one of those days.

What do I do when those days hit? Well, for me personally, first, I cry. Tears have always come easily to me, which has been both a curse and a blessing. And now that I have had a good cry, I want to climb back into bed even more, because as we all know, that can be very draining.

But deep down, I also want to get past this roadblock that has me feeling overwhelmed and ready to give up on lots of things right now.

So, I found myself writing an email to someone, dumping out all of my woes and frustrations, which did three things.

1. It let me see that the things I am upset about really are valid (or not...).
2. It got it out of my system, keeping me from holding on to it. When I hold on to things like this:
   a. I start seeing myself as a victim and having a martyr mentality (which no one around me appreciates, for good reason).
   b. I am affected physically, and my body starts to shut down. The longer I hold on to it, the longer it takes me to recover.
3. I found I gave myself a different way of looking at it, and possible solutions to get around some of these frustrations.

After I reread the page and a half that I had written to my friend, I canceled the email instead of sending it! Why? Because she really did not need to have me dump on her like that, and I felt better, so it didn't need to be sent.

The next time you are feeling that overwhelming sense of, "I can't do this! I can't go on!" or "I give up!" I suggest having a good cry (if you are like me), and then tell someone in writing what is going on inside you. You don't have to be an author or good at grammar. Just write it out. Write to *me*, if you want to.

When you read through what you have written and have had a release, do not send it, for the same reasons I didn't.

And then if you need to go back to bed, do that, too. Because this grief journey really *is* about you, especially if you are in the first couple of years and in survival mode.

Reflection: On a scale of 1-10, where are you right now on feeling like you want to give up? No matter how low that number is, please allow yourself to be encouraged that it *is* possible to get into the higher numbers eventually.

What is something you can physically do as self-care before the end of the day to release some of the pressure to make you feel better? I suggest something physical, because that will spill over into making us feel better emotionally, mentally and even spiritually. It doesn't have to be big, either. How about a walk around the block; or a nice warm bath with candles; or only eat two cookies instead of eight. I can't emphasize enough how important self-care is in our grief, especially when we don't care one bit about what happens to us.

He strengthens those who are weak and tired.
Isaiah 40:29 (GNT)

February 3

Feeding Your Soul

I know it can be really hard to do, but it is important to find ways to feed our souls (which is our mind, our emotions and our will) as we grieve the deaths of our children. Fortunately, there are several ways of doing that. One of them is through the gift of music.

God created music to be a pathway to the soul. What we choose to listen to will affect our emotions and will either keep us in that place of deep grief and darkness, or help us see a glimmer of light and hope to take a step forward.

I have made myself several play lists on YouTube. When I find a song that makes me feel hopeful, I add it to my "hope" list, which I will play through when struggling with feeling hopeless. I have a "peace" list for when I am feeling the turmoil of my grief, a list of songs that allow me to miss Becca when I need that release, a list of just instrumental music, and so on.

Another way to feed our souls is through reading. Maybe you aren't a reader by nature, but reading is truly a great way to "meet" other bereaved parents who will confirm:

- You are not going crazy with early dementia.
- Still being a mess (even after a few years) is normal for someone who has lost a child.
- All of those confusing things you are being told by well-meaning people around you just aren't true.
- *Things will eventually get better.*

When Becca first died, I was hesitant to connect with others who were a mess like me. I thought it would make me worse. And unfortunately, there *were* some that I talked to who were stuck and told me I would always be a mess, and there were books I read that came across as though my life would never be worth living again.

However, I refused to believe those things, and kept looking for those who would give me hope. It turned out, they are out there, and now I am one of them, writing books to offer hope to other grieving parents who are looking for it, while still acknowledging the suffocating darkness that comes with the death of a child.

Reflection: Have you stopped listening to music? Maybe it's hard for you to connect with worship music right now, but there is still so much out there that can give you strength when you need it. I highly recommend that you put together a few music lists you can play when you are struggling.

Take a minute and think about where your greatest struggles are. Talk to God about it and ask the Holy Spirit to help you put a couple of music lists together. Maybe have a list called, "Can't sleep" with music (or people you like to hear teach) that you can play at night when needed or make some lists like the ones I mentioned. There is no right or wrong music, as long as it helps you take the steps needed for that moment with that struggle.

> *He is my strength, and He is the reason I sing;*
> *He has been there to save me in every situation.*
> *Psalm 118:14 (VOICE)*

February 4

Extremely Forgetful

Extreme trauma and deep bereavement, such as the death of your child, changes a person. It literally makes physical changes in us, including chemical changes in our brains, which totally affects our thoughts and how our minds operate.

I became so forgetful it drove me crazy, especially the first two or three years. I would get so frustrated with myself at the things I would forget, things I would misplace, things I did not or could not remember and at my constant confusion and fuzziness. It took me quite a while to find out that was a normal part of intense grief.

I started speaking over myself according to 1 Corinthians 2:16, "I have the mind of Christ" and 2 Timothy 1:7, "I have a sound mind". Eventually the fog began to clear, and I wasn't quite so scattered and forgetful.

After several years, I have to be honest and say I still don't have a clear mind like I did before. It can be very frustrating at times. Friends have tried to encourage me by saying things like "Oh, I forget things too." But this is not the same thing as just getting forgetful with age. We have been through a traumatic event, and our minds just freeze, forgetting how to function at times. I keep giving it to God and do not allow myself to be stressed out about it.

What was happening with me physically and in my mind during the worst of my grieving period those first couple of years seemed so much greater than my strength to get through it. In a very real sense, the mental and emotional "energy" of grief saps brain power and leaves a person quite disoriented and unable to hold a thought for very long.

Getting our minds back is a process! It takes time. Do not try to look too far ahead. It is exhausting and overwhelming. Do the next thing you can do, whatever it is, no matter how small it is—that's it. Just one thing at a time. You have permission to give yourself lots and lots of grace, *especially* when others do not!

Reflection: I truly mean it when I say to give yourself grace on this journey, especially when you get frustrated with yourself for things that are out of your control (like the grief fog we struggle with). May I suggest praying those same two scriptures over yourself.

Also, ask the Holy Spirit for extra protection from your forgetfulness. For instance, yesterday I was in a downtown area of a large city with a pareavor who is barely in her second year of grief. She went to purchase something but was surprised and confused to discover she did not have her wallet. Walking back to the car to get it, she discovered it was just sitting on the roof of her car, with *nothing missing*. I believe that was God, looking out for her!

I know it is so very frustrating but be encouraged that the worst of it will begin to pass, usually around the third or fourth year.

For God has not given us a spirit of fear,
but of power and of love and of a sound mind.
2 Timothy 1:7 (NKJV)

February 5

A Wise Investment

Sitting alone to "chat" with the Lord and just be in His presence, anywhere from a few minutes to several hours a day is one of the things that pulled me out of the darkness quicker than anything I could have done. I am no spiritual giant. But somehow, I knew that no matter how much pain I was in, God was the only hope I had of surviving the devastating and horrific blow I had received in this life.

Quiet time is not an excuse for the lazy, but a wise investment for the diligent. (Priscilla Shirer)

I love this! No guilt trip about whether we have a daily "quiet time" or devotional time with God. Just the simple truth that it is an investment. It is an investment into ourselves for the exact moment and place we find ourselves in, and also for the unknown future.

It is in this place where we feel His grace flow freely, and where our spirit and soul receive a measure of healing, (even though we often don't feel any of that healing because it takes so long, and the wound is so very deep). Needed adjustments are made within ourselves, in relationships, and in the confusing and painful circumstances.

I personally felt like Peter, after people were offended by something Jesus said and the entire crowd walked away except for the His immediate followers. Jesus asked them, "You do not want to leave too, do you?"

No matter where you are in your grief journey, I pray you have the same answer. "Lord, to whom shall we go? You have the words of eternal life" (John 6:68).

I often like to read different versions of scriptures that speak to me. Here are how four of them translate John 6:68.

- You have the words of real life, eternal life. (MSG)
- You have words that give life that lasts forever. (NLV)
- No one but you gives us the revelation of eternal life. (TPT)
- You [alone] have the words of eternal life [you are our only hope]. (AMP)

Reflection: Even if we are angry at God and blaming Him for what happened, it's okay to have it out with Him and have "chats" with Him about it. It doesn't have to be a set time, but whenever you have the urge to say something to Him, just say it. And if you have the chance, take a minute and be silent to see what He speaks back to you in reply. Listen for that still small voice. It will probably feel like it comes from your own thoughts, but it is not something you would have thought of yourself.

Try it right now. Tell God how you feel, or ask Him a question, and then sit still. Sometimes it works better to write it down, and then let your pen flow with whatever comes to your mind. Do not try to edit it; don't try to change it. Just let the words flow until nothing else comes. Then go back and read it to yourself. When I do this, I am often amazed at what is on the page in front of me, and I know there is no way I thought of those words. If He does it for me, He will do it for you because I am not any more special to Him than you are.

Come near to God and He will come near to you.
James 4:8 (NIV)

February 6

It is Okay to Rest

We bought and moved into our house on wheels, the summer of 2018 and pulled out that October. I distinctly remember sitting in the passenger seat, looking behind me, and thinking how surreal it was that Dave was driving our house! (I still feel that way at times several years later.)

Honestly, the transition went even better than we thought it would and it has been extremely rewarding. But even though that first year in the Hope Mobile went great, I realized there were some things that got lost in the transition that I needed to get back into my life. One of the big ones was to remind myself that there are times that it's okay to just rest.

We need to realize that just like someone who has had major surgery needs time to do nothing but rest and recover, we need to rest and recover from the "surgery" of our child being cut off from us. It isn't a matter of "getting the victory" over it, which is an area I struggled with. I felt guilty that first year for not being able to get the victory over my sadness and move on, in grieving the death of my daughter. I now know that is crazy, and don't want you to struggle with the same kind of guilt.

February

It is easy for me to convince myself that people are counting on me, so I must stay on top of things, not giving myself the same grace that I tell others to give to themselves.
I need to remember I am in this for the long-haul, and that keeping up with doing things for those I am serving can be hard on me. There are times when I need to take off to get some rest and refresh myself, to be able to effectively minister to other pareavors in their grief. There are also simply times I need a break for my own grief, of losing my daughter from this earth.

We all need times of rest, not just those first few years, but for our time remaining here on earth.

Reflection: It's easier to give someone else grace who is going through a difficult circumstance than give grace to ourselves, isn't it? As moms, we can tend to feel guilty for not doing more. As a grieving mom, that guilt can be amplified, because we are usually doing *so* much less than we did before.

If you have other children, or things like responsibilities at work, finding time to rest (or just plain crash) can be a really hard balance to find. The thing to remember is that you must take care of yourself, even if we don't want to (or we tell ourselves we just can't). Right now, just take some deep breaths, and allow yourself to rest in the quietness of this moment.

> *Then, because so many people were coming and going that*
> *they did not even have a chance to eat, he said to them,*
> *"Come with me by yourselves to a quiet place and get some rest".*
> *Mark 6:31 (NIV)*

February 7

A Heart Transplant

When Becca died, it felt like my heart wasn't just broken, but it had shattered into millions of pieces and could never be put back together. It literally hurt and affected other parts of my body, including my mind. I wondered if I would literally die from a broken heart, and I even wanted to be gone from this world. (I think almost all of you can relate?)

I now know that is "normal" grief for a parent who has lived through the death of their child and that it is considered traumatic grief for a parent who has had to bury their child.

How is it even possible to live with our hearts damaged so deeply they can never be put back together the way they were before the death of our child? Here is something I wrote in my journal five months after my heart and life were shattered.

> *I have been thinking about how I am in the process of healing from a heart transplant.... When I think of what I know of Becca's 3 surgeries, I can see the parallels. I am recovering from heart surgery, and it's okay to have the all-over emotions that I do right now. It will get better as I heal! Thank You, Holy Spirit.*

The heart is a vital organ. If the heart is not working right, the entire body is affected. That isn't just our physical heart, but the heart of our soul and emotions. When our heart is "taken out" from the death of our child, we are going to have to allow lots of time for our healing, and during that time, learn how to actively move toward our healing (just like being in physical therapy after a literal heart surgery).

Some days moving toward our healing means staying in bed and sleeping, allowing ourselves the rest needed to recover. Other times we *must* get up and do the painful therapy needed to move toward strengthening, if not for ourselves, for those who love us; those who want and *need* us in their lives.

Reflection: Take a few minutes to allow The Great Physician to hold your heart, gently and lovingly doing the needed surgery to repair the brokenness. See yourself as a patient, healing from a needed heart transplant, allowing Him to be at work on healing your very deeply wounded heart.

Is it time for rest, or is it time to push through on the therapy, doing something that may be difficult, but necessary? When we are weak, He is strong. And with how weak we are, that must be some strength!

He sent His word and healed them, and rescued them from their pits.
Psalm 107:20 (TLV)

February 8

Light in Our Place of Darkness

After we lost Becca, I began to study the physical changes deep grief causes in our bodies. I wrote about it in my book *Come Grieve Through Our Eyes*.

> *I did not know until a year and a half after Becca's death that a person can literally have a broken heart. It affects the left ventricle, even changing the shape of the heart, as part of the heart temporarily enlarges and doesn't pump well, while the rest of the heart functions normally or with even more forceful contractions. And as a note, based on the research I have done, it happens almost exclusively with women. It causes heart attack-like symptoms, and is called broken heart syndrome, stress-induced cardiomyopathy or takotsubo cardiomyopathy (based on its official discovery in Japan). Other names for it are transient apical ballooning syndrome, apical ballooning cardiomyopathy, and, Gebrochenes-Herz-Syndrome. With all of those names, how did I not know it existed?*

The deep grief of the death of our child also compromises our immune system and causes our brains to "misfire," bringing much confusion, disorientation and forgetfulness that is very scary at times. It can be so bad, that many of us think we have an early onset of Alzheimer's disease. I was still somewhat dealing with those things five or six years later (and still do, when there is a trigger than affects me deeply).

There are no words to describe the suffocating darkness we find ourselves in after our child dies. For most parents, especially the mothers, it can take several years to see much of anything penetrate through the darkness. And it doesn't help when people start telling us after a few months that we need to start getting past our grief, or that we should be "over it" by now.

Grief is not an event; it is a process. And grieving the death of a child is definitely a life-long process.

I am so very thankful that the death of our children did not blindside God. He knew the exact moment each of our children would leave this earth, and He also knew the darkness that would come over us and had a plan to bring light into that darkness through the Holy Spirit living inside us.

Reflection: In His love, mercy and compassion, God made a way for us to have life again, beyond the death of our child. But it starts with His Light, making such a tiny pinhole we often don't even realize it is there.

If the Holy Spirit is in you, God's light is in you. Take a minute and allow that light to penetrate the darkness. Close your eyes, picture His light and His glory flowing through every part of your body, including your heart and your mind. Let it flood your soul. Then thank Him that He has not left you in your place of suffocating darkness.

You, Lord, keep my lamp burning;
my God turns my darkness into light.
Psalm 18:28 (NIV)

February 9

Still Angry

"I will say I am still very angry at God. I've not been able to pray any longer. My heart aches for God at the same time my anger prevails." This was part of a recent email I received, from someone who lost her son over four years ago.

One of the things I hear about the most from pareavors, is how much they struggle with anger. It can be especially hard to quiet ourselves in the presence of God, and to try to shut down our thoughts for Him to be able to fill us with peace, because we are so filled with our pain.

We also tend to gravitate toward bathing our pain in pain. And sometimes we have to step outside of that and figure out how to steep ourselves in something that's good.

Maybe it's music, either listening to it or playing an instrument. Maybe it's art or doing a craft of some kind. It's not necessarily just sitting down and praying or trying to read your Bible, but it is immersing yourself in something that is constructive, not destructive.

The bottom line is that it is normal and okay to be angry with God for not stopping the death of your child. But you need to go through the process of working out that anger, because you cannot work through your grief without also working through your anger. One of the best ways to help with that is to immerse yourself in things that are good.

When we immerse ourselves in positivity instead of negativity, it changes how we look at things, and that's a powerful place to start.

Reflection: If you haven't talked to God about your anger, go ahead and do it right now. Let Him know how angry you are. Then ask Him to show you what activity you can do that will begin to diffuse some of that anger; something constructive that when you are done, you feel good about what you have just accomplished.

There is a scripture in Philippians 4:13 that you might not be too happy with right now, but we need to be reminded of its truth. You and I can do whatever we need to do through Christ, who gives us the needed strength. You really can do anything with *God's* strength. That's a big deal in this whole process, knowing that we have a God who is stronger than anything, no matter how weak we feel in all of this.

> *I let everything that's going wrong spill out of my mouth; I spell out all my troubles to Him.*
> *Psalm 142:2 (VOICE)*

February 10

Death Cannot Separate Us!

I am so thankful that *nothing* can ever separate us from the love we have for our children, because that love is what continues to keep us connected to them, even if they are not here to be able to receive that love.

I am also thankful that nothing can separate God from the love He has for *His* children, and yes, that reminds me of Romans 8:38-39. Once again, I see a verse in the Bible that I have been familiar with for many, many years that now takes on a whole new meaning since Becca died.

This passage of scripture gives a list of all the things that cannot separate us from God's love. I know (and have been keenly aware since Becca left this earth) that the list includes distress and tribulation, and even says neither life nor death can separate me from His love.

But what I specifically noticed now that I didn't before, was that it also says, "things present or things to come." Um... ya... I have no idea how many times I have read that verse in total agreement over the years with a resounding "AMEN!" not knowing that "things to come" meant the death of my daughter.

February

Wow! That means that waaaaay before my child transferred to her eternal home ahead of me, I was in agreement that when it happened, it was not going to separate me from my Father's love for me! In other words, I am not going to believe the lie that God does not love me and is horrible at being God, or is not a good Father, because my child died before I did.

I have been called to KNOW the love of God which goes beyond comprehension... and that also has a new meaning, doesn't it? We cannot comprehend how a God who IS love would allow such a horrible tragedy in our lives.

The bottom line to all of this is that it is totally my choice to either believe, or not believe, that absolutely nothing that happens in my life means God's love for me has changed.

I can choose to decide He must not love me like He says He does and remain angry, bitter, resentful and miserable; OR I can choose to accept that I just don't get it because His love for me is beyond what I can comprehend and make sense of. That means it is impossible to be separated from it, which is a huge blessing in my darkest time, because I can lean into that love and draw peace, comfort and strength.

Refection: Not being able to be separated from God's love is a lot like the love we still have for our child. Just because they cannot directly receive it, does not mean it went away. We will *forever* love our child. And just because we cannot directly feel God's love does not mean it went away. He will *forever* love us. Love is not always based on feelings. It is based on commitment and believing, when those feelings are not there.

One way God has proven that we can never ever be separated from His love was to make sure that our physical separation from those we love isn't permanent. God the Father allowed His own Son to die a torturous death so that we will not be separated from our children, or from Him.

Selah - pause and think on this. Absolutely nothing can separate us from loving our own child, and absolutely nothing can separate God from loving you, His child.

> *So now I live with the confidence that there is nothing in the universe with the power to separate us from God's love. I'm convinced that his love will triumph over death, life's troubles, fallen angels, or dark rulers in the heavens. There is nothing in our present or future circumstances that can weaken his love. There is no power above us or beneath us—no power that could ever be found in the universe that can distance us from God's passionate love, which is lavished upon us through our Lord Jesus, the Anointed One!*
> *Romans 8:38-39 (TPT)*

February 11
Taking Back Your Health

When we are in a place of emotional stress, it is usually all we can do to handle life day-to-day (or even minute-by-minute). It is very common during that time to stop taking care of our bodies.

But I have discovered, unfortunately, that is one of the worst things we can do, because our emotions are so tied up in our physical health. Think about it. When we are getting enough sleep, eating healthy food that is fuel for our bodies and moving around (even if it is just getting out for a walk), we feel so much better. I know I sure do.

At first, when the tragedy takes us to our knees, we don't have much of a choice. Our body just kind of seems to take over as a response to the intense grief. Some of us find ourselves eating unhealthy "comfort foods" constantly. Others discover they don't eat anything at all for many days. Some of us can't seem to stay awake and all we can do is sleep. Others want desperately to sleep, but even with sleep aids it still seems to elude them.

Me? I slept a lot and grabbed the comfort foods, which put an extra 30 pounds on my body. Several years later, I am still struggling to get my health back under control.

February

But we all get to a point where the fog starts to lift, and we are left with the reality of the depth of our pain and horrific loss. Many of us continue in the pattern we found ourselves in, convincing ourselves we are helpless to stop.

I want to encourage you that is not true. What is usually happening, is that we see ourselves as a victim of the circumstance and let that become our identity. (My identity became, "I am the mother of a child who died.") As long as that is our identity, we will continue to believe things won't change, and will continue to struggle, both emotionally and physically.

At some point, we all come to a place where we are faced with a choice. "Do I want to stay a victim and let that become my identity? Or do I want to figure out how to climb out of this pit of darkness and back into a place of hope and light and life?"

Reflection: Is it time for you to make that choice of staying a victim or climbing out of the grief pit? Even if you aren't at that place yet and are still in those early times where the grief consumes you, it is possible to start making your way out with teeny tiny baby steps, by taking back your health.

What is one small thing you can do, that you have let go? I'm not talking about making a commitment to doing this thing every day from now on. What can you do today, and maybe tomorrow? Then tomorrow ask yourself the same question.

If you miss a few days, do not feel guilty. When you are ready again, just do one small thing toward taking back your health. Just keep working toward it, because it is worth the effort, no matter how small, as it begins to build.

You have shown me many troubles of all kinds. But You will make me strong again. And You will bring me up again from deep in the earth.
Psalm 71:20 (NLV)

February 12

The Health Struggle

If you are ready to start climbing out of the pit and get back to living again, here are three suggestions to help you start going in the right direction.

1. Take a daily stroll. I know we don't feel like it, but it does so much to release stress and keep our bodies in better working order.

2. At least once a day, chose something healthy to eat instead of reaching for that indulgent item that you will pay the price for later. I know that is easy for me to say and much harder to do. Something that might help is a change in perspective. I can either "treat" myself to those brownies or that ice cream, or I can "treat" myself to something that will be fuel for my body. Usually once I take the first bite of the healthy item, it tastes good because my body is craving the nutrients and I am glad I chose what I did... usually....

3. Build in times of rest, including going to bed early or sleeping in late. Whenever we face a crisis, our adrenal glands (the built-in "fight or flight" mechanism we each have) are working overtime in a big way. You can become critically ill if they burn themselves out. Rest is one of the only things that counters the work they are doing on your behalf.

We don't get to choose how our body reacts to a shocking tragedy. But what we can and need to do is look to God for how to not abuse our bodies during this time and ask Him what we can do to help our bodies come back into alignment with being healthy. He knows what we need, each day, each moment. Then, do your best to follow through with the nudges of the Holy Spirit.

The last thing I want to say is to not be hard on yourself for letting your body somewhat fall apart. *You have been in survival mode.* Just take one day at a time and keep stepping in the right direction.

February

Reflection: It is a process to become physically healthy again after a tragedy strikes our lives. Our physical health is so important because of how it affects our mental, emotional and spiritual health. When our body is out of whack, all the rest is so much harder to keep under control.

In the beginning of my grief journey, I found that it just wasn't in me to take care of myself. When I was ready, I had to bring God into it, asking Him to show me what I needed to do, and when I needed to do it. Because I asked Him to help me with this, when I felt a nudge to do something (like drink a glass of water, go out for a short walk, stand up and stretch, take a nap and don't set a timer to wake myself up after a certain time, etc.) I did my best to follow that nudge, believing it was the Holy Spirit directing me.

Take a minute and quietly ask God to do the same for you. While you are at it, ask Him to help you become more aware of those nudges and to follow through when they happen, believing that He is at work, helping you in this area also.

> *The Father is sending a great Helper, the Holy Spirit, in My name to teach you everything and to remind you of all that I said to you.*
> *John 14:26 (VOICE)*

February 13

Love is Always a Risk

February is a month where "love is in the air" with Valentine's Day. Personally, I always used this day to love on my kids, since I do not feel like Dave and I need a day set aside to show our love for each other. I would buy them each a card and a little gift that would be sitting on their plate for supper, along with making a fun meal that ended with some kind of heart-shaped dessert.

One reason the pain is so deep after the death of our child is because our love for him or her doesn't go away when they leave us. The love we have for our children lasts forever. In fact, for most of us, the love for our child who is no longer here continues to grow. Those who have not lost a child could never understand. How could they? I'm not sure I understand it myself, but it's true. My love for Becca has continued to grow stronger. Maybe it's that whole, "Absence makes the heart grow fonder" thing.

We grieve deeply, because we love deeply. That is one of the risks of love. Think about it. Love is a risk, because to love someone is to allow ourselves to be vulnerable, running the risk of not being loved in return. We understand that with adult relationships, but our kids are different. We expect our children to love us in return because of how deeply we love them and because of the special bond we share with them. So, when they are gone from this earth, and that love can no longer be returned, it is extremely painful.

Our child is forever a part of our very being, no matter how far away from us they are. He or she is forever in our hearts and in our thoughts. And thankfully, our separation is only temporary, because God, in His deep love for our child and for us, made a way for that to be possible.

Reflection: Consider praying this prayer with me: *Lord, my deep grief is a reminder of my deep love that cannot be poured out on my child right now or returned. But someday we will be together again, and all this stored up love will be dumped on my child! While I am waiting, I ask that right now, you would give my child a big hug from me, and love on them in my place. Thank you.*

If you were to buy a little Valentine gift to show your child how much you love and miss them, what would it be? It's okay to picture yourself giving him or her that gift and imagine giving each other a great big hug. It's also okay to let that liquid love run from your eyes, as you feel the deep love that has grown even more since they left.

> *So you have sorrow now, but I will see you again and*
> *then you will rejoice; and no one can rob you of that joy.*
> *John 16:22 (TLB)*

February 14

Love and Grief Go Hand-in-Hand Now

If you read yesterday's entry, you know that for well over 30 years, I have used Valentine's Day as a day to love on my kids. I always bought a little gift (and often a card) for each one, wrapped it and set it by their place for supper (or breakfast as the kids got older and I knew someone would not be home for supper because of sports and other activities).

Once they started having kids, it transferred to the next generation. I would have the "grands" all come over for a fun time and give them a little something.

But now we live in our motor home, and we are not in Wisconsin to be able to celebrate Valentine's Day with them. I still get a little something and ship it back home to the grandkids. I just can't seem to help it. I love to love on my family in special ways like that.

However, because I have always made Valentine's Day about my kids and grandkids, it also gives me another holiday day that can be a trigger, causing me to miss Becca deeply.

Valentine's Day is a day to let people around us know how much we love them. And that is why love and grief go hand-in-hand. The pain of missing our child and not being able to pour that love out on him or her is every bit as deep as the love we have for them.

We can see that as a positive thing if we choose to. The reason we are such a mess is because of how much we love our child, and that is a *good* thing to have that much love for your son or daughter.

You will probably notice me asking you this question several times throughout this book, but if you knew your child only had the amount of time on earth they did, would you have chosen not to have them at all? I know I sure wouldn't. I would rather have had that time with Becca as my daughter, than to not have had her in my life at all to avoid this pain. I am guessing you feel the same way, no matter how short that time was.

Reflection: Go ahead and both love on and grieve your child this Valentine's Day in whatever way is meaningful to you. Maybe make him or her a valentine or play a special song for them. Ask God to help you feel the warmth of your love for the blessing of having your child, to outweigh the grief of missing them, even if it is just for a brief moment. I will be praying for it to be so. But if not, that is okay. Remember, love and grief go hand-in-hand for us now until we are with them again.

> *Love knows no limit to its endurance, no end to its trust,*
> *no fading of its hope; it can outlast anything. It is, in fact,*
> *the one thing that still stands when all else has fallen.*
> *1 Corinthians 13:7-8 (PHILLIPS)*

February 15

The Hole in Our Hearts

The summer of 2019 was pretty rough for me. At the end of July, we lost a grandchild from a pregnancy loss. In June, six weeks before that, my dad left this earth. Then the beginning of August, Dave's mom passed away, to be with her husband of 65 years, (who went to his eternal home the previous summer).

Within eight weeks, Dave and I each lost a parent, and we lost a grandchild. These are three more holes in our hearts, with deep losses that cannot be filled. The thing is, we would not want to fill them. The reason the pain is so deep is because the love for them is so deep.

I was surprised at how much I cried when finding out our grandchild would not be making an entrance into this world. But since that time, I have had a thought that makes me smile. It really hurts to know that Becca has all these nieces and nephews she has not met. She does not get to love on them and have fun with them, and they do not get to have their fun-loving aunt in their lives. However, Becca has a niece or nephew in heaven to love on and have fun with that *we* have not met, and our parents have another great grandchild to enjoy!

There is no doubt about it. It is quite difficult to have our families and those we love deeply, split into two different places. Not just different states, or different countries, but entirely different realms. But one-by-one we'll all cross over there, and we will be together forever.

We grieve deeply because we love deeply. The holes we carry in our hearts are a reminder of our love that has nowhere to go right now. But those holes will be filled, never to be there again.

Reflection: I think about how often during my life I heard the description that we have a hole in our heart that only Jesus can fill. We try with all kinds of things the world has to offer, but it's like trying to put a square peg in a round hole, and it just doesn't fit.

We can do the same thing with the painful loss of our child. We can try to fill the pain and void with things that are not good for us in excess, like comfort foods, being on social media, lots of shopping, wine/alcohol, and even working out constantly at the fitness gym.

The one thing that is impossible to do in excess, is continually bringing it all to God, and rest in His loving embrace. Is there anything that you are doing to try and numb the pain that is not good for you? Hand it over to God, asking Him to help you look to Him for your needed healing. Fill that void with more of Him.

He heals the broken hearted and binds up their wounds
[healing their pain and comforting their sorrow].
Psalm 147:3 (AMP)

February 16
Rest is Needed for Recovery

I like to go for morning walks, especially if we are parked at a campground that is surrounded by the beauty of nature. One time at a place in California, we were in a valley, surrounded by mountains. I usually stayed on the trails along the bottom, but one morning I found myself drawn on a trail that led upward.

Quite often I was paying so much attention to the path and my steps, that I was missing the view, so sometimes I would stop and take a look to enjoy what was around me. It reminded me how it is the same with us. We are so consumed by our grief (and rightly so, especially those first twelve to twenty-four months) that we don't see what is going on around us. There *are* good things all around us; things we can still be thankful for. Sometimes we have to force ourselves to put our grief on pause to look for those things.

I also used those times of looking around at the view to get rested before continuing to walk further up the mountain, which made me think about how our grief is a lot of hard work! It can take everything we have just to be in survival mode. It's okay to rest when you are weary, when triggers hit hard, and you don't have any energy to do even the simplest things like take a shower or put a frozen pizza in the oven.

In the natural, the greater the injury, the more time is needed to rest for recovery. If someone has had open heart surgery, the body needs a lot of rest, for many weeks, to help with the recovery process. We gain strength when we rest. And as someone who has faced the death of your child, it is one of the worst emotional traumas a person can go through on this earth. You need a lot of rest to help with the recovery process of your shattered heart.

Refection: Rest is not only okay, it is what you *need*, in every area, physically, emotionally, and yes, even spiritually in some ways. I remember my father-in-law saying, "Sometimes the most spiritual thing you can do is get some sleep!" I love that, and totally agree!

February

But rest does not always mean sleeping (or zoning out in front of the TV). We can rest by going to a beautiful spot in nature and just relax, taking in the beauty. We can rest by getting a facial or a massage. We can rest by grabbing a warm chamomile tea and reading a fiction book that can take us out of our reality for a while. We can rest by taking a bath, surrounded by candles.

Stop right now and ask yourself what you can do to rest. What makes you feel more relaxed, just by thinking about it? Now make plans to *do* it within the next 3-5 days.

Rest in the Lord and be willing to wait for Him.
Psalm 37:7 (NLV)

February 17

One Step at a Time

Yesterday I shared about finding myself taking a trail up a mountain for one of my morning walks. The next day, I found myself on a different trail, going up a different mountain. The climb to the top was taking much longer than I thought it would. I was getting quite tired, and I started hoping I would meet up with the path I was on the day before, which would be a quicker way back down.

I kept going, thinking things like, "That path should be just around this next bend." As I continued going forward, looking for that other path, I eventually found myself at the very top of this new mountain. As I looked to my right, I was shocked to see that waaaayyyy down below me was the top of the mountain where I had stood the day before. I had no idea that I was climbing that much higher!

It was rather exhilarating, looking around at the beauty beneath me and all around me. And yes, it was a relief, knowing the reason I was so tired was because I had climbed a much bigger mountain.

As we keep walking on this grief journey, one step at a time (sometimes one breath at a time) there will come a day when we suddenly discover that we are doing better than we ever thought we could or would. At the time though, it feels like we can't go on and things will never get better.

Keep going. Keep climbing. If you need to take a break and sit it out for a while, that is okay. We all do. Then give yourself a pep talk, cheer yourself on, stand up and take another step. It will be so worth it when you can look down on where you have been, seeing how far you have climbed when all you did was take one step at a time.

Reflection: Take a minute and picture yourself at the top of a mountain, looking all around. What do you see? How do you feel? Think about what it took to get there. Then equate that to your grief journey. Picture yourself feeling like you are at the top of life and can conquer anything. Because you can. You have been through the worst of the worst, and not only survived, but are learning how to live again!

It feels good, doesn't it? I know you are not there, and you will have to come back to reality, but at least you now have a goal to reach for, knowing it is possible. If I can do it, so can you.

> *The Lord makes firm the steps of the one who*
> *delights in him; though he may stumble, he will*
> *not fall, for the Lord upholds him with his hand.*
> *Psalm 37:23-24 (NIV)*

February 18

The Trap of Self-pity

Our grief can easily turn into self-pity. Self-pity is being self-centered. We know this, but often we don't care. However, self-pity is a major trap and one of the enemy's favorite tools to keep us in our dark place of pain, unable to find our way out.

One form of self-pity is that we won't allow God to minister to us because we feel like we don't deserve it. We are so busy blaming ourselves for what happened, we pass judgment on ourselves, pushing God away as our source of comfort and our way out of the darkness. I want you to think about the fact that none of us deserve anything from God. This is no exception. Salvation is a gift. Grace is a gift. Blessings from Him are a gift. Our children are a gift from Him, and so is the comfort and help He wants to give us now that our children are with Him instead of us.

It is one thing to feel sorry for yourself, but it takes it to another level when we try to get other people to feel sorry for us. If you have given in to this mentality, sooner or later people are going to get tired of you wanting their sympathy.

We can make a great show of suffering in order to arouse the people around us to give us their sympathy and to feel sorry for us. Yes, we are a victim of the enemy and what he brings to this earth, but that does not mean that we have to have a victim mentality. There is a big difference between, "You should feel sorry for me because my child died" and "I am still deeply missing my child." If you are thinking, "People *should* feel sorry for me!" then you may need to honestly consider if you are one who has moved from legitimate grief into self-pity.

If people are not giving you what you want in this area, don't get angry with them. Go to God to get what you want and need. He will sit with you, He will hurt with you, He will encourage you in ways you don't expect. He will sustain you. He will be your rock, your anchor, and your strong tower of protection from the attacks of the enemy while you are so vulnerable.

Here is something that may be hard to receive. We have a good reason, but that does not mean we have a right to stay in the place of self-pity, because God sent Jesus to pay the price to set us free from all shame, all guilt, and every reason we could possibly have to remain feeling sorry for ourselves.

You do not need others to feel sorry for you. You need to hand it all over to God so He can help you get out of the darkness and back into the light, learning how to live a life of meaning and purpose.

Reflection: You may not realize it, but through our grief, God is working in us the gift of compassion that will flow out of us, so we are able to walk with others who are hurting. But when we invert that gift and turn it into self-pity, we pervert that gift to the point of it being idolatry, because everything becomes about us.

Grace is a word that is so full of meaning that it is hard to put just one definition to it. I heard a great definition recently that said grace is accepting the unacceptable. When we admit that we cannot help ourselves, God does something amazing.

God gives us the ability and anoints us to help someone else. But when all we think about is *What about me?* we cannot receive God's gift of grace to help others. In allowing God to flow through us to help someone else, we throw the door wide open for our own needed breakthrough. The choice is yours. I hope you choose grace, instead of self-pity.

> *So now we draw near freely and boldly to where grace*
> *is enthroned, to receive mercy's kiss and discover the grace*
> *we urgently need to strengthen us in our time of weakness.*
> *Hebrews 4:16 (TPT)*

February 19

Grief is Like...

There are many ways to illustrate what grief is like. Depending on when you picked up and started this book, you have probably already heard me talk about how our grief is like learning how to recover from an amputation, and that I had a front row seat to watching someone live this way, since my daughter had her little left leg amputated at only three years old.

Here are three more comparisons.

February

1. Grief is like carrying a rock in your pants pocket. At first you are *very* aware of it, as it bangs against your leg with every movement. After a long time, you are aware it is there, but it does not affect you as deeply all the time. Then you move on to times where you consciously forget it's there as you go throughout your day.

    Sometimes we reach into our pocket to grab something else, and as our hand feels the rock, we remember… There are times we will put our hand in our pocket because we want or need to feel the rock, and there are other times we pull the rock out to hold it and look at it, and then it goes back into our pocket. Even if we change pants, the rock will still go with us.

2. Grief is like the ocean waves. You feel like you have been shipwrecked and there are huge waves crashing over you with no mercy. Every time you try to come up for air, all you can do is get a quick gasp, only to be tumbled around by another wave crashing over you. When you think you can't take any more (multiple times), the waves finally start coming further apart. At least now you can catch your breath.

    Eventually the waves are not as big, making it easier to get back to the top. Calmer waters eventually come. There will still be waves and storms that send you swirling, but each time you get better at maneuvering through them, knowing they will end, and the calmer waters will come once again.

3. Grief is like carrying a backpack of rocks up a hill. At first you cannot move under the weight, as you look up to where you need to go. With much struggling, you begin to work your way forward. After a while, you are able to take some steps, even though at times you stumble backward. Eventually, you discover that you are walking up the mountain. It's hard, but you're doing it.

    As you continue, the backpack of rocks becomes easier to carry as your strength builds. There are times you need to take a rest. Some rests are relatively short, and others take longer because of feeling the full weight you are carrying once again. The longer you climb, the easier it gets, and the fewer rests you seem to need. But you will always continue to have the backpack of rocks to carry, and the effects of it.

Grief is hard work. Fortunately, it does get easier, even though we will deal with it for the rest of our time here.

Reflection: Do any of these illustrations resonate with you? Pick the one that you can relate to the most, and picture yourself working through the illistration, eventually getting to where it is easier. You may even want to find a tangible item (or a picture) and put it somewhere you can see, to remind yourself that it will get better.

> *We are pressed on every side by troubles,*
> *but not crushed and broken. We are perplexed*
> *because we don't know why things happen as*
> *they do, but we don't give up and quit.*
> *2 Corinthians 4:8 (TLB)*

February 20

When You Feel Like You are Falling Apart

There are those who would tell us it is our choice to either lean on God for strength or fall apart, but that did not work for me. I did both. I leaned on God *while* I fell apart.

Those who have lost a child understand there are times when the intense grief of those first few months and years will emotionally and physically take over, and we really have no choice in the matter. We can't function no matter how much we try or how much we may want to.

February

On those days, the only thing I could do was to cry out to God, and in that place of trauma, He never rejected me. I still occasionally have times like this, and when I call out to Him in my pain and weakness, He still comes in to give me the strength I need, moment by moment, until I can function again.

We all tend to find ways to bring ourselves comfort in our deep grief, and it is very easy to do so in unhealthy and even harmful ways. Doing things to continually numb ourselves from the pain will only prolong the grief and even intensify it.

Sometimes we may do some of these things because we just need to shut down for a while. And that is okay! But we want to monitor ourselves to make sure it is not a substitute for going to God to help us get through this.

Lean on Him, *while* you fall apart. He is there for you, in your anger, confusion and pain. His love for you is so deep that He is keeping your tears in a bottle. They are valuable to Him. He sees, He knows, and He cares. Someone who sacrificed His own child to save yours and mine is worth leaning on.

Reflection: One thing God so graciously shared with me in all my times of sleeping so much was the reminder that He never sleeps or slumbers. He could still minister to me while I was sleeping. And He can and wants to do the same thing for you. When you go to sleep at night, ask Him to bring healing to your soul while you are sleeping. He does not need us to be awake.

> *God lives forever! You can run to him for safety.*
> *His powerful arms are always there to carry you.*
> *Deuteronomy 33:27 (NIRV)*

February 21

You Need Something to Keep You Going

Spiritual leaders are important in our lives, but they do not replace the Holy Spirit. Something is very wrong when a spiritual leader becomes God's voice in a person's life, and when that leader tries to override a woman's Godly husband. But during my time of intense grief, I allowed both of those things to happen, and it nearly destroyed me.
I am sharing this with you because I do not want you to allow what was done to me, to happen to you.
As I continued to grieve deeply, weeks and months after Becca died, the man who was my pastor at the time put me in a place of "rest" and isolation, believing I was having a spiritual melt-down, since I was having such an emotional struggle after Becca died. This forced place of "rest" went on for weeks and then months.

I would spend hours and hours in my little prayer room under the basement stairs, mostly sleeping and crying. I would read my Bible, pray for a while, cry, and then sleep some more. That became my life because I had nothing to go back to, since the pastor would not allow me to have any kind of ministry or leadership role in the church, totally misunderstanding the grief I was working through.

Although Dave wholeheartedly welcomed a season of rest for me after Becca's passing (even sending me on a cruise to relax and get away) when the weeks turned into months and he saw me spiraling even further into despair, my husband became very concerned. He saw how wrong it was for me to be kept in this prolonged place of "rest", knowing I needed to return to the things God had called and anointed me to do in ministry, which would allow the Holy Spirit to flow through me to others as part of my healing.

It is really hard to go back to work, especially if it is a job that needs you to be mentally alert and clear-headed. I know many parents have no choice but to return to their jobs immediately, and their grief fog even causes some of them to lose their jobs. I am really sorry if that has happened to you.

However, we need something to keep us connected. Something that was part of our lives before our child died. Even if we don't want to, and we do it on autopilot, we need something to keep us going.

Reflection: My husband had a week or two off work, but then he had to go back. About a week after the funeral, my youngest son went back to school. The rest of the kids also got back to their previous life schedules of work or college. Were they all in a fog? No doubt about it. But even just going through the motions of life from before Becca's death helped them. I did not have that, and it nearly killed me.

What do you have in your life that keeps you going? Taking care of a pet? Going back to work? Taking care of other children? A knitting group? If you have not picked anything back up, ask God to give you the strength to do so, and then push yourself when He gives you the needed nudge. Sitting in our grief day in and day out is like atrophy for an unused muscle after an injury. It doesn't feel good when you first start moving, but as you continue, it will get easier, and you will be glad you did.

If you have something you are already back to doing, and feel like giving up, don't! Lean on God to give you the strength to push past the worst of it, until it is part of your routine again and does not take as much effort.

> *I pray that from his glorious, unlimited resources he will empower you with inner strength through his Spirit.*
> *Ephesians 3:16 (NLT)*

February 22

Self-care is so Hard!

I know in the darkest depth of our grief, we are in survival mode. When people around us throw out something like, "Make sure you take care of yourself," our thoughts go in all kinds of directions, but we usually respond with something like, "I will."

Survival mode stinks, doesn't it? We can barely function, much less even think about "taking care" of ourselves. And if you have other children, it takes everything you have to barely take care of them. Plus the guilt that comes with not being able to do this fully in the way they need, can add to the heaviness of our grief.

I remember those days well. I also look back and realize that sometimes what I excused as grief was self-pity. If I wanted to eat a bunch of ice cream to make myself feel better, that is what I did. I deserved it. After all, my daughter died. But it never made me feel better because it did not change the fact that she was gone and was not coming back.

At the beginning, I also did not slow down. Other grieving parents are probably the only ones who will understand when I say I couldn't function at home, but if it was job or ministry related, I was all in with a fervor. (I was still a leader in an international children's ministry and administrator of their online school.) I know part of it was being on autopilot, and part may have been not wanting to let other people down by letting my grief get in the way.

Don't guilt yourself into having to continue in a ministry if you need the rest and the break. Sometimes we need to continue, as it gives us a reason to get up and out the door and a reason to keep living. But other times it is out of feeling obligated and guilty from other people telling us it's what we need to do (those who have never lost a child, I might add), when what we really need is to rest and have lots of time to process our grief and deep loss.

When I look at it now, I have absolutely no idea how I was able to coordinate a children's ministry training trip to Africa less than a year after Becca died and do it again the next year. But it cost me dearly, and

I am still paying for it. I ended up with severe adrenal fatigue with a difficult recovery, which still kicks in and affects my being able to function at times.

Almost a decade later I am also still struggling with getting over twenty pounds back off, from how I just let myself go and didn't care.

So, my word for you today is that if at all possible, *dig deep* and CARE about yourself. Do not make excuses like I did. Do not take that third and fourth piece of cake or eat that entire bag of chips. Make yourself take a simple walk around the block a few times each week.

I know that first year or two we don't want to be here, and we don't care what happens to us. But there are plenty of people who *do* care and still want and need us around. Eventually you will care again, and the more you let yourself go now, the harder it will be to get your health under control.

Reflection: Self-care is hard, but much of it is a mindset. It is just as easy for me to choose to munch on an apple as it is to munch on a stack of cookies. I get to choose if I am going to go for a short walk before I climb back into my bed for the afternoon.

What is something that you know you tend to give in to, that isn't good for you, but you don't really care? Think of something you can do to counter-act it, and then ask God to help you change the way you are seeing it and start making better choices.

> *Dear friend, I pray that you may enjoy good health and that all may go well with you, even as your soul is getting along well.*
> *3 John 1:2 (NIV)*

February 23

Liquid Love

A few days ago, as I was spending time with the Lord, I got a picture in my mind (some believers refer to it as a vision) that was pretty incredible. I saw an image that I knew was Jesus, sitting behind a potter's wheel. He was shaping the clay on the wheel, and it was His tears that were wetting the clay as He formed it. Wow! Take a minute and let that sink in!

We don't know why He did not stop our children from leaving this earth ahead of us, knowing how much pain it would cause. We probably won't know, until we can see the full picture like He can, and like our children can, who are on the other side of eternity, no longer bound to this world like we are. But He hurts deeply for us and with us! As we cry, He is crying with us, in our darkness and pain.

Tears are a big thing to God. In Psalm 56:8 we are told that God keeps our tears in a bottle. I often say we are going to have some of the biggest bottles in heaven! And when we get to heaven, we are told that God Himself will wipe away the tears from our eyes. Revelation 21:3-5 says, "I heard a voice thunder from the Throne: '...They're his people, he's their God. He will wipe every tear from their eyes. Death is gone for good—tears gone, crying gone, pain gone—all the first order of things gone.' The Enthroned continued, 'Look! I'm making everything new.'" (MSG)

What a glorious day that will be. It reminds me of the hymn that says, "When we all get to heaven what a day of rejoicing that will be. When we all see Jesus, we'll sing and shout the victory."

But until then, allow your tears to continue to be the gift they are; a release valve for the pain and suffering we all go through here, and the liquid love that will continue to pour out as we miss our children, waiting to be reunited with them, never to be separated again.

February

Reflection: I am so thankful the Bible lets us know it is okay to cry, especially because Jesus cried. He is our example. If Jesus shed tears over something painful, we know it is okay for us to cry as well.

Here is something to think about. Our tears are not just our liquid love for our child, but they are His liquid love for us as well. He is crying with us and through us. As you think about this, I pray that He will pour out His love on you in a way that you know it is real, and that it brings peace and comfort in the midst of your pain and sorrow.

Then tears streamed down Jesus' face.
John 11:35 (TPT)

February 24

Take Off and Go Somewhere

I am sitting at a beautifully wooded campsite while writing this and have just come back from a morning walk through some of the campground. Something that struck me is how busy this place is on the weekends, and how quiet it is during the week, because there are so many people who "get away" for the weekends, and then on Monday, it is back to work.

Why do we do that? Why is it so many of us (myself included) have to "get away" to force ourselves to pull away from the day-to-day business of life, and just relax, or *make* time for fun, or to reflect on where we are in life (even if it is in an extremely painful place)?

I believe a change in atmosphere somehow flips a switch in our brains, causing us to think differently. We are somewhat forced to have a different perspective.

Six weeks after Becca died, I ended up going on a cruise by myself. My husband and I *love* cruises, but this time I literally cried while waiting to pull out, sitting on this incredible ship, not knowing how I was going to "endure" this time completely alone.

It turned out to be one of the best things I could have ever done for myself, causing me to spend so much time reflecting, talking to God, allowing Him to minister to me, and lots and lots of crying. At the same time, just being able to step out of my room and have things to do to occupy myself when I needed a break was perfect. Not having to cook, but just grab something already prepared whenever I was hungry, was a bonus. (Even better – I didn't have to clean up the kitchen or do the dishes!)

I know that not everyone can hop on a cruise ship like I was able to do. But I'll bet there is a place within a couple of hours of where you live with a little cabin you could rent, even if just for the weekend. Or someone has a tent you could borrow. Or....?????

When our child dies, there is something that can help us turn the corner and begin to come to a needed place of healing, moving toward living again without numbness, suffocating tears and constant stabbing pain. It is a change in our perspective. Getting away will help do that. No plans, no agenda, just away by yourself.

Believe me, I know that may sound scary and horrible!!! But you just may discover, like I did, that God uses it to bring a greater measure of healing than you thought was possible. Even if you go back home not feeling any differently, I can pretty much guarantee that a deep work was done in you, that you will eventually be able to look back on and say, "I am so glad I took that time away because..."

Reflection: Stop and think about a time in the past when you were able to just get away, and the peace and joy it brought you. Where did you go? Can you get there again? Or is there somewhere else you can go that will help you with the rest and recovery process? Do not put it off. Don't make excuses. You *need* this!

(Note: GPS Hope has weekend retreats and is part of a yearly grief cruise. To find out more about how to join us, go to our website gpshope.org and look under the "Events" tab.)

My beloved spoke and said to me, "Arise, my darling, my beautiful one, come with me.
Song of Solomon 2:10 (NIV)

February 25

Trusting God Again

We are all very aware that we do not always get the answer we want to prayers we have prayed. And sometimes that makes us angry with God, insisting He did not hold up His end of things. We may even decide that we are not going to trust Him anymore because we do not understand why He didn't step in to save our son or daughter and why He would allow such pain in our lives.

You are probably familiar with Job in the Bible. In the pain of losing all ten of his children, losing all of his finances and having painful boils, he states that even if God killed him, Job would continue to put his hope and trust in God (Job 13:15).

When I discovered that statement many years ago, (way before Becca died) I made it my own. And I continued to do so after Becca died, through the tears and anguish, both to God and to myself. There are times it is not easy to say it or feel that way, but I say it anyway. "God, even with my daughter being taken from me on this earth, I will trust You."

I would encourage you to make the same statement. You may ask, "How can I say that when I don't believe it?"

You can say that because it is true by faith. Remember when Jesus went to a girl who had died and was laughed at because He told the people she was not dead but was "sleeping" (Matthew 9:24)? There was no doubt she was dead, but Jesus was speaking by faith what He knew to be true. Her spirit was not dead. He was calling her spirit back into her body to bring life back to her on this earth.

Reflections of Hope

Romans 4:17 tells us that God gives life to the dead and calls things which do not exist as though they did. That is what Jesus was doing, and that is what we can do also in Him.

So, go ahead and say it. "It does not matter what happens to me on this earth. God, I will still trust You."

Reflection: In speaking this out, you are speaking what does not exist, hoping to see what God has already done to make it true. Even if you do not feel it immediately, I can guarantee it will break something off of you, especially if you continue speaking it, because a new level of freedom happens when we surrender completely to the God who loves us more than we could ever imagine.

If we want to be able to live again beyond the death of our child, we will have to make that choice to begin looking past our pain and trust His love for us. Make the choice, and the feelings to back it up will eventually come.

Even if the fig tree does not blossom and there are no grapes on the vines, if the olive trees fail to give fruit and the fields produce no food, if the flocks die far from the fold and there are no cattle in the stalls; then I will still rejoice in the Eternal! I will rejoice in the God who saves me!

Habakkuk 3:17-18 (VOICE)

February 26

Birthday Blues

I am not talking about having the birthday blues for our child's birthday. I am talking about our own birthdays. This may not make sense to those around us, but having the birthday blues on our birthday is very real.

February

Friends and family may understand our sadness on the anniversary of our child's death. They may understand that Mother's Day can be painful for us. But our own birthday? Yes!

We know there are others who want to celebrate the day we came into the world. But one of the most important people in our lives is not here to celebrate with us. While we may get cards and gifts from others, we cannot help but think about the child we will not be hearing from.

No signed card. No gift. No phone call. No hugs. No "Happy Birthday!" No voice singing with the others...

Birthdays are supposed to be happy days, (thus the saying "*Happy* Birthday") with people being extra nice to you, spoiling you, and having positive reflections. Instead, it can be a day of not wanting to be around anyone, difficulty getting anything done, weepy, no appetite, and just wanting to stay in bed and get the day over with.

Is there anything we can do? Yes, I believe there is. First of all, we must realize that much of this is a mind-set. We may not want to still be here, but we are, and there are people around us who are very glad about that. I will go so far as to say there are people in your life who *need* to celebrate how thankful they are that you are still here. It may be that they just aren't sure how to approach it with you.

May I suggest the week before your birthday, make a plan for that day. If you want to be around people, there is nothing wrong with reminding others that your birthday is coming and you are hoping and praying for a good day. You can also take the initiative and make plans with specific people. (Just putting out there, "Hey I will be at such-and-such place for my birthday if anyone wants to join me," is probably setting yourself up for being alone. Most people just don't respond to generic invitations like that.) If you prefer quiet and solitude, then plan ahead for it. What movie are you going to watch? What book are you going to read? What trail are you going to walk on? What special something are you going to eat?

The night *before* your birthday, I suggest taking some "me" time. Pamper yourself. Do something that makes you feel special. Treat yourself. Do what you can to climb into bed with a sense of relaxation and contentment about doing something special for yourself.

On the day of your birthday, if you need to, set a "sadness" time limit. Allow yourself time to think about and miss your child, but set a timer so that you do not wallow in it, with a plan of exactly what you will do when the timer goes off to pull yourself out of it.

Obviously, these things will not make the pain go away, but my prayer is that it will ease the day and make it more bearable.

Reflection: You are a masterpiece. You are worth celebrating. That's it! I will say it again. YOU ARE A MASTERPIECE AND YOU ARE WORTH CELEBRATING! You may be a messy masterpiece, but you are God's masterpiece. I guarantee that He is celebrating you, probably dancing a jig with your child, too!

And now if you will excuse me, I am going to celebrate my birthday today, because even though Becca isn't here to join me, I am a masterpiece and worth celebrating!

> *The LORD your God is with you; his power gives you victory.*
> *The LORD will take delight in you, and in his love*
> *he will give you new life. He will sing and be joyful over you.*
> *Zephaniah 3:17 (GNT)*

February 27

It Ain't Instant

We live in a society where we expect instant results. Cooking on the stove is not fast enough, so we zap our food in the microwave. People spend lots of money to update to the fastest internet and phone connections. We even have things like instant rice, instant oatmeal and instant mashed potatoes! Unfortunately, there is no instant fix for our grief; no magic wand to wave over us to make the pain go away.

February

Healing of any kind from a deep wound takes time, whether it is physically, mentally, emotionally or spiritually. And we often feel like it's taking too much time. How often have you been told to take it easy after an injury, and in your impatience, you overdid it, taking yourself backward in the healing process?

Our grief can be the same way. Being in the dark is not fun. In fact, it can be scary and depressing. We want to be better. We want out, and we want out now! So, we convince ourselves that we are "fine" and push ourselves more than we should. It can be the smallest thing, like running a bunch of errands on the same day instead of spreading them apart. We used to be able to do that with no problem and find ourselves believing that it should not be an issue However, in a few days (or sometimes weeks) we find things crashing down around us, and wonder why, when we thought we were doing so well.

Healing takes time, but it will come. God is at work. Often the work is so deep, that we cannot see it or feel it. But if you have invited Him into this process, you can be sure that He is there, doing what needs to be done on your behalf. We need to work with Him, by not forcing ourselves to try and do what we used to be able to do, while in a deep recovery process.

Reflection: When you get a glimpse of light in the darkness, don't try and stumble your way toward it so you can push yourself through it. Be thankful that you see the light and embrace it, right where you are. Instant does not mean better. In fact, there is a noticeable difference between something like instant tea or coffee, compared to brewed.

Most people prefer the taste of food that has taken much time and preparation, to something that was made from an instant mix. It is the same with us as we are in a place of healing. You will carry a better "flavor" if you allow God to do the healing in His timing, than to try and do it yourself faster, which usually results in set-backs and more frustration.

Are you trying to work toward an instant healing, or allowing the time that is needed? Ask God to help you be a good "patient" in the recovery process.

> *But those who wait for Yahweh's grace will experience divine strength. They will rise up on soaring wings and fly like eagles, run their race without growing weary, and walk through life without giving up.*
>
> Isaiah 40:31 (TPT)

February 28

There's No Place Like Home

One day a phrase from the Wizard of Oz just popped into my mind. "There's no place like home!" My thought was, "Wouldn't it be nice if it was as easy as Dorothy in the Wizard of Oz to just click our heals three times and everything would go back to the way it was and be good again?"

Immediately I realized that it was not really that easy for Dorothy. Before that could happen, she went on a difficult journey. She had to fight the wicked witch and was attacked by flying monkeys. She had to boldly defend her friends who were under attack. And then after all that, Dorothy was hugely disappointed to find out the wizard (whom she thought would have all the answers and help her get back home) was just a man behind a curtain.

But it was *that* journey that made her realize she had what she needed all along.

We are all on an extremely difficult journey. Many struggle with wanting answers. We want to know if God is so good, why does he allow so much suffering and evil in this world? But maybe that isn't what we really need.

Maybe we don't need to fight God for the answers as much as we need to fight with everything in us to hold on to the goodness of God in the middle of all these unanswered questions.

Maybe our focus is not supposed to be on demanding God to give His explanations for our suffering, but to create communities around that suffering, helping us to absorb it and be transformed by it to learn about grace and true love in a way that was not possible before.

Maybe as we wrestle with God, we need to be like Jacob and tell Him, "I won't let you go until you bless me!" realizing that we just may be on the edge of a greater blessing than we knew was even possible to have (if not in this lifetime, in the next when we are reunited with our children again).

Maybe, just maybe, God did not do this *to* us, but in His incredible mercy He is taking what the enemy meant for evil to destroy us, and is turning it into something *for* us that causes us to see with new eyes, like Dorothy had when she returned to reality from the dreamed-up land of Oz.

Let me share with you some of the scene when the fairy godmother appeared to tell Dorothy about the ruby red slippers on her feet.

Fairy godmother: You've always had the power to go back to Kansas.

Dorothy: I have?

Scarecrow: Then why didn't you tell her before?

Fairy godmother: Because she wouldn't have believed me. She had to learn it for herself.

Hmmmm.... wow. That is pretty powerful.

There is no place like home. Our kids may not be able to come home here with us, but some day, we will be going home to them. What a wonderful day that will be!

Reflection: There are so many of us on this journey ahead of you that can tell you these things, but you are on your own journey, and must get to the point where you can believe it for yourself.

What you need, you have had all along because God Himself lives inside you. It is a matter of getting to the point where you can be okay with what you do not know, realizing you don't need those answers to have peace. You can even learn how to live a full life again while being here on earth without your child. You can get there, because you already have inside of you everything you need, and you have others on the journey with you to help.

> *Everything we could ever need for life and godliness*
> *has already been deposited in us by his divine power.*
> *2 Peter 1:3 (TPT)*

February 29

Leap Day

Some Christians will try to tie "leap day" into taking a leap of faith. Not me.

Why? Because many of us are struggling just to take baby steps! We feel like every time we take two or three steps forward, we fall down, just like a little one trying to learn how to walk.

The development of a child seems to match our own development in grief, after the death of our son or daughter. It is almost like we are starting all over. Just like a baby, that first year we can be unable to function, depending on others to do all the things we just can't do for ourselves.

Then we try "walking", and we feel like a failure. It seems we just can't get anywhere, no matter how hard we try. And many times we just sit there and cry in our frustration and pain.

Then as a toddler, we can get around a bit, but it is awkward, and we still fall. Sometimes it really hurts, and other times we bounce right back up again.

Our grief years quite often match the age of a child growing into adulthood. When I first heard this, I was six years old in grief years.

February

Now I am eleven. I kind of feel like the big sister, making sure my younger siblings are being taken care of and leading the way from my own whopping eleven years of experience!

Reflection: How about you? How old are you in grief years? Can you see a similarity to a child at that age? Does it allow you to go a bit easier on yourself, knowing you are just an infant, or are learning to crawl or to walk?

"Grief years" is not something we ever thought about before our own child died. Do not expect to leap forward but know this is a long process and you are right on track.

You taught me how to walk with care so my feet would not slip.
2 Samuel 22:37 (VOICE)

March

March 1

Another New Month

We have just started a new month, and that makes me think of new hope. Not all of us feel that way, though, so I thought I would try to help with that just a bit.

1. A new month often brings new weather, and in this case, it is getting us closer to spring! Those of us who are in the cold northern states truly appreciate this. I think about how winter makes everything look so dead, and it can really affect our mood. However, it is just a season, and new life always returns, no matter how harsh or how long the winter has been.

   So, it is a wonderful reminder that no matter how long or how deep into darkness our grief has taken us, at some point, "spring" IS coming with new life and new hope.

2. A new month brings new opportunities. Some of you may not see this as a good thing, especially when it is a month with a date that is very difficult. But it still brings new opportunities to do something different that will possibly take some of the sting away. If you know it is going to be difficult, ask yourself what you can do differently that will help. Maybe change the focus from dwelling on your painful loss, to thinking about your child's gain, and do what you can to picture him or her in heaven and what it is like for them. If you have to go to an event you are dreading, what can you do to bring your child with you and have others celebrate their life with you for a moment?

   So, a new month does bring new opportunities to move toward a healing that allows you to learn how to live in hope, light, and even move toward having meaning and purpose again. You may think that is impossible, but those of us who at one time thought it was impossible as well, are here to encourage you.

3. Sometimes we dread going forward, because we feel like it is taking us further away from our child who has left this earth. I

have shared this before, but it is worth repeating. God graciously pointed out to me once (when I was almost panicking feeling that way) that I am not getting further away from Becca, but I am getting closer to her. Each day I am here brings me one day closer to being reunited with her again!

So, a new month brings us that much closer to seeing our children again. Hoorah!!!!

A new month *can* bring new hope, new light, new life, and new possibilities.

Reflection: How about you? Does at least one of these make sense to you? Ask God to speak to your heart in a way that you can receive, to take the edge off of "new" having a bad connotation to it. New does not have to mean putting your child behind you. New can bring good things, which is God's plan for you.

See, I am doing a new thing! Now it springs up; do you not perceive it? I am making a way in the wilderness and streams in the wasteland.
Isaiah 43:19 (NIV)

March 2

A Brief Flash of Time

A previous acquaintance of mine, who is now a friend, lost her twenty-two-year-old son, Josh, in a car accident six months after we lost Becca. I love what she wrote:

Do we sacrifice the joy of having children to spare us the pain that occurs if we lose them either by death or rebellion? I think not. The joy we receive from our children outweighs any pain from the loss. I would take my twenty-two years with Josh over and over again with the same outcome if that was the only way I would have the honor of being his mother.

Going through all this has spread a little light onto why our Father in heaven would create this world and allow us to have our own free will. He knew we would rebel and He knew the only way to save us from ourselves would be to sacrifice Himself on our behalf. He also knew the joy of creating us in His own image would outweigh that pain.

The love we feel for our children, as all-consuming as it seems, is only a speck of the love our God has for us.

Try to imagine that...it's impossible to comprehend.

Kathy Pelton

How about you? Does your pain outweigh the joy of having your child in your life for the short time he or she was here? Do you wish you had never had him or her because of the suffocating darkness you found yourself in after their death? Probably not.

If you are like Kathy (and myself), you would go through it again because of how special your child was and how deeply you love him or her. That is why the pain is so deep; because the love is so very deep.

And to think God's love for us is even deeper; that the *joy* of having *you* with Him in eternity was worth the painful sacrifice and death of his own son as the price for that to happen.

Reflection: It doesn't seem like it now, but life here is just a brief flash of time compared to all of eternity, which is where we will meet up again with our children.

Can you think of a time of waiting for something that seemed like it took forever then, but looking back it seems that time was so quick compared to now? I feel that way about my 100-day count-down until my wedding day. Dave and I have now been married for thirty-nine years, which now makes those one hundred days of waiting seem like almost nothing.

I think that is how it is going to be when we join our children. No matter how long we have waited, it will seem like nothing in comparison to all of eternity that we will be with them. So not only can we carry the joy in our hearts of having had them as our children for a short time here on earth, we can also carry the joy knowing that after a "short" painful wait, we will have the rest of eternity together!

Let us run the race that we have to run with patience, our eyes fixed on Jesus the source and the goal of our faith. For he himself endured a cross and thought nothing of its shame because of the joy he knew would follow his suffering.
Hebrews 12:2 (PHILLIPS)

March 3

When Will it Stop Hurting so Much?

I have yet to meet a freshly grieving parent, within the first couple of years after the death of their child, who does not want to know, "When will this stop hurting so much?" It is so very hard, and we don't think we will ever be able to live again without that crushing, all-consuming pain.

This may sound really strange, but there is somewhat of a release in accepting the fact that this is normal for losing a child, and to allow yourself to rest in God to bring His healing in His way and His timing. (And just an FYI, it is usually in such small increments, that we can't see or feel it happening for quite some time.)

When Dave & I were dating, and he wanted to propose, He kept hearing God say "Wait". Dave decided to study the word and found out one of the Biblical meanings is "a carved work".

I believe within the waiting process of our painful grief, God is doing a very deep carved work in each one of us; something that goes way beyond anything that makes sense in the darkness.

I remember during those first couple of years how I would go to God over and over again with my pain, my wondering, my feeling so worthless and useless in my paralyzing grief, and over and over again He would tell me it was okay, to just rest in Him, lean on Him, cry to Him, and more than anything, to trust Him, and the deep work He was doing in me.

One time I even heard God ask me, "Can you hold on in this place? I AM here with you!"

My response was, "Lord, whittle away. I will wait while You do this carved work, whatever it is...just be my strength and my hope through it, please!"

Another time, He led me to Philippians 4:4-8. Verse 8 says, "Finally, brethren, whatever things are true, whatever things are noble, whatever things are just, whatever things are pure, whatever things are lovely, whatever things are of good report, if there is any virtue and if there is anything praiseworthy—meditate on these things."

I actually wrote down each portion of this verse and then made myself think of those things and write them down, such as "whatever things are true." I wrote a whole page of what was true in my life, truth based on what God says. I went through the whole verse that way.

Every slight shift in perspective would help pull me a little bit more out of that place of pain and darkness, to a place of being able to function again, and eventually feel like life was still worth living.

Reflection: I highly suggest you do the same thing for yourself. You might be surprised at what you come up with, and how it begins to give you a slightly different perspective that begins to give you a pinhole of light in your darkness.

I wish I could tell you that at a specific point in time, the deep suffocating pain will stop. But I can't. What I *can* tell you is that **it will**. Not as soon as you want it to, but it will. How do I know? Because it happened to me, and countless other parents who did not think it would happen to them.

Summing it all up, friends, I'd say you'll do best by filling your minds and meditating on things true, noble, reputable,

> *authentic, compelling, gracious—the best, not the worst;*
> *the beautiful, not the ugly; things to praise, not things to curse.*
> Philippians 4:8 (MSG)

March 4

Is My Child in Heaven?

This is a topic I am passionate about, for sure, because there are way too many parents who have this unnecessary fear!

If you are tormenting yourself with the thought that your son or daughter might not have made it into heaven, let me say that you don't know that. You do not have all the information that God has.

God's love for your child supersedes your love for him or her. How can it not? He IS love itself. God planned for, and knew your child, before you were even in your *own* mother's womb! The love we have for our child is so very deep, but His love for us and for our children is beyond what we can even comprehend, (as stated in Ephesians 3:19). I don't know about you, but it is taking me a lifetime to learn about His love, and I feel like I have barely scratched the surface. I am so thankful that He loves Becca even more than I do, because He can love her with a perfect love, when I was unable to in my own human limitations.

Each one of us is created with His desire to have an intimate relationship with us, not just here on earth, but for all of eternity. I believe God is big enough to have made every opportunity possible for your child to accept Him before leaving this earth, and it could easily have happened during a time you know nothing about. It could have happened when he or she was young, in a very simple child-like faith and they didn't know how to explain it. They could have received the gift of salvation as a teen but didn't want to tell you for various reasons. And it most definitely could have happened at the moment of his or her death.

In God's world, He is not bound by time, and remember, God IS love itself. He is drawing us closer to Himself every second of every day. (If we *don't* know Him, He is drawing us to discover and receive Him, and if we *do* know Him, He is drawing us closer to know Him in deeper ways.)

It is the Father's will that no one perishes in an eternity without Him. When you put all of this together, it would be *impossible* for God to abandon your child, while at death's door! I believe with everything in me that He was there, with one last wooing for your son or daughter to receive His love and the gift of salvation through Jesus, if they had not already done so. All it takes is the simple heart response of "Yes!"

So, give that fear to God, trusting that He took care of it. Not having the information that you want to have, doesn't mean it did not happen at some point in his or her life.

Reflection: Fear and faith come from the same place; it comes from the unknown. Fear of the unknown brings torment. Faith in the unknown brings peace. We get to choose if we are going to live in the torment of fear, or if we are going to live in the peace of trusting God in what we do not know.

I think it is easier to believe your child is in heaven than to believe or wonder if he or she is not. You can rest in the knowledge that God did everything He could, including that last second of your child's last breath, bringing your child to a place of repentance and receiving the gift of salvation. Trust and believe that God reached out with the gift of salvation, and your child grabbed ahold and accepted it. The Holy Spirit wants to give you peace in believing, so ask for His help, if you are still struggling.

If you already have the assurance that your child is in heaven waiting for you, would you please take a minute and pray for those who are reading this and are struggling with and being tormented by their fears? Pray that they will be able to choose faith and have the peace they are longing for.

He does not want any to perish but all to come to repentance.
2 Peter 3:9 (TPT)

Note: There is *so* much more I can share with you, as an assurance that you can have hope that your child is in heaven waiting for you, instead of being tormented by fear and doubt. I asked my friend, Pastor Lynn Breeden (who lost a five-year-old son over thirty years ago), to join me in a podcast on this topic. She has the same passion, of bringing hope to pareavors who are living in fear that their child might not be in heaven. Some of the things we talked about were:

- *Nothing* can separate us from the love of God, according to Romans 8:38-39.
- Suicide is not the unpardonable sin and *does not* disqualify a person from an eternity in heaven.
- It is God's will that no one perishes into an eternity without Him
- We can see in the Bible that God's desire for mercy and grace are much greater than His desire of judgment.

You can go to gpshope.org/podcast/18 to hear this discussion, and to have Pastor Lynn pray over you.

March 5

Getting into Right Alignment

We are made in the image of God as a three-in-one being: spirit, soul and body. We are a spirit, we have a soul (which is our mind/thoughts, our emotions, and our will) and we live in a body.

Another way to look at it is that we are spiritual beings, having a physical experience while living here on this earth and our soul is in the middle, deciding what this life is going to be like for us, based on the decisions we make and how we react and behave to what this life throws our way.

As a children's minister, I used to do an illustration of how our soul can affect our spiritual walk. I would ask three children to come up and take ahold of a rope with one hand, all facing the same direction. The one in front represented our flesh, the one in the middle was our soul, and the one in back is our spirit. When told to walk forward, they all moved smoothly together.

Then I had the child who was in the back (our spirit) turn around and face the other way, to represent when we receive Jesus into our lives. Now when they all walk forward, there is a tussle, with the spirit being dragged by the soul and the flesh. When the soul decides to turn around and line up with God's spirit inside us, now the flesh becomes the one getting pulled, and doesn't have the power it used to, as being the one in charge.

Here is where things get interesting. The soul is the deciding factor of which direction is going to have the most pull and decides if that person is going to walk toward God, or toward their own flesh. In other words, what we feed into our soul is going to determine much of the day-to-day mind set of our lives. The best part is that when our soul follows the spirit long enough, the flesh will eventually turn around and line up with the other two, realizing life is easier and better that way.

I think you can see where I am going with this. What you align your soul with, is what will determine how quickly you are able to get out of the darkness and get back into the light, learning how to live a life of meaning and purpose again. It will also help pull you out of those downward spirals we can easily fall back into. Getting into right alignment means that instead of living from the devastating fact that "my child died", we can learn to live from the place of thankfulness that "my child lived", and still lives!

Reflection: God is always at work in us, through the Holy Spirit, to help us come into right alignment. That does not mean it is easy. And it doesn't mean that if you are struggling (or don't even care, because your loss is so fresh) that you can't or won't get there.

Ask God what you can do to feed your soul, causing it to turn away from the despair and hopelessness of the flesh, turning toward God's hope, strength, comfort and light. It may be so simple that you don't think it will make a difference. That one small thing might not, but one thing built on top of another will start to pull you in the needed direction of having meaning, purpose and even joy in your life once again.

> *May God himself, the God who makes everything holy and whole, make you holy and whole, put you together — spirit, soul, and body—and keep you fit for the coming of our Master, Jesus Christ. The One who called you is completely dependable. If he said it, he'll do it!*
> *1 Thessalonians 5:23 (MSG)*

March 6

The Shackles of Unforgiveness

There are so many people we need to forgive when our child dies. Some of us tell ourselves we cannot forgive, but this is just not true. Forgiveness is not based on our emotions, on whether someone deserves to be forgiven, or whether or not someone is sorry. (But I also want to say that forgiveness does not replace justice or someone facing the consequences of their actions.)

Forgiveness is for our own freedom. If we choose not to forgive, our anger and bitterness not only affect us physically, emotionally and spiritually, but we are cutting off a necessary piece to work toward the needed healing of our shattered hearts.

I believe that making the choice to work towards forgiveness on such a deep level needs extra oomph, and that comes with our words. Words are powerful. God created this world with His words. And our words can deeply affect the outcome of things happening in our lives.

In my book *When Tragedy Strikes*, I provide the words to pray or speak forgiveness over the different people in our lives we may need to release:

- Our child for leaving us

- Those who directly or indirectly were involved with their death
- Those who have hurt us in the grieving process
- God, who could have stopped what happened

In one of my online grief support courses, I added two more:

- Ourselves
- Those who are not grieving the same way we are

There are many pareavors who share with me that they are not ready to forgive certain people (especially a person directly responsible for their child's death) or forgive themselves. I will not shame you or try to convince you that you have to do so. You are on your own grief journey, and when you are ready, God will be there to help you with it.

Reflection: The spoken word is powerful. Often, if we are thinking about something, when we hear someone else say what we are thinking, it gives life and power to our thoughts.

Forgiveness is not based on how we feel about the situation or the person. It is a gift we give ourselves, to take off the shackles of anger, bitterness and regret. As a parent struggling with grieving the death of your child, you deserve to be set free from the chains that are keeping you bound in this prison.

Look at the above six possible groups or people that may be holding you hostage to your grief by your unforgiveness. Speak out your forgiveness to each one. Choosing forgiveness is usually a process and a choice we make over and over again until we are fully released. It's like putting in the key and turning it over and over again, until the shackles finally fall off.

Even if you don't feel like you have anyone to forgive, I recommend speaking each one of them out loud at least once. Doing that often brings an extra measure of release that we did not realize we needed.

Bear with each other and forgive one another if any of you has a grievance against someone. Forgive as the Lord forgave you.
Colossians 3:13 (NIV)

March 7

Having Hope

I have been listening to a lot of Joyce Meyer podcasts the past month. Her straight-to-the-point teachings are what I really need right now. This morning I heard her talking about hope, and how you cannot have faith without it. Her definition of hope is a *positive expectation*. It isn't like, "I hope God gets me through this." It is believing that He will, whether we can see Him at work or not and no matter how we feel.

The bottom line is that we are going to have faith in something. We either believe that God is able to somehow get us to the other side of this trauma to be able to live again, or instead, we believe that He doesn't want (or He isn't able) to get us out of the suffocating darkness and pain. That means we will be stuck in this place for the rest of our lives.

Believing that God is able and that He will somehow get me to a place of living a life of meaning and purpose again, is what worked for me. It was not easy, but it's where I decided to put my faith, and made the choice to have hope (a positive expectation) that He could and would get me to that place. This has not been just my own personal experience. Hundreds of other pareavors I have met over the years have experienced the same thing.

Question: Do you have something that is working better?

Is choosing to let your mind meditate on the darkness, the anger, the unfairness, the regrets and all the "Whys?" working for you? Is that bringing you peace? Is it giving you a glimmer of light that sparks hope in your heart? Is it helping you climb out of the dark pit you were hurled into? Is it helping you to live in a way that honors the life of your child?

Choosing to throw it all back at God and asking Him to help you may not ease the pain right away. But I can guarantee that if you continue to do this every time those dark thoughts come your way, eventually you will begin to see a path that will lead you out of the torturing darkness.

Hope is real because God is real. He is the giver of hope, and He has already given it to you because He is in you. The seed of hope is in you. You can have a positive expectation that God will get you out of the darkness and give you a life of meaning and purpose again. Just because you cannot see it or feel it right now, doesn't mean it does not exist.

Reflection: Yes, we may go back and forth for a while, but each time through the darkness, we see the path again, it will be brighter and easier to stay on it longer. Choose to fix your mind on the things that will bring you out, not keep you stuck. Ask God to help you, and then keep choosing it.

Also, stay connected with other pareavors who will encourage you and walk with you, until you are ready to share the same message of hope with another pareavor who needs it! You may not think that will ever happen, but hope changes everything!

> *We have this certain hope like a strong, unbreakable anchor holding our souls to God himself. Our anchor of hope is fastened to the mercy seat in the heavenly realm beyond the sacred threshold.*
> *Hebrews 6:19 (TPT)*

March 8

The Process of Learning to Rest

After Becca died, I discovered *so* many scriptures that I had either misunderstood, or they took on a whole new meaning to me, such as Matthew 11:28-29 where Jesus says,:

> *Come to Me, all you who are weary and burdened, and I will give you rest. Take My yoke upon you and learn from Me, for I*

am gentle and humble in heart, and you will find rest for your souls. (NIV)

There are lots of theological teachings on what Jesus meant by this, including what it meant for Jesus, as a rabbi, to say this. But that is not what I want to share with you. My personal revelation of these two verses did not mean that Jesus would make my life easy, but that being yoked together with Him is being yoked to that place of rest for my soul; that He would help me carry this heavy burden which is impossible for me to carry on my own.

I rediscovered Psalm 23 in The Complete Jewish Bible translation, that promises to *restore my inner person*, and that if I *pass through death-dark ravines, He is with me*; and that *His grace and goodness are still pursuing me every day of my life*. God kept pointing out to me that He wanted me to rest in Him and in the deep love He has for me during this dark time when I felt so devastated, lost and confused.

This is not to say at some point I have it all figured out and now continually live from a place of rest. I wish God would just speak a command and make it all better, taking away the pain and replacing it with constant peace and rest, but it has not happened that way. Learning how to live in that place of resting in God has been a process. The pain can still be pretty intense at times, making me feel like I am going backward, losing that peace and the place of rest.

Would we rather have our child back? Absolutely. But that is not going to happen here on this earth. So, we might as well allow God to love on us and be at work in us, so that their death is not wasted in our lives.

Reflection: How are you doing in the "resting in Him" department? What does that even mean? It is when we determine to let go of our anxious thoughts, our fears, our doubts and our anger, by allowing the presence of His peace to push it all away, even if it is just for a moment. It is breathing in deeply, thinking of how wonderful it will be when we see our child again. It is letting God know that even if you are angry and don't understand why this happened, you trust Him to get you through it. It is acknowledging that you can't do this without Him and letting yourself emotionally fall into His arms as He holds you.

Entering into His rest is not a time and position, but sometimes that is where it starts. You might want to get on your knees and take a minute to tell Him you need Him to help you carry this burden, allowing you to find rest for your soul. Then wait, and let Him meet you however He wants to come to you. Even if you do not feel any different, if you keep at it, you will eventually feel the heaviness lifting as you feel Him helping you carry the load.

> *Then Jesus said, "Come to me, all of you who are weary and carry heavy burdens, and I will give you rest".*
> *Matthew 11:28 (NLT)*

March 9

The Second Year

As I started hearing from other bereaved parents, I discovered I was not the only one who struggled even more in the second year than the first one. There does seem to be an underlying generic timeframe that many of us pareavors can fall into.

The first year is a painful fog, full of numbness, confusion, pain, and disbelief. All the "firsts" hit us hard. The first time he or she is not with us for *each* holiday or yearly family event, the first year they are not here for their birthday and of course, the first anniversary of their death.

I thought the second year would be easier, because I had already gone through everything once. As pareavors just starting out on this horrific journey, we do not think it is even possible, but the second year of being without our child can be worse than the first year in some ways. I hope that is not the case for you, but I want to be up front and honest that it is a possibility.

Why does that happen to so many of us?

Well, for me personally, that first year I braced myself for all the "firsts," plus I was still in that fog of trying to figure out if this had really happened. The second year caught me off guard as the fog began to lift. Round two of all those yearly events no longer had the blessing of numbness to block the full depth of the pain. When that initial shock finally wore off, it caused the weight of my loss to hit me full force, with a heaviness and darkness that left me wondering if I would ever get through it. I remember thinking how desperately I wanted the pain to end, afraid that it never would.

The third year for many of us becomes more livable. We are starting to accept the finality and painful fact that our child will never again be with us at any of these events. We are starting to resign ourselves to the fact that no matter how much it hurts, we must figure out who we are without our child. Some of us even begin to see glimmers of hope; that we can still have joy and happiness in the life we are living with those who are still here whom we love, and who love us.

After saying all of that, I also want to emphasize that we are all on our own individual journey.

Unfortunately, there many parents who remain in the "second-year level" for quite a long time. They take many more years to get to the place of painful acceptance, which is necessary to be able to start rebuilding their life in a way that brings peace, joy, love and laughter back into their lives. (For instance, I personally know someone who waited over four years before they could even bring themselves to have a tombstone made for their child's grave.)

Let me say it again, because it is so important. *NO ONE* is on the same timetable of grieving the death of their child.

Reflection: Do not look at any dates to compare yourself with where others are in their grieving process and use it as some sort of a timeline to force on yourself. We are all on our own individual timeline and need to go through the process at our own speed. Yes, there are some "patterns" (for lack of a better word) that some of us seem to fall into, but don't expect yourself to fit into that.

Right now, take a few minutes to release yourself from any shame or guilt you have put on yourself (or have allowed others to put on you) that you are not as far along in the grieving process that you think you should be. Give yourself grace to walk your own necessary path. As long as you are putting one foot in front of the other, taking each day as it comes, you will get there.

> *Let us hold unswervingly to the hope we*
> *profess, for he who promised is faithful.*
> *Hebrews 10:23 NIV*

March 10

Knowing Why Will Not Bring Peace

There are many pareavors who feel like God betrayed them and they can no longer trust Him. We believe we *might* be able to trust God again if He would tell us why He allowed such a horrible thing as the death of our child in our lives.

And what if He told us why? Do we really think our response would be, "That makes so much sense! Thanks for telling me. Now I can move on and not be in as much pain or turmoil about it." I doubt it! The truth is, if He were to give us a reason why, it would not be a good enough reason for us, and we would argue with Him against the answer He gave us.

Have you ever been in a situation where one of your children demands to know why you won't let them do something, and you know they won't understand (or like) the answer? Usually, they just want to know why, so they can argue with you on why your reason is not good enough! At that point, what is the typical response as a parent? "Because I said so!"

I wonder if God is saying something similar, in a much gentler way, when we ask Him "Why"?

Because I did. You just have to trust me...

March

Like I said, having an answer to our why question probably won't be very helpful, because it will not seem like a good enough reason. Understanding will never bring us peace. That is why we are told to lean on God's understanding.

Refection: I have found that instead of questioning God's character, I get much further by leaning into Him for the strength I need. And the way I lean into Him is by praying something similar to this:

Thank You for Your love. Thank You for the strength You have for me. Thank You for the life of (__my child's name__) and for his/her release into Your glorious presence.

Thank You, Daddy, for letting me just be with You and rest in your arms! Pour into me what needs to be poured in, for You know what I need more than I know myself.

Thank You, Father, that our mortality is swallowed up by life. That means (__my child's name__) is in the real world now! She/he is living the reality of eternity with You, Father God, and with Jesus! And thank you that someday, I will be joining him/her.

Remember, your peace will not come from the answer to your question of "why," but in your decision to trust the One who sees and knows beyond what your mind or emotions can understand.

I've told you all this so that trusting me, you will be unshakable and assured, deeply at peace. In this godless world you will continue to experience difficulties. But take heart! I've conquered the world.
John 16:33 (MSG)

March 11

Working Through the Anger

Many pareavors are angry with God for allowing their child to die. You may be one of them. After all, God could have stopped it. We all know that.

I am going to say something that may shock you. Being angry with God is a healthy, normal reaction to something that is so earth-shattering, and life-altering, and He is okay with the emotion of anger. God wants us to vent and to share, to pour out our hearts to Him; to wail, to cry and to have us demand to know why. We even see that in the Bible, such as David in the book of Psalms.

I think the hardest part of this is that we long to know the answers why, but we don't get to know those answers. In our humanness, we have a need to understand it. Somehow, we have to make sense of it, and I don't know that there is a "make sense of this." I don't think that we get to always know the answers most of the time, if ever, this side of heaven. So, obviously, it is easier to be angry at God, because He seems to be the one who is in charge of all this.

God can take your anger, and He is probably the best person to be angry at, because He understands us. His shoulders are pretty broad, and He can handle whatever we throw at Him, including our angry and ugly accusations. When we're crying out to Him, we're talking to Him. He wants our communication, whether it's good, bad or ugly, it doesn't matter. He just wants us to talk to Him.

It is like when we are angry with our spouse or someone close to us. Sometimes we have to have it out with them to be able to work it all out. It can be the same thing with God because it is a relationship. So, if we are angry at God, we need to have it out with Him, and work our way through it.

Reflection: You have probably already done a good job of letting God know how you feel about the death of your child and how mad you are at Him for not stopping it. But after you do that, how often have you then quieted yourself in the presence of God and given Him the opportunity to fill you with His peace that goes beyond our understanding, smack dab in the middle of your pain?

The bottom line is that it is normal and okay to be angry with God for not stopping the death of your child. However, you need to go through the process of working out that anger, which includes letting Him speak to you and fill you with His presence within your brokenness and deep wounds. Open the door to give Him opportunities to love on you in a way that does not make sense. And remember, it is a process, not a one-time fix.

> But in my distress I cried out to the Lord; yes, I prayed to my God for help. He heard me from his sanctuary; my cry to him reached his ears.
> Psalm 18:6 (NLT)

March 12

As a Husband and Father

(By Dave Diehl)

Even within my own deep painful loss, as a husband and father, I quickly learned how vitally important it was for me to make allowances for my family members, especially my wife, in the way they processed their grief.

We all handle grief in different ways and on different timelines. My other four children all grieved in different ways and some longer than others. They all still have times when they miss Becca immensely. I encourage all of them to allow each other the space they need to grieve in their own way and not expect the others to grieve in the same way they themselves do.

This is especially true for us husbands in regard to our wives. If you are like me, as I suspect many men are, I did not always want to talk about it. I preferred to keep my feelings to myself, except with a few close people.

My wife, on the other hand, seemed to wear her grief on her sleeve. Laura would post all sorts of feelings on Facebook. I would every so often, but nothing like she did those first couple of years. (So much so that I knew it made some people uncomfortable, even though she always pointed to God as her source of strength.) I would sometimes think *is this normal* or *is my wife having some major issues here?*

Laura has a very deep and close relationship to God. She amazes me with her insight, yet here she was struggling, even though she knew without a doubt where Becca was and the glory she was experiencing. Was it normal for this to be so hard and go on so long? The truth is, absolutely! Pretty much everything is "normal" when it comes to grieving the death of our child, it seems.

At one point it occurred to me that often people, myself included, criticize those who post too many feelings on Facebook. I wonder, though, what we would think of King David's posts if he were one of our "friends." The Psalms look quite a bit like some Facebook postings, and they are plastered with his feelings!

If you are a father who has faced the death of your child, and you are frustrated that your wife is still deeply struggling, let me be very real with you here. In most cases, it will take our wives months or years to "get on with life" the way we imagine they should. It is not our place to determine what that looks like; ours is to simply love, care for, and protect her during this time, however long it may be.

Reflection: Do you wear your grief on your sleeve, or do you keep it very close and personal? (Or does it depend on the moment and who is around you?)

It is easy for those around us to judge the way we are working through our grief (including our spouses) when it looks different from them or makes them uncomfortable, which can be very hurtful. If that has happened to you, ask God to help you to forgive them for not understanding. Do not allow their judgement to become an added roadblock to fighting your way out of the darkness. (And if this has not happened to you, send up a prayer for your fellow pareavors who are struggling with it.)

> *Be kind and helpful to one another,*
> *tender-hearted [compassionate, understanding].*
> *Ephesians 4:32 (AMP)*

March 13

Laughter and Tears

I am sitting at my sister's house as I write this. Dave and I were able to stop and visit for a day and a half on our way through her area. As always, when we get together, no matter how short (like this time) or how long the visit, we always manage to get in both tears and laughter.

It amazes me how both of these can go together so often. But that is not always the case. When our child first dies, the laughter seems to be gone forever. We do not think we will ever laugh again. And when we eventually have something that makes us want to laugh, we can feel guilty.

In thinking about this, I decided to look up what I wrote about the word laughter in my book *My Grief Journey*. Here is what it says.

> *How can we possibly smile, or ever be happy again after our child dies? Just the thought of it can make us feel guilty.*
>
> *But we can, and not only that, it is exactly what we need to do. And we need to reintroduce fun and laughter into our lives, because laughter is medicine to the soul.*

> *If it was reversed (like we all wish it was) would you want your child to remain isolated, depressed and hopeless, believing that life was not worth living without you? Of course not! When we stop and think about it, most of us know in our hearts that our child would not want us to live our lives out that way either.*
>
> *It's okay to have hope. It's okay to smile. It's okay to laugh and enjoy life again. From one pareavor to another, I give you permission.*

Yes, when your soul has a reason to smile and even to laugh, I give you permission. It is very true that laughter is like a medicine to our souls. Not only does God tell us that, but medical science has backed God up and proven it as well.

Reflection: It does not do any good for me to give you permission to laugh again, if you do not give it to yourself. It really is okay to lean into a funny moment and let the laughter be released. If this is an area you struggle in, ask God to help you let go of the unfounded guilt that you should not have.

Don't worry about leaving the tears behind. They will return soon enough. But for right now, let's take our "soul medicine" today and find something that will make us laugh, allowing our laughter to be the needed release that God intended for it to be.

> *A happy heart is good medicine and a joyful mind causes healing, but a broken spirit dries up the bones.*
> *(Proverbs 17:22 (AMP)*

March 14

Our Self-talk

As we work our way through the deep grief and darkness, it is important to be aware of our thoughts and our self-talk. So often we find ourselves using the words "never" and "always".

- I will always be a mess.
- I will always be sad and depressed.
- I will never be able to be happy without my child here.
- I will never be able to celebrate Christmas again.

Here is a big one: I will never be able to forgive _____. (Fill in the blank; it might even be yourself.)

When our child dies, there are so many people we need to forgive. It may be the person who caused it, people around us who are hurting us in our grief, ourselves (for not being able to stop it), our child for leaving us, and yes, God. Unforgiveness is extremely heavy baggage we carry around. Forgiveness is not for others, to let them off the hook, but to release ourselves from them, lightening our load. Forgiveness is not usually an "I can't" but an "I won't", often because that person caused such a deep hurt that we think they don't deserve to be forgiven.

Any of the "always" or "never" thoughts that we think are because we cannot see through the darkness. And until we can see light, we tell ourselves it won't ever happen.

But what if...? What if that light is on its way? What if you are *not* the one-and-only person that God *isn't* able to help since the creation of the world, after the death of their child? What if thousands of others who have lost their child thought the same thing and found out they were wrong?

Hope! Hope is a powerful word. And as long as there is God, there is hope! If nothing else, believe that as long as there are other pareavors offering encouragement, there is hope.

Reflection: Your active mind. It is either thinking positive thoughts or negative thoughts. Do your best not to let it become the devil's playground with fear, doubt, lies and anxiety.

When you find yourself struggling with so much overwhelming darkness and negativity, remind yourself that His light is still in you. The seed of hope is in you. Switch out your own negative "never" and "always" with His. He has told you that He will *never* leave you and that He is *always* with you. This is not based on how you feel. Nourish that seed of hope that is dormant in you by speaking the truth. It will begin to sprout and will push its way to the surface so that you can start to believe it.

> *Let my words and my thoughts be pleasing to you, Lord,*
> *because you are my mighty rock and my protector.*
> *Psalm 19:14 (CEV)*

March 15

Difficult Events

There are going to be times when attending a joyful or celebration event will feel like a slap-in-the-face reminder that your child is not here; that he or she will not be part of something they should have been right in the middle of. This will continue for many years such as weddings or a baby shower that would have directly affected your child in some way.

I have found there are a couple of options when invited to something like this.

One is that instead of making my absence about me, I let those hosting/attending know that my absence is about *them*. I do not want to dampen or possibly ruin the celebration for them and those attending by how deeply I still love and miss my child. Be completely honest and tell the host, "You are working so hard to make this such a nice event, but I just don't know if I can keep the tears at bay and would rather not take away any of the attention that belongs to _____."

The other option I have found that seems to surprise people, is to ask if there can be a way to include your child. Can a toast be made to your child (and possibly others who have also passed on and are missed)? Can there be a photo placed somewhere? Can a book be set on a table where those attending can write a memory or a note to your child, letting him or her know how much they are missed? Yes, there will probably be some moments of tears, but doing something like this can give a sense of relief, as it gives you the needed grace and permission to miss your child.

When I know my daughter will be acknowledged in some way, it helps bring a healing comfort in the midst of the pain to know others miss her as well, and have not forgotten her. Will there be tears? Probably. Do I care? Not anymore. They are tears of a love that will never be quenched until I am with her again, and I don't care if people around me understand that or not.

Reflection: First, please release the guilt of not attending functions that are too difficult, no matter how long ago your loss has been. Accept the fact that those who have never lost a child just aren't going to understand. How could they? I know I sure didn't, until it happened to me.

Then think about what events are coming up in the next few months. A wedding? Someone's graduation party? A 50th birthday celebration? Do not stew over it and leave the host hanging. Pray, make a decision whether or not you will be going, and rest in God's peace with that decision. It isn't about what others think you should be doing, it is about what you and God know you need, based on where you are in this journey.

> *God our Father loves us. He is kind and has given us*
> *eternal comfort and a wonderful hope. We pray that*
> *our Lord Jesus Christ and God our Father will encourage*
> *you and help you always to do and say the right thing.*
> *2 Thessalonians 2:16-17 (CEV)*

March 16
I Can't See Any Good

When my husband, Dave, graduated from college with a Computer Science degree, he wanted to get a job to stay in the area and not relocate. The only job offered to him locally, after several months of searching, was with a non-profit organization. The pay was miserably low, and it was difficult to make ends meet. However, the employer made up for it in insurance benefits, which was not a big deal to us at the time. But God knew that within the next few months we would need those benefits.

That was when Becca (who was only three years old at the time) was diagnosed with cancer, had her leg amputated, and went through nine months of chemotherapy. During that time her medical bills were easily in the hundreds of thousands of dollars, but we only had to pay less than $1000 of the medical costs! When we look back, the job God provided that did not seem like it was meeting our needs, turned out to be exactly what we needed with incredibly good insurance, which far outweighed our need for better finances.

Each time a terrible event happens in our lives, we can get upset at God, even angry, wanting to know why He allowed it. But for many of us, as we continue on and are able to look back, often we can actually see God's hand was in it. We may not have been able to see Him at work in the middle of the crisis, but now that we are further down the road, we can connect the dots and see how God used that situation to bring direction we might not have even known we needed at the time.

So, in other words, when we are questioning, "God, why did you let this happen to me?" His answer could very well be, "I did not let it happen *to* you. I let it happen *for* you."

You may be thinking at this point, "There is no way I can read this and have Laura tell me the death of my child was something God did *for* me." And I am not about to say that!

I have been in that place of suffocating darkness myself after the death of our daughter and have told God to just kill me now and take me off this earth. I am not going to tell you that God did not stop your child from leaving this earth as something good He did for you. However, we need to realize that the death of our child did not blindside God. He knows what we cannot possibly know. He can see what we cannot see.

Our lives will never be the same. *We* will never be the same. But within that, we can make sure the death of our child is not wasted. We can allow God's love to wash over us, to heal us, and to take the change in us and use it *against* the enemy who brought death into this world.

I know there will not be enough "good" that comes from the death of our child that will outweigh the desire we have to still have him or her here with us, or remove the pain. But we need to keep our hearts open so that God can show us how He will keep His Word, bringing good things into our lives again.

Reflection: I recently heard an illustration that might help. When we make a cake, the ingredients by themselves don't taste very good. No one wants to eat a mouth full of flour or eat a raw egg. But when you put all the ingredients together, you have something good. Many of you reading this are still waiting for more "ingredients", to see how anything good can possibly come from the death of your child.

If you can't see any good yet, that means God isn't done yet. Ask Him to help you be able to see when "ingredients" start being added to your life, so that you can once again taste and see that He is good.

Taste and see that the Lord is good;
blessed is the one who takes refuge in him.
Psalm 34:8 (NIV)

March 17

I Don't Want to be Here

"So kill me, God! Do it now, please!"

This was what I wrote in my journal, two months after Becca died. I didn't think I could take the horrific pain and suffocating darkness anymore.

I hear and see quite often other freshly grieving parents feel the same way I did. We are not usually suicidal; we just don't want to live anymore. A part of our very being has been cut off from us and the pain is too great to continue living.

For most of my adult life, I wanted to live to be 100, like a few of my relatives. (There is longevity and good health on both sides of my family, so there is a fairly good chance of it.) But after Becca died, I took that off the table and decided the sooner I was out of here, the better!

A few months later I wrote a journal entry thanking the Holy Spirit for giving me a reason to stick around. That reason was for specific people I still had in my life, and some of the things I realized I really didn't want to miss out on with them. I had a glimmer of a reason to continue living and ended my entry by writing:

With that new hope and revelation, I can once again claim verses like Psalm 91:16: "With long life I will satisfy him."

I still felt like it was a stretch to believe God would *satisfy* me. I mean, how was that possible with my daughter no longer here on this earth? But I was feeling the seed of hope sprouting inside of me, and I was going to do what I could to water and nurture it.

Most of us know in our heads that we have other people to live for. But it takes a while for our hearts to get past the horrendous pain, to be able to comprehend it in a way that becomes a lifeline for us.

So, if that is how you are feeling, just know that you are not the only one! And know that there is hope to get beyond it.

Reflection: We are all on our own timeline, so don't expect to feel a certain way by a certain time. Very few parents I know have only taken several months to feel like they want to stay here and continue living out their lives; for most it has easily taken well over a year or more.

To help get you there, pull out a piece of paper and write down at least five people who still want you and need you in their lives. (Don't tell yourself no one needs you or would even miss you. That is the enemy feeding you lies!) What are some things you know that are in their future that it might be kind of nice to be there to see or be part of? Write those things down next to their names. Now put that in a place where you will see it once in a while.

The important thing is that even if you don't think it can possibly happen to you, make sure you hang on to those of us who felt the same way when our child died but are now moving forward with our lives. Let us be your hope for you.

For I know the plans I have for you," says the Eternal, "plans for peace, not evil, to give you a future and hope—never forget that."
Jeremiah 29:11 (VOICE)

March 18
Lies Keep Us Bound

People tend to act on their feelings, based on what they believe. Many people live out of their feelings, and feelings do not always equal the truth. To put that a different way, just because I have feelings about something, no matter how strong, does not mean my feelings are necessarily based on the truth.

We all know that a child's perception of a situation can be quite different from the reality of what actually happened. A child may be heart-broken because of an event in their childhood. Then at some point in their adult life, that child hears the explanation of what really happened, which was beyond what they could understand at the time. They may even find out what they thought was horrible as a child, was done for their benefit. Now they can look at what was once very painful as a child who had limited understanding, through the eyes of reality instead, allowing them to start letting go of the painful emotions that were attached to that event.

To change your behavior, which is driven by your emotions, you must know and understand the truth. It is truth that will set you free. To experience victory in any area of your life, you must overcome limiting beliefs in that area.

Do I believe God killed my daughter to use it in some way in my life? ABSOLUTELY NOT! Do I believe that God allowed the natural consequences of a fallen and sinful world to take effect, not stopping it, even though many people were praying for her healing? Yes, I do. Do I still give Him permission to do what He wants to do as God, instead of what I want Him to do, because He can see so much more than I can see? ABSOLUTELY!

I have chosen not to change my thoughts and beliefs on who God is because I did not get a prayer answered the way I wanted Him to answer, no matter how painful it may be.

Reflection: Too often we sit back in our pain and grief and wait for some sort of miracle to happen in front of us when the miracle is already inside us. The miraculous isn't something we strive for; it is something we were created for.

A miracle needs to take place in each one of us after the death of our child. It is something only God can do, and that is to set us free from the suffocating dark pit we found ourselves thrown into. Since the truth sets us free, ask God what lie you are believing. Allow Him to speak truth into your shattered heart and mind, to set you free from that lie. This is not a one-time fix, but a slow release, as we learn to walk in that truth and are then ready to receive the next truth He has to share.

For if you embrace the truth, it will release true freedom into your lives.
John 8:32 (TPT)

March 19

Helping Others Understand

A question I get asked a lot is, "How do I get the people around me to understand why I am still grieving the death of my child so deeply?"

Let me warn you, this might be hard to read, because of how deeply true it is. There may be some triggers here, but there is something you may want to consider sharing with them to help a bit.

Have you had one of your parents die? Maybe a grandparent, aunt, uncle, or a good friend that you were really close to? Have you quit missing them? At certain times of the year, or when something triggers a memory, does your heart ache, and do you maybe cry a few tears?

That is how we feel every day because every day there are triggers, reminding us that our child is no longer here with us.

For instance:

- *When someone asks us how many children we have*
- *We see their favorite cereal that we will never buy for them again*
- *When we hear a song they used to dance silly to or sing loudly to*
- *On the first day of school every year*
- *We want to show them something we bought that they would get a kick out of but... we can't...*
- *Every holiday (especially Mother's Day/Father's Day)*
- *On their birthday and on their anniversary death date when they left this earth forever*
- *During a thunderstorm because they loved (or were scared of) storms*
- *Our favorite sport team plays, and we no longer hear him or her cheering with us or ranting with us*
- *When something funny happens and we want to tell or show our child and then remember... we can't...*

I know we desperately want those around us to extend grace in our horrible loss, allowing us to grieve deeply the way that we need to and is *normal* for someone who has lost a child. Unfortunately, way too often that does not happen. The people around us want us to get back to normal and go on with life, giving the impression they think it's no big deal our child has died.

Grieving the death of our child is something that we don't want to go through either. But we don't have a choice. We will miss them for the rest of our lives here on earth.

How could someone who has not had their child die possibly know what it is like? Plain and simple, *they can't*. Which is why it is so important to connect with those who *can*.

Reflection: Tears are a gift from God. I know you may have felt like you cry way too much, and they are more of a curse. But we underestimate the healing they bring to our souls. We are very wounded, so it is going to take a lot of tears to wash away so much of this pain.

With that being said, it is good to have an explanation for those who truly want to know why we are still struggling. May I suggest you reread what was written for today, giving some time to think through what you can share with others who think you should be past being so sad all the time. Yes, I know there will probably be more of those darn tears as you do this, or even as you share your reason(s) with others. But each tear is bringing you closer to the measure of healing you are longing for.

> *When Jesus saw her weeping, and the Jews who*
> *had come along with her also weeping, he was*
> *deeply moved in spirit and troubled.... Jesus wept.*
> *John 11:33, 35 (NIV)*

March 20

Feeling Anxious

Much of this book was being put together during the COVID19 worldwide pandemic. With this unusual event, many found themselves with a lot of extra anxiety. For many, it also caused their painful grief to rise to the surface even more. Some of you may have even lost your child during this terrible time. If that is the case, I am so very sorry!

Since Becca died, God has really been working on me in the area of being anxious. I used to tell myself I was not worried; I was just anxious. But there really isn't much difference, is there? Both of them are being concerned in a negative way about something in the future that we probably don't have much control over.

Both fear and faith come from the same root – our thoughts and emotions about the unknown future. So, that means we get to choose.

Am I going to be anxious and worry about a possible future event that I will probably not be able to change? Or am I going to trust that even though the worst possible nightmare has happened in my life, God is still taking care of me and will continue to be the peace in my storms (or the hurricanes) of my life?

Fear brings torment. A trusting faith brings peace.

Which one are you going to choose and fight for? Better yet, which one are you going to choose and *surrender* to?

Reflection: For quite some time now, I have been making the shift that my trust in God is not based on the outcome of a situation. My trust is now rooted in my relationship with the One who holds the outcome and has the final word in everything; the One who has a plan to right every wrong ever done here on this earth. It may not be in my own desired timing, but it will happen.

What is something you are anxious about right now? See yourself giving it to God. Watch Him take it and set it gently aside, and then come and put His arms around you, holding you tightly. Feel the warmth of His love melt away the anxious thoughts, the worries, and the cares, as you melt into His arms, feeling deeply loved, protected, and secure.

> *Don't fret or worry. Instead of worrying, pray. Let petitions and praises shape your worries into prayers, letting God know your concerns. Before you know it, a sense of God's wholeness, everything coming together for good, will come and settle you down. It's wonderful what happens when Christ displaces worry at the center of your life.*
> *Philippians 4:6-7 (MSG)*

March 21

From Winter to Spring

Many of my friends say that fall is their favorite season. I do love fall, with all of its splendor in the north when the trees turn all those beautiful colors. It can be breathtaking! However, spring is my favorite season. I love watching what looked old and dead come into full life with so much green and watching an endless array of colorful flowers begin to blossom.

Have you noticed in the spring how things seem to have their own time to bloom? Some growth comes out right away, and others take a lot longer, even making us wonder if it is going to happen at all.

This can be like our grief. We all feel like winter has come into our lives. And the further north you live, the more you experience what that is like. Nothing grows. Everything is brown and drab. And it seems to go on and on, like it will never end.

But spring *always* returns! Some years it is later than others, but it happens. Little green buds start coming out on the trees. The grass goes from brown to green. Farmers start planting their fields and little shoots begin to rise from the brown dirt. Flowers start to bloom. Robins begin to appear, along with butterflies and bees.

March

Many years ago, there was a bush in our front yard that normally had beautiful deep pink flowers on it, but for a couple of years, it stopped blooming and looked like it was dying. So, toward the end of summer one year, I chopped it down to almost nothing, and waited for spring. To my amazement, it grew back and was full of more beautiful flowers than it *ever* had in the years before!

You may feel like you have been chopped down to nothing and will never "bloom" again. You may think you will live the rest of your life, feeling like it is winter. But spring always comes! Your life is not over. It may take a while, but there is still life in you to be lived, and it can and will be beautiful again.

How do I know? Because you have the Seed of hope living in you. Because God's resurrection power is at work in you. Just like you cannot see the work being done in a seed under the ground, you may not be able to feel or see God at work in you, but that is okay. One day it will break through, and you will start to see and feel the warmth and beauty of life around you.

Reflection: Look around you. Can you see any signs of spring yet? Spring will come in full force, just like it always does. And just like new life is all around you, it is happening inside you. It might be a while, but you will bloom again.

Close your eyes and lift your face upward. Imagine feeling the warmth of the sun on your face as you let it relax you. Then imagine feeling the warmth of the Son surrounding your heart as you let Him give you peace. See that seed of hope stir, as it is nourished by His love.

Oh, that we might know the Lord! Let us press on
to know him. He will respond to us as surely as the
arrival of dawn or the coming of rains in early spring.
Hosea 6:3 (NLT)

March 22

Is God in Control?

As I was praying for those parents who are connected to GPS Hope recently, I wrote the following as I felt God was speaking softly to my heart for some of you.

My child,

I know you are angry. But the basis of that anger is fear. Fear that you have no control over your life or those you love. Fear that what you believe might not be true. Fear that I am not who I say I am and that I am not really in control, either.

I assure you, the world is in My hands, but that doesn't mean I control. You see, there isn't any difference in "control" and "being in control".

"Being in control" means manipulating, and that is evil. That is the enemy.

I give freedom. I give peace. I AM love itself, and it is impossible for love to control or manipulate. I gave this world to man, and man has corrupted it. I will walk with you through the evil and corruption, until you join me here, where evil and corruption are not allowed.

With your own children, if you were to control their lives, it wouldn't be from true love. It would be from a selfish fear that wants to keep them captive. You want to determine what will happen to them so that both you and your child won't have to go through pain. (And yes, there is a difference between building parameters of safety and outright control. You don't raise your child in a cage to control them. You find ways to protect them and teach them how to be safe, allowing appropriate freedom within that.)

There are three ways to force a person to do what you think is best for them or what you want them to do; manipulation, intimidation, or domination. Do any of those show love? I cannot do any of those things, because I AM love itself, which makes it literally impossible for any of those to come from Me.

Just like a good parent would do, I will be there with you. I will encourage you. I will bind up your wounds. I will speak words of truth, to bring peace and comfort. The ONLY control you have on earth is over yourself. You get to choose where your thoughts take you. Do they take you to darkness, anger, false blame and bitterness? Or do they take you to truth, life, peace, trust, light and hope?

You get to choose who you will serve in your soul and in your mind. Death, or life? I want you to choose life, so I am at work. Even when you can't see Me, you can't feel Me, you can't hear Me, I am at work to bring light into your darkness. To bring hope into your hopelessness. To bring purpose and meaning back into your life. To bring you joy that you didn't know was possible.

Choose life. Choose love. Choose Me. I will get you through this without "being in control", without manipulating you, without using intimidation tactics, and without being a tyrant and placing demands on you by dominating you. I will do it with pure and perfect love, which is what your child is experiencing in all of its fullness.

I love you, more than you can comprehend, because I AM love. You would not have love for your child if I was not in it, because it is impossible to love without my presence. I AM love. Choose to open yourself to that love so that you can receive what I have for you while you are waiting to be reunited with your child.

No, I am not "in control" because I AM LOVE!

Reflection: I think today's reading is its own reflection. Read it again. And again. And again. Fold the page back, put a special marker here, so that you can come back to it when you need the reminder.

> *I hear the Lord saying, "I will stay close to you,*
> *instructing and guiding you along the pathway*
> *for your life. I will advise you along the way and*
> *lead you forth with my eyes as your guide.*
> *Psalm 32:8 (TPT)*

March 23

Peace and Pain Together

The pain of losing our child always seems to be with us. Even if I am not emotionally feeling the pain at the moment, it is still there. It is almost like a physical chronic pain. There are times you are so used to having the pain that you don't even realize you are feeling it.

During the first few years after my daughter Becca's death, God gave me many reminders to rest in Him and His ways that did not make any sense. It was a hard thing to do, because I could not see any light in my darkness or understand why God was allowing so much intense pain. He would share His reminders to just "be" and to rest in Him in so many different ways. He would remind me to take a breath and breathe in His love and peace; or to cling tightly to His hand, reminding me to look at Him whenever my circumstances overwhelmed me.

Let me say here, though, that the pain is still pretty intense at times, and I can feel like I am going backward as I lose that peace and the place of rest I am fighting to keep. For instance, at one point, Becca's husband dropped off four plastic tubs on our front porch that he no longer wanted. They all contained things of Becca's that were special and important to her, along with some of her medical equipment and other not so good memory items.

It was *really* hard to go through those bins. But the thing that left me in a crying mess for the next few days was when I discovered her wedding dress smashed in the bottom of the last bin. It felt so cruel, so careless. *My daughter's life has been reduced to four plastic bins*, I thought.

But instead of allowing myself to go in that direction, I told myself the truth. Her life was so much bigger than these four bins. However, it was another door of finality I had to painfully work through, and once again make a conscious decision to rest in who God is, within the painful circumstance.

I have now learned that peace and pain can both reside in us at the same time. Whether I am consciously feeling the pain or not, an underlying peace seems to travel side-by-side with my pain. It is definitely the peace of God that goes beyond any understanding, and I am so thankful that He offers it to us and gives it freely.

I wish God would just speak a command and make it all better, instantly removing the pain and replacing it with constant peace and rest, but it doesn't happen that way.

Reflection: Learning how to live in that place of peace is a process that becomes part of our journey and learning to rest in God is a must if you want to get out of your place of darkness.

That means spending time alone with Him. You do not even have to talk to Him, just "be" with Him, in your pain, your anger, or your darkness. Don't feel guilty about taking as much time as you need to be intimate with the One who loves you like crazy and wants to get you out of the suffocating pit and onto the path of living again. Spend intimate time with Him. Lots of it.

Spend some time with Him right now. See Him reaching past the pain in your soul and shining His Light on the peace in your spirit. Let Him show you the way out by resting in the fullness of Himself.

Peace I leave with you; My [perfect] peace I give to you; not as the world gives do I give to you. Do not let your heart be troubled, nor let it be afraid. [Let My perfect peace calm you in every circumstance and give you courage and strength for every challenge.]
John 14:27 (AMP)

March 24

I Know How You Feel Because...

Something I have noticed, is how rare it is to hear a parent who has lost a child say to another pareavor, "I know how you feel." We know the pain is too individually deep to know how another parent feels. Each relationship between the child and the parent is so unique. I could never know how you feel, just like you could never know how I feel. Even if we lost a child in a similar way, such as a car accident, or the same form of cancer, we won't tell anyone who is grieving, "I know how you feel because..."

And yet, it is amazing how quickly someone who has never experienced the death of a child will tell us they know how we feel. "I know how you feel. I was devastated when my grandma died because we were really close." Or, "I know how you feel. I lost my husband several years ago and I thought I would never get over it" (said while holding on to the arm of her new husband).

When a grieving parent is told something like this, the reaction it raises on the inside of us is oftentimes instant anger. We do not mean to feel that way. But to compare your loss with mine is so very, very wrong! I am sorry, but to tell me you know how it feels to bury my child because your aunt died and she practically raised you, is not the same thing. Painful and tragic? Yes, for sure! Does it feel the same as my pain? Sorry, but no.

This is a very painful subject for parents who have lost a child to death; to have another person say they know how it feels to lose a child because they lost... (and it has nothing to do with losing a child). Those who have lost both a child and a spouse, or a child and a parent, etc. will say the loss of their child has taken them to a place of much darker and intense pain, and that place of darkness and pain stays with them for way longer.

Do people need to work through the grief of these kinds of losses? Definitely! But don't try to tell me because you have suffered a painful loss that you know how it feels to have my child die, having part of my very being cut off from me.

Reflection: We know the death of a family member or close friend can cause deep pain and trauma in a person's life. We are not minimizing other losses. All we are asking is for people to not compare losses, and not to tell anyone who has experienced a devastating loss (especially someone who has lost a child through death), "I know how you feel because..."

Here is another way to look at it, that may help. Those people are trying to relate with you through the deepest pain they have ever felt, because they want you to know that they are hurting with you. The way they worded it may not be correct, but their heart is hurting deeply for you, remembering how deeply they hurt when their loved one died. Ask God to help you not to bristle when someone compares their grief and tells you they know how you feel.

You can even take it further by asking Him to give you a gracious and kind reply, realizing they are hurting with you, based on the deepest loss they have experienced.

You're familiar with the old written law, 'Love your friend,' and its unwritten companion, 'Hate your enemy.' I'm challenging that. I'm telling you to love your enemies. Let them bring out the best in you, not the worst. When someone gives you a hard time, respond with the supple moves of prayer, for then you are working out of your true selves, your God-created selves.
Matthew 5:43-44 (MSG)

March 25

God Didn't Forsake You

When Becca died, I knew better than to blame God, but I did have to fight with myself about it. I know that God is not the cause of death; the enemy is. But that did not take away the immense pain and darkness and how lost and alone I felt.

Here is one my journal entries, showing my struggles with anger and frustration, over a year-and-a-half after Becca died:

6/26/13: Holy Spirit, why the despair? Why the weeping? Why the anger? For days now...why? What is going on internally that is causing all of this? I throw myself at Your mercy and cry out HELP ME! And I'm so angry that I am even struggling like this! I feel so fake! How can I be a Spirit-filled Christian and be struggling like this? How can I spend time with You for hours in some seasons and be like this? How can I be putting this prayer room to so much use and be so much in my flesh?

The enemy wants us to believe we are alone, but that is a lie. God will never leave us and never forsake us. You may be thinking, "If that is true, why did He let my child die? He *did* leave me. He *did* forsake me!"

Many grieving Christian parents go through a time where they get angry with God and turn their backs on Him. They can't believe in a God who would take their child from them. But Jesus warned us we would have tribulation in this world (John 16:33).

God did not leave me. He carried me through it. I cannot say He walked with me—I don't think I did much walking for quite some time. God is not my crutch to prop me up; He is my wheelchair to carry me, and He certainly did during that painful dark time. I am guessing that right now, God is carrying you, like He did me. If you can't see that now, you will some day when you look back.

Refection: Yes, God could have stepped in and saved our child, and that is beyond what I can understand. I have a finite mind. I don't know why He did not save Becca, and I don't know why He didn't save your child.

But what I do know is there is no greater time for our need to have God at work in our lives than the death of our child. Without God there is no hope. And without hope, we will be stuck in our pit of despair.

We get to choose whether we move toward God, or we move away from Him. But when we move away from God, we are moving away from the One who can give us the greatest strength possible to get through this. Don't fight Him. Even if you are still angry and confused, *choose* to move toward Him, and accept His strength to carry you.

By the way, God also did not leave Becca. He was with her as she crossed from my world into His. And He was there with your child also. He didn't forsake them; He received them and welcomed them into His life-giving presence.

> *Brothers and sisters, we do not want you to be*
> *uninformed about those who sleep in death, so that*
> *you do not grieve like the rest of mankind, who have no hope.*
> *1 Thessalonians 4:13 (NIV)*

March 26

Taking Communion

When I had my little prayer room under the basement stairs (in the house we sold to my son), I kept matzo crackers and grape juice handy so that I could occasionally have a time of reflection of what the death of Jesus personally means to me. This became even more meaningful after Becca's death.

I would start by putting on some meaningful worship music, allowing myself to be immersed in His presence. It was always a sacred time that often came with tears, as I allowed the Holy Spirit to remind me how deeply God loves me.

It is mind boggling that He came to this crappy world for the purpose of dying an excruciatingly painful and shameful death, so that I would not have to be permanently separated from Becca and eventually my other children, my grandchildren, Dave, our parents, my sister and others I love deeply. He also did it to set me free from the chains the enemy puts on me while here on this earth!

Reflection: If you have never had your own personal communion time, thinking it must be served to you by church leadership, let me just say that cannot be supported anywhere in the Scriptures.

I encourage you to take some time right now, gather whatever you have available for the elements, and allow God to minister to you in a *deeply personal* way as you remember His death, burial and resurrection through taking communion. I believe God will meet you in a very precious and sacred way.

> *He was despised and rejected—a man of sorrows, acquainted with deepest grief. We turned our backs on him and looked the other way. He was despised, and we did not care. Yet it was our weaknesses he carried; it was our sorrows that weighed him down. And we thought his troubles were a punishment from God, a punishment for his own sins! But he was pierced for our rebellion, crushed for our sins. He was beaten so we could be whole. He was whipped so we could be healed.*
> *Isaiah 53:3-5 (NLT)*

March 27

Winter Doesn't Last Forever

I don't know about where you live, but around here this year it sure feels like it is taking a long time for spring to fully arrive. I was reminded of that once again when I looked out my kitchen window and saw my

March

first robin this year. Back in Wisconsin, that has always been a sure sign of spring for me, even though they will probably get some more snow!

Whether I am just more antsy than usual in wanting warm weather and the beauty of colorful flowers and green trees and grass, or if it is truly a bit late some years, it makes me think about how anxious we can be in our grief, as well.

"When will I stop hurting so bad?"

"I don't think I will ever enjoy life again."

These are things we think and say, especially the first two or three years after the death of our child.

Things are so colorless, and we feel bitterly cold and dead inside. We can't see a way out, thinking this is how it will be for the rest of our lives.

I have had several moms tell me that they did not think they ever would or could get past the darkness, but now two years, or three years, or five years after their child's death, something is stirring inside them that they want to start feeling alive again. I see this as a sign that the "winter" of grief is coming to a close, and the new growth of spring is on its way.

There is no right or wrong amount of time for us to be in that dark suffocating place of grief. But wherever you are on this journey, I pray that this spring will give you a sign as a reminder of hope, that just like God made the sun to rise every morning, and spring to always follow winter, that He made a way for you to have life again after the death of your child, even if you can't imagine it to be so.

Reflection: Depending on the year, it is close to the day we specifically remember Jesus' death and resurrection. Even if you are angry at Him for not stepping in and saving your child from leaving this earth, I encourage you to take a moment to thank Him, that at least He made a way for you to be with your child again very soon, never to be separated again, because of what Jesus came to earth to do in reconciling a sinful decaying world to Himself.

Until that day comes, I hope you will also join me in being thankful that the winter season is coming to a close and spring is on its way, both physically in the seasons, and emotionally in our grief.

My love speaks and says to me, "Get up, my love, my beautiful one, and come with me. For see, the winter is past. The rain is over and gone. The flowers are coming through the ground. The time for singing has come. The voice of the turtle-dove has been heard in our land. The fig tree has its fruits. The flowers on the vines spread their sweet smell. Get up, my love, my beautiful one, and come with me! O my dove, hidden in the rock, in the secret place in the mountain-side, let me see you. Let me hear your voice. For your voice is sweet, and you are beautiful".
Song of Solomon 2:10-14 (NLV)

March 28

The Key of Forgiveness

Forgiveness is a key God has given us that will unlock prison doors. It is kind of like the master key that works in any lock.

Forgiveness is not based on whether that person deserves to be punished. It is not based on our feelings. It is not something we do for the other person who has wronged us. Forgiveness is a gift that you give to *yourself*, to unlock your *own* prison door and set *yourself* free.

Many years ago, I discovered something about elephants that I like to share when I am out speaking. You may have seen one tied by a rope to something that is not very secure, causing you to wonder what would happen if that elephant broke away and started running.

When it is still a baby, the owner will tie a chain around its leg, securing it to something he or she can't pull away from. That baby will try to pull away for weeks, and eventually give up, believing it is impossible. Once the baby has that mindset, as soon as that elephant feels anything put around his leg, he won't even try to get away, believing he is trapped.

That is how I see many of us with our refusing to forgive. We tell ourselves that we *can't* forgive someone. Maybe it is the person who was directly or indirectly the cause of our child's death. Maybe it is someone

March

who has hurt us deeply by not being there for us or saying something inappropriate. Maybe you can't forgive yourself and are convinced that it was your own fault because you should have _____ (fill in the blank).

Forgiveness is the foundation of rebuilding your life with hope and healing. We can only get so far in learning to live again when we refuse to forgive someone. It keeps you attached (like the elephant who doesn't know it can get free) and keeps you being dragged through the emotional mud by that person, even if they don't know or don't care. But then, who is it really hurting - that person, or yourself? Because refusing to forgive is like drinking poison and expecting the other person to die.

Reflection: Who do you need to forgive? How about if you take a step in that direction? Please do not say that you can't. Be honest. Either say you are not ready to forgive them yet or admit that you are making the choice to just plain be unwilling to forgive because you think they deserve your anger and hatred.

If you don't want to stay stuck there and are ready to use the key to unlock yourself from this prison, ask God to help you to start the process to forgive. Forgiveness is not based on your feelings. it is based on doing what you know you need to do. The feelings of freedom may come immediately, or they may take a long time. But the best and most powerful way to get there is to speak your forgiveness out loud. Say it over and over again until you find yourself walking in the freedom of unforgiveness.

> *Since you are all set apart by God, made holy and dearly loved, clothe yourselves with a holy way of life: compassion, kindness, humility, gentleness, and patience. Put up with one another. Forgive. Pardon any offenses against one another, as the Lord has pardoned you, because you should act in kind.*
> *Colossians 3:12-13 (VOICE)*

March 29

Is Jesus Lord?

I don't remember exactly what it was, but many years ago I was asking God to change or fix something happening in my life. In my spirit, I heard Him ask me which prayer I wanted answered. I was not sure what He meant.

In my heart, He reminded me of my consistent prayer of giving Him permission to do whatever He needed to do in my life, to get me where He wanted me to be. He then let me know that whatever this was I was praying for Him to "fix" was something He wanted to use in my life to get me where He wanted me to be.

So, at that point I needed to make a decision. Did I want God to answer this immediate prayer and take me out of my misery and fear, or did I want Him to answer the other prayer by allowing the situation to do a work in my life—getting me to where He wanted me to be?

As I said, I do not remember what that situation was, but I do remember I took the "fix it" prayer off the table and stayed with my prayer of "do whatever You want to do, to get me where You want me to be." I had no idea that a few years later, as I continued to make choices allowing him to truly be Lord of my life, it would mean Becca would have an earlier departure from this earth than me, and how dark, heavy and painful the grief would be.

We have now passed the ten-year mark of Becca's earthly departure. Does it still hurt? YES! A LOT! Do I still trust God enough to continue keeping Him in the place of Lord in my life? YES! Because I don't know any other way to get through the rest of my time here on earth without her! And I am so very thankful that I do not have to make a choice of either leaning on God or falling apart. I lean on God *while* I fall apart.

Reflection: Making Jesus Lord of our lives is easy, until we find ourselves in a place like this valley of death. We didn't mean we were giving Him permission for something like this, did we? It can be really hard to understand why a "good" God allows such horrible tragedies in our lives. Joni Ericson Tada says it like this: *Often God allows what he hates, to accomplish what he loves.*

How about you? Are you afraid to continue allowing God to be Lord of your life, since your child died? Remember, God sees what we cannot see, and He knows what we do not know. He *does* answer our prayers, based on the big picture of eternity, which we cannot see from our limited view on this earth. And He *is* Lord of this earth, whether we acknowledge it or not. The question becomes, "Is He still *my* Lord?" Raise your hands and tell Him that He is. How else are you going to make it for the rest of your time here on earth without your child?

> *With all your heart you must trust the Lord and not your own judgment. Always let him lead you, and he will clear the road for you to follow.*
> *Proverbs 3:5-6 (CEV)*

March 30

God's Goodness

Have you stopped to think about the fact that God's specialty is bringing life from death? It is doing the miraculous – something only He can do, which includes making good on His promise we read in Romans 8:28 to work out everything we go through here on earth for our good.

God did not fail you. What happened to your child was not God's fault. In fact, He told us that in this world we are going to have trials and tribulations. Receiving His incredible gift of salvation is our golden ticket into the next realm. It is not a golden ticket for giving us a perfect life here on this earth. That would be a bribe, not a relationship.

My friend, Sara, who lost her daughter and only child says it quite well.

> *If I want to blame someone or something, I turn my anger on the devil. He's the one who brings disease, destruction, and*

> death, not God. God is the One who comforts me, strengthens me, helps me--daily, hourly, even minute-by-minute. He keeps me putting one foot in front of the other. He is faithful and trustworthy to be my light in the darkness, my peace in the storm, and my comfort in deep sorrow.

God wants to bring triumph from your tragedy. He wants to help you to be an overcomer. How can we do that, if we don't have anything to overcome? How can we have a testimony without a test? "God saved me by keeping something bad from happening," might be something to be excited about, but the real testimony is, "God gave me life again after my soul died and was buried with my child."

That is a true miracle which happens in our lives because of God's goodness.

Reflection: Most of us struggle with Romans 8:28 after the death of our child. What good could *possibly* come from the death of our child???? I have a friend who, after the death of her son, has said: *Maybe "all things working together for good" doesn't meet our definition of good, but God's.*

If we continue to read beyond verse 28, we find where God tells us that absolutely *nothing* can separate us from His love. His love is good. His love is kind. His love brings comfort. His love casts out fear. What do you need from Him today? It is wrapped up in the goodness of His love that has an abundance of everything we need.

> *The Lord is good, a strength and stronghold in the day of trouble; He knows [He recognizes, cares for, and understands fully] those who take refuge and trust in Him.*
> *Nahum 1:7 (AMP)*

March 31

God Wants to Establish You

In 1 Peter 5:10,11, God says He will establish you. What does that mean? It is to be unshakeable, unmovable like a tree firmly rooted. That does not sound like us, after the death of our child, does it? We can get there, though. Let's look at three ways He wants to establish you.

1. One thing He wants to do is to establish you on the right path. Proverbs 4:25-26 tells us, *Let your eyes look straight ahead, and your eyelids look right before you. Ponder the path of your feet and let all your ways be established. (NKJV)*

   We also know that our steps are ordered by the Lord (Psalm 37:23). He also wants to make your crooked path straight (Isaiah 42:16).

   We may feel lost, but if we stick with Him as closely as possible, God will make sure we are on the right path.

2. He wants to establish you in the purpose you still have for your life. Ephesians 2:10 tells us that we are His workmanship, His handiwork, His work of art, His masterpiece; and God prepared ahead of time good things for us to do, and gave us the ability to be able to do them within our union with Jesus.

   We may feel like our purpose here on earth died with our child, but that just isn't true. The death of your child did not blindside God like it might have you. He knew before your child was conceived that there were things for you to do after he or she left this earth, and He wants to show you what those are so that you can live them out.

3. He wants to establish your words lining up with His Words. Job 23:10, 12 says, *He knows the way that I take; When He has tested me, I shall come forth as gold. ...I have treasured the words of His mouth More than my necessary food. (NKJV)*

   If we put an importance on His personal and intimate words to us, we will find that His words become our words. Not words that try to corner Him as we demand answers, but words that allow Him to be our steadfast rock in our time of desperation, allowing us to learn how to live a life beyond just surviving, but thriving.

God wants to help you to become immovable and unshakeable. Will you let Him do that for you?

Reflection: There is one more area I want to share, which may be the most important one. God wants to establish you in His love. Take your time in reading the following scripture, pausing after each phrase, to take it in like a wonderful aroma.

That He would grant you, according to the riches of His glory, to be strengthened with might through His Spirit in the inner man, that Christ may dwell in your hearts through faith; that you, being rooted and grounded in love, may be able to comprehend with all the saints what is the width and length and depth and height— to know the love of Christ which passes knowledge; that you may be filled with all the fullness of God. Ephesians 3:16-19 (NKJV)

I also recommend that you pull out whatever you use to look up scriptures and take a look at this verse in other translations. Let Him truly establish you in His love, being unshakeable, unmovable and firmly planted.

> *And after you have suffered a little while, the God of all grace, who has called you to his eternal glory in Christ, will himself restore, confirm, strengthen, and establish you.*
> *1 Peter 5:10 (ESV)*

April

April 1

Hold On Pain Eases

I remember at least a year after Becca died telling God I just wanted to stop hurting so bad! I could not see an end to the pain, because I knew I would never stop missing her.

This morning as I was praying for you in this same area, God began to have me speak hope over you. A song came on my computer that was a great reminder that He has not left you or turned His back on you. It talks about how a light is coming for the heart that holds on, and that there will be an end to the troubles and heartaches of this earth. But until that day comes, God will never let go, in the calm or in the storm, in the highs or in the lows.

This song is not just about God holding on to us, but it is also a declaration about our holding on to Him. It goes on to say that even when I walk through the valley of the shadow of death, and get caught in the storms of life, His perfect love is casting out my fear. I know He is near, so I won't give up and I will still praise Him.

I have had more times than I could ever count when I am singing praise to him with my heart breaking and tears running down my face.

If you are angry at God for allowing your child to die, that's okay. You have a lot of company, and I believe with all my heart He is okay with that also. He knows the pain of having a son die a cruel and torturous death. He knows we are frail humans with finite minds that do not understand His ways.

But the sooner you can make a decision to run *to* Him instead of away from Him within that anger and pain, the sooner your shattered heart will begin to be put back together, and the pain will ever so slowly begin to ease.

Reflection: Our hearts will never be whole while we are here on this earth because a piece of our hearts will be missing until we are reunited with our children. But we *can* live a life worth living again.

I encourage you to grab hold of HOPE; the hope Jesus died for you to be able to have. **H**old **O**n, **P**ain **E**ases. If you hold on to Him with everything you have, I promise you, the pain eases. Ask Him to help you to hold on until that begins to happen.

In hope against hope Abraham believed.
Romans 4:18 (AMP)

April 2

Full of Life

When our child dies, we have to go through at least one memorial service of some kind. For some of us, we could not even think about standing up in front of others to share something during the service. Others find the strength to do so, whether it is the grace of God or our numbness (or a bit of both) that enables us.

I, personally, fell into the second category. The numbness was definitely there, because for almost three years afterwards, I did not remember what I said at Becca's funeral, and it really bothered me. To make it worse, I could not find the paper with my notes.

I was so happy when it showed up, and kind of surprised at what I found written, because my own words that I spoke at my daughter's funeral were an encouragement to me, and they still are for me today. I want to share something from that with you, in hopes of bringing you some encouragement as well.

Becca is actually now more alive than we are!

We are not physical beings having a spiritual experience. We are spiritual beings having a physical experience. That means what is happening in the spirit realm is more real than the physical realm we are living in, which is why I could say, as soon as Becca's spirit left her body, that she is more fully alive than any of us still here on earth. The same is true for your child as well.

Yes, we all go through the numbness of being in survival mode, for the first two or three years. We can't find our way out of the suffocating darkness; we just want to stop hurting so much and most of us just want to be done here. I am not discounting or minimizing that at all. But there comes a time down the road when we can begin to make some choices in our grief and one of those is choosing our perspective.

When I think of my loss, and how much I miss my daughter, I can still fall into the darkness of grief. But it helps tremendously when I remind myself of something else I shared at her funeral:

- *We are blessed beyond the curse of death.*
- *This is not a permanent separation.*
- *I will see my child and others again.*
- *God's promise is that the glory revealed in us cannot even be compared to our suffering.*

I believed those words when I spoke them at Becca's memorial service. I believed it in the blackness of my depression and in the crushing darkness of grieving Becca's death. And I still believe it with every fiber of my being today.

Reflection: I admit, it can be difficult to live from a place that is beyond the one we are in right now. I am not saying that what we see, hear and feel is not real, or doesn't matter. But there is a spiritual realm which was already present before this world was ever created, and it will continue when this world is no longer here.

If you struggle with the reality of "this world is not my true home," you might want to ask the Holy Spirit to make the spirit realm more real to you, making heaven and the throne room more of the true reality that it is. Read books and articles about it. Ask God to give you dreams about it. Allow Him to help you live more from the place of being a spiritual being than living from the place of a physical being. It really will make a difference in living from a place of hope and light.

> *You, however, are not in the realm of the flesh but are in the realm of the Spirit, if indeed the Spirit of God lives in you.*
> *Romans 8:9 (NIV)*

April 3

Choices

Most of the time, we choose what we *want* to believe. I can choose to believe there is no God or He would have saved my child. I can choose to believe that if there is a God, He is not good and He isn't fair or He would have saved my child. Both of those options leave me feeling angry and empty.

I have chosen a third option. There is a God, His thoughts and ways are so much higher than mine, He loves me with a perfect love, and even though I do not understand why He has allowed this to happen, I still trust Him with my life both here on earth and for eternity. This option has brought me to a place of peace, rest, hope, and life again—even within the pain.

It is possible to choose to trust His love for you, even when you cannot see it or feel it. Not only is it possible, but it is a necessary step to get through the suffocating darkness into a place of light.

I would like to share something God spoke to my heart, that is just as true for you as it is for me.

> *I have a love for you that is so special and so deep and so unique that I can't love anyone else with it. It is a love that is only for you! No one else can receive it because it is yours and yours only!*

As a parent who has lost a child, I have gone through the trauma, grief, and darkness that come with it. I am also someone who was able to plant a seed of hope in my life that is now growing into a tree of life. It feels like a completely different tree from before my daughter, Becca, died, but it is alive and sprouting and starting to bear some fruit.

Death is a part of life. We will all die at some point. As painful as it is, some of us will have children who leave this earth ahead of us. The question is, how are we going to choose to live the rest of our lives when they are gone and there is nothing we can do to bring them back?

I have chosen to trust God and continue to trust God, knowing He could have healed Becca but did not, allowing her to go to her eternal home ahead of me. He has a purpose and a plan that I cannot see or know about, because He is God and I am not.

Reflection: Go back and slowly read what God spoke to my heart, hearing God speak this truth directly to you. Read it several times if you need to. Read it out loud. Keep reading it, until the truth of it breaks through and you know in your heart that because of His incredible, extravagant love for you, you *can* trust Him.

And then while being wrapped up in His love for you, ask yourself, am I going to choose to remain in my pain and darkness so that everyone remembers I had a child who died, or am I going to choose to work through my grief so that I can live in a way that reminds everyone that my child lived, and his or her life mattered?

I am praying that you choose to learn to live in a way that honors the life of your child.

I have loved you with an everlasting love.
Jeremiah 31:3 (NIV)

April 4

The Sting of Death

There is a verse we hear every year around this time, and it is another one I really struggled with after Becca died. 1 Corinthians 15:55 (NLT) says, *O death, where is your victory? O death, where is your sting?*

I begged the Holy Spirit to please explain this to me because I can tell you *exactly* where death's sting is after the death of my daughter! I know His Word is true, but this just was not true in my life - not even close! God did not answer that prayer right away, but one day when it was not even on my mind, He began to speak to me about it.

Whenever we are dealing with a bee sting, one of the first things we do is make sure we get the stinger out. My understanding is that sometimes the stinger remains in the skin and continues to release its poison until it is pulled out.

Right now, we still have the stinger in us. The pain from the "poison" of our child's death is still affecting us and will continue, until we join our child on the other side of eternity. That is where the "sting of death" will be pulled from us, and we will no longer be under the effect of that poison and continue feeling the pain of our child's death.

As I read the scripture in multiple Bible versions, I discovered what the Holy Spirit had spoken to my heart is exactly what this verse means. Starting in verses 53-54, The Contemporary English Version says it this way:

> *Our dead and decaying bodies will be changed into bodies that won't die or decay. The bodies we have now are weak and can die. But they will be changed into bodies that are eternal.* **Then** *the Scriptures will come true, "Death has lost the battle! Where is its victory? Where is its sting?"*

Did you notice I emphasized in the above scripture when that will happen? It is when our own physical bodies are changed into eternal bodies. At that point, death will have completely lost its power to hurt us. It will be gone! *The stinger has been pulled!*

I hope that thought encourages you. I know it does not help for the sting you are feeling right now but hang on, because there *will* come a time when this scripture becomes true in our lives.

Reflection: Our children have already had the sting of death removed from them. They are no longer affected by the dark things of this world. When I join my daughter and you join your child, we will be able to look down at Satan and laugh at him, because we will be able to say, "Death where is your sting? I don't have it now and you can't get me with it anymore!"

When I think about it, why should we wait? Why not tell the devil that now? Read the following through a few times, allowing the truth of it to sink in. Then when you are ready, declare it out loud.

> *Satan, I may feel the sting of death now, but you don't have the final word in my life, or my child's life! That stinger has already been pulled from my child and someday it will be pulled from me as well. When that happens, I will be dancing in victory with my child, and with Jesus, who defeated you for all of eternity when He died, went to hell snatching the keys of death from you, and walked out from the grave to remain alive forever. I may not feel like rejoicing right now about the day God will take away the sting of death from me, but I will someday. Until then, I choose to thank Him for this amazing gift that is mine to receive when my time here is over.*

When the perishable has been clothed with the imperishable, and the mortal with immortality, then the saying that is written will come true:
"Death has been swallowed up in victory."
I Corinthians 15:54 (NIV)

April 5

More Than Wishful Thinking

When someone says they hope something will happen, it is usually wishful thinking. "I *hope* it won't rain this weekend." "I *hope* they figured out what is wrong with my car." "I *hope* my puppy doesn't get much bigger."

The world's definition of hope is so much different than what God means when He uses the word hope. Have you ever thought about how crazy it would be that when God talks about hope in the Bible, He was talking about wishful thinking?

- Psalm 33:22 *Let your unfailing love surrounds us, Lord, for our wishful thinking is in you alone.* (NLT)
- Psalm 94:19 *When doubts filled my mind, your comfort gave me renewed wishful thoughts and cheer.* (NLT)
- Jeremiah 17:17 *You alone are my wishful thoughts in the day of disaster.* (NLT)
- Romans 5:5 *Now wishful thinking does not disappoint, because the love of God has been poured out in our hearts by the Holy Spirit who was given to us.* (NKJV)
- 1 Thessalonians 4:13 *... We don't want you to grieve like other people who have no wishful thoughts.* (GW)
- Hebrews 6:19 *This wishful thinking is a safe anchor for our souls.* (NLV)

That is almost laughable, right? And yet, that is quite often how we interpret God's hope, without even realizing it. When God talks about hope, He is talking about a confident expectation. It is the seed we plant that grows into faith and trust.

A great example is a little girl who hopes she will get married someday. That is the wishful thinking kind of hope. But one day a young man comes into her life, they fall deeply in love, and he gets down on one knee with a question and a ring. Her getting married is no longer wishful thinking. It is something she actually starts planning for with anticipation, knowing it is coming. There is a confident expectation that she is going to get married.

God's hope is so much more than wishful thinking! It is something we can count on, knowing He is at work and has not abandoned us in our greatest time of need.

Reflection: Let's look at the previous verses, putting in God's definition of hope; a confident expectation in God's power, His love, and His ability and desire to bring us out of the darkness and back into light, giving us a life of meaning and purpose again.

- Psalm 33:22 *Let your unfailing love surrounds us, Lord, for our hope (confident expectation) is in you alone.* (NLT)
- Psalm 94:19 *When doubts filled my mind, your comfort gave me a renewed hope (confident expectation) and cheer.* (NLT)
- Jeremiah 17:17 *You alone are my hope (confident expectation) in the day of disaster.* (NLT)
- Romans 5:5 *Now hope (confident expectation) does not disappoint, because the love of God has been poured out in our hearts by the Holy Spirit who was given to us.* (NKJV)
- 1 Thessalonians 4:13 *...We don't want you to grieve like other people who have no hope (confident expectation).* (GW)
- Hebrews 6:19 *This hope (confident expectation) is a safe anchor for our souls.* (NLV)

Wishful thinking will not get you out of your black hole of grief, but true hope will; the anticipation and confident expectation that God will pull you out of the suffocating darkness and put you on a path of life that leads you to fullness and satisfaction in walking out the destiny and purpose He still has for you.

Now faith is confidence in what we hope for
and assurance about what we do not see.
Hebrews 11:1 (NIV)

April 6

Submission Versus Surrender

"All to Jesus I surrender..." These are the beginning words of a hymn I sang in church throughout my childhood and into my teen years. What I have come to realize is that the word "all" really does mean *all*.

I have also come to realize that surrender is not the same as submission. What is the difference? I personally think it is a heart issue. Submission is more of a: *Fine! Whatever! I'll do it your way!* It's being in agreement, but more because you *have* to. Have you heard the story about the little boy who was standing on his chair at the dinner table, and was forced to sit down to eat his supper? He told his mom, "I'm sitting on the outside but I'm still standing on the inside!" That is a funny, but good illustration of submission.

Surrender is done because you *want* to make the choice to be in agreement. It may be out of fear, or hurt, or something you talk yourself into, but it is not done in anger and resentment. Of course, the best illustration we have of surrender is when Jesus was in extreme emotional turmoil in the garden of Gethsemane. He was thinking and praying about his soon coming torture and being murdered on an execution stake. Jesus not only surrendered, but was in complete and total abandonment when He came into agreement with His loving Father by saying from His heart, "Not my will, but Your will be done."

Let me ask you something. At some point, have you made Jesus Lord of your life? Have you sung it in a song? Have you made a congregational declaration that "Jesus is Lord"? Have you even directly told Jesus at some point that He is Lord of your life and Lord of your family? I am guessing the answer is yes to at least one of those, if not all of them. Then guess what? That trumps *everything*!

That does not mean it is easy. Jesus *knew* what was coming, and yet in His deep struggle, He put aside his own pain and surrendered to the horrific challenge facing Him. That amazes me! Would we have had that same heart of surrender if we had known what was coming with our child? Most of us struggle with surrendering our shattered heart to our loving Father after the death of our child, much less if we had known beforehand what was going to happen.

Many of us have had our faith in God shattered after the death of our child. That is because our faith was in getting God to do something for us, like He is a genie in a lamp. But faith is not a formula in figuring out how to twist God's arm to get the answer we want to our prayers, so we don't have to face heartache and trials. Faith is trusting in God even when the answers I want don't come. It is knowing intimately the one to whom I pray. It is being like Jesus, who fought His way to be able to fully surrender to a *loving Father*, who is so much bigger than what we could ever comprehend on this side of eternity.

Reflection: Right now, you may be in a place of submission, instead of surrender. You feel like your only option is to submit because He is God and you are not, but you are angry and confused.

I don't want to sound harsh, but if Jesus is truly Lord of your life, it means you have chosen to be in a place of surrender to whatever comes your way here on this earth, trusting that your loving Father knows what He is doing in the scheme of eternity. *Not my will, but Yours be done.*

The hymn I shared at the beginning goes on to say, "...all to Him I freely give. I will ever love and trust Him, in His presence daily live." Invite the Holy Spirit to help you fight your way to a place of surrender, because there is so much more peace when your heart is at rest with letting God be God and Jesus be Lord, even when it does not make sense and your heart is shattered.

> *Let my prayer be as the evening sacrifice that*
> *Burns like fragrant incense, rising as my offering to*
> *you as I lift up my hands in surrendered worship!*
> *Psalm 141:2 (TPT)*

April 7
He Is Still There

I love when we have a campsite with the Hope Mobile along the water. Over the past few years, we have been blessed to have several spots on either a lake or a river. When that happens, I always do my best to make time for sitting outside to enjoy the peace and beauty.

There can be paths along those lakes or rivers. I remember one specific time that I was walking on a path along a small river in Florida. Sometimes the path would move away from the water, and I could not see it at all. Eventually I could see some of the river through the trees. I might lose sight of it again for a while, and then suddenly a full view would open of the river's beauty. The entire path was like that. I never knew as a walked along if I was going to be able to see only a little of the river, none of it, or the full beauty of it.

That is a lot like our hope, especially those first few months and years. At first, we might not see any hope at all, of ever getting past the darkness and being able to live without our child. Eventually we get a quick glimmer of hope, only to lose it again. Then something happens and we feel full of hope, but it goes away as quickly as it came. Then another glimpse...

I ended up writing a verse in a song about my walk along the river and how God is always with us, even when we cannot see Him. I realized the sun is another example of this. Here is the second verse of that song.

> *You are light, like the sun in the sky,*
> *As I am walking in this place of grief.*
> *Sometimes I can see you clearly,*
> *And the warmth I feel gives me so much hope in my future.*
> *The storm clouds come but I keep walking.*
> *Then a ray slips through the clouds and I can see,*
> *That the sun is still there, and I keep walking.*
> *When out of nowhere, the full sun bursts through again,*
> *In all of its warmth, and I am full of hope again.*
> *I'm reminded that He promised to lead me,*
> *To be my light on any dark path.*

And I keep walking, I keep walking.

The sun is always there, whether you can see it or not, or feel it's warmth. In the same way, hope is always there, whether you can feel it or not, because the Seed of Hope lives inside you.

When a seed is planted, it takes a while in the natural for a seed to break open, work its way through the soil to be seen and keep growing. I am confident that the Seed of Hope, which is inside you, is breaking open and working its way through the dark soil of your heart, on its way to peeking through and continue growing where you can feel and see it.

Reflection: This is another opportunity to use the God-given gift of our imagination. Take a minute to picture yourself as a seed, planted deep in the ground. It feels like you are dead because nothing is happening as you are buried under the heaviness of the soil. Now allow the faithfulness of the sun begin to warm you, and a trickle of water begin to refresh you. See yourself responding to the continual faithfulness of the sun and the water, finally breaking free of the heavy darkness.

Now look outside. Is the sun shining, or is it behind clouds? Or maybe it is on the other side of the world right now because it is nighttime. Let a lifetime of knowing that the sun is *always* there and will *always* shine again at some point be a tangible symbol – a glimpse - of God's love and care for you, along with His ability and desire to help you through the darkness. *Always.*

> *And this hope is not a disappointing fantasy, because we can now experience the endless love of God cascading into our hearts through the Holy Spirit who lives in us!*
> *Romans 5:5 (TPT)*

April 8
The Painful Domino Effects

Seven years after my daughter's death, there were still some pretty deep fallouts. To be honest, it so deeply affected the siblings and the chain reaction had gotten so bad, that we could not even all be together for Christmas. I call that kind of thing a domino effect. The first "domino" goes down, and it causes a chain reaction of more things falling down.

So, what do we do? I have learned over the years there are really only two things we *can* do.

The first one might seem like a cop-out, but it really is our first line of defense, and that is to pray. Only God can heal broken hearts. Only God knows the depth of pain of everyone involved and what it will take to heal and repair any broken relationships. We must open the door to let Him work, by surrendering it all to Him and giving Him permission to do whatever He needs to do. (And then letting *Him* work.)

The second one is to love. That can be easy to say, but very hard to do, when we feel that we have done nothing to deserve the way we are being treated. But we cannot make excuses and say we are giving "tough love" when it is really a reaction from our own hurt. The saying, "Hurting people hurt people" is very true. Loving those who are causing us so much pain cannot be done in our own strength. And that takes us right back to prayer.

Two of the very painful domino effects in my life as a result of Becca's earthly departure have been resolved, and it was done in the way I have shared above. Through my own stabbing pain, with the grace and strength of God, I have prayed and loved (not perfectly, for sure) until I saw the fruit of healing and restoration.

To be honest, I am writing this as a reminder to myself that this is what I need to continue doing in one domino effect that feels like it is escalating in the wrong direction, instead of getting better. And while I pray and do my best to give love whenever I have the chance, I will remind myself that nothing here is permanent. One day, even if it is not here on this earth, all of our relationships will be restored. In the meantime, I am doing my best to not focus on what I see, but on what I can't see, believing and trusting that God is working behind the scenes.

Reflection: Do you have any domino effects in your life from your child leaving this earth? Maybe it is something with your job. Maybe it is someone close to you, like a parent or spiritual mentor, who is nowhere to be found when you need them more than you ever have, causing other issues. Maybe it is your spouse, grieving so differently than you which is causing dominos to fall. Or maybe yours are like mine, watching your other children behaving in ways you never thought you would see.

Right now, open the door to let Him work, by surrendering it all to Him and giving Him permission to do whatever He needs to do. Then ask Him to help you stay out of it, letting *Him* work. Be determined to only step in and do something if you hear clearly from God that you should do it. Now that you have given it to Him, trust that He is at work, even if you cannot see any results.

There is always hope, and that is what I am holding on to. How about you?

> *Pour out all your worries and stress upon him and*
> *leave them there, for he always tenderly cares for you.*
> *I Peter 5:7 (TPT)*

April 9

"God is Good All the Time." Really?

Have you been in a church service where someone says, "God is good all the time," and the congregation responds by saying, "All the time

God is good"? I know some people who refuse to say it because it makes them cringe in unbelief.

I don't care for it either, but it's not because I don't believe it. It is because we each have our own definition of what that means to us. For many Christians, it means God won't let anything really bad happen to me in this life. So, when a tragedy happens (like our house burning down to the ground, or the death of our child), we decide He isn't really good, because a good God would not do this to me.

Times of suffering are when the devil majorly attacks our thoughts. "If God really loved you, you wouldn't have to go through this." "If God was really good, He would not have let this happen." The truth is, both believers in Christ and nonbelievers can face extreme hardships. Being a Christian does not mean we won the lottery to a trouble-free life here on this earth.

The difference is, those of us who have made Jesus Lord of our lives have someone to give us peace in the storms. We have someone who will walk with us, giving us comfort and direction. We have someone who is working on our behalf to make sure we are not destroyed by the tragedies but are delivered through them. We have someone who is working that devastating loss into something that can bear good eternal fruit. We have someone who can bring joy back into our lives again.

We have someone who cares so deeply that He allowed His Son to be brutally beaten and endure a torturous death, so that we could be reunited with our children forever. The act itself of Jesus being beaten and hung on a cross was not good, but the eternal fruit of Jesus entering hell to snatch the keys of hell and death, and His resurrection certainly was good!

It is very common to struggle with one's faith after the death of their child. It may be for just one day or it may be for several years. In the midst of our pain and darkness, we all have to reevaluate who we *thought* God was, which can open the door to find out who He really is, while discovering a much deeper meaning to the phrase *God is good all the time, and all the time God is good.*

Reflection: So, the question remains: Is God good all the time? The enemy who is trying to get you to turn your back on God (the same enemy who brought death, pain and darkness into this world) wants you to think no, He is not good. That is why Satan is the *enemy*. He has plans and tactics to turn you away from God and His love for you and your child, and he knows the death of your child makes you an easier target.

But the fact is, God defeated this enemy in the eternal realm so that we can defeat Him, too. And because of that, hopefully you do not want to be deceived and come into agreement with the enemy.

So, yes, God is good. We may not understand the "why" this side of eternity, but we can trust in the eternal goodness of God. Say it out loud, and say it with conviction, to get the enemy to start backing down. "God is good!"

> *When he heard this, the boy's father cried out with tears, saying, "I do believe, Lord; help my little faith!"*
> *Mark 9:24 (TPT)*

April 10

Salvation is So Much More

Jonah was a prophet who was trying to get away from God. He literally got on a ship that was going in the opposite direction of where he knew God wanted him to go. As they were sailing, the ship he was on found itself in a violent storm, and it was decided the reason was because they had this prophet on board who was trying to get away from God's plan for his life.

The Bible tells us Jonah was thrown into the sea by the ship's crew to stop the storm and the Lord sent a great fish to swallow the prophet. Jonah felt like he had been thrown out of God's sight, but he was determined to call out to God for help anyway, looking to God as his deliverer in an impossible situation.

Even at a time when things looked totally hopeless, Jonah had hope. "While I was fainting away, I remembered the Lord, and my prayer came to you in your holy Temple....Salvation is from the Lord," Jonah 2:17(NASB). (You can read his entire prayer from inside that fish in Jonah chapter 2.) God caused the fish to spit Jonah out on dry land, and wouldn't you know, it just happened to be on the shore of where God wanted Jonah to be in the first place!

The Lord is always ready to offer us salvation as well. With Jesus being the ultimate and final sacrifice, salvation is an ongoing deliverance for us who have received that special gift purchased for us. You may be thinking, "But my child wasn't delivered!" That depends on our perspective of what the Deliverer came here to do. Just like the early apostles thought Jesus came to be a worldly king and conquer the evil worldly empires, we can think He came to remove all effects of sin and destruction in our personal lives while we are here on this earth.

Salvation is more than a golden ticket to have a good life. It is more than just getting into heaven. Salvation is offering us ongoing deliverance from the effects of the tragic and traumatic things that happen to us while we are here on the enemy's playing field. The death of your child does not stop God from being able to get you back to living a life of meaning and purpose again.

We often think it is a bad thing that we cannot get away from God, but that isn't true. It's a very good thing that we can't, because it means we cannot run away from His peace, His comfort, the love He wants to pour out on us, or anything else that we need after the death of our child. That, my friend, is the deliverance He gives us. That is part of the total package of salvation which we have chosen to receive.

Reflection: We might be able to see what God did in Jonah's life as love and grace, but it is much harder to see it for our own lives. Many of us have told God in the past that we have given Him everything and that He is Lord of our lives. That means we gave Him permission to not stop the tragedies of this world from affecting us, if He knows it can be something that will get us where He wants us to be in our lives. And that

Reflections of Hope

"something" usually ends up being in a more intimate relationship with Him that goes beyond what we even knew was possible.

Even at a time when things looked totally hopeless, Jonah had hope. When He did not think God could hear him, he prayed anyway. Just because you can't feel Him when you pray, does not mean He isn't there or He isn't listening. It's just that our darkness is so dark, it keeps us from being able to see His light for a while. Keep talking to Him. Don't give up! One day you will find yourself coming out of the dark pit and back into the light.

Where can I go from your Spirit? Where can I flee from your presence? If I go up to the heavens, you are there; if I make my bed in the depths, you are there. If I rise on the wings of the dawn, if I settle on the far side of the sea, even there your hand will guide me, your right hand will hold me fast. If I say, "Surely the darkness will hide me and the light become night around me," even the darkness will not be dark to you; the night will shine like the day, for darkness is as light to you.
Psalm 139:7-12 (NIV)

April 11

We Were Warned

Recently I heard someone share John 16:33 in a version that made me want to dig into it a bit deeper and see how other versions of the Bible worded it. *I have told you these things so you may have peace in Me. In the world you will have much trouble. But take hope! I have power over the world!* NLV

Instead of continuing to write my own words, I am going to share some of these other versions with you and pray that you are encouraged and strengthened by them.

April

> *I have told you this so that you will have peace by being united to me. The world will make you suffer. But be brave! I have defeated the world!* (GNT)

> *I've told you all this so that trusting me, you will be unshakable and assured, deeply at peace. In this godless world you will continue to experience difficulties. But take heart! I've conquered the world.* (MSG)

> *I have told you these things, so that you can have peace because of me. In this world you will have trouble. But be encouraged! I have won the battle over the world.* (NIRV)

> *And everything I've taught you is so that the peace which is in me will be in you and will give you great confidence as you rest in me. For in this unbelieving world you will experience trouble and sorrows, but you must be courageous, for I have conquered the world!* (TPT)

> *I have told you these things so that you will be whole and at peace. In this world, you will be plagued with times of trouble, but you need not fear; I have triumphed over this corrupt world order.* (VOICE)

This sure blows holes in the "faith" teachings (that I was part of at one time) that pulls out verses telling us if we have enough faith, we can ask God for whatever we want and we will have it!

Jesus' promise was not that we would never face suffering, pain and tragedy while in this world. In fact, He did just the opposite, warning us that these things *would* happen. His promise is that because of Him, we can learn to have peace in the midst of the turmoil while here, and that He comes out victorious in the end, which means that we will also, if we stick with Him.

This life isn't where everything is made right, and it is important to remind ourselves of that fact.

Reflection: Aren't you glad that someday we will also leave this damaged world behind and live in that permanent place of Jesus' victory? But in the meantime, we can learn to live in our own internal personal victory through Him, that is not based on what has happened.

If there are any parts of this verse that you struggle with, I urge you to take it to God and ask the Holy Spirit to give you the needed revelation of truth that will give you hope, release His peace inside you, and strengthen your heart.

You *can* keep going, because He isn't just with you, He is *in* you, and He has conquered death and the grave! The death of your child wasn't just the end of his or her time here on earth, it was the beginning of a glorious eternity in heaven!

Now may the Lord of peace Himself grant you His peace at all times and in every way [that peace and spiritual well-being that comes to those who walk with Him, regardless of life's circumstances].
2 Thessalonians 3:16 (AMP)

April 12

Our Suffering

Philippians 3:10 talks about how we want to know Christ more, and that we want to know Him in His resurrection power. That sounds pretty exciting, doesn't it? What Christian would not want to have that? In fact, some of us may have heard a lot about the authority and power we have in Christ and spent time putting those things to use over our child who died. We spoke and decreed healing and protection over them. We "claimed" and prayed verses in the Bible over our children about their well-being and having God's favor and blessings in their lives.

But that verse goes on to talk about also knowing Him in the fellowship of His sufferings. We don't like to read that part, do we? Why would we want to suffer on purpose? How would that help us live a victorious Christian life?

Let's think about that. There cannot be a resurrection without a death of some kind, and the greater the darkness is (caused by death), the greater

April

the power is that will be used to bring us back to a place of light and life. Here is the amazing thing. Do you realize that bringing life from death is one of God's specialties? I am not talking about the resurrection of our child who is alive in heaven, but bringing *us* back to life after the death of our child!

When our child dies, we feel like we have died with them. I have heard it said, "They just forgot to bury me." Many experts will say the greatest trauma a person can go through is the death of one's child. Every parent seems to know that is probably true, because something tells us that the worst thing that could probably ever happen to us is to have one of our children die. And now that we have a child who died, we *know* that is the worst thing that can happen.

God willingly put Himself through that. He gave up His son to die an excruciatingly painful death. I do not believe God turned His back on Jesus at that time because of the sin Jesus was carrying. After all, God did not turn His back on Adam and Eve when they sinned. He does not turn His back on us when we sin, including before we were saved. But I could see why God might have turned his face away for a brief moment because He couldn't bear to watch His son die such a horrible death, even though He knew the purpose behind it.

We have an opportunity to know Jesus (and Father God) in a way that most others never will. We get to know Him in His sufferings! What an incredible honor that God would put us that close to His heart! It is the closest we could possibly be, and because we can know Him in such a deep place of suffering, we also have the opportunity to know Him in His resurrection power that many others won't experience either.

Reflection: When Jesus was hanging on the cross and cried out, asking why God had forsaken Him, Jesus was quoting something David had written while going through a dark time. God had not left David, but the darkness he was in made it feel that way. Personally, I really don't think God turned away from Jesus. As He took on every single sin ever done by anyone who had ever lived or was yet to be born, it was such an intense suffocating darkness that Jesus could not see His Father or sense His presence. Does that sound familiar; being in such a dark place that you wonder where God is because it feels like He is not listening to you and has turned His back on you?

Just like God did not walk out on David, or Jesus, He has not walked out on you. This is not based on what you feel, it is based on the truth of His promises. And just like you have the privilege of knowing Jesus in His sufferings, you will also have the incredible privilege of knowing Him in His resurrection power in a whole new way! There *is* life after death, including the death of your own soul. Allow the truth that God is still with you to begin to sink into the depth of your very being.

And I continually long to know the wonders of Jesus more fully and to experience the overflowing power of the resurrection working in me. I will be one with him in his sufferings and I will be one with him in his death. Only then will I be able to experience complete oneness with him in his resurrection from the realm of death.
Philippians 3:10-11 (TPT)

April 13

Their Birthday is so Hard!

Forever 29. Everyone reading this knows exactly what that means.

Today, April 13th, is Becca's birthday. She would have turned 40 her last birthday. Wow! How is that even possible? I have a hard time wrapping my head around it, or imagining Becca that old.

I should have already called her to make plans. "What are you doing for your birthday? Do you want me to make something for you and your family to come over here for supper?" I should have already gone shopping for the ingredients of her favorite cake – chocolate filled angel food.

It doesn't help that the further away we get, it seems the fewer people want to continue celebrating with us, which really hurts. Far too many people question why we still want to find a way to acknowledge our child's birthday when they are no longer here with us, don't they? The reason is pretty simple. It is because when a human being is created and comes into the world, it is a big deal! Just because he or she is no longer on this earth does not erase that fact, or our memory of it, nor does it take away our instantly fierce and intense love for the little bundle of joy that came into our lives that day.

The day our children entered the world was a special gift from God, and it should be celebrated, even if no one wants to join in. You may want to do the same thing every year, such as bake their favorite cake. If no one wants to share it with you, take it to a homeless shelter and let them know it is in honor of your child's birthday. (The people there know what it is like to be going through a rough time. They will appreciate your thoughtfulness and probably want to hear you share about your son or daughter.)

You may want to do something different each year, depending on the circumstances. That is what I do. One year I got my guitar out and wrote a song, honoring the day our children came into this world and into our lives. (It is called *I Remember Well*, which has since been recorded.)

I'm not sure yet what I will be doing this year, but Happy Birthday Becca! I celebrate the day you entered this world, with all the emotions that now come with it, but most of all with the same deep love I had, and will always have, for you.

Reflection: How do you feel about your child's birthday? Some of you may not want to celebrate your child's birthday because it is just too painful to not have them here. I understand that, but I want to gently remind you that your child's life is still worth celebrating. Please ask the Holy Spirit to help you still see the blessing of this very special day when it comes.

It doesn't mean you won't cry, or not feel your heart breaking. It just means you are acknowledging the gift given to you, and showing how thankful you are that you got to be your child's mom or dad, no matter how short that time was.

And you do not have to wait for his or her birthday. You can take time right now to celebrate in your heart and thank God for the gift of the day your child came into this world.

> *You formed my innermost being, shaping my delicate inside and my intricate outside, and wove them all together in my mother's womb. I thank you, God, for making me so mysteriously complex! Everything you do is marvelously breathtaking. It simply amazes me to think about it! How thoroughly you know me, Lord! You even formed every bone in my body when you created me in the secret place; carefully, skillfully you shaped me from nothing to something. You saw who you created me to be before I became me! Before I'd ever seen the light of day, the number of days you planned for me were already recorded in your book.*
> Psalm 139:13-16 (TPT)

Note: I *love* to help pareavors celebrate their children's birthdays and do so by announcing them on my Grieving Parents Sharing Hope podcast. If you would like me to share your child who is no longer here with our thousands of listeners, the week of his or her birthday, go to gpshope.org/birthdays and submit the needed information.

April 14

Three Needed Shifts

Our perspective has a whole lot to do with our healing process. First, we need to have a perspective of hope that it is even possible to find our way out of the suffocating darkness. Quite often that comes by seeing others who have been in that same place after child loss but are now living a full life within the sadness of missing their child.

Our perspective also has a lot to do with how quickly we will get through the horrific darkness and stabbing pain. If we feel hopeless, we won't do anything to move in the direction of learning how to live a life of meaning and purpose again, in a way that honors the life of our child.

I want to share three things that might help to shift your perspective in a way that will move you in a needed direction.

April

1. I know some of you may not want to admit this, but the Bible is right when it tells us in Philippians 1:21, "To die is gain!" I am not talking about us, but our child's gain. Yes, I know our children died before they could experience some important "milestone" things on this earth. But what they have gained *far* exceeds *any* experience this world could have given them! When we can shift our focus to being happy and excited for them at what they have gained, it eases some of our pain.

2. This life is not permanent. Our time here on earth is only like a blink of an eye. It is a *teeny tiny* dot on the line of eternity. Where we are going has *none* of this world's heartache, turmoil and separation. We need to make a shift to having more of a vision for the permanency of eternity than we do this "vapor" of life that is here today and gone tomorrow that James 4:14 talks about.

3. God is *always* good. Here the needed shift comes when we understand that "good" does not mean He gives me whatever I want, whenever I want it. Good means that God makes His decisions through the view of eternity, which I don't have. He sees what we cannot see, and knows what we don't know, and if we can't see anything good yet from what has happened, it means God is not done yet.

Reflection: It is not time that heals; it is what you do with your time. Saving one dollar at a time in a piggy bank doesn't seem like much, but each time you add another dollar, it grows. Adding one dollar at a time can eventually turn into literally hundreds, or even thousands of dollars.

It may not seem like you are doing much, but the smallest change in perspective means there will be a small change in your thoughts, which will eventually change your actions. It won't happen right away. In fact, the shift will probably build so slowly that it will seem like a "suddenly" when a breakthrough comes.

One shift in perspective for me, personally, happened about three years in. At the beginning, when I thought of my loss, I would cry to the point where I could hardly breathe. Eventually, I made myself start thinking about Becca's gain instead of just being selfish about what I lost, and letting my mind imagine what it might be like for her in heaven. I realized that letting my happiness for my daughter be stronger than being distraught for myself, moved me in the direction of peace. Now, it is much easier to naturally think of Becca's gain, so that I can not only function, but live a fulfilled life until it is my time to join her.

Take a minute and ask the Lord to help you get your "piggy bank" started with a tiny shift in at least one perspective.

> *I pray with great faith for you, because I'm fully convinced that the One who began this glorious work in you will faithfully continue the process of maturing you and will put his finishing touches to it until the unveiling of our Lord Jesus Christ!*
> *Philippians 1:6 (TPT)*

April 15

It is a Slow Process

I learned very early how important it was to rest in God by just being with Him. I did not have to do anything but be loved on and comforted. This is the place I want you to find as well, as early as possible.

In those early weeks and months, I would try to sit in His presence with worship music on (sometimes just instrumental music, sometimes with the words), allowing myself to just soak up His love for me. But most of the time I would find myself thinking about Becca and crying all over again. I once asked God during that time, "Am I truly resting in You? My mind goes to my daughter so often!" His answer to me was worth sharing because I believe it is for you, as well.

> *You are in a process—remember slow and steady? See it as the process it is and allow Me to love on you. See Me as the Good Shepherd I am, loving on My little broken sheep!*

April

What I want to share with you next may be hard for you to understand, but I pray you will see it clearly in a way that brings you some freedom and peace.

We are all broken. Deeply broken. In fact, I remember feeling so very shattered that I did not even think it was possible to find all the pieces, much less have God put them all back together. But as I continued this journey, I began to see and understand that brokenness can be a gift. When we know and admit how broken we are to God, from a place of being vulnerable and no longer fighting Him, we can experience an incredible depth of His love in a way that we did not even know was possible here on this earth. And I am in awe of it.

If you are not there yet, that's okay. It took me quite a while, too. Just know that it is possible, yes, even for you. He really is a Good Shepherd, ready and waiting to love and help bring healing to His deeply wounded sheep.

Reflection: I love to read Psalm 23 in The Complete Jewish version. I love picturing myself being led by the Good Shepherd, lying down in lush meadows and sitting beside quiet waters. One of my favorite lines is, "He restores my inner person". It goes on to say that His love chases after us, every day of our lives.

Spend time with Him, and as you do, don't be overly concerned about your thoughts and where they lead you. Just keep coming back to that place of letting His love catch up to you, embrace you and restore your inner person. It is a much slower process than we want it to be, but it is so very worth it!

> *He offers a resting place for me in his luxurious love.*
> *His tracks take me to an oasis of peace, the quiet brook of bliss.*
> *That's where he restores and revives my life.*
> *Psalm 23:2-3 (TPT)*

April 16
Broken Can be Beautiful

Have heard of or seen Kintsugi "golden joinery", also known as kinsukuroi "golden repair"? This is how Wikipedia describes it.

> *It is the Japanese art of repairing broken pottery by mending the areas of breakage with lacquer dusted or mixed with powdered gold, silver, or platinum, a method similar to the maki-e technique. <u>As a philosophy, it treats breakage and repair as part of the history of an object, rather than something to disguise.</u>*

Wow! I love that last line! It reminds me of something I read recently about the verse in 2 Corinthians 12:10 that says when I am weak, He is strong. What I read got me to start thinking about something I had not realized before, that God does not want to come down into our weakness. He wants to bring us up into His strength.

That first part seemed a bit wrong to me at first, until I realized there is a difference between God becoming something *in* us and being *with* us. God cannot come *into* our weakness to be part of us there because God is not able to be weak.

However, He will stay *with* us in our weakness and sorrow and tears. He joins us there to cry with us and wipe the tears. We are like a child who has fallen and been badly hurt, and our Father picks us up and carries us. The only way we can continue is in *His* strength because we do not have any of our own.

His strength not only gives us hope and light, but gives our lives meaning and purpose again, just like a piece of pottery that has been put back together and repaired with gold, making us even more valuable than before. After all, we are now learning how to live in a way that honors our child and still gives their life meaning and purpose.

It's like our child is the gold God uses on the broken vessel! Think about it. Our children are some of our greatest treasures and right up there as the most valuable thing in our lives. Yes, I know the true "correct answer" is that it is God's love that holds us together, and that is very true. But the way I see it, God is the "glue" that makes us whole and complete again, within our brokenness, and our children are the gold that makes our brokenness stand out and be so beautiful and valuable.

Yes, broken can be beautiful as we surrender to the hands of the potter, allowing Him to rebuild our shattered lives.

Reflection: Let's look at that line again: ...*it treats breakage and repair as part of the history of an object, rather than something to disguise.* So often we feel like we need to wear a mask to disguise how broken we really are. But we do not have to do that with each other as pareavors, and especially not with God. Our brokenness is part of who we are now. The question is, are you going to allow God to not only put those pieces back together, but to make something beautiful that will honor both your child and Him?

> *And then, after your brief suffering, the God of all loving grace, who has called you to share in his eternal glory in Christ, will personally and powerfully restore you and make you stronger than ever. Yes, he will set you firmly in place and build you up. And he has all the power needed to do this--forever! Amen.*
> *I Peter 5:10-11 (TPT)*

April 17

I Don't Want to Go to Church

I hear from so many pareavors about how they do not want to attend church services anymore or be part of the church institution. Many of them know they need God to get them through the darkness, but going to a weekly service is something they just can't do.

I get it. I have to admit that I can still have a hard time sitting through a church service. Why? I used to love "going to church". I loved being part of various ministry teams. I loved corporate worship. I loved a good message that challenged me to be all I could be for His glory.

As I spent some time really thinking about why this is, I believe for many of is us, it is because a church service seems so impersonal and shallow after losing a child. What we need from God (and others) is more than being part of a two-hour weekly routine of singing a few songs, taking an offering, hearing the announcements, listening to some preaching, and then being dismissed.

We need more than being led by a group of people with polished music from a platform. We need more than sitting in rows of chairs facing someone giving a sermon (that we cannot relate to) with Bible verses on a screen behind them, as people around us nod their heads along with giving an occasional, "Amen".

We also do not want to hear stabbing testimonies about how God miraculously spared someone's life, when we did not get to have that testimony about our child.

Not everyone struggles in this area. Some of you are going to a weekly place of fellowship where you are embraced in your grief and are being strengthened and encouraged. If that is the case, I am truly glad that you have such a huge blessing. Unfortunately, that is not what most of us have experienced.

Like I said, meeting with a local group of believers every Sunday morning used to be something I looked forward to and was very satisfying for me... but now it can feel very empty. But that does not mean I am not getting fed, that I don't still worship Him with music, or that I am not in fellowship with other believers. As a matter of fact, meeting with other pareavors (especially when we have our GPS Hope and Healing retreats) can leave me feeling just as refreshed as the "down time" I occasionally give myself.

Jesus Himself tells us (in Matthew 18:20) that where two or more are together in His name, He is smack dab in the middle of it. Christ's church is anywhere believers are together. So, if you are one who

April

struggles with showing up every week for a service in a particular building, just remember, you cannot *go* to church when you *are* the church.

Reflection: Christians are quick to say that the church is not a building, it is the people, and yet we still seem to put the emphasis on routine meetings in a building built for that purpose. In the New Testament, the original Greek word that gets translated as "church" is the word *ekklesia* which means a gathering or assembly. The early Christians got together as an informal, family-style gathering.

As pareavors, that is what is refreshing to us and what we need, more than anything. Not to be in a formal setting with a planned routine that makes us feel invisible, but to *be* the church, getting with other believers who know how to weep with those who weep (Romans 12:15), and how to encourage and build each other up in our own individual and unique journey.

Take some time and talk to the Lord about this. If He is nudging you to be part of a local fellowship, then trust Him and do your best to go when you can. But if you are not feeling a push in that direction trust Him in that also, and don't let others guilt you or pressure you into something that God is not directing you to do.

For where two or three gather together as my followers,
I am there among them.
Matthew 18:20 (NLT)

April 18

God's Word

I have shared this before, but after the death of my daughter, a scripture that I have seen for many years (sometimes my entire life) quite often takes on a new meaning. Please allow me to share another one of those verses with you. Romans 15:13 states:

> *Now may the God of hope fill you with all joy and peace in believing, that you may abound in hope by the power of the Holy Spirit (NKJV).*

Joy, peace, and hope are a "filling" by God Himself. But I need to come into agreement with this and make it very personal.

In other words, I need to speak God's hope into my hopelessness! I claim it as mine, just like I would claim my diamond ring if it had been stolen and it showed up at the police station after the thief was caught. I think you can agree that our hope, which may have been lost (or just plain stolen) with the death of our child, is more valuable than a diamond ring! So, claim your right to it. Get it back! Repossess it, by telling yourself and the darkness you are in, that hope belongs to you.

You may not "feel" hopeful immediately. And it may continue to come and go at times. But the more you remain steadfast in determining that hope belongs to you, the more it will grow and take hold.

And then, from that place of hope, do the same thing for peace. After all, it is yours to take back from the enemy who stole it from you! Then go on to claim your joy back. I know that one really seems impossible, and for me, it has been the longest to claim and receive. But it can happen, because just like hope and peace, it was stolen from you and Jesus paid the price to return it to its rightful owner.

Hope, peace, and eventually joy once again? Yes, it is possible. Romans 15:13 says it is in believing, and if you can't quite believe it can happen, it's okay, because Jesus and I have enough belief for you, until you have your own!

Reflection: The spoken word has so much more power than something that is just in our thoughts. I want you to say the following out loud with me: *I pray the God of hope will fill me with all joy and peace in believing, so that I will abound in hope by the power of the Holy Spirit (who is in me).*

Which one do you need the most right now? Belief? Hope? Peace? Joy? Say the verse again, putting the emphasis on that one piece.

Say it again, this time with your emphasis on the word "fill". Now say it one last time, slowing down and taking in those last few words, "by the power of the Holy Spirit who is in me".

Remember, God's Word is active, alive and powerful. It does not return to Him empty. Right now, more than ever in our lives, we need to make sure we allow His Word to do its powerful work in us.

> *For the word of God is living and active and full of power [making it operative, energizing, and effective]. It is sharper than any two-edged sword, penetrating as far as the division of the soul and spirit [the completeness of a person], and of both joints and marrow [the deepest parts of our nature], exposing and judging the very thoughts and intentions of the heart.*
> *Hebrews 4:12 (AMP)*

April 19

Why Am I Still Here?

Please believe me when I say that I know the indescribable pain of having my child die. Day after day I wanted something to happen to me that would take me out of this world. I wasn't suicidal, but I sure did not want to be here anymore! I could not imagine living the rest of my life in so much pain, without my daughter here by my side. But in God's totally amazing love and grace, He did not answer that plea and allowed me to continue here on this earth. Yes, you read that right!

Let me say it again, just a bit differently. *It is His deep love and eternal grace that keeps us here, when all we want to do is be done and go to our eternal home to be with our child.*

It took several years, but I can honestly say how thankful I am that God did not answer my plea for death to take me. Why? Well, there are all kinds of reasons I have now, but truthfully, one of the main reasons is that I would not be here to encourage *you*!

Along with thousands of other pareavors, I made the transition of not wanting to be here, to being okay with it, and finally getting to where I actually *want* to stick around here for a few more years. If I can, you can, too. You *can* have hope that it will not always be like this. That is, unless you continually choose to remain in the blackness of deep grief here on earth.

I know at the beginning there isn't a choice. Grief just overtakes us because death is a huge loss, and the death of a child is not normal, and the most devastating loss we can experience on this earth according to most experts.

But the death of our child is not where God reaches His limits to be able to bring light into darkness, nor did it blindside God. He has a plan you probably cannot see right now. He can and *will* help you come out of the darkness and back into light and life again, if that is what you want.

It will probably take longer than you think it should or want it to, and there can be many "setbacks," but I can tell you, it is worth the fight, when you are ready to learn how to live again here on earth until you are greeted by your child with a huge hug and the words, "Welcome home!"

Reflection: Think about people in your life who are important to you. Is it a spouse? Someone at your place of fellowship or a special Bible study? A parent? A coworker or neighbor? Other children or grandchildren? Get a piece of paper (especially if you are still in that place of not wanting to be here), write down each person, and behind their names, write down all the good things you can think of yet to come in their lives that you would miss out on if you were not there with them. (If you already did this from the March 17th Reflection, get out that piece of paper and look at it, reminding yourself of these things, and even possibly adding to it.)

I understand you may have the thought, "I wanted my child to be part of these things, too! Why would I want to be there without him or her?" Unfortunately, you cannot change that, and I *know* it hurts! But you can get to the place where the gladness of still being here with those you love, outweighs the pain of knowing your child is missing the earthly events because they are part of the heavenly ones.

Put this paper somewhere that you will see every once in a while, and even continue to add to it as you think of people or events. Eventually, you will realize you no longer need the paper.

> *The thought of my suffering and homelessness is bitter*
> *beyond words. I will never forget this awful time, as I grieve*
> *over my loss. Yet I still dare to hope when I remember this:*
> *The faithful love of the Lord never ends! His mercies never cease.*
> *Great is his faithfulness; his mercies begin afresh each morning.*
> *Lamentations 3:19-23 (NLT)*

April 20

I Just Want to Scream

My guess is that many people were so wonderfully supportive for the first few days and even a few weeks after your child died. But at some point, everyone else's life has gone back to normal, and you just want to scream at them, because your life is still at a screeching halt. How can the world go on, as if nothing happened?

I get it. I remember feeling that exact same way.

People who have not faced the loss of a child may tell you that you need to move on, that you need to get past it, or that you need to find a way to have closure. These are all people who do not want to see you in so much pain, and they mean well, but to say it bluntly, they don't know what they are talking about.

- Your child will always be part of you, so you won't be "moving on."
- Only having the precious memories of your child *instead* of your child makes it impossible to "get past it."
- Having your future taken from you in the love and legacy of your child means there will not be "closure."

However...

- It *is* possible to have hope in the midst of your intense pain.
- It *is* possible to have light break through the darkness.
- It *is* possible to laugh and have joy in your life in a new way.
- It *is* possible to live a life of meaning and purpose again.

It will probably take longer than you want it to. That is okay. Give yourself lots and lots of grace and allow yourself lots and lots of time, even if those around you don't. Let me rephrase that; *especially* if those around you do not.

It may not seem like it now, but you can (and will) eventually learn to live again without your child here on earth. It will look a lot different than you had planned, and there will be many reminders and new situations causing you to stumble around again for the rest of your life. (Some of us call them grief attacks.)

Sometimes you will be forced to give in to your limitations of grief. Sometimes you will learn how to work around it. And yes, there will be times you will be able to soar above it. There is no right or wrong way. It is whatever way works for you at that moment in time. And there are lots of us who doubted it ourselves but have learned how, who are cheering you on.

Reflection: At some point, you will join the rest of the world living out life. As a matter of fact, you may even be a random person that a freshly grieving parent sees and wants to scream at, "How can you be going on as if nothing happened, when my child is dead?" Come to think of it, is it possible that you have looked at a stranger who is a pareavor, not knowing they have been right where you are, when you wanted to scream at those around you who were going on with their lives? Hmmm....

Not only is it possible to learn how to live again, but it is probable, if you stay connected with pareavors who have figured out how, and if you do whatever it takes to stay connected to God. But for now, just rest, knowing that you are surrounded by bereaved parents who have been right where you are, and that you have our hearts, our love and our prayers.

> *Likewise the Spirit helps us in our weakness. For we do not know what to pray for as we ought, but the Spirit himself intercedes for us with groanings too deep for words.*
> *Romans 8:26 (ESV)*

April 21

Offering a Hand of Hope

Hope. Without it, we cannot move forward. That is true of anyone, but especially for pareavors. Unfortunately, we have been dealt such a huge blow that we often don't believe hope is ever possible. Just a glimpse of hope can be a long time in coming.

It is easy for someone on the outside looking in, to be able to see hope in someone else's future; but hope is not something that can be forced onto another person. When you are the one on the inside, trying to dig yourself out of a black pit you were hurled into, hope is almost impossible to see, much less believe in, and it sure doesn't help to have those who never lost a child try to pump hope into us.

The best way for a grieving parent to find that hope they so desperately need is to hear from other parents who have been where they are, who can offer a hand of hope to them from their own experience. You will find that almost every single one who made it through that initial suffocating darkness, acknowledge that their hope came from God, who is the giver of all hope. (They may have been angry at Him and pushed Him away for a time, but eventually realized they needed Him to get through it.)

Dr. Norman H. Wright is one of those pareavors offering hope to those on the path behind him. Here is something he has to say. "It's okay if you don't feel like there's any hope at this time. Coming up, there will be that day where that little glimmer of hope begins to weave its way into your life and then it begins to grow and to expand."

Hope. It is something we all need. No one can truly live without it, and there are lots of us pareavors who want to help you find yours.

Reflection: We know that Jesus went through a horrible torture and death for us, but it wasn't just to pay the price for our sin. It was also for times like this, so we can be reassured that we can be reunited with our children, never to be separated again.

It's like your child went away on a very long trip to a beautiful exotic place. It is so incredible that descriptions and pictures could never capture it for someone who has not been there to see it for themselves. It is such an absolutely perfect place, that our children won't be coming back to us in this old decaying world, but we *will* be joining them at some point.

I read something from a bereaved parent once, who said to find hope and peace, she "just fell into the lap of God and let Him heal her". There *is* hope for you to grab ahold of and hang on to, that it is possible to not only just survive, but to thrive once again. But if you can't find hope for that right now, you can at least have hope for that glorious reunion. Take a minute to fall into God's lap, thanking Jesus for the incredible sacrifice of His own life, so that we can live with our children forever in such a wonderful place.

He heals the wounds of every shattered heart.
Psalm 147:3 (TPT)

April 22

Is it Impossible?

I remember the first time a grieving parent told me "You may have been able to get to that place, but I don't ever see myself getting there." It was the second year after her daughter's death and I had just tried to talk her out of getting rid of all her Christmas decorations, since she believed she would never ever celebrate that holiday again.

It is natural for a grieving parent who is feeling the full weight of their deep loss, to believe it will be impossible for them to ever have a life worth living again. In fact, I do not think I have ever met a grieving parent who did not struggle with feeling that way those first few months or years.

Do you remember the angel's response when Mary asked how she could become pregnant as a virgin? "For with God nothing is or ever shall be impossible," Luke 1:37 (AMP). And we have something powerful that Mary did not have. We have the Spirit of God actually dwelling inside us... full time... 24/7... So, if He is in each one of us, then nothing is too difficult or impossible when we turn it over to God who is living inside us.

Do I still struggle? Without a doubt! I had almost a month-long "funk" before what would be Becca's 37th birthday. Last week I felt melancholy, going back to feeling like it did not seem possible that she was really gone (and finally let myself have a good cry, which I had not done in quite a while). On the day she had been gone for ten birthdays I cried all day.

But that spark of hope never leaves me. I will not let it. I have hope that it will get brighter again. I have hope that God has joy and laughter in my life again. I have hope that this is only temporary, and I will see Becca again!

Reflection: Hope is in me, because the Giver of Hope is in me. The same Giver of Hope is in you, which means hope is in you. And the Giver of Hope is in my friend I shared about, who thought she would never celebrate Christmas again. I was glad to hear that she got rid of some things, but not everything at that time. It took a couple more years, but she is back to putting up a few decorations, and doing some of her Christmas baking again. She did get to that place she thought would never happen from her place of hopelessness and darkness.

Tell yourself out loud, "If Laura can do it, if her friend can do it, and if others can do it, so can I!" Ask the Holy Spirit to help you say it with belief, no matter how small it may be. It probably won't happen as fast as you want it to, but by the power of the Holy Spirit, hope will abound someday. If not here, then for sure when we are there with our children in His glorious presence forever! But when we think about it, hope won't be needed then!

For with God nothing [is or ever] shall be impossible.
Luke 1:37 (AMP)

April 23

What Are You Focusing On?

You probably already know this, but what you focus on is what will grow, first in your thoughts, and then in your words and actions. That is true in any area of our lives.

I understand when our child dies, the grief is all-consuming. We can't help it. We are in shock. We have faced one of the worst traumas possible in this life, and many of us also have PTSD. The reality of what happened is something our mind knows, but our heart is in disbelief, and it takes a long time to process. But there does come a time where life starts to "distract" us from our grief, and we get to choose whether to go with it for a short time, or to dismiss it and remain focused on the grief and our very deep loss.

When those opportunities happen, if you continually choose to focus on the pain and earthly loss of your child, it will continue to grow and continue sucking you under, feeling like you will be tossed around by the crashing waves forever, unable to catch your breath. What a terrifying thought, and yes, I remember having them!

Those life distractions are times when you can come out from under the waves to catch your breath, and we need to take them whenever possible. But you can do even more than that. You can even get to the point where you can make a conscious decision to think about what and who you still have in your life. When you take time to think about, *focus on*, and give thanks for what or who you still have, your love for them (and still wanting to be part of their lives) is what will begin to grow, and eventually it will help bring you out of that deep dark suffocating place.

Obviously, we did not get a choice about the death our child. But we each have a choice for ourselves while we remain here on earth. Life or death. When life wants to pull you up to the surface occasionally, are you going to refuse, choosing to continue living as though you are dead? Or are you going to take advantage of the chance to breathe? As you make that choice again and again, you will eventually find yourself focusing more on, and being thankful for, the life your child lived, instead of being stuck in the pain of his or her death.

Reflection: One reason this is so important is because our thoughts become our words, and words are extremely powerful. We see that all through Scripture.

Sometimes our decisions need to go beyond what we are feeling. Ask Him for the needed strength to push through your dark thoughts to speak the truth of what God says. Ask the Holy Spirit to help you focus your thoughts more often on life, instead of death. We can't just wish this pain would not be so intense. We cannot keep saying we will never get better or will never be able to live without our child here with us. Ask God for help to speak His truth and His life into your thoughts and into your pain, no matter how much your feelings are the opposite.

> *For the weapons of our warfare are not merely human, but they possess the divine power to destroy strongholds. We demolish arguments and every proud pretension against the knowledge of God, and we compel every thought to surrender in obedience to Christ.*
> *2 Corinthians 10:4-5 (NCB)*

April 24

Feeling Helpless

Being helpless is such a horrible feeling, especially when it comes to our children. And we have faced the ultimate extreme feeling of helplessness; we were not able to protect our child from death. Oh, the pain and guilt of being such a horribly bad parent!

Or were we?

Neither *life nor death* are in our hands. Think about it. God is the one who gives life within the womb. We may engage in the act of intimacy, but only God can create that little life when things connect physically, putting a soul and spirit inside a teeny tiny human being before we even know he or she is there! That is pretty amazing, isn't it? So it really isn't us that brought life into the world, it is God, through us. The giving of life really is not in our hands as much as we might think it is.

April

We don't think about that as often though, do we? Here is another thought. When God forms a life inside the mother, He knows exactly how many days that life will have here on this earth. Yes, each of our days are numbered, including the life of our children, the nanosecond they are conceived.

We may cry out, "That's not fair!" May I remind you, many things are not fair in this fallen sinful world, especially from our viewpoint? And that is also what can make us feel so helpless; we really cannot control much of anything about life or death.

Personally, I have made the hard choice not to feel helpless, but to be hopeful. I am determined to stay connected to God, believing that He is truly good all the time and not just when I get my own way. I believe with every fiber of my being that my daughter is with Him in the safest and most wonderful place possible, and until I join her, I will move forward toward being happy and fulfilled in this life.

So how do we break the bondage of feeling helpless? We surrender to the fact that our lives are truly in God's hands, from conception to death. We do everything we possibly can to stay connected to the One who is the giver of life, not just life here on earth, but everlasting life.

Reflection: Remember, our children are more full of life now than they ever were here on this earth! Yes, I want Becca here with me, and yes, I still cry because it hurts, and I miss her *so very much!* But I also want my daughter to be happy and whole, which she is! I don't have to feel helpless, like I was a bad parent because I could not stop her death. The issue is that I didn't know the number of her days here on earth would be that much less than mine.

We were not given that information when our children were born, and that is a *good* thing, isn't it? Take some time to give to the Lord that feeling of helplessness and guilt that you were a bad parent for letting your child die. It was not anyone's "fault" including God's. We each have a different number of days to be lived out here on this earth. Our children fulfilled their time here, no matter how short that was, and are now joyfully waiting for us to join them, when *our* numbered days here are up.

> *Stay joined to me and I will stay joined to you. No branch can produce fruit alone. It must stay connected to the vine.*

> *It is the same with you. You cannot produce fruit alone. You must stay joined to me. I am the vine, and you are the branches. If you stay joined to me, and I to you, you will produce plenty of fruit. But separated from me you won't be able to do anything. If you don't stay joined to me, you will be like a branch that has been thrown out and has dried up.*
> *John 15:4-6 ERV*

April 25

Hope Can Turn into Blessings

Until Becca died, I did not know such suffocating darkness even existed. I didn't know anyone who had lost a child, so I started connecting with others through things like Facebook pages and reading books, but much of what I found was hopelessness.

I knew that my life would never be the same, but I could not come into agreement that it would always be dark and not worth living. I refused to believe this was now my full-time identity. I did not want to live the rest of my life as a "victim" of what happened to me!

As horrific and devastating as her loss was, I did not believe the death of my child was where God reached His limit, and He was unable to help me work through it to be able to do more than just survive day-by-day for the rest of my life. In other words, I knew I had to have hope, because without hope, we cannot move forward.

Shortly after Becca died, somewhere I heard or read the words "Spiritual blessings come wrapped in trials." I wrote a note saying, "The loss of a child is an awfully deep trial to wrap a blessing in!" These unexpected words from God were immediately spoken into my heart: *I know, because My Son died, and it was wrapped in the blessing of you!* Wow did that hit me hard!

My plan became to receive those blessings! Like Jacob wrestling with the angel, I told God I would not let Him go until I started to see some of those blessings in my life! It hasn't been easy, but it seems to have

April

worked. And I will say that YOU are one of those blessings, as God gives me the privilege and honor to walk with others who have lost a child, being a reflection of His hope.

Reflection: In order to have hope, one thing we need to do is hit head-on the fact that God's plan *is* to bless us. You may be familiar with Jeremiah 29:11 where God says, *I know the plans I have for you, to prosper you and not to harm you, plans to give you hope and a future* (NIV). We may feel like He lied to us in this verse. But God's plan *isn't* to harm you. God's plan is to give you hope when the enemy steals from you and tries to destroy you. His plan is to bless you with good things beyond what the enemy has done (especially when you don't think it is possible) and to give all of us a wonderful future *beyond* this world, with our children and others we love.

Remember when I said I had to fight for those blessings here on earth? You probably will too. Let it start with acknowledging that He *wants* to bless you, He *has* blessings for you, and that you do still have a good future both here on this earth and the one to come with your child.

> *God wants these great riches of the hidden truth*
> *to be made known... The secret is this: Christ in*
> *you brings hope of all the great things to come.*
> *Colossians 1:27 (NLV)*

April 26

I Lost My Friends

When our child dies, we are surrounded by family and friends who hurt with us, cry with us and pray with us. Some of them will sit with us or call to see if there is anything we need. We often get a couple weeks' worth of meals brought to our house.

Then three months, six months, twelve months later, it seems some of those same people start hinting that maybe it is time to pull ourselves out of our grief pit and start to move on (or they outright tell us that). Two or three years later, many of those people who were with us when it happened almost seem to roll their eyes if we are "still" bringing up our child, especially when it is something that brings us to tears. (That is, if those people are still in our lives, since they seem to start avoiding us or just plain scatter.) That hurts, doesn't it, and we want to know why?

Does it really matter why they no longer want to be a part of our lives? What if their reason does not make sense to us? We are not going to argue that excuse out of them and knowing their reason probably won't make us feel better. Do you really have the energy and perseverance to try to help them understand how much you need them right now? I sure don't.

The best thing we can do is to forgive them and let them go. In doing that, we release ourselves to begin to heal from this wound our friends and family did not intentionally give us.

The interesting thing is that two years, three years, five years, ten years later, when someone who did not know us when we went through that awful loss, finds out we had a child who died, there is so much compassion and care voiced to us. They may even find a tear or two in their own eye, thinking about what we have gone through.

Why is that? I am sure I could sit and try to analyze it and come up with a reason. Instead, I want to call attention to it, so if you are in that place where you do not like to talk about your child because you know the people around you are tired of hearing about it, take a risk and open up to someone who does not know that about you.

At the very least, don't feel like you have to run and hide if you get hit with an unexpected grief trigger when you are around people who may not know this part of your life. Let those who are with you know why you are tearing up and invite them to join you in that sacred place of missing your child. You just might be amazed at how they will enter in, think about your child with you, and comfort you during that moment!

Reflection: This is something that almost every bereaved parent has eventually experienced; that when we have grief triggers, those who did not know us when our child died seem to have more grace and compassion for us than many of those who knew us when it happened.

It would be easy to see this as something discouraging, but I want you to see it as something to bring you hope. There will still be those who will hurt with you, cry with you and remember your child with you. It's just they might be people you have not met yet.

If you feel caught in this place of those around you not wanting to hear about how you are still missing your child, ask God to bring people into your life who will have compassion and allow you the needed grace to share your child with them.

> *So if there is any encouragement in Christ, any comfort from love, any participation in the Spirit, any affection and sympathy, complete my joy by being of the same mind, having the same love, being in full accord and of one mind.*
> *Philippians 2:1-2 (ESV)*

April 27

I am Afraid I Will Forget

As we are raising our children, it is normal that we do not think of them every minute of every day. There are *lots* of times throughout our day that our children are not continuously on our minds. Depending on the season of life and the ages of our children, we can go many hours without thinking about them.

For instance:

- During work (or you would be fired)
- While out with friends (or they would stop wanting to spend time with you)
- Watching a movie with our spouse (and there are definitely other times when our kids are *not* on our mind)
- Practicing something we want to get better at (we are concentrating on what we are doing)

Reflections of Hope

All that changed, didn't it, when our child died? It's like our minds won't let go, and the negative results of the list above becomes a reality, including things like losing friends and sometimes even our job.

Why am I bringing this up? So that you know it won't always be like this. Eventually your mind will begin to think of other things occasionally. And that is okay!

It's okay to have several hours at a time when you don't think about him or her. And when that happens, you don't have to feel guilty about it! If you did not have your child on your mind every waking moment when he or she was here, why do we feel like we are betraying our child by not thinking about them every minute, now that they are no longer here on earth? The answer is: you aren't.

When your mind begins to release you from thinking of them every waking minute, that doesn't mean you are forgetting your son or daughter. That is absolutely impossible! It just means you are moving out of the darkness and toward hope and light again in your life.

Reflection: When we are deeply in love with someone, we don't think about them every second of every day. We may feel warm fuzzies, smile a lot, and have a spring in our step and a sparkle in our eye, but that is how our soul is reacting to the person we love and want to be with. Should the person who is causing us to feel this way be jealous of the fact that they are not in every thought we think? Of course not.

When we are in deep grief, our soul reacts to the child we love and want to be with. We cry, we feel numb, we can barely function. As day-to-day life begins to reform around us, we will have moments that we do not consciously think about our child. When that happens, it doesn't mean you have forgotten him or her, any more than someone who is in love has forgotten that person when they do not consciously think about them.

Release yourself from any guilt you may have, thinking you are a terrible parent for not continually thinking about your child who is no longer here with you. I guarantee it does not mean you are starting to forget them. He or she will always be part of your heart and soul, even when they are not in your thoughts.

So now there is no condemnation for those who belong to Christ Jesus.
Romans 8:1 (NLT)

April 28

The Pain of Missing My Child

Yesterday we looked at how we did not think of our children every waking moment when they were alive, so it is okay when we start transitioning into not thinking of them every waking moment now that they are no longer with us here on earth. Today I want to talk about something that might almost seem like the opposite of this.

Some people wonder why we still want to celebrate their birthdays or why we still share pictures of them or still talk about our child who is no longer here with us.

Well, when our children do something like stay somewhere overnight, or go to camp for a week or on a short-term mission's trip, we miss them. We think of them, we wonder how they are doing and what they are experiencing. We look forward to seeing them again! And we talk about them. We do not stop talking about our child just because they went away for a while.

Why in the world would we stop missing or stop talking about our child just because he or she is no longer here on this earth? If anything, it should make us miss them even more, because we don't know when we will see them again, and we know we won't be getting phone calls or seeing updates on social media about what they are experiencing. (Wouldn't that be awesome???)

And of course, we will continue to talk about them because they are still part of us. It's just that the things we have to say are based on our memories of when they were here with us. Plain and simple, we will miss our children deeply until we see them again. And something would be wrong with us if we did not.

But missing our child is not the same as constantly thinking about them. It's okay *not* to think of our child 24/7, because we didn't do that when they were here with us, either. However, there is an undercurrent of an ache in our hearts *because* we miss them.

At the beginning it is like a deep pain that can be debilitating. We can't get away from how much it hurts. It even keeps us from sleeping, and when we can fall asleep, it is very restless because that pain is still felt.

There is a very long healing process, and it does get much better, but it never fully goes away. Eventually we can be so used to it that we don't even notice it at times, just like a chronic pain. Certain times will cause the pain to flare up, even to the point of not being able to function again, but for the most part, the more time that goes by, the better we get at learning to live and move around it.

Reflection: Thinking about and missing our child who is no longer here with us, is something that is now a permanent part of our lives. Since we only have memories, and we no longer get to envision our future with them here on earth, why not take some time and imagine what your future will be like when you are both in heaven? What are you doing together? What has he or she been doing to help prepare for your arrival?

It may come with tears, it may come with smiles, or it may come with a mixture of both. Just because our future here is not what we thought it would be, does not mean we have to be robbed of still imagining a future with our children.

> *You must not let yourselves be distressed—you must hold on to your faith in God and to your faith in me. There are many rooms in my Father's House. If there were not, should I have told you that I am going to prepare a place for you? It is true that I am going away to prepare a place for you, but it is just as true that I am coming again to welcome you into my own home, so that you may be where I am.*
> *John 14:1-3 (PHILLIPS)*

April 29

A Vulnerable Target

When our child dies, we are such a vulnerable target for the enemy. We are confused, angry, and all the other emotions you are now very familiar with. We can struggle with doubts of God's goodness, asking questions along the line of:

- Does God really even exist?
- Is there really a heaven?
- How could He be real if He is so cruel by allowing so many terrible things to happen in this world?

One of the enemy's top objectives is to make us think all the horrible things that happen to us here on earth is God's fault, and that He really is not who He says He is. Satan is out to do that by planting doubts in our mind, just like he did with Eve at the beginning of time. Satan is a lying, deceiving, killing, destroying thief, and then he gets us to blame God instead of himself for what has happened.

God is in the business of redeeming and restoring what the enemy corrupts and damages. So maybe we are not looking at it through the right eyes. We are trying to humanize God, which just is not possible.

I would go crazy if I believed Becca's life was over; that she is nothing but dust now and I will never be able to hug her, or hear her laugh, or see her ever again. I get so much more peace from believing that there is a God, and He sees the big picture. God knew the exact second Becca's heart would stop, and when her last breath would be taken.

He knows that about me as well. God lovingly put a plan in place before that ever happened so that we could be together again. He was there to meet Becca when she crossed over, and He and Becca will be there to meet me when I cross over.

I just cannot believe that this is all there is, and once we die, there is nothing left of us. I have seen too much to try and believe there is no God. The only way I can keep going is to know that our life here for all of us is only temporary. As Wayne Jacobson said to me once, it's like we are in the lobby, and the real show is on the other side of the door, behind the curtain. But waiting in the lobby sure is hard when our child is on the other side, isn't it?

Reflection: Death is a part of life. Unless we are here when Jesus returns, we will all die at some point. As painful as it is, some of us will have children who leave this earth ahead of us. The question is, how are we going to choose to live the rest of our lives when they are gone and there is nothing we can do to bring them back?

During grief, people either move toward God or away from Him. But when we move away from Him, we are moving away from the One who can help us the most. God wants to walk with us through this valley of death. He wants to give us comfort. He wants to give us strength. He wants to give us hope. These are all things we desperately need. But if we choose to move away from Him, we will continue to desperately need these things.

This is a time to get as close to God as you possibly can so that He can take the worst of the hits for you. Let Abba Father hide you in Himself as you grieve and gain strength, for as long as it takes.

> *Stay alert! Watch out for your great enemy, the devil. He prowls around like a roaring lion, looking for someone to devour. Stand firm against him, and be strong in your faith.*
> *I Peter 5:8-9 (NLT)*

April 30

No Longer a Victim

I am definitely a victim of the death that tore my child away from me, and so are you. This is something obviously none of us chose. But once it happens, we tend to embrace the identity of being a victim in our horrific pain and darkness. We want people to know this is who we are, and we want people to know about our child whom we can no longer introduce to them in person.

As bereaved parents, we all need to stop playing the victim card at some point. I am sorry if this sounds harsh, but please know I am not talking about those first months, and even the first two or three years when the darkness is suffocating and the pain is immeasurable; that time when we literally have to remind ourselves to breathe, much less know how we can possibly live a life beyond the death of our child. I am talking about when we find ourselves choosing to feel sorry for ourselves and want others to feel sorry for us, too. (This is actually self-pity and will send you even deeper into the pit you have found yourself thrown into, just like it did to me.)

You have to get to the point where you want out, more than you want to stay there, no longer wanting the death of your child to be the identity of who you are. You have to want to see the light of hope. The rays of this light can reach any depth, but it usually starts with just a tiny dim illumination. As you continue focusing on that small light, without even realizing it, the light will start to pull you up, until you can grab the hand of the giver of that Light.

The only way out of being a victim is to change your identity. No one else can do that for you. And the first part of it is to admit that is where you are, and that eventually you are there because you choose to be there. I am not saying you chose to be a parent who lost your child. What I am saying is that if you are purposely hanging on tightly to the identity of being a parent who has lost your child (even if it is only to yourself) you are choosing to allow yourself to remain in self-pity as a victim, instead of allowing yourself to begin to rise above it.

I really do understand it! The loss of our child shakes us to the very core of our being. The grief is more than intense; a part of us has died with our child. And we truly were a victim of the worst thing life can throw at us. But it is not a place we have to camp out and stay for life, unless we want to. We all get to a place down the road (and that time and place is different for each one of us) where we must make a choice. And I am here to encourage you that it is possible to consciously decide that while we will never forget our child and will not let others forget, we will not live the rest of our lives buried under the label of victim and the crippling limitations that gives us.

Reflection: You may need to ask yourself: Am I going make a choice to continue getting my identity from the painful circumstance that my child died, or am I going to make a choice to get my identity from the truth that my child lived, choosing to live in a way that honors my son or daughter's life?

I am so very thankful being the victim of the death of my daughter no longer defines who I am today, and I pray you desire to have the same freedom.

> *At last we have freedom, for Christ has set us free!*
> *We must always cherish this truth and firmly*
> *refuse to go back into the bondage of our past.*
> *Galatians 5:1 (TPT)*

May

May 1

Honored to be Your Mom

My child,
Flesh of my flesh,
Soul of my soul,
Part of my very being,
I had an instant deep and fierce love when I first saw you.
My heart was yours, and I knew I would give my very life to protect you.

And yet, here I sit, with the suffocating pain and darkness of knowing I was unable to protect you from death.

So now I find that just as deep and intense as my love for you, is the deep and intense pain of my grief in living without you. And yet I know that somehow, I must.

How? How God? How do I go on with a piece of my very being gone from this earth?

As I ask and seek for this help, God in His tender love, compassion and faithfulness reminds me that I do not have to live without you.

You are forever in my heart and my thoughts, and forever a part of my very being; our separation is only temporary. You have just moved on to our eternal home before me and have unpacked and settled in, waiting for me and the rest of us to join you.

This is not a final good-bye. It is an "I'll see you later." When I have the thoughts that I would give anything to see you again, to hug you or hear you laugh, I realize that *I will!* Maybe not as soon as I want to, *but it will happen!*

So, I will wait. I will wait with hope, expectancy and even excitement to see you again. Every day I am here on this earth means I am one day closer to that desperate need I have as a mother, to love on you.

And while I wait, I will choose to live my life in a way that is full, full of love, full of peace and contentment, full of laughter. And yet I know it will also still be full of pain and longing. For I have now learned that all these things can live inside of me together.

I am honored. I am honored and blessed to be your mom, and I imagine and dream of our reunion someday, filled with love and joy that goes beyond words to describe it.

But until then, I will have good days and bad days. I will have days filled with happiness, and days filled with pain. And all of those days I will continue to miss you with every fiber of my being.

By Laura Diehl

Reflection: I don't know about you, but as soon as the calendar turns to May, my immediate thought goes to Mother's Day, and how much I do not like that day, for so many reasons.

On this first day of May, let's take some time to think about how blessed and honored we are to be the parent of our very special child. Notice I did not say we *were* the parent, but that we *are* the parent. You *are* the mother or father of your child, even if he or she is no longer here on earth with you, and that is something that cannot be taken away from you.

Then take a minute to "imagine and dream of our reunion someday, filled with love and joy that goes beyond words to describe it". Guess what? It is going to be even better than what we can imagine!

> *"I will make new heavens and the new earth, which*
> *will last forever," says the Lord. "In the same way,*
> *your names and your children will always be with me."*
> Isaiah 66:22 (NCV)

May 2

Bereaved Mother's Day

Did you know there was such a thing as Bereaved Mother's Day? It comes the first Sunday in May, the Sunday before Mother's Day, and is a day to remember and honor those of us who have had to travel the difficult road of being a mom whose child has passed from this earth.

This day was started by Carlie Marie in Australia, based on the death of her son, Christian, whom she gave birth to, knowing he had already died in her womb a few weeks previously. She felt drawn to create International Bereaved Mother's Day to help heal hurting mother's hearts. This was in 2010, so it is fairly new. Carlie intended it to be a temporary movement, believing that sometime in the near future there will be no need for this day because *all* true mothers will be recognized, loved, supported and celebrated on Mother's Day itself.

I don't know about you, but I do not want this to be a temporary movement. Yes, it would be wonderful if Mother's Day was handled differently by most of the people around us. But it is also wonderful to have a special day set aside for all of us mothers who have a child no longer here with us; a day set aside to share our child with family and friends, to make sure he or she is never forgotten by others.

To me, having a day set aside like this is also a way to have a day that does not take as much away from my other children wanting to celebrate my being their mother the following week. It kind of frees up my aching heart, since I am able to celebrate being Becca's mom the week before Mother's Day, while also allowing myself to lean into the painful reoccurring "fresh" grief this time of year.

The sad and yet wonderful thing is the fact that there is a day for us! We get to be acknowledged for our empty arms and being a mom of a child who is no longer here with us.

Reflection: Many bereaved moms will draw or paint a heart on their hand on this day, writing their child's name inside it, to remind those around us that every day we still carry the love for our missing child in our hearts.

I encourage you to take advantage of this day coming up (or if you are a dad, encourage your wife to participate). Do whatever you want or need to do, to acknowledge the love you have for your child as a bereaved mom. If family and friends will join you, great! If not, there are plenty of moms who will, including us here at GPS Hope. On Sunday, go to our Facebook page and share your child with us there. Post a favorite photo of the two of you together, a picture of the heart drawn on your hand with his or her name in it, what you miss about them... whatever you want to share!

Have a sacred Bereaved Mother's Day, doing whatever you need to do. Both grieve and celebrate being the mother of your child who is no longer here on this earth.

> *May the Lord bless you and keep you. May the Lord show you his kindness and have mercy on you. May the Lord watch over you and give you peace.*
> *Numbers 6:24-26 (NCV)*

May 3
The Chain Reaction of Our Beliefs

People around us who have never lost a child will tell us that time heals, which is why they think we should be over the death of our child after a year or two. Any bereaved parent who has been on this journey for many years will tell you it is not time that heals. It is what we do with our time that moves us in the direction of a measure of healing.

At some point, you will be able to choose, and even train, where your thoughts to go. Taking control of your thoughts will affect the choices you make, which affects what you do with your time, which affects the healing process of getting out of our suffocating darkness and learning how to live again.

Let's think about this. Your beliefs drive your thoughts.

Your thoughts drive your emotions.

Your emotions drive your actions.

We can think of it like a train, with our beliefs being the engine, and our actions being the caboose, with our thoughts and emotions being the train cars in between.

For instance, I can believe that if I ever get out of this darkness and pain, it means I am forgetting my child. My thoughts will line up with that belief, telling myself that over and over again. Those kinds of thoughts keep us surrounded by darkness and depression because we believe it is the truth, and we know what our actions are when we feel that way.

How about if we back this train up? Let's go to the engine of this train that is driving us: our beliefs.

Not a single one of us who is experiencing life again after the death of our child has forgotten our child, in the least bit. We have discovered that it is not our pain that keeps us attached to them, it is our *love* for our son or daughter that keeps us connected! It is impossible to forget our child, and the sooner we believe that truth, the sooner our thoughts will begin to change, which means our emotions and our actions will begin to move us toward being in a better place with our grief.

But just a warning, it is work. It's something we have to do on purpose, and is a process that can take a long time. Even when we understand and start making the effort, there will be plenty of times we fall back into that suffocating darkness. Just keep going. Let that engine of your thoughts keep driving the train, and you will get there.

Reflection: You do not have to know how it can happen. All you need are thoughts that maybe, just maybe, it is possible to get past the worst of this. Moving toward that truth will cause you to start to think, "Others have done it, and maybe I can too." Then those thoughts will eventually start to affect your emotions, which in turn will drive your actions and often your reactions, also causing the grief triggers not to run as deeply or as often.

It is possible. Not only is it possible, it is probable, if you will believe the truth that will set you free. Ask God to help you believe.

> *Let us then be eager to know this rest for ourselves, and let us beware that no one misses it through falling into the same kind of unbelief as those we have mentioned.*
> *Hebrews 4:11 (PHILLIPS)*

May 4

Individual Timeline

When my daughter died, I had never lost a close or immediate family member. That means I had absolutely no grid whatsoever for my grief. I know there is no loss that compares to the depth of pain we experience from the death of our child, but I did not know that at the time. And since I didn't have anyone in my life who had lost a child who could walk with me and tell me that what I was going through was normal for the loss I was experiencing, it left me feeling really alone and scared.

Many of the books I read back then, or groups I found to connect to on social media, left me feeling worse instead of better, because there were so many who were still in their place of darkness, several years later, saying it never gets any better. I wasn't trying to compare myself to them, I was just looking for hope, and it was very difficult to find.

We cannot compare our grief to other losses, and we cannot even compare our grief to each other's losses. We also cannot compare our grief process with each other. Do *not* look at any dates to see where I or others were emotionally in our grieving process and use it as some sort of a timeline to force on yourself. We are all on our own individual timeline and need to go through the process at our own speed.

After saying that...

For those who are close to that one year mark, just know it is normal for the days leading up to it to be pure torture, for so many reasons. You may think that you just can't make it through. You can't breathe, you can't function. That is normal... and yes, you will make it through.

For those who are close to the two-year mark, you may be feeling like you are done and that you *really* won't make it, because you thought it would be better by now, and in some ways, it is even worse than the first year. That is normal... and yes, you will make it through.

I just want to say that if you feel like it is taking too long to get out of this tormenting pain and you know you cannot possibly live the rest of your life with this much suffocating torture, that is normal. You are not the only one who has felt this way... and yes, it will eventually get better and yes, you will make it through.

Reflection: As I said, I was not trying to compare myself to someone else's grief. I was looking for hope. I was looking for the hope that I am doing my best to hand to you! You have a choice to make.

1. You can either decide it will not get better, and there is no hope and give up.
2. You can decide that even though it is so dark you can't see any hope, you are going to believe it is there somewhere, and reach out for it.

I will be very honest. You will need to *keep* reaching out for it until you can see it and feel it for yourself. Until then, I and many other pareavors will be that hope for you, so *don't give up*!

Surely there is a future, and your hope will not be cut off.
Proverbs 23:18 (ESV)

May 5

We Get to Choose

When I go to the cemetery to visit my daughter's gravesite, I have to drive through an older section in the front of the cemetery. Many of those tombstones never have any decorations or any visitors. Why? Because they have been there for so long that no one knows who they are and there is no one left to miss them.

The truth is, whether I like it or not, many years down the road, that will also be the case with my daughter's grave, and mine, and yours, and everyone we love. If you are like me, I have no idea who my great-great-grandparents were. I have the names of some of them, but never actually met them. I knew some of my great-grandparents in my childhood days, but very few of my great aunts and uncles.

It can make me cringe and feel sick to my stomach when I think about the possibility of people forgetting Becca. I don't care so much if they remember *me*, but I want them to know who my children are when I am gone. I am guessing you are the same way.

So, what do we do? How can we make our children more than just a tombstone in a cemetery, or ashes in an urn? How can we let others know our child was here, and make sure his or her legacy outlives us, even when their time here on earth did not?

The first thing is getting to a place where *we want to live* in a way that honors the life of our child. Our grief is real. Believe me, I know the suffocating blackness takes over in the beginning, and we have no choice but to be in that place of darkness. But at some point, you *will* see a tiny glimmer of hope that it just *might* be possible to learn how to have a full life beyond the death of your child.

The question is, when that happens, will you grab ahold of it tightly and fight to keep it, or will you let it pass you by? Will you choose to learn how to live again, so that your child can continue to live through you, or will you choose to remain emotionally dead, keeping anyone from knowing your child lived?

Reflections of Hope

Reflection: When you begin to realize that it is possible to be able to live beyond the death of your child, you have a choice to make. Am I going to live out my life in a way of hopelessness and despair that honors the *death* of my child, or am I going to find a way to rise above this darkness and live my life in a way that honors the *life* of my child?

I hope you can see that choosing to remain in a place of darkness and bitterness, which keeps us from living out our own lives, will not serve the purpose of honoring the life your child was given, no matter how short his or her life may have been.

Yes, we can choose hope and light and life and then slip back into the darkness. I have done it many times. But when that hope comes to you once again, grab it like a rope and let it pull you back out of the dark pit. Choose life. Choose life. Choose life, as many times as it takes until your life has meaning and purpose again. Choose life in a way that honors your child and leaves him or her a legacy.

> *Today I have given you the choice between life and death, between blessings and curses. Now I call on heaven and earth to witness the choice you make. Oh, that you would choose life...*
> Deuteronomy 30:19 (NLT)

May 6

Hindsight

We can learn a lot from hindsight, can't we? We can also learn from the hindsight of others when we do not have our own yet. Many of us pareavors who have been on this journey for several years want to offer our hindsight, in hopes that you will learn from our mistakes and regrets on how we dealt with things after the death of our child.

Here is one of those things.

May

Please do not expect your friends and family to remember your child's birth date or death date like you do. You are setting yourself up for frustration and even anger by expecting others to be affected as deeply as you were by your child's death, including remembering exact dates. That is not a fair expectation.

There is nothing wrong with reminding people that your child's birthdate or their departure date is coming up. It will also help them understand why you are even more sad or depressed during that time, because no one is a mind reader.

Here is another thing to pass along that many of us have learned in hindsight. We would have tried harder to focus more on the good memories instead of the painful ones.

I understand that at the beginning, it feels like all our memories are painful, because that is all we have now. But it is possible to push through that and begin to think of the memories as something you treasure. Personally, when I allowed myself to wallow in what I lost, I would spiral deeper into that black abyss of suffocating darkness, pain and tears. (It can still happen if I let it.)

When I forced myself to think of what I had been blessed with through having Becca as my daughter for the years she was here, it would pull me up and out, even if it was just for a short time at first. It caused me to be grateful to have been her mom, and to have the relationship we did.

True thankfulness dispels darkness, and no one can deny that. So, learning to focus on being thankful for what I had instead of focusing on what I did not have, was a huge help.

Please don't look back in hindsight, wishing you had done these things when they were suggested to you from those who have been where you are. Instead, look back with satisfaction that you *learned* from those who have been where you are.

Reflection: Which one of these two things seems to tug on your heart the most? What are you going to do about it?

If it is trying not to be sensitive about others not remembering dates, I am guessing there are probably a small handful of people you would like to share your heart with, when it comes to those "sunrise" and

Reflections of Hope

"sunset" dates. Contact them and let them know. Decide how you can include them in your time of remembering. Save yourself added heartache from making the assumption that since they don't remember the date it means they don't care.

If you struggle with meditating on what you lost instead of what you gained by having your child in your life, make sure you don't compare how you did not get as much time with your child as someone else. I guarantee that whatever amount of time we each had with our children before they left this earth wasn't enough.

Those first couple of years can be brutal. So can years three, four, five and on if you do not want to grab ahold of the hope being offered to you by other pareavors. Do not let that be you. Learn from our looking back, wishing we had done some things differently.

> *Through the heartfelt mercies of our God, God's sunrise will break in upon us, shining on those in the darkness, those sitting in the shadow of death, then showing us the way, one foot at a time, down the path of peace.*
> *Luke 1:78-79 (MSG)*

May 7

Difficult Days and Events

Mother's Day is now one of the most painful days of the year for most of us moms.

Many of us will stay home and not go to church. Some of those reasons are:

- It messes so much with our identity and hurts too much to be "recognized" by being asked to stand or being given a flower when we have a child no longer with us.

- We are afraid we won't be able to hold ourselves together and we don't want to be the "Debbie Downer" at church of what others see as a happy day.
- We don't want people who mean well saying stupid things to us, making us feel even worse.

Many of us feel guilty, because we still have other children who want to honor us and celebrate us on Mother's Day, but all we can think about is the one who is not there.

I have a friend who has been without one of her sons for thirty years, and she still struggles with this day.

Let me stop right now and say that I am so very sorry for those of you who have no other children. I cannot even begin to imagine how hard this day is for you... my words just seem so very empty and unhelpful...

For me, personally, I have found the best thing I can do is get away somewhere during the day by myself and have a good cry. Giving myself permission and just letting the tears flow seems to be much more helpful than having a massive headache from trying to fight it all day. Purposely allowing the dam of tears to break feels like the grief has been given an outlet, giving me the capacity to receive the love from my other children.

But it isn't just Mother's Day, is it? This time of year seems to be full of events that we don't want to attend because our child should be part of them; graduations, recitals, banquets, proms, weddings, showers, family reunions, etc. It can seem endless.

What can we do?

First, I want to give you permission to say, "I'm sorry, but I won't be coming." If you just can't, then you can't. Those hosting may be upset, offended, or ignorantly trying to persuade you to change your mind by telling you it is what you need, and it will be good for you. Only you can make that decision, but if you do not attend that event, all of us pareavors are behind you. We get it!

The other suggestion is to put a plan in place. This can be an exit plan, a short "excuse me" plan, or find-a-way-to-include-your-child-in-the-event plan. ("If you want me to come, please do this for me, so that we can remember and honor my child who should be there with us.") There are lots of ways to do this without making others feel like you are turning the event into being about your child.

These difficult days and events are now part of your life. But they will get easier as time goes by. Well, most of them anyway.

Reflection: For the rest of our lives, people will not understand us because of our decisions not to attend certain events here and there. You may even judge yourself, which you should not do.

What about any events coming up in the next few weeks? What will you do? Take a minute and begin to pray about what you believe God will give you the strength and grace for, and what you need to just avoid at this point. He knows where you are in this journey, and He will not judge or condemn you for missing your child so much.

Depend on the Lord and his strength; always go to him for help.
1 Chronicles 16:11 (NCV)

May 8

Expect the Unexpected

I am a parent who took a lot of trips to the gravesite for probably a year or more. One day while I was there, the med-flight helicopter flew over me. I totally lost it and found myself sobbing uncontrollably. Later, I wrote on Facebook about what had happened, and a friend told me it was a sign of PTSD (Post Traumatic Stress Disorder). I guess it made sense, since Becca had three med-flight rides within the last eighteen months of her life.

The last year and a half of Becca's life she also had around a dozen ambulance rides because of her heart issues. For many, many months after Becca passed, whenever I heard an ambulance I would freeze in panic and my mind would immediately question, "Where is Becca?" And of course, there was always the realization of where she was, and the siren was definitely not for her.

The first year of special dates is always difficult for anyone who has lost a loved one, but for a parent who has a child missing it can be almost unbearable. For us, Thanksgiving came first and brought with it the memory of how the year before, Becca had insisted on hosting the family, even though she was wheelchair bound and how proud she was. Then came Christmas, Becca's favorite holiday, and then the pain of the first time she was not there to celebrate her birthday, Mother's Day and so on. Eventually it came around to the one-year anniversary of her death.

Everyone grieves differently, and I wanted to be sensitive to that. Some of the family wanted to get together and celebrate her life, and others did not want anything to do with that. I was torn, and to be honest I don't even remember what ended up happening that first year for her birthday or the anniversary of her death.

The part I do remember, though, is a precious memory I now share with Becca's daughter. That first year, my granddaughter asked what we were doing for her mom's birthday. Knowing how some of the family did not want to do anything, I suggested I come to her school for lunch on that day and bring birthday cupcakes for the two of us. She was thrilled, and we continued doing it for a few years (until she hit Middle School and didn't want to continue).

One thing I have learned is that there are seasons of grief "recovery". What worked for us to get through one year may not work the next. We may start a tradition for something like their birthday, which goes for several years, and then suddenly for no reason, it just seems to fall apart.

Expect the unexpected. Take it year by year, and don't be surprised if things change over the years on how you deal with certain dates or events. You will change how you feel about certain things, and those around you will change how they feel. There may come a time where something you used to do that was important is no longer a big deal. There may come a time when something is still extremely important to you, but it isn't to anyone else, and you will need to learn to be okay with it.

Do what you need to do to get through each event, realizing it may change from year-to year or over time.

Reflection: Do you feel overwhelmed by reading this? I want to make sure you understand I am not saying your child will not be as important to you over time. That will never happen! In fact, most of us will say that the love for our child continues to increase over time. This may sound really strange, but it is almost like the increased love starts to push out the constant pain – there just isn't enough room for our hearts to hold both anymore, and the growing love for our child wins out.

I *am* saying how you feel about it, and the thoughts you think will eventually change, which may cause you to need to change some of your actions. It is not good or bad. It just is. Ask God to help you tuck this information away somewhere, so that when these things happen, you are reminded that it is just another "normal" part of our journey, and to give yourself and those around you grace.

> *Grace and peace to you many times over as you deepen in your experience with God and Jesus, our Master.*
> 2 Peter 1:2 (MSG)

May 9

Why Did God Do This to Me?

Let me start out by saying that God did not do this to you.

Yes, for some reason (which we may never know this side of eternity) a specific horrific tragedy of the death of our child happened, to each one of us reading through this book.

No one is exempt from difficulties and tragedies in this life, including Christians! We are going to deal with pain and suffering in this life because we live in a fallen sinful world. God tells us this over and over again in His Word, and so did Jesus.

We are not immune to these things hitting us. We've got to understand that, so that *when* these things hit us, our faith is not shattered, and we fall apart and blame God! He did not promise us a trouble-free life while we are here on this earth. But God did promise that He would be with us through those times.

It may not seem like it right now, but God is not against us. He *does* have something for each of us. God has light and life that penetrates and shatters the suffocating darkness and intense pain. He has a peace for each of us that goes beyond anything we can understand. This peace causes us to delight in His mercy and grace in our lives within the horrible earthly tragedies and losses.

So, don't give up. Don't give up on life. Don't give up on hope. Don't give up on happiness, laughter and joy. Hang on, one day, one minute, one breath at a time.

Reflection: We want to know "Why?" don't we? But even if God told us the why, it would not take away the pain and it probably wouldn't make sense to us. We would just argue with Him that His reason wasn't good enough to not stop our child's death.

There are some answers we just are not going to have this side of heaven. Once we allow ourselves to be okay with not having the answer to our "Why?" here on earth, some of our anger will fade, along with some of the darkness, and we will see a glimmer of light and hope in our lives.

I believe our children know the "why" because they now have God's view, and they are cheering us on! Spend some time thinking about the fact that your child is now in eternity, not limited by earthly knowledge, and that he or she is okay with being in heaven. What would your son or daughter be telling you as an encouragement while you are still on earth, knowing you have more of your life to live before joining them?

I have told you these things so that you won't abandon your faith.
John 16:1 (NLT)

May 10

It's Okay Not to Be Okay

Before we moved into the Hope Mobile, whenever I sat at my desk I was surrounded by memories of my daughter, Becca. Some days those memories would make me smile, and other days they would once again bring me to tears.

Holidays and special events definitely have this same issue. Some years are filled with tears, and others are filled with warm memories that bring smiles and even laughter. And I have learned that it's okay.

It's okay to be smiling one moment and crying the next.

It's okay to be able to go to one event and but not go to the next event.

It's okay to want to talk about my child with someone who misses her, or to not want to talk about my child right now to anyone.

It's okay to fall apart and be a mess because something triggered a wave of grief, and it's okay to be a mess with no explanation.

It's okay to finally have a burst of energy one day, and the next day not even get out of bed.

It's okay to not be okay! Let me say that again, a little louder this time. Especially as a bereaved parent:

IT'S OKAY NOT TO BE OKAY!

And that is encouraging. Well, maybe not to those who have never faced a deep loss like ours. But if you are anything like me, this was a relief when I found out it is not only okay to be like this, but it is *normal!*

It gave me so much hope to know that there are other bereaved parents who seem to have figured out how to live without their child, who were once in the same "not okay" place that I still find myself in at times.

Reflection: Our grief, after the death of our child, is like being on a roller coaster. In the dark. It not only goes up and down, but also goes upside down and backwards. Our emotions are all over the place, and we never know what is coming next.

It's okay to feel like you are not doing it right because you aren't going through your grief in "stages" like some people say we should. In fact, I would be concerned for you if you are working your way nice and neatly through them. There is no rhyme or reason to everything we feel, so please let yourself be okay with not being okay. Also, remember as you are terrified and screaming, there are many of us on the same ride with you. We are all doing this together.

> *God is a safe place to hide, ready to help when we need him.*
> *Psalm 46:1 (MSG)*

May 11

The Shattered Pieces

When my daughter died, I remember feeling so very shattered that I did not think it was possible to *find* all the pieces, much less have God put them all back together. But as I continued this journey, I began to see and understand that brokenness can become something beautiful.

Just like the Kintsugi I talked about on April 16th, (the Japanese art of repairing broken pottery by mending the areas of breakage with lacquer powdered gold), God truly can put me back together in a way that I am still both valuable and beautiful in my brokenness. He truly can restore our souls.

When we use the word "restore" we think of getting something back to the way it used to be, which we know is not going to happen, is it? However, when God restores, He wants to go beyond making something the way it used to be. He will take what is broken, put it together again and make it even more beautiful than before it was broken.

Reflections of Hope

Let me say that again in a different way. Most dictionary meanings of the word "restore" is basically to return something back to its original condition. But that is not God's definition. All through history up to this very day, when God restores, He makes sure to go beyond the original condition and makes it even greater or better.

I am not talking about our situation; I am talking about us. He will take the shattered pieces of our life, glue them together with his love, and make them strong in the places where they were once weak. As you walk with Him through the darkness, you truly can come out the other side better and stronger in so many ways.

Reflection: Do a search on images of Kintsugi pottery. You will see every piece is very unique and beautiful in its brokenness. Each one of us will have different areas in our lives that will become stronger and more beautiful as we give Him all the shattered pieces we can find and let Him find the ones we can't.

Ask Him to restore you like Kintsugi; broken, yet beautiful and valuable in your brokenness.

> *Let my passion for life be restored, tasting joy in*
> *every breakthrough you bring to me. Hold me close*
> *to you with a willing spirit that obeys whatever you say.*
> *Psalm 51:12 (TPT)*

May 12

They Just Don't Get It

If you have had this book for a while, you may have already read through the March entries. On March 19th, I talked about how to

May

explain to people what it is like to have a child die, and why it is so hard to "get over it."

Today I want to offer another way to explain it. Once again, there is a trigger warning because of how deeply true it is, but I don't think it will hit as deeply as the reading in March.

So, if it might be a trigger, why am I putting it in this book that is supposed to be reflections of *hope*? Because tears bring healing. And with how deeply we have been wounded, it is going to take lots of them to wash our souls of the darkness and pain. (If you are one that doesn't cry or cannot seem to cry, that's okay. God is working to bring your healing in other ways.)

Here we go. This is what you can share with that person who just doesn't get it.

If we go on a weekend trip, or are gone for several days on a business trip or a get-away of some kind, we usually check on our kids because we miss them and want to know they are doing okay, right?

When our child goes somewhere for the week (like summer camp) we miss them and can hardly wait for them to come home so we can hug them tight and hear their stories. It is considered normal to miss a child deeply if they are gone for a lengthy time, such as being on a month-long mission's trip, living out of state for college, or going into the military. However, within that long separation, there is still communication in some way, such as texting, Facetime, Skype, Zoom, emails, and even fun things like Snap Chat.

How would you feel if you could not do any of that? How would you feel if your child left the country, for two years? It would be hard, but you would be okay, knowing at the end of those two years he or she would be back. How about if they were leaving for ten years and you absolutely knew there would be no way to communicate with them? Would you be a bit of a mess for at least part of that time?

What if that were for the rest of your child's life? You knew for sure that you would *never ever* talk to them, *never* see them, *never ever* again hear them laugh, never hear them say, "I love you", never know what they look like as they age, and you would *never* ever again be able to hug them or give them your love?

Welcome to our world. Only yours is just imagining it. Ours is reality. For the rest of our lives. Period.

Reflection: There are those who want to know why you are still struggling because they are truly concerned for you, and then there are those who want to know why because they are selfish and want you to be there for them and want you to go back to being who you used to be. It's usually pretty easy to tell the difference.

If you have one or two people in your life who truly care and have been there for you in needed ways, take a moment to thank God for them, and be sure to tell them thank you. If you don't, ask God to bring someone like that into your life.

Then take a minute to thank God that He made a way to be reunited with our children so that our separation is *not* forever.

> *What a wonderful God we have--he is the Father of our Lord Jesus Christ, the source of every mercy, and the one who so wonderfully comforts and strengthens us in our hardships and trials. And why does he do this? So that when others are troubled, needing our sympathy and encouragement, we can pass on to them this same help and comfort God has given us.*
> *2 Corinthians 1:3-4 (TLB)*

May 13

Trying to Be in Control

In the English language, the word "love" is such a generic word. We use the same word to say, "I love that color," to "I love a good storm," to saying "I love you" to someone very special in our lives.

May

"Pain" is a generic word, also. There are so many different kinds and levels of pain. Just like when our child was born we did not know that we could love so deeply, when our child died, we did not know that we could feel pain so deeply.

Sometimes, instead of moving toward God's light and giving Him that pain, we try to stay in control. We try hard to make our own safe little world so nothing else will happen. But that will not lessen our pain, and it definitely will not bring us peace, because it is impossible to be in control of everything.

I think of how the government is constantly passing new laws to "make us safe." But there is no way there can be enough laws to make us completely and totally safe, eliminating all possible harm or death. It is the same with each of us. There is no way you can have all the control, so that nothing else bad will happen in your life. We have an enemy who will make sure that is not the case, and will try hard to get you to blame God in the process.

Many Christians have the false belief that if you are grieving or in pain (physically or emotionally), it is because you are not giving that thing to God, or you "don't have enough faith." But having peace does not mean the pain will automatically leave.

One surprising thing I have learned is that peace and pain can reside together in me. We don't have to choose between leaning on God or falling apart. We can lean on God *while* we fall apart, allowing Him to give us that miraculous peace that goes beyond our understanding.

It's okay that it does not make sense to us. I am just thankful He paid the price for it to be possible.

Reflection: At this point, the safest and most healing thing we can do is to lean into God as much as possible.

Climb up on His lap as your Daddy. Let Him wrap His arms of love around you like a blanket that warms your heart. If you can't feel His presence or His peace, ask God to heighten your awareness of Him. Think of the words in a familiar Christmas song, "Be near me, Lord Jesus, I ask you to stay, close by me forever..."

Let these words be the cry of your heart.

> *Now may the Lord of peace himself give you peace
> at all times and in every way. The Lord be with all of you.*
> 2 Thessalonians 3:16 (NIV)

May 14

Isolation

Even before Becca died, one thing God has taught me over the years is how a desire to be isolated because something painful has happened in my life is something the enemy tries to put on me. He causes me to not want to be around people, because it is even easier for him to pull me in a downward spiral, eventually not even wanting to spend time with God.

When a wolf goes after a herd of sheep, it goes after the one who is on the outer fringes – the one who has isolated itself from the others. It is a much easier prey. So here is my warning. Do not isolate yourself. I understand not wanting to attend church services or family events. But do you best to not totally isolate yourself from other pareavors, especially those who are further down this road than you are.

Let me clarify though, that there is a difference between spending time alone and isolating yourself.

It took me almost three years before I spent time with other bereaved moms. At first, it was because I could not find anyone in my area who had lost a child. Then, after a while, I didn't want to find anyone. I was a mess, and I did not want to be in a group of people who were a mess like me! I didn't want to sit around crying and boohooing with others about our children dying, feeling even worse when I left than when I arrived.

As I was coming up on the three-year anniversary of Becca's death, I made myself go to a conference I heard about in a nearby state. It was a three-hour drive, and I had to arrive the night before. Sitting in the hotel room by myself, my hotel phone rang. It was Lynn Breeden, the host of the event, asking me if I wanted to join her and her team for dinner. I

May

was scared. I was depressed. Everything in me screamed, "RUUUUUUN!" But I found myself saying yes and heading downstairs.

I was immediately embraced with warmth and love and acceptance. I felt like a long-lost sister! I am tearing up right now, just thinking about it.

That weekend was a huge turning point in my taking steps toward healing. I discovered it was actually *comforting* to be around a group of people who were a mess like me. We didn't just sit around and cry. We shared our children with each other. We laughed. We heard words of hope and encouragement, and yes, there were tears. But when they came, I did not have to explain or make excuses. Everyone there completely understood.

So please, do not be afraid to connect with other pareavors, especially those who can be a guide, walking with you out of your darkness and back into a place of hope and light again. And if there are no groups in your area, there are many ways to connect online with the GPS Hope community, or others who are doing just that.

Reflection: Can you tell the difference when you are needing to be alone with your grief, and when you are isolating yourself in a way that is not good for you? Are you like I was – not interested in connecting with other bereaved parents because you were afraid they would make you even more sad and pull you down even further?

I am very sorry to say that there are some individuals and groups who do that. If you have not connected with others who have lost a child and can walk with you in a way that brings hope, don't give up. God wants to bring people into your life who will walk with you, right where you are in a way that does not make your path feel even darker. How do I know that for sure? Because that is what God has called me (and others) to do.

Ask God to help you put aside your fears (or false expectations) and find a group that wants to be part of your journey. Believe me, we are here!

When I am afraid, I put my trust in you.
Psalm 56:3 (ESV)

May 15

Not in My Plan

When Becca was born, it was not in my plan for her to have cancer. It was not in my plan for her to have heart issues. It was *definitely* not in my plan for her to die at age twenty-nine!

As we are all very aware, we do not always get what we plan or what we want in life. In fact, we can probably think of a lot of things that have happened, or not happened, that were not in our plans or what we thought our lives would be like.

While God did not *do* any of it *to* you, for some reason, God decided to make it part of His plan *for* you. He can see the future you cannot see. Before you were even born, God knew your days here on earth would be more than your child's. He put a plan in motion for your life, beyond the life of your child's, even before your own parents or grandparents were born. That is kind of crazy to think about, isn't it?

Even though it wasn't in our plan, it was in His. He knew when our child died that He was not going to let it be the final work of the enemy in our lives to take us out of commission for the rest of our time here on earth. He knew, even before we were born, the horrible place it would take us to and had a plan in place to bring us back into the light again, not to just barely survive but to thrive.

Yes, it will look very different than what *we* had planned. But it did not take God by surprise, and it looks exactly like He planned. He knows how long you will be in this dark place and knows each word, each thought, anything you see or hear that will help you get back to learning how to live again. He knew the setbacks and the grief triggers, and none of it messes up His plan to get you to a good place again.

God still has a plan for every single one of us. You can have hope, because it is a plan that has blessings for you (and me) that we don't even know about yet! Would we rather have our child back? YES!!!! For sure! But since that is not an option at this point, I am going to do whatever I need to, to make sure that I grab ahold of God's plan, and suffocate the enemy for what he did, instead of letting him continue to suffocate me!

May

Reflection: God will not allow the painful things in your life to be wasted. He will make sure there is a purpose in your pain! I know it might seem absolutely impossible for that to happen, but one of God's specialties is to do the impossible.

I suggest starting to ask Him how He plans to do that. You probably won't get an answer right away. You might not even see an answer for weeks or months. Don't let yourself be anxious about it or think it will never happen. Just keep going, one day at a time. Do what you can do each day, no matter how much or how little that is. Keep reminding yourself that God has a plan, and He is at work, even when you cannot see it or feel it. Once you can believe this truth, you will be well on your way to receiving the light, life, peace and blessings God has for you beyond the darkness and pain.

I'm feeling terrible—I couldn't feel worse! Get me on my feet again. You promised, remember? Barricade the road that goes Nowhere; grace me with your clear revelation. I choose the true road to Somewhere, I post your road signs at every curve and corner. I grasp and cling to whatever you tell me; God, don't let me down! I'll run the course you lay out for me if you'll just show me how.
Psalm 119:25, 29-32 (MSG)

May 16

There Are No "Stages" of Grief!

One of the things we often hear about, after the death of our child, is what is called the "Five Stages of Grief", which are: denial, anger, bargaining, depression, and acceptance.

I am telling you there is no such thing! Does that make you feel relieved? Even many counselors do not realize these five stages were introduced in a book called "Death and Dying" by psychiatrist Elizabeth

Kübler-Ross, back in 1969. It was inspired by her work with terminally ill patients, as her reflection of what they go through in facing their own mortality when diagnosed with a disease they cannot recover from.

It was *not* a pattern for grieving the death of a loved one. They are not stops where we hang out on some kind of grief timeline.

As a matter of fact, it seems that later in her life, Kübler-Ross noted that these five stages are not a linear and predictable progression, even for the terminally ill, and that she regretted writing them in a way that was so misunderstood.

So, if you have been concerned that you have not been following these five stages of grief, you can be greatly relieved!

Our grief is more like being the pinball in a game you never wanted to play, changing to extremes in an instant, having multiple opposite feelings going on inside us at the same time, with lights flashing and bells ringing! For most of us, when we find out that feeling like we are going crazy is considered normal for someone whose child has died, it helps ease the burden a bit of thinking we are "doing it wrong".

There is no such thing as a wrong way to grieve, especially when it is your child who has passed. The death of one's child is a trauma. You are the only one who can determine what grieving your child needs to be for you. Those first three years or so can feel much more like that pinball being shot around than some grief stages we are neatly working our way through.

Reflection: At some point, the messiness of our grief will start to become untangled, like a knotted-up ball of yarn. Doesn't it make sense that it will take quite a while though, knowing you are dealing with traumatic grief? Many of you have PTSD as well. This whole thing is a process, and it takes so much longer than we want it to. But those of us who were there ourselves at one time, and are now further along, can assure you that it will happen.

It's also good to know that when the messy tangled ball of grief seems to come back here and there over our lifetime, the mess is smaller, and untangles more quickly. Take a minute and picture a messy tangled up ball of yarn, and then imagine someone untangling it as they knit it into a beautiful blanket. Allow yourself to realize that what you have just pictured is *you!* God *will* take that mess and turn it into something useful and beautiful in time.

> *As for me, all I need is to be close to God.*
> *I have made the Lord God my place of safety...*
> *Psalm 73:28 (ERV)*

May 17

Survival

If you have faced a deep loss before, grieving the death of your child may seem so much worse, and you may think you are going crazy. Or you may be like me and had no grid for deep grief, having never lost an immediate or close family member.

Either way, you may have times where you find you are literally forgetting to breathe and have to remind yourself to take a breath. Your body is out of whack; your mind is full and empty at the same time. Your sleep is off. Often times you can't stop crying, and it might even seem like everything around you looks gray and colorless. You can forget things, even as simple as how to peel an orange or find yourself panicking because you suddenly forgot how to get home from the store you have shopped at for ten years.

You do not know how you can go on living, and probably don't want to, which makes no sense to your mind if you are happily married or have other children still here, or a ministry or a job you love. You are barely in survival mode, and don't think it is possible to get out of the darkness, much less to a place of wanting to live without your child. You may be convinced it is impossible to have a life with purpose and meaning ever again.

Reflections of Hope

Let me assure you, *all* of this is normal. Once again, those of us who have traveled this road ahead of you have felt all of that ourselves. And I am sorry to say that you must go through this like the rest of us did. There is no way around it and there is no timetable.

Now let me share with you two of *the* most important things you need to know. You *will* survive. You are not alone!

Reflection: I did not know this kind of darkness even existed until the death of my daughter. So I, along with so many others who have lost a child from this earth, understand the horrific darkness that you find yourself in. We cannot know exactly how you feel, but we are familiar with the darkness that sucks us under and holds us down, feeling like we are suffocating in a way that cannot be put into words.

We also didn't know that God's love is so deep that it really can penetrate this darkness! It may take a while because we are so numb and in so much pain. (Strange how that happens, isn't it?) But not only can it happen, it will happen.

Do not give up! Ask Him to help you be okay with how long it is taking. Trust the process of going through it, knowing that so many of us who have been in that place of suffocating darkness are on the other side. If we can, you can, too. You can and will come out on the other side into a place of light and a life with meaning and purpose once again, *because of your child's life*, not in spite of their death. It will not be easy but hang on to the hope that it can be done.

> *The Lord himself will go ahead of you. He will be with you.*
> *He will never leave you. He'll never desert you.*
> *So don't be afraid. Don't lose hope.*
> *Deuteronomy 31:8 (NIRV)*

May 18

Letting Go of Guilt

My friend Denee was tortured with guilt for over a year and a half after her daughter took her own life with post-partum blues. Our daughters knew each other growing up, through school and local church activities, but it has only been since they both died that Denee and I have gotten to know one another on a deeper level.

When presented with the truth that God was asking her to trust Him beyond all of her unanswered questions, it took another eight months before she was ready to do so. I know many of you who are reading this have been in that same place for much longer.

I would like to share something Denee wrote.

> *On our daughter's birthday, I was finally able to say, "Lord, I don't get this, and this is so wrong and there are so many unanswered questions, but I trust you." There are things that happen in this life that are so painful and tragic and wrong, but as Papa said in* The Shack, *"Just because I can bring incredible good out of incredible tragedy doesn't mean I orchestrated the tragedy."*
>
> *God is good and He is faithful and He is the healer of the brokenhearted and He WILL give beauty for ashes! I trust that!*

There are a couple of things that are important to realize when we struggle with guilt over our child's death. First, guilt does not serve us well. The "if only's" and deep regrets do not change anything. In fact, as long as we are in that frame of mind, we are continuing to feed the darkness and depression we all face after the death of our child (especially one who ended his or her own life whether it was intentional or unintentional).

Another thing to accept is that the solution is not in ourselves. Denee had to let go and trust the One who holds life and death in His hands, just like all of us need to. God loves both you and your child more deeply than any of us can comprehend.

Unfortunately, many of us have a misguided definition of faith, which makes all of this even more difficult, and can be part of the guilt we find ourselves trapped in. True faith is *not* getting the answers we want (or we "claim") to our prayers. True faith is trusting Him when certain prayers are not answered in the way we prayed, believing that He can see what we cannot see, and knows what we do not know.

Coming to a place of acceptance that God did not cause the death of our child, is where many of us have to start. Then we need to accept the fact that He had a reason for not stepping in and stopping our child's death that will not make sense to us on this side of eternity.

It is important for us to grasp that this life and what we can see, hear, touch and feel, is only temporary. Our child is on the other side of eternity, and we will be joining them some day. Thankfully, our extremely painful separation is *not* permanent. We can release the guilt, knowing our children are in the safest, most wonderful place possible. Yes, I know we would much rather have them here with us, but wanting that, and hanging on to guilt because they aren't, will not change it. So, we might as well make a decision to let it go.

Reflection: I encourage you to do exactly what my friend Denee did. Do not rely on your own strength or desire to trust God with the most painful thing you have ever faced. Be honest with Him. If you are like Denee, tell Him, "I want to trust you. Help me!" And if you are not to that point of wanting to trust Him, tell Him! And then ask Him to help you to *want* to trust Him.

Thousands of other bereaved parents, along with myself, have come to the same conclusion as Denne; God is good and He is faithful. He is the healer of the brokenhearted and He *will* give beauty for ashes!

We trust that! And you can, too.

> *Create in me a pure heart, O God, and renew a steadfast*
> *spirit within me. Do not cast me from your presence or take*
> *your Holy Spirit from me. Restore to me the joy of your*
> *salvation and grant me a willing spirit, to sustain me.*
> *Psalm 51:10-12 (NIV)*

May 19

Eternity

We tend to think that eternity starts for our lives when we leave this earth. But eternity does not just start for us when we die. We are all eternal beings right now because it starts as soon as we are conceived. That means eternal, resurrection life is available to us all now, in this life here on earth. Jesus came to bring God's resurrection power into our lives *while* we are here on this earth, not just after we die and leave this earth.

Each of us has a set number of days here on this old earth, and then we move on to the glorious side of eternity. Our child's time here was much too short as far as we are concerned, and we were supposed to go first. But the fact remains, our child has now moved on to his or her permanent home and is more full of life than we are!

For reasons we do not understand (or like), our children left this side of eternity and crossed over where we cannot see or be with them temporarily. They no longer have a life to live with intentional purpose here on earth. So now it is important that we continue moving forward in *our* earthly purpose, so that when we join our child who is waiting for us, we will hear the wonderful words, "Well done, good and faithful servant...Enter into the joy of your lord" (Matthew 25:21 NKJV).

Emmanuel, God with us, is something emphasized during the Christmas season. But it is important to remind ourselves of this wonderful fact all through the year, especially for those of us who have been hurled into such a suffocating dark pit of grief.

Yes, there *is* hope in your future. But not just your future in eternity after you die, but in eternity now, while living out your time here on earth. There is hope in your future because He *is* Emmanuel, God with us. Not only is He the coming King who will be riding on a white horse in the clouds, but He is here with us now, dwelling inside our very being, comforting us, guiding us, and bringing light back into our darkness.

Reflections of Hope

Reflection: If you were to see pictures of baby Jesus in other cultures, you might be surprised. To the Africans, Jesus is a little black baby. To the Chinese, He has slanted eyes and yellow skin. To the Germans, He has big blue eyes and yellow curls. To the Mexicans, He has olive skin, brown eyes and dark hair. What is so awesome about this is that Jesus is so real, so personal, that He belongs to each of us. He really is Emmanuel, God with us.

Would you please join me in this prayer?

> *Thank you, God, for the hope we can have in our future, not just when we leave this earth, but while we are still here, as we navigate our purpose without our child here with us. Help us to see that eternity has already started for all of us and that we are closer to our kids than we realize, because You are eternal, and You are in us. Amen.*

I know God has made everything beautiful for its time. God has also placed in our minds a sense of eternity; we look back on the past and ponder over the future, yet we cannot understand the doings of God.
Ecclesiastes 3:11 (VOICE)

May 20

Abiding

I believe the reason I was not angry with God when my daughter died is because I learned many years ago to abide in Him when our family went through a very traumatic event that lasted for several years. It was during this time, God taught me something by using Psalm 91:1-2.

> *He who dwells in the secret place of the Most High, shall abide under the shadow of the Almighty. (NKJV)*

I used to think *dwelling* and *abiding* were the same thing, and that this verse was just kind of repeating itself. But the Holy Spirit was gracious

May

and showed me something that helped me so much during that very dark time in our lives. It was also a help when I was blindsided by Becca leaving us when her heart gave out.

First, let's look at what a dwelling place is. It is your home. It is where you live and do much of your day-to-day life.

To abide means:

- to wait for
- to endure without yielding
- to bear patiently
- to accept without objection
- to continue in a place
- to remain stable or fixed

This means that when we *choose* to live and dwell in God's presence to the best of our ability, we will remain stable, in a fixed place under God's place of shade. Being in His shade does not mean we won't be in the heat. It just means we will have a place to get out of the worst of the heat trying to beat down on us.

To abide has much more to do with *being*, not doing. It is a place of rest, not striving to get God to do something, but resting in what He is already doing behind the scenes after placing our painful circumstance in His hands. Because I had learned this several years earlier, when Becca died, even though everything came crashing down, I was able to remain fixed on Him being my source of everything I needed.

If you did not have that revelation before your child died, it doesn't mean you missed out and it's too late for you. You can still put yourself in a place of rest, dwelling and abiding in Him.

Reflection: We have a granddaughter who often sleeps with her hands behind her head. We have pictures of her sleeping this way as an infant and on through the years. We call it "Alainah position". It is a position of complete rest. Right now, I would like you to go into "Alainah position". Put your hands behind your head, lean back and rest.

Let God know you don't want to keep striving to get out of this place of darkness, but you want to learn how to rest in what He is doing behind the scenes after placing this whole suffocating dark mess in His hands!

If you are not fighting Him, you can just rest in who He is, knowing that He is working on giving you a firm foundation for your life. He is taking you off of shifting sand and putting you on the Rock!

> *He that dwells in the secret place of the most High shall abide under the shadow of the Almighty. I will say of the Lord, He is my hope and my fortress: my God; in him will I secure myself.*
> *Psalm 91:1-2 (JUB)*

May 21

Miracles

I used to teach preschool, and the easiest description of the word "miracle" I could come up with to share with those three-year-olds was "something only God can do." Some of us have been taught that miracles were only for Bible times (which is how I was raised with my dad being a pastor) and some of us were taught that God still does miracles today (which is what I came to believe as an adult).

No matter what your belief is in this area, we all wanted a miracle for our children, to keep them from dying, whether it was healing them from a sickness or an accident of some kind, or praying protection over them to keep them from deathly harm. Obviously that miracle we wanted did not happen.

Quite often we are looking for a miracle to happen physically, like a healing or protection from an accident; in other words, stopping someone (like our child) from leaving this earth through death. But even

May

before my daughter died, I often thought there are so many times we underestimate the miracle that happens *inside* us.

That has become even more true for me after Becca's death. I think the greater miracle is often so much more than what happens to us physically. It is what happens inside us, especially when we are in such a dark place in our grief. We think it is impossible to get out of the darkness or to ever be okay living without our child here with us.

But that is where the truest miracle happens. It is happening so deeply inside us that we cannot see it or feel it for a very long time. It's like a seed that is underground. Just because we cannot see anything happening, does not mean the seed is dead. It may be dormant for a while, but at some point it will start forming a shoot inside itself that will eventually work its way to the top of the soil where life can be seen.

The growing of a seed into a plant is a miracle. It is something only God can do. Yes, we can water the seed and make sure sunlight reaches it. Those are both needed. But life sprouting from a seed is God's work. Breathing life into you after the death of your child is something only God can do. There are things we can and need to do, to give God something to work with, but He is the one that brings life from death. Both for our child who is on the other side of eternity, and for us, who feel like we died when our child died.

Reflection: God works one of His greatest miracles when He brings our heart back to life after our child leaves this earth before we do. Just because God did not give us the miracle we wanted that would have kept our child here with us, does not mean He will not do a miracle to bring light and life back to you.

You may feel like you don't want to live here without your child. You may feel like you want to figure out how to live again, but do not see how that is possible. You need a miracle - something only God can do. Be bold and ask Him for one. After all, He has already done the miraculous work of making a way for us to be with our child again, forever!

Jesus responded, "What appears humanly impossible is more

> *than possible with God. For God can do what man cannot."*
> *Luke 18:27 (TPT)*

May 22

Music

I occasionally hear from parents how their love for music, singing, or worship used to bring them so much joy, but after the death of their child it is something painful in their lives. One parent wrote, "Since my son died, I can't listen to music at all. It sends me into hysterics."

For me personally, music has been such a part of my life since I was very little, that I cannot imagine not being able to have it in my life, especially in my darkest time. This is an area that I cannot relate to, but that doesn't mean I don't want to acknowledge those who do struggle with it.

Music is a pathway to the soul. God created it that way. We know from scriptures that Lucifer (whom we now call Satan) was created with pipes and was a leader of worship before the earth was created (Ezekiel 28:13). We also know he was cast out of heaven because of his pride, thinking he should be worshiped along with God.

That means one of the greatest tools the enemy has, is music. Satan is out to do anything he can do, to distort music as the pathway to our soul, using it to pull us away from God instead of toward Him.

Music did bring me immense pain when Becca died. I especially had a hard time with songs about heaven because it felt like a slap in the face reminder of my loss, but I knew I needed music in my life since God created it as a pathway to our souls. I believed it would also wash over my soul, bringing a measure of healing I so desperately needed. I forced myself to worship, with tears running down my face, sometimes crying too hard to be able to sing any words. It was like an open wound that painfully needed to be cleaned out before the healing process could even begin.

After maybe two to three years, I began to transition from thinking about the pain of my loss, into what my daughter gained. The more I imagine her joy in where she is and who she is with, the less painful it is for me. There are even times I am happy and excited for her!

Music affects us all differently after the death of our child. If you are like me and others, it is good to know that you are not the only one who struggles with it.

Reflection: If you are one who cannot listen to music, ask God why, and then let Him show you exactly what is behind your pain, beyond your initial grief. He may speak to your heart as you pause and wait, or He may show you a few weeks from now, when you are not even thinking about it. And it may surprise you that what you thought was a simple answer ("I already *know* why!") has more behind it than you realized.

God wants to set you free from the pain of not being able to be ministered to, through something so powerful He created for the purpose of encouraging your soul. Rebuke the enemy so that he will flee from you and ask the Holy Spirit to help you be willing to endure the cleaning out of your open wound, so that the healing balm of music can begin to do its work.

Praise the Lord! For it is good to sing praises to our God;
for it is pleasant, and a song of praise is fitting.
Psalm 147:1 (ESV)

May 23

Come and Rest

I want to go back to a scripture we looked at in March. In Matthew 11:28-30, Jesus says:

> *Come to Me, all you who are weary and burdened, and I will give you rest. Take My yoke upon you and learn from Me, for I am gentle and humble in heart, and you will find rest for your souls. For My yoke is easy and My burden is light. (NIV)*

We may have a hard time with that last sentence because what we are dealing with is anything but easy and light! Six weeks after Becca died, I was reading and meditating on that scripture, and here is what I wrote in my journal.

> *11/29/11: Being yoked together with You is being yoked to that place of rest.*

Two weeks later, God began to apply that revelation to my life as two different people specifically suggested I go on a cruise. One was a man of God who visited our church. He sensed a deep heaviness on me, not knowing my daughter had just died, and felt I needed to go on a cruise to rest and help ease the burden I was carrying.

With last minute plans, I went off by myself to the Caribbean for a five-day cruise. My eyes were red from all the crying I was already doing before we even pulled out of the port! There was a lot of time spent crying in my room, just allowing myself to be in His presence.

At one point I asked myself why I had such deep-rooted sadness and sorrow and pain? Looking back, I know how absolutely ridiculous that question was. But I was trying so hard to walk out my faith in "victory" and did not have anyone who had experienced the death of their child to help me sort out my confusion. I could not see that this was a natural part of grieving, especially only being a few weeks out from the trauma of my child's death. I thought something was wrong with me and I wanted to know where it was coming from so I could get past it.

May

Let me share something the Holy Spirit spoke to my heart during those days on the ship.

> *Laura, when you get thrown into the deep waters, there is turmoil and thrashing at the beginning. You either drown or you swim. You have learned to swim, but not only to swim, but to float in trust and rest. And it does not matter if the waters get deeper, because you are resting on top. Others around you can panic or try to help you, but you know—deep calls to deep. The deeper the waters, the more secure you are in your trust of Me. That is great faith!*

I came away from that cruise in a better place in my grief. Yes, there was still a lot of suffocating darkness. Yes, there were still buckets and buckets of tears the next few years. Yes, I still begged God to just take me out of this world so I could join my daughter. But it was a time that God really did a *deep* work in my heart, and I am thankful for that time away with just me and the lover of my soul, as I allowed Him to love on me deeply in the midst of my horrific painful loss.

Reflection: Jesus tells us to come to Him with our shattered hearts and our heavy burdens. He promises to help us learn what rest really means. The best thing I ever did those first couple of years was to constantly shut myself in with God, cry, and pour my heart out to Him.

If at all possible, I highly recommend taking a few days away from everyone and all of your daily responsibilities and just hang out with God, whatever that looks like. Don't say you can't, and don't put it off. You *need* this time away so God can pour out His love on you and bring you to a place of rest, above the pain and turmoil.

But right now, take a minute and meditate on the same scripture below in the Message version. Ask the Holy Spirit to bring you to a needed place of rest, that goes beyond the pain and turmoil. If He can do it for me, He can do it for you.

> *Are you tired? Worn out? Burned out on religion? Come to me. Get away with me and you'll recover your life. I'll*

> *show you how to take a real rest. Walk with me and work with me—watch how I do it. Learn the unforced rhythms of grace.*
> Matthew 11:28-29 (MSG)

May 24

Our Faith

We all know God could have stepped in and saved our child from dying. In fact, there were several times Becca should have died throughout her life, and God spared her over and over again. So why didn't he do it again on October 12, 2011?

Our friends, Bob and Linda, lost their son Lukas, in a single car accident. His friend was driving late one night. They crashed, and he walked away, not telling anyone that Lukas was still back at the scene hurt and unconscious. Eventually the accident was discovered, and Lukas was taken to the hospital. After several days, his parents were told he would not be able to recover, and they had to make the horrible decision to take their son off life support. (The friend was tried in court by the state and is serving time, because Lukas probably would have lived if he had received immediate medical attention.)

The accident happened on an Easter weekend, and many area churches that were packed with people for Easter services were praying for Bob and Linda's son to recover. Obviously, those prayers were not answered.

Since that time, Linda has pointed out to others that the Bible is filled with miracles and stories of hope. The eighth and ninth chapters of Matthew are full of miracles of healing:

- Healing at Capernaum
- Driving out demons
- A girl restored
- A woman healed

- Healing of the blind

In John chapter eleven, Jesus even raised his friend Lazarus from the dead.

One reasons so many of us have a hard time reading the Bible after our child dies is because we read about the miracles, which are supposed to bring us hope, but we did not get our miracle, so instead of hope, it makes us confused and angry.

All of those feelings do not show a lack of faith. In fact, if anything, it shows that we *have* faith. We know God could have stopped it. We just do not know why He didn't. If it helps, I want to remind you that the book of Psalms is full of asking God questions like "Why?" and "How long is it going to be like this?".

These are all things that we have to work our way through. Some of us take longer than others. Many of us start taking steps to trust God again, but then get caught up with the anger and confusion and asking God all those questions again.

We want answers! We want God to explain Himself to us. We want to make sense of something that will never make sense this side of heaven. This is all part of the grief journey we are on. It is also part of our faith journey.

Reflection: Corrie Ten Boom (a woman who survived a holocaust concentration camp) said, "When a train goes through a tunnel and it gets dark, you don't throw away the ticket and jump off. You sit still and trust the engineer."

Losing one's child is a true test of our faith. Not faith in getting God to do what we want Him to do, but in trusting Him when those answers do not come. After the death of our child, life is pretty dark, and it feels like we will never see light again. But I want to tell you not to jump off the train, because you can still trust your Engineer.

Remember, being angry at God does not show a lack of faith. It shows that you *do* have faith because you know He could have stopped it. The bigger issue is, will you *still* trust Him? After all, He made a way for us to be together again forever, knowing this was going to happen.

> *The Lord is there to rescue all who are*
> *discouraged and have given up hope.*
> *Psalm 34:18 (CEV)*

May 25

Strength and Stability

After the death of our child our world has been completely shattered and we desperately need strength and stability. In our heads, we know that comes from God, but in our hearts many of His promises can now seem very distant.

Isaiah 61:3 is a familiar verse to many of us, which tells us that God will give a crown of beauty for ashes, the oil of joy for mourning, and a garment of praise for the spirit of heaviness. But did you know there is more to the verse?

It goes on to say, "... that they will be called oaks of righteousness, a planting of the Lord, that he may be glorified." (ESV)

We can look at this verse in four different sections (which I did, on my podcast in episode 184) but today I am just going to share my thoughts on how we will be called oaks of righteousness. Some versions simply say trees, but it is not just any tree. So, why an oak tree? Let's look at some of its characteristics.

- It starts with such a small beginning as a tiny acorn, but it grows to become one of the largest and strongest trees.
- The growth of an oak tree is very gradual. It can be so slow that you do not notice it year-to-year. Then suddenly you realize how big it has gotten and how much it has grown.
- Oak trees go through seasons. In the spring they bud with new growth; in the summer they are full of green leaves; autumn causes the leaves to change color, eventually falling to the ground and leaving a dead-looking tree through the winter.

- It endures storms, great winds, ice and snow. It also absorbs the sun and the rain. All of this is needed to bring an oak tree to its place of full maturity.

This is an amazing picture of us. We truly can go from our place of deep grief, despondency, despair, hopelessness, and even feeling like we have died ourselves, to being like a fully mature tree, producing fruit.

It starts out so small, and that little acorn has to be buried in the ground. Breaking out of the shell and popping to the surface takes so long that we think it has died. We think we have died along with our child, and they just forgot to bury us. Plus, it can take so long to feel joy and meaning again that it confirms the darkness of our thoughts that we will never get back out into light and life again.

The growth can be so slow that we don't think anything is even happening.

Even though there is no apparent life in us, we are just dormant for our season of deep grief.

You and I eventually become stronger through the storms, as we continue to soak up provided nourishment. In that place of maturity, an oak tree buds and blossoms, producing fruit, and so will we, even becoming a place where others can come for shelter.

You may not feel like it, but you are a mighty oak tree, with the ability to become strong and stable after something as horrific as the death of your child.

Reflection: Did you know that oak trees can be found around the globe, growing in all kinds of different soil types, rainfall levels, temperatures, and elevations?

That tells me that no matter the situation of our child's death (including losing more than one child or your only child, through murder, drug overdose or suicide, a long illness, or completely unexpected) we *can* get to a place of growing and flourishing again.

You are an oak tree, planted by God, who is making sure that you will come to a place of thriving again, based on both who He is and who we allow Him to be for us in this process. Not only can you become stable and strong again, but through the battles that leave us scarred, we can stand in even more strength and stability than ever before.

> *Jesus looked straight at them and said, "There are some things people cannot do, but God can do anything."*
> *Matthew 19:26 (CEV)*

May 26

Our View

We may feel like we are trapped in this world, but that is not the case. We are in it, but this is not our permanent home. We are citizens of heaven, which is where our children are. We are in a higher kingdom that is both above us and in us that we need to be part of while still here on earth.

When our child dies, we usually only have one lens to view life through, which makes everything very dark. We are pretty blind to anything else around us, and it is a struggle because we are left feeling like we are just stumbling around in our darkness.

We need to see something better. We need to see some light and so much more than what you and I may be seeing right now. We need to see the Kingdom of God more clearly. We need to understand who God is for each one of us in this situation. We need a lens change to help us see that God has not abandoned us and that He is still for us, not against us.

Having the mind of Christ is not about trying to spiritualize our thinking. It is about learning to live in the space of who we are now and who we are becoming through the Holy Spirit. Yes, the Holy Spirit is still at work in your life. He has to be, because He lives inside you, and will not allow you to remain in darkness.

I know you probably feel like you died the day your child did. There is no denying that part of us did. However, there is still life in us because He is in us. I am still alive in Christ Jesus, and so are you.

Living in the Kingdom of God is more powerful than any circumstance we face here on this earth, but we don't have to wait until we get to heaven to have life in His Kingdom. We are in this world, but we are not of this world. We are citizens of a different world, and it is a world that is full of life.

Reflection: I know it may seem like just the opposite right now, but that is because your lens is still dark from the grief. There is no shame or guilt for that. It is what it is. The enemy has given you a huge blow, and it puts us in a place of darkness that is beyond what can be described.

Even in the darkness, God wants to take you from glory to glory (2 Corinthians 3:18). Being changed from glory to glory involves our vision and how we see things. Our soul can still be in darkness, while our spirit is finding and connecting to the light.

How do we do that? By spending time with Him and continually asking Him to see Him in all of His glory and beauty. Do not look with your soul and your feelings. Look with your spirit. Allow Him to breathe fresh life into you. As you begin to see Him as He truly is, the darkness in your soul will begin to lift.

Open the eyes of their hearts, and let the light of Your truth flood in. Shine Your light on the hope You are calling them to embrace. Reveal to them the glorious riches You are preparing as their inheritance.
Ephesians 1:18 (VOICE)

May 27

When Will I Stop Crying?

Some of the worst triggers that catch me by surprise are when I think I see Becca somewhere and get smacked once again with the crashing realization that it cannot possibly be her. For several years, motorized scooter carts in a store triggered the thought of my daughter. Even just hearing someone the next aisle over in one of those carts can give me a shocking reminder of my loss. I have had to fight tears so many times when I am out shopping because of triggers like this.

Sometimes I "win" and can escape without crying, and sometimes I don't, as the tears spill down my cheeks. (I will say that it has gotten much better over the years.) I have often wondered why I don't ever see anyone else in the store who looks like they are crying. Am I the only one who struggles with grief triggers out in public like this?

The first year of special dates is always difficult for anyone who has lost a loved one, but for a parent who has a child missing, it can be almost unbearable.

Because this takes so many of us by surprise, I feel it is important to share this more than once in this book. What I was not expecting was to have the second year be harder than the first! I see two reasons for this. First, I braced myself for those one-year markers. I knew they were going to be hard, so I tried to prepare myself for them mentally and emotionally. The second year it felt like I was caught off guard. *I have been through this before; it should be better this year*, I thought, but when those dates came, they hit me like a brick wall.

The second reason is that I was still in such a fog of unbelief the first year. As the fog started to lift that second year, the loss was hitting me with full force. By the third year (for me personally) it was turning into more like a very painful acceptance, trying to figure out how to live this new life without my daughter.

I feel like I need to say this to the parents who are still in deep grief. Do NOT look at any dates to see where I or others were emotionally in our grieving process and use it as some sort of a timeline to force on yourself.

I want to remind you that we are all on our own individual timeline and need to go through the process at our own speed. Yes, there are some "patterns" (for lack of a better word) that some of us seem to fall into, but don't expect yourself to fit into that. Give yourself grace to walk your own necessary path and know that it is normal to shed many, many tears.

Reflection: It has taken me almost my entire lifetime to learn that tears are a gift from God.

Jesus knew that when His dear friend Lazarus died, it was only temporary. And yet we know Jesus wept. If you want to cry, go ahead and cry as hard as you need to. Let your tears be the gift God gave them to be, allowing them to wash away some of the pain.

It may feel like you will be like this for the rest of your life. I assure you, while there will always be tears, they do eventually come further apart. Whenever they come, do your best to see them as the gift they are, both washing away some of the pain, and letting you know that you will never be able to forget or stop loving your child.

> *He will take away death for all time.*
> *The Lord God will dry tears from all faces.*
> *Isaiah 25:8 (NLV)*

May 28

Freedom From Bitterness

Many of us are angry after our child dies. Anger can turn into bitterness, which leads to resentment. It is an ugly progression. This is an area where we need to do everything we can to guard our hearts and keep it from happening.

Bitterness hurts you and those around you. It takes you off the path of moving in the direction of your needed healing. We cannot control the thoughts that come into our mind, but we can control what we do with those thoughts. We can dismiss them and get our mind onto something else, or we can turn those thoughts over and over again in our mind, allowing them to take root in the depths of our soul.

Reflections of Hope

When bitterness and resentment take root, it usually leads to depression. We start feeling sorry for ourselves, allowing our soul to spiral downward even deeper into our pit of darkness, pushing everyone away from us, which causes the downward spiral to continue out of control.

If the only thing you can see in your future is pain and darkness, then don't look there. For many of us, all we can handle is one day at a time. In fact, often we can only handle one hour at a time, or just work on taking the next breath.

There is hope though. You can be free from bitter thoughts. It takes giving your mind to the Holy Spirit, allowing Him to show you how to change your thoughts. When you are thinking about the past in all of its pain and horror, let Him give you something else to think about in your past that was good. When you are thinking about the future and the pain of who won't be there, let Him give you something to think about in your future that is eternal and exciting.

God wants to be in your thoughts. He wants to help you learn to think on the good things to come in your life, both here and in eternity. He wants to help you keep your grief from turning into bitterness, resentment and depression.

Reflection: These dark thoughts are part of the grieving process, but we do not have to give in and camp out at any of them. Stop and take a minute to ask yourself what are the thoughts about your child's death that makes you angry? Where you can feel bitterness and resentment creeping in? Is it someone who thinks you should not be grieving so deeply for this long? Is it thinking about the future events your child won't be here for?

If you know ahead of time what triggers you in this direction, it will be easier to recognize it and refuse to let it creep in. Call out the enemy for what he is trying to do, and lean hard into God's love for you. Ask the Holy Spirit who lives inside you to take over your thoughts. Take it one thought at a time, and fight until there is a release from that bitterness.

> *Above all, be careful what you think*
> *because your thoughts control your life.*
> *Proverbs 4:23 (ERV)*

May 29

The Enemy Did This

Before we were born, God knew everything that was going to happen to us in our lives. He knew we would mess up from time to time, and already had a plan in place. He also knew we would have hard things thrown our way from the enemy of our souls.

A few months after my daughter died, my sister's house burned down to the ground. Their family of seven lost everything except the clothes on their back and the van they had driven to church that night. The only way Diane and her family have been able to work through this traumatic event and come out on the other side with victory and joy, is because they refuse to let their loss become the enemy's gain. She has made the choice to not let the past be a mortgage to her future. She refuses to be chained to the devastation of the loss by feeling sorry for herself, but is going forward; pressing into what God still has for her life and her family.

I realize losing a house and everything you own isn't the same as losing our child. But it is still devastating and a huge trauma. There are so many special things that can never be replaced. And how do you *completely* start over, when you don't even own something as small as a paper clip or a spoon?

It is up to us, to choose to take those things and see how they fit into what God has for us. A turning point is when we realize our destiny is not so much about what we get handed in life, as it is what we do with those things we are handed.

We choose what we believe. But believing something does not make it true. Sometimes what we believe is based on false information. But don't let that thought discourage you. Every time I ask God to show me a lie I have chosen to believe, He reveals something to me. That is a good thing, because it means I can get rid of it and secure even more freedom in my life to live from a place of contentment, as well as fulfill my purpose.

Reflection: When our daughter Becca had cancer at three years old, we had a pastor who helped us to not blame God but see it for what it truly was; an attack of our spiritual enemy trying to "steal, kill, and destroy" us (John 10:10).

We had a choice to make. We could believe this was God's fault and be angry with Him for what had happened (or for not taking away her cancer) or we could be angry at Satan for bringing sin and sickness into the world which affected our daughter in this horrible way. We chose to pull together and fight the true enemy, instead of God or each other, and are so thankful we did!

I made the same choice when Becca died, twenty-six years later. And I am so thankful I did!

Too often, our false beliefs hold us back from going forward in fulfilling God's incredible plan He still has for our lives. Ask God to show you what your false beliefs are, and then allow Him to take them from you, replacing each one with His truth.

You will know the truth, and that truth will give you freedom.
John 8:32 (VOICE)

May 30

Reunited

"My little daughter is dying. Please come and put your hands on her so that she will be healed and live," Mark 5:23 (NIV). This was spoken by a man named Jairus, who fell at Jesus' feet. We read that Jesus got up to go with him but was stopped by the woman who had the issue of bleeding, touched the hem of his garment and was healed.

People came to Jairus during that time and told him his daughter had died and there was no longer a reason for Jesus to come.

We can have that same reaction. "My child is dead. You did not stop it. Don't bother with me now! Leave me alone." Jesus did not listen to that then, and He is not listening to it now. Jesus told this father not to be afraid, but to believe. What was he to believe? That he would see his daughter again. That she was not really dead.

Now I know Jesus raised this girl from the dead on the spot, and we did not get that. But we do still get the promise that our child is not really dead. He or she transferred to our eternal home in glory ahead of us. They are more alive than we are! Their bodies have put on immortality. They are living in the fullness of God's abundant love and perfection.

God wants to redeem us in a different way than He does with those who maybe had a miracle and did not lose their child - the miracle *we* wanted.

We have the opportunity to know Him like very few get to. We get to know Him in His sufferings. He lost a son to a brutal torturous murder. He knows what it is like to have a child die, He also knows what it is like to get him back, and we will too! Just not here and now. In the meantime, we can know Him in a depth that others do not, and it gives us a glimpse into how much he loves us. Would you be willing to have your child die to save someone else. He did! He went through that so we would not be separated forever from our children and others we love.

Jairus only had to wait maybe a couple of hours before he saw his daughter alive again. We don't know how long our separation will be, but once we are reunited with all of eternity ahead of us, I am convinced it will seem like a nano-second.

Reflection: Our child's departure from this world has changed us. We will never be the same. And eventually, we get to choose what that looks like. Our child was given to us as a gift, not as a right. The question is: What kind of a person do you want to become as a result? Do you want to be your child's parent, stuck in the place and event of his or her death, or do you want to allow God to redeem it, and learn how to live in a way that honors his or her life!

We may not have been given our child back to us here on earth like Jairus was, but they will be given back to us. Death is not the end. It is a door to the next life. Let us live in glorious anticipation of that day!

I tell you the truth the time is coming and is already here when the dead will hear the voice of the Son of God, and those who hear will have life.
John 5:25 (NCV)

May 31
Comparing Our Losses

I hear from parents who desperately want to see their child in a dream. Sometimes other family members will have dreams about their child and then tell the parent about those dreams, which gets them even more upset. "I am the mom! I loved her more than anyone! Why am I not seeing her? Why don't I get to have that?"

Some get frustrated when they find out another pareavor had a dream about their own child, because they so desperately want to see their own child also. "Why do they get to have a dream about their child, but I don't have a dream about mine?

May

There are pareavors who are angry because their child died suddenly, unlike those who "knew their child was dying and got to say goodbye". Other parents had to watch in horror and agony for weeks while their child slowly slipped away getting weaker and weaker and finally struggling to even be able to breathe. They are angry about how their child had to suffer like that, along with having those traumatic haunting memories, and would rather have had a sudden loss.

"Why did you get 29 years with your daughter, and I only got to have seven years with mine? At least you got to watch her grow up and know what she was like as an adult for a few years. I didn't get to have that." On the other hand, yes, I had the blessing of seeing my daughter as an adult. I also got to know what it was like to turn the corner from a rough childhood and *very* rocky teen years to having my daughter become one of my best friends, and then have that ripped away from me.

I could continue with more of these questions, wanting to know why we did not get to have it like someone else, but I am sure you get the idea.

There just aren't going to be answers to most of these questions on this side of heaven. But they are questions we still need to ask; to hammer them out until we get to the point where we are exhausted asking and resign ourselves to not knowing, which will allow us to move past them.

If you are not there yet, it's okay. You may still be fresh in your grief, which can be up to five years. These may sound like empty words, but keep hanging in there, one day, one breath, one tear at a time, while doing what you can to not torment yourself with how another pareavor got something with their child that you did not get.

Reflection: When I am asked how to help someone who has lost a child, I tell them not to ever start a sentence with the words "At least...". Don't bother saying whatever it was you were going to say, because it will hurt more than it will help.

While it is extremely rare for a pareavor to tell another pareavor, "I know how you feel because I lost my child, too", in our minds, we can still compare our loss with other pareavors. So, I want to make the same suggestion to you. If your thought starts with the words, "At least they..." then dismiss it from your mind immediately, knowing there are probably pareavors around you who have their own "At least..." thoughts about your loss.

These comparisons can keep us in a place of bitterness and turmoil, which you know is not a good place to be. Ask the Holy Spirit to call attention to when you think these thoughts, so you can begin to get rid of them.

> *All they are doing, of course, is to measure themselves by their own standards or by comparisons within their own circle, and that doesn't make for accurate estimation, you may be sure.*
> *2 Corinthians 10:12 (PHILLIPS)*

Just for the record, I feel like I had it both ways with my daughter's death, as far as watching it happen and yet also being suddenly. Let me explain. I had been home for three hours after visiting her at Madison University Hospital. She was getting dismissed the next morning, but I had a feeling in my gut that something wasn't right, and I needed to get back up there. She died while I was driving the 50-minute trip there! I missed Becca's death by maybe 30-40 minutes. If I knew something was off, why didn't God at least let me get there first?

For the last eighteen months of her life, I had to watch her go through more traumas than most people have in a life-time. She had at least a dozen ambulance rides and three emergency helicopter rides. She had two open heart surgeries (one was to give her a six-pound pump to run the left side of her heart which was run by a computer and two big batteries strapped around her waist), she had a stroke, was revived from Sudden Cardiac Death, survived being in the Trauma ICU with Sepsis with all of her organs shutting down.

Becca was in the hospital more than she was home that last year and a half. I sat with her for many days, multiple times when she should have died, but each time she fought and lived! And yet, the night before being dismissed as healthy enough to go home, she died suddenly and unexpectedly.

Life here is not easy, and it is not always fair, but God will always be our Anchor if we let Him.

June

June 1

Dads Grieve Differently

We have heard that our grief journey is personal and there is no wrong way to grieve. We may wholeheartedly agree with that statement, until it comes to our spouse. Then we think that he or she is doing it wrong!

Sometimes I get emails from a newly bereaved mom, asking how she can get her husband to do a better job of grieving. They want to know how to get their husbands to open up and talk to them about it or know how to convince him to go see a counselor.

As women, when most of us have a problem, we need to talk about it. Our brains never stop thinking. Every thought is connected to a bunch of other thoughts, so talking helps us sort it out by being able to segregate that issue to deal with it better. We aren't necessarily looking for a solution, we just need to be able to think our thoughts out loud to help us clarify how we feel and what we can do about it.

Did you know that most men only talk about a problem if they think the other man, they are talking to can help fix that problem? We all know that unless someone can bring our child back, this is an issue that cannot be "fixed." A dad does not need to talk about it. He needs to process his deep loss in different ways, which to a wife may look like avoiding the grief.

I read about a woman who was concerned that she had not seen her husband cry since the death of their child and he kept coming up with major projects in the intense heat outside, like renting a tiller and starting a garden. Those who understood how most men seem to grieve differently than women, assured her that unless he was doing something to endanger himself or others (like excessive drinking or explosive anger) that it was okay because this is how he was dealing with the pain and processing his grief.

By nature, men are the protectors and have a hard time showing what they perceive as weakness, but I am absolutely certain the dads are hurting. I am also certain that Father's Day will increase the pain and

June

grief these men are feeling. In fact, my husband, Dave, says it is *the* toughest day of the year for him concerning Becca's loss.

If you are married, you might want to make sure you give your husband some space to grieve on his own on Father's Day, whatever it looks like for him, which will probably be much different than how you needed to grieve on Mother's Day.

Reflection: When it comes to grieving the death of our child, we tend to offer our spouse our own best solution. We women want our husbands to talk about it, since that is what helps us. The men want us to stop immersing ourselves in things that remind us that our child is gone, not realizing it is one of the ways we need to process the reality of what has happened.

All of us really do grieve differently, and it is most obviously seen in a husband and wife who are grieving the death of their child. Ask God how you can support your spouse in the way he or she needs to grieve and process your joint loss.

If you are not married, ask God to give yourself grace to grieve however you need to, especially when it does not make sense to anyone around you.

*So stop being critical and condemning of other believers,
but instead determine to never deliberately cause a brother
or sister to stumble and fall because of your actions.
Romans 14:13 (TPT)*

June 2

God Was not Punishing You

One of Job's greatest desires was for his children to be right with the Lord. His children were known for gathering at each other's houses to party for their birthdays. Every time, when they were done with their festivities, Job would arrange for them to be purified and make sacrifices for each one of them, in case they had sinned and cursed God in their hearts.

Then one day, Job lost all ten of his children in one blow, literally, as the house they were all in crashed down on them in a windstorm. Not only that, but Job lost all of his wealth and finances, and then lost his health as he got a disease with big painful boils on his skin.

Like Job, some of us have also had horrible things hit us right after (or shortly before) the death of our child, which can cause us to question God even more. "Wasn't the death of my child enough?" As bereaved parents, we may have a lot of "why" questions for God after our loss(es) like Job did. One of those questions can be, "What terrible thing did I do to deserve this?"

Job's friends insisted he made God angry by doing something wrong, but there was absolutely nothing Job did that "opened the door" for the enemy to have a right to mess with him, as some of us have been taught. Job wanted some answers, especially since he was convinced that he had done nothing wrong to bring these horrible tragedies in his life.

I want to *assure* you that you have not either. How can I say this, not knowing what is in your past?

In Job 9:33, Job lamented that he wished there was someone to arbitrate between himself and God. Job did not have someone like that, but you do! If you have received the gift of salvation, every wrong thing you have *ever* done, no matter how bad, had the penalty canceled when Jesus took it on Himself while hanging on the cross.

Reflection: God sees you and me as righteous in the blood of Jesus. Your relationship with God has been made right in Him. The death of your child was *not* a punishment for some past sin. We may still suffer the natural consequences of bad choices, but the price of punishment was paid *in full* over two thousand years ago.

However, that does not make us immune from the evil that is in this world because of Satan. There is righteous suffering that is the result of unseen, spiritual conflicts between the kingdom of God and the kingdom of Satan; between the kingdom of light and the kingdom of darkness, of which we often get caught in the middle, while we are still here on earth.

It doesn't mean we have to like it, or even be okay with it. But we hang on, knowing God tells us He will bring good out of everything we go through (Romans 8:28) and somehow will turn it around to benefit our life while bringing Him glory and bringing down the enemy.

God did not "allow" your child to die as a punishment for something in your past. Sit with that thought for as long as you need to, until the truth of it pushes out the lie. If your question of "why" is based on your past, let the answer of "NO" be settled once and for all.

> *But God, being [so very] rich in mercy, because of*
> *His great and wonderful love with which He loved us,* [5]
> *even when we were [spiritually] dead and separated from*
> *Him because of our sins, He made us [spiritually] alive*
> *together with Christ (for by His grace—His undeserved favor*
> *and mercy—you have been saved from God's judgment).*
> *Ephesians 2:4-5 (AMP)*

June 3

Curse God and Die

She is most famous for telling Job to "curse God and die." Who is it? Job's wife. The one who birthed all ten of the children who died together in a huge windstorm.

Most of us moms have the experience that our husbands are a bit more "practical" about their grief. They bury themselves in their work. They do not want to talk about it. If they cry, it is not usually around us, and we don't know about it. But just because they grieve differently, does not mean they aren't grieving at all or are not dealing with the deep loss. There are good and valid reasons for the different ways men and women grieve that I am not going to get into here. (You can find blogs and podcasts about this at gpshope.org.)

As moms, many of us don't care who sees how much pain we are in after the death of our child. I know for me, I put out some deeply emotional social media posts that made Dave, my husband, uncomfortable. I never got angry and blamed God for what happened to my daughter, but I have to be really honest and say I don't know how I would have been if I had lost all five of my children at the same time.

Knowing how common it is to have that struggle of being angry at God for allowing the death of one's child, I can understand the response of Job's wife to her husband who was refusing to blame God. Because the book of Job is all about Job's response to his tragedies, it is easy to forget that these things happened to his wife as well. She is also a victim of what Satan had done and was really having a hard time with her husband's blind acceptance of the tragedies that happened to them both.

In the second chapter of Job, it seems her view is that watching her husband remain devoted to God is a cop-out and that he should challenge God, even if the consequence of that was his death. Her statement was obviously made from a place of very deep grief when she threw out at him, "Are you still maintaining your integrity? Curse God and die!"

He answered her with "Shall we accept just good from God and not trouble?" Did that make her fume even more? We don't know for sure. What we do know is that Job realized it would not help at all to blame God, and all it did for his wife was cause her to be a bitter woman, toward God and those around her, including her husband.

Reflection: Most people are not looking at what Job's wife said through the eyes of someone who has had a child die, so she is pretty much hung out to dry by those who read that one sentence about her. No one seems to think about the fact that this mother lost all ten of her children at the same time! I believe her response of telling Job to curse God and die was out of that place of deep dark suffocating grief.

Many of you have experienced that same kind of anger at God, for allowing your child(ren) to die. I know it is a heavy burden to carry, and to question God is normal and valid. However, we need to ask ourselves, do we want to be known as being an angry and bitter person? Will that bring honor to our child, or to God, who is not the source of death, but the redeemer of it?

I hope and pray that you decide to allow the Holy Spirit to dig out any root of bitterness, so that you can learn how to live out your life with meaning and purpose, instead of living in an empty shell just waiting to die.

Guard against turning back from the grace of God. Let no one become like a bitter plant that grows up and causes many troubles with its poison.
Hebrews 12:15 (GNT)

June 4

Back and Forth

At my daughter's funeral, I drew on God's strength to stand up front and speak, sharing encouraging scriptures that were being an anchor to me those first few days. People were amazed that I was so strong. We all know what happened next. Just like every pareavor, I crashed hard into that deep suffocating dark pit of grief.

Some days I felt like I could lean on God, knowing somehow, He would get me through. Other days, I knew there was no way I could make it through life one more minute and begged God to take me to go be with Becca.

Guess what? Job did the same thing. As we look at Job again, we see him going back and forth with standing firm in His belief that God is righteous and good, and then questioning God's character.

We read his very first response in Job 1:20-21 where he fell down and worshiped God, blessing His name in the midst of the horrible tragedies. Believe it or not, some of us were like this when our child first died. We acknowledged His sovereignty and goodness, even though we did not understand why this has happened.

But then we see Job take a dive down and we watch him struggle back and forth. Let's look at some of it. (Note: I have paraphrased his words and added the scripture reference in case you want to see it for yourself.)

- God, why didn't I just die when I was born? I would be at peace right now! (3:11)
- Why doesn't death come for those who long for it? (3:21)
- What I feared and dreaded the most has happened! (3:25)
- God does incredible things that we cannot even comprehend, including lifting up those who are mourning. (5:9-11)
- My pain and anguish are beyond what can even be measured! God's arrows are in me. I can't take any more of this! (6:1-9)
- God, you made me with your own hands. Why are you destroying me like this? (10:8)

June

- Even if God kills me, I will continue to put my hope and trust in Him. (13:15)
- God knows me. He knows my heart and when He has tested me, I will come out like gold that has been purified in the fire. (23:10)
- God does whatever he wants. That is why I am terrified of Him! My heart can't take any more. (23:13-16)
- In chapter 28 Job reminds us that some of the most valuable things come from the depths of darkness.

I think you get the point. What I want us to realize, is that even in going back and forth, Job seemed to know that all his blessings were from God, and that rejecting Him would mean there was no possibility of future blessings. He may have questioned God, but Job did not push Him away and close the door.

Reflection: I received so much new revelation that was very encouraging in reading Job from the perspective of a parent who has had a child die. There are many things we can relate to in the book of Job.

What was Job's final conclusion? "I know that You can do anything, and that no plans of Yours can be withheld from You. I am sorry that I have spoken of things that I did not understand. I used to know *about* You, but now I really truly *know* You" (My short paraphrase of Job 42:1-5).

If you want to have Job's conclusion (which included being blessed with a full life once again), then maybe you should repeat Job's words and ask the Holy Spirit to make them a reality in your life. *I know that You can do anything, and that no plans of Yours can be withheld from You. I am sorry that I have spoken against You about things that I really don't understand. I thought I knew you, but I want to truly know You in an intimate way in all your wonder and goodness. And as I do, please bring the blessing of meaning and purpose back into my life.*

> *Oh, that we might know the Lord! Let us press on*
> *to know him, and he will respond to us as surely*
> *as the coming of dawn or the rain of early spring.*
> *Hosea 6:3 (TLB)*

June 5

They Didn't Understand Either

In all his complaints, pain and confusion, it is interesting that Job did not turn his back on God. He falsely accuses God of causing the death of his children, the loss of his finances and his painful boils, but he knows that even within all of what he is going through, God is the only One who can give him any kind of restoration, hope or peace.

So much of our darkness is because we have a hard time seeing any perspective except our own pain of the earthly loss of our child. We have plenty of examples in the Bible, besides Job, who were given an assignment by God or had a painful tragedy happen, that made no sense.

People like:

- Abraham, being told by God to offer his only son Isaac as a sacrifice on an altar. This son was God's promised heir that took many years and a literal miracle to be conceived.
- Moses, who was instructed to free over a million slaves, leading them through a desert to a promised land of goodness. These people were complaining and ungrateful, no matter how many miracles God did for them.
- Gideon, when facing hundreds of thousands of the enemy's armies, was told to whittle his army down to only 300 men who were armed with horns to blow and a lit torch inside a pitcher!
- Mary, the mother of Jesus who accepted the assignment of being a pregnant woman out of wedlock and the shame that came with it (including a possible stoning) and the ridicule of saying she was impregnated by God's Spirit and not by any man.
- The apostle Paul, who was compelled to bring Jesus to the Gentiles, which brought him beatings that left him as good as dead. In his travels, he also had multiple accidents and injuries that should have taken his life over and over again.

Because we read about them in the Bible as history, it is easy for us to see what God was doing in their lives with eternity in mind. But it could

June

not have been easy for them living it out at the time, not knowing God's eternal perspective or the whys.

The Bible is a record of dozens of people who did not understand at the time why God was allowing something tragic to happen to them. Some were delivered in their lifetime, and some were not. Heaven is *filled* with those who could not see the full picture of what God was doing with the tragedies in their lives while here on earth, but can understand and see it clearly now, *including our children*.

Reflection: Hebrews 11:39-40 gives a list of people who were commended for their faith, yet none of them received what had been promised to them while they were here on earth. That is not what we want to hear, is it? We want to have the results of those like Abraham, who did not have to follow through with sacrificing his son, Isaac, or to be like Job who had his life fully restored while still here on earth, but that is not always the case.

I find that Job's final response to God was pretty amazing. While Job was still struggling with all his deep losses, in Job 42:2, he acknowledges that God can do anything, and that no purpose of His can be withheld from Him.

God's plans and purposes are beyond what we can know or understand. You are still in safe hands. You are still valuable, and there is still a purpose for your life. Some day you will be one of those who look back and can see what God was doing through your child leaving this earth ahead of you. Let's choose to trust in that plan, even in the pain and the confusion after the death of our child. If Job can, after all of his huge losses, we can, too.

> *Job answered God: "I'm convinced: You can do anything and everything. Nothing and no one can upset your plans. You asked, 'Who is this muddying the water, ignorantly confusing the issue, second-guessing my purposes?' I admit it. I was the one. I babbled on about things far beyond me, made small talk about wonders way over my head."*
> *Job 42:1-3 (MSG)*

June 6

Choosing to Trust

Those of us who have lost a child can have major struggles with trusting God. We may have prayed daily for God's protection over our children, trusting He would answer that prayer because of our unwavering faith. We may have fasted and prayed for a sick child, fully believing we would see Jehovah Rapha, God our Healer, in action.

People around us may have told us something like, "Keep praying in faith. God is going to heal your child," which brought encouragement at the time. Or how about since that horrible day hearing something like, "Hang in there. God knows what He is doing, just trust Him."

We often want to shout, "I DID trust God, and my child died!"

First, let me say that you are allowed to question what God is doing in your life. Surprised? Abraham did, Jonah did, Elisha the prophet did, the twelve apostles did... get the picture?

We have prayed for protection or healing for our children, and that prayer was not answered the way we thought it should (or would) be. Yes, my daughter's death sent me into a suffocating darkness that I did not even know existed. But trusting God and refusing to let go of Him in the midst of my pain, which was so deep I would sometimes forget to breathe, is what got me where I am today.

It reminds me of when Jesus asked his disciples if they were going to leave him like the rest of the crowd did, when He said something difficult that made no sense to them whatsoever. Peter's response in John 6:68 (NLV) was, "Lord, who else can we go to? You have words that give life that lasts forever."

After going through the kind of tragedy we have experienced, trusting God again does not usually happen in just one decision, but in making the decision over and over again. It can be a process, and that is okay. Just do your best to make the decision each time to trust Him, no matter how you feel, and when things do not make sense. After all, isn't that what trust is?

Reflection: Where else can we go? God does not just have eternal life for us in heaven, but He still has a full and meaningful life for us here on earth. I encourage you to choose to make that decision to trust Him as often as you need to, so that God can wrap you in His hope, His comfort, and yes, even His peace. Ask Him to shift your perspective to see things in a different way. Trade the anger and blame, so you can receive the love of the Father that your child is now basking in.

Think about it. Our children now know how trustworthy He is! They can see the full picture that we cannot see!

God has everything you and I need to help guide us out of the darkness of our suffocating grief. You *can* choose to trust Him in the midst of the pain. And I'll bet your son or daughter would tell you the same thing.

> *Lean on, trust in, and be confident in the Lord with all your heart and mind and do not rely on your own insight or understanding.*
> *Proverbs 3:5 (AMPC)*

June 7

Words from a Bereaved Father

(By Dave Diehl)

I have written many checks before, but I never dreamed I would be writing a check to pay for my daughter's burial plot! I could barely see through my tears to sign it.

I believe most of us men tend to compartmentalize everything in our minds, almost as if everything in life has its own little box and we only take out one box at time. For the most part, I was able to take out my work box and stay there, but grief had just shattered my "Becca box" into a million pieces. I tried to sweep my grief into a grief box, but the problem with grief is that it cannot stay in a box! Somehow those shattered pieces find a way into all the other boxes. These pieces tend to appear out of nowhere and not always at convenient times.

It was not easy, and there were times at work I would close the door to my office and allow myself to tear up and grieve some more. So, if you're reading this and you're a father who has lost a child and you tend to compartmentalize, I encourage you to allow yourself those moments to grieve. Grieving is not a sign of weakness; it is a way for us to heal.

All holidays bring some difficulty as we celebrate them, such as Christmas, New Year's, and family birthdays including our child's. My first Father's Day after Becca died was especially different for me. Becca was the child who made me a father when she was two and I adopted her. I vividly remember her bringing me donuts for breakfast in bed for my first Father's Day.

My first one without her was extremely difficult. I had four other children whom I loved dearly and spent the day with, but I needed to spend time at her graveside that day as well. It was probably the longest time I ever stayed out there, crying tears of pain that she wasn't with us anymore and tears of joy for all the funny memories. I needed to allow myself that time of grief.

We all do, including us fathers!

Reflection: More people are starting to acknowledge the loss of a child on Mother's Day. Not as many think of bereaved dads on Father's Day.

As a bereaved dad, I want to personally recognize how difficult this day can be for you. It is one of the most difficult of all "dates" for me regarding the loss of my daughter, Becca. One thing I do on Father's Day is to ask God to tell her how much I love and miss her and to give her a big hug and kiss from me. I have no doubt that He does that for me and will do it for you, too. Just ask Him.

I honor you this Father's Day and pray that you will feel the love of our Heavenly Father's arms around you, as He comforts you as a Father who understands. Laura and I want you to know you have our hearts and our prayers.

Remember your promise to me, your servant. It gives me hope. You comfort me in my suffering, because your promise gives me new life.
Psalm 119:49-50 (ERV)

June 8

The Rain

Yesterday morning I was sitting out in the rain. Well, not really sitting in it, but sitting under our awning, watching it. It was a bit chilly and damp, but I enjoyed it for a good hour.

Quite often when it rains, we see it as a nuisance. Going from our car to a building we get all wet. It can wreak havoc on outdoor summer plans. Too much of it can cause flooding, etc. But I found myself thinking about how nourishing the rain is and thanking God for how He designed all of this to work; how water used to come from the ground and did not come from the sky until the flood in Noah's time; how it all goes back up and comes down in a cycle; how it does what it is designed to do to nourish life, and so on.

As my thoughts continued to wander, I kept coming back to the different opinions and perspectives we can have on something as simple as the rain. This eventually brought my thoughts to the difference in perspectives we can have on everything here, including the death of our child.

At first, the darkness and grief overtake us and overwhelms us. But after a year or two, or sometimes more, we find ourselves getting to the point where we get to make choices. Am I going to keep myself in this dark place, or am I going to fight my way out? If I decide it is time to fight my way back into the light and figure out how to live a life with purpose and meaning again, how do I get there?

Much of it is changing our perspective. There are so many thoughts that can be changed and seen from a different viewpoint. For instance, Becca is more alive than I am right now, in heaven in a perfect body, surrounded by God's glory! Wow! It is kind of hard to feel sorry for myself when I am so happy for her!

When it rains, do you usually think of how it affects you in a negative way? Maybe occasionally you can stop and remember why we need it, and also let it remind you that there is more than one way to view the death of your child.

Reflection: As parents, we always find ourselves sacrificing for our kids and putting them ahead of ourselves. But when our child dies, we are consumed by what we lost, and have a hard time comprehending what they have gained.

Every time I ask God to change my perspective on Becca's death, He amazes me within the next few days by revealing something that moves me toward another measure of peace and healing in my soul. I'll bet if you ask, He will do the same thing for you!

> *Pursue the things over which Christ presides. Don't shuffle along, eyes to the ground, absorbed with the things right in front of you. Look up, and be alert to what is going on around Christ — that's where the action is. See things from his perspective.*
> *Colossians 3:2 (MSG)*

June 9

Our Beliefs

Our emotions drive our actions. The way we are acting (or reacting) to the death of our child is based on our emotions. Our emotions run very deep. There is so much pain. There is so much confusion. There is darkness and a feeling of hopelessness. That is normal and natural. But that is not where we have to stay.

My emotions (which cause my actions) are driven by my thoughts. I can think things like *I will never get past this*, or *I will always feel this way*.

June

Why do we have these kinds of thoughts? It is because those are our beliefs, and our beliefs affect our thoughts.

I know some parents even have the thought *I don't <u>want</u> to get past this*, which is usually because they equate the pain of grieving their child with remembering their child. They are afraid that if they quit hurting so much, they will forget their child.

This is an example of how your beliefs drive your thoughts. If you believe that staying in your pain will keep the memory of your child alive, then you will continue in that emotional state of despair and not be able to live a life of peace, hope, and fullness that includes walking out your God-ordained destiny.

Let's step back and look at the whole picture, putting it all together. Your beliefs affect your thoughts. Your thoughts influence your emotions. Your emotions drive your actions. (You may want to go back and read that a bit more slowly.)

When our child first leaves this earth, it can feel like everything goes black. All our beliefs, thoughts, emotions and actions get thrown into one jumbled mess and it is almost impossible to sort it all out. But we do. We start to sort it out before we even realize it. Based on various things, such as who we connect with and our previous beliefs about God and life, we begin to have certain beliefs about our grief and our huge loss.

Do you have even a glimmer of hope that it is possible to live again? Thousands of parents have walked this path ahead of you and picked up the shattered pieces of their lives. While missing their child deeply, they have learned how to be part of the lives of the people who are still here in a fulfilling way. Can you open yourself up to that possibility?

Refection: What you allow yourself to believe can be crucial to how soon you are able to get out of the darkness and to a place of learning to live life again with meaning and purpose. What is your thought when you read that you can learn to live a life of meaning and purpose? Is it something like *I don't know how, but someday I am going to get there...* Or is it more like *I doubt if that will ever happen...*?

Reflections of Hope

If it is more like the second one, ask the Holy Spirit to help you start to believe that maybe, just maybe, if others have gotten out of this suffocating darkness, then possibly you can too. Those kinds of thoughts will start to affect your emotions as hope grows, which in turn will influence your actions. You will also find that it affects your reactions, eventually causing the grief triggers to not to run as deeply or as often.

You get to choose what you believe. The truth is, you *can* learn how to live a life of meaning and purpose again, and truth sets us free.

> *Why am I so overwrought, why am I so disturbed?*
> *Why can't I just hope in God? Despite all my emotions,*
> *I will believe and praise the One who saves me, my God.*
> *Psalm 42:11 (VOICE)*

June 10

For God's Glory?

So often we read in the Bible that we are to give God glory, or that things happen so God can be glorified. As Christians, we are told that our purpose here on earth is to bring God glory. I know it can seem impossible to find a way to bring Him glory through the death of our child and have even heard people say that can seem almost narcissistic on God's part.

We need to understand what God's glory is, though. In Exodus 33:18, Moses made a bold request to God. He said, "Show me your glory." Do you know what God's response was? He replied to Moses, "I will make all my goodness pass in front of you," (verse 19, NIRV).

Yes, God's glory is His majesty and splendor, but more than anything, it is His goodness. He is SO good that it shines from Him in a way that is blinding and powerful enough to kill our earthly bodies. How do I know this? Because God told Moses he would honor his request and then had him stand in the crack of a rock. It says God covered Moses' face as He went past, so that Moses only saw the backside of God's glory and goodness so that he would not die (verses 20-23).

God's goodness is not solely based on if we get what we want here on earth. God's goodness is based on who He is for all eternity. We have a hard time understanding or comprehending that, but I picture our kids yelling down to us how good God is, letting us know that we will see it for ourselves someday, but they want us to believe it now.

Here is a question that may be tough to answer honestly. Would your child really want to come back, after being immersed in the fullness of God's goodness that is so bright that it is blinding to those who are still in our earthly bodies? Do you really believe what they are missing out on here is better than what they are experiencing there?

God allows in His wisdom, His love and His *goodness* what He could easily prevent with His power. We need to realize that God's glory and goodness is not just based on our limited earthly experience as we are looking through eyes of being earthly based instead of heaven bound. Thankfully, our lens is only temporary. God sees through a lens of eternity, and now, so do our children.

Reflection: So how do we get to where we can believe that somehow, God can still be glorified through something so horrible? You can start by making the same request Moses did. "Show me your glory, Lord."

Ask Him questions like, "Who do You want to be for me now, that You could not be for me at any other time in my life?" "How do You want to show me Your goodness in way that I did not even know was possible?"

Then allow God to reveal His glory through His goodness to you that goes so far beyond the death of your child. I believe if you do that with a sincere heart, He will begin to open your eyes to things you have not been able to see up to this point that reveal His goodness, which will be revealing His glory. Eventually, He can truly be glorified as His goodness is being displayed through each one of us.

You are good, and the source of good; train me in your goodness.
Psalm 119:68 (MSG)

June 11

Waiting...

Some of us lost our children quickly and unexpectedly. Some of us lost our children through a long, drawn-out illness.

My daughter went through ten years of severe heart issues that included at least a dozen ambulance rides and three med flight helicopter rides the last eighteen months of her life. She survived a pregnancy and labor when the doctors gave her a 50/50 chance of survival because they just did not know what her heart was going to do. She lived through three open heart surgeries. (One was to put in a pump to run the left side of her heart, and another was to take it out after a bizarre incident that made the pump start shorting in and out, shocking her heart over and over.) She had a stroke that caused permanent damage, was brought back to life after seventeen minutes from SCD (Sudden Cardiac Death), plus survived being in the Trauma Life Center when all her organs shut down from sepsis (blood poisoning).

This girl was a walking miracle that started when she was only three years old, getting bone cancer, having her little left leg amputated, and going through nine months of chemo. She was the only survivor of the children who were in her hospital getting treatments at the same time. The chemo she had at that time is what caused the heart damage that plagued her those last ten years.

And then on the evening of October 12, 2011, her heart just randomly gave out and she died! As strange as it may sound, I was blindsided. So many people prayed and fasted for her, some of them since she was three. I really believed that God was either going to miraculously heal her heart, or she was going to be able to get the needed heart transplant. But after ten years of waiting, that did not happen, and then I was left waiting in the darkness, struggling to even want to live without her here.

When my husband, Dave, and I were dating, God kept telling him to "wait" to propose. Dave did a study on the word wait and found out one meaning is "a carved work."

In our darkness, I believe we are waiting a long time because God is doing a carved work. He will even let us believe that He has betrayed us and be angry with Him as He is at work in our darkness. He continues though, knowing that someday we will understand. And that "someday" may not be until we are reunited with our children.

Dare to tell God that you are going to wrestle with Him until you see something good in your life *because* of the earthly departure of your child. Fight for it. And realize sometimes that fighting is learning how to rest in Him while He is at work preparing your personal miracle, which is something only He can do in such a place of darkness and pain.

Reflection: So often we think our life is not as valuable as our child's life was. We are older. They had more to live for. They had more talents and abilities than we do. Why would God receive my child into His eternal presence ahead of me, when they deserved to live more than I do?

None of us can understand God's ways, especially when it takes us to such a dark place, and it all seems so very unfair. But as you wait in the darkness, God is doing a carved work in you. It is a work that is so deep, no one can see it, including you. But you can be sure that what He is doing outweighs how insignificant you may think you are. Rest in the waiting. Allow God to do the work that He knows will make you shine, both for Him, and for your child.

And stop telling yourself that your child deserves to be here more than you do. When we think about it, we are also saying that we deserve to be in heaven right now more than they do. Hmm...

*Wait for the Lord; be strong, and let
your heart take courage; wait for the Lord!
Psalm 27:14 (ESV)*

June 12

Fighting with God

This is one of those times I want you to hear from another pareavor whom I have spent time with. Dennis Apple feels called to walk with others who have found themselves as a member in this unwanted club, also.

Dennis, who was a pastor when his son died, shares in his book *Life After the Death of My Son* how he was disappointed and angry with God. Dennis says he was "hanging out near the back door of my faith," and for a long time he refused to say or sing the phrase, "God is good all the time."

How did he get past that? Dennis states as he came to a crossroads, he asked himself a couple of questions: *Do I believe there's a sovereign God who knows and sees all, including my suffering over the loss of our son? Am I going to trust in this sovereign God whom I don't always understand?* After wrestling with these questions for a long time, he was able to say through painful tears, "Yes, I believe in Him, and yes I will trust Him."

His wife, Beulah, also made a conscious decision after several years of deep grief. Did she want to remain in this same dark place she had been in for almost five years, or did she want to come out of it and make the best of her life and her family that was still here? She chose to "lay aside the garment of grief and mourning, sweep up the ashes that surrounded her, and go on." It was a turning point for both her and their marriage.

When we see and know others who have faced the death of their child who not only survived, but are somehow living a life of meaning and purpose again, it gives us hope that somehow, it must be possible.

A word of caution, though. Make sure you are connecting with pareavors who will acknowledge your grief, but also be a light of hope that you can and will get past the suffocating darkness. We all know our lives will never be the same, but some parents are stuck in that darkness, telling others behind them that they won't ever get out, either. Keep looking until you find those who give you the hope you need.

Reflection: Are you like Dennis, "hanging out near the back door" of your faith? Does it feel impossible to believe that God is good after the death of your child? But at the same time, you know the only way to make it through this horrific darkness is to lean on the One you feel betrayed you, which increases your anger?

I am praying you do not wrestle with this for five years like Beulah did. Right now, at this exact moment, you can make the same decision that many others before you have made. You *can choose* to do whatever it takes to work your way out of the darkness and make the best of your life and to be part of the lives of those who are still here.

The longer it takes you to make that choice, the longer you will remain in the suffocating darkness and the harder it will be to find your way out. If you have already said yes to that decision, this is your chance to recommit, not looking at the darkness you are still fighting, but looking at the light you are moving toward.

Taste of His goodness; see how wonderful the Eternal truly is.
Anyone who puts trust in Him will be blessed and comforted.
Psalm 34:8 (VOICE)

June 13

A Dad's Guilt

(By Dave Diehl)

The Father's Day after Becca's death was without the child who made me a daddy. Most dads have their first Father's Day with an infant, but

Laura's daughter, Becca, was already two years old when we got married and I adopted her six months later as my own.

I vividly remember my first Father's Day after we were a family. My new little girl woke me up early with a kiss and said, "Happy Father's Day, Daddy!" as she handed me a plate full of powdered sugar donuts and climbed up into my bed and we ate them together. She had a way to melt my heart, as our children often do.

When Laura receives an email from a grieving dad, she usually passes it on to me. Quite often he is expressing guilt that he feels like a failure for not protecting his child from death and his family from the devastating effects of it. I think this is something that we *all* deal with to some extent or another. However, as a man, we have a God-given protective instinct over our wife and children that runs very deep.

It took me a few weeks to even start to recognize my own loss of Becca, as my first instincts were to try to protect my wife and kids from the pain they were going through. As a father, it guts us to the core to feel so helpless like this. But the truth is, by listening to our family, loving on them and giving them grace during this season, it is actually protecting them and helping them in the way they need. You are not failing them; it is quite the opposite.

I believe all of us deal with guilt of not being able to help our child that passed; and for some, the circumstances surrounding our child's passing can add even more shame and guilt, and the feeling of failure. But I also know without a doubt that you did everything you could with the information you had at the time.

Guilt and shame are the weapons of the enemy of our soul. He wants to bring more death out of our child's death. We are all extremely vulnerable during this time and he knows it. So, one thing that helps me is to remind him and myself, that Jesus took ALL my shame and GUILT upon Him! I will not pick it back up; it is not mine to bear. It is on His shoulders now. I am so thankful for that.

Of course, it does not mean it's not still a battle at times, but I continue to remind myself of that. I also remind myself of the amazing fact that, in terms of eternity, we will see our kids again sooner than we think.

Reflection: If you're struggling with guilt and all the "what ifs" and "should haves," give all those things back to the Lord to carry, and give yourself grace. That is one of the reasons He died for us, to take our guilt and shame. It is His to carry now, not yours.

Do not just accept it as a thought in your head but take the time to let it sink into your heart and the depths of your very being. God wants you to know... no, let me rephrase that... God *needs* you to know that in Him, you are not a failure! He paid a very high price to make sure of that.

> *O Lord, you are so good, so ready to forgive,*
> *so full of unfailing love for all who ask for your help.*
> *Psalm 86:5 (NLT)*

June 14

Our Treasure in Heaven

Often when I read my Bible, I see many verses with a totally different set of eyes since Becca died. That happened once again, fairly recently, when reading Matthew 6. It says in verses 19-21:

> *Do not store up for yourselves treasures on earth, where moth and rust destroy, and where thieves break in and steal. But store up for yourselves treasures in heaven, where neither moth nor rust destroys, and where thieves do not break in or steal;* **for where your treasure is, there your heart will be also.** (NASB)

Our children are our greatest treasure here on earth. So, when they leave this earth and head to their eternal home before we do, a huge piece of our heart goes with them. Wow! No wonder we just want to be done here and go to be with our child! *Where your treasure (child) is, there your heart will be also.*

Before Becca died, I wanted to live a very long and fulfilling life.

After Becca died, for the first couple of years I just wanted to be done here and would beg God to take me. It didn't seem to matter that I had my wonderful and loving husband, four children and two grandchildren (at that time) still here to live for. I wanted out of here, and the sooner the better.

As time went on, and the intense pain began to be absorbed in a way that allowed me to somewhat function again, my greatest desire to just be done here began to subside as well.

And now the way I feel is that I don't care either way. I can stay, or I can go. I know I have a life to live that is still wonderful (five more grandchildren have been added since then) and fulfilling (with the incredible blessing of walking with other grieving parents through GPS Hope). But I am also ready to go, when God decides it is my time, whenever that is.

Reflection: I remember almost a year to the day after Becca died, telling a friend that I felt guilty because I was more excited to get to heaven to see Becca than I was to see Jesus. Her reply? "But Laura, you have made a deposit there!" So, if you are in that place of wanting to be taken from this earth to be with your child who is no longer physically here, just know that Jesus Himself told us that where our treasure is, our heart will be also.

I am 99% sure you won't always feel that way, eventually being like me and getting to the point where you have no feelings about it one way or the other. When it happens, it happens. You will have discovered you have a life to live that still has good things in it. It might take a while, but you can look forward to when you feel that way.

> *The thief's purpose is to steal and kill and destroy.*
> *My purpose is to give them a rich and satisfying life.*
> *John 10:10 (NLT)*

June 15

Our Prize

Something I have come to realize in a much deeper way than ever before, is that God is not just "out there" somewhere. He is actually inside me. Because I have invited Jesus to be Lord of my life, the Spirit of God dwells in me. I don't have to wait for God to come to me from somewhere out there. I can quiet myself and listen to His still small voice from inside me, speaking peace, bringing comfort.

Whatever I need, He is already inside me to meet that need. The amazing thing is that He is also sitting on His throne at the exact same time, and I can come boldly to that throne of our gracious God to receive His mercy and find His help which I so desperately need (Hebrews 4:16).

Here is another scripture that has helped me continue moving forward.

> *Brothers and sisters, I do not consider myself yet to have taken hold of it. But one thing I do: Forgetting what is behind and straining toward what is ahead,* " *I press on toward the goal to win the prize for which God has called me heavenward in Christ Jesus.* (Philippians 3:13-14 NIV).

This does not say we are forgetting and leaving our children behind us. That will never happen! I see it as an encouragement to "press on toward the goal," which to me is learning how to live a full and meaningful life again, with the "prize of the upward call" being eternity with Him and with my child (and others I love) who are patiently waiting for me to join them.

Looking forward to what is still ahead is a huge comfort to me. It does not erase the pain of now, but over time it helps to ease it, for sure. And the longer I remain here, the more excited I get that I am getting closer and closer to that prize, and my daughter!

Reflection: As I found myself struggling so deeply with the horrific thought of getting further and further away from Becca, I asked God to help me by giving me His thoughts. He so graciously showed me that the truth is actually something totally different from how I was seeing it.

Every day I live on this earth brings me closer to my own departure date, and *closer to* Becca, *not* further away from her! That truth set me free! I still have moments when I have those painful thoughts, and they can still make me cry. But I am not overwhelmed by them, as I now believe a truth that is deeper than my pain: I am getting closer to her, not further away from her.

Let that thought begin to break through your pain, bringing you the peace and comfort that the Holy Spirit wants it to bring.

> *... in our moments of impatience let us remember that hope always means waiting for something that we haven't yet got. But if we hope for something we cannot see, then we must settle down to wait for it in patience.*
> Romans 8:25 (PHILLIPS)

June 16

Closure

I was recently listening to a podcast about the topic of being focused and heard something that made me go hmmmm.... I had to hit the pause button and really think about what I had just heard. Let me share that thought with you in my own words.

> *Closure is not walking away from something and shutting the door behind you. It is about replacing a negative with something more powerful in your thinking, in your perspective, and in your words. It's about moving on from where we are, and if you do not do closure properly you are going to keep going around in circles.*

It is more about who we are becoming, than what is happening around us. If we don't allow change within ourselves, we will not get the closure we are looking for. We are looking for rescue, or answers, or revenge, instead of identity and release of that thing having hold of us. The key is to ask God to see things with His perspective instead of our own.

You might want to read through that again slowly, stopping to think about each sentence after you read it.

I talk a lot about our perspective; about asking God to help us see things with different lenses, specifically to see things the way He sees them. What I had not really thought through, until hearing this recently, was how the change has to come from inside us, based on our identity and who we are becoming.

There is no getting around the fact that we are a different person after the death of our child. Not only is there a "before and after" in the timeline of our lives, but there is also a "before and after" in who we are as a person, and at some point, we get to choose what that looks like.

Who is it we are becoming? Are we going to be bitter, or better? Are we going to continue going around in circles in our darkness, anger and bitterness? Or are we going to close the door on that part of us, finding ways to replace it with things that will change our thinking, our perspective and our words, taking us to a place of light, and living a fulfilled life again?

Yes, it will look very different, but it can be done.

That, my friends, is the true closure we need in our lives after the death of our child. Not putting our child behind us, but holding their life in front of us in a way that moves us forward to a place of living a life with meaning and purpose again.

Reflection: Let's get the closure we need on the darkness that keeps us unable to function. Ask God for help. Ask to see things through His eyes and with His perspective. Ask Him to put His thoughts of hope and light in your heart and mind instead of drowning yourself in your own thoughts of darkness.

One last thought: If you do not like the word closure, use a different word. What you decide to call it is not as important as the action and movement you take in the direction of getting out of the darkness of death and back into the light of life.

> *May my words and thoughts please you. Lord,*
> *you are my Rock—the one who rescues me.*
> *Psalm 19:14 (ERV)*

June 17

It's Not Just the Good Stuff

One thing I have done to help rebuild my trust in God, is to slowly shift my thinking to Becca's gain instead of my loss. For instance, I don't like it when other people tell me, "But she *is* healed now!" Duh! I know that, but that was not what I meant when I was praying for her, and I still want her here with me! Telling me that does not "fix me" or make me feel better.

However, when I am by myself, allowing the Holy Spirit to be my Comforter, I can start to receive that truth. She really is healed now, dancing with both legs, has no more trouble breathing and a strong heart that will never give out again. She is done going through the painful trials and traumas of this world. She is safe. She is whole in body, soul and spirit. I also believe she is waiting for me with great anticipation! I can even find myself thanking God that my daughter is safe, and whole, and happy!

Am I totally healed and back to "normal?" No way! That will never happen. But I am leaning on God in this painful journey, and it is not based on what I can see or know, but the exact opposite. It is based on what I cannot see and what I do not know, because that's what trust is.

I can choose to believe there is no God or He would have saved my child. I can choose to believe that if there is a God, He isn't good and He isn't fair or He would have saved my child. Both of those options leave me feeling angry and empty. I have chosen the third option. There is a God, His thoughts and ways are so much higher than mine, He loves me with a perfect love, and even though I don't understand why He has allowed this to happen, I still trust Him with my life both here on earth and for eternity. This option has brought me to a place of peace, rest, hope, and life again—even within the pain. (When Tragedy Strikes)

In other words, I have learned that *choosing* to continue to trust God here on earth with temporary painful things I do not understand gives me so much more peace than *choosing* to remain angry and being determined that He is not trustworthy.

Reflection: We often spend much of our time thinking about what our child is missing with their early departure; things we got to experience but they did not, especially if there were things that we know our children wanted to do, but never had the chance. We can even torture ourselves with it, becoming physically ill with the thoughts of all the wonderful things they are missing out on.

Let's take a few minutes and do the opposite. How about thinking of some specific *negative* things they are missing out on? What are some things that might even be devastating to your child, if he or she were still here with you? They could be things happening culturally; something going on with a family member; grieving your death when it is your turn to go; even a tragedy that might have happened to them in their future that was unplanned.

Don't let these things pull you down but allow them to give you a moment of thankfulness that your child isn't just missing out on the good, but they do not have to experience the bad and the outright evil that we are still dealing with here.

Good people pass away; the godly often die before their time. But no one seems to care or wonder why. No one seems to understand that God is protecting them from the evil to come.
Isaiah 57:1 (NLT)

June 18

Those Darn Grief Triggers

In 2019, I spent most of May, and half of June, watching my dad slowly fade away until he finally crossed over to see Jesus and join Becca and the rest of his family. (He was the last of four siblings.) I had the privilege of being there when he took his last breath, along with my sister and his wife of twenty-nine years. We were all cheering him on and loving on him.

My dad was eighty-three and had been ready to leave this world for quite some time, especially after his granddaughter died. Even as a retired pastor, he struggled with "survivor's guilt," frustrated with the fact that he had lived a full life, but Becca still had so much to live for (including her nine-year-old daughter) and he was the one still here. Our family could see that her death took a lot out of him and was surprised he made it another seven years.

The funeral was so much harder than I thought it would be. I knew a boutonniere from Becca's wedding would be pinned to his suit, but when I saw him and that sprig of flowers on his lapel, I just lost it big time with wailing cries. I had another breakdown saying "goodbye" before they closed the casket. The tears and deep emotions were not so much for my dad. I was very thrilled for him, as he had been wanting to see those pearly gates for several years now. But it felt like a slap-in-the-face reminder that my daughter was already there, and they were enjoying being together again.

With that deep of a grief trigger, I knew I had a choice to make. I could wallow in it, taking the next few days or weeks continuing to allow myself to drown in the pain of not having Becca here (which I honestly considered doing). Instead, I decided to tap into what I was feeling and write another song. I will share the words of the full song on another day, but I love the chorus which says:

> *A lifetime here is not enough for us to be together,*
> *So, God has made a way for it to be forever.*
> *But until that day comes*
> *I won't make it through by letting go,*
> *But holding on tight to the memories I treasure.*
> *This is not good-by, I'll see you later.*

I think you will agree with me, writing these words and putting them to music was worth not staying in bed and climbing out from under my blankets. (Although I did still have some tears here and there as I was grieving the earthly loss of my dad, which triggered missing my daughter.)

Grief triggers can be brutal, can't they?

Reflection: How about you? Have you had a grief trigger that you were able to turn around by something you realized (like a change in perspective) or something you did? If you have, make sure you acknowledge the importance of being able to do that in moving toward a greater measure of healing. If you have not, don't allow yourself to be discouraged. If you notice, what I shared was seven years after Becca died.

When something hits you hard as a grief trigger, I give you permission to take it easy for a while. Those around you may not understand how deeply it affects us physically, emotionally and mentally, but those of us who have lost a child understand how so many things can be tied to our loss. You need to take care of yourself, and you need to give yourself permission to do so when others around you do not.

> *God, listen to me shout, bend an ear to my prayer. When*
> *I'm far from anywhere, down to my last gasp, I call out,*
> *"Guide me up High Rock Mountain!" You've always given*
> *me breathing room, a place to get away from it all, A lifetime*
> *pass to your safe-house, an open invitation as your guest.*
> *Psalm 61:1-4 (MSG)*

June 19

Three Things

Today I want to share three specific things you can do to help you get through the first couple of years after the death of your child. These are talked about here and there, throughout the daily readings, but it might help to see them together.

1. **Perspective** - ask God to give you His perspective on something that is plaguing you with fear, anxiety or panic because of your limited view. God has done that for me so often, and it really helps to see these intensely painful thoughts through His infinite eternal eyes instead of my own limited earthly ones.

2. **Do your best to stop the "What ifs" and "Whys"** - They serve absolutely no purpose. They will not bring your child back and can send you spiraling down further into that suffocating pit. These thoughts just bring torment.

    Instead, start asking God "How?" How is He going to help you get through this? How is He going to get you to want to live again without your child? How is He possibly going to take something this horrific and bring anything even *remotely* good from it? (Those are the questions He likes to answer.)

3. **Start a thankfulness journal** - What we focus on will consume us. Allow yourself to start seeing the good things that are still around you. Every night, make yourself write down at least three things you can be thankful for.

    It could be as small *as I noticed a bird chirping today for the first time since my child died,* or *I walked by a bakery and it smelled good,* or *I didn't start crying today until I got into the shower instead of when I first woke up.*

These will only slightly ease the pain, and sometimes we can't feel any release at all when we try moving in a direction that brings a measure of healing. But I promise you, if you keep doing it, you will eventually notice a change taking place very deep inside. Keep going, and you will be able to see light in the darkness and hope in your hopelessness.

June

Reflection: Don't just read today's entry without following through on something. Which one of the three things seems to speak to you the most?

If it is asking God to change your perspective, write yourself a note where you will see it, to remind yourself. (It can be as simple as writing the word PERSPECTIVE.) If it is changing your why questions to how, do the same thing. Write a note with the word HOW and put it somewhere you will see it as a reminder. If it is to start seeing the good things that are still around you, write a note on your shopping list to get a pretty journal to begin writing down things you are thankful for.

In our grief fog, we can be extremely forgetful, so right now, whichever one you choose, take the time to write a note as a reminder, so that you don't forget to follow through.

> *Lord, when doubts fill my mind, when my heart is in turmoil, quiet me and give me renewed hope and cheer.*
> *Psalm 94:19 (TLB)*

June 20

Nature Reminds Us

One recent summer, the Hope Mobile was parked in the San Diego area. The campground was in a valley, surrounded by mountains. Several of the mornings I went for a walk, and every time I took a path leading outside the campground, it took me up one of those mountains. The first path I took went up a very small one. It was so small I would call it more of a hill. But it did give me quite a nice view at the top.

The second one I climbed was quite large, and I did not even realize how high I was getting until I reached the top and looked out around me, getting a beautiful view of the bigger mountains still around me and the campground below me.

The next day, when I reached the top of a third mountain, I was shocked to be able to see that the spot where I had been standing the day before was quite a distance below me, and the campground was waaaay below me. And this time the view around me was exhilarating!

The beauty I was surrounded with those last two days, both on the climb and especially at the top, left me in complete awe of God's majesty and power. It refreshed my belief that if He created all of what I was seeing, then He can certainly take care of me and all that comes my way while I am here on this earth. I found myself singing in worship to Him, and spending time casting all my cares on Him before working my way back down.

A few days later, Dave and I took a drive to be able to spend some time walking the beach along the Pacific Ocean. As I looked out at those waves and the vastness of all that water, I was reminded of how great God really is, and how His love is as wide and deep as the ocean. Seeing the power and majesty of the ocean reminded me once again how incredible the power and majesty is of the One who created it.

Looking up at the heavens at night and seeing all those stars, planets and the moon can have the same effect on me. The vastness reminds me how great God is and how He is able to take care of me through the storms of life.

Believe it or not, He is taking care of you, too.

Reflection: Being out in nature and seeing the beauty He created helps us see things from a needed perspective. I want to encourage you to get outside and enjoy the beauty around you. It does not have to be big mountains or the ocean. Allow yourself to be in awe of whatever you see and hear, and even feel. Then allow yourself to be refreshed in the presence of the One who is so much greater than the creation you are enjoying.

It may not seem like it, but He has you in the palm of His hand and will not let go of you. He is walking this journey with you, and He has a plan that you can't see right now. He can and will take care of you every step of your journey here on earth. Getting out in the wonder, beauty and amazement of nature will help stir up that truth in you. Even right now, I'll bet if you open a door or window, you will hear or see something that will remind you how big our God is, and that He is not limited in being able to help you get through this darkness.

> *I look to the mountains; where will my help come from?*
> *My help will come from the Lord, who made heaven and earth.*
> *Psalm 121:1-2 (GNT)*

June 21

Where is God?

God's promises of faithfulness are not based on what He *does* for us, but who He *is* for us while we are living out our time here on this earth. The time of perfection is yet to come. So, why do we start out here? Why does He put us through all this? Why can't we all just be born in heaven and skip all this crappy and painful stuff?

Starting out in heaven does not mean we would love God and fully understand His love. Look at what happened with Lucifer. He puffed himself up with pride, and one third of all the angels followed his lead and were cast out of heaven!

Living here on earth is where we get the opportunity to experience His goodness in a way the angels cannot. (Yes, I saw some of you roll your eyes.) Think about it though. We get to know a depth of His love personally. He loves us so much and has such a strong desire to be with us that He made a way to live inside our very being! The angels will never know what that is like. They know His holiness and majesty. They know Him from His throne room, but we have the opportunity to know Him in a place of internal intimacy.

God has let us know that His desire is to be as close to us as possible and given all of Himself to each one of us. It is up to you and me to decide how much of Him we want. He can, and wants to be our constant companion and the source of everything we need during this time.

The real question for many of us is not "Where is God?" The question is "Where am I?" I can walk out on Him very easily, and many of us do. We ignore Him, as though He is no longer with us, but that is never the case because He still dwells inside us.

I would like to say that I have learned not to live this life based on my feelings, but on knowing that not only is God surrounding me with His love, but He is also in me, shattering the darkness with His light. The truth is, I still live life based on how I feel, more than I care to admit.

But within that, I choose to hold on to the belief that even though I might *feel* God is far away because I don't see light in my place of darkness, that God is behind the scenes, working in ways that have not reached me yet. I hope you decide to choose the same thing, because it is the truth, whether you feel it right now or not.

Reflection: In Zechariah 2:5, the prophet is talking about the city of Jerusalem or Zion. Zion is a symbol of His church (not replacing the Israelites, but a symbol). Knowing you and I are the church, we can take hold of this verse, letting us know that God is a fire around us, and His glory is in the midst of us.

We will not experience the fullness of His glory until we are with Him and our children. But that does not mean we have to wait. In Colossians 1:27, not only are we told that Christ, the hope of glory is *in* us, but that God wants us to know this! I believe God knows that we need to experience some of it here, which is another reason He is in us and wants us to know it in a very real way.

Jesus told us that from our belly, living waters will flow (John 7:38). I don't know about you, but I sure need those living waters to flow over me. Why not right now?

If you can, find some soft instrumental music to play. Let's take a few minutes, put our hands over our belly, close our eyes, and imagine His life flowing through us. Picture God Himself inside you, warming your very being with His love. Let it wash over you, releasing the tension, pouring peace over you within the pain. Allow yourself to breathe in the fragrance of His grace, and breathe out the anger, doubts and fears.

Where is God? He is *in* you because He is *for* you. Let's keep reminding ourselves of this, especially when we are in our darkest moments.

> *Then, when that happens, we are able to hold our heads high no matter what happens and know that all is well, for we know how dearly God loves us, and we feel this warm love everywhere within us because God has given us the Holy Spirit to fill our hearts with his love.*
> *Romans 5:5 (TLB)*

June 22

The Power of Our Thoughts

God has been reminding me through several ways how important my thoughts are. Our minds are the biggest battleground in every way, including spiritually and emotionally. When I am discouraged over something, if I allow my mind to justify my dark thoughts, I find myself continuing to spiral downward rather quickly.

If I think I can't, then I can't. It is that simple. It keeps me from even *trying* to pull myself back up.

If I truly believe with every fiber of my being that I cannot ever get past survival mode in a way that allows me to function again (much less somehow live a thriving life once again), then I am correct, I cannot.

Let me say that we *all* feel that way at the beginning. And when I say beginning, I mean the first year or two. I have had grieving parents during that time tell me, "You may be living life again, but I won't ever be able to." But as the days, weeks and months go by and they stay connected in various ways with those who are further along on this journey, they begin to see a slight glimmer of hope that just *maybe*, it *might* be possible. That glimmer of hope can go dark very quickly, but it will find itself poking through their darkness again at some point.

Reflections of Hope

When that happens (not if), grasp hold of it and hang on as tightly as you can, knowing it will come and go for quite a while. The more you seize that hope and hold on for as long as possible, the quicker it will start to return, and it will begin to stay longer.

If you think you can't, you can't. Instead, grab this hope and make it yours. And if you cannot even do that, grasp those of us who have that hope for you.

Reflection: Did you know that neuroscience has proven our brains can be rewired, based on our thoughts and beliefs? If we think something long enough, the pathways in our brains will start new paths to begin to turn that thought into a firm belief. It is called neuroplasticity. There is a lot of information out there on this subject that can be found easily with some internet research.

All you need, to give that glimmer of hope a start, is a willingness to say, "I can't see it now, but maybe down the road I might..." In other words, hope in the fact that there might be hope. God can work with that, and He will.

> *So I wait for the Eternal—my soul awaits rescue —*
> *and I put my hope in His transforming word.*
> *Psalm 130:5 (VOICE)*

June 23

God's Will

A precious friend of mine shared with me this past week that she grieved for three years about not being able to have children. She started out praying for "God's will" and then got to the point that she ached for a

June

child so badly she did not care about God's will, she just wanted a child and would pay the consequences later.

This way of thinking caused her to become hard hearted. When God broke her, causing her to have a soft heart toward Him again, she was able to pray for His will again in her life, even if it meant never having a child. Excitingly, she became pregnant, but then lost the baby during pregnancy. Talk about cruel, right? But because she had wrestled with that issue, in her deep pain and grief, she was able to trust God to get her through it. (She has since been blessed with three more children, but she has also gone through breast cancer, which became another level of trusting God.)

This friend told me it was because of each thing she went through that she was able to pray and trust God through the next trial.

Another close friend, who lost her son-in-law by suffocation in a grain bin accident several years ago, has talked to me about her struggle with the issue of God's will and prayer. What is the point of praying at all, if God is just going to do what He wants, including not stepping in to save someone or protect them?

She has concluded that even though we don't like the "Christianeze" answer (because people throw it around in a flippant way), God *does* answer our prayers. However, just because it is not the answer we wanted, it does not mean He isn't good or that He didn't answer.

We need to keep praying because it is more about our communication and relationship with Him than it is about "having enough faith" to force things to happen the way we want them to. I also believe if God backed us up by giving in to everything we prayed for, we would make a mess of things because we are so selfish and don't see (or care about) the big picture! His will is not always our will, and we need to get to the point where we are okay with that as we continue our life here.

Reflection: The only way you would allow your child to go through intense pain (such as my daughter's amputation at three years old), is if you knew the outcome outweighed the pain. God is your Father, and the Father of your child. He has the same heart. He sees beyond the pain of our child's death, into the eternal outcome, which somehow will far outweigh our pain at some point.

Have you become hard hearted because God did not answer your prayers the way you wanted, concerning your child? The enemy is the one who comes to kill, steal and destroy. Jesus came to bring life. Our child's life did not really end. They just received their transfer ahead of us. As painful as that is for us now, is it really that horrible of an outcome for them? Our will for our children is for them to be healthy and happy, which they are. (I know we just wanted it to be here with us.)

Ask God to help you have the heart, "Not my will, but Yours." It will move you away from the anger and bitterness toward a place of peace and rest.

> *Father, if you are willing, take this cup of agony away from me. But no matter what, your will must be mine.*
> *Luke 22:42 (TPT)*

June 24
A Lens Change

A lens is a pretty simple thing. It either bends light, so we can see something more clearly, or it reduces the light so that what we see is misrepresented in some way. Lenses can either help us see better, or they distort the view and cause us to see something differently than what is actually there.

We all have lenses that we see life through. It is our perception, or what we believe about something, and we change those lenses throughout our lives. Those lenses, either increases or decreases the reality of our relationship with God.

After the death of our child, it is almost like we have gone blind. It seems we have no lens to see much of anything except our grief and the darkness of our earthly loss. But I assure you that even in the darkness, you still have a lens you are looking through. Not only that, but you also get to choose what lens you will continue to look through as time goes by. The lens you choose now, will greatly affect how you begin to see, once the darkness starts to lift.

- Our lens is either a truth that sets us free, or it is an error that keeps us captive and prevents us from a deeper encounter with Him.
- Our lens will lead us into fear, or it leads us into a new understanding of God's love for us.
- Our lens can cause us to remain a prisoner of our past, or lead us into living in a way we didn't think was possible, living a life of meaning and purpose once again.

Seeing clearly is important, not just physically but also mentally, emotionally and spiritually. That sounds like a lot, doesn't it? But the good thing is that all you need to do is put yourself in the hands of the eternal eye doctor, who can help you see things more clearly in each area of your life.

It does not happen all at once. It is a gradual change. Think of it like when the eye doctor gives you two choices, repeatedly. (Can you see better with number one or number two? How about now – one or two? How about now...?)

God is there to help each one of us see what we need to see. But it starts with allowing Him to begin giving us the needed lens change that will help us see more clearly through the eyes of eternity.

Reflection: Something God has been trying to get me to understand recently is that the struggles I am in do not start with me. They start with Him! Everything starts and ends with God! Our lens change is not about us. It is about seeing who God is and who He wants to be for us. We are constantly having a lens change as we walk in relationship with Him, and the death of our child needs the biggest change of all.

I don't know about you, but I need to see something better. I need to see more than what I am seeing right now. I need to see the Kingdom more clearly. I need to understand who God is for me in this situation. I need a lens change. How about if we ask God for a new prescription, together? Then let's allow Him to be at work as He adjusts our eyesight.

> *To worship God in wonder and awe opens a fountain of*
> *life within you, empowering you to escape death's domain.*
> *Proverbs 14:27 (TPT)*

June 25

A New Look at Something Familiar

It really does seem like *everything* in our life is now defined by "before" and "after," doesn't it?

Reading the Bible after Becca died has changed a lot for me, as the Holy Spirit gives me new insights that I would have never seen "before." Recently, while reading in Matthew, I had another one of those discoveries, in what many of us refer to as "The Lord's Prayer" found in Matthew 6:9-13.

Jesus' disciples asked Him how to pray, and so Jesus gave us this as a model. I realized for the first time that Jesus did not tell us to pray for protection over ourselves or those we love. I am not saying it is wrong to pray for that. There is plenty of scriptural basis for it, and I have prayed for protection over myself and those around me on a regular basis. However, if that did not make the cut, and Jesus didn't tell us to pray that way, there must be a reason.

He suggested we pray for:

- Our Father to meet our daily needs.
- For forgiveness when we fail (in the same way we are to forgive others who fail and deeply wrong us).
- Help keep us from sinning when we are tempted.
- To deliver us from evil (or from the effects of the evil one, which is not the same thing as "Don't let anything bad ever happen to me").
- To allow His Kingdom to be released and His will to be done here on earth the way it is done in heaven.

June

What all of that means to me, personally, is that we are praying to allow God to be God in our lives, no matter how it affects us temporarily here on earth, knowing that it is so very different in heaven, where our permanent home is. If I have said or sung that Jesus is Lord of my life, then I need to be prepared for whatever that means. But no matter what happens, it is made very clear that our Father will provide what we need, whether that need is physical, emotional, mental or spiritual.

I do not believe for a second that God caused the death of any of our children. That would be impossible, because God IS life. There is no death in him whatsoever. But for reasons we cannot see or understand, he allowed the sinful corruption of this earth to take its course, as His will in heaven was to have our child precede us.

After all the suffocating darkness and painfully deep grief of losing Becca from this earth, I am now to the place where I look forward to the day my child will be there to greet me when it is His will in heaven to allow *me* to go to my permanent home.

Reflection: If you cannot shift your perspective there yet, that is okay. But in the meantime, realize that while it is a good thing to pray for protection over our children, it isn't that God failed us and did not answer our prayer. He *did* answer us, but it was a different prayer of making Him Lord and wanting His will to be done on earth *as it is in heaven.* That means at times we do not know how our prayers will be answered, and where it will take us.

But as long as we hold on to Him, even in our anger and pain, He will provide what we need for as long as we are still here on earth.

Pray like this: Our Beloved Father, dwelling in the heavenly realms, may the glory of your name be the center on which our lives turn. Manifest your kingdom realm, and cause your every purpose to be fulfilled on earth, just as it is in heaven. We acknowledge you as our Provider of all we need each day. Forgive us the wrongs we have done as we ourselves release forgiveness to those who have wronged us. Rescue us every time we face tribulation and set us free from evil. For you are the King who rules with power and glory forever. Amen.
Matthew 6:9-13 (TPT)

June 26

The Spirits of Our Children

One night, Dave and I went out to supper with a couple who recently lost their son. The mom asked me, "Do you think our kids' spirits can come back and visit us?" She shared a situation where both she and her mom had an impression that her son was at a profound event at the same specific place for a few seconds, very happy with what was happening. There was another time this mom sensed her son's presence in a very real and tangible way.

These are not "flaky" people. They are very rooted and grounded in their relationship with the Lord and are spiritual leaders and pillars in the Body of Christ. They are sensitive to the voice and presence of the Holy Spirit.

First, let me say that God makes it very clear that we are NOT to go to mediums or try to call up the dead (Deuteronomy 18:9-11). That is dangerous and opens the door for the demonic realm to approach and deceive us, letting darkness have an influence in our lives disguised as light and hope. But that is not what I am talking about here.

I know strong Christians who are positive they occasionally feel the presence of the spirit of their loved one who died and no longer has a bodily form. These Christians have not sought after them as a spiritual being. They are not going to psychics or mediums to try and hear from their loved ones. But at some point, usually quite unexpectedly, they suddenly just "know" that their child or loved one is in the room with them, usually *very* close by.

I do believe that it is possible that our children's spirits have opportunities to visit us, for the specific purpose of bringing comfort, peace, or whatever our need is for that moment. And there are places in the Bible that support this. For one thing, we know there are spiritual beings, angels and demons, all around us. We are surrounded by a spiritual realm that is even more real than the earthly realm we live in. Remember when God opened Jacob's eyes to see a ladder reaching to heaven with angels ascending and descending, found in Genesis 28:12?

June

So, if our children are no longer contained by their bodies, isn't it possible that God occasionally allows them to ascend and descend as spiritual beings also, if there is a purpose for it?

Then there is the time in Matthew 17:1-3 when Moses and Elijah came to earth to speak with Jesus before His death. And how about the "great cloud of witnesses" that Hebrews 12:1 talks about, referring to the entire previous chapter of those who had died? Is it just those in Hebrews 12 who are in that group, or is it everyone who has died and now has full access to the Father as a spiritual being without bodily limitations?

We are not to seek for our children to come back to us to give us a sign of some kind. We are to seek God, allowing Him to give us the comfort and peace that we need. And if He chooses to pull back the veil to let our child come visit for a specific purpose, then He is more than capable of doing so.

Reflection: If you are like me, you have concerns about allowing yourself to be deceived, simply because you want to believe something that might not be God's truth. I have learned over the years that when I take anything I am questioning to God, I always ask Him to show me the truth, and not to allow me to be deceived. I believe God honors that heart, and the Holy Spirit will help me sort it out without going down the wrong path on the questions I put before Him, including this one.

If this is something you have wondered about, take it to God. Ask Him to not let you be deceived. Then make sure you are seeking His presence and not your child. I do not know if you will have your child's spirit ever visit you or not, but don't let that desire take you away from God, who wants to be here for you in your place of grief.

*All these many people who have had
faith in God are around us like a cloud.
Hebrews 12:1 (NLV)*

June 27

Regrets

Because I had gotten some emails on the topic, one day I decided to ask on our GPS Hope Facebook page if there were those whose child believed their life was going to be cut short, or felt like they might leave this earth soon. I was surprised at how many responded with a story confirming this.

Looking back, I believe my daughter knew she was going. While I was on a ministry trip, Becca ended up in the hospital for a routine IV diuretic treatment. I talked to her daily on the phone and each time she would ask me when I was coming home. I would remind her "on Wednesday" and always offered to come home early. She would decline my offer, but the next day would ask me again when I would be back.

The day I flew home, I went directly to see her in the hospital. For part of our visit, she wanted me to anoint her with oil and pray for her (I am an ordained minister) and she wanted me to kiss her on the forehead. (That was a bit strange, but she was always a bit fun and quirky.) I left the hospital to head home with my luggage and less than four hours later she was gone.

Let's turn the corner now and look at a different direction. I know there are some of you who have children who made it clear that they did not want to die, and those memories haunt you. Some of you are angry because God did not seem to care and let your child die anyway, even though people were praying for their healing or protection.

Why does any of this matter? What is the point of talking about all of this?

For me, it reminds me that our children all had different circumstances, but they still died. We are all still here without them. For some, realizing their child knew and gave some indication brings a measure of peace. For others, it brings torment since they can now look back and believe they should have known and done something. Some of us had a chance to say goodbye (even though we might not have known it at the time like me with Becca). Others are really upset because they did not get that chance.

Whether our child seemed to know they would not live a long life or did not; whether our child let us know they didn't want to die early, or we never had that conversation, we *all* have regrets and things that we wish we had done or said differently looking back. But regrets don't serve us well, do they?

Reflection: As horrible as it might sound, as the saying goes, "it is what it is." I guess we could say, "It was, what it was." My prayer is that if any of the things in today's reading have tormented you, that you will be able to release it, replacing those dark thoughts with a changed perspective, allowing yourself to move in the direction of a greater measure of healing.

Let go of the regrets. Release them. They will not change anything and just continue to torture you. When those things start plaguing you, tell yourself, "There was nothing I could do about it, and my child is not holding anything against me." As a matter of fact, start right now, by saying that out loud. Your child has released you. God has released you. It is time to release yourself.

> *Those who enter into Christ's being-here-for-us no longer have to live under a continuous, low-lying black cloud. A new power is in operation. The Spirit of life in Christ, like a strong wind, has magnificently cleared the air, freeing you from a fated lifetime of brutal tyranny at the hands of sin and death.*
> *Romans 8:1 (MSG)*

June 28

It is a Fulltime Job

For those first few months up to two or three years, grieving the death of our child is like having a fulltime job *with overtime!* It consumes us. It takes everything we have, whether we want it to or not. It drains us, leaving us to feel like there is just no way we can go on.

Eventually, our grief becomes more like a fulltime job, thankfully without all the constant overtime. It usually sneaks up on us around three to five years into our grief, and we don't even realize it at first.

Just like a fulltime job, grieving the death of our child is still the greatest part of our life. It still drains us and exhausts us, but now we have times of reprieve, as if we are clocking out for a while. We can go out and do something without feeling like we are on the verge of falling apart. We can join certain activities or family events (even if we are not ready to stay the whole time) and have some smiles and laughs without feeling guilty. We can watch a movie and actually enjoy it, instead of just staring at the screen, oblivious to what we are watching.

We clock back into our fulltime job of grieving afterwards, but it is not all-consuming anymore, although we can still slip into overtime for a few days (even weeks) here and there.

Then, after several years of hard work, we find ourselves able to go down to part-time grief. However, we are always "on call" because our grief is like an undercurrent, ready to surface in a split second. Sometimes we know there is something coming that will be a trigger, and other times we get slapped with it out of the blue with no warning, in a place we least expect it.

When that happens, we clock back in to increase our grief work time. Sometimes we are clocked in for a few minutes or hours. Sometimes it is for a day or two. And there are occasional times, when we need to go back to fulltime, such as when our child should be graduating with their classmates, or a wedding happens that our child would have been in, or a death in the family of someone close to us. That happened to me when my dad died, several years after Becca's death. I was out-of-sorts for a few weeks, having a hard time focusing and functioning. Then seven weeks later my mother-in-law, whom I loved dearly, passed away in her sleep, which did not help at all!

I am so glad to be back to part-time right now. But I know there will continue to be times when it goes back to fulltime for a while, and unfortunately, also overtime. But thankfully, that is very rare at this point.

Reflection: Where are you right now? Are you on overtime, fulltime, or part-time grief? It is all hard work, but the overtime is just outright brutal! If that is where you are, what can you do to give yourself a short break now and then?

We cannot stop the overtime until that work project is complete, but we can and need to take as many breaks as possible, no matter how short they are. The Holy Spirit knows exactly what you need and when you need it. If you feel a prompting to do something that does not make a lot of sense (obviously nothing harmful), then follow through on those promptings. You just never know how it will lift your load just a bit.

> *He gives power to the faint, and to him*
> *who has no might he increases strength.*
> *Isaiah 40:29 (ESV)*

June 29

Out of Order

It is bad enough to have a child die, but to have the death be because your other child murdered him or her? What a mess! But we read in Genesis 4:1-8 that is exactly what happened to the very first couple God placed on this earth, when Cain murdered his brother Abel out of jealousy.

I cannot even begin to imagine what that was like for Adam and Eve. Not just to have one son murder the other one, but to know that they had *never* experienced death! It had never happened before. That must have been such a shock for them to have a son who was lifeless, discovering that is what it meant to "die."

We know Adam lived a total of 930 years. The Bible tells us he was 130 when his son Seth was born who came after this murder, so Adam must have lived close to 800 years here on earth without his son, Abel. That also blows my mind, because I don't know how I can bear ten, twenty or thirty years here without my daughter!

I find it amazing that the first death in the Bible is one of the worst things that could ever happen to a person; and not just the death of one's child, but a son murdering his brother! And yet, the entire history through God's Word is one of hope that goes beyond any death, or the circumstance surrounding that death. This was because Jesus came and died his own horrific torturous death so that when we leave this earth, we continue to live with our loved ones, never to be separated again!

Aren't you glad God shortened the lifespan of humans, so that we won't have to wait several hundred years to see our child again?

Reflection: One of the things we hear others say, and have probably even heard ourselves say, is that the death of one's child is out of order. We are not supposed to bury our children, they are supposed to bury us!

And yet, the very first death that happened here on earth was not the death of Adam or Eve (the first parents) but the death of their son. Is it possible that God was trying to show us that literally from the beginning of time, there are going to be children who die before their parents do? There is no easy way to say this, but maybe it is not quite as "out of order" as we thought. Selah. (Pause and think about that.)

Apparently for some of us, it *is* God's order. Ask the Holy Spirit to help you not go there the next time you find yourself thinking this, or hear yourself or someone else say that, and instead thank Him that you would not have to wait as long as Adam did to be reunited with your child.

> *I don't think the way you think. The way you work isn't the way I work." God's Decree. "For as the sky soars high above earth, so the way I work surpasses the way you work, and the way I think is beyond the way you think.*
> *Isaiah 55:8 (MSG)*

June 30

There are No Words

Sometimes when I respond to emails sent to me, I find myself writing something that needs to be shared with more than just the recipient of the email. This is one of those times.

We all know that unless you have lost a child, the people around us cannot possibly know what it is like. There just are no words to describe the darkness and the pain. It consumes every part of us, causing us to be unable to function most of the time. Sometimes we even forget to breathe. We can't even describe it to each other, but we know what it is like because of our own experience.

Guess what? We can take that knowledge and turn it around to think about what heaven is like! Unless we have been to and seen heaven for ourselves, we cannot even possibly begin to imagine what the beauty of it is like; what it feels like to have such indescribable peace, freedom from all pain of any kind, and receive love that makes us feel like we are so clean and pure that we could fly!

I have always believed that heaven is beyond what can be described or comprehended. I have reminded myself and others that Romans 8:18 talks about how the glory to come cannot even be compared with the suffering we go through here, and that means it must be SOME glory based on how deep our suffering is from losing a child!

But even more than that, our kids are there!

Until the email I found myself writing, I had never stopped to think about the fact that just like I can't describe to someone the pain and darkness that the death of one's child throws you into, our kids would not be able to describe to us the total peace, perfection and glory they now live in!

Wow! I know I would rather have Becca here with me... or would I? Would I really prefer her to be here in this crappy world that seems like it is falling apart right before our eyes instead of in a place that is so absolutely phenomenally awesome that it cannot even be put into words?

Years ago, I would have said, "I don't care! Her place should be here with me!" And if that is your response, you are normal, and there is no judgment or shame coming at you from me for feeling that way!

But just know, it is possible to get to the point where we are happier for them, than we are hurting for ourselves, at least most of the time.

Reflection: Let's use our God-given gift of imagination right now. Imagine yourself in heaven, amazed by seeing colors that you did not even know existed. Try picturing a beautiful meadow that is so gorgeous, it can't even be compared to the most beautiful one you have ever seen (with your own eyes or in a picture). Try seeing yourself walking on streets made of gold pavement, and a huge gate made of the most illustrious pearl that you did not even know was possible to be so beautiful.

Pretty hard to do, isn't it? All of it is so much beyond what we can imagine or what can be explained to us in a way that we can understand. Just like our pain is beyond what anyone can understand, heaven is wonderful beyond what we can understand. That is *home* and we will be there someday with our children who are experiencing it now. Yay for them!

If you still cannot get excited for your child beyond the pain of missing them, it's okay. Wherever you are right now is the right place for you. Once again, give yourself *lots* of grace in this journey.

However, as it is written: "What no eye has seen, what no ear has heard, and what no human mind has conceived" — the things God has prepared for those who love him".
1 Corinthians 2:9 (NIV)

July

July 1
Living a Life of Purpose

I was recently talking to a bereaved parent who said to me, "I want to get to a place of living with meaning and purpose, but how do I do that? How do I figure out what that purpose is now?" There is no easy answer. However, there will probably be a path of breadcrumbs. Let me explain what I mean by that.

What or to whom are you now drawn? It may be something you enjoyed doing before your child died, but for many of us, it changes, and we might think it is weird and makes no sense. Here are a couple of examples.

I love to speak and give presentations that impart something. In other words, I love to teach. I also love to travel. When Becca died, that did not change (although I had to step away for a while from my international children's ministry to work through the darkness of my grief). I am back to speaking and traveling, but instead of the subject being the passion of children's ministry, it is a passion and love of walking with other grieving parents from a place of darkness back to a place of light and hope.

I have a friend who became an ordained pastor after the death of her son. Her level of compassion to "shepherd" others through life and help them to know God better in both sorrow and joy seemed to be birthed out of what she went through. I am pretty sure the thought never crossed her mind to become a pastor before her little boy died.

So, how did we both know what our purpose was after the death of our child? It was just a natural progression. We found ourselves being drawn to something and allowed the pull to move us down the path to where we are now.

Maybe you feel drawn to return to the hospital where your child spent time with a lengthy illness. It is a painful thing to think about, much less actually go there, and yet you cannot explain the desire to do so. Maybe, just maybe, as you follow the inner pull and keep going where you feel drawn, even when it does not make any sense, it will lead you to where you eventually find yourself living from that place of meaning and purpose.

It might be helping others who are dealing with the same thing you went through. Or you may find yourself working toward making something safer, bringing public awareness to an issue, raising funds for needed emergency equipment, etc..... The list is endless.

Some parents I know end up doing exactly what they were doing before, but now have a much greater inner purpose for what they love doing.

So, if you are wanting the life of your child to make a difference in this world through you, just keep going, one day, one step at a time. I fully believe it will lead you to that place of purpose and meaning.

Reflection: Take a few minutes and think about what you may feel drawn to right now. It may be a certain group of people, it might be a place, it could be a situation, maybe a hobby of some kind, or it may be nothing at this point.

The important thing is to not pressure yourself and feel like you are doing something wrong if you feel stuck in this area. It can take several years for the fog to lift enough to discover that you are being drawn to something that could feel like it is giving your life purpose and meaning once again.

May he grant you your heart's desire and fulfill all your plans!
Psalm 20:4 (ESV)

July 2

God Uses Nature

One year just before Christmas, my oldest son had me watch online while some oysters were being opened for the gorgeous pearls inside. There were five of them, and he informed me that these pearls were my Christmas gift.

If you don't know how a pearl is made, they form when an irritant works its way into an oyster. As a defense mechanism, the oyster's body takes defensive action. The oyster begins to secrete a smooth, hard crystalline substance around the irritant to protect itself. Layer upon layer of this coating, called *nacre,* is deposited. This process requires a sufficient amount of time (generally three to five years) for a thick layer of nacre to be deposited, resulting in a beautiful, gem-quality pearl.

One day I found myself in tears thinking about how deeply touched I was to have something tangible in my hands to remind me of the hope I have in what God can still do with my life. God promises to take something so horrible as the death of my daughter and turn my shattered life into something of beauty that was still valuable and worth living!

Right then and there, I knew I wanted to find a way to give the same "gift" of this gorgeous symbol of the hope we have in Him into the hands of other pareavors. For several years we had what we called Pearls of Hope for this purpose. I found myself writing something to send with each pearl, reminding us that even though it feels like it, we did not die along with our child.

Here is part of what I wrote:

> *You have had something way beyond "an irritant" invade your life. You have had to face the death of your precious child. And now you have the opportunity to allow God to do a far greater miracle in you than He does in an oyster, which is to allow Him the time and tools needed to make something beautiful out of something so horrific.*

July

> *Yes, it can happen. Not only can it happen, but it will happen, if you allow the One who sees what you cannot see and knows what you do not know to be at work, deeply hidden in your heart and soul, where no one else has access. He wants to use this tragedy to make you highly valued; a rare and valuable gem, glowing with His love and glory unlike anyone else on earth.*

YOU are a precious and rare gem. You may not feel like it right now, but as you continue on your journey, you will realize that yes, you are still valuable. It is *because* of the deep never-ending love you have for your child that you can have hope as to your rare beauty and value.

Reflection: There are many things God teaches us through the nature that He created. For example, a butterfly coming out of the cocoon is a beautiful picture of how working our way out of bondage and darkness makes us strong.

As parents who have faced the death of our child, we are that butterfly in a cocoon. But many of us do not want to come out. Even if we do, we often believe that getting out is close to impossible, as we feel too weak to keep fighting. But we must. Some of the strongest, most caring people that I know are pareavors who have fought their way out of their cocoon of bondage and darkness.

Pearls, butterflies and ...? Ask God to speak to you through His creation, giving you the hope and strength that you need to keep going.

> *So we're not giving up. How could we! Even though on the outside it often looks like things are falling apart on us, on the inside, where God is making new life, not a day goes by without his unfolding grace.*
> *2 Corinthians 4:16 (MSG)*

July 3

What We Gain

At some point in those first few years, I made a conscious decision that as long as I am still here, I refuse to let my daughter's death keep me from living. I refuse to live in a shell, waiting to die just to go be with her. I have fought and will continue to fight to have a full life, enjoying my other children, my growing legacy of grandchildren, my marriage, and the calling on my life to embrace other grieving parents in their pain and be a light of hope in their darkness.

After my daughter passed from this earth, I experienced the exact same desire as most of you. I wanted to die and be done here. This is where another change in perspective happened for me.

Instead of continually thinking about how I wanted to die, I started to see that there were some good reasons to stay around here a while longer. I went even further and realized I don't *have* to live; I *get* to live! Here are a few of the good reasons we *get* to live here a bit longer.

- We get to live in a way that honors our child and keeps their memory alive!
- We get to join arms with other bereaved parents who are some of the most incredible people on this earth.
- We get an exclusive front row seat to the depth of God's love for us, as we realize that God Himself chose to suffer the death of His own Son in exchange for an intimate relationship with us.
- We get the opportunity of knowing Christ in His sufferings at a depth most Christians do not, which means we will also know him in the fullness of His resurrection power in a greater way.
- We get to know the depth of the reality that this world truly is not our home and to live life with eternity in mind, more than being caught up and entangled with the things of this world.
- We get the joy of knowing that we have made a precious deposit in heaven and have one of our greatest earthly treasures there waiting to welcome us to our eternal home.

I will admit that the last one may seem a bit far-fetched. But as I picture Becca in heaven and all the things she is experiencing (including people she has met and is talking to), I get excited to think that my daughter is one who will be showing me around and introducing me to people. Something inside me just knows that the joy and pride that she will have when I arrive will make all this pain disappear. It warms my heart and puts a smile on my face.

The pain of burying my daughter will always be an undercurrent that can explode into my life at any given moment. But so is the peace that goes beyond anything I can ever understand.

Reflection: I hope you don't get tired of being told how important our perspective is. I still need to remind myself of this, when I take a dive down into my grief, compounded by life's difficulties, so this is just as much for me as it is for you.

You may not be able to comprehend the list of things you just read. That's okay. It took me a few years. Just know that it is possible to see through different eyes as you continue this journey. May I suggest something? Pick one of the "get to" perspectives that is a bit of a stretch and ask God to help you get there.

> *I am leaving you with a gift—peace of mind and heart. And the peace I give is a gift the world cannot give. So don't be troubled or afraid.*
> *John 14:27 (TLB)*

July 4

Honesty Can Bring Freedom

In our deep grief, we tend to withdraw and pull away from people. There is definitely a time for that, especially when we are doing it to spend time with the Lord. But don't continually push people away, because there are some who can give you the comfort and encouragement you need.

We are so good at putting on a mask, telling people we are fine. It could be because we want people to stop tiptoeing around us, which reminds us of our painful loss. Maybe it is because we do not want them to try and fix us, or we feel that if we keep talking about our child, no one will want to be around us.

For some of us, we put on our so mask often that it causes us to fool ourselves into thinking we are okay, when we are not. But it is important to be honest with yourself about how you feel.

One way you can be honest with yourself is in a support group. Most of us need to be in a group specifically for grieving parents. If you cannot find one in your area, try looking for one that meets online. If you can't find a group, or don't feel you are ready for one, get a journal and start writing in it. You can write whatever you want, knowing that no one is going to be reading it.

If you cannot be honest with yourself about how you are feeling, you will not be able to be honest with those around you. Believe me, I understand how you may not want to unload on a coworker during your lunch break or tell a cashier at the store how you are really feeling when she dutifully asks, "How are you?". But when someone who cares asks how you are doing (like a trusted friend), you may be surprised how much of a load is lifted for that day, or that moment, by being able to share honestly how you are feeling.

Reflection: Take a minute to be honest with yourself and evaluate your emotions right now. Are there things you have not admitted to others (or even to yourself)? Maybe it's because you believe that a Christian should not have so much anger or have so many doubts. Maybe you feel guilty because you have started to laugh on a rare occasion, or because you are starting to have times where life distracts you from remembering that your child died.

We all have to work our way through the bad and the ugly when it comes to our grief. There is no way around it, and trying to wear a mask to hide us from ourselves, only prolongs the journey. Being honest with yourself means that you will be working your way toward a needed healing to be able to live and function again. Remember, the truth sets us free.

> *Two people are better off than one, for they can help each other succeed. If one person falls, the other can reach out and help. But someone who falls alone is in real trouble.*
> *Ecclesiastes 4:9-10 (NLT)*

July 5

Finding Your People

In our place of grief, we need people who will help us move forward in a way that is not pushy, but supportive. This may be a group that we were part of when our child died, or it may become a totally different group of people. For me, it has been a few different groups that I was never part of before.

A few years ago, I went to a conference for authors and entrepreneurs. I was surrounded by over two hundred kindred spirits who have a personal message to share and are moving forward in taking their message to those in the world who need it.

I cannot begin to tell you what these few days did to boost the desire to allow God's fire of purpose to burn brightly in me once again. Yes, it is a completely different purpose than it was a few years ago, of traveling to the nations for children's ministry and trainings. But it is a flame that was fanned to new proportions, feeling like a blazing fire of determination to not let Becca's death be wasted; to reach as many bereaved parents as possible with the message of hope, helping each pareavor find their personal path to a fulfilled life of purpose beyond the pain.

Oftentimes, our deepest pain becomes our greatest purpose. That has definitely been the case for me and, if you allow it, can be the same for you. How do I know? Because of those I rubbed shoulders with at that conference. Each one there had a story to tell, and many have told it by becoming an author with a published book, including several who have faced the death of their child (or children).

Every person was there because they were choosing to surround themselves with others who would impart into them what is needed to make their purpose as effective as possible. Each one chose not to become isolated in their pain, but to take the risk to reach out and help others behind them on the same painful journey they found themselves on, and yes, some of them were fellow pareavors.

How about you? Where are you on this grief journey of pain to purpose? Don't stay on a path that keeps you in total darkness, pain and fear. Make a choice to take at least one step toward light, hope, and a fire in your soul once again. It can take a while to get to the point of wanting it, and it will be something you have to fight for. When those two things come together (a desire to have it and a willingness to stay in the battle to win the war), you will find yourself standing on a different path; the path of learning how to live a fulfilled life with meaning and purpose beyond the death of your child.

Reflection: If you are ready, ask God to connect you with a group who will help you find a purpose from the pain of the death of your child. If you are not quite ready for that step, I pray that I have convinced you that at some point, it will be important to find and grab hold of a group of people who will help you move forward by discovering and walking in your unique purpose, with your gifts and talents.

You *can* do it, because I did it, and I believe in you!

We are confident that as you share in our sufferings,
you will also share in the comfort God gives us.
2 Corinthians 1:7 (NLT)

July 6

This Used to Really Sting

This year is more than half over. Does this make you feel relieved, or does it sting? I know for me personally, when I first lost Becca, a thought like that went beyond a sting. It took my breath away.

So why would I bring it up and risk the possibility of doing that to you? Because I want to encourage you that it does get better! It will not always be like this. Yes, it takes time. And I am not saying the untruth that "time heals all wounds." I firmly believe that it is what we *do* in that time that starts to bring us out of the suffocating darkness and back into light and being able to live again.

Do I miss Becca? Absolutely, with every fiber of my being! But I am now in a different place than the first two or three years of being without her. Now, knowing we are beyond the half-way point of the year doesn't take my breath away. It doesn't sting or make me feel relieved. It is just a fact that gives me a pause of reflection and then I carry on.

This is a journey, a process, we are all in. We are all at different places and we will all hit various milestones at different times. But we are all in this together!

Time definitely means something different than it used to, doesn't it? Once again, our perspective has a lot to do with where we are on this journey. Being half a year further from our child's death means we are also half a year closer to being with them again.

Reflection: In today's reading, I said that it is what you do with your time that will bring the needed measure of healing. I want to make sure you know what I mean by that. Yes, there are things we can do, like spending time with other pareavors who understand and can encourage us, or starting some sort of fund raiser to bring awareness to a cause in our child's memory.

But in those first two or three years, often what we need to do the most is to just "be." We need to sit and stare at nature, absorbing what is around us such as birds chirping and chipmunks scurrying. We need to go for a walk and allow God to walk with us in the silent pain.

I have found through the years that there are times I need to come back to that place of "just be." It seems we will always be a bit fragile when it comes to our child, and many times I take on too much, forgetting that I am not the person I once was, and things come crashing down on me. If you need some time to "just be," I give you permission. Others do not have to understand. You don't even have to understand. That is okay. Take however long you need to "be" and allow God to restore your inner person.

> ... he leads me by quiet water, he restores my inner person...
> Psalm 23:2-3 (CJB)

July 7
Survival Mode

Yesterday I talked about how we go through times when we need to not "do" anything but just "be." However, I realize that many of you have responsibilities and commitments each day, and it does not matter how much you want to push them aside, it is just not an option.

Most of us are in survival mode those first couple of years. We live on autopilot, going through the motions. People see us functioning and tell us how strong we are and how they could never go through what we are going through (as if we had a choice in the matter). They don't see us fall apart every night and how nonfunctioning we are in the privacy of our homes. Those who have other children at home have the responsibility of their care, and we feel guilty for doing such a bad job.

This is all part of the process of going through traumatic grief. As much as you don't like it and feel like you should be doing better, it is normal. Do not let others compare you to when they lost a parent or close friend, concerned that you should be doing better by now. You should

July

also not be comparing yourself to where I was on my journey by a certain time, or any other pareavor.

Your relationship with your child, how he or she died, your personality, etc. will affect how long you are in survival mode and how long it takes to get to a place of being able to function again, and then keep moving to learn how to live a life of meaning and purpose again.

I can assure you that if you are in survival mode for several years, there is nothing wrong with you, other than the fact that you are going through the trauma of having your child cut off from you and it takes everything you have just to make it through the next minute.

Reflection: There is just no way around it. Survival mode is a frustrating place to be, especially when you have daily responsibilities that suck out of you what little energy you have.

Remember those people who said, "Let me know if you need anything!"? Make a list of your daily responsibilities and consider asking some of those people to take care of several items on your list. Be honest with them, letting them know that you are still in survival mode, even if you are in your second or third year.

To help them understand that you are in a normal place of grief after the death of your child, give them an article about the trauma of losing one's child. Send them to the page *I Know a Grieving Parent* on the GPS Hope website (or one of the blogs). Give them a book like *Come Grieve Through Our Eyes* to read, so they can see how normal it is for someone who has lost a child to still be struggling deeply for up to five years.

Then ask God for the strength to help you fulfill your remaining responsibilities each day in a way that is needed for those who are depending on you.

> *From the end of the earth will I cry to You, when my heart is overwhelmed; Lead me to the rock that is higher than I.*
> *Psalm 61:2 (NKJV)*

July 8

Scars are Reminders

Around the age of three, I got my ankle caught in the spokes of a bicycle. The injury turned into a staph infection, taking me out of the world of childhood play for quite a while. We have pictures of me sadly sitting by a pool with my left foot dangling in the water and my right leg bandaged up (and covered with a plastic bread bag to make sure it stayed dry) while my sister and cousins are having fun playing and splashing around. Even though I totally recovered, I still have a scar on my ankle and always will.

A few years ago, I was cut open for a hysterectomy and was quite surprised when it took me many weeks to be able to function and take care of my family again, instead of them taking care of me. Once again, I have a permanent scar, reminding me of what I went through.

Just like a physical scar, there are things that happen in our lives that cause emotional scars. The scar of the death of our child is definitely one of those events. It is like my daughter's amputation. The scar on her stump from her missing leg is a lot like the emotional scar we carry when our child has been cut off from us on this earth (much more than the scar on my ankle).

But the comparisons don't stop at the scar of the injury.

Did having a staph infection in my ankle keep me from ever swimming again? No way! I love to swim and be in the water (especially in warm places with beautiful beaches). Did having an amputation keep Becca from running and playing with the other children? No, it did not. It may have slowed her down and caused her to adapt to how she ran and how she played, but it did not stop her.

Does the death of our child mean our life is over, and we will never be able to live a full life again? No, it does not. We need time to go through a "recovery" process (for lack of a better word) and need time to learn how to function with our child no longer here, but it does not mean we will never be able to function again.

July

Reflection: We will go through times when everyone around us is splashing and playing while we are unable to participate because of our wounds. We will go through times when we cannot function and have to wait for more healing. We will go through times when we have to adjust the way we do things.

We will forever bear the scar of our "amputation" and always have reminders that part of us is missing. But we are not permanently injured to the point of being out of commission for the rest of our lives. If you are in the first one to three years of grief, this may sound impossible. But I assure you, it is not.

Do not give up. Don't give up on life. Don't give up on hope. Do not give up on happiness, laughter and joy. Hang on, one day, one minute, one breath at a time. Our scars are reminders of what has been taken, but that does not mean we won't be able to live a life of meaning and purpose again. It will look different, but it is possible! Even if you do not believe, right now say it out loud. "It *is* possible for me to live a full life again. It will look different, but it is possible."

> *For I will restore health to you and your wounds I will heal, declares the Lord, because they have called you an outcast,*
> *Jeremiah 30:17 (ESV)*

July 9

Beauty for Ashes?

In Isaiah 61:3, we are told that God will give us a crown of beauty for ashes. How is that even possible? As I was talking about this to a group of pareavor moms, one of them said, "I would rather keep the ashes!"

It does come across as God saying He will take away the memory of our child and replace it with some sort of beautiful thing that is even better, doesn't it? But is that what God is really saying here? I don't think it is.

Reflections of Hope

The ashes represent a sorrow that is so deep, it causes us to step out of life for a while. Back in Old Testament times, when one faced a horrific loss, they would sit around with ashes on their head. (Don't ask me where that came from because I don't know and did not want to do the research.)

There are several people in the Bible who did this.

- Daniel, when the Israelites had been taken in captivity to Babylon.
- Tamar, when she was raped by her stepbrother and left with no hope for her future to become a wife or mother.
- Joshua and the people, when they were losing a war and the warrior men were being killed.
- Job, who lost all ten of his children in a windstorm when the house they were in collapsed on them.

Okay, we see this, but what is the "ashes for beauty" thing that Isaiah is talking about?

Here is how I see it for us as pareavors. We have many identities in life, and one of the best is to be a mom or a dad! It plays one of (if not *the*) most major roles in life we can ever have, and yet it is not our core identity. At the very deepest part of our being, and the most important and relevant identity we have is to be a son or daughter of the Most High God, Creator of the entire universe! He is the God above every other god, and the King above any other King who has ever been or ever will be.

That means we are royalty. We do not have to keep the ashes on our heads. We do not have to stay in this place of suffocating darkness, barely surviving. God is offering us the opportunity to get up and learn how we can still have a good life that is based on being His child, instead of remaining hopeless based on losing ours.

Yes, God still has good and wonderful things for us. It is not to replace our child, but to replace the intense darkness and pain of losing them temporarily while we are still on this earth. He has a crown of beauty for the ashes we are wearing. God does not just see us in the present, but He sees us in the present/future. He sees that crown of beauty on us, even if we cannot. The question is: Do you want to make the exchange He is offering you?

Reflection: It makes my heart hurt when I receive emails from parents who insist they will never be happy again because their child was their *entire* life, and they are so angry at God because He knew that but "took" their child from them anyway. If that is you, I want you to think about what you are saying and thinking, because that means your child was raised to the place of God Himself in your heart.

I do not believe for one second that God took your child from you because he or she was more important. However, I do believe God allowed the natural corruption of this world to take its course, and is now wanting to use this pain to reveal Himself to you in wonderful ways that You have never known Him, because you put the love for your child above your love for Him, and His love for you.

In Daniel 9:3 we read, "So I set my face to the Lord God to seek Him by prayer and supplications, with fasting, sackcloth and ashes" (TLV). I encourage all of us to take a few minutes and seek God's heart, knowing He is love itself, telling Him we are sorry for doubting that love because of our pain and lack of understanding the why, and asking Him to give us His crown of beauty to wear instead of our constant sorrow and pain.

> *Then, by constantly using your faith, the life of Christ will be released deep inside you, and the resting place of His love will become the very source and root of your life.*
> *Ephesians 3:17 (TPT)*

July 10

Mourning Versus Grieving

We are going to stay in Isaiah 61:3 today and look at the second part, which tells us that God will give us the oil of joy for mourning.

Reflections of Hope

Believe it or not, right after I wrote that sentence, since I had just been sitting for over an hour as I wrote yesterday's entry a I decided to take a break with a short walk. I did not return until seventy-five minutes later because it turned into long walk! I am so glad I went, because it gave me exactly what I needed to be able to share my heart in this reading.

Before I share what happened on my walk, let's talk about the difference between mourning and grieving. In talking to a group of moms, we all agreed that to us, mourning was the deep initial raw kind of pain when our child dies, and it is difficult to even function. We can have that for quite some time. Grief is when that initial suffocating pain begins to subside. We still have pain beyond words while at the same time being numb, but we can begin to function again. We notice life going on around us in a way that doesn't send us into anger or back to withdrawal.

When I looked it up, I was surprised to find out that mourning is the outward expression of a deep loss, such as wearing black clothing, a black band on your arm, etc. Grieving is the internal turmoil and pain we feel with our deep loss.

In other words, mourning is the outward show of the inward pain of loss. We may not wear black like they used to, but we still show on the outside of us what is happening on the inside of us, don't we?

So, is Isaiah 61:3 telling us that God wants us to put on a mask, pretending like we are no longer mourning, but are happy and joyful, putting this all behind us? It feels like that is what a lot of people want us to do, so they can be more comfortable with our grief, or maybe I should say be comfortable with our mourning.

I believe this verse is talking the about outward show of where we are internally. I know it seems like we will never have true joy again, but now let me share with you about the walk I just returned from. (Just as a note of reference, we are in Washington right now.)

I love berries, all kinds of berries! Back home on our Wisconsin campground site, we have wild black raspberries growing. When they start getting ripe around the end of June, I often just walk over and pick a bunch to eat on the spot. My two oldest granddaughters will come over and we will pick enough berries for me to make a pie.

July

Did I mention that I love berries? On my walk, I found a little path that went through a beautiful grove of trees that of course I just had to follow. It led me to a bigger path that I continued to walk on. When it branched off to the left, in my head I just simply said, "God, which way should I go?" My heart told me to keep going straight. It happened a second time, and as I continued straight, I was suddenly surrounded by blackberries! It was wonderful and I was like a little kid, all excited about these berries, grabbing some to eat every few steps.

The next time the path turned, I felt a nudge to take the turn, and the berries not only continued along that path, but I found myself in an area that was so beautiful I had to stop and take it all in.

It seems like such a small thing, but it brought so much joy to my heart, that I smiled all the way back to the Hope Mobile with a spring in my step and a lightness in my heart. That was definitely trading any outward show of mourning while missing Becca, to an outward show of my internal joy at the little kiss from God I had just received.

Reflection: In the Bible, often when you see oil, it is a representation of the Holy Spirit. So, if God is giving us the oil of joy for our mourning, it is a reminder that we already have joy inside us though the Holy Spirit. If you are like me, it feels like any joy that had grown in my life before, was chopped down and stomped on.

But that seed is still there. It may be dormant, but it is still in us, so we need to do what we can to water and nourish that seed. He wants to give you the outward expression of what is going on internally, and His desire is to bring joy back into your life. It is a process and takes time, but it can happen.

Remember to occasionally ask God how He wants to help you nourish that seed of joy in you, knowing it may be as simple as going for a walk. Be open, and be ready, because you never know when a moment of joy will burst through. When it does, grab it, express it, and thank God for His Spirit that is growing joy in you once again.

> *You did it: you changed wild lament into whirling dance;*
> *You ripped off my black mourning band and decked me*
> *with wildflowers. I'm about to burst with song; I can't keep*
> *quiet about you. God, my God, I can't thank you enough.*
> *Psalm 30:11 (MSG)*

July 11

Replacing our Heaviness and Despair

Okay, time to dig into the next section of Isaiah 61:3, where it says God will give us a garment, (a mantle or covering) of praise for the spirit of despair and heaviness.

I am very aware of what our praise and giving thanks to God does for our soul and spirit, including those of us who are in deep grief. If you have not read any entries on these things yet, you will at some point. However, have you ever noticed that this is not a conditional promise? This verse does not say, "If you praise me, I will do something for you in return."

What if it means we are to tap into God's praise for us? What if He wants to cover us in His love as He sings over us, rejoices over us and praises us for just throwing ourselves at Him with the simple and sincere cry of "Help me!"?

Think about in the natural when you are bummed about something or just having an off day, and a stranger gives you a sincere compliment. Or maybe a friend blesses you by giving you something unexpected. Doesn't that life your spirits and make you feel better?

What if that is what God was talking about when He says that He will give us a garment of praise to help release our spirit of despair? That idea changes things dramatically. It is not always about my praising Him, but sometimes it is about realizing that He is praising me... wow... Let's look at the full verse before going on.

> *"to provide for those who grieve in Zion— to bestow on them a crown of beauty instead of ashes, the oil of gladness instead of mourning, a mantle of praise instead of a spirit of despair. Then people will call them "Oaks of Righteousness", The Planting of the Lord" in order to display his splendor.* Isaiah 61:3 (ISV)

Do you see how it ends? We are told that God will do these things for us so that we will be like oak trees, planted by God Himself. Why oak trees?

How often have you seen an oak tree uprooted? Not very often. Also, think about how oak is one of the most sought-after woods for sturdy furniture. It is strong, its roots grow deep, and it is steady and dependable. That is something I need in my life, and so do you.

God's faithfulness to us is astounding. The promises He gives us when we are in the deepest, darkest pit possible can not only lift us out, but bring beauty and joy back into our lives, lifting the heaviness and making us sturdy and secure.

Reflection: A tree can grow back from a stump and become a full tree again. It happens because the roots are still there. This is a beautiful picture of how we can also live a full life again, after we have been cut down by the death of our child.

To nourish those roots, allowing some growth to happen, take a minute to picture God praising you. He is coming to you with a warm smile, telling you how proud He is of you because you are simply coming to Him for help, strength and comfort. Picture Him placing on you a beautiful covering. Feel the warmth of it, as it wraps you up like a strong loving hug. Sit in His love and His praise for you for as long as you need, and don't forget to come back to it when you need an extra dose of encouragement on this grief journey.

For there is hope for a tree—if it's cut down,
it sprouts again and grows tender, new branches.
Job 14:7 (TLB)

July 12
When You Feel Stuck

Something I learned about a few years after Becca died is called the RAS filter (Reticular Activating System). It is what our subconscious looks for, based on what our conscious thoughts are thinking. For instance, have you ever thought about buying a certain car, and you start seeing them all over, when you never noticed them before?

That was your RAS filter. Those things were always around you, but your subconscious knew that was an important piece of information that your mind has been thinking about, so it makes sure you noticed it as possible valuable information. (Our subconscious weeds out billions of pieces of "useless" information, based on what is in our conscious thoughts.)

This also affects our thoughts about non-concrete things. So, if my conscious thoughts are that I am an overweight ugly woman, my RAS filter will weed out the things that do not apply to that thought, and make sure I see the things that support that belief about myself.

Our minds are an amazing creation that God has gifted to us, and too often we do not realize how much control we have in that area of our lives. The input regulates the output, and God made it that way!

> *What you focus on is what you will grow. So if you continue to focus on the pain and loss, it will grow until it is ready to consume you and overtake you. But if instead you think about, focus on, and give thanks for what or who you still have, that is what will begin to grow, and eventually it will bring you out of that deep dark place. You may not think so right now, but you can actually get to the place where you celebrate your child's life, instead of being stuck in the pain of their death.* -When Tragedy Strikes

Please know that I am not talking about those first two to three years when we can't help but have our deep and traumatic grief take over almost everything. I am talking about when we find ourselves starting to choose where our thoughts and feelings are going to go.

The question you need to ask yourself is: Do I want to be a victim and remain being the parent of a child who has died, or do I want to step beyond that identity and be a parent who is thankful for the life of my child, no matter how short it was, and honor my child's life with my own life?

July

Reflection: I have learned to do something to help reset what I focus on and would like to suggest you try this yourself. Write down on a piece of paper, "I am choosing to close my RAS filter to...." And then list three to five negative things you no longer want to focus on. These can be things that allow you to stay in a place of depression, that may not even be related to the death of your child. Remember, they can be things you feel are true, but you want to change your view and shift the way you see it and think about it.

Then write down, "I choose to open my RAS filter to see...." And list three to five good things you want to start focusing on. These should be things that will lift you out of the darkness and back into the light; things you know in your head should be true, but your heart is not lining up to it yet. This list could be endless, but limit yourself to five things, to make sure you don't put yourself on overload.

Then put these two lists in a place where you will see it as a reminder, so that your RAS filter will start to reset. Remember, God created us (and even told us) to renew our minds!

> *Don't copy the behavior and customs of this world, but let God transform you into a new person by changing the way you think. Then you will learn to know God's will for you, which is good and pleasing and perfect.*
> *Romans 12:2 (NLT)*

July 13

Waiting on God

When Dave and I were dating, he asked God a few times about proposing to me, but he kept hearing the word "wait." After a while, he decided to do a bit of a study on the word wait. He discovered that one of the Biblical meanings is "a carved work." In other words, in the waiting process, God was doing a very deep carved work in both of us, so that we would fit together more tightly in a marriage.

We had no idea what was ahead of us and are very thankful for that carved work done in us, not just before we were married, but also continuing to be at work during our marriage.

There have been many times since then that I have needed to wait on God, as He does a deep work that is often hidden from my view. I probably don't even need to say that Becca's death was definitely one of those times!

Let me clarify something. I do not believe for one second that God caused Becca's death. What I believe with every fiber of my being is that when God created this world, he turned it over to man, giving each human being a free will to make choices because that is what love does.

Mankind messed things up from the very beginning, and now we all deal with the sin and corruption that is here as a result. In other words, each person has a free will to make choices, and those choices can literally be deadly to others.

In Becca's case, it was the decay, corruption and illness that the enemy was able to release on this earth (because of man's choice to sin) that so deeply affected our daughter in getting cancer and later having heart failure because of one of the chemo drugs.

Trusting God with our lives does not mean that nothing bad will ever happen to us. What it means is that *when* these horrible tragedies happen, He is with us, every second, even when we cannot see Him or feel His presence.

Reflection: As we wait on God to bring us through, resting in Him, crying and screaming at Him, and allowing Him to be God in the middle of our mess, He is truly doing a carved work that is hidden from our view.

I want to encourage you to keep waiting. Through the pain, the suffocating darkness and the grief that is so deep it has no words, He is with you, and He is at work. I promise, because He promises. The other reason that I know He is at work in you is because He has been at work in me. I could not have made it this far without Him doing a

July

carved work in my pain and darkness. He did it for me and He will do it for you!

Meanwhile, the Eternal One yearns to give you grace and boundless compassion; that's why He waits. For the Eternal is a God of justice. Those inclined toward Him, waiting for His help, will find happiness.
Isaiah 30:18 (VOICE)

July 14

Our Other Children

(Note: If you lost your only child, I am so very sorry. Please feel free to go straight to the reflection if today's reading might be too hard of a trigger.)

Parents who have lost a child are shell-shocked, as their whole life has been jarred, turned upside down and inside out. Everything in them shuts down. They are living on autopilot at best. They are in survival mode, and if they have other children, it takes everything in them to be at some sort of a minimal functioning level to be there for their other children.

Most siblings, if not all, will say they lost their parents along with their brother or sister, for quite some time. Many of these children say their parents' deep grief cause them to struggle with feeling like their parents wished it were they themselves who died instead of their sibling (not realizing their parent's grief would be just as deep if it had been them). I personally experienced one of my children telling me this. It ripped my heart out, but I am glad she felt like she could voice her feeling that way to me.

Often the siblings find themselves asking questions like, "Why am I still here? Why wasn't it me? What did I do wrong for this to happen to my brother/sister?" And they can have hidden fears, wondering who is next. (I had a cousin who wrote that on his calendar after two older siblings died.)

The siblings, no matter the age, are often overlooked as someone who is suffering a very deep loss. If it was a child on the younger side who died, the emphasis of care and concern is for the parents' loss. If the death was an adult, the emphasis is on the spouse's loss and the children of the one who died.

I even know of a sibling being told, "Thank goodness it wasn't your husband or one of your children," as if that makes the loss any less painful. Talk about not validating the deep and intense life-long loss!

I will confess, until this hit our own family, the heavy loss suffered by grandparents when a grandchild dies, and siblings when they lose a brother or sister is something I was unaware of. In a way, I wish I was still unaware of it. But then I would not be here with you right now.

Reflection: One mom who lost her only child and has become a precious friend, will use this kind of reading or conversation with other pareavors, to help with her struggle of not having any children now. "At least I don't have to deal with those kinds of issues."

We all have different losses, and different things to overcome based on the details of our personal loss such as the circumstances of our families, how our child died, their age, etc. All of those differences do not diminish anyone else's pain or struggle as pareavors. The one thing that still unifies us all is the fact that we are pareavors; a parent who has had our child ripped away from us through death.

Please take a minute to ask God to be with those who are specifically struggling with being there for their other children. And then send up a prayer for those who are struggling because they have no other children.

Now rest in the fact that *you* have been prayed for by all the others who are reading today's entry!

Do not forget to do good and to help one another...
Hebrews 13:16 (GNT)

July 15

Making a Choice

There is so much out there from grieving parents who are stuck in their grief, telling other grieving parents that their lives will never be the same; that it will always be dark, and life will never be worth living again without their child. I personally refused to believe that.

I knew that my life would never be the same, but I could not come into agreement that it would always be dark and not worth living. I had four other children and grandchildren. I had a calling on my life and an international ministry. I knew I had the Seed of Hope and Life living inside of me. As horrific as it was, I did not believe that the death of my child was where God reached His limit, and He was unable to help me work through it in triumph to live a victorious life over my enemy.

However, after saying all of that, it is extremely traumatic, and it does take months and years to work through the painful loss of our child being taken from us, starting to see light in our darkness. It is a choice, and yet it isn't. Only those who have faced this blackness will truly understand what I am trying to put into words.

At first, the darkness overtakes us whether we want it to or not. But eventually we get to start making choices as to whether or not we are going to stay in that place. There are those who choose to fight their way out, and those who don't. There are those who choose to die emotionally, and those who choose to find a way to live. Those of us who make the choices to fight and to live, do so at different times in our journey.

When we come to the place where we decide to *choose* life and joy, it is a choice we have to make over and over again. It is something we have to hold on to with tenacity. There are many times we think it is never going to happen. But it *can* be done, and it is so very worth it!

Reflection: Please understand that when I say it is a choice that we have to make, I know we cannot be pushed into making it. And of course, as you have seen by now, each one of our paths is so very unique. There is no way "one size fits all" in this journey of losing a child.

Once again, I am asking you to take these desires and needs to God, even though He already knows them (and you have probably done it so many times already). There *is* a breakthrough for you! Every time you cry out to God, He moves more of the darkness so that His light can start to shine through. It happens so slowly that we cannot even tell anything is happening. Let Him help you to hang on, and He will come through for you.

> *Depend on the Lord; trust him, and he will take care of you.*
> *Psalm 37:5 (NCV)*

July 16
If They Can, So Can You

I know how hard it can be to believe that it is even possible to have joy or happiness in your life ever again. I don't want you to think I am by myself in believing that can (and will) happen, so I want to share with you what a couple of other pareavors (their names have been changed) have said about this.

Sheri talks about how her daughter has been gone longer than she was here. As she put it, "My grief did not hold its shape like concrete." She says it is a process that we move through. I love that! Sheri encourages others to *choose* to heal, and it will happen. Be intentional about it. Follow the path, step by step until you find yourself in that place.

Lauren thought she would never have joy in her life ever again. She struggled for ten years after the death of her nineteen-year-old daughter. One day she made a conscious decision to finally start moving forward. It was during the Christmas season, and she bought herself stocking hangers that spelled out JOY. She started seeing the word joy everywhere. (Remember the RAS filter I talked about on the 12th?) A

July

friend even gave her a coffee cup with the word joy on it. Lauren realized that joy really was all around her if she wanted to see it.

She started seeing it in her son, at her work, and finally in herself. A couple of years later, when her son got married, he needed some Christmas decorations, so she went through some of hers and gave him the JOY stocking hangers. She had to laugh at herself when she realized that she was giving away her joy!

Lauren says that having joy again after the death of your child is hard to achieve and you have to work at it. She struggles with feeling like she wasted so many years by staying in that dark place, but also acknowledges that it took that long for her to be ready to want to live again.

These are two more pareavors who have chosen to fight and to live their lives in as much joy and fullness as possible without their child here on earth. They are doing their best to encourage pareavors who can only find negative words of doom and gloom, that they can also choose to fight through the darkness to get back into the light of life. If you are not able to make that choice yet, you will, and we pray it will be sooner and not later.

Reflection: I want to share one more pareavor's thoughts with you. Helena shares that you cannot change what happened. All you can change is how you let it affect you. She feels saddened when she hears of pareavors who, after many years, seem to be unable to find a glimpse of hope in their life without their child. She believes that does not need to be the case.

Helena lost her son to suicide, and toward the end of that first year, even though she was in so much pain and missed him terribly, she was determined to enjoy her other children and friends. She admits how guilty she felt at first, but realized she owed it to those who were still in her life, to her beloved son and to herself, to carry on ahead. She told herself, and now tells others, that life will never be the same, but it goes on, and you get to choose how happy you will be with what has been handed to you.

Picture a "DO NOT PARK" sign. Let that be a message to you. It is right to grieve deeply; you have been through a trauma. But please do not stay parked in your pain. Make a conscious decision to move toward living a life again with joy, meaning and purpose. And know that I have prayed for you to have the strength and endurance needed to get there.

> *Then he turned my sorrow into joy! He took away my clothes of mourning and clothed me with joy.*
> *Psalm 30:11 (TLB)*

July 17

Help Getting Out of the Pit

"Time heals all wounds!" is not a true saying, especially when it comes to the death of our child. I believe 100% that it is what we *do with our time* that brings a measure of healing. Today, I want to help stir your thoughts as to some things other pareavors have done with their time that has moved them in the direction of getting out of that horrible dark pit.

Some have picked up an old hobby or started a new one. I know someone who got the equipment and went back to the days when she used to make pottery. Another friend started refinishing furniture and making wood signs with sayings and now has her own indoor booth at a high-end market boutique to sell them.

Finding a hobby will help you begin to take your thoughts off your loss for a while. Yes, the sadness will still be there, but it is helpful to be able to have your thoughts occupied with something that your hands are doing. Sewing, gardening, get back to stamping, coloring, do paint-by-numbers, start a collection of something, take an auto mechanics course... the options are endless!

A second thing I would like to suggest is to volunteer somewhere to help others. This one is a key that many grieving parents find successful. There is something about helping others that lifts your heaviness a bit and opens your heart to warmth and goodness.

Serve at a homeless shelter, volunteer at the local animal shelter, donate some time at a food or clothing bank. Help raise money for an

July

organization that has a special place in your heart because of your child. There are so many great organizations that need feet on the ground to keep their doors open.

The last one is a big one; get a pet. I know of several grieving parents who got a pet to help comfort them and bring some joy into their lives after the death of their child and cannot say enough about how much it has helped them, both emotionally and physically. (Most of the pareavors I know got dogs. I am a cat person, myself.)

I know you may feel like you do not have the energy to do any of those things. It is one of those vicious cycles and the only way out of it is to make a conscious decision to move in the direction of doing *something*. Once we make that effort, it will begin to pull us in the needed direction, causing some of the needed healing for our well-being.

Reflection: After Becca died, Dave took me shopping to replace my guitar that I loaned out many years ago and never saw again, as it was hocked for drugs. I started writing songs again, specifically for those who are grieving, and have now made a CD. Talk about doing something with your time that brings a measure of healing!

Please don't say that you just can't do anything. Take a few minutes right now and really think and pray about what you can start to do that will pull you up out of your pit, even for just an hour or two every few days. I am not talking about joining a gym and working out five days a week! Something simple but touches you in your soul.

God knows what that is, and I believe that in the next few days or weeks, He will show you exactly what it is.

Keep asking, and it will be given to you; keep seeking, and you will find; keep knocking, and the door will be opened to you.
Matthew 7:7 (CJB)

July 18

You Are Amazing!

Can I share with you two things that amaze me about bereaved parents?

First, we are good at *not* telling another parent who has lost a child, "I know how you feel." People who have not lost a child try to tell us they know how we feel because they lost their _____ (fill in the blank).

When I was in those early months and still very raw, that would make me angry, and I had a hard time not getting snippy with them. We know that if they have not lost a child, they do *not* know how we feel, and how dare they try and compare the loss of our child with a very different kind of loss!

I eventually realized that when someone compares their loss to the death of my daughter, that person is trying to empathize by sharing the deepest, most painful loss they have faced. Now it is easier for me to appreciate it as their way of showing kindness by trying to relate to my pain and can just let it go instead of feeling offended.

As pareavors, we know that the loss of one's child is so deeply personal, we don't even say to *each other*, "I know how you feel," even if our child died the same way. I don't know how you feel. I know how I felt and the very dark place it took me to. But your relationship with your child was unique. Their age and way they died was different than what I experienced. We may say, "I lost my daughter the same way." But we don't tell each other, "I know how you feel because I lost my child, too."

I love that about us.

Which brings me to the other thing that amazes me. I have found that pareavors are some of the most compassionate people on the face of the earth. Let me clarify that. I am not talking about how we no longer have any bandwidth whatsoever for drama.

I am talking about when we hear a story about how another parent lost their child, so often the thought goes through our minds, "Wow! I can't imagine losing my child *that* way!" We are so full of compassion and care for each other. We are immediately drawn into their story and will let them talk about their child. As pareavors, we are some of the only ones who are not only willing, but *want* to hear about another parent's child who is no longer here.

I am truly honored to be part of a group of people who have faced such a deep loss that have such an instant deep bond of love for each other. When you find out someone is a fellow pareavor, there is an instant connection and our heart goes out to them, whether it happened last week or thirty years ago.

You are amazing!

Reflection: I know we would rather not be amazing in this way. We would rather have our son or daughter here with us and still be ignorant as to what it is like to grieve the death of our child. But since that is not the case, you might as well "own" how awesome you are to the rest of us in this "unwanted club membership."

Your child made you amazing, both through his or her life, and through his or her death. Right now, say out loud, "I am amazing!" Acknowledge that because your son or daughter was amazing, it makes you amazing. You are special. You are loved. *You are wanted and needed by the rest of us! YOU ARE AMAZING!*

I praise you because you made me in an amazing and wonderful way.
Psalm 139:14 (NCV)

July 19

Our Eternal Purpose

We may tend to think that our child did not get to fulfill his or her purpose because they left this earth before we did. But we do not know that. God had a plan in place for them, as well as for us, before they were even conceived.

Reflections of Hope

I have really been thinking and praying about this a lot lately. How is it that God created each one of us with a plan and purpose for our lives, but our child fulfilled that purpose so much earlier than we did? And how were they able to do that if they died at a very young age or even in the womb? What if our child died while in rebellion? Does that mean that he or she missed fulfilling God's purpose for their life?

God tells us He knows the plans He has for us (Jeremiah 29:11) and He knows the numbers of our days here on earth (Psalm 139:16 and Job 14:5), yet we know the enemy comes to kill, steal and destroy (John 10:10). So, did the enemy stop God's plan for the lives of our children? But the Bible also says that no plan of God's can be withheld from Him (Job 42:2).

I can go round and round on these things and my mind just cannot seem to land on anything that makes sense of it all... except....

We are only looking at our time here on earth, but God is looking beyond that into eternity. Could it be that we see our purpose as something we "do" here on earth, but God looks at our purpose through the eyes of who we *are* from the day we are conceived, right through to our entrance into heaven and beyond? Are we looking at our purpose as something external and based on the natural realm, when our true purpose is spiritual and eternal?

Just because I don't understand why my child died, does not mean there is no purpose in it. What if our child's purpose was done here on earth, but it is continuing in eternity? What if the purpose of our child's death here on earth was to influence our lives so deeply that we touch others in a way that affects eternity on their behalf? For instance:

- Ann started an organization going into schools against bullying after her child died by suicide because of being bullied.
- BJ and Doug led a sign language choir that travels around the world as they minister to grieving parents after the death of their son and a pregnancy loss.
- Kelly wrote a book and started a ministry to those who have faced pregnancy loss after her own losses.
- Dave & Dee hold a yearly run for Q-T heart disease and donate heart defibrillators to local businesses after their daughter died in her sleep from this.

July

- Angelique has recorded a powerful song that her son wrote two weeks before dying, and the songs she now writes, sings and records have a much deeper message for those who are hurting and lost.

I could go on for several pages, but you get the idea. We might see these things I shared as God's purpose for their life after the death of their child, but I also see it as the eternal purpose of our child continuing here on earth through us.

We do because we are. We are the parent of our child. We are filled with God's spirit. We may still be here on earth, but we are eternal beings with an eternal purpose.

Reflection: Today's reflection is simple but profound. Spend some time thinking about how we usually see a purpose for life as something that we do while here on earth, but since we are spiritual beings, our purpose is so much more than that.

Just because your child is no longer here with you on earth does not mean their purpose for eternity has been fulfilled. How will their life and death continue to affect others for eternity through you? This just might also become your eternal purpose.

You saw me before I was born and scheduled each day of my life before I began to breathe. Every day was recorded in your book!
Psalm 139:16 (TLB)

July 20

I Don't Think I Can Make It

I heard a message recently from a pastor who had a great illustration. As a college basketball player, he dislocated his finger. It was popped back into place, and a splint put on, to help it heal properly. He was told that it would be painful and awkward, but not to take it off early before the designated number of weeks.

At some point, Pastor Freddie decided it was not worth going through the pain of letting it heal in the splint and took it off. He now lives with a permanently crooked right index finger.

Going through the healing process of grieving the death of our child is extremely messy and beyond painful!!! And when I say "healing," I don't mean going back to the person we used to be. That is impossible. I am talking about a healing that allows us to function again and even learn how to live a fulfilled life beyond the death of our child.

My husband, Dave, had quadruple bypass surgery when he was only 48 years old. Yes, he is "healed," but will forever bear the scars from that surgery and will take medications and live a certain lifestyle for the rest of his time here on earth.

Did our daughter "heal" from her amputation? Yes, and no. She was never the same little girl, physically or emotionally. But she did "heal" in a way that allowed her to live a full and happy life, even with her limitation of only having one leg.

No, you will never be the same. But you can allow a healing that will bring you to a place of having meaning and purpose, and yes, even happiness, in your life once again. And you do not have to go through the process alone. There are lots of other pareavors who want to walk with you through the messiness and the pain, encouraging you, crying with you, and celebrating the smallest of steps toward that hope and light.

Reflection: One time I told God I felt like I was having heart surgery with no anesthetic and wanted to be done! I heard Him speak to my spirit that yes, it was painful, but He was doing a deep work and He asked me not to get off the operating table. Now, looking back, I am glad that I stayed put and worked my way through it, but I didn't know if I was going to make it at the time.

I want to encourage you that no matter how painful, do not try to get around the grief by ignoring it, or drowning it out with busyness or other things. I guarantee that it will come back later with the possibility of destroying everything and everyone you still love.

I know it feels like you are not going to make it, but you can do it. Please do not take off the splint (and stay on the operating table).

> *And I am sure that God who began the good work within you will keep right on helping you grow in his grace until his task within you is finally finished on that day when Jesus Christ returns.*
> *Philippians 1:6 (TLB)*

July 21

Who Will You Be Meeting?

I have been crying all morning. My son and his fiancée just lost their child that she was carrying. As I write this, she is back in the surgery room getting a D&C. God met me, right where am in this place of new grief, opening my eyes to see something I had never thought about before. I hope it encourages you the way it did me.

One thing I can struggle with is how Becca only got to know one of her nieces here on earth. There are now several nieces and nephews that will not have their Aunt Becca as part of their lives here. But this morning, I found myself sending the following text to my son.

I just had the thought, Becca may not know her nieces and nephews here, but she knows the ones that are there with her and I'll bet she was there to greet them front and center and threw them a heck of a welcome party!

(Anyone who knows me knows that I just used some of my strongest language right there!) To think that Becca is enjoying having a niece or nephew up there with her, that none of us got to meet... how exciting and fun for her!

What a thought, though, isn't it? Our children may be missing out on things here, but there are things we are missing out on that they get to be part of! Plus, our children are part of the welcoming committee for those we love when they cross over!

Yes, I know we would rather have them here with us, hands-down! But I am so excited for the day it is my turn to go, and Becca is there to meet *me* front and center, and to see the party she and Jesus have worked on together, just for me! And she will get to introduce me to that grandchild I did not get to meet here!

Reflection: How about you? Can you imagine what that will be like to have your child be there to meet you when it is your turn to cross over? Who will he or she introduce you to? Maybe it will be someone you have read about in the Bible, or in a history book, or maybe someone who was martyred for Christ. Maybe it will be a family member who died before you were able to meet them. If that doesn't put a smile on your face, does it at least stir up a bit of joy in your heart?

No, it does not remove the heaviness, and it can all come rushing back strong. But even a few moments here and there of reminding ourselves of what is in our future is so very worth it!

> *...We crave for all that is mortal to be swallowed up by eternal life. And this is no empty hope, for God himself is the one who has prepared us for this wonderful destiny.*
> *2 Corinthians 5:4-5 (TPT)*

July 22

The Dividing Line

We know that when our child dies, there is a dividing line of before and after and we will never go back to being the same. There is nothing like seeing your child in a casket and burying them on that day, or to take home your child's ashes in an urn. There is nothing more life-shattering and it changes you *profoundly.*

I have realized that it is the same in our relationship with God. There is a dividing line of before and after in our relationship with Him at that point and it will never be the same, either.

There is a common hymn that is sometimes sung at funerals called *It Is Well with My Soul.* Every time I hear it, I get emotional, especially knowing the story behind the song. Horatio Spafford lost a young son to pneumonia in 1871. The same year his business was ruined in the Great Chicago Fire. Two years later, he sent his wife and four daughters on a ship to England, planning to join them after finishing dealing with his lost business. He received a telegram saying there was a shipwreck and only his wife survived.

Most accounts say that as Horatio was on a ship to join his wife, the captain let him know when they were in the area the ship sank with his daughters, which is when he wrote the words. The first verse says:

> *When peace like a river attendeth my way, when sorrows like sea billows roll; whatever my lot, thou has taught me to say, 'It is well. It is well with my soul.'*

It is a song that I can connect to because it was written from the pain and grief of losing his four daughters in a single tragedy. It speaks to how I felt when Becca died. It was a sorrow that was so deep. I had never felt anything like that, and I had no idea there was a place that dark.

I am sure there are many of you reading this thinking, "How can anyone possibly say it is well with my soul when God allows things like this to happen? I don't see myself *ever* getting to that place!"

Reflections of Hope

One thing I have learned over the years is that faith and trust are really the same thing. It is a belief in something you cannot prove at the moment. It is making a choice to believe in something we cannot physically see, hear, or touch.

We cannot trust someone we don't know. We do not trust total strangers because we don't know them. The more we know somebody, the more trust we can have in that relationship. I think what happens is that we *thought* we knew God pretty well, based on things we were taught. When our child dies, we suddenly find out that almost everything we thought we knew about God was wrong.

That puts us on a journey to discover who God really is. As we fight our way through the darkness, we find out there is a stability in God. We discover how incredibly faithful He is and that His comfort goes beyond anything a person can give us. He is *so* much bigger than we ever knew He was and most importantly, there is a deeper love that surrounds us than we ever understood before or can comprehend even now.

All those things we *thought* we knew about God? It's like now we *know*. We know the depths of God's love and who He really is, more than ever before.

Reflection: That is the before and after in our relationship with God. I know it can take a while to get there. Many of us go through a time of anger and want nothing to do with Him, even wondering if He really exists. It is okay and normal to feel that way and have those kinds of questions and reactions.

For myself and so many other pareavors, now that we are far enough on this journey, we have learned that God really *can* be trusted and that His love goes far beyond what we ever experienced before. It is different, but it is so much deeper and richer now.

If Horatio Spafford could open His heart back up to God after all he went through, you and I can too. It can be well with your soul, and your relationship with God can become so much more than it ever was before. Ask the Holy Spirit to help you believe it is possible.

And may you have the power to understand, as all God's people should, how wide, how long, how high, and how deep

His love is. May you experience the love of Christ, though it is too great to understand fully. Then you will be made complete with all the fullness of life and power that comes from God.
Ephesians 3:18-19 (NLT)

July 23

Fighting for Joy

Recently I found myself in a place of contentment, even though it was the week of Becca's birthday. There was a peacefulness that is hard to describe. I was not falling apart and was okay with where I was on my life's journey. I had spent almost a year praying for and fighting to have joy back in my life again. Not just moments of happiness here and there, but to live from that place of having joy as an undercurrent along with the undercurrent of the pain of missing my daughter.

Around that same time, someone told me how much happier and at peace I seemed than the last time they saw me, which was wonderful to hear because it confirmed to me that I was truly allowing God to be at work in me.

There are a lot of studies and thoughts about the difference between joy and happiness. I see happiness as when we feel good about our outward circumstances, and joy is feeling content about our inward circumstances.

We can have a moment when we smile or laugh at something, but inwardly we are still in darkness. We can also have a moment of painful tears, but inwardly we are at rest. That is because happiness is outward, while joy is inward. Happiness is soul fruit. Joy is spiritual fruit.

You may be at a place where you find it appalling to even think about having joy in your life again after the death of your child. But it is good for you to know that at some point down the road, you will become weary of the heaviness and weary of thinking that is who you need to be, as a way to not forget or not betray your child.

The original Greek word in the Bible for joy is the word *chara*. It is a state of mind and an orientation of the heart. For most of us, our mind knows that our child is gone, but our heart is having a hard time accepting it. The sooner our heart lines up with our mind and starts to accept the fact that we will not see our child again until we join them in the fullness of God's glory, the sooner we can start to move in the direction of having joy in our lives again.

Reflection: I may not be happy with my circumstances, but I can still have an inner joy and contentment, knowing this is not permanent and that God has an incredible plan that is beyond what I can comprehend right now.

Psalm 16:11 tells us that God will show us the path to life, and that His presence in our lives will give us joy once again. Turn this verse into a prayer, asking God to make it a reality that it is okay to have joy back in your life It may take quite a while like it did for me. But having joy in our lives is so much better than having time drag by ever so slowly, remaining a victim in the darkness. It is worth going for!

> *You direct me on the path that leads to a*
> *beautiful life. As I walk with You, the pleasures are*
> *never-ending, and I know true joy and contentment.*
> *Psalm 16:11 (VOICE)*

July 24

The Truth

When God created us, He did an amazing thing by making us in their (Father, Son and Holy Spirit) image. One of the ways He made us in their image is by allowing us to think our own thoughts. He does not control our thoughts, even though He could. He even allows us to think that He is the evil one.

July

I remember times when my kids blamed me for something and were angry with me when I was not the one who caused the pain, or my decision was based on something I could see that they could not. It is the same way with God. He allows us to have our own thoughts, even if we believe a lie about Him. That is how much He loves us. He does not force us to trust Him or love Him. He lets it come from our own choice and our own thoughts.

The truth is, the only powers great enough to keep me from living out my kingdom inheritance here on earth are lies and deception. It is *not* the death of my daughter, or any other tragedy that I have experienced in my life. And in case you need to be reminded, believing a lie is just as powerful as believing the truth.

Whether we believe it or not, the truth is that we are secure in God and His blood covenant through Jesus. Even if we falter through life, even if we are angry with Him, He remains holding our hand, walking with us. In fact, I believe there are many times in my life He has just plain carried me when I was too wounded to walk.

Do not let the enemy take the greatest pain and darkness you have ever faced and turn it into a lie that God does not love you, or that He has turned His back on you. Don't let your feelings override the truth that He is with you in the darkness and will continue to be with you, because the truth always sets us free.

Reflection: The best way I know to get out of the enemy's sticky web of lies is to still your soul, quiet your own thoughts, and ask God to give you His thoughts. You need to be transformed - totally changed - by the renewing of your mind (Romans 12:2). Allow God's thoughts to speak softly to you in the depths of your being to set you free from the turmoil. Sit quietly in His presence, letting His thoughts reprogram your thinking.

If you are angry with Him, you may not want the truth to penetrate the lies of the enemy. Allow His love to break down that wall so that He can set you free from being chained to the darkness of your grief.

> *Don't give the slanderous accuser, the Devil,*
> *an opportunity to manipulate you!*
> *Ephesians 4:27 (TPT)*

July 25

I Miss Me

There are some people around us who want us to stop grieving, get over it and get back to being ourselves, but that is not going to happen. We will never be the same person we used to be, and our friends and family are not the only ones who miss the old us. *We* miss who we used to be.

Everything changes, and that includes who we spend time with. It is very rare for a pareavor to keep the same group of friends after child loss. Why? Because most people drift away (or just plain cut us off), and that adds to our hurt and makes us feel even more alone.

A couple of years ago, the Holy Spirit showed me something that I would like to share with you. I saw a man walking on a road with some friends. He was struggling, and when they came to a bench, the group waited for him as he sat down to rest. This happened a couple more times, but the third time, the group decided to go on without him, convinced that he would catch up with them later.

As the man was still sitting, another group came by and stopped. They invited him to join them and waited for him to be ready to continue. Each time the man had to rest again, they were happy to sit with him and keep him company. Soon the man realized that this new group of people were his true friends and the ones he wanted to continue traveling with, no longer feeling like he needed to catch up to the first group.

I think it is obvious from this "vision" that the ones who are the most willing to walk this journey with you are those who understand what it is like to lose a child from this earth. You may feel like you are just living

July

in a shell, waiting to die because you know the old you is gone and not coming back. You think life is not worth living anymore.

Other pareavors are not looking for the old you to return and are happy to show you that living a meaningful life is still possible as you learn how to live again in this new environment of child loss. Look for us and connect with us, so that we can walk this journey together.

Reflection: The question often becomes, "How do I connect with other pareavors to get this kind of support?" The most effective is going to be a local support group for grieving parents. Check with your hospitals, hospices and funerals homes and of course search the internet for anything close to you.

It is even more difficult to find a support group that is faith based. If you have not been able to find what you are looking for, consider starting your own. Mine started by just having a small group in my home, to talk about our kids and some of our struggles. Often, I would just find something in a book to read out loud and then we would talk about it.

I know of several moms who just get together on a regular basis to have lunch together. They meet at a restaurant or in each other's homes. There is no agenda, they just have a time of fellowship sharing their hearts, their struggles and their kids with each other.

Is God nudging you to meet with other pareavors? If so, it is because He knows they can be His arms of love around you in a tangible way. Do not put it off. If you are already connected, ask God to put a pareavor in your path who needs your group.

Therefore encourage and comfort one another and build up one another, just as you are doing.
1 Thessalonians 5:11 (AMP)

July 26

Our Identity

A very important benefit of Christianity is the tremendous sense of identity we have that comes from knowing Jesus Christ in a very personal way. But that identity can come crashing down around us after the death of our child, because we feel like God betrayed us.

It seems we only thought we knew who God was, and who we are in Him. In church, many of us have heard a lot about what it means to be "in Christ." But we don't hear nearly as often what it means that Christ is in us, and how to live from the revelation that God Himself, in all of His glory, is living inside us. We may know that in our heads, but do we really get what that means?

When Jesus died, His blood was sprinkled on the mercy seat in heaven once and for all, on our behalf. God's very presence no longer remained behind a curtain, which is why the veil was torn in two from top to bottom.

We are no longer separated from God by a curtain. Those who accept the work of the blood of Jesus are seen as righteous. Our spirits are in right standing with God and the very being of God dwells, or "tabernacles," inside us. WE are now the temple where God's Spirit rests!

That means we do not have to try to reach "out there" somewhere, trying to get ahold of God. When we believe in the price Jesus paid for us on the cross, His Spirit comes to live, or dwell, inside us. We only have to quiet ourselves and listen to Him from within our own spirit. I can live from a place of rest, knowing He is inside me and will comfort me deeply, guiding me with His wisdom and loving kindness.

Reflection: God has so much to say to you, and to me. Much of it has to do with who He is inside us, and how to live from that place. To go forward in the fullness of God's identity in us, we have to let go of our own identity, the one that has been shattered, by the death of our child.

It is not about what I do or don't do. It isn't about what has happened to me. It is all about who I am, with God Himself residing inside me. Take some time to allow God to speak to you from inside your own heart where He dwells. He knows what will bring you comfort and hope and wants to be with you in your pain.

> *You realize, don't you, that you are the temple*
> *of God, and God himself is present in you?*
> *1 Corinthians 3:16 (MSG)*

July 27

At His Feet

Yesterday I started talking about how we feel like we lose our identity after the death of our child, including who we are as a believer in Christ, especially when we feel like God betrayed us by allowing our child to die.

In the reflection, I said, "In order to go forward in the fullness of God's identity in us, we have to let go of our own identity; the one that has been shattered, by the death of our child." I want to share something that might help you with this.

Let me ask you something. When you "go to the feet of Jesus" where do you see yourself? At the cross? That is a place of forgiveness, which has already been given to us.

Jesus is not on the cross. He is sitting on a throne at the right hand of the Father (Hebrews 12:2). Ephesians 2:6 tells us that we are seated there spiritually as well, since we are in Christ. That is where my daughter and your child are as well. (If that is something you struggle with, be sure to turn to March 4th and read that entry right now. You can also listen to a podcast I did on that subject. Go to gpshope.org/podcast/18.)

When I started seeing myself at the feet of Jesus at the throne, which is where He is now, it put me in a totally different place of identity! His throne is a place of majesty, power, and authority. His throne is a place of glory, and my daughter is right there, seeing it all with her own eyes! That makes me want to live from that place of identity even more.

I do not want my identity to come from where Becca *was*, but where she is now. I don't want my identity to be "my daughter died," but "my daughter is alive!" I am guessing that is what you want as well.

Reflection: I understand that it takes time to get to that place. I know full well that we are each traveling our own journey of grief after the death of our child. I know it takes way longer than we want it to, and the darkness closes in on us, whether we want it to or not.

But I also know there is light on the other side of the darkness. I am here to poke a hole in that darkness:

- so that a glimmer of hope can get through.
- so that eventually you, too, can have one of the deepest, most fulfilling revelations possible on this earth.
- so that your identity is not based on earthly circumstances, but on who Christ is in you.

He is the hope (the confident expectation) of glory, living inside you. It is the same glory our children are experiencing in all its fullness.

Is there a song you like (or used to like) about His glory? Sing it to Him right now, picturing Him sitting on the throne while you are at His feet.

The Son is the dazzling radiance of God's splendor, the exact expression of God's true nature—his mirror image! He holds the universe together and expands it by the mighty power of his spoken word. He accomplished for us the complete cleansing of sins, and then took his seat on the highest throne at the right hand of the majestic One.
Hebrews 1:3 (TPT)

July 28

Shattered Dreams

After Becca died, I was on autopilot for the first couple of years, still ministering and traveling nationally and internationally. When the reality of the deep loss and the suffocating darkness of the grief eventually began to seep through, I could no longer function physically or emotionally and had to step down from that ministry.

I spent hours, weeks and months in isolation while trying to find other bereaved parents ahead of me on this path who could pull me back into a place of hope, light, and life again. Back then, almost everything I found (books, Facebook groups, etc.) was all darkness and hopelessness, telling me that I would never get out and that life would never be worth living again.

However...

- I refused to believe and come into agreement that the rest of my life here on earth would remain in darkness and not be worth living.
- I refused to remain emotionally crippled in a way that kept me from being part of the lives of my other children and growing clan of grandchildren.
- I knew God was not blindsided by Becca's death the way I had been.
- I did not believe the death of my daughter was where God reached His limit, and He was unable to pull me out of my black pit and back onto the path of life again.
- I knew there was a Seed of Hope living inside me.
- I knew there was still a calling on my life.
- I did not want to just survive in a shell waiting to die, but wanted to get to a point where I could thrive in my life once again.

I did not know how, or what my life would look like, but I did not want more death; I wanted life! After all, bringing life from death is God's specialty.

Not only did God come through with these things, but He went above and beyond what I ever thought I would do with my life even before Becca died, turning me into an author of multiple books, becoming a podcaster and starting what has become a national and international ministry for other bereaved parents!

Becoming an author has been a dream of mine since I was young. And this new dream of reaching as many pareavors as I can to offer hope and encouragement is a dream that is bigger than me, bigger than any one person. It is a God-sized dream.

Right now, wherever you are in this grief journey, I am guessing that just about anything would be a God-sized dream. That's okay. In fact, that is more than okay, because when it happens, you will know that God's hand is still on you.

Reflection: If you can't see any dreams for the future, my next question is, do you want to? If your answer is not really, or you aren't sure, I suggest you go back to the list of statements I made (refusing to believe my life was no longer worth living, knowing there was still a calling on my life, etc.), making them your own.

Say them out loud.

"I refuse to believe..."

"I refuse to remain..."

"I know there is..."

"I do not want to..."

Print them out and post them some place where you can see them, reminding yourself every day of the truth; truth that will bring a new level of freedom within the grief.

I am not saying these things will cause the pain to go away or put you on some fast-track of getting to the other side of the deepest darkness. But they can be a spark or a key, cracking open the door to light. And as you continue, that door will open further, revealing hope, dreams and purpose once again that goes beyond the death of your child.

When hope is crushed, the heart is crushed,
but a wish come true fills you with joy.
Proverbs 13:12 (GNT)

July 29

Changing the Why Question

We want to know why. "Why did this happen to my child?" "Why didn't God stop it?" "Why didn't I do something different to keep it from happening?" Are you getting any answers to those questions? I didn't think so.

When terrible things happen in our lives, we often want to know why. That is a normal question to ask, but how many times in the past have you had something happen that seemed bad or wrong, finding out later it was actually God at work, doing something needed that you could not see at the time?

One of the first times I remember that happening to me was when Dave and I first got married. There were so many college students coming out with computer degrees back then, that in our area it was next to impossible to get a job without experience. He was told to go to Chicago or another big city, get some experience, and then come back to our area.

Dave did not feel like that was what he was supposed to do. A local company finally hired him as their sole programmer and computer department. The difficult thing was that it was for a nonprofit company, and they did not pay much at all. I also had to work, and we were barely scrimping by.

What the company did though, was offer really good medical insurance as a benefit. We had no idea when Dave took that job how much more we would need the insurance than the money. Becca was diagnosed with cancer, had her leg amputated and went through nine months of chemo. The total cost was well over seven-hundred thousand dollars by the time it was all done, but only around $1,000 of that came out of our pocket!

When Dave first got hired, the salary offered to him was very disappointing and frustrating, but the Lord knew what He was doing when the door was opened for that job. God was not trying to back us into a corner or punishing us for something in our past. He was doing something *for* us that we could not see right away.

The question of why, hardly ever gets answered on this side of life, and continually asking why doesn't serve us well. The longer we don't get an answer, the more frustrated we can get, which can turn into anger and bitterness. You might as well admit it; even if He told you why, it probably would not seem like a good enough answer, and you would just argue with Him. It is probably time to let go of the "why?" and ask a better question.

Reflection: What is that better question? The question I have found to ask God instead is "How?" "How are you going to get me through this?" "How are you going to help me want to live again?" How are you *possibly* going to work something good out of something so horrible?"

I can hear God's answer. "I am glad you asked. Let me show you." God probably won't answer the question of why, but He will delight in answering the question of how. So go ahead. Start asking Him how, and do your best to leave the why for when you join your child and it will either make more sense, or it will no longer matter.

Come, see the glorious things God has done.
What marvelous miracles happen to his people!
Psalm 66:5 (TLB)

July 30

Did He Really?

I had something hit me full force this morning. It stunned me and left me in tears. It is something I have known my whole life, but for some reason, I had eyes to see the depth of what it means in a way I never have before.

I don't think I would have ever seen the magnitude of this, if I did not have a child die. The suffocating pain and darkness that came with her death is what makes this so clear, almost eleven years later.

As I type these words, I am praying that somehow, the Holy Spirit will give you the same deep revelation, so that you can realize the depth of this as well, and what it means to you, personally.

In past cultures, we know that child sacrifice was done to appease some sort of deity, or even to prove their loyalty to a tribe. I cannot even begin to imagine being willing to murder my child to HOPEFULLY make some god happy enough with me that my life would go okay, or to hope that some other tribe would honor their word to not hurt my people. Child sacrifice goes a step further than human sacrifice, because we know how important our children are to us and how much we love them. They are an extension of our very own being, so sacrificing one's own child proved how devout they were by giving up their own child.

For many years I have been so very thankful that I never lived in those times, or in any of those cultures. Even before Becca died, I just cannot picture myself (or anyone for that matter) being so connected to a higher being that I would murder my child for my own gain. I especially cannot ever imagine doing that after Becca died, knowing how deep the pain is. It makes me sick to my stomach just thinking about it!

But people have done that for thousands of years. Fortunately, it is not very common in today's world to sacrifice one's own child, but there are still countries, such as Uganda, where abducting a child for sacrificing is still happening.

Why am I painting such a dark and bleak picture. Isn't this supposed to be a book of hope?

Because I realized that Jehovah God, OUR God, does not require us to sacrifice our children to Him. Instead, He did the exact opposite. Instead of asking us to sacrifice our child to prove ourselves to Him, He sacrificed His child to prove Himself to us!

Let that sink in... to prove how deep His love and commitment to us is, He sent His own son down here on earth to be a sacrifice on our behalf. When I look at it this way, I have a hard time wrapping my head around this. He was willing to go through the pain of watching His own son die a torturous death, as a sacrifice offered for me... for YOU... for each one of our children.

What an amazing God He truly is!

Reflection: Would you ever consider offering your child to be a sacrifice to prove how committed you are to something or someone? To show how deeply you love them... that they are just as important to you as your own child? Nope! Me either!

But that is what God did for us. There is nothing greater God could have done, to prove His love for us than to sacrifice His child for you and for me. He allowed His child to take our place on the altar, to pay the price for our sins, both past, present and future. His child took on all of our guilt and shame when God sacrificed Him for us!

If that does not prove how much God loves you and your child, I don't think anything will. Even if you don't "feel" the depth of this and what it means, I urge you to tell Him thank you. After all, it is this same sacrifice that also makes a way for us to be with our children again.

> *For God has proved his love by giving us his greatest treasure, the gift of his Son. And since God freely offered him up as the sacrifice for us all, he certainly won't withhold from us anything else he has to give.*
> *Romans 8:32 (TPT)*

July 31

Together Forever

There was beauty here until you left, but now it's hard to find,
Especially through all the tears I cry.
But I know that where you are there is beauty beyond words.
And I am glad for you, at least I try.

There is just a bridge between us, but the toll is very high.
The only way to cross it is to die.
You went on ahead, there was no choice on when.
And I feel left alone to wonder why.

A lifetime here is not enough for us to be together,
So God has made a way for it to be forever.
But until that day comes
I won't make it through by letting go.
But holding on tight to the memories I treasure.
This is not good-by, I'll see you later.

When it's time for me to pay the toll and cross that same old bridge
Those left behind may wonder why.
But you and I will both be there together forever.
And when it is their turn to cross, one-by-one they'll come join us,
With no more asking why.
And finally, we'll all be there together forever.

A lifetime here is not enough for us to be together,
So God has made a way for it to be forever.
But until that day comes
I won't make it through by letting go.
But holding on tight to the memories I treasure.
This is not goodbye; I'll see you later.

And you and I will both be there together forever.

(Written and copyrighted by Laura Diehl)

Reflections of Hope

Reflection: Isn't that a wonderful thought? God knew that even if we left this earth before our child did, that our time here with our son or daughter, and those we love, would not be enough, so He made a way for us to be together forever! That is how good He is and how much He loves you and your child.

Right now, get out a pen and paper, and write down some of the thoughts you had as you read through the words of the song. Just write three or four lines, putting your heart onto paper. Then sing what you wrote. Yes, that is what I said. Sing those words out! It does not have to sound good. You are the only one who will hear it. Just put notes to your words, letting it sink in and bring a bit of healing to your soul.

> *Christian brothers, we want you to know for sure about those who have died. You have no reason to have sorrow as those who have no hope. Then, those of us who are still living here on earth will be gathered together with them in the clouds. We will meet the Lord in the sky and be with Him forever. Because of this, comfort each other with these words.*
> *1 Thessalonians 4:13, 17-18 (NLV)*

August

August 1

Something You Can Count On

Zephaniah 3:17 has been one of my favorite verses for many years. It tells us that God is in the midst of us, that He renews us in His love and that He actually rejoices and dances over us with singing, which is an amazing thought to me.

I have come to realize that God is not just excited about me when I'm happy, or only when I am excited about Him. There are no conditions or limitations to His excitement over me. As a matter of fact, my Bible tells me that He is even closer to me when I am bruised and broken and have a crushed spirit (Psalm 34:18).

Many Christians have been taught that God has a wonderful plan for their lives. We think that means our life is going to be great—full of fun, laughter, sunshine—and nothing bad will ever touch us. But that is man's interpretation.

Jesus warned that we will have hard times but promised that He will be with us to help us through them. He said those who mourn will be comforted (not that we will never mourn). He said we will always have the poor with us (He did not end poverty at that time). These are the kinds of things the Holy Spirit will use the most, to draw us closer to Himself and to have the opportunity to know Him more intimately than we ever knew was possible. And He will bring us to a place of being victorious if we let Him.

God's love for us is the one stable thing that we can count on in the life we are living here on this earth. Not only does He love you, but He is right smack dab in the middle of your grief with you, and He is excited about you, knowing your future and the good things He still has for you.

He is the foundation we have built our lives on. Most foundations of a building are unable to be seen. That does not mean it's not there. A building might fall, but the foundation remains. Our lives may have fallen apart, but the foundation of Christ is still there. We may not believe it, we may not be able to see it or feel it, but He is still there, firm and steady.

Reflection: God does have a plan for your life. "For I know the plans I have for you, declares the Lord...to give you a future and a hope." Jeremiah 29:11. One translation says, "I have plans to give you a future filled with hope."

Your future is full of hope. It can also be filled with wonder and amazement at the goodness and faithfulness of God, through both the incredible blessings and the painful tragedies because through both, we have the opportunity to see His powerful hand at work in our lives.

He is your anchor, your rock, your firm foundation. He is also a very present help in time of trouble and the giver of hope. Ask Him to open your eyes to see those things in a very real way. And not only can you have hope in your future here on earth, the most truly wonderful part happens when we leave this sinful world and move to eternity with Jesus. And just think, as a side note, we have someone very dear and close to us who has beat us there.

My body and my heart may grow weak. God, you give strength to my heart. You are everything I will ever need.
Psalm 73:26 (NIRV)

August 2

Like A Fish Out of Water

I'll bet you are a somewhat like me; when your child died, you felt like a "fish out of water" as the expression goes.

I recently got to see a similar visual, but it was a swan out of the water. I had no idea how hard it is for a swan to walk. It was almost painful to watch the swan try so hard to put one foot down and then the other, to maneuver its big body on those two small legs and feet. But once that swan was in the water, it was a totally different picture. The beautiful swan was now in its element and glided gracefully across the pond.

It made me think of us as humans. We also function so much better in our God-created element.

We feel like we were violently ripped out of our element when our child died. It is so important to eventually figure out what our new element is that we can begin to flow in. Hint: it usually has something to do with keeping our child's memory alive in a way that honors them and helps others, like my friends:

- Connie is carrying on what her son started with "traveling Bibles" being left for people to find, record where they found it, write a special message inside and place it somewhere else for the next person to find.
- Janice, who wrote a memoir book about her daughter Dawn's battle with cancer, and the lessons Dawn taught others as she battled for her life here on earth.
- Marcella developed the Comfort Cub for infant and pregnancy loss after her son lived for a few minutes after birth. It is now also being used for those in trauma and other situations where comfort is needed.

Most parents do not start something as big as what is listed above. There is usually something local they are drawn to in a way that helps people in their own community that they never paid much attention to before the death of their child. *Anything* you can do for others that makes you feel less like a "fish out of water" is a good thing.

Reflection: After your child's death left you so deeply wounded, have you been able to find yourself getting comfortable in new element that makes life a bit easier? If you haven't yet, that's okay. We are all on individual timetables. When you are ready, either God will begin to reveal something to you, or you may find yourself just stepping into it so naturally that you do not even realize it is happening.

And some day, instead of being like that swan, walking clumsily across the grass, you will find yourself gliding across the water. But even when that happens, it is good to remember that we will *all* still occasionally climb out of the water and struggle walking through the grass.

For I am about to do something new. See, I have already begun! Do you not see it? I will make a pathway through the wilderness. I will create rivers in the dry wasteland.
Isaiah 43:19 (NLT)

August 3

Music is a Key

Music is a pathway to the soul. That is something I learned as a teenager.

In high school, I started occasionally turning my radio from the local Christian station to a local rock one, and eventually that was pretty much all I listened to. As an impressionable youngster (I didn't think so at the time), it made me weak enough to give in to what I knew to be wrong, and I became pregnant the summer out of high school (which caused me to give back scholarships and be unable to attend a Christian college that I had been accepted into).

God redeemed everything greatly, in His wonderful grace! But it is something I can look back on, knowing that the music I consistently listen to can change how I view life. I am not judging anyone in what they listen to. I still enjoy turning the station occasionally and will play songs that are "non-Christian" that speak to my soul (or my mood). But I am still very aware of how music affects my soul, and therefore my spirit.

I had another dose of that this morning. I stumbled on a song that broke something in me, bringing me a new level of freedom in this unwanted journey that we have all found ourselves on. One song led to another, and a good hour later, I felt like I could take on the world with God by my side!

I want to encourage you to pay attention to the music you are feeding your soul with. God designed music to move us, to change us, to uplift and encourage us. If it is not doing that, then maybe you need to change your "station" and listen to those songs that you have been avoiding, knowing how they used to pull you up when you needed encouragement from Him.

For some of us, worshiping God after the death of our child seems impossible. However, there are plenty of songs you can listen to that will give you hope, reminding you that God is always with you through the dark times in this world; songs that will move you toward Him in your pain and confusion, allowing the Holy Spirit to give the desperately needed comfort you need, placing you on a path of healing.

Reflection: I highly suggest making a playlist of songs that you can turn on when needed and just let them play through. I have several playlists with different topics, such as peace, trust and hope. As a matter of fact, I have made my YouTube list of *Songs of Hope* public, in case you want to check it out.

I also have a list of songs about heaven. It reminds me that Becca is in a good place, making me feel closer to her, thinking about what she is seeing and experiencing. These songs also remind me that I will be there with her someday, because God has the final word!

Another powerful topic is resurrection power. I sobbed listening to David Phelps version of *I've Just Seen Jesus* thinking of how Becca must have felt when she saw Jesus, and how some day that will be me, joining her. *We Shall Behold Him* and *He's Alive* are a couple more really good ones with the same singer.

Yes, you may cry. A LOT. But they are healing tears, and just may cause some needed shackles to drop off.

And whenever the tormenting spirit from God troubled Saul, David would play the harp. Then Saul would feel better, and the tormenting spirit would go away.
I Samuel 16:23 (NLT)

August 4

Guilt is Not Necessary

Sometimes it helps to know that other pareavors have the same struggles. Here are some of those things we all seem to struggle with at times:

- Having a hard time remembering people's names – both those we just met and even acquaintances before our child passed.
- Not being able to follow through with responding to text messages, emails, or answering phone calls.
- How much it hurts when we see people around us doing things with their family, or even hearing them talk about it.
- Not wanting to go out with others when you used to enjoy it.
- The reality of our child's younger siblings become the same age, and then older, than our child who died.

Please don't feel guilty if you can relate to any of these, or something similar along these lines. It is normal to struggle with emotions and other things we never had issues with before. You are not a terrible person. You are a pareavor – a parent who has been robbed of your child from this earth. You have been through a trauma and are in recovery.

It is also good to know that other pareavors have not remained stuck in the same places you may be struggling in. Some of the areas many of us have been able to get unstuck are:

- No longer feeling guilty that I laughed or enjoyed something.
- Realizing that it is okay that my child was not the first thought on my mind when I woke up.
- Discovering things in my life that I can still appreciate and be thankful for.
- Figuring out that it is not betraying my child by learning how to live again without them here with me.
- Knowing that even though life is very different now, it can still be good.

As you move into these same things, you do not need to feel guilty. You have enough to deal with, without adding guilt to the mix. It's okay to let it go. I give you permission. In fact, I urge you to say goodbye to guilt so that you can move forward much easier in the needed healing process.

Reflection: Many of us go through our day just wanting it to be over, hoping tomorrow will be better. I know of someone who lost three children and came to realize in doing that, she was letting her days slip away in a wasteful way. She made a conscious decision to learn how to live again saying, "It's our personal choice, as life stops for no one."

I know of another mom who felt guilty the first day she did not feel crushing heartbreak. But then she remembered that her daughter was full of laughter and life and light. This mom chose to begin to find ways to fill her days with those things.

When we do choose to move toward a measure of healing, desiring to bring laughter and joy into our lives once again, it is hard work. It is a battle. It can be exhausting. Choosing to focus on the blessings we have, and leaning into the sweet, instead of the bitter, can be extremely difficult.

But it can be done, and it is so very worth it! Even if you are not ready to make that choice right now (or don't think it is possible for you like it was for others), at least tell yourself and God that you want to get to that place.

> *And so now, I entrust you into God's hands and the message*
> *of his grace, which is all that you need to become strong.*
> Acts 20:32 (TPT)

August 5

He Still Lives in You

God is not just "out there" somewhere. He is living and dwelling inside us. He does not come and go, based on how we feel. The Spirit of the

August

Living God who created the entire universe does not just surround us, He is *in* you and He is *in* me!

Because I have invited Jesus to be Lord of my life, the Spirit of God dwells in me, which also means the Seed of Hope is in me. It is the same for you. We do not have to wait for God to come to us from somewhere out there. We can quiet ourselves and listen to His still small voice from inside us, speaking peace, bringing comfort. Whatever we need, He is already inside us to meet that need, including what we need to water that seed of hope to make it grow.

A little over a year after Becca died, in one of those times when I became still to hear God talk from His place of living inside me, I heard Him speak to me about the way I was thinking. I wrote down in my journal what I heard Him say:

Let's go back to perspective. You have been stuck on how difficult your life has been. I want you to spend some time meditating on the good, on the blessings, on the wonderful and joyful things. Let's "reprogram" you and your thought process!

Our thoughts are so very dark when our child dies. All we can think about is the child who is no longer here with us, and everything that goes with it. We try to make sense of it and want answers. But to get through the suffocating darkness and be able to live again, we cannot lean on our own understanding.

If you want to go forward with peace in your heart (that runs next to the pain), then you will have to acknowledge that He is God, and you are not. His ways and His thoughts are so much higher than ours. In the stillness of listening to His voice inside you, God probably won't answer the question "Why?" while you are here on earth, but He wants to direct your path into *how* you can still have a life of purpose.

Reflection: Believing a lie is just as powerful as believing the truth and speaking out those beliefs will make our thoughts even more solid, whether it is the lies, or the truth. Just because you have thoughts or feelings about something, no matter how strong, does not mean they are necessarily based on the truth.

Proverbs 3:5-6 tells us that God will direct your path. He will show you the way out of the darkness and back into a place of light. He will guide you from a place of hopelessness to a place of hope. He has not abandoned you. He still lives inside you. He is, and He has everything that you need.

Seek for the truth in your thoughts and perspective, because the truth sets us free from being chained to the darkness of our grief. Let Him show you the way out, by showing you more of Himself, as He lives inside you.

> *Trust in the Lord completely, and do not rely on your own opinions. With all your heart rely on him to guide you, and he will lead you in every decision you make. Become intimate with him in whatever you do, and he will lead you wherever you go.*
>
> Proverbs 3:5-6 (TPT)

August 6

A Sacred Moment

I am not sure if you know who Mitch Carmody is, but for many years he was one of the most known and sought-after speakers in the world of bereaved parents, having given his life to those who are grieving, after the loss of his nine-year-old son, over thirty years ago. (He has now "retired" from most of his traveling and speaking.)

A few years ago, Mitch posted a video. The only way I can describe it is that he allowed us to enter a sacred moment in time for him and his wife. They had just signed the papers to sell their farm that they had lived on for over two decades and were moving to another state. Together, they decided it was time. After thirty years of still having many of their son, Kelly's, possessions in a large trunk, they pulled out a few items and then burned the entire trunk with most of the items still inside

August

(which included the blanket he died in, and all the condolence cards received) instead of taking all these mementos with them.

It made me so thankful to have people like this ahead of us. Those who are willing to let us know things like:

- It is okay if you still have your child's room the same way, years later.
- It is normal to hang on to as much as we can of our child who is no longer with us on earth for years and years and years.
- There is no timeline and no right or wrong way to grieve and remember our children.

Those ahead of us also help reassure us that no matter what we save or don't save of the items that belonged to our children, or if we move away from the cemetery our child is buried in, that we will *always* carry our children deeply in our hearts. Nothing will ever be able to change that.

So, I just want to assure you that your heart will tell you when (or if) it is time to enter into this same kind of sacred moment. And to also assure you that when it comes (and I understand that sometimes that decision is made for us, such as moving and having to pack up their bedroom, or start giving away their things to make room for a growing family) that it does not mean you are moving on without your son or daughter, or that you are leaving your child behind. It just means you are stepping into another level of healing, because you know *that you know,* **that you know** your child is still with you, and the physical mementos are not as needed as they were before.

Many of us get pressured from family and friends that it is not healthy to leave things the same way for so long, or to hang on to so many of our child's belongings. But how could they possibly be the judge of that since they have never lost a child? Your own soul, and the Holy Spirit in you, will know when it is the right time to have that sacred moment.

Reflection: Here is a quote from Mitch.

> *In grief we stand on the edge of darkness, at times afraid to take that next step...having faith is knowing that we shall find something firm to stand on to, or we will be taught how to*

> fly... We live in one sphere of existence, our loved ones who have died in another but with faith, the desire and undying love we can connect at the seam where our worlds meet. Dreams may die, but their spirit does not, nor does their memory.
>
> We substantiate our loved one's life, by how we live ours.

I love how he says we will either find something firm to stand on to, or we will be taught how to fly. All of us have things from our children that we are just not ready to part with. That is okay. Just ask for the Holy Spirit's help so that when it is time, you have the faith needed to know that you will be okay. You will still have the memory of your child with or without so many of their belongings.

> *Don't expect anyone else to fully understand both the bitterness and the joys of all you experience in your life.*
> *Proverbs 14:10 (TPT)*

August 7

If Only...

We can learn how to be better or stronger by looking back at past mistakes, but living with regrets is not something God has for us. God is not one who looks back. He is always in our now and wants to help us to look toward the future with hope.

We need to realize that God knows each one of our hearts and beating yourself up with thoughts like, "If only I had known I would have..." or "I should have..." only fills you with painful laments that will not allow you to have any kind of peace or hope.

You did the best you could at the time with the knowledge you had. How do I know that? Because as a parent, that is what we do for our children. We can all look back and see now what we may not have been

August

able to see at the time. But living in a state of regret or wishing you had done something differently does not change anything. It certainly does not bring our child back.

I can tell you as a parent of five adult children that I look back with regret at the many mistakes I made with all of them. I used to almost put myself on the witness stand and accuse myself of how terrible a parent I was, playing scenes in my mind of moments I did not handle something in a calm or Godly way.

When our child dies, our moments of bad parenting are amplified, because now we cannot tell our child how sorry we are for when we messed up. We tend to do that as a punishment to ourselves. We feel we deserve to remain miserable because we blame ourselves for not being able to do more or be more.

If you had a friend who was beating themselves up because of mistakes they made as a parent, what would you tell them? That they are right? That they need to wallow in it and make sure they stay there in that place as a punishment? Of course not! Then why do we do that to ourselves?

It is easy to see that kind of nonsense with someone else, but much harder to see it in ourselves, isn't it? So let *me* tell you, STOP IT! You are not to blame for what the enemy brought to this world and the way it affected your child, you and your family. Let yourself off the hook, just like you would for someone else.

Our thoughts of blame and self-condemnation will continue to torment us, until at some point, we let them go, or we will forever be brought to our knees from the bullying pain these thoughts bring. What is done is done. What is gone is gone. We may not be able to have what the world calls "closure" to the death of our child, but there can and should be closure to our regrets and "if onlys."

Reflection: This is another area where we need to learn how to change our thoughts. Instead of dwelling on the difficult moments of parenting, try thinking about the good times; those moments of laughter and being in awe of being the parent of your child. You might also want to ask the Holy Spirit to lead you to a scripture to meditate on to pull you up when the "if onlys" start sucking you under.

I am pretty sure your child has already forgiven you and released you from all of these things. And when you join him or her, those regrets will be totally wiped away forever. Why wait until then? Release yourself from them right now.

> *Brothers and sisters, I know that I still have a long way to go. But there is one thing I do: I forget what is in the past and try as hard as I can to reach the goal before me. I keep running hard toward the finish line to get the prize that is mine because God has called me through Christ Jesus to life up there in heaven.*
> *Philippians 3:13-14 (ERV)*

August 8
Our Kids are Safe

Much of this book was written during the COVID19 epidemic. During the height of it, one day while brushing my teeth, it suddenly hit me that Becca does not have to deal with *any* of this! She would have been at high risk and probably struggled with the mask mandate. She was claustrophobic, plus her lungs would often fill with fluid because of the heart issues, and the mask would have made it even harder to breathe. I am sure I would have been constantly fighting worry and fear for her at a whole new level.

Let me say here that if you lost your child during the shut-down, I am really sorry. I have heard some gut-wrenching stories from parents who either could not be there with their child when he or she passed, or were unable to have a funeral/memorial service with friends and family. My heart goes out to you!

I know we would all much rather have our children here with us. But in the midst of something like a pandemic virus that affects the entire world, there is one area where we can be at rest. Our children who are not on this earth with us are now safe from any kind of dangerous disease or virus that can quickly spread like COVID19. That is something we can be thankful for, even in the middle of the terrible pain of missing them.

August

Jesus is the Alpha and Omega, the beginning and the end. He has the final word on everything. And we need to remind ourselves that this world is only our temporary residence. Anything that happens here is not final. It is just part of the journey (an extremely painful journey for those of us who have experienced child loss) and our kids have transferred out of this falling-apart world ahead of us.

I know we would rather be the ones gone, with our children continuing to live out their lives here on earth. But since that is not what happened, we can at least be thankful they have been spared any further agony of the fall-out of this sinful and decaying world.

Reflection: We don't know the details of what the future holds, but we do know Jesus told us that things are going to get pretty bad before He returns.

For me, personally, when I am honest with myself, I realize it is pretty selfish of me to insist that I should have been in heaven first, while Becca remains here trying to navigate the difficulties of this world. We tend to think about the good life experiences our children are missing like not graduating, or not getting married or not watching their own children grow up, or not having grandchildren. It isn't very often we think about the bad, horrible and traumatic things they will not experience.

I am not saying it is wrong to grieve those things, wishing our children had been able to experience them. Please do not feel guilty for hurting (or even being angry) about it. We *need* to work through that.

It is all in our perspective. While I still miss Becca deeply, I have learned to ask myself, "Why would I want her here instead of there? Especially when things are going to continue to get worse." Please take some time to consider the fact that in the place of missing those earthly experiences, our children are having an even better experience. They are in a glorious place, full of love, light, no worries, no cares, no sickness and no more death. Take a minute to picture your child loving life there, knowing that he or she is missing out on the destruction of this world.

> *For see, I am creating new heavens and a new earth—so wonderful that no one will even think about the old ones anymore.*
> *Isaiah 65:17 (TLB)*

August 9

We Get It...

Those around us who have never walked in our shoes have a hard time understanding *many* things that still affect us deeply after the death of our child. Those who have lost a child from this earth are the ones who will understand.

We change when our child dies, not just emotionally, but it takes a toll on you physically.

We get it...

The death of your child leaves a gaping hole that cannot ever be filled.

We get it...

It is bound to affect one's marriage. Whether it strengthens the marriage, or tears it apart, the death of your child cannot help but affect the love-of-your-life relationship that you do day-to-day life with.

We get it...

I have two plots picked out for Dave and myself as close to Becca as I can get. If you are like me, you want to be close to your children in life or death, even if you know it is just his or her body (whether buried or ashes).

We get it...

You need to know that the life of your child mattered and somehow still affects other lives for the better. Some of you connect to a cause, based on how your child died. Others put scholarship funds in place, write books or start organizations. You might have something permanently placed in a public venue in your child's name. You are determined that your child's life and legacy will live on.

We get it...

Crowds make you uncomfortable. You do not feel like being social and do not want to just hang out with friends.

We get it...

August

Things you used to enjoy no longer hold your interest.

We get it...

Life will never be the same. You will never be the same.

We get it...

Reflection: After the first few years of suffocating darkness and painful grief, you can turn a corner and start to smile at the memories and the joy your child brought into your life. But you will never be beyond shedding fresh tears for the deep pain of missing your child.

We get it...

You thought, "Others might be able to get to that place, but I never will."

We get it...

It affects your relationship with God. Some of you immediately drew your strength from Him, and some of you will do so only after your anger gets you nowhere and you turn to Him in desperation. The death of your child can't help but affect your relationship with God.

We get it...

Not only do we get it, but God gets it. Give yourself grace to be wherever you are in this journey in your relationship with Him. I am pretty sure that God is giving more grace to you than you are giving to yourself. Take a moment and rest in knowing that He is okay with your confusing thoughts and swirling emotions. Tell yourself that you will make it. No matter how you feel right now, somehow, you will learn how to live life the way the rest of us have, because we get it, and we made it.

Lord, you know the hopes of the helpless.
Surely you will hear their cries and comfort them.
Psalm 10:17 (NLT)

August 10

Grief Recovery?

Several years ago, in my searching for how to deal with my grief from my daughter's death, I came across an article called "Grief Recovery." As I started reading it, I discovered it was for any kind of loss including jobs, moving, pet loss, death, divorce (or any kind of breakup), starting school, etc.

It talked about how recovery is when we can have memories without the pain. I had a hard time reading it without getting angry. It is just impossible to compare grieving the death of a child to all these other things. I'm not saying those things are not painful and that there is not a level of grief involved, but this article was basically saying after you grieve the right way, you can move on with life and put the past behind you.

I might be able to move forward, but it is not by putting the death of Becca behind me! She will always be in front of me. Our children are our legacy. They are supposed to keep going when we leave this earth. Even if she is not with me anymore, I cannot leave her in my past and go on without her.

The things that trigger us and remind us of our loss can come unexpectedly out of nowhere and bring back the memory, accompanied by intense unwanted pain once again.

Grief recovery for a bereaved parent? No, not really. Yes, it is possible to get to the point where we can have memories without the pain. It happens gradually, but for the rest of our lives there will be times where the pain returns, because all we have are the memories of our child. The goal is to have that happen less and less, but it is naïve to think we will get to the point where we no longer feel pain within the memories and therefore have "recovered," as the article I read suggested.

Like someone with an amputation, we will never fully recover. But we *can* eventually learn how to live around it, adapting our life to that part of us missing, and we *can* eventually have many memories that bring a smile to our hearts instead of stabbing pain.

Reflection: Have you gotten to that place yet, where a memory of your child pops up and there is a warm, happy feeling inside instead of pain and tears? Maybe a smile started to form, but then it was immediately replaced by the familiar sting of loss.

Many of us feel like if the memories do not come with pain, it means we are starting to forget our child. Nothing could be further from the truth! That will never ever happen. I want to ask you to try something. Let's practice. Think of a fond memory with your child, and instead of leaning into the loss, lean into the memory itself. Let the warmth and fun into a piece of your heart, even if for only two or three seconds.

Every once in a while, try it again. You will find at some point that it becomes easier. No, you won't ever fully "recover," but you can get to the point where those memories hurt less often, until the hurt only happens occasionally instead of the other way around.

Honor me by trusting in me in your day of trouble.
Cry aloud to me, and I will be there to rescue you.
Psalm 50:15 (TPT)

August 11

Already Thinking About the Holidays?

At this point in the year, we can already be starting to think about the upcoming holidays. Even though it is still months away, we can begin wondering how it will be for me this year and what I will do this time around. To everyone else, holidays might seem like a long way off yet, but not for many of us. It can be especially daunting if your child's birthday and/or death date falls during that time.

Seeing holiday decorations in stores can cause a stab in our hearts now, instead of the fun it used to be. Just getting invited to a holiday event can feel like a slap-in-the-face reminder that your child is not here; that he or she will not be part of something they should have been right in the middle of.

What should you do when the invitations to these events start coming your way? Sometimes, especially those first two or three years, we need to graciously decline. I recommend doing your best to let those hosting/attending know that your absence is because you are thinking about *them*. If you think it might help, write a note to the host, like the following, and if appropriate, give her permission to read it to the group at some point.

It may seem unreasonable to you that I am still in such deep grief. The fact is, I am, and I can already tell that this (name of event) will be what I call a "grief trigger," causing me to miss (child's name) in such a very painful way that I won't be able to just pretend that I am fine. Since I do not want to detract from or dampen the joy of this special time, please excuse me. Thank you for extending that needed grace. I love you and will be thinking of you.

The other thing is to just plain go away for a period of time during a difficult holiday. I know *many* families who do this. They plan a vacation or a get-away during their worst part of the holidays. (Wouldn't it be nice if we could go away for the entire last two or three months, and not come back until sometime in January?)

There is a third option for some of the events, which is to ask if your child can be included in some way at the holiday party or event. (When you get to November 6th, you will find a list of suggestions.) Knowing that your child will be acknowledged in some way helps bring a healing comfort in the midst of the pain to know others miss them too and have not forgotten him or her.

Will there be tears? Probably, but doing something like this can give a sense of relief, as it gives you the needed grace and permission to miss your child. Plus, I don't much care anymore if I cry in front of others. I know they are tears of a love that will never be quenched until I am with my daughter again, and I don't care if people around me understand that or not.

Reflection: On a very practical note, our bodies affect us more than we often realize. If our bodies are out of whack, our emotions will be even more out of whack. So, if you are attending an event that will be difficult, make sure leading up to it that you make yourself get plenty of rest/sleep, eat healthy and drink plenty of water to avoid the myriad effects of dehydration.

As a final word, do *not* let others who have never lost a child put a burden of guilt on you! Be sure to take some time to release yourself of any guilt for not attending functions that are too difficult, *no matter how long ago the loss has been.* You do not need to carry unnecessary guilt on top of your grief!

> *Blessed be the Lord, who daily bears us up; God is our salvation.*
> *Psalm 68:19 (ESV)*

August 12

Finding the Real Us

Growing up, one of my favorite stories was *The Velveteen Rabbit*. In fact, I named one of my own stuffed bunnies Velveteen, and would often sleep with it at night.

In case you are not familiar with the story, this little stuffed bunny with velveteen fur becomes a boy's favorite toy, which he plays with, talks to, and cuddles with each night. The stuffed bunny thinks he is real, because when the nanny complains that the boy is making too much fuss over a toy, the boy tells her it is because his little bunny is real.

Eventually, the boy becomes sick with scarlet fever, and the well-worn and much-loved bunny is taken with the bedding to be burned. A real tear trickles down the face of the bunny, which immediately grows a flower with a fairy in it. Because the bunny was so loved and was real to the boy, she turns the velveteen rabbit into a real live bunny, to go live with the other rabbits in the woods.

Let me share an exchange in the nursery between the wise old Skin Horse and the Rabbit.

> "What is REAL?" asked the Rabbit one day...
>
> "Real isn't how you are made," said the Skin Horse. "It's a thing that happens to you... It doesn't happen all at once. You become. It takes a long time... Generally, by the time you are Real, most of your hair has been loved off, and your eyes drop out and you get loose in the joints and very shabby. But these things don't matter at all, because once you are Real, you can't be ugly, except to people who don't understand." (*The Velveteen Rabbit* by Marjorie Williams)

You might already see that there are several similarities in this story, to our journey as a pareavor.

First, it reminds me that working through our grief is a process. As the Skin Horse said, *It doesn't happen all at once...It takes a long time."* It takes years, as a matter of fact.

One day, the stuffed rabbit was on the ground while his boy played. Several rabbits discovered him as they came out of the woods.

> *"He hasn't got any hind legs! He doesn't smell right!"* the wild rabbit exclaimed, jumping backwards. *"He isn't a rabbit at all! He isn't real!"*

I don't know about you, but many of us feel like the people around us just don't get it. They do not validate our loss, because we are so different than they are. They hop away and leave us, not understanding why we are the way we are.

The Velveteen Rabbit is also a story of hope. He went from a place of devastation and being thrown away as useless, to becoming real. I certainly felt devastated and totally useless. I felt like my soul died when my daughter died. But I did not stay that way and you won't either.

Who would have thought that a popular children's story would parallel our journey as a bereaved parent?

Reflection: *The Velveteen Rabbit* is a story of going from being ugly to being real. As I came out of the darkness and back into a place of hope and light, I began to see both myself and others differently, along with a depth I did not have before. It was almost like I went from being who I was, thinking I was "real," to being who I am now, on the other side of the suffocating darkness after Becca's death.

To become "real," like the velveteen Rabbit, we are being taken through a very ugly place. We may feel like we have been left in the burn pile, seeing no hope of surviving. But as our tears spill out as liquid love, God is at work. He will not leave you in that place. He wants to make you alive in a new way. Give Him permission to do so, and remember, it won't happen suddenly. It takes much longer than we want it to, but it will happen.

For the Lord is the Spirit, and wherever the Spirit of the Lord is, there is freedom. So all of us who have had that veil removed can see and reflect the glory of the Lord. And the Lord--who is the Spirit--makes us more and more like him as we are changed into his glorious image.
2 Corinthians 3:17-18 (NLT)

August 13

A Great Gift

Yesterday, I shared about a favorite childhood story, *The Velveteen Rabbit*, with some of the similarities from it to our journey as pareavors. I want to share one more thing with you. The book ends with the boy playing outside the following spring, seeing a rabbit that looks very much like his stuffed bunny that was destroyed.

> *But he never knew that it really was his own Bunny, come back to look at the child who had first helped him to be Real.*

Our children gave us a great gift. The gift to become truly real. I know so many parents who are much further on this journey than I am, who have said they would not want to go back to being the person they were before their child died.

Why would they say that?

Because our child changed us. Both their life and their death.

We tend to look at how dark our life became after our child's departure, but there are also ways we have grown and are growing (or will grow), *because* of our brokenness. For me, I tend to not fret over the smaller things as much as I used to. I am much more aware of the present moment, knowing that is really all I have. My compassion for those who are hurting is way more than it ever used to be.

And because Becca had life, there are things she did that taught me something or showed me the way to being a better person, such as watching how she had a way of accepting everyone (whether she agreed with them in life choices and opinions or not) and how she was able to bring so much laughter while she was deathly ill her last 18 months. Watching Becca live life with only one leg and not letting it limit her, gives me motivation to push through my own difficulties instead of giving in to the obstacles that come my way.

How about you? Some of you may not have gotten to this point yet, because your child's departure is still too fresh and your grief is still very dark and deep, but is there something you like better about yourself now since your child died? Is it easier to let go of toxic relationships? Are you more aware of what is really important in your life now? Are you now easily able to say "no" when people ask you to do something, when before you always said "yes?" Do you no longer feel guilty about putting your own needs first?

If you can't see anything yet, it does not mean it won't or has not happened. It just means you can't see it yet.

Reflection: Here is another thought. We often talk about how we are forever changed because our child died, but I want to ask: *How are you different now because your child LIVED?* What are the new lenses your child's life gave you, helping you to see the world with a different view than you had before?

What did your child's life teach you? As the wise old Skin Horse said: *Once you become real, you can never become ugly again.*

The life that pleases me is a life lived in the gratitude of grace, always choosing to walk with me in what is right. This is the sacrifice I desire

from you. If you do this, more of my salvation will unfold for you.
Psalm 50:23 (TPT)

August 14
Changing Your Thoughts

The world is so very different from when I grew up, and I am sure you can say the same thing. Respect and honesty were part of our culture. It was much safer and not full of division and violence like it is now. It seemed like diseases and viruses were not running as rampant as they are now.

These days and times of uncertainty did not take God by surprise. He cannot be caught off guard, because He sees and knows everything, from the beginning of creation all the way to when He creates a new heaven and a new earth.

Which means the death of our child did not blindside God. In His eyes, we still have a life to live. He has a plan for us, and believe it or not, it is a good plan. Does it seem next to impossible to believe that? How can a good plan for our future be one that is without our child in it? Or one with such bad things happening around the world?

I had to learn the reality of the truth that my plans are not God's plans. His ways are not my ways. His thoughts are not my thoughts. I have grown into a deeper faith in how awesomely powerful my God is. That He really can take something as horrific as the death of a child, and somehow, miraculously, bring good from it. (Let me just add, if you cannot see any good yet, it means God is not done yet.)

As I mentioned a couple of months ago, neuroscience (the study of the nervous system in the brain) has proven that we become what we focus on. Our brains do not control our thinking, but our thinking actually controls our brains, even to the point of rewiring our brains in what we believe, how we feel and how we act. (If this is new to you, or you did not look it up on the internet when I mentioned it in June, you can do a search for neuroplasticity for a lot more information.)

This is important to know, because if my focus is on my loss and the terrible things happening, I cannot rise above it to face my future. But if I do my best to focus on my promised future, then it is easier to rise above the loss and uncertainty, allowing me to step forward into that future and the good things God still has for me.

In other words, we can focus so much on what we don't have, that we can keep ourselves from seeing or believing that God still has good things for us in our future while we are still here on earth. That is called hope!

Reflection: Even when this world is in chaos and things like COVID19 becomes a world-wide pandemic, God already knows how it will affect each and every one of us, and He has a plan.

The question is, will I choose to see through my own eyes of anxiety and fear, or will I choose to do my best to trust God and His plan, knowing that He sees what I cannot see, He knows what I do not know, and reminding myself that this world is not my true and final home.

I want to encourage you to ask the Holy Spirit to help not to live by your feelings of fear, hopelessness and depression, but by your choices of turning to God and choosing to believe that He is holding you and will bring good things into your life again. It can make a big difference in how you move forward.

> *... be inwardly transformed by the Holy Spirit through*
> *a total reformation of how you think. This will empower*
> *you to discern God's will as you live a beautiful life...*
> *Romans 12:2 (TPT)*

August 15

Deep Grief Leaves Deep Scars

I did not realize it at the time, but having a front row seat to my daughter having her leg missing was a good illustration for us, as bereaved parents. Having our child die is like having an amputation; a part of our very being has been cut off from us. The wound is severe, but it will eventually heal. However, there will always be a scar, reminding us that a part of our very being is missing.

Did having an amputation keep Becca from running and playing with the other children? No, it definitely did not! It may have slowed her down and caused her to adapt to how she ran and how she played, but it did not stop her.

Did having a staph infection in my ankle from a bike accident keep me from ever riding a bike again? No way!

Did having quadruple bypass surgery at age forty-eight keep my husband from permanently doing things like holding and playing with his grandchildren, or starting new adventures like selling our house and learning how to drive a 38-foot motor home that we live in full-time? Nope!

When these horrible things happen, including something as terrible as the death of our child, does it mean our life is over and we will never be able to live a full life again? No, it does not. We need time to go through a "recovery" process (for lack of a better word) and need time to learn how to function with our child no longer here, but it does not mean we will never be able to function again.

- We will go through times when everyone around us is splashing and playing while we are unable to participate because of our wounds.
- We will go through times when we cannot function and need another measure of healing.
- We will go through times when we have to adjust the way we do things.
- We will forever bear the scar of our tragedies.

- We will always have things that trigger reminders of our deep loss.

But we are not permanently injured to the point of being out of commission for the rest of our lives.

Our lives will never be the same. *We* will never be the same. But within that, we can make sure the tragedies in our lives are not wasted by leaving us incapacitated. And that includes the tragedy of the death of our child.

We *can* allow God's love to wash over us, to heal us, and to take this change in us and use it against the enemy who brought death into this world. And just think, *all* our scars will disappear someday, both the physical ones and the emotional ones, when we join our children in that place where there is no more pain, no more sorrow, and all of our tears will be wiped away.

Reflection: Until that day comes, it is important to remember that the reason wounds heal is so that we can continue living. Yes, our scar reminds us of what happened, of who was cut off from us, but it also reminds us that *our* life isn't over. There is still more living to do, if not for yourself, then at least for those who love you and still need you in their lives, and for your child who is no longer here.

We can (and need to) learn to *live* with our scars in a way that honors our son or daughter, not in spite of our child's death, but because of his or her life. Take a minute and ask the Holy Spirit to show you how to work with Him in healing your wound, so that you can get to that place as quickly as possible.

See, God has come to save me. I will trust in him and not be afraid.
The Lord God is my strength and my song; he has given me victory.
With joy you will drink deeply from the fountain of salvation!
Isaiah 12:2-3 (NLT)

August 16

Does God Choose When We Die?

What are your thoughts about this statement?

> *God is the one who gives life within the womb, and God chooses when each person takes their last breath.*

Some may feel like the wording that God "chooses" when each of us will die, is scary and disturbing because it implies that God organized or orchestrated our child's death.

The Bible is very clear that God knows when each of us will die. Psalm 139:16 tells us that all of our days are ordained by God and written in His book That also means He knows how we will die. Does that mean we have no control over when we will die? I think it is yes and no.

First, we have to remember that the enemy is the one who brought death into this world. God is the giver of life. When God created man, He gave us a free will. We get to make choices, both good and bad, but living in a world that is influenced by Satan greatly affects those choices. A person can choose to take their own life because of the hopelessness they feel. A person can drive while drunk and end someone else's life by that choice. Someone can choose to do something risky (including having a potentially dangerous occupation) that ends their life.

Living in a fallen, sinful, corrupt world also affects us in ways we do *not* get to choose. No one chooses to have cancer or any other debilitating disease, but sickness and disease can grab ahold of us, drastically altering our physical and mental abilities, eventually taking someone's life.

This is a tough topic, because there are times God steps in and miraculously spares someone's life. He did that for my daughter several times over the years, especially the last 18 months of her life. I have no answer for why He did not keep her alive the night of October 12, 2011. When God does not stop a person's body from shutting down (whether it was from sickness, risky behavior, or by their own hand intentionally or unintentionally), in a sense, He is choosing when that person leaves this earth and passes on to the other side of eternity.

God is omniscient. That means He knows everything, including the exact moment our child would take their last breath, before he or she was even born. He also knows what is in the future for all of us still here on earth. Nothing we can do will change what God already knows will happen, including the choices we will make that will shorten or lengthen our lives.

Reflection: So, does God choose when we die? I guess it depends on how you look at it. God knows what will happen in each of our lives, without robbing us of our God-given freedom to make choices. Sometimes those choices become literally life-or-death. Sometimes God intervenes and sometimes He does not, for reasons that make no sense to us at all on this side of eternity.

"Choosing" may be a poor choice of wording, but God views death in a very different way than we do. He sees it as precious, because someone He loves very much is coming home to meet Him face-to-face and move into a phenomenal place that He has prepared just for them. We may not understand or have all the answers, but we can rest and abide in the One who does.

> *His loved ones are very precious to him,*
> *and he does not lightly let them die.*
> *Psalm 116:15 (TLB)*

August 17

Where Am I Putting My Faith?

As Christians, sometimes we can think that we are exempt from the sorrow of the world. We tend to see God like a genie in a lamp, where we can just rub the right way and He will pop out and say, "Your wish is my command. What would you like me to do for you?" However, it does not work like that. If I could pray and God would pop out and give me whatever I wanted, then He's not God anymore. I am God because He must do whatever I am telling Him to do.

Whenever we insist that God answers our prayer the way we want Him to, we are off track. The reason to pray is to get ahold of God Himself, not pushing Him into giving me the answer I want.

Obviously, our prayers were not answered the way we wanted them to be answered, or I would not have written this book and you would not be reading it. But I can still say that God is good. I may have lost my Becca from this earth, but I gained more of God in all of it. I gained a relationship with God that is different than it ever would have been if I had not been on this unwanted path.

Would I trade all that to get Becca back? I have to say that yes, when I am in the deep pain of missing her, I would. But that is not how it works. Fortunately, there has been a tradeoff. Because of what I have gone through, my life is richer and goes deeper because God is more real than before, which is a gift. It is also a gift that I am blessed not to have to worry or be concerned about Becca like I am my other children.

My friend, Lynn, lost her young son over thirty years ago to a very aggressive cancer. Here is how she answered, after a grieving mom asked her how she could be so happy.

> *I have four other boys right now, that are going through hard things in life. They've had broken marriages and struggled. I pray over them every day, but I don't ever worry about Joel and where he is, and if he's okay. I know where he is. I know he's being raised by the best Daddy there is. Do I want him here? Yes. But is it a comfort to know where he is? Yes. It is.*
>
> *I think that's the cool part of all of this; we gain and grow in our relationship with God, and it is different. I can say that even through all of this, God is still good. God still answers prayer. God is still in our prayers, whether they're answered the way we choose or want them to be or not.*

There is something good that God has for each one of us beyond the death of our child, but it is hard for us to see that when we are in such a dark place.

One of the things I have learned is that if our faith is in the answer to our prayer, we are going to fall apart, because we are not always going to get the answer that we're wanting, or that we are praying for. But I can stand if my faith is in knowing so intimately the One to whom I am praying, that I can trust Him with the answer no matter what it is. My faith is not going to be shattered, because it is not based on getting a certain answer.

Reflection: Has your faith been in getting the answer you want to your prayers, or has your faith been in the One who sees and knows everything, and answers based on the view of eternity and His immense love for you and your child? One will make you angry, confused and blame God. The other will bring peace in the middle of your pain.

God paid a high price to make sure we are with Him in perfection and glory when we die. He can be trusted to answer your prayers in the right way, not just based on our time here on earth, but for all eternity. Ask Him to help you trust Him with the answer that you did not want.

> *He that did not hesitate to spare his own Son but gave him up for us all—can we not trust such a God to give us, with him, everything else that we can need? ...Christ died for us, Christ rose for us, Christ reigns in power for us, Christ prays for us!*
> Romans 8:32,34 (PHILLIPS)

August 18

Do not Stay Stuck

I am living proof that you do not have to be stuck between your past and your future. You can be full of God's love and be content, knowing your value does not come from what you do or what has happened to you. You can know that your value comes from who you are in God, and who God is in you. You can still have purpose in your life and live in victory over everything that the enemy uses to try and take you out.

Believe it or not, the worst tragedy of my life brought one of my greatest revelations. For quite a while after Becca died, I could only see myself as a mom who had lost her child. The intense grief was suffocating. I allowed my huge loss to define me as a person.

Since everything was such a blur for so long, I can't tell you when or how it happened, but by the grace of God, I finally had a breakthrough of understanding that my identity was not tied to my circumstance of being a grieving mother. Also, by the grace of God, that started to release an even deeper revelation; that my identity is not based on anything but who Christ is in me – that hope of glory.

You may not feel like it, but you are also still full of God's glory, even in the darkest time of your life. You do not have to stay stuck in the pain of your past, but you can live from the place of the life of Christ in you.

Reflection: In looking at Isaiah 62:3 which says, *You shall also be a crown of glory in the hand of the Lord.* (NKJV) I have asked myself, why is the crown in His hands? I believe it is so that He can place us where He wants us. So that He can put us in His place of choosing, to rule and reign on this earth. It also means that we are still in His hands, which is a good thing.

If you and I are living from a place of true Kingdom identity, we will be okay with that. I don't mean that we won't grieve and there won't be immense pain. But we won't stay stuck in our identity that our child died. We will learn to live from the place of, "My child lived and is still alive, thanks to Christ who gave them the gift of salvation and who is living in me."

There is so much freedom in living from a place of surrendering to God's plans as you are aware that He dwells inside you. Ask Him to give you that same revelation that He gave me, that your identity is not tied to being a bereaved parent, but is wrapped up in Him, your hope of glory.

You'll be a stunning crown in the palm of God's hand.
Isaiah 62:3 (MSG)

August 19
And it Came to Pass...

Back in July, I shared how many grieving parents (myself included) want to scream when we see that other people's lives are still going on, when ours has come to a screeching halt after the death of our child. I talked about sitting in my car at a stop light, watching people walking, people in cars around me having conversations, and cars driving past me as if the world was okay.

Eventually (and by eventually, I mean two to three years), I found myself running those same errands without the sense that because my world had come to an end, everyone else's should, too. Until...

When my daughter died, I had no grid for facing a deep loss. Dave and I had been blessed to have all four of our parents with us up to that point. Three years ago, we lost the first of our four parents when Dave's dad died unexpectedly from a heart aneurysm. Dave and I became instant caregivers to his mom, whose dementia and other health issues needed someone with her 24/7. For three months we took shifts, living with her as we jumped through all the hoops going through the process to get her placed in an assisted living facility.

Life once again came to a standstill. I saw what looked like life going on as normal for those around me, while my world had been turned upside down. My son and his family purchased their first home, and we were not able to help them move or get settled much at all. My youngest son moved as well, and we were not able to help him, either.

Dave and I had just purchased the Hope Mobile and were in the process of downsizing to be able to move into it, to go on the road full time for GPS Hope. That not only came to a halt, but I also found myself bringing back to the house things I had already moved to the motor home. Our oldest son was buying our house, and that came to a standstill as well, since we could not move out, as Dave and I were taking turns being full-time caregivers to his mom.

I knew I would be able to get through this new situation that had me at a complete standstill, because I had already faced the worst thing that could happen in my life and had come out the other side, able to live again when I did not think that was possible.

I am honored to be someone you and others can look at, wondering how I ever got past Becca's death to be able to live again. And a few years into this journey, I believe that you will have others wondering that about you. Plus, you will know, like I did, that you can get through anything else this world throws your way.

Reflection: "And it came to pass..." Those can be some of the most encouraging words in the Bible. Some translations say, "in time..." or "after that..." In other words, it won't always be like this.

If you are frustrated that life is going on while you feel so very stuck, I want to remind you to think of it a little differently. It is actually a good thing to see life going on around you, because that means you are surrounded by people whose lives also came to a standstill, but they have been able to move forward at some point. And that includes bereaved parents like Dave and me, who were once in that same place of suffocating darkness of child loss.

I am not saying that life goes on as normal, the way it was before the death of your child. That would be impossible. What I am saying is that if you keep going, one day, one hour, one breath at a time (and I know sometimes it feels like you can't), at some point down the road you will find yourself feeling a stirring of being alive again. Just keep watching those who are ahead of you as a hopeful reminder that just maybe, it can happen to you also, and thank God for putting us in your life.

> *What a wonderful God we have—he is the Father of our Lord Jesus Christ, the source of every mercy, and the one who so wonderfully comforts and strengthens us in our hardships and trials. And why does he do this? So that when others are troubled, needing our sympathy and encouragement, we can pass on to them this same help and comfort God has given us.... in our trouble God has comforted us—and this, too, to help you: to show you from our personal experience how God will tenderly comfort you when you undergo these same sufferings. He will give you the strength to endure.*
> *2 Corinthians 1:3-4, 7 (TLB)*

August 20

I Just Want to Die

Debbie Reynolds was a famous actress whose career spanned almost seventy years. You may be more familiar with her daughter, Carrie Fisher, who played the part of Princess Leia in the Star Wars series.

When Carrie died in 2016, her eighty-four-year-old mother passed away the very next day. Her son, Carrie's brother, believes his mom died of a broken heart. The last words she spoke, fifteen minutes before having a severe stroke that claimed her life were, "I miss her so much, I want to be with Carrie."

For several days after Debbie's death, I saw many bereaved mothers writing things like:

- Why did Debbie Reynolds get to die, and I didn't?
- She is so lucky she doesn't have to go through what the rest of us have to.
- I still want to die, and it has been over three years since I lost my daughter.

Many Facebook groups for grieving parents were posting about how the world finally gets to see that having a broken heart from the death of a child is a real thing.

I wish God would just speak a command and make it all better, but it just doesn't happen that way. As much as I want Him to, God has not brought a giant eraser and removed the pain of my daughter's death, and obviously He has not honored my many requests, those first few years, to leave this earth to go be with my daughter.

Instead, He is teaching me how to walk through it, leaning on Him and allowing Him to carry me when I have no strength. After all, isn't this supposed to be a big part of our Christian walk? We realize more and more how much He loves us, so that we can deepen our trust in Him, knowing we can depend on Him to help us with what we need to be

August

able to get through this life (especially something so difficult as the death of our child).

Since my daughter died, so much of my Christian theology has been challenged and shifted. It isn't because I am twisting things around to confirm new thoughts and beliefs, but because I have new lenses which bring so much clarity to old beliefs that I was taught, but no longer see as truth.

So many scriptures have new meaning to me now. Not the ones being quoted at me as Christian clichés, but verses that the Holy Spirit breathes life into when I am being held in His arms in the depth of my darkness and pain.

Reflection: What is the difference between Debbie Reynolds and each one of us? To put it very bluntly, she got to die, and we didn't. But in joining Carrie, it meant she had to leave behind and miss out on the lives of those she loved who were still here.

I know that we don't care and tell ourselves no one will really miss us that much and there is nothing left for us to live for here. That means you are believing the lies of the enemy. If you have the Holy Spirit in you, you have life in you and a reason and purpose for still being here.

Don't let this make you feel guilty for feeling that way. We all do those first few months and even years. Just be sure you are not giving in to the hopelessness and lies that are bombarding your thoughts and speak God's truth to yourself. "God still has me here because there is more life for me to live. I *will* get out of this darkness with His help and live a life of meaning and purpose again. And I won't give up until that happens!"

...what seems impossible to you is never impossible to God!
Matthew 19:26 (TPT)

August 21
Honoring Our Child

Once we emotionally make the decision to fight to come out of our dark pit of grief, we can begin to see how to do that in a practical way that can honor the life of our son or daughter. Doing this also helps us continue choosing not to remain in that place of suffocating darkness.

Here are just a few ideas of easy ways we can do this:

- A memorial brick - Our local Rotary Gardens has a memory lane where this can be done, as well as Lambeau Field (where the Green Bay Packers play, a team of which Becca and our family are avid fans and owners).
- A bench on a trail - We have an "ice age" trail through our entire state, and people can have a bench put along the path with a plaque honoring the memory of a loved one,
- A tree in a park - There are many parks that would love to have a beautiful tree planted and will allow an "In Loving Memory Of..." plaque to be placed at the foot of it.

All three of these can be a place you can go to remember your son or daughter; a place that will help you reflect on memories of their life, as opposed to being in a cemetery (or staring at their ashes in an urn) which tends to cause more painful thoughts of their death.

My husband, Dave, and I had the opportunity to do something quite different. Since I was a leader in an international ministry for many years, which has taken me to Africa several times, it gave me connections and friends in several African countries. Dave and I wanted to find a way to better the lives of others, as a way to honor Becca and keep her memory alive. We gave money to some missionary friends who lived in the extremely poor country of Burundi. They passed the money on to a family to start a little kiosk type store to support their family. As far as we know, their business is still going and bringing this family in Burundi, Africa, hope and life!

Someday, all of us who are alive right now will be long gone, and eventually, no one will be left who knew us. But there are things we can

August

do to make sure our children will be thought of and remembered by many, extending beyond our own lives when we leave this earth to join them.

I refuse to let Becca become nothing more than an undecorated tombstone when I leave this earth. I am going to make sure her life and legacy live on for others. How about you?

Reflection: I have a friend whose daughter died while in high school. A memorial bench was placed for her on an open walkway to the football field. This mom cannot go there, because she knows she would sit on it and cry, and it would be too awkward. Be sure to take something like this into consideration when deciding what to do to honor and memorialize your child somewhere, but also know that you will get to the place where you won't cry every time you think of your child.

Another option is to place a brick for your child around a statue called the Angel of Hope (based on the book *The Christmas Box* by Richard Paul Evans). This is a specific place for those who have lost a child, so when you visit, if someone else comes, you know why they are there and have an instant connection. These statues are in many cities around the nation, but if there isn't one in your area, maybe that is even a project you could take on, getting one placed.

Do some research and find something you can do, to give yourself a place to go that will help you remember your child's life instead of their departure.

...give honor and respect to all those to whom it is due.
Romans 13:7 (TLB)

August 22

Feeling Out of Control

We do not like it when things are out of our control, and the death of our child is by far the greatest time that has ever happened in our lives. You may be trying hard to get some sort of control back in your life but are finding it is next to impossible.

Our bodies seem to be doing their own thing and breaking down on us. Our thoughts are all over the place. Our emotions are totally out of whack and uncontrollable, which can make you feel forgetful, foggy, overwhelmed and disoriented. Even your response to these emotions can feel out of your control and confusing. We sure can relate to Job, when he said, "Would that my anguish were weighed, laid on a scale together with the disaster I've suffered! For there is not enough sand in the seas to outweigh it! It's no wonder my untamed words are but *incoherent* stammering." Job 6:2-3 (VOICE).

Life cannot be controlled, which includes our debilitating grief when our child dies. Anger and frustration often come as a result. It may help to look at our definition of life. We might believe "life" is when we get a good report from the doctor, or when our relationships are going well. When those things don't happen, we blame God, and he becomes the enemy. But God Himself *is* life through Jesus. He told us in John 14:6, "I am the Way, the Truth, and the Life." If we think we know what we need to have to live and it does not include God, then we have a wrong definition of life.

When God's definition of life collides with your definition, you will get frustrated or angry, and might even try to leave God out of your grieving process. But doing it on your own will make it extremely difficult and drag things out much longer.

We want to figure out how to get our lives back under control. Since that is not going to happen, what are your other options? God wants you to give that control to Him, so that He can help you navigate you through this.

Reflection: Think of a time you went somewhere and got terribly lost and had no way to guide yourself. Now think of a time where you had no idea where you were going, but you had someone with you who was familiar with the area (or building) and went with you, guiding you to where you needed to be.

That is how we are in our grief. If we continue to push God away, angry that our life is in His control instead of our own, we will continue to wander, lost in our grief. If we allow the Holy Spirit to walk with us, He will guide us back to a good place and you will be empowered, through His power.

Jesus: I am the path, the truth, and the energy of life.
John 14:6 (AMP)

August 23

To Live or Die

In Philippians 1:21, the apostle Paul makes a statement that is translated in many versions, "to live is Christ, and to die is gain." I recently decided to study this out a bit, and here is what I found.

First, Paul used the word Messiah, not Christ. Why does that matter? Well, they both mean "the anointed one," but *Mashiach* (Messiah) carries with it the additional weight of the promised deliverer. The Messiah was the one the Israelites were waiting for to deliver them from bondage and bring restoration.

Knowing this made the phrase, "to live is Christ" take on a new meaning that brings me a new wave of hope and thankfulness, even many years after Becca's death. When I do my best to stay connected to Jesus through the Holy Spirit, He carries a specific anointing to be my deliverer. His powerful anointing continues to bring healing and restoration to my shattered heart.

What about the phrase "to die is gain"? We believe this in our own lives because when our child dies, we want to die and go be with them. In fact, we feel like we have already died and are just living in a shell, waiting for it to give out so we can be done here.

However, let's look at this from our child's perspective. I have to ask myself, if it is true that to "die is gain," what did my child gain?

You and I have children hanging out in incredible glory and perfection; no sickness, no pain (physical or emotional), no hurtful rejections... I think you get the idea and could build on this list. When I take time to think about what my daughter has gained, I can start feeling happy for her, which eases my pain some.

Another thing I discovered when studying this verse is that the original word which is often translated "gain" is *revach*, which also means to profit. Our children gained even more life than they had here. Everything that is good was multiplied beyond what we can imagine. There was a huge profit made for them.

When I look at this verse on how God originally said it through Paul, it is so much more than the blanket statement that I have always skimmed over. It is to give us eyes for both those who have gone on ahead of us, and for ourselves who are still here. To live, is to take on Christ, in all His anointing and all His promises to be our deliverer. That is what He wants to do and who He wants to be for you.

Reflection: Going back to Philippians 1:21, let me put all of this together, using several translations of the Bible, combined with my own words.

For me to continue living means that I am connected to the One who promises to deliver me and continue to bring healing and restoration to my shattered heart. Being alive here on earth means that through Christ, the Messiah, there is still a way to have fullness and joy again, along with a reason to keep living. Death just means we gain even more of Him. It is like our children have won the biggest jackpot possible!

You can live in a way that is full again, because Christ is in you, who is the hope of glory. He is life itself. Ask Him to make good on this in your life, knowing it might take a while, but it can and will happen if you keep leaning into Him.

> *Living within you is the Christ who floods you with the expectation of glory! This mystery of Christ, embedded within us, becomes a heavenly treasure chest of hope filled with the riches of glory for his people, and God wants everyone to know it!*
> *Colossians 1:27 (TPT)*

August 24

It's Your Choice

You get to choose what you believe about what happens to us when we die. Many Christians start to have doubts, wondering if there really is a heaven and wonder if their child is really there waiting for them. That just brings torment. I want you to think about this. You are the one who gets to make the decision to believe that there is a God, and that when our child died, they gained something wonderful.

I recently heard it described that it is like we are on a path with our children, but we have a child who has gone further down the road out of our sight. We are still on that same path together, and at some point, we will catch up to him or her.

God made a way for our earthly death not to be final. Plus, He not only walks on this same path with us, but He will also carry us when needed, while offering His anointing and His promise of everything we need as we travel through this very deep, very dark valley.

In other words, we need to see God as one who comes along beside us with deep sorrow and compassion, not as someone to blame who caused the death of our child. It is much more helpful when we see God as the rescuer in our story, rather than the cause of our pain by something He did or did not do.

Too often we have a fairy godmother view of God, and we get mad when He doesn't wave His wand and make all the bad things go away. I think of Dorothy in the Wizard of Oz. Glinda could have told Dorothy at the very beginning how to get back home, but she didn't. Dorothy had to go through a difficult and scary journey first. At the end of her journey, before telling her how to get home, Glinda asked Dorothy what she had learned on that journey.

Just because God does not remove all the evil attacks on our lives does not mean He is not involved or doesn't care. God isn't just sitting back watching our lives unfold like a movie in front of Him. He is actively involved as everything in our lives unfolds, and because He is, there are good things that can come from the tragedy of the death of our child while we are on our journey. But if we only have our eyes focused on the tragedy, we will miss it.

Reflection: God did not cause the death of our child. The broken world we live in throws these things our way. Yes, we know that He could have stopped it from happening, but from His view (and our child's) we are still on the same path. Our son or daughter is just ahead of us, where we cannot see or be with them.

Someday, we will catch up. In the meantime, ask God, as you continue to live out each day, "please show me the meaning my life has on this journey. My life here has not ended, and I need to know what you want to do through this as something good."

Remember, you get to choose whether or not to believe there is so much more, both here and to come. I hope you choose to believe in what will bring you peace and will open the door for you to move toward a greater measure of healing. After all what is the alternative?

Help us to remember that our days are numbered,
and help us to interpret our lives correctly.
Psalm 90:12 (TPT)

August 25
Some Will, Some Won't

Among grieving parents, the subject often comes up about signs from our children or being able to connect with them. The pain is so deep, and the longing is so very real. Death seems so final. Our minds cannot comprehend never seeing, hearing or touching our child again – at least here on this earth.

It is very normal to long to see our child; to want to hear them laugh, see them smile, be able to talk to them. I don't know why some do and some don't, but I have had the blessing twice where God has rolled back the curtain of heaven, and I have been able to see Becca there.

I did not pursue it, and I did not beg God for it. I especially did not have those experiences by going to a psychic. I personally believe that is very dangerous. Let me tell you why. There is a spirit world, with a Kingdom of Light and a kingdom of darkness. Those spirits that are not in God's kingdom of light are out to deceive and destroy us as God's creation.

They were around your child here on earth. They know things about your child that other humans will not know. I truly believe that when a psychic "brings up" our child from the dead, it is actually an angel of darkness (a demon) pretending to be our child. They will tell us things that only you and your child would know (from a physical earthly point of view) to convince you that it is your child communicating.

That gives us a false comfort, while drawing us into the world of darkness without realizing that is who we are following. Then when all hell keeps breaking loose in our lives, we cannot figure out why, and keep going back to talk to our child for more comfort, not realizing that by doing so, we are continually inviting that darkness into our lives.

Some of us will see our children in our dreams, and some will not. We can get angry when others are having dreams about our child, and we don't. Some of us will feel their presence at times, and some will not.

Some will have direct signs that have a special meaning to them with their children and some will not.

This is an area where I just don't have any answers as to the why. But once again, "Why?" or "Why not?" is a question that is very rarely answered here on earth, because we either would not be able to comprehend the explanation, or we would just argue because it would not seem like a good enough reason.

I wish I could give you something that would make all of this go away and bring your child back to you, even if just in your dreams, but I don't have that kind of power. However, I do have the power of prayer, and I am praying that God will be as real to you as your child is, and that will be enough for you as you continue this unwanted journey.

Reflection: God is spirit. Your child is spirit and now fully in the spirit realm. You are spirit, and God's spirit lives within you. That means *God* is the connection between you and your child.

Seek God, not your child, since He is the connection between you and your son or daughter. The Holy Spirit in you knows the desire of your heart and He will give it to you if He knows it will truly help you and is what you need. If necessary, ask the Holy Spirit to take that desire away and replace it with a deeper desire for Him. Only He can bring you the peace and comfort that you truly need.

At least we know that if we don't get any kind of encounter with our child while still here, we will be with them again, and when we are, we will never be separated.

We must never stop looking to Jesus. He is the leader of our faith, and he is the one who makes our faith complete.
Hebrews 12:2 (ERV)

August 26

Loneliness

Loneliness and isolation seem to be a big part of our grief journey. We are often torn, because sometimes we find that while we want to be alone, at the same time, we don't want to be lonely. We can convince ourselves that unless we are with others who understand us because they have also lost a child, we will continue in our loneliness.

There is something you can do to pull yourself out of that ache of loneliness, and that is to reach out to someone else who is hurting. I know it may not be easy, and it could take months before you are ready to help someone else in need, but at some point, you will find that you need to stop thinking about what you have lost and start thinking about the needs of those around you.

It could be as simple as taking flowers to an elderly neighbor or offering to watch someone's pet while they are on vacation.

Even if you are in the early weeks or months of your own grief, you could send a letter with a card to someone else who has lost a child, letting them know where they can find some resources or get support by connecting with other pareavors who will walk this journey with them. Just knowing there is someone out there who has also experienced the loss of a child and has reached out to them can be a lifeline.

To get out of the trap of loneliness, you are going to have to take some sort of action. Those of us who have been in those early months of grief understand how hard that can be and understand if you just aren't ready yet. We also know that being around other people is not what we are longing for; it is being around people who care, and who will allow us to be whoever we need to be, at any given moment, in our grieving.

That is why pareavors gravitate to each other, and why helping someone else can be so important, both to you and to them.

Reflection: When you reach out to others, it causes your own hope to start rising within you. Take some time and honestly evaluate if you could find a way to help someone else. Be honest with yourself whether you just don't want to because it sounds too difficult, or you truly can't. This does not have to be reaching out to another pareavor if that could be a trigger for your own grief. But don't just dismiss the idea, either.

If that is the case, then ask God to show you someone who could use some help in a different area. Don't count something out because it feels too small or unimportant to you. It may be exactly what they need to pull them out of their own place of loneliness or discouragement, which will lift you up as well.

> *If you offer yourself to the hungry, and satisfy the need of the afflicted, then your light will rise in darkness, and your gloom will become like midday.*
> *Isaiah 58:10 (NASB)*

August 27

The Enemy's Objective

We may not realize it, but we try to humanize God by accusing Him of manipulating this world, which brings Him down to our level of having a sinful nature. He is not cruel. God is not capable of doing something like allowing horrible things to happen to only some of us, and then being selective on who He helps and who He does not.

One of the enemy's top objectives is to make us think all of the tragic things that happen to us here on earth are God's fault, and that He really is not who He says He is. The enemy is out to do that by planting doubts in our mind, just like he did with Eve at the beginning of time. Satan's specialty is lying, deceiving, killing, destroying, stealing from us, and then getting us to blame God instead of him.

God's specialty is restoring and redeeming what the enemy corrupts and damages. He loves us, even through times of doubt, anger, bitterness and blaming Him. So, if you are angry and blaming God for the death of your child (or for not stopping it), you might be looking at things from the enemy's blinding perspective.

Everything that happens to us here is *very* real. However, there is something that is even more real, and that is where our children are. This is not final. As Wayne Jacobson said, it is like being in a theatre and we are still waiting in the lobby. The real show is on the other side of the door, behind the curtain.

I would go crazy if I believed Becca's life was over; that she is nothing but dust now and I will never ever see her again or be able to hug her or hear her laugh. I get so much more peace from believing that God sees the big picture; that He knew the exact second Becca's heart would stop, and her last breath would be taken.

He knows that about me as well, and He put a plan in place before that ever happened so that we could be together again. He was there to meet Becca when she crossed over, and He and Becca will be there to meet me when I cross over. The same is true for you and your child.

There is nothing cruel about that. Our kids just got let into the show before we did.

Reflection: Why didn't God answer our prayers to keep our children safe? One thing I have learned is that there is a difference between situational prayers and relational prayers.

In the Old Testament, the people had to pray situational prayers. They did not have their own personal relationship with God through the Holy Spirit living inside them. We have the opportunity to pray relational prayers. What do I mean by that?

When something happens, even as horrific as the death of our child, we have a chance to draw closer to Him in intimacy. We can ask Him things like, "Who do you want to be for me through all of this?" "What is it about You that I don't know yet, that will help me?"

God is all about relationships. He wants to have an intimate relationship with you. That does not mean that we should not take our needs and desires to Him. But God wants to be more than just someone we place an order with, like we do at a fast-food restaurant. He wants to sit and commune and be in fellowship with us. And the closer you get to Him, the harder it is for the enemy to deceive you and get you to blame God for the destruction he himself caused.

> *But Lord, your nurturing love is tender and gentle. You are slow to get angry yet so swift to show your faithful love. You are full of abounding grace and truth. Bring me to your grace-fountain so that your strength becomes mine. Be my hero and come rescue your servant again!*
> *Psalm 86:15-16 (TPT)*

August 28

When God Seems Distant

A lot of pareavors share with me that when they pray, it feels like their prayers are not getting anywhere. They are not feeling God's presence or His love. When they try to read their Bible, there is no life in it.

I know this is fairly common, and as I was praying for those of you who are struggling with this, I saw a picture in my mind of a clogged shower drain. It was covered with debris, and no water was able to get through. I then saw a hand come in and begin pulling the debris aside so the water could begin to run through the drain.

When our child dies, the darkness is overwhelming. Not just for a few days or weeks, but for months, and even a few years for many of us. We are numb, and nothing seems to be able to touch us except the intense pain.

But God reaches in and begins to clear away the darkness and the layers that keep us from seeing Him or feeling Him. It may take quite a while since there is so much debris and several layers that need to be cleared. We can't tell anything is happening, but it is. The water will begin to trickle. You will begin to get glimpses of Him, His love for you and how He is hurting with you.

The night Jesus was betrayed, He told Peter that Satan had asked to sift him like wheat, but Jesus had prayed for him, that Peter's faith would hold strong (Luke 22:31,32). According to Hebrews 7:25, Jesus is doing the same thing for you. Jesus Himself is interceding for you. God may seem distant right now, but He is with you, and He is fighting for you.

Do you know what else Jesus told Peter that night? Jesus told him that when he had turned back (been restored), to strengthen others, which is exactly what Peter did. God works in mysterious ways. He has used my daughter's death to cause me to reach out and be a comfort and light of hope for others who find themselves hurled onto this same path.

God may seem distant, but He is not. He did not leave Peter, He did not leave me, and He did not leave you. Darkness is not an indicator of where God is not, but where He *is*. He is right there in the darkness with you until the debris is cleared and you can see and feel His presence once again.

Reflection: As you keep crying out to Him, He continues to clear away the darkness, and more of His love and His presence gets closer to where you can see and feel Him again. And when you can't cry out to Him anymore, just rest. Let Him do the work and clear out the darkness from His side. At some point, the drain will begin to clear, and you will start feeling a refreshing in your soul. So, do not give up.

Why does it take so much longer for some of us? I don't know. But I do know that He is faithful because I have seen it over and over again. He will not stop until you are back into the light, living a life of meaning and purpose again. After all, you have Jesus Himself interceding for you!

He can save fully and completely those who approach God through him, for he is always living to intercede on their behalf.
Hebrews 7:25 (PHILLIPS)

August 29

Going to Church

This may not be your experience, but I cannot even tell you how many parents share with me that they are not going to Sunday morning church services anymore after their child dies. It is such a painful place for so many reasons. Unfortunately, one of those reasons is because of our well-meaning Christian friends who want to fix us by quoting Bible verses at us.

It fascinates me that we all say Christ's church is His people, not a building; and yet if a Christian doesn't show up at the same building every Sunday, they can be labeled as a backslider, or even rebellious. But after the death of our child, there are many of us who need something deeper and more real than the routine of a Sunday morning service, which includes taking sixty seconds to greet the people around you as a time of "fellowship".

God's love can reach us any time and any place. Anyone who has accepted Jesus as their Savior has the Holy Spirit living inside them, which means He is in us to lead and guide us in our individual and personal walk with Him. Yes, we need each other, and we are told not to forsake the assembling of ourselves, but when that was written, "church" was an organic, living, breathing Spirit-led family. It was not what the Western culture has made it to be, as a weekly routine in a building used for the purpose of sitting in rows facing a platform to be led in a planned service.

Let me stop and say that I am *not* anti-church! I have met God deeply and been moved and changed many times while in a church service. God shows up and will move through whatever format we make available to Him.

I just want to remind you that YOU are the church. If you cannot go to a building to sit through a service, that's okay. God will still meet you right where you are. This just might be a season in your life where God will show you His love in new and powerful ways that do not depend on an institution - a building where believers assemble every Sunday.

For those of you who are attending services and getting nourishment, fellowship and support, I hope you know how blessed you are. Unfortunately, that is very rare for a pareavor.

Reflection: Jesus Himself told us in John 8:36 that if He sets us free, we are really truly free. You are free to follow His leading. If that means walking into a building every week with a worship team and a pastor preaching the Word, then that is what you need to do. If that means stepping back so the Holy Spirit can be your teacher, bringing a healing that is needed outside the four walls of a building, then that is what you need to do.

Either way, make sure you are doing it because that is how the Holy Spirit is leading you, based on your intimate relationship with Him. Others do not have to understand. You don't owe anyone an explanation. This is between you and God. You are free in Him!

A slave can't come and go at will. The Son, though, has an established position, the run of the house. So if the Son sets you free, you are free through and through.
(John 8:36 MSG)

August 30

Goodbye or Hello?

On October 12, 2011, I was working my way home from a children's ministry conference in North Dakota. Becca was back in the hospital for a routine treatment to take off the extra water from her weakening heart. While I was away, every day we talked on the phone, and Becca would ask me when I was coming home. I would tell her, "Wednesday" and ask, "Do you want me to come home early?" She would always tell me no.

The first leg of my flight home arrived late to the airport, and for the first time *ever*, in many years of travel both nationally and internationally, my name was being paged in the airport as a final boarding call. I ran as fast as I possibly could, pulling my carry-on wildly behind me through the maze of people walking. As I turned the corner of my gate, they were starting to close the door and I hollered out to them.

They stopped, scanned my ticket and down the ramp I went. I was barely able to breathe and as I started to look at my ticket to see where my seat was, a kind flight attendant told me not to worry about it and to take the empty seat right in front of me, and another one brought me a bottle of water.

My daughter, Kim, picked me up from the airport and we drove straight to the Madison University Hospital. There were some unusual things about that visit, that looking back on now, Kim and I were sure Becca was saying goodbye without coming right out and saying that she knew she was leaving us.

As I was walking out of her hospital room with plans to return the next morning for her being dismissed, we gave each other the "I love you" sign. Three hours later, she was gone.

I understand that there are many of you who do not have this kind of story. You did not get to say goodbye like I did (even though I did not know I was saying a final goodbye at the time). I am so very sorry... I truly am. I hesitated to share this because you know I don't want to bring more pain, frustration or anger to any of you.

But then I realized we will *all* get to say HELLO!

No matter how abrupt their leaving was, or how blindsided we were, each one of us will have a joyful reunion someday with our child.

I know that does not take away the pain of them not being here with us. I can still cry some heavy tears with pretty good sobs. But I try hard to not wallow in the pain of missing her, and instead, imagine what it will be like to see Becca again. It isn't always easy, but it is what I aim for.

Reflection: It is natural to spend a lot of time thinking about the details of our child's departure. But that only keeps us in a dark place, being tormented by something that is over and done. We are the ones reliving it in a painful way. Our children certainly are not!

I want to encourage you to take a minute and picture your "hello." Even if it comes with tears, it is still much better than tormenting yourself with the tears of their departure. Instead, start thinking about the reunion. Ask God to help you make the shift of meditating on the goodbye with darkness and depression, to meditating on the hello with excitement and glory.

> *We may weep through the night, but at*
> *daybreak it will turn into shouts of ecstatic joy.*
> *Psalm 30:5 (TPT)*

August 31

Choosing Forgiveness

Unforgiveness affects our relationship with God, which is why it is so important not to let our hearts be poisoned by it. When our child dies, there are so many people we need to forgive.

We need to forgive anyone and everyone who had anything to do, even remotely, with the death of our child. Oftentimes, we have to forgive ourselves, because we are convinced there is something we could have (or should have) done differently, which would have prevented their death. And many of us have to forgive our child for dying. (To someone who has never experienced the loss of the child, that might sound crazy or even horrible. But those of us who have had to live through this understand how that is possible, for various reasons.)

> *When it comes to the death of our child, including the circumstances around it and the domino effects it may cause, we can discover we don't have what it takes within ourselves to*

> *forgive. But God already knows that, and He has made a way for us to be able to forgive in His strength—a strength far beyond our own.* (When Tragedy Strikes)

The act of choosing forgiveness is not based on emotions or how we feel. It is based totally and completely on a choice we make. When we choose to forgive, we begin working our way toward healing, peace, and yes, it is possible to even have joy once again. If we choose not to forgive, the unforgiveness grows into anger, resentment, and bitterness. It becomes a toxic poison in our lives that we release on everyone around us.

If that describes you, I urge you to make the choice to forgive those you have refused to forgive up to this point. It is not easy. It might even seem impossible, especially if the root of bitterness has gotten a deep enough grip in your heart. But if you don't want to live out the rest of your life in this kind of turmoil and misery, it is a choice you must make. It does not affect the other person, but it will destroy you.

Reflection: Making the choice in our minds to forgive does not immediately affect our heart and the feelings that go so deeply within us. But when we choose to forgive over and over again, making a conscious choice, sometimes even saying out loud, "I choose to forgive," eventually our hardened heart will begin to soften, and we will start to feel a change within us.

Do not let unforgiveness run your life. It will ruin and destroy you, leaving a path of wounded people whom you love. And if your unforgiveness is rooted so deeply that you don't even *want* to forgive, God can help you with that as well. Just be honest with Him and ask Him to give you the desire to forgive, so that you will not remain in this place of darkness, depression, and bitterness. He wants to give you hope. He wants to give you light. He wants to bring life out of the death that has happened within your soul and your very being, and He will if you will let Him.

> *Be careful that none of you fails to respond to the grace which God gives, for if he does there can very*

August

easily spring up in him a bitter spirit which is not only bad in itself but can also poison the lives of many others.
Hebrews 12:15 (PHILLIPS)

September

September 1

It's Taking So Long

Don't be surprised or disappointed in yourself if you feel like you are going backward sometimes in your grief. I remember how often I felt that way. I would have what I considered a good day. Maybe I didn't cry that day. Maybe I was not in such a daze, and I was able to function with my family a little bit. Maybe I was finally able to run several errands in one trip before being too exhausted, causing me to return home before I was finished.

Then the next day I would just fall apart. I could not function. I was back to crying and feeling numb. Sometimes I could not get out of bed, much less leave the house. There were times I could handle something okay, but the following week the exact thing would turn me into a mess again, such as hearing a certain song on the radio. It felt like every time I took one small step forward, I would find myself taking three giant steps backwards.

At the beginning, it feels like you have died yourself and that you are just living in a shell. It feels like every part of you is completely out of your control. But then *ever so slowly,* you start to see a tiny bit of progress. When that happens, it might continue, it might just plain stop, or you may find yourself feeling like you are going backward and that you've lost any progress you thought you were making.

This is typical for all of us in our place of deep grief. There is no rhyme or reason to any of it and there is no timeline.

Some of you may be thinking, "I haven't even started going forward. I just keep going backwards." If you feel like you have not moved forward at all, do not allow yourself to get discouraged, because you will! You will get to a point where you begin to see yourself making progress and be able to handle things better than at the beginning.

Just give yourself a lot of grace and don't compare yourself to where you are with other bereaved parents that are on this journey, especially the ones who are way ahead of you that have been on this journey a lot longer. It does not matter where anyone else is in their journey, because we are all untangling our own messy ball of grief.

Reflection: If you have struggled, wondering if it will always be this way, ask the Holy Spirit to show you the tiny things that are happening, showing that you *are* working your way through it.

It may be something as simple as a stranger smiled at you in a store and you were able to smile back, or the fact that you thought about baking some cookies. It could be that you realized how beautiful some flowers were, or you discovered yourself humming. Maybe you were able to replace a negative thought with a more positive one. Just picking up this book to read today's entry is showing that you are moving forward in some way.

Keep bringing your darkness and your pain to God. Rest when you need to rest. Push through if it is something you feel you need to do. These are all steps of moving forward, whether you feel like you are or not.

Take courage, all you who love him. Wait for him to break through for you, all who trust in him! Psalm 31:24 (TPT)

September 2

Believing in God's Goodness

What determines God's goodness? Is He good because He answers my prayers the way I want Him to? What makes a person good? Is it because they give us what we want to make us happy? Or are they good because they know how to make right decisions for everyone involved? Are they good because they are not willing to compromise in the moment, but hold fast because they see and know the greater good further down the road?

I find it makes me sad when people walk away from God, deciding that He is not a good God because He didn't give them the answer they wanted to a prayer. God is not a vending machine where we put in the prayer, push a button, and the solution we want drops out for us.

We have a young granddaughter who is being taught to say please and is learning that just because she says "pleeeeease" doesn't mean she automatically gets what she wants.

When you ask someone for something, they have a choice to say yes or no. When we ask God for something, He has the choice to say yes or no. Did I want Him to say yes and allow Becca to stay here on this earth? Of course I did, with every fiber of my being! As a matter of fact, I believed He was actually going to heal her heart, either through a miracle or through a heart transplant. I was totally blindsided when she died—even though she was very sick.

But I have chosen not to change my thoughts and beliefs on who God is, just because I did not get a prayer answered the way I wanted it to be answered, no matter how painful it is. That is a big part of what trust is; still believing in the goodness of someone when what I see or feel does not make sense at the moment, no matter how much it hurts or how wrong we think it is.

Your emotions may be telling you that you cannot trust God and that He is not good. However, decisions made based on emotions are quite often wrong. I encourage you to make the difficult choice to trust Him, not based on whether or not you get what you want but based on the fact that if you cannot see His goodness in your situation yet, it means that He is not done working on your behalf.

We all have choices to make about trusting God. We ask our children many times to trust us, *especially* when our decisions cause them pain (and we know what they don't know and can see what they cannot see). God is asking the same thing.

Reflection: A greater measure of healing will begin to happen when we decide that we are going to believe in His goodness and trust Him with our lives once again.

The choice is yours. Are you going to make it based on anger, resentment or frustration? Or are you going to move beyond that, believing He knows how to make right decisions for everyone involved, and that He was not willing to compromise in the moment, but held fast because He sees what we cannot see, and knows what we do not know? Even if it does not happen here on this earth, we *will* see the fullness of His goodness when we are with Him and our children once again.

I am not saying it is easy, but it is possible.

> *I am expecting the Lord to rescue me again, so that once again I will see his goodness to me here in the land of the living.*
> *Psalm 27:13 (TLB)*

September 3

I Did not Understand

When the only beef we have had are McDonald's burgers, and someone invites us to have a steak, we can refuse because we love those burgers so much and can't imagine that anything could taste better! We don't want to miss out on that delicious juicy burger and be disappointed in the steak. (Just go with me here, okay?)

But once we bite into that perfectly grilled and seasoned steak, we realize the incredible flavor we were missing out on all that time and now prefer a good steak instead of a fast-food burger.

So, what does this have to do with our grief? In Romans 8:18 we are told that the glory to be revealed cannot even be compared with the suffering we go through here on this earth. I really truly believe that!

I remember growing up when my dad was watching the news, that sometimes he would grumble, saying things like, "The world is getting so bad that Jesus will have to come back before we hit the 1980's!" That would get me so upset because I wanted to graduate, get married and have kids. I wanted to go to college and get a teaching degree. It wasn't fair that I would miss out on all of that. (And yes, I would beg God not to send Jesus back until I could do all these things that I longed and dreamed of doing.)

Now I realize I felt that way because I did not understand what is waiting for me - the glory, the beauty, the perfection, the pure love that almost melts a person and makes them feel completely whole and so much more!

I honestly believe that once we get to heaven, we will feel so complete and whole, saturated in love, filled with peace and joy beyond what we could ever imagine, that all of those things we so desperately did not want to miss out on, here on earth, will no longer matter one bit.

I also believe our children feel that way now. Remember not wanting a McDonald's hamburger anymore after tasting a perfectly cooked steak? I think what they are experiencing in heaven far outweighs what they may not have wanted to miss out on here on earth.

God's promise of glory far outweighing the suffering that we experience here is not just for us and the suffering we have been through in losing our children from this earth, but it is for our children as well. The glory they are now experiencing cannot even be compared to any suffering *they* may have had here, or anything *they* may have missed experiencing because of their short time here on earth.

Reflection: If you are a parent who struggles with what your child never got to experience here on earth, I suggest you pause and imagine what he or she might be doing in heaven right now. Think about some of the things your child liked to do here, and then picture him or her laughing and exhilarated at doing them, being far better at it there than they ever were here.

Is that scriptural? No, but there are two things I know.

1. God gave us the gift of imagination. As adults, we are so much better at imagining the bad instead of the good, so let's use that gift for good instead of bad.
2. We know, based on the glimpses that John and a few others had, that the Bible cannot tell us everything about heaven, because it is just too much. So why not imagine it to be the things we love here? If we are wrong, we know it will be even

better than what we pictured!

So, I say, use the gift of imagination that God has given you and go for it, especially if it helps pull you out of a place of painful disappointment and regret. Remind yourself that what your son or daughter is experiencing in heaven far outweighs what they may not have wanted to miss out on, here on earth.

> *This is how I work it out. The sufferings we go through in the present time are not worth putting in the scale alongside the glory that is going to be unveiled for us.*
> *Romans 8:18 (NTE)*

September 4

They are Not Lost

Do you have a special memento or something that reminds you of your child, that you keep close to you? I have a special pinky ring, engraved with Becca's name. It has a heart in front of her name and a butterfly behind it. One day I realized it wasn't on my hand. I looked everywhere I could think of and decided it must have gone down the sink drain with some dish water. It just devastated me.

Over a year later I was cleaning out my knitting bag to start working on a knitting project for Christmas gifts. There was the ring, lying in the bottom of the bag! I was so happy my ring showed up that it brought me to tears.

We can be very attached to things that helps us feel like our child is still close to us in some tangible way. Maybe you have never even considered getting a tattoo, but now you have one for your child. You might have a necklace that you never take off containing some of his or her ashes. Maybe it's something in your wallet. We each seem to always have something on us or close to us that reminds us of our child and makes us feel close to them in some way.

Losing my ring and finding it again after so long, and in such a random place, made me wonder; if something like this brought me to tears, what is it going to be like when I finally see Becca again? What is it going to be like when we get to see our kids; not just something that reminds us of them or something that makes them feel close to us? We won't just be looking at or holding an object anymore, but we will actually be seeing them and holding them, pouring out our love on them again! That is going to be incredible, isn't it?

For the rest of our lives, we are going to have moments when we are thinking about what we have lost. It is hard. I wish God would take a giant-sized eraser and take away all the pain of missing them, but that just doesn't happen. We talk about losing our children (or child loss), but aren't you glad that your child isn't really lost, but is in a safe place where you will "find" him or her again?

Reflection: What is that tangible thing you either have on you, or keep close to you, that makes you feel closer to your child? Touch it right now, and as you do, remind yourself how wonderful it is, to only need it as a temporary comfort. It is a momentary substitute for the real thing, which is still in our future.

Pray this with me: *Thank you, Father, that our children may be "lost" from this earth, but they are not lost in the sense that we don't know where they are. Our children are with You, safe and secure and someday we will find ourselves with them and with You for all eternity, never to be lost again.*

For though I am far away from you my heart is with you...
Colossians 2:5 (TLB)

September 5

I Should Have Known

Here is part of an email on a topic that I frequently receive.

> *I feel tremendous and overwhelming guilt that somehow, myself or his father, could have saved my son. The constant questions of "What ifs" or "Was there something I could have done different to save him?" is hardest thing to live with.*

My answer to these kinds of questions is usually pretty simple and straightforward. "No! If there was anything more you could have done, you would have done it!"

There is a man named Jerry Sittser, who lost his mom, wife and a four-year-old daughter in a head on collision with a driver who crossed the center line. Jerry was driving their vehicle and he understandably tormented himself with the same kind of questions, such as, "What if I hadn't insisted that it was time to leave when I did?" "What if I had lingered a little bit longer at a couple of the stop signs on the way out?"

We ask these questions as if what happened to our child was our fault! Looking back, we think somehow, we should have known, so that we could have intervened in some way or done more than what we were already doing.

Most of us don't like the fact that we cannot see our future to be able to alter it or change it in some way, especially in this issue of the death of our child. We don't like not knowing; but the thing is, we don't know what we don't know. Punishing ourselves by living in regrets and tormenting ourselves with the "what ifs" does not bring our child back. It does not change the past.

We cannot change what has happened in the past, but we can decide how we are going to live out our future. Are you going to decide to live in a shell waiting to die as you continue to torment yourself with these things? Or, are you going make the decision to figure out how to live your life in a way that honors your child, and that shows the rest of your family that your child who died isn't the *only* person who is important to you?

Reflections of Hope

That is so critical to do, because our other children, our spouse, or other close family members and friends get the message that the child who died is the only person who mattered in our life. While that child may have been one of the *most* special people in your life, he or she was not the *only* special person. It is important for us to find ways to live so that isn't the message that those around us receive.

You would *never* allow a friend whose child has died to blame themselves. Don't do it to yourself! Let yourself off the hook, just like you would anyone else.

Reflection: We all go through regrets, and we question ourselves and torment ourselves after the death of our child, wondering if we could have done more or missed something we should have seen. Like I said, the answer is no, because you would have done something if you had known.

You need to let yourself off the hook, just like you would insist on someone else letting themselves off the hook. As someone I hope you consider a friend, *I* insist that you let the wondering and the guilt go. Say it out loud. "I release myself. I will not continue beating myself up for something I did not know."

I hope and pray that you will release yourself from these tormenting thoughts and questions, in order to be able to navigate toward hope and light and even meaning and purpose again. If you don't think it is possible, look to those who thought the same thing but have eventually been able to do it, as an encouragement.

> *Whenever our hearts make us feel guilty and remind us of our failures, we know that God is much greater and more merciful than our conscience, and he knows everything there is to know about us.*
> *1 John 3:20 (TPT)*

September 6

The Intimacy of Prayer

Prayer.... *What's the point? Prayers did not keep my child from dying, even though I based my prayers on scriptures in the Bible. So why bother praying anymore?* This is one of the greatest struggles I hear about, in conversations with other bereaved parents. Here is part of one email I have received on this subject.

> *We are told to "Ask and ye shall receive."*
>
> *When prayers are "answered" or miracles happen, we praise and thank God. But, when people die despite prayerful petitions begging to save them, people quickly say that it just wasn't God's plan. It feels like God is always off the hook.*
>
> *Are the answered prayers and miracles part of God's plan, too? Were those miracles going to happen anyway? Or did people actually influence God and change his plan with their prayers and fasting? If I'm "meant to" be hit by a semi-truck while driving the kids to school, should I bother asking God to 'please keep us safe today' during our morning family prayer?*
>
> *I'm struggling to see the point of prayer if our prayers have no influence on God?*

I will admit, this is something that Dave and I both struggled with, even years after the death of our daughter. I continued to pray and have conversations with God but could still find myself hesitant when putting requests before Him for things like healing or protection for my family.

When Becca was diagnosed with bone cancer in her leg at only three years old, people were fasting and praying for her. I also honestly believed the more people I told that God was going to heal her, the more it showed how much faith I had, so God was obligated (according to His Word, so I thought) to heal my daughter! But it did not work that way. Becca still had her little left leg amputated and went through nine months of chemo. This sent me on my own journey about this "prayer of faith" stuff!

Years later, when Becca was married and became pregnant, she was put in the hospital at around five months along and given a 50/50 chance of surviving the labor and delivery because of heart damage caused by the chemo. I didn't understand why I was crying so much when they wheeled her back to get the baby out early. My husband nailed it when he said, "It's because we don't know which direction we are going to have to trust Him for."

Becca lived for another nine years. When she died, it felt like I was put on yet another journey concerning faith and prayer. Something about the death of our child seems to do that to all of us, doesn't it?

There is something about prayer I thought I already understood that I am finally starting to grasp. I am beginning to understand in a much greater way that prayer needs to be a two-way communication as part of my intimate relationship between me and God. I did not realize how much I use prayer to talk to God, assuming I know what His will is, based on the situation, not based on His relationship with me.

I am getting much better at laying my petition before Him, knowing I will be thankful if He answers the way I am hoping, but also praying that He gives me strength for whatever lies ahead, thankful that He will *always* answer that prayer!

Reflection: We need to remind ourselves that in Matthew 5:4, Jesus said that those who mourn will be comforted, not that we wouldn't have death and difficult things affect our lives. Just because God did something one way for someone else, does not mean that is how He wants to do it for me or for you.

He does not want our relationship to be conditional on our end, based on whether or not He does what we want Him to do. He wants us to learn how to be in intimate fellowship, thankful that He always has the final word on every situation in our life, while being who we need Him to be in everything that life and the enemy throws our way. That is a gift I never fully appreciated until now. Ask God to open your eyes and your heart to the same wonderful gift.

September

Look at how much encouragement you've found in your relationship with the Anointed One! You are filled to overflowing with his comforting love. You have experienced a deepening friendship with the Holy Spirit and have felt his tender affection and mercy.
Philippians 2:1 (TPT)

September 7

Our Fuzzy Brains

As you are aware, our brains do not function well *at all* after the death of our child. But you may not be aware that the grief from the death of our child is considered traumatic grief, and actually causes chemical changes in our brains that produce the confusion and fuzziness. So, it isn't just emotional, it is also literally physical.

Shortly after Becca died, I started parking in the same area all the time at stores that I shop at frequently to prevent that feeling of panic trying to remember where my car is. I still park in those same areas, over a decade later.

Several years into my grief journey, my fuzzy brain allowed me to wear my fuzzy slippers from my condo room to the swimming pool with my granddaughter. (We both had a good laugh when we saw what was on my feet at the pool!) And then a few days later, I discovered the same slippers were on my feet as I was starting to wheel the luggage cart out to the car as we checked out of the unit. I laughed at myself again and took a picture of my feet and sent it to my granddaughter.

I know at the beginning, it can be very unnerving to feel like there is no information in your brain to even draw from, even to do things that should be automatic. (I once heard of a grieving mom who forgot how to peel an orange, and someone else who put an entire watermelon in the freezer and discovered it days later.)

Many of us wonder if early dementia is setting in. I sure wondered that for quite some time, but now I know that it is just "grief brain," and I can laugh at my stupid forgetfulness... well, most of the time.

If you struggle with this as well, give yourself lots of grace, and try to get to the point where it doesn't bother you anymore, realizing that is just part of who you are now. Others around you may get frustrated by it and not understand, but we get it, and we love you, fuzzy brain and all!

Reflection: From what I am learning, unfortunately, it never fully goes away. Even eleven years later, if I have a deep trigger, which includes the days around the death date, I still have times where I just do not think straight.

There are some things we can do, like use essential oils, or take certain supplements to help our brain function better. But there is just no way around the grief fog at times. It is something that happens to all of us. Let that be a relief to you, instead of a discouragement.

Want to know something good about it? All these years later, whenever I am forgetful, I can always blame it on grief fog. That's my story and I am sticking to it!

> *I'm bruised and broken, overwhelmed by it all;*
> *breathe life into me again by your living word.*
>
> Psalm 119:107 (TPT)

September 8

He is Sustaining You

In Matthew 4, we read how God spoke with an audible voice from heaven how pleased He was with His Son. Immediately after that, Jesus was *led by the Holy Spirit into a wilderness* where Satan attacked Him at a very weak and vulnerable time.

While Jesus was there, He was without food for forty days. Talk about being extremely vulnerable physically, emotionally, and mentally! This is when Satan came to him in full force, trying to use a time of weakness to trick Jesus into turning the stones into nice warm, fresh bread.

Jesus' famous reply was letting the enemy know that God said we need more than just earthly food to sustain us. We need the bread of life that will sustain us for the long term.

You are still alive because God is sustaining you. You may be at that place where you don't want Him to keep you alive. I was there myself when Becca died, so I get it. But God *is* life, and you being alive means that God is sustaining you, even though it may not feel like it. Sometimes, it is just by helping us take the next breath. That breath comes from God, and even if you don't want that next breath, the fact that you are still breathing and still here, means that God is still sustaining you through the hurt and darkness. He is there *with* you.

I imagine Jesus was struggling, wondering where His Father was in all of this, especially knowing the Holy Spirit had led Him to this difficult circumstance. But I notice that Jesus did not answer Satan based on how he felt. He answered on what He knew to be God's words. Many of us do not feel God's presence or hear His voice because of the dark wilderness we are in. It is so hard to make our decision about where God is, not based on how we feel, but based on what God says about never leaving us or forsaking us.

We may be in a wilderness, but God has not abandoned us there, no matter how much it may feel like it. He is with you. It is so important to be able to grab ahold of this truth. Even if you cannot see it now, when you get further down this road you will be able to look back and see that He really was with you.

Reflection: There was nothing in the law of Moses saying that what Satan was asking Jesus to do was wrong. After all, He was within days of turning water into wine. The temptation to Jesus was not, "You are directly asking me to sin." The temptation was asking Jesus to do something his own way to meet His desire and needs, instead of being led by God within the intimate relationship with His Father.

I know some of you have a hard time reading your Bible. Maybe it is time to try again. It can be helpful to read in the book of Psalms, since David was so good at sharing from a place of rawness and how he felt in places of darkness, writing in a way we can really relate to. But then he often goes from there into how good God is for being with him, taking care of him and going before him, while in that pit of despair.

Just like Jesus said, we are sustained by the word of God. If you cannot seem to read the Bible yet, He can still speak to you in other ways. Ask him to open your ears to hear what He wants to say to you in the context of His heart and being in an intimate relationship with Him. That is an individual thing for each one of us.

> *Your words are what sustain me; they are food to my hungry soul. They bring joy to my sorrowing heart and delight me.*
> *Jeremiah 15:16 (TLB)*

September 9

The Misuse of Scripture

The enemy used scripture to try to get Jesus to make a wrong choice. In Matthew 4:6 Satan comes to Jesus and tempts Him by saying, "If you really are who you say you are, then prove it by jumping off this building because God says (in Psalm 91) He will send angels to keep you from getting hurt." (That is my personal paraphrase.)

Satan was misusing God's own word against Him! I love the answer Jesus gave. "The scriptures also say..." and He threw one right back at the enemy to counter how God's word was being misused.

We often find ourselves in a conflict like this about what the Word of God says. The Word says that He is our healer. The Word says He is our provider and protector. The Word says our prayers have power. The Word says all it takes is a little bit of faith to make things happen.

September

But when our child dies, none of that seems true anymore and we struggle with praying or believing God's Word anymore.

Satan jumps on this. "If any of that were true, God would not have let your child die." Satan is a master at playing the "if" game to put doubts in our minds. He did it to the first humans God created and he did it to Jesus. Why wouldn't he do it to you and me as well?

Just like Jesus refuted scripture with scripture, we need to do the same. Yes, those scriptures of healing and protection are there, but it is also written that we are going to have trials and tribulations. There are no promises that having Jesus in our lives means He will continually work miracles to wipe away all potential problems while we are here on this earth.

Matthew 5:45 says, "For he gives his sunlight to both the evil and the good, and he sends rain on the just and the unjust alike" (NLT).

We know God's promise in Romans 8:28 that says, "So we are convinced that every detail of our lives is continually woven together for good, for we are his lovers who have been called to fulfill his designed purpose" (TPT). Why would God promise to work things out for our good, if there is never anything bad? There *are* good things from God still to come that you cannot see yet.

Reflection: Don't let the enemy suck you down even further by making room for the "if God really..." doubts. There are counter scriptures that will strengthen and help you and will be what you need as an anchor and speak truth into your life.

If you need to find some of those scriptures, do a search on words like rock, tower, strength or refuge. Copy out a few of the verses that will help you refute the doubts that the enemy tries to tempt you with.

The name of the Lord is a tower of strength;
the upright man runs to it and finds refuge.
Proverbs 18:10 (NCB)

September 10

God Cannot Be Manipulated

When Jesus was led into the wilderness to be tempted by the enemy, we know Satan waited until Jesus was at a very weak and vulnerable time after going without food for forty days. The second temptation he brought to Jesus was to throw Himself off the highest part of the temple to prove that Jesus was who He said He was, and to prove that God would "honor His Word".

Satan already knew without a doubt that Jesus was God's Son here on earth in the flesh, and he also knew that God keeps His Word. There really was nothing to prove. But when we are in a fragile and vulnerable time in our lives, the enemy can get us to believe and do things we normally would not believe or do.

If Jesus had thrown Himself off the temple the way the enemy was taunting Him to do, it would have been a situation of trying to force God's hand to honor that one scripture that the enemy quoted from Psalm 91 of the promise for protection.

Jesus recognized that the enemy was using scripture, trying to get Him to manipulate God. He responded with reminding Satan (and probably Himself) "It also says not to put the Lord your God to a foolish test!" (Matthew 4:7 TLB). Jesus jumping off the temple would have been doing his own thing, while having the presumption that God was going to send angels to catch him.

We often do the same thing by holding one or two verses up to God, trying to force His hand to do what we want Him to do. We build our comfort zones so that we do not really need God in our lives. We just need Him to maintain our comfort and not let anything rock our boat. Taking a scripture, applying it to our expectation, and believing God is going to make everything good in our eyes and keeping us in our comfort zone, is putting God to a foolish test. It is also manipulation.

There is a difference between standing on a promise that God has given me for a specific situation, and throwing a verse in God's face to try and strong-arm Him to get Him to do something for me. God does not manipulate, nor can He be manipulated. Manipulation comes from the evil one, and we are on his playing field, following Satan's game plan when we use scripture in a presumptuous way like Satan did with Jesus.

I am so thankful that we serve a God who is not into manipulation and who always has our back, even when it does not serve our comfort zone. I hope you are, too.

Reflection: We know that bailing our kids out from a bad situation is not always the best thing for them. Yes, it keeps them comfortable, but that is not always what is needed. Likewise, God does not always rescue us from our circumstances, but He definitely walks with us through them.

There are times, like the death of your child, that He wants to save you *through* it, not from it. There is a huge difference. As He does, you have an opportunity to get to know Him intimately in a deeper way that most others do not get a chance to know.

There is a larger purpose unfolding that is beyond what makes us happy or keeps us comfortable. Take a minute and ask the Holy Spirit to help you learn to live by what God is doing, which will take you off the devil's playing field of trying to manipulate Him, while guiding you into a deeper truth of who God is and how you will be able to touch others with that truth.

> *Even when your path takes me through the valley of deepest darkness, fear will never conquer me, for you already have! Your authority is my strength and my peace. The comfort of your love takes away my fear. I'll never be lonely, for you are near.*
>
> *Psalm 23:4 (TPT)*

September 11

The Most Painful Loss

One of the times in the Bible where we see a group of people losing children all at once, was the last of the ten plagues in Egypt which can be read about in Exodus 11. It was the death of all firstborn sons when Moses was delivering the Israelites from slavery. Let's back up a few years, though.

I find it interesting that Moses himself survived a genocide. It had been decreed by a previous Pharoah that every Hebrew male baby that was born must be killed by throwing them into the Nile River. Most of us know how Moses survived. He was hidden in a basket, floating on the same river that was supposed to be his deathbed. The Pharoah's daughter found him and raised him in the palace. (All of this can be found in the first two chapters of Exodus.)

Now, many years later, by the decree of God through Moses, the firstborn son of each Egyptian family dies. Exodus 12:30 (NIV) states, "there was loud wailing in Egypt, for there was not a house without someone dead." At that point, the Egyptians begged the Israelites (who were their slaves) to go away.

I think this final plague shows God's agreement that the death of a child is the most painful grief and loss that we can experience here on this earth. Here is something that boggles my mind, though. God allowed Himself to go through that experience when He sent His Son Jesus to die, taking the punishment of our sins on Himself. Father God put Himself through the worst thing a parent can go through, to show the depth of how much He loves us.

Those who think that God is not a loving Father because He allows all these horrible things to happen, do not fully understand love. Love does not create robots, demanding and manipulating others to do everything their own way. Love allows mistakes. It allows consequences. And love is there to bring comfort and peace *within* those painful things that happen to us, because true unconditional love refuses to force its will own on someone else.

September

It is hard to take our eyes off our own pain to understand that God is looking at the full picture of mankind through the lens of eternity. If we think God is only a good Father when He does not let bad things happen here on earth (like the death of our children), it means we still do not understand that He is looking at the full picture with eyes of love.

God knows that the earthly death of our child is not the end. He knows we will be together again. *He willingly let His own Son die a brutal death to make sure that happens because of how much He loves you and your child.* Who does that? Would you? I certainly wouldn't! But God did. Through the suffocating pain of our own loss, we can trust in that kind of love.

Reflection: The sun rises on those who are evil and on those who are good. Rain falls on both the just and the unjust. Jesus Himself tells us this in Matthew 5:45. This means there are times when sin and corruption implode on itself, and those who are innocent are affected, often more than the one who caused the trauma to happen.

If we do not make Jesus Lord of our life, there are going to be difficulties in our lives. And guess what? If we *do* make Jesus Lord of our life, He outright tells us that there *will* be difficulties in our lives (John 16:33). The difference is, when we make Jesus Lord of our lives, His very Spirit lives inside us, which means we have access to peace within our pain. We have the seed of hope in us. We have light that will break through at some point and shine in our place of darkness. We can have joy and laughter within the sorrow. We have comfort and wisdom and the ability to see blessings within the storms of life.

Do what you can to stop fighting Him on how unfair it is, and instead allow Him to be with you in the pain and darkness, knowing that there *will* come a day where He will have His vengeance and it will all be made right.

> *The Lord will be your everlasting light,*
> *and your days of sorrow will end.*
> *Isaiah 60:20 (NIV)*

September 12

Getting Answers from God

We want answers and we want them now! We want (or feel like we need) God to explain Himself to us, telling us why our children left this earth before we did.

I think the bottom line is that we try to make sense of God with our finite brains and limitations, but that is just plain impossible. We want God to answer to us, which is just as futile as a teenage daughter arguing with her parents, wanting them to answer to her. How can they? How can they explain that they see what their teenager cannot see, and know what their daughter does not know, in a way that makes that teen satisfied with the answer? And how can God possibly explain to us through His lens of eternity in a way that makes some sort of sense, causing us to be okay with what has happened?

My husband, Dave, got a four-year degree in Computer Science. (It was so long ago that he even had to do a computer punch card program for one of his classes. Yikes!). His entire 30-year career was with programming computers, fixing computer programs and crashes, or internationally managing others who were doing it.

There are times I ask Dave (who is my personal geek squad) to do something for me, and he has to tell me it can't be done. I always want him to explain why, because it seems like he should be able to find a way, since he is a computer programmer by profession. He often sighs, knowing that at some point I will get totally lost and not understand what he is trying to explain to me. (Interpretation: I get really frustrated, because it still doesn't make any sense to me...)

I am pretty sure the same thing would happen if I were to ask a nuclear scientist a question on how something worked, because it is beyond what my mind would be able to follow or comprehend. God is greater than any computer techy or nuclear scientist, so what makes me think I would be able to follow or comprehend God's explanation, either?

I still occasionally find myself caught in the struggle of wanting to know why. When I find that happening, I sometimes ask God what it is about Him that I don't understand yet, because when I try to lean on my own understanding, I can get all messed up. I want and need to see things from His perspective. What if I don't get an answer to that right away? Then I have decided to continue to believe that He sees what I cannot see, and knows what I do not know, and I will continue to share my heart with Him, trusting that someday, it will all make sense.

Reflection: We often try to bring God down to our level because we want to understand His actions. We want to know why He does what He does. That is like the Israelites. They knew the acts of God, which left them always grumbling and complaining, but Moses knew His ways (Psalm 103:7).

There is a big difference between knowing the actions of God and knowing His heart. When we go beyond knowing the acts of God and press in to knowing His ways (in other words, His heart), we *can* still trust that He is good and He is faithful, even in the deepest and darkest pain we can face on this earth. Are you looking at God through the lens of knowing His actions, or the lens of knowing the heart of His ways? Not needing an answer to the question of why, can make a big difference in moving forward in a needed measure of healing.

Show me how you work, God; School me in your ways.
Psalm 25:4 (MSG)

September 13

Events that Trigger

This week is our oldest son's birthday.

What I do not share very often is that our three-year-old daughter, Becca, was diagnosed with cancer on my due date with this baby. I went ten days overdue, with my water breaking around 3AM while sleeping in a chair next to Becca, who was going to be coming home from the hospital that morning after her first round of chemo. (She had not been home for two weeks since the testing and her diagnosis.)

The labor was only about forty-five minutes from the time my water broke, and the delivery was very rough. It was discovered the baby was coming feet first, but he came so fast there was no chance to do a C-section. They almost lost both of us because he was so large (8 pounds 10 ounces), and the cord was being pinched as he got stuck coming out.

My doctor did some heavy duty yanking and pulling to save us both. I was in *so* much pain during those life-and-death moments and so weak and sick afterwards, since there was no time for an epidural or pain meds. We did not realize how close we came to death until a nurse talked to us about it the following day.

For the next nine months, I hardly ever saw my newborn son, since much of my time was spent an hour away, staying with our little girl at the hospital while getting her chemo. Her amputation made her stays there even more of a challenge.

It was years later when we found out that the long-term effects of one of the drugs Becca had been given was heart damage, which is what eventually caused her death.

All of that to say, it is impossible to think of the day our son was born without thinking of Becca and what we were going through with her during that time, which ultimately caused her death, twenty-six years later.

So, what do we do when our child's death date falls during a time when we should be celebrating something important? Or a celebration is a trigger to our deep loss?

I make time to acknowledge the pain of the "bitter" however I need to. Each time it might look different, but it almost always comes with tears at some point. (As a matter of fact, my eyes are filling with tears right now as I type this.) After allowing myself this time, I then do my best to lean into the "sweet" instead of the bitter. I put my attention and focus on whatever good thing is in front of me.

Yes, there may remain an undercurrent of sadness, but I refuse to let things like my son's birthday be overshadowed by something horrible that cannot be changed, no matter how painful a reminder it may be.

He needs to be celebrated and loved on. Not only does he need it, but I need it as well!

Reflection: I need these event reminders that even though there will be bitter times for the rest of my time here on earth, my life is not just bitterness. There is still sweetness and there are still good things to live for and enjoy.

I have found that the more often I choose to put as much focus as I am able on the sweet, the bitter becomes more tolerable and happens less often. That does not mean it is easy, but with determination, it can be done. I have also discovered that it eventually gets easier to choose the sweet most of the time, although I admit that I still have my moments of leaning into the bitter, and sometimes I still just need to have a good hard cry!

Bittersweet... that is us for the rest of our lives. Which one are you going to choose to focus on, as often as possible? I hope you join me and choose the sweet. The bitter happens enough on its own. Let's do our best to ask God for the desire and the strength to lean into the "sweet" during those times. Are you with me?

> *Let the sunrise of your love end our dark night. Break through our clouded dawn again! Only you can satisfy our hearts, filling us with songs of joy to the end of our days.*
> *We've been overwhelmed with grief;*
> *come now and overwhelm us with gladness.*
> *Replace our years of trouble with decades of delight.*
> *Psalm 90:14-15 (TPT)*

September 14
Spirit to Spirit

We are three-part beings. We have a soul (our mind, will and emotions), we live in a body, but we *are* a spirit being. Jesus was very clear that He was leaving this earth so that the Holy Spirit could come (John 16:7). He lives inside us when we believe and receive by faith that Jesus died for our sins and was resurrected. We are the temple of the Holy Spirit (1 Corinthians 6:19), so our spirit is fully connected with the spiritual realm, whether we are aware of it or not.

In John chapter ten, Jesus says His sheep hear and know His voice and follow Him. As Christians, we are supposed to be sensitive to the Holy Spirit, growing in knowing His voice, so we can grow in our direct communion and fellowship with Him. It is a Spirit-to-spirit connection. So, if we are aware of God's presence, is it that far off-base to occasionally be aware of the presence of our child's spirit, who is connected to Him, Spirit-to-spirit as well?

Let me say I believe there are times when God knows we need encouragement, so He will send us a sign that relates to our child, but it is not him or her. For example, let's say a grieving parent is floundering hopelessly in the suffocating darkness of their grief. A cardinal comes and sits within three feet of them. For whatever reason, some parents will think their child came to visit them as that cardinal. There is no scriptural ground that anyone's spirit comes back in the form of an animal. However, I do believe that God, in His deep love and compassion, sent that cardinal to give peace and comfort, because of a special connection and meaning.

One thing that I become more aware of with each passing year, is how much I do not understand about God. Even having the Bible to read and study His vastness, His majesty, His glory or His love, it is all beyond what I can comprehend or wrap my head around. Paul tells us in I Corinthians 13:12 that we see in part, and we know in part. We cannot see the full picture, because what we see here on this earth is like looking through a dark glass.

September

Yes, I know we have both the Word and the Holy Spirit to teach and guide us, but there is not a single person here on earth who does not have blind spots and wrong beliefs in some areas. None of us knows *all* truth. But we are constantly being taught by the Holy Spirit, who lives inside us, having our eyes opened to more light and more truth, which continues to set us free from false beliefs.

Reflection: If you want to feel connected to your child, I suggest getting as close to God as possible. We fellowship and communicate with Him through our spirits. Having a deep connection with God as Spirit-to-spirit means you are also still deeply connected to your child.

It does not mean you will feel your child's presence, although I believe at times that does happen through God's spirit. But the closer you get to God, the more peace you will have because your trust in Him will grow as He loves on you and communicates to you.

Personally, I don't believe in seeking signs from my child. I believe in seeking God. Remember, you are already connected to the spirit realm because of His spirit inside you. Seek Him, and you will find all that you need to get you through the rest of this journey.

> *From now on, worshiping the Father will not be a*
> *matter of the right place but with a right heart. For*
> *God is a Spirit, and He longs to have sincere worshipers*
> *who adore Him in the realm of the Spirit and in truth.*
> *John 4:23-24 (TPT)*

September 15

I Keep Walking

Back in April, I shared a verse to a song I wrote. It was about how the sun is always in the sky, but we cannot always see it or feel the warmth of it, and how that can be like God in our grief.

I also shared a specific incident that caused me to write this song. One day, taking a walk, the path kept coming and going next to a stream. When I could not see the water, sometimes I could still hear it. There were also times I could not see it or hear it at all, which made me think the trail had taken me away from it. Then suddenly the water would be next to me again.

I started thinking about how that is like our grief at times. Many of us start out in such a place of darkness that we cannot see or hear God. But as we keep going, day-by-day or even minute-by-minute we get glimpses of Him, reminding us that He is still with us.

Today I would like to share what became the first verse and the chorus of this song.

> *You are water, like a stream in the woods*
> *As I am walking in this place of grief.*
> *Sometimes I can see you clearly*
> *And the beauty I see gives me so much hope in my future.*
> *I lose sight of the stream, but I keep walking.*
> *Then I hear a sound and get a glimpse*
> *That the stream is still there so I keep walking*
> *When out of nowhere, the river is there again*
> *In all of its beauty, and I am full of hope again.*
> *I'm reminded that He promised to lead me*
> *Beside still waters and restore my soul.*
> *And I keep walking, I keep walking.*
>
> *As I keep walking remind me of Your love.*
> *Remind me that Your grace and mercy are following me.*
> *As I keep walking remind me that You're here.*
> *Remind me this world is not my permanent home,*

And I'll keep walking, I'll keep walking.

If I can't see You, I'll keep walking.
When I can't feel You, I'll keep walking
Because I know You are here, so I'll keep walking.

Reflection: Some of you may think you have not had any glimpses of God. I believe you have, but just not recognized it. Reading this book is a getting a glimpse of God and His love and care for you.

Once we start realizing God is faithful in giving us those little signs, we get to choose how we react to them. We can either be frustrated and upset that it was only a glimpse and absorb the darkness again, or we can be thankful that we at least got a glimpse and allow it to give us a spark of hope.

I recommend being thankful because that opens our eyes to see even more.

Even when we are too weak to have any faith left,
he remains faithful to us and will help us...
2 Timothy 2:13 (TLB)

September 16

Making God Choose

Many parents are hurt and upset, feeling betrayed by God for not answering their prayers of healing for their child. How could God possibly say that He has so many good things for us and then allow something like this to happen in our lives? Was God lying to us? Was He deceiving us and just trying to make us think that we would have a good life if we received the gift of salvation? Now that we did, is it like a bait-and-switch and we really don't get what we thought we were going to get, or what He told us we were going to have?

There is a teaching in the Body of Christ that if you have enough faith, God will answer your prayer the way you want Him to. But when we think about it, there must be more to it than that, especially if my prayer collides with your prayer.

Let's say there is a mom in a hospital begging God for her son to get a kidney transplant because he will die soon if a transplant doesn't come through. There is another mom who faithfully prays protection over her children every day, not knowing that her daughter is the perfect match for this boy's kidney.

Which prayer is God going to answer? The one who goes to church more often? The mom who pulls out her Bible and reads it more than the other mom? Do the prayers of a parent who is on the weekly worship team have more weight than a parent who serves monthly in the nursery?

If one of these parents is going to have a child die, there must be more than just some sort of balancing scale of who is a "better Christian" or "You have whatever you believe or ask God for." God is *so* much bigger than some formula that we plug in and get what we want like a vending machine.

Just like your prayers don't outweigh someone else's to get what you want, another person's prayers won't outweigh yours and cause calamity in your life when those prayers collide. That is a good thing.

Reflection: We often make the mistake of believing that God's goodness is based on getting what we want in life and not ever having anything too difficult happen to us or our families. However, if you think about a relationship between a parent and a child, that parent is not a good parent because they give their child whatever the child wants. He or she is a good parent for looking at various angles and *not* giving in to that child's desires if they know it will have unwanted short or long-term effects.

I understand that many of our children were not in a situation where there were directly colliding prayers like I described. However, we have no idea what kind of a chain reaction was either avoided or set off that will affect others deeply for eternity because of our child's departure.

Just because we do not understand, doesn't mean that God is not good. Ask God to help you change from seeing Him as a bad Father through the eyes of child who does not understand the painful circumstance, to seeing Him as a good Father who is always there to pick up the pieces of your shattered heart.

> *And I will ask the Father, and He will give you another Helper (Comforter, Advocate, Intercessor—Counselor, Strengthener, Standby), to be with you forever— the Spirit of Truth, whom the world cannot receive [and take to its heart] because it does not see Him or know Him, but you know Him because He (the Holy Spirit) remains with you continually and will be in you.*
> *John 14:16-17 (AMP)*

September 17

Our Promised Miracle

When Jesus walked this earth, He did *so* many miracles in his three years of ministry time. He also warned His followers that we are going to have trials and difficult things happen in our lives while we are here on earth.

Have you ever noticed that when Jesus talked about sending the Holy Spirit, He said the Holy Spirit would be sent to be our Comforter, not to be a constant miracle worker like Jesus was? Most Bible translations use the word Comforter, but it is also translated as Counselor, Helper, Advocate, Strengthener or Companion. Still nothing about helping us be like Jesus in the miracle-working department.

Don't get me wrong. I believe God still does miracles. I also believe that quite often we are praying for some outward miracle of a changed circumstance, when so often the miracle God wants to do is *inside* us through the power of the Holy Spirit.

I think what God does to bring us through to the other side of the worst possible thing that could happen to us, is a miracle. We don't think we are ever going to be able to get out of the suffocating darkness. We don't think we are ever going to be able to enjoy life again. The place we are in is just too dark, too heavy, and too deep of a pit.

Wouldn't it be a miracle if God could pull you out of this? Wouldn't it be a miracle if you got to the point where you were okay to go on living without your child here? Wouldn't it be even more of a miracle if you *wanted* to live a life of meaning and purpose again while you are waiting to be reunited with your child?

Does that seem impossible? Welcome to the world of miracles!

Many of us have been taught that we need have enough faith to see miracles happen. But how much is enough? If that is all it takes, then it seems we did not have enough faith to keep our child from dying.

Faith isn't being presumptuous in telling God what the outcome should be. It is in knowing intimately and trusting the God who holds the outcome in His hands. It is believing that if He does not do the outward miracle that I want or think I need, that He will do a miracle on the inside of me to get me through it. In other words, faith is trusting in God to do the miraculous, based on His course of action, not mine.

Reflection: I know this is a difficult thing to understand. We all know God could have stepped in and saved our child from leaving this earth so early, but He didn't. That does not mean that God did not step in and do a miracle.

Maybe the person He wants to save is *you* in a way you never even knew you needed. After all, God already did a miracle for our child by meeting them at the transfer point and welcoming them to a place of absolute perfection that our minds cannot even begin to comprehend.

Ask the Holy Spirit to open your mind and heart to the miracle that He wants to do in and through you, and to also accept the fact that He did a different miracle for your child than the one you wanted. If you keep going, you will eventually make the same discovery I did; that even in the pain and the darkness of the death of my daughter, I experienced a miracle-working God whom I trust more now than I ever did.

> *But when the Father sends the Comforter instead of me—and by the Comforter I mean the Holy Spirit—he will teach you much, as well as remind you of everything I myself have told you.*
> *John 14:26 (TPT)*

September 18

Heaven

As a pareavor, I have five things that I think are important about the subject of heaven.

1. Being a spiritual person does not automatically erase the painful effects of our child leaving this earth ahead of us.
2. Some parents have a fear of not knowing if their child is in heaven.

   > *I believe God is big enough to have made every opportunity possible for your child to accept Him before leaving this earth. This could easily have happened during a time you know nothing about (including crying out to Him at the moment of death)... Not having the information, you want to have doesn't mean it did not happen at some point in their lives.* (When Tragedy Strikes)

3. You are not a terrible person for having a stronger desire to get to heaven to see your child than to see Jesus. You have made an extremely valuable deposit there!

4. When we arrive, we get to hear stories from others about our children and what they have been doing there. Can you imagine Moses coming up to you, laughing about something your child did that he just has to tell you about? Wow! Now there is a thought! Our children are hanging out with so many incredible people that are history to us, but real life to them.

5. We need to remember that it is a good place! So good, that anyone who has had the privilege of getting a glimpse of it cannot describe it. It's kind of nice to know that there is an opposite to the pain we feel that is so dark we can't describe it. Makes me think of Romans 8:18 that says the glory to be revealed cannot even be compared to the suffering. That must be some glory, and our children are experiencing it!

Reflection: I know we would rather have our children here with us. Hands down, no question about it! But since that is no longer an option, why not think about what heaven is like for them? While they were here with us, we always wanted good things for them, right? We would willingly sacrifice to make sure they were well taken care of and happy.

Well, now God is doing that for us. And I don't know about you, but I am positive He is doing a better job of it than I did. Plus, I no longer feel the need to worry about Becca, or pray tearful prayers over her life, because I know that she is safe, whole, and full of joy.

I know this does not erase the pain of missing our children, and we still want them with us. But it certainly takes some of the sting to think about things from their viewpoint now. Let's spend some time today thinking about where our children are, instead of where they are not.

So we do not set our sights on the things we can see with our eyes. All of that is fleeting; it will eventually fade away. Instead, we focus on the things we cannot see, which live on and on.
2 Corinthians 4:18 (VOICE)

September 19

Why?

Every step on our life journey is a step of trust. We either trust in others, in ourselves, or in God. Trusting completely in others, or only in ourselves, will eventually fail. But when something horrible happens in our lives (such as the death of our child), we often tell ourselves we cannot trust God unless we know the "why."

I often use my own experience as a parent to help me understand my heavenly Father. Are there times I need my children to trust me without giving them an explanation? Of course. Are there lots of reasons I might not tell them why? Yes. I also know there are times my children have asked why (or why not), not because they really want to know, but because they want to be able to argue against my reason, whatever that reason is.

We can have the same attitude with God. Even if He told us why He allowed this tragedy in our lives, it would not be a good enough reason in our intense pain and darkness, and we would just want to argue with Him on how wrong He was to do this to us.

Understanding will not bring us peace. That is why we are told to trust in God and not in our own understanding (Proverbs 3:5). For some reason, we often think that if *we* can figure things out, *we* can be in control. But the relief felt does not last very long because soon there is something else that we are trying to make sense of.

During deep grief, people either move toward God or away from Him. But when we move away from Him, we are moving away from the One who can help us the most. God wants to walk with us through this valley of death. He wants to give us comfort. He wants to give us strength. He wants to give us hope. These are all things we desperately need. But if we choose to move away from Him, we will continue to desperately need these things. This is a time to get as close to God as you possibly can.

Reflection: The picture I get is one of a distraught child crying uncontrollably as a father bends down to pick up that child. The child is so upset that he is kicking and screaming and fighting his father. Eventually, the child runs out of strength and relaxes in the embrace of his loving father. And now that child can receive the comfort, strength, and hope that he wants and needs.

It is the same with us. We often fight the One who can give us the very things we need. Instead, we need to quit fighting Him, receive His embrace, and allow Him to carry each of us in His strong arms of love.

*Trust in the Lord with all your heart.
Never rely on what you think you know.
Proverbs 3:5 (GNT)*

September 20

Tossed in the Storm

In Luke chapter eight, we read about how the disciples were out on a boat when a huge storm came. The boat was filling with water and the disciples were terrified that it was sinking, and they were going to die. Where was Jesus? He was with them, asleep in the boat!

Isn't that how we feel when our child dies? We know that we are sinking, and we feel like Jesus is sleeping, not doing anything to help us. We want to wake Him up to stop the storm like He did for the disciples.

What did Jesus tell the disciples after He stopped the storm? He asked them where their faith was. "Where is your trust in me?" Even when it feels like Jesus is asleep, He is still in charge of the wind and the waves and when the time is right, He *will* get up and calm your storm.

We want God to show up in a certain way, and when He doesn't, we think He is not there with us. We have expectations of Him, and when God doesn't do things our way, we think He has abandoned us. Jesus thought God abandoned Him while hanging on the cross, but I don't believe that was true.

I have always been taught that God turned His back on Jesus because He was a holy God and could not look at or be around sin. If that were true, God would not have come into the garden looking for Adam and Eve after they sinned. It is our own guilt and shame that separates us from Him, not our sins which have been paid for in full! When Jesus cried out while hanging on the cross, asking why God had forsaken Him, He was quoting King David in Psalm 22:1. God did not abandon King David, God did not abandon Jesus, and God has not abandoned you.

Isn't it interesting that God knew the storm would come while they were out on the water, and yet He didn't warn them in some way not to get into the boat? When we allow God to be God, and learn to rest in that, there is a sweetness that comes in. There is beauty in fighting your way through the night as you rest in Him. Do not fight for answers. Don't fight to stay angry. Fight for a place of surrender and a place of rest within the dark and tumultuous storm of grief.

Jesus is in your boat with you through the storm. If it feels like He is sleeping, just curl up next to Him and sleep with Him. Let His peace become your peace while the storm rocks your boat.

Reflection: In Matthew 14 and Mark 6, we read about another time the disciples were out on a boat when a big storm came, but this time Jesus was not with them. Instead, He came toward them walking on the water. Peter wanted to walk with Him, so Jesus told him to come on out. Peter got out of the boat and started toward Him, walking on the water, but as soon as he focused on the storm, Peter started to sink. Jesus was right there to help him.

The only thing that keeps you from drowning in your pain is Jesus. However, the only thing that keeps you from Jesus is the pain. So, the question becomes where is your focus? If you continue to focus on the storm and the pain, you will sink. If you do what you can to focus on Jesus being there with you in the storm, knowing He *will* calm it for you at some point, you will be okay.

When Peter wanted to walk on water, Jesus didn't reprimand him for saying, "IF you are Jesus...." He just said, "Come!" He is saying the same thing to you as He did to Peter.... Come.

> *Jesus said, "Come!" So Peter got out of the boat and walked on the water toward Jesus.*
> *Matthew 14:29 (GW)*

September 21

A Place of Surrender

I have many pareavors ask why they do not see or hear God, or feel His presence like I did, or like others they have heard about. For me, one of the keys has been surrendering.

I spent more time resting in Him than I did wrestling with Him about why my daughter died or demanding to know why He let her get cancer when she was only three years old (which started the whole thing). I decided even more than why, I needed to know *how* I was going to possibly get through this suffocating darkness and pain to be able to live a life of contentment, meaning and purpose again. I surrendered. Instead of fighting God on the why, I wrestled with Him on the how.

There is no button to push to just suddenly surrender. But we can offer the invitation to ourselves to move toward a place of surrender. We can set the table. How do we do that? I believe the best way is by coming before God and just being in His presence. Let Him know that you have nothing to say. You are done talking. Just focus on something like the beauty of the nature in front of you or think of a word that you can focus on such as the word Shalom (the Hebrew word for peace, rest, wholeness) and then trust that in the silence, that God is at work doing what needs to be done deep inside of you.

We need to cultivate an environment where surrender is most likely to happen, which is usually in the silence of just letting God be God on the inside of us. There is a real grace in allowing ourselves to just be. It puts us in a place to receive, and receiving is so much easier than trying to manufacture what we need! "Jesus, you are the Prince of Peace. You are my peace and I surrender to and come under that covering of peace that you have for me, as you live inside me."

Even in a place of surrender, the pain and darkness are not lifted immediately like we want them to be, but God is with us in that place. That is what makes surrender bearable. There is something beyond myself that is holding everything together, so I can trust Him to hold me together, too. If I am left to myself, I will continue to spiral down, but connecting to someone so much bigger than me is an anchor that will get me through the worst of this storm.

You can either put yourself in a place of surrender, or you can be an angry and resentful person, causing the pain and darkness to continue for even longer. The choice is yours. I highly recommend the place of surrender.

Reflection: One of the things that causes suffering is resistance to suffering. Until you surrender to the hurt and what caused it, you cannot find healing. The posture of surrender and acceptance to the fact that our children are no longer here with us on earth is taking a huge step toward finding our way out of the suffocating darkness and pain that feels unbearable.

Ask yourself what God is inviting you into, because embedded in every circumstance there is a divine invitation to move into a new and deeper place with Him. Please hear my heart of love and gentleness behind what I am about to say. These are the cards you have been given. What are you going to do with them? Are you going to fold, or are you going to do some trading so you can play and win? We really can trade anger, pain and darkness for purpose, meaning and joy. We may have found ourselves playing a totally different game, but we can still win.

Even when bad things happen to the good and godly ones, the Lord will save them and not let them be defeated by what they face.
Psalm 34:19 (TPT)

September 22

Our Emotions

After the death of our child, we are filled with strong emotions that we did not even know we could have. Others around us don't understand why we cannot just let go of things like seething anger or deep sorrow. They think we are choosing to hang on to them, or not relying on God enough.

For those first several months (I am talking up to even twenty-four to thirty-six months), those emotions overtake us. If that is the case for you, it is okay to admit that is where you are. Just because others who have never lost a child don't understand, you do not have to try to deny or feel guilty about the emotions you are having. As a matter of fact, experts will say that the only way out of the deep suffocating grief is to lean into those emotions.

That seems like the last thing we want to do, isn't it? But the only way to get past them is to go through that valley of the shadow of death. Don't try to push those feelings away but lean into them. Let yourself feel what you need to feel.

After a while, you will learn how to lean in but not let it highjack you. You will realize that what happened is what happened, and there is nothing you can do about it. You may even be able to observe those emotions compassionately from a distance as you give yourself the grace to grieve.

As we allow ourselves the needed space to feel what we need to feel, those emotions will eventually start to subside a bit and give you some

September

space to breathe and live again. When those emotions come back and overtake you, lean in again. Fighting it prolongs getting through it.

When you are not living from a place of anger, regret and other negative emotions that all come with the death of our child, it opens you up to a place where you can begin to see a future that is not full of pain, but one that can still have meaning, purpose, and even contentment and joy again.

It also makes it easier to receive what God has for you. God has, and is, everything we need. It is easier to receive than to try and manufacture it. Surrendering to Him allows the door to be opened for those things to start growing in us until they start manifesting, or we begin to see the seedling pop through. But just like in the natural, it still takes quite a while for a tree to fully grow and start to bear fruit.

Until then, you need to know that others have been right where you are. You are not alone.

Reflection: One of the things that keeps us in such a difficult place emotionally is continually wanting to know why it happened and thinking how unfair it was for our child to die. "Why *me*? Why *my* child?" Here is another way to look at that. "Why *not* me? What makes me think I deserve to be exempt more than others from deep suffering while here on this earth?"

Sometimes a different perspective can help us with our emotions. It is never a sudden fix, but a process. The only way out of the darkness and emotional turmoil is plowing through it. Just like a really bad storm, it will eventually pass. There may be a lot of damage and rebuilding will need to take place, but it will not always feel like this.

God, you're such a safe and powerful place to find refuge!
You're a proven help in time of trouble— more than
enough and always available whenever I need you.
Psalm 46:1 (TPT)

September 23

I Want to Quit

The devil is always trying to throw us into a pit. With the death of our child, he succeeded throwing us into a deep one. Then he lies to us, telling us we can never get out.

Do not believe the lies of Satan that you will never get out of this dark pit that he has thrown you into and that life will never be worth living again. God is no respecter of persons, and what He does for one person He will do for anybody. The promises of God are for all of us, so if you know of even one person who has been able to get out of that place after the death of their child, then you can be there, too.

Let me say it again. You can be there too! You may feel like giving up, but I want to remind you that God's mercy is new every single day. Quitting is not an option.

I recently heard a story about a donkey who fell into a deep pit. The owner decided the donkey was so old, it was not going to be worth the work and the effort to get him out, so he asked a couple of neighbors to help him throw dirt in the pit to just bury the poor thing. At first the donkey sounded very pitiful as they shoveled in the dirt, but then it got quiet. They figured it had already died and kept shoveling in the dirt to finish burying the animal.

The men did not realize that as they threw the dirt down on the donkey, it would shake the dirt off its back and get on top of it. As they threw down more dirt, the donkey would shake it off and get on top of it. That old donkey did it long enough, refusing to give up, until eventually he was able to climb out of the pit on top of what was supposed to put him under.

Jesus is an expert at getting people out of the pit they find themselves thrown into by the enemy. The Good Shepherd, Jesus Himself, said that He will leave the ninety-nine for the one. If you are the one, He is coming for you, to get you out of your place of darkness!

No matter what pit you get thrown into, if you are a man or woman of God, He can pull you out and lift you up to a place you never thought

September

was possible. God will even use the exact thing the enemy tried to use to take you under, to pull you back up in a way that you did not expect. After all, God brought Jesus out of the grave after snatching the keys of hell and death from the enemy who put Him in the grave!

God's hand and favor (yes, His favor) is on you, no matter what the enemy does to you. So don't give up. Do not quit.

Reflection: Joseph was someone who literally went from a pit to a palace. His jealous brothers had thrown him into a pit with plans to kill him, but instead sold him as a slave to a passing caravan going to a different country. God was at work in Joseph's life for many years, to the point where he was second in command to the Pharaoh of the strongest nation on the earth at that time.

When Joseph's brothers were forced to go to him and grovel at his feet to beg for food for their families in a time of famine, his response (in Genesis 50:20) can be our response as well, to the one who put us in our pit. "What you meant for evil and harm, God intended for good, that I may be in a position to...."

You probably don't know what that position is yet, but you can still fill in the blank with something like "that I may be in a position to kick your devil back-side big time some day!" Go ahead! Let him know right now that you are not staying down there. Then give the Holy Spirit permission to work His resurrection power in your life to get you out of that pit.

He lifted me out of the pit of despair, out of the mud and the mire.
He set my feet on solid ground and steadied me as I walked along.
Psalm 40:2 (NLT)

September 24

The Enemy Wants You Hopeless

All of us are goal-oriented people. Think about it. We are always moving toward something we want in life. That is a good thing because those goals give us something to look forward to. It is called hope.

When our child dies, all our goals that had to do with that child dies with them, which seems to carry over into every part of our lives. We lose hope that life is even worth living without the plans we had for, and with, our child. When we don't have any hope, we don't see a future, and it puts us in a vicious cycle which is hard to get out of.

The enemy wants to keep us in that place of hopelessness. He wants us to think that the darkness will never end. He tries to get us to give up on even trying to get out of the pit we have found ourselves hurled into. He wants to keep us defeated, which will happen if we believe his lies that it is God's fault we are in this place and believe life is not worth living anymore.

God does not bring harm. He does not do bad things to us. God knew this would happen, and He still has good things for you on the other side of the darkness. No pit of darkness can hold you forever because of what Christ did for you. If you make a conscious decision to dig in your heels, determined not to roll over and quit, but decide you are going to get from the pit to the palace (like Joseph did) and not let the enemy stop you, God will step in and get you there.

Every trial and difficult thing I have been through is what has made me who I am today. I have heard Joyce Meyer say that victory with God is not a ride on an escalator. It is a walk of faith, one step at a time. We may not understand it, but if we put our trust in Him, He will take what the enemy meant to take us out, turn it around, and use it to trample the enemy and use it for something meaningful and good in our lives.

I am not saying that we will get to the point where we think the death of our child was something good that happened in our lives. That just will not happen. But if we keep leaning into Jesus and the victory that He gained for us through His death on the cross, He will take this horrific tragedy and cause something good to come from it.

God is totally amazing in that way! He doesn't cause the bad things to happen in our lives, but He takes those bad things and turns them into something good that will help us be able to move forward, wounding the enemy that caused it, making him ineffective. It is like taking the enemy's weapon out of his own hands and using it on him with full force! Who would not want to do that?

Reflection: Hope is a belief of confidence and trust that somehow, someway, God is going to take what happened and work it out for something good in your life. Look for the little, tiny glimpses of light that God is at work, pulling you out of the pit. They are there to encourage you while you are still down there as He is working behind the scenes.

Hold on to the spark of hope it gives you that God is doing the impossible of bringing you out of the darkness back into the light. He is pulling you out of the pit the enemy put you in and is heading you to the palace of His goodness, where life will have meaning and purpose again.

*As for you, because of the blood of my covenant
with you, I will free your prisoners from the waterless pit.
Return to your fortress, you prisoners of hope.
Zechariah 9:11,12 (NIV)*

September 25

Was It God's Fault?

As I was looking at some of the parents in the Bible who had lost a child, I came across a scripture that seemed to go totally against what I believe about God, and even what I have shared with others about God's goodness, and how He does not cause death.

I am referring to 2 Samuel 12:13-15 that says God struck King David's child with an illness, causing him to die. This is something that goes against what we know about God being a loving Father. It also seems to conflict with other scriptures, which can cause lots of pain and confusion in the death of our own child, such as Deuteronomy 24:16 (NIV) which says, "Parents are not to be put to death for their children, nor children put to death for their parents; each will die for their own sin." Or there is Ezekiel 18:20 (NIV) that states, "The one who sins is the one who will die. The child will not share the guilt of the parent, nor will the parent share the guilt of the child."

These were instructions to the Israelites as part of their laws. We may read those verses and think that God does not keep His own word because He did punish David's child for the sin of his father.

Let's look at this a bit further. First, only God can go beyond every situation and see the eternal results, which gives Him the right to make a different decision than the one He tells man to make. Secondly, we see death as a punishment, something bad. But for a seven-day old infant, how is going straight to heaven and skipping the part of being on this earth a punishment? That baby went from seven days of living on earth, to living in God's glorious presence forever!

Psalm 116:15 tells us that God sees the death of one who belongs to Him as precious. Second Corinthians 5:8 reminds us that to leave our body is to be home with the Lord. In Philippians 1:21, Paul rightly believed that to leave this earth by dying is a huge gain. It is a profit, or a promotion.

We act like death is the worst thing that can ever happen to our child, but is that really the case? Maybe, death is the best thing that could have happened to them, because now they are in a place of perfection and love beyond what we can comprehend here. I am pretty sure they do not regret missing out on milestones here on earth like we do for them.

Yes, it is *the worst* thing that could have happened to *us*, but not to them. Whether the death of our child was caused by God directly or by natural circumstances, the bottom line is that they got to go ahead of us. It was a promotion they received before we did. They got to jump the line! I truly believe that when we get to join them, either everything will finally make sense, or it just won't matter anymore.

September

But until then, we are left with allowing God to pick up the pieces of our shattered hearts and hold them gently in His hands.

Reflection: There are going to be scriptures we do not understand and don't know what to do with. Some scriptures seem to contradict each other. There are some verses that seem to contradict what has happened in our life, with what we thought we know about God, which could be where the answer lies. We think we know who God is, but there is always more to learn about Him.

If what we think we know about God pushes us away from Him, then we need to pray to discover the truth, because knowing who God really is will draw us closer to Him, not push us away from Him.

I am not a Biblical scholar and don't have the theological answers to why it seems God contradicts Himself, but we do know that peace comes when we choose to trust Him, in spite of what does not make sense from our limited view and painful circumstances. I have chosen to stay in relationship with Him because I don't know of any other way to make it through my time here on earth.

> *That is why we never give up. Though our bodies are dying, our inner strength in the Lord is growing every day. These troubles and sufferings of ours are, after all, quite small and won't last very long. Yet this short time of distress will result in God's richest blessing upon us forever and ever! So we do not look at what we can see right now, the troubles all around us, but we look forward to the joys in heaven which we have not yet seen. The troubles will soon be over, but the joys to come will last forever.*
> *2 Corinthians 4:16-18 (TLB)*

September 26

A Very Wrong Statement

"God won't give you more than you can handle!"

Why do people say this? There are so many tragic things that happen on this earth that are way beyond what we can handle, especially the death of one's child!

It certainly doesn't bring any kind of comfort. And it is not in the Bible anywhere! The closest thing to it is in 1 Corinthians 10:13, where we are told that God will not allow us to be tempted to sin beyond what we can handle, and always provides a way out of that temptation.

Plus, saying that God won't give us more than we can handle, puts the blame on God for something He did not do. How are we supposed to trust God, running to Him for peace, comfort and healing if He is the one who did this to us? Think about it this way; if someone punches us in the face, how easy would it be to turn to that same person for comfort for what they did to us, as the one who caused our pain?

God did not bring death and evil into this world. God is not the one who gave us this horribly painful circumstance. We live in a sinful world. Evil and corruption are all around us, and we are not immune to it while living here on earth, even as believers in Christ. God let us know that and wants to walk with us through this dark valley. He hurts with us, collecting our tears. He wants to love on us and comfort us, which is exactly what we need. He also sent Jesus to conquer death so that our separation is not permanent.

I remember talking to my friend, Sara, as Dave and I were staying in her home. She had lost her only child, Jeanette, six years earlier. We both agreed that if we had to choose between 1) Using God as a magic genie to get whatever we wanted to avoid suffering, or 2) Knowing Him and experiencing His love more deeply and intimately than we ever knew was possible within our suffering, we would both choose the deeper relationship with Him and His incredible love. Do we wish it came some other way than through the death of our children? Of course!

It's okay if you are not to a point where you feel that way. It is also okay not to agree with such a wrong statement that God will not give us more than we can handle.

Reflection: One of the songs I sang often in my younger years had a line in it several times that said, "God can do anything but fail." Think about that. One thing that God *cannot* do is to fail. We may think He has failed us by not stopping the death of our child, but that is because we are seeing it through our heart of pain and limited human perspective of what we have lost here on earth.

The truth is, the death of our child *is* more than we can handle, but that does not have to be a bad thing. Just like Sara and myself, and countless other pareavors, you can eventually get to the same place of being thankful for a much deeper level of knowing Him and experiencing His love more intimately than we ever knew was possible here on earth.

Then Christ will make his home in your hearts as you trust in him. Your roots will grow down into God's love and keep you strong. Ephesians 3:17 (NLT)

September 27

Does it Really Matter?

Many pareavors who have been on this journey for a while will do their best to give hope to those just beginning, encouraging them that it is possible to eventually live a life of meaning and purpose again. We know that each of you will get to the point where you realize the importance of living purposefully. If you have been reading this book for a while, you have probably read that from me several times now.

Reflections of Hope

There is a popular poem by Linda Ellis called *The Dash*. It is about a man who spoke at a friend's funeral. He mentioned the two dates that will go on the tombstone, which are the birth and death dates. But then he went on to talk about the small dash between those two dates, which represents the life lived.

I know we wish that the life our children lived, represented by the dash, had much more time and many more events in it. But that is not what I want us to focus on today. I want to talk about our own "dash." In this poem, several questions are asked that I think are good for us to think about in our own lives.

At this point, I don't think we have to ask ourselves if we are putting things ahead of people. Worldly possessions have already taken a back seat to what is truly important in life, so that is not much of an issue for most of us after the death of our child. But we can ask ourselves if we are treating others well. Are we showing appreciation more often and loving those around us more deeply, knowing how fleeting life can be?

Are we treating others with more respect and compassion? Are you doing what you can to make the lives of those around you better? Are you occasionally giving a smile to those around you who may need such a simple thing to keep going themselves?

What will your eulogy say as to how you lived out your "dash?" Would you be pleased? Would your son or daughter who is waiting for you be able to proudly say, "That's my mom!" or "That's my dad!"? I think that is something to not only think about, but to aim for.

Reflection: Yes, I want us to pause and ask ourselves: How am I living my dash? Am I fighting my way out of the darkness, back to a place of light, and hope and purpose again, in a way that honors my child, and honors the One who created my child and me?

These are not just significant dates for our children, but someday they will be for us as well to those left behind. Let's do our best to make sure that *our* dash matters, not just before the death of our child, but after their death as well. I want the *full* dash to count, for Becca, for me and for the rest of my family. How about you?

*We've passed through fire and flood, yet in the end you always bring
us out better than we were before, saturated with your goodness.
Psalm 66:12 (TPT)*

September 28

Being Convinced

When everything is going great and I am getting all my prayers answered the way I want, it is easy to believe that God is faithful, that He is good, and to choose to trust Him with my life. But it is totally different to still believe He is faithful and good, continuing to trust Him when something horrible happens, like the death of my child.

If you are like me, for many years I was a "good Christian" and "claimed the promises of God" like praying protection over my family. And I saw Him answer those prayers over and over again. So, when my daughter, Becca, died, does that mean God did not keep His promises? Does it mean that He is not faithful and that I can no longer trust Him?

I can offer no easy fix or solution to this often painful dilemma after the death of one's child, although it is very black-and-white. We either believe God is good and Satan is evil, or we do not. We either believe that God *isn't* big enough and has *not* won the final victory over sin and death, or we believe that He is *more* than enough, and the death of my child is not where God reached His limits. Somehow, He has a way out of the suffocating darkness of grief *because* of His deep love for me, and I am determined to hold on to Him with everything I have until He gets me to that place.

There is freedom in surrender. There is peace in trusting. That may not make any sense, but isn't that part of what makes Him God? So often, life here on this earth will not make any sense with our limited minds. We need to get to the point where we are okay with the fact that there are some answers we will not get on this side of eternity.

Reflections of Hope

Living life here on earth without my oldest daughter has been an extremely painful challenge. And in working my way through the grief, I have discovered that God is not who I thought He was. He is way better than how I limited Him before. He is more compassionate, more loving, more faithful... more *everything* that is good and what I need, to get me through my remaining time here until I am reunited forever with Becca.

I pray you will make the same discovery.

Reflection: Do you feel separated from God's love? Romans 8:38-39 says something that most of us quoted and believed before our child died.

> *For I am persuaded that neither death nor life, nor angels nor principalities nor powers, nor things present nor things to come, nor height nor depth, nor any other created thing, shall be able to separate us from the love of God which is in Christ Jesus our Lord* (NKJV).

Think about it. We used to truly believe with all our hearts that nothing, including death or things to come, would be able to separate us from God's love. Now we are in that place of death and "things to come" that we had no idea would happen. Let me say that it is just as true today as it was before your child left this earth. Absolutely *nothing* (including your doubts, thoughts, feelings confusion, anger or blame) can separate you from God's love. Ask the Holy Spirit to help convince you of this fact.

> *For I am convinced that nothing can ever separate us from his love. Death can't, and life can't. The angels won't, and all the powers of hell itself cannot keep God's love away. Our fears for today, our worries about tomorrow, or where we are–high above the sky, or in the deepest ocean–nothing will ever be able to separate us from the love of God demonstrated by our Lord Jesus Christ when he died for us.*
> *Romans 8:38-39 (TLB)*

September 29

Sorrow and Suffering

Sorrow and suffering. Those two words often seem to be together, but they don't even begin to describe how we feel after the death of our child.

I was having it out with God about this one day. The depth of the pain was unbearable. I knew that somehow, I had to get past it; that I could not go on living this way in such deep darkness and depression. I also knew I had to be the one to allow myself to release it but did not know how.

Shortly after, somewhere I heard or read the words "Spiritual blessings come wrapped in trials." I wrote a note saying: "The loss of a child is an awfully deep trial to wrap a blessing in!" God's unexpected answer followed as a whisper in my heart, "I know, because My Son died, and it was wrapped in the blessing of you!"

Wow! You might want to read that again. God knows how a blessing can be wrapped in a huge dark trial, because when Jesus died while hanging on that execution stake, it was wrapped in the blessing of having you (and your child) live with Him for all eternity!

God knows deep sorrow, which includes watching His son be brutally beaten and murdered. And within that sorrow, He carried ours as well. Obviously, Jesus knew sorrow and suffering as well, to the point of being in such a dark place that He thought Father God had turned His back on Him as His Son.

Sorrow and suffering are companions to us in this life. No one is immune. Yes, I understand that for those of us who have lost a child, these two things run deep and seem to be able to outlast us. But someday, we will discover that as they have traveled this journey with us, we leaned on them a lot to help get us through the darkness.

Why do I say that? Because the only way out of our place of pain and darkness is to go through it. We cannot push them away, no matter how much we want to. We need to put our hand in theirs, allowing them to lead us out. Let your sorrow melt into His sorrow. Let your suffering be absorbed by His suffering. When you do, you will begin to see to the other side.

Reflection: The book of Psalms is full of laments. David knew how to press into the sorrow, taking all of it to God as he went through the different emotions of his own grief (including having both an infant and an adult son who died). One of the ways to allow sorrow and suffering to lead us is to talk to God about it, like David did. If you are angry, tell Him. If you are sad and depressed, share that with Him. No matter how you are feeling, tell those things to the One who understands and is there in the darkness with you.

One day, these two companions of sorrow and suffering will give way to the companions of joy and peace. When we experience the fullness of them, like our children are now experiencing, we won't even recognize or remember what our old companions were like!

And everything I've taught you is so that the peace which is in me will be in you and will give you great confidence as you rest in me. For in this unbelieving world you will experience trouble and sorrows, but you must be courageous, for I have conquered the world!
John 16:33 (TPT)

September 30

G.R.I.E.F

Using G.R.I.E.F. as an acronym, here are five of the most important things I believe you need to remember on this grief journey.

G - *Give yourself lots of grace.* Don't compare where you are on your journey with others. Do not put yourself on a timetable. Don't expect too much from yourself, because you are going to be forgetful and you will feel like you are crying all the time. Be kind to yourself.

September

Give yourself lots and lots of grace and allow yourself lots and lots of time. There is no right or wrong way. It is whatever way works for you at that moment in time.

R - *Release yourself from the guilt,* especially the "should haves," and "if onlys." If you had a friend who was blaming themselves for their child's death, you would tell them not to. That is a terrible burden for your friend to put on themselves, so do not do it to yourself.

Why wait until you are with your child to release yourself? Release yourself from the guilt right now. Do not say *I can't.* You are choosing to hold on to it as a way to punish yourself. Regrets and guilt do not serve you well. It just keeps sucking you under.

I - *Ignore those who want to try to fix you.* They mean well, but if they have not lost a child, they cannot possibly know what you should or should not be doing. People who have not faced the loss of a child may tell you that you need to move on, that you need to get past it, or that you need to find a way to have closure. These are all people who do not want to see you in so much pain, but to say it bluntly, they don't know what they are talking about.

E - *Engage with other pareavors.* Those of us who have lost a child can help you know that everything that you are thinking and feeling is normal. We can be your hope for you when you do not have your own, be a light in your place of darkness, and can be an encouragement that you *can* learn to live a life of meaning and purpose again. Pareavors need each other, to have others around them who "get it."

F - *Find a way to honor the life of your child.* The ways we can honor our children are endless. Finding a way to honor the life of your child will help in not staying stuck in their death, which was a moment in time; an important and devastating moment for sure. But I don't want to live my life from the position "My daughter died." I want to figure out how to live from "My daughter lived, and her life mattered."

So those are the five things I think are important for each of us to remember who have lost a child

G – Give yourself a lot of grace.

R – Release yourself from guilt.

I – Ignore those who are trying to fix you.

E – Engage with other pareavors.

F – Find ways to honor the life of your child.

Reflection: I realize none of these five things specifically brought God into the process, but that is because God needs to be woven into each one of these.

G – You can give yourself grace because God is giving you grace.

R – You need to release yourself from guilt because God is not holding anything against you. In fact, Jesus paid a very high price – his own life – to make sure that you are released from all shame and all guilt. Holding on to your guilt is like denying that Jesus went to the cross and died for you.

I – You can ignore others who are trying to fix you because God is the only one who can take the shattered pieces of your heart and bring them back together.

E – Just like the Holy Spirit led you to this book, He wants to help you connect and engage with other pareavors who can walk this journey with you so they can be His words of hope and His arms of love wrapped around you.

F – God has already made a path for you to walk on, that will help you find ways to honor your child while giving you a life of meaning and purpose.

God said, "My presence will go with
you. I'll see the journey to the end."
Exodus 33:14 (MSG)

October

October 1

I Just Don't Understand

With all the whys, the anger, the suffocating darkness and confusion, it is easy to blame God for what has happened to our child. We question how God can call Himself a loving Father or possibly tell us that He is a good God. We don't understand, and it is normal and okay to bring our questions and emotions to God, no matter how dark they are.

The other day, I saw someone's Facebook post that spoke volumes to me about this very thing. "You do not realize what I am doing, but later you will understand." Yes, this was Jesus speaking, in John 13:7. It struck me so deeply that I had to get out a Bible and read these words for myself!

This world we are in is *not* permanent, but it is here to prepare us for the place that is. That means everything that happens here is with eternity in mind. However, our view of it is with very limited sight, which can be confusing until the veil is lifted and we are on the other side with our child.

I believe with everything in me that our children, who are now on the other side of the veil, can also see everything clearly, and understand what we do not understand. They are cheering us on, knowing that when we join them, not only will we understand, but the pain will be completely behind us as the glory of eternity explodes all around us.

Until then, I have a choice. I can choose to continue blaming God or others for what has happened, remaining a victim of this horrible trauma for the rest of my life. Or, I can make a decision that I refuse to stay in this place, taking responsibility for learning how to fight my way out of the darkness in a way that honors the life of my child and that makes life livable again.

This is a good reminder for me personally, whenever we hit another anniversary year of Becca leaving us here, which happens this month. As I go through the next few days, while there will be many tears, I will do my best to remind myself that this separation from Becca is not permanent and someday I will understand.

Reflection: I recently heard a podcast with Wayne Jacobson who said something that I think is worth passing along. "Pain is not the antichrist. Pain does not prove that God has left us. God is with us through the things that cause pain in this world, and it is like the hurt of a surgeon that is bringing you back to life, not the hurt of a mugger beating the tar out of you to steal something from you."

While it is very true that we don't understand the why, we can choose who we are going to blame, which greatly affects the rest of our time here. When you blame God, it keeps you connected to the enemy, who is very happy to take advantage of it, keeping you trapped in your pain and darkness. When you blame the enemy (who is called the enemy because he wants to take us down by causing pain and confusion), then it begins to break that hold, allowing God to be the surgeon you need, bringing you back to life. May I suggest that you choose to put yourself in the hands of the surgeon, not the mugger.

> *Jesus replied, "You don't understand now what I am doing, but someday you will."*
> *John 13:7 (NLT)*

October 2

We Get to Choose

I find it very sad when people walk away from God because of the pain caused in their lives when He did not give them the answer they wanted to a prayer. Once again, may I remind all of us that God is not a vending machine where we put in the prayer, push a button, and the solution we want drops out for us.

We all have choices to make about trusting God. We ask our children many times to trust us, *especially* when our decisions cause them pain and they don't understand why we would do that to them. Like a good father, God is asking us to trust Him as well.

I do not want to be like the crowd we read about in John chapter six, who just came to Jesus for what they could get from Him (to see another miracle after getting fed a free lunch) and then walk away because there was something about Jesus that seemed too hard to understand. I want my heart to be like Peter's. When Jesus asked the disciples if they were going to leave Him, too, Peter's response was, "Where else could I possibly go? You have what I need!"

I have found that my attempts at being in control of my own life (or those around me) to "fix" things does not work. My attempts to control God to "fix" things the way I want them fixed, so I do not have to deal with pain and suffering, don't work either. I only see two other options.

I can either blame God for something I do not understand and walk away like many do, or I can decide that He is the only one who can find a way to somehow redeem this mess into something that can make life livable again.

I hope you will join me in believing in what He promises, that even if it doesn't happen here on this earth, we *will* see the fullness of His goodness when we are with Him and our children once again.

Reflection: Your emotions may be telling you that you cannot trust God and that He isn't good. However, decisions made based on emotions are quite often wrong. I encourage you to make the difficult choice to trust Him, not based on whether or not you get what you want, but based on the fact that if you cannot see His goodness in your situation yet, it means He is not done working on your behalf.

Let me say that again so it can sink in. If you have not seen anything good yet, it is because God is not finished yet.

> *For now we see obscurely in a mirror, but then it will be face to face. Now I know partly; then I will know fully, just as God has fully known me. But for now, three things last — trust, hope, love; and the greatest of these is love.*
> *1 Corinthians 13:12-13 (CJB)*

October 3

Is God Punishing Me?

Did God allow your child to die as a punishment for something you did wrong? I can answer that question with one word. NO! No, God did not kill your child as a punishment for something you have done wrong, or to teach you some sort of a lesson.

Here is part of a recent email that you may be able to relate to.

> *I'd say one of my greatest struggles right now is feeling guilty because God probably was, or is, trying to teach me a lesson. I have thoughts at times that I'm so bad that God took away my child and I'm living here with so much frustration and pain to make me learn my lessons.*

Does that sound like a good father? "I am going to make something horrible happen to my child so I can teach them a lesson." Is that what a good parent does?

A good or wise parent does not cause heartache and horrific things to happen in our lives just so we can learn our lesson, and that is not what God does either. If God killed the children of parents who did wrong or bad things, I don't think many of us would be here, because our own parents have done sinful things. Wouldn't there be a much higher death rate in the children of criminals who are behind bars, if God specifically allows our children to die as a punishment for the wrong things we have done? It just does not work that way.

Reflections of Hope

We often don't think logically when in such a deep place of grief, but hopefully you can see how that question does not make any sense.

We are all sinners. If you have accepted and received the *free* gift of forgiveness offered to us through the death of Jesus on the cross, *all* your sins have been paid for! It's not a hit or miss. It is not "Jesus paid the price for some of my lighter sins, but I still have to pay the price for the worst things I did wrong. God had my child die, because when His son died on my behalf, it did not cover everything."

We know that is not true. That even sounds a bit absurd, doesn't it? And it is just as absurd to think our Heavenly Father would cause something so horrible as the death of our child as a way to teach us some sort of a lesson that we need to learn. Can we learn lessons through the painful things we are going through? Yes, if we are teachable and don't want our child's death to be wasted. But the purpose of our child's death was not to punish us or to teach us something.

Reflection: Jesus left this earth so that the Holy Spirit could come and live inside each one of us. One of the "job descriptions" of the Holy Spirit is to be our teacher, but He is also our Comforter.

We can learn and grow in deep ways because of the dark things we deal with here on this earth, but God did not orchestrate any of it for that purpose. He knew what would come our way before we were even born, and He already had a plan in place on how the Holy Spirit would be able to use it in our lives to bring deep growth in ourselves and in our relationship with Him.

If you have had this type of negative thoughts plaguing you, give them over to God once and for all, inviting the Holy Spirit to be who He wants to be as your teacher and your comforter.

Love never brings fear, for fear is always related to punishment. But love's perfection drives the fear of punishment far from our hearts. Whoever walks afraid of punishment has not reached love's perfection.

1 John 4:18 (TPT)

October 4

Bittersweet

When our child passes through this life ahead of us, the pain is more than can be put into words. But as life around us goes on, we eventually (and I use that word very loosely) learn how to function with that piece of our heart missing. But every event that should be worth celebrating is now bittersweet. It seems that the sweeter the moment in life, the deeper the sting is in our hearts because our child is not with us to share that moment.

When those grief waves come, it is important to lean into it, allowing yourself to feel the pain, like a valve allowing the pressure of grief to be released. And the fresher the loss, the more painful pressure there is that needs to go somewhere. In fact, it may be one constant release for many months.

We all come to a point somewhere down this road, where we get to make a choice. Am I going to keep that painful loss in the forefront of my life, leaning into the bitterness of my earthly loss, or am I going to find ways to lean into the sweetness of life that is still all around me? If you are ready to move further away from the bitter, let me share with you something that helps me lean into the "sweet" during those times. When I feel the heaviness of grief trying to come in, I will pause and think of my beautiful Becca in heaven, dancing on two legs, with Jesus. She is in the greatest celebration of all (which means she is not really missing out on much here compared to what she is experiencing).

I will remind myself that this earth is not my permanent home. I tell myself that at some point, life on this earth won't matter, and we will all be united for eternity. What a glorious day that will be! Focusing on my child's gain, and the fact that this world is not permanent, allows me to lean away from the bitter and into the sweetness of the moment.

Reflection: This whole bittersweet thing is part of our lives now, whether we want it to be or not. Our whole life feels like we have been split in two. It is like a tree. Your children are not "who you are," but they are part of the trunk of the tree. They spring from the very roots of who you are. As a tree, you have been struck with lightening and have been split in two.

This wound in the tree causes it to pull from the roots to a new depth, never before known to that tree. There will be a sealing of that wound, but it will be forever scarred. Over the years it may leak sap at times, but it will heal and go on to have fruitful, flourishing branches, providing life for others who depend on the tree and love it.

You need to know that there is deep healing for deep wounds.

> *Look how you've made all your devoted lovers to flourish like palm trees, each one growing in victory, standing with strength!*
> *Psalm 92:12 (TPT)*

October 5

The Changing Seasons

Life is lived in seasons. Some of our seasons bring small changes, and some are huge. Six years after Becca died, Dave and I went through another huge, unexpected change of a season in life.

Two years before that, we started hearing God tell us that GPS Hope needed to purchase a small motor home. We thought it would be used to travel in for a few weeks at a time as we spoke and ministered to grieving parents. We spent literally hundreds of hours researching on the internet and window shopping at RV dealers around the nation as we traveled by car on ministry trips, to figure out what would fit our needs. We did not know when it would happen, but we wanted to be faithful to position ourselves when He said it was time.

Then in May of 2017, He told us it was time, but He also told us there was more to it than what we first thought. He spoke to both of our hearts that we were to sell our house to one of our sons and start looking for something we could live in full time! Um... excuse me????

The craziest part is that after looking at motor homes for almost two years, within ten days of hearing God give us this new information, we found the perfect pre-owned motor home in great shape for its age, very low mileage and the asking price was half the value and well in our price range! We absolutely fell in love with it, and knew it was our new home on wheels. Every detail started falling in to place, and by that October, we became "full timers" on the road for GPS Hope.

As each one of us continues here on this earth without our child, we are going to go through seasons of change, whether we like it or not. Some will be small, and others may be huge. Either way, life goes on, and the rest of the world keeps going.

At the beginning, that really hurts! But in the long run, it is a good thing, because we realize that those around us who have also faced the deep grief of losing their child managed to move with the changes and seasons of life. Seeing others who were able to live again beyond the death of their child, gives us hope.

Reflection: Seasons will always change. Spring always follows winter, and summer always follows spring. I believe one reason God did this was to be a reminder of His faithfulness in our lives.

As we come into the fall season, let it be a reminder to you, as a symbol of hope that a new season is coming. If you are still in the winter season of your grief, it's okay. Just know at some point, the season will change, and spring will come. God says so in His Word and backs it up in His creation.

There is a time for everything, and everything on earth has its special season.
Ecclesiastes 3:1 (NCV)

October 6

Rescuer

The other day I was listening to a contemplative message. She was taking us through Matthew 16, when Jesus asked the disciples, "Who do people say that I am?" His followers gave a few answers, and then Jesus asked, "Who do *you* say that I am?" In verse sixteen, Simon Peter responds with, "You are the Christ, the Son of the living God."

As I continued listening, the question was presented to us personally. She told us to picture Jesus standing in front of us, asking that question, and to give Him our personal answer. "Who do you say that I am?" The answer that arose in me immediately was "rescuer," which surprised me. Not because I don't believe it, but because of how strongly I do! It has become the story of my life.

Starting as a child, one of my very first memories was standing at my front door around three years old, crying, and seeing it open. What I know about what happened is based on what my mom and sister tell me, as everything before and after that is not in my recollection. I had just fallen out of my second story bedroom window and landed on the ground below, and was standing at the door crying, waiting for someone to unlock the door, and let me back in the house. I had no broken bones and was not even sore the next day.

My life has been one rescue after another. Sometimes physically, sometimes mentally, sometimes emotionally and sometimes spiritually. Even when I claimed promises in scriptures, fasted and prayed to stop something bad from happening, God has rescued me from that dark place I did not want to be in.

When bad things happen to good people, we see God as the villain instead of the rescuer. We can think, "If God is love, he would have not let this horrible thing happen." We need to realize that is a presumption on our part, with limited understanding, based on the pain it brought into our life.

God's presumed inactivity does not compromise His love. God gave every human the gift of choice. Not just choices on doing good or bad (which affects people around us), but He gave us the freedom of choice as to whether or not we will choose to believe that even in our pain and confusion, we will trust Him with the final outcome.

Authentic love is produced by choosing love.

Let me try and explain what I mean. Giving in to everything our child wants does not show love. It shows that I am selfish and only thinking of myself. I want my child to like me. I do not want to put up with the fit my child will throw if they do not get what they want. It is all about how it affects me.

However, if I am thinking of my child beyond how it will affect me (including causing them to be angry with me from misunderstanding the intent and love behind it) I will do things differently. "No discipline is enjoyable while it is happening—it's painful! But afterward there will be a peaceful harvest of right living for those who are trained in this way," Hebrews 12:11 (NLT). That is authentic love.

Let me be very clear, I am NOT saying God killed your child to discipline you in some way. What I am saying is that love does not force, it allows choice, or it is not love. We see this when we look at things from the opposite direction.

In their limited ability to understand, my child can decide he or she does not want anything to do with me, allowing their hurt and anger of not getting what they wanted to push me away. Authentic love will continue to be there for the child, even if it is from a distance by the child's choice.

Aren't you glad God loves us with an everlasting love? Even when it does not look or feel like love, He cannot help but love you with authentic love that allows you to choose when you will come back into His arms to receive that love.

Reflection: How do we know when someone truly loves us? Is it when we get them to give us everything we want, no matter how it affects anyone else? That is not love, it is manipulation. Authentic love is when someone sticks by us in the good and the bad.

God is not our "sugar daddy." He is our rescuer in this world of sin, corruption and evil, even to the point of eventually rescuing us right out

Reflections of Hope

of here to be with Him and our child and other loved ones away from all this pain and suffering.

So, why do we have to be here first and go through all this?

Think about this... how can we truly know authentic light and love without pain and darkness? After all, the angels had nothing but His glorious presence, and yet Lucifer's pride rose up against God and one third of all the angels followed him. Being with God first does not guarantee eternity with Him. Being here first, allowing Him to be our rescuer, does!

How are you ready to answer Jesus' question, "Who do *you* say that I am?"

> *Those who know the Lord trust him,*
> *because he will not leave those who come to him.*
> *Psalm 9:10 (NCV)*

October 7

God's Ultimate Favor

Is there more than one kind of favor with God? This is something I have been meditating on for two or three years now. Here is something I have realized about Moses and the Israelites that helps me to understand this better.

The experiences and incredible miracles God performed for the people of Israel never translated into faith and trust. Instead, the people attacked God's character. They accused God of delivering them from bondage just to see them die in the desert (Exodus 16:2-3). Moses' attitude was different. No matter what obstacle they faced or how impossible it seemed, He knew and relied on the goodness of God to bring them through once again.

Moses knew how important God's favor and blessings were to Israel because His supernatural interventions had saved their lives multiple times. He also knew that these miraculous blessings had more of a purpose than just sustaining and saving the Israelites.

In Exodus 33:13, Moses makes a pleading request of God. "If it is true that you look favorably on me, let me know your ways so I may understand you more fully and continue to enjoy your favor..." (NLT). Moses knew that the ultimate favor of God was not found in the physical blessings He provided for His people, but it was in knowing and having an intimate relationship with the Lord himself. The ultimate favor of God was to know and trust the loving, merciful giver of those blessings.

The Israelites could have experienced God's glory, just like Moses did. The Lord wanted to be close to them as well, but their bitterness toward Him from going through difficult and seemingly impossible things prevented it.

We may not realize it, but every Christian has the same choice. We ultimately choose between seeking God's unlimited favor of a good life or seeking His ultimate favor of knowing Him and the depths of His love in an intimate and very personal way.

When we see God as a golden ticket to a good life, of course we are going to be angry and bitter at Him when something devastating happens. When our desire goes beyond just wanting the physical blessings and constant supernatural protection here on this earth, to wanting to know God and his ways in the deepest, most intimate way possible, then it is easier to grab Him with everything we have. We become like Moses, refusing to go forward without Him (Ex. 33:15).

There is so much more to know of our great God than earthly blessings and keeping tragedy away from us. He wants us to know his glorious presence in every realm of life, especially in the depths of the darkness of grieving the earthly departure of our child.

Reflection: We can easily confuse God's unlimited favor of blessings and good things in this life with God's ultimate favor, to know Him intimately and having the fullness of his presence always with us, no matter what we are going through, good, bad, or outright ugly and evil.

Reflections of Hope

The people of Israel chose to limit themselves to knowing God through His acts, but Moses chose to know the ways and character of God. That makes all the difference in whether or not we believe that we can still trust Him with our lives after something as horrible as the death of our child happens.

Even in your darkness and despair, I hope you can muster up the courage to say the following with me: *God, let my life be defined by your ultimate favor - to know you for who you are, like my child knows You now. That what I desire for the rest of my time here on earth!*

Now then, I pray, if I have found grace in Your eyes, show me Your ways, so that I may know You, so that I might find favor in Your sight.
Exodus 33:13 (TLV)

October 8
Getting Out of the Trap

Grieving the death of our child is a lot of hard work. It consumes us emotionally, mentally, physically, and even spiritually. It doesn't help when we are surrounded by people who do not understand the depth of our loss and offer us advice or try to fix us, instead of doing their best to validate what we are going through and just be there with us.

There are so many emotions that go beyond the intense stabbing pain of missing our child. Guilt, blame, fear, anger and jealousy are just some of those intense feelings rolling around inside us. No wonder we are so exhausted all the time!

There is no easy way around the pain. Part of the internal struggle is that our mind knows our child is no longer here with us, but our hearts just do not (or cannot) accept that fact, which keeps our minds from being able to process it all.

October

Grief is not a sickness. If you have a cold, you may feel miserable for a few days, but then it goes away, and you are right back into living life again without giving a thought to how miserable you were just a few days ago. That is impossible to do when it comes to the loss of our child.

Even though it is impossible to forget about our child and the pain of missing them, I do want to address a trap that is easy for us to fall into with our grieving. Some parents cling to their negative emotions because they feel that working toward letting go of the pain means they are betraying their child. They feel guilty if they start to see life with any kind of hope, or if they feel anything positive.

I want to assure you that moving past the darkest part of your grief is *not* moving on without your child or betraying them. It is just keeping yourself trapped in the painful event of their death, which is preventing you from being able to enjoy your child's life. Why would you not want to learn how to enjoy your child once again and the wonderful blessing they have been to you, instead of being in turmoil and painful darkness whenever you think about him or her? That is not who they were, and I hope when you really think about it, that is not how you want to be attached to them for the rest of your life.

You are the only one who can choose to move back into the darkness when positive thoughts and feelings come your way. You are the only one who can allow yourself to choose to lean into those good thoughts and feelings. I know at first, we do not have that choice because the grief and darkness consume us. But keep working at allowing yourself to recognize and accept some of those positive emotions when they come. Be patient, giving yourself lots of grace, and eventually you will get out of the trap and learn to live in a place where sorrow and joy can live side-by-side. You will not be betraying your child, but loving them by honoring his or her life with light instead of darkness.

Reflection: Sometimes we need to literally give ourselves a break from grief. I assure you, it will be there when you get back. So, have that coffee with a friend, go to that live show you wanted to see, walk through the zoo with someone young and excited to be there and join their excitement, do one of those painting classes.

I am giving you permission to "live" outside of grief for an hour or two. You may be so fresh in your grief that there is no way you can. That is okay, too. I totally understand. But you are not betraying your child if you do. Who can you call that will do something with you but not make you feel like something is wrong with you for being where you are in the grieving process? We all need a break. Do not feel guilty, just take it. Like I said, the grief will still be there when you get back.

> *Anxious fear brings depression, but a life-giving word of encouragement can do wonders to restore joy to the heart.*
> *Proverbs 12:25 (TPT)*

October 9

The Promises of God

We have been taught about the promises of God, and most of us know that we can "claim" those promises for ourselves and our children. That is one reason our faith is shattered with the death of our child. It seems that God did not keep His promises to us.

Many years ago, the Holy Spirit showed me something about the Word that might help a bit in this area. There are times God is speaking to a specific individual or group of people, but we take that scripture and try to make it apply to ourselves.

For example, the scripture often called "The Great Commission" found in Matthew 28 (and variations of it in Mark 16, Luke 24 and John 20) is where Jesus says to go into all the world and make disciples. Many of us have been told this is a command of Jesus to all of us. But was it really? In Matthew 28, Jesus specifically also says to "baptize them in the name of the Father, Son and Holy Spirit."

So, if this is a command from Jesus to every believer, aren't we in sin if we have not gone to other nations to make disciples and if we have not baptized these followers? (Fortunately, I have been to many nations, and even baptized people in a muddy Ugandan river, so I'm good! How about you?) I believe Jesus was giving this instruction to the specific group He was addressing at that moment. (I am not saying we are off the hook of sharing Jesus, but I believe, according to other scriptures, it looks much different from what we may have been taught.)

Another example of taking a scripture and applying it personally is after the devil himself caused Job to lose all his children, all his wealth and his health, Job stated "The LORD gave, and the LORD has taken away; Blessed be the name of the LORD" (Job 1:21 NKJV). People take that as God's view, as if He said it Himself. Did God really say, "I give, and I take away. I bless Me!"? No, this was Job's limited understanding of God, not God Himself talking.

I share all of this to say there are promises of God that we have also been taught to "claim" that have either been taken out of context or we do not look at the fact that it was spoken to a specific person in a specific situation. Without realizing it, we try and make it apply to us in our situation as a way of manipulating God to do what we want Him to do. Then when that doesn't work, we blame God for not keeping His promise.

Instead of taking His Word out of context, or taking a promise made to someone else and claiming it is God's personal promise to me, let's stand on the promises of God that *are* for us as His church and His bride. Most of those promises are not to keep anything bad from happening to us while we are here on earth, but that He will be faithful to be with us, giving us hope and strength, while helping us to learn how to overcome the trials and sorrows we will face.

Reflection: Hebrews 6:18 tells us it is impossible for God to lie, so it isn't that God did not keep His promises. It is that we had a wrong understanding of something we thought was a promise. I encourage you to find some of His promises to stand on that truly are from God to you.

One of them for me is written to His church in Romans 8:18, which tells me the sufferings of this present time cannot be compared with the glory that will be revealed in me. Knowing how great my suffering has been, that must be some *incredible* glory that will be revealed to me at some point!

How about the promise of Jesus telling us He will never leave us or forsake us found in Hebrews 13:5? That is not a promise based on conditions. It is set and firm, no matter what we choose to do or not do, or based on how we feel about Him.

Holy Spirit, help us find the real promises God gave to us, so that we can stand on them in Your truth, knowing you did not betray us or lie to us. Amen.

> *These two things cannot change: God cannot lie when he makes a promise, and he cannot lie when he makes an oath. These things encourage us who came to God for safety. They give us strength to hold on to the hope we have been given.*
> Hebrews 6:18 (NCV)

October 10

What Goes Up Must Come Down

Depending on when you started this book of daily reflections, you may have already read about the walks I took in California that took me up some mountain trails and some of the things God showed me during those walks with the similarities to our grief journey. Today I want to share with you another one of those thoughts.

Part of these walks went up the mountains gradually, making the climb fairly easy. But other parts were steep, and could even get rocky, making it a lot more work and leaving me a bit more winded. A couple of times on the steepest parts, I stopped to catch my breath before continuing.

When I reached the top, the view was fantastic! It was so worth the climb, and I stayed for quite a while taking it all in, feeling renewed and energized. But, as wonderful as it was, there was no way I could permanently stay there. I had to work my way back down to the Hope Mobile.

That's when I realized how similar this is to our lives. We can work and strive to climb up above our circumstances, and when we hit those mountaintops, it is great! But unfortunately, we don't get to live in that place. We eventually find ourselves back at the bottom of the mountain.

Being at the bottom of the mountain does not equate to being at the bottom of life. It does not mean we are living in a place of misery and hopelessness. We do not live most of our lives on mountain top experiences, but being at the bottom of the mountain can still be a good place with joy and laughter mixed in with the pain and tears.

We can be thankful there will always be new mountains to climb along our way that will renew and refresh us with that beautiful view at the top, even after being in the deep dark valley of death. So, go ahead. When the opportunities come, climb the mountains, and enjoy the view at the top. Fight for it, because we all need those mountaintop moments, and they are so worth it!

Just make sure to remind yourself that going back down does not necessarily mean you are heading to a bad place. It's simply the place we live life most of life, both the bad and the good.

Reflection: I am sure there have been times in your past where you found yourself in an extremely difficult place, not knowing how you would be able to enjoy life again. I am also pretty sure God walked with you through that time and brought you through the other side with joy in your life once again, even occasionally giving you mountaintop experiences.

I know that none of those times compares to where you have found yourself after the death of your child. However, we can still remind ourselves of those times, telling ourselves that He has done it before, and He can do it again, even if you don't see how it is possible.

Many of us ahead of you will tell you those mountaintop experiences in life can still happen. If you haven't had a chance to climb one of those mountains yet, hang in there. It will come if you just keep walking, one day, one step at a time.

> *Though I have fallen – I will arise.*
> *Though I sit in darkness, Adonai is my light.*
> *Micah 7:8 (TLV)*

October 11

Is My Child Sad?

A grieving parent who is barely two years into this journey, recently shared with me that God obviously knew their child's death would bring so much darkness and pain into their lives and yet He allowed it anyway, and then asked if I thought their child could "be happy with our Lord in Paradise, seeing the unending heartbreak and tears left behind." I thought it was a great question and decided to share my thoughts on this with other grieving parents who might be wondering the same thing.

Yes, God knows what losing our children will do to us, both short-term and long-term. For most of us, the first few years are full of a suffocating darkness that cannot be put into words. Also, for most of us, it is impossible to see ourselves back in any kind of light to live a life worth living, much less ever feeling happy again.

So, does this cause your child in heaven to be sad for how much you are hurting? I believe your child sees the same picture that God sees; the same one that you and I *cannot* see right now. She or he is on the other side of eternity and can see beyond the darkness of our "now" here on earth.

Because God is in eternity, He sees the beginning, the middle and the end all at once. He sees the future that we cannot see. I believe since our children are now on His side of eternity, their focus is on the future when we will join them and how much we will love it, not on our earthly timeline of where we are now and the intense pain their early departure has given us.

In fact, I think it is impossible for them to be sad for us because Revelation 21:4 says, "He will wipe away every tear from their eyes; and there will no longer be death; there will no longer be sorrow and anguish, or crying, or pain; for the former order of things has passed away" (AMP). If they are painfully missing us, it means heaven is not what God said it is.

Isn't that what we have always wanted for our children; for them not to feel sorrow and anguish or pain? We may want our children here with us, but they are experiencing something far better than we could have ever given them here.

Reflection: I happen to know that the parent who sent me the email had a child with life-long health issues and the parents were the caregivers to that child well into her adult years until she passed. When something like this is the case, it can make it difficult to use our God-given gift of imagination to picture our child totally healed and whole, since we only knew them with their disabilities and limitations. But I believe the Holy Spirit can step in and help us see them in that way.

Instead of using our imagination to picture our child sad and lonely without us, let's use it to picture our child ecstatic in joyful anticipation, knowing what they will be gaining and super excited beyond what can be put into words that someday he or she will be there to meet us upon our own arrival into that glory that God promised. I don't know about you, but I would much rather my child be full of joy than sorrow, so why not picture them that way?

> *He will wipe every tear from their eyes, and there will be no more death or sorrow or crying or pain. All these things are gone forever.*
> *Revelation 21:4 (NLT)*

October 12

Their Heavenly Birthday

Like the rest of you, that first year after Becca's death was *so* very painful. For me (and many of you as well), the second year was shockingly worse, as if that were even possible! The third year was still painful, but the reality of having to learn who I was without my oldest child was setting in. The fourth year I did "okay," but the five-year-thing had me a mess and *very* fragile once again.

What is it that made the fifth year so hard for me? Is it because five years seems such a long time? Is it because buried somewhere deep within me I knew this was just the beginning? Is it because I had tried for the last three years to make sure my other children did not think I loved Becca more than them, so at home I did my best to pretend I was fine 95% of the time? Is it because my previous son-in-law, Becca's husband, took down her Facebook page saying five years was long enough and our family needed to move on (like he had with a new wife and a son they already had together)?

Or is the real reason the simple fact that I gave birth to her, raised her for eighteen years, had her for one of my best friends for the next eleven years, and then in one moment's time it was all taken away from me, and it just plain hurts, no matter how long it has been since she left us?

I find myself crying out to God at how desperately I still need Him for this grief that I still struggle with. And what comes to me in the quietness of my soul is that a change in perspective can be very powerful.

Here are some of the things God reminds me of that can ease my pain and make life livable again.

> 1. I am not getting further away from Becca with each year. I am getting closer to her, as each day brings me closer to my own departure to be with her again.
>
> 2. It is only stuff. Yes, it is Becca's stuff that I no longer have access to when my son-in-law dumped it all, and removed her Facebook page, but no one can take away the part of her that

lives forever in my heart, my mind, my memories... my very soul! (By the way, my son was able to get his sister's page back as a memorial page.)

3. While twenty-nine years was not long enough, it still happened! I was blessed with this daughter who brought so much joy (and many challenges with her stubbornness) to my life. I can honestly say I would rather have had her for only twenty-nine years than to not have had her at all.

I still cry, I still hurt (sometimes very deeply), but I also rejoice that this life is only temporary.

Reflection: The anniversary of our child's death is also the day of what some call their "heavenly birthday," which is today, October 12, for Becca. This entrance into heaven for her meant a new body with both legs, since her left leg was amputated because of bone cancer at age three. Instead of her earthly limitations and suffering with a damaged heart due to the long-term effects of the chemo, she now has a heart that is perfect and strong. She did not get someone else's used heart in a transplant that she so desperately needed here on earth. She got a brand new one that will never go bad on her again.

You may have had a child who was healthy, and you are not able to have the kind of perspective of thankfulness for their new body, like I do with Becca. But that means your child won't ever have to experience anything like that here on earth. No long terminal sickness, no accident that causes permanent damage, and no more going through the evil and corruption of this world.

Does that take away the pain of not having them here with us? Of course not! But it can help us shift from dwelling on our painful loss to being happy for them, because of their incredible and glorious gain.

Painful grieving? Yes. But without hope? No. So with that, on this day each year, I will make sure at some point to celebrate with her and say, "Happy heavenly birthday, Becca!"

> *So we do not look at what we can see right now, the troubles all around us, but we look forward to the joys in heaven which we have not yet seen. The troubles will soon be over, but the joys to come will last forever.*
> 2 Corinthians 4:18 (TLB)

October 13

I Can't Stop Crying

Someone recently asked me, "How do newly bereaved mothers get through this? I can cry at any moment. I work on my yard just to stay busy, then I cry most of the evening. I cry all the time and I can't stop unless I'm doing something to keep my mind off my child and the death of my child."

I want to say that is so normal! How can we not cry when our child isn't here with us anymore? Crying is good. It may not feel like it's releasing the pain, but it is, and it is washing our soul.

Think about it. We love our children. That love has not stopped, but we no longer have a place for that love to go. We want to love on our child but he or she is not here, so it's like our tears are that love; a liquid love that is just spilling out of us because we don't have anywhere for this love to go anymore.

The constant crying will lessen. It usually takes a long time, even a couple of years. I don't want to discourage you and I hope it does not take that long for you, but I just want to let you know, it might. It might take a couple of years for things to really begin to feel like you are not crying all the time.

When that starts to happen, do not beat yourself up for feeling like you are going backwards if you start crying again. You will probably realize one evening that you didn't cry at all that day. You might even go for a few days with no tears, and then you spend the next week crying every day again.

It is normal for us to start moving forward and then feel like we are right back where we started, but that is not what is happening. You are on a journey, and this is part of the process. We all have to work through our grief. There is no way around it. I am sorry, but it does come with a lot of tears because of how deeply we love and miss our child.

There are going to be things that hurt for the rest of our lives, but it does get better. It takes longer than any of us want it to, but you will get there, so just continue the process. Keep going, one tear at a time.

Reflection: I want to share part of an email with you from someone who thought they would never stop crying or get out of the darkness and suffocating pain.

> *I was driving down the road yesterday and I found myself smiling and singing. It became obvious to me that I was actually happy and in a good mood. I saw the light!!! I think I have come to the point that I am beginning to live again. It has been such a very dark journey and many times I didn't think I was gonna make it. But thanks to God's unfailing love and patience, I believe I have.*

You will have the same experience! You will get to the point where you are not crying every day. You *will* make it through. If you cannot believe that yet for yourself, I will believe it for you, just like I did for the pareavor you just heard from who has come out of the darkness and back into a place of light and living again.

> *Death once stared me in the face, and I was close to slipping into its dark shadows. I was terrified and overcome with sorrow. I cried out to the Lord, "God, come and save me!" He was so kind, so gracious to me. Because of his passion toward me... he restored me.*
> Psalm 116:3-5 (TPT)

October 14

From Bitter to Better

In case you are not familiar with the story of Ruth in the Bible, let me summarize it. When there was a famine, Naomi moved with her husband and two sons from Bethlehem (in Israel) to another country. While there, her sons got married. Before any children were born, Naomi's husband and both of her sons died. When Naomi decided to move back home to Bethlehem, one of her daughters-in-law, Ruth, insisted on moving with her.

When they returned, Naomi told her friends and family not to call her Naomi (which means pleasant), but to call her Mara (which means bitter), "because the Almighty has made my life very bitter. I went away full, but the Lord has brought me back empty. The Lord has afflicted me. The Almighty has brought misfortune upon me," (Ruth 1:20-21 NIV). She is pretty raw, telling it exactly how she sees it. Can you relate?

Through God's hand, Ruth found favor from a man named Boaz, who begins to provide food and protection for them. When Naomi found this out, she told Ruth, "Why, God bless that man! God hasn't quite walked out on us after all! He still loves us, in bad times as well as good!" (Ruth 2:20 MSG).

Naomi was about as low as you can get, living in a foreign land where she lost her husband and both her children. She blamed God for all the losses in her life. But eventually, Naomi was able to see that God had never stopped showing her love and grace. So, even when she was in that deep, dark place, where she could not see God's hand, that did not mean that His hand was not still on her life with love, blessings and favor.

I think a lot of us are like Naomi in that sense. "My life is bitter. There is no reason to live. God has done this to me, and I don't want to be here anymore." We do not realize that God's loving hand is still at work in our lives, like it was in Naomi's, and that He still has favor and blessings for each one of us as well. We are like Naomi, just trying to survive. But also like Naomi, God wants to help us get beyond that and be able to thrive.

October

The Bible is full of men and women in traumatic and tragic situations, including those who have lost children. The Bible is also full of reading about how God made Himself known to them through those difficult things. He was faithful to walk with them, teaching them how to overcome the pain in this world while learning how to live a good life that goes beyond those tragic events. God is the same yesterday, today and forever. He never changes. If He did it for all of them, He will do it for all of us!

Reflection: It might be helpful to think about your life as a book. The chapter you are in right now is a bad, very dark, very long chapter. But it is not the entire story; it is one chapter. God will be faithful to you in this chapter, just as He has been for others throughout all of history that we read about in the chapters of the Bible.

Even if you cannot see it, even if you can't feel it, He is still at work. He is always at work. He *is* the way out. He has the hope that you need. His love is always for you and His grace is always at work in your life. Thankfully, you will not always be in this chapter. My question is, how can you allow God to help you finish this chapter well, so that you do not have to stay here in this place of barely surviving any longer than necessary?

> *I remember my affliction and my wandering, the bitterness and the gall. I well remember them, and my soul is downcast within me. Yet this I call to mind and therefore I have hope. Because of the Lord's great love, we are not consumed. For His compassions never fail. They are new every morning. Great is your faithfulness. I say to myself, "The Lord is my portion; therefore, I will wait for Him." The Lord is good to those whose hope is in Him; to the one who seeks Him. It is good to wait quietly for the salvation of the Lord.*
>
> *Lamentations 3:19-26 (NIV)*

October 15

God Is not Done Yet

Can you imagine being a married woman and the king calls you to his castle? He is the king so you cannot refuse, and you end up pregnant with his child. When he cannot cover it up by bringing your husband home from war to sleep with you, he has your husband murdered (making it look like a war casualty) and then brings you into the castle to become one of his wives. When you have the baby, the infant only lives for seven days. Yes, this happened to a woman named Bathsheba with King David, and we can read about it in 2 Samuel chapters eleven and twelve.

As the mom, wouldn't you be furious with the king and blame him for everything? It is all his fault. Right? And yet the Bible says that King David comforted his wife, Bathsheba. That means she had to have allowed them to come together to grieve the death of their child. One of the ways David comforted Bathsheba, was that he was intimate with her.

She became pregnant again and gave birth to a son and they named him Solomon. King Solomon was a rainbow baby. Isn't that something? King Solomon, the wisest king who ever lived, was a rainbow baby. That just amazes me. Even within this terrible story of what surrounded Bathsheba's first child, God had a plan to bring something good from the situatIon.

We all know that our children who have left this world can never be replaced. I know there are some of you who have had a beautiful rainbow baby. I also know there are some who have lost a baby while it was either in the womb or shortly after birth and were never able to have another child. Some of you lost your only child and a few of you have lost more than one, or even all your children.

Romans 8:28 is a verse I struggled with for a while when Becca died, which tells us God works everything out for our good. My thought was, "How is it even remotely possible to bring something good from the death of my child?" It just seemed so impossible. Something I heard during that time was, "If you haven't seen anything good yet, it means God isn't done yet."

October

The incredible thing is that I have found this to be true! So, keep holding on because God's mercy, faithfulness and goodness are still over you. Let me also say that it is okay to be angry with Him and at the same time still know that you need Him. I know it can be a struggle, but every time you can surrender to Him again, give Him the shattered pieces of your heart. Let Him hold you. Let Him comfort you. Let Him bring good things back into your life once again.

Reflection: My friend, Crystal, held her newborn baby as she died, just a few hours after being born. Her little Madeline remains an only child, as Crystal has not been able to have more children. In her own words, "I began to understand I couldn't spend the rest of my life mad at everything and everyone for having what I wanted. I had to lift myself out of the anger, sorrow, and depression. I couldn't continue living my life waiting to die." God gave her a wonderful way to carry on little Maddie's legacy that is helping others heal from their own loss. Once again, good has come from the devastating blow of child loss.

There *are* good things He still wants to give you and to bless you with as you continue to walk out this journey with Him. He did it for David and Bathsheba, for Crystal, for me, and for literally countless other pareavors. Open your heart, allowing Him to bring you the peace and the comfort you need, realizing His goodness to you can come in many ways and will look differently for each of us.

Night's darkness is dissolving away as a new day of destiny dawns.
Romans 13:12 (TPT)

October 16

A Weapon Against Doubts

I recently saw somewhere that the Biblical meaning of temptation is *a trial in which we have a choice of being faithful or unfaithful to God.*

Reflections of Hope

When Jesus was here on earth, he was fully man and was tempted by the enemy. Every time that happened, He had the same choice we do, whether to be faithful to God or not, no matter what He was seeing or feeling.

The third temptation Satan brought to Jesus in the wilderness, before He started His ministry, was showing Him all the nations of the world, telling Jesus he would hand them all over if Jesus would bow down and worship him just one time.

I have often wondered how that is even a temptation. Of course, Jesus is not going to bow down and worship Satan! But let's think about this. God gave this earth and everything on it to man, and man turned it over to Satan. That means this world belongs to the enemy. Jesus came to open the way for us to take it back and to walk out the Kingdom of God here on earth.

Jesus could have gotten it all back directly from Satan, without having to go through horrific torture and being brutally murdered, while carrying the guilt and the shame of all our combined sins. When I really think about it, that was quite the offer. Satan was telling Jesus, "You won't have to go through all of that. You don't need to do it the Father's way. I will hand it all over to you, if you just do this one thing."

Satan wants you to think that you don't need God either. "If God really is who He says He is, why didn't He stop your child from dying? If God is good, why did He let this happen?" The enemy will try to convince you that you will do better staying mad at God or pushing Him out of your life. "Do it *my* way and I will give you what you want."

Remember, the Biblical meaning of temptation is a trial in which we have a free choice of being faithful, or unfaithful, to God. I know we feel like God was unfaithful to us, but that is not true. That is what the enemy wants us to believe. He is called the enemy for a reason. He comes to steal, kill and destroy whatever he can, to make us start to doubt and believe lies about God.

Those doubts will make it hard to seek for hope and strength from God's Word, which is what the enemy wants, because His words are one of the greatest weapons we have against the enemy. That is the weapon Jesus Himself used, so the enemy is going to sow seeds of confusion and doubt to keep you away from that weapon, so that you cannot use it against him.

The weapon of the Word is just as powerful in your hands as it was for Jesus. Do not let him convince you otherwise!

Reflection: The Holy Spirit is with you in your wilderness, just like He was with Jesus. Don't choose to live by your feelings while in this difficult place. Choose to live by what God says, whether you can feel it is truth in your darkness or not. He *will* bring you out! Stand your ground and choose to remain faithful to God by continuing to hang on to the promises of His faithfulness.

> *Embrace the power of salvation's full deliverance, like a helmet to protect your thoughts from lies. And take the mighty razor-sharp Spirit-sword of the spoken word of God.*
> *Ephesians 6:17 (TPT)*

October 17

I Prayed and Fasted

Let's talk about King David again and the baby he had with Bathsheba (2 Samuel 12). When the infant died, David's attendants were afraid to tell him that the child was dead. He had been fasting and praying for God to spare his son's life, and they were afraid he would do something desperate.

David heard them whispering among themselves, asked if the child was dead, and was told yes. At that point, David got up from the ground, cleaned himself up, put on fresh clothes, went to the temple, and worshiped God.

Reflections of Hope

I know what it's like to storm heaven, fasting and praying on behalf of my child who was facing death with an illness; first when she was only three years old with cancer, and again years later when she needed a heart transplant. But I admit that I did not have David's heart when Becca died. I did not understand why out of all the times her life was spared (and there were *many* over the years), this time it was not. But I did not get angry at God. Angry at the enemy? YES! But I knew God was the only hope I had to get out of this darkness.

I felt like I died and needed God to bring life back to me. I knew the only way that was going to happen, was to hold onto Him with everything I had, trust Him with the painful, confusing mess, and allow Him to minister to me, pulling me out of that darkness. It was not easy. It took a long time.

The peace we so desperately long for comes when we get to the point where we can surrender ourselves to God's love and comfort, even within the pain. That is what I see David doing. He trusted God immediately to make a right decision in the earthly death of his son, no matter how it affected him personally.

I am amazed that David was able to worship God and go back to functioning normally right away. It took me many months (I am talking two to three years) before I felt I could function again on a somewhat normal level.

When our child died, that was an event, a very painful event. Grief is the process of working through that event to get out of the suffocating darkness, back to a place where we can live again. We all get to that place in our own time. I sure wish my timing was like King David's and I am guessing you do, too.

Reflection: After spending time worshiping God, David went home and requested food. His attendants asked him why he was acting that way. They were very confused because when his son was alive, he cried and refused to eat, but after his son died, he got up and wanted to eat.

David's answer is one that I think we all need to spend some time thinking about. "While the child was still alive, I fasted and wept. I thought, 'Who knows? The Lord may be gracious to me and let the child live.' But now that he is dead, why should I go on fasting? Can I bring him back again? I will go to him, but he will not return to me."

We cannot bring our child back. No matter how angry we are with God, with ourselves, or with anyone else, our child will not be back with us here on this earth. Choosing to stay in our place of darkness, taking on the victim mentality that my child died, is not going to bring him or her back.

They will not return to us, but we will go to our children someday. That is why we can grieve with hope.

*Those who have been ransomed by the Lord will return. They will enter Jerusalem singing, crowned with everlasting joy. Sorrow and mourning will disappear, and they will be filled with joy and gladness.
Isaiah 35:10 (NLT)*

October 18

The Fear of Letting Go

Back in January, I shared what can be a familiar movie scene that played out in my mind one morning as I was praying for those connected to GPS Hope. Here is the scene.

Person standing above a mountain or building ledge: *Let go and grab my hand!*

Person dangling dangerously in the air: *I can't!*

First person: *You have to!*

After a final glance downward, the person in danger of falling, releases her grip on the ledge and frantically grabs the hand reaching down to her.

This scene is so familiar, that I had to laugh when I saw it in a TV show that Dave and I were watching, within a week of originally writing that.

Today, I want to share a second thought about that familiar movie scene, which is about letting go of the past and moving into the future. I am not talking about letting go of your child and moving on without him or her. That is impossible for us to do!

What I mean is that while we are still here on earth, our child's life is now behind us, but he or she is still in our future. It's like we are clinging to a ledge with everything we have, trying to keep from losing our child. As long as we are clinging to the past in a way that keeps us attached to the painful death of our child, we cannot release our grip to grab ahold of the fact that we still have a future with him or her.

It is a leap of faith from one unknown to another.

One leaves us dangling over the edge of a cliff, holding on in our own strength and determination, while the other leaves us with God holding us, pulling us away from that terrifying place and into His arms of comfort, peace and love.

It is almost like as soon as we let go, there is a bridge that connects the two. Our memories start to become treasures, instead of a stabbing pain, as we realize the truth that this is not the end, that God loves us so much that He made a way for us to be together again, forever. This reminds me of a line from the song I shared on July 31st, *Together Forever.*

> *But until that day comes, I won't make it through by letting go, but holding on tight to the memories I treasure, this is not goodbye I'll see you later.*

Reflection: I encourage you to use every ounce of strength you have to grab ahold of the future that God has already given you, which includes being together with your child once again. But in order to do that, you will have to release your grip on the painful event of the death itself, so that you can be thankful for your child's life, both the one they lived here on earth and the one they are continuing to live in heaven.

It is not the pain of missing them that keeps us connected. We can never forget our child; that is impossible. It is our love for them, and it is the fact that our separation is only temporary, and we will see them again!

> *Don't worry or surrender to your fear. For you've believed in God, now trust and believe in me also. My Father's house has many dwelling places. If it were otherwise, I would tell you plainly, because I go to prepare a place for you. And when everything is ready, I will come back and take you to myself so that you will be where I am.*
> *John 14:1-3 (TPT)*

October 19
Faith in God's Power

1 Corinthians 2:9 says, "No eye has seen, no ear has heard, and no mind has imagined the things that God has prepared for those who love him" (GW). This was a verse that used to be so exciting to me! God has more for me than I could ever imagine! Wow! How awesome is that? Lay it on me, God!

Let me just say, the darkness and pain of my daughter's death was definitely more than I could have imagined, and it is not awesome, it is horrible!

But wait...let me share with you what I have discovered. This verse is not talking about the great life we are going to have with awesomeness and wonderful things being poured out on us continually. It is talking about the mystery of the death of Jesus, and how God was going to use it so that our "faith would not be based on human wisdom but on God's power" at work in us (verse 5). Now that is a real wow; much deeper than the shallow "bless me with all kinds of good stuff, and I will follow You" kind of belief in God.

Verse 12 tells us that we did not receive the spirit that belongs to the world. Instead, we received the Spirit who comes from God so that we could know the things which God has freely given us. So, what has God freely given us?

How about for a start:

- Comfort
- Peace in the storms (or tsunamis) of life beyond our own understanding
- Hope
- Joy that goes beyond our circumstances
- Triumph and victory over tragedy
- Resurrection power and life from death

I now see these verses in 1 Corinthians (and Ephesians 3:20 that says God can do more than we can ask or think) as more of a promise for those of us who have been thrown into a place of deep darkness. It is God's promise that He is going to bring us out of this place in a way that we cannot see, hear, or even imagine right now. This new understanding makes a whole lot more sense to me than using these scriptures as a u-rah-rah-Go-God type of verse to be excited about Him being some sort of Santa Clause bringing us all kinds of fun presents.

I choose to believe the richness of the full depth of 1 Corinthians 2:9. My eyes cannot see, my ears cannot hear, and my mind cannot imagine what God is going to do with my darkness, but God can. He will do so much more in my life, as He starts to bring glimmers of light into my darkness.

Reflection: I know it may not seem like it, but God's power *is* at work in us. Verse 14 reminds us that the natural man does not receive the things of the Spirit of God. The sooner we make the shift of not looking at things with our natural eyes but seeing them through the Spirit of God who lives inside us, the sooner we will find ourselves coming out of the darkness.

But remember, this is a journey, and it usually takes much longer than we want it to or think it should. There is no timeline for this. I have chosen to believe not only that He can, but that He *will* bring life from death itself, no matter how long it takes. After all, that is His specialty! Will you join me in believing this?

> *What we have received is not the spirit of the world.*
> *We have received the Spirit who is from God. The Spirit*
> *helps us understand what God has freely given us. ...In fact,*
> *such things can't be understood without the Spirit's help.*
> *1 Corinthians 2:12,14 (NIRV)*

October 20

A New Thought

How can I trust God when He betrayed me like this? Let me say that our perspective has everything to do with how this question is answered, which probably shifted drastically at a time when you needed God more than ever in your life. So, to shift our perspective in this once again, either a new thought needs to be introduced and received, or an old one reclaimed.

Here is one of the new thoughts I had. During a worship song at a church service one day, I realized that if I bring God into my battle (including the battle of my fears and my darkness) then I will win, because it is impossible for Him to lose! He is the Alpha and Omega, the beginning and the end. God has the first and last word in my life, and He also has it in the life of my child.

God has never entered a battle where He came out as the loser, and He never will. As soon as I see God on my side and not as the enemy, and ask Him to fight for me, I know somehow in the end I will come out victorious!

I never thought about it until Becca died, but the very first person on this earth to die was Abel, the son of Adam and Eve. He was murdered by his own brother. So, a child dying before the parent dies has been happening since the beginning of the fall and corruption of mankind. No one is exempt from the possibility.

Reflections of Hope

Even before creation, God had a plan to win the war Satan started. Wars have many battles, and each battle is different. War also has civilian casualties. Anyone who lives on this earth is a participant in this war. In 2 Timothy 2:3, Paul talks about suffering as a soldier in Christ's army. In a war, whether a soldier or a civilian, some walk away with only minor injuries and setbacks, some are injured for life, and some lose their lives.

It is the same in the spiritual realm. There are many battles, and each battle is different. There are soldiers and there are civilians. There are some who walk away with minor injuries and setbacks, some are affected for the rest of their time here, and some lose their lives here on earth.

However, the final outcome is that He will win the war, and we ARE on the winning side. This is not permanent. You will come out victorious in the end, if not here, then when you become a casualty of war and get to leave this earthly battleground.

Reflection: It may feel like the war has been lost and God did not fight for you, but remember that this is only one battle. I know it feels like the wounds from this battle will never heal, and you are out of commission for the rest of your time here on earth. I am here to tell you that is only true if you give up and accept that fate.

Is this a new thought you can take hold of, causing you to move closer to God and what you desperately need from Him, or maybe a belief that you need to reclaim? Spend some time thinking about this, allowing the Holy Spirit to direct your thoughts and shift your beliefs in a way that allows you to move toward trusting Him again and His perfect love for you and your child.

Jesus is the Captain of the Hosts of Heaven. If you let Him, He will lead you into a place of victory in total triumph over the enemy who took out your child from this earth. Who would not want that?

> *Be prepared. You're up against far more than you can handle on your own. Take all the help you can get, every weapon God has issued, so that when it's all over but the shouting you'll*

still be on your feet. Truth, righteousness, peace, faith, and salvation are more than words. Learn how to apply them.
Ephesians 6:13-16 (MSG)

October 21
Losing Faith in God

Many of you write to me, letting me know that you are not sure what to believe about God after the death of your child. You are not sure if you even want to (or can) believe there is a God because you had faith that God would protect your children. You believed He would not allow horrible things to happen to you or your family because you served Him, went to church, read your Bible, prayed, etc. When your child died, it made God seem like a liar, if there even is a God.

Second Corinthians 5:7 is a familiar verse to most of us. It says that we walk by faith, not by sight. Here it is in several different translations.

- For we live by trust, not by what we see. (CJB)
- Indeed, our lives are guided by faith, not by sight. (GW)
- It's what we trust in but don't yet see that keeps us going. (MSG)
- Our life is lived by faith. We do not live by what we see in front of us. (NLV)
- The path we walk is charted by faith, not by what we see with our eyes. (VOICE)

Now let me tell you what is in front of and behind those familiar words.

"So we are always confident, knowing that while we are at home in the body we are absent from the Lord. For we walk by faith, not by sight. We are confident, yes, well pleased rather to be absent from the body and to be present with the Lord," (2 Corinthians 5:6-8 NKJV).

Reflections of Hope

WOW! Those seven words *we walk by faith, not by sight* are sandwiched in between the gift of knowing, by the grace of the Holy Spirit, that when we leave this earth, we are with the Lord.

Our children are with the Lord, and some day we will be joining them! How can I not believe in a God who had an incredible plan set in place before He even spoke this world into existence? A plan that keeps my child safe in a place too wonderful to be described, while I finish my time here. I can know, by the witness of the Holy Spirit inside me, that when I am absent from my body and go to be with the Lord, I will be reunited with my child, never to be separated ever again!

Reflection: Just because we cannot understand God in our place of pain and turmoil, does not mean that God is a liar. He cannot lie. There are many things about God that we do not understand. God and His ways are a mystery to us as His creation while here on this earth. We will abandon Him if we make our decisions based on what we see and how we feel. That is where faith comes in. But even if we walk away from Him, He will not walk away from us in our place of need.

How about you? Will you join me in making the choice to live by faith that we will be with our children again, and not by what we see now, which is a temporary separation? I am not saying the pain of missing them will go away, but the anger and fear you may be carrying can be exchanged for peace and thankfulness.

> *Now the power that has planned this experience*
> *for us is God, and he has given us his Spirit as a*
> *guarantee of its truth. This makes us confident,*
> *whatever happens. We realize that being "at home" in the*
> *body means that to some extent we are "away" from the*
> *Lord, for we have to live by trusting him without seeing him.*
> *We are so sure of this that we would really rather be "away"*
> *from the body (in death) and be "at home" with the Lord.*
> *2 Corinthians 5:6-8 (PHILLIPS)*

October 22

Our Anger

Many pareavors become very angry with the death of their child. When left to grow and fester, anger becomes bitterness and resentment. It poisons us and taints our view of life (and death). Anger and bitterness never make anything right. It never brings satisfaction and will keep you stumbling in your darkness on this grief journey.

Let me back up a bit and say that your anger is legitimate. There is nothing wrong with feeling angry. When our child dies, we feel a great injustice has happened. We are not supposed to bury our children, they are supposed to bury us. The dreams of the future with that child have been abruptly shattered. We all feel like it should have been us, not our child. How can one not be angry?

When we are full of anger, we can even feel like we do not care who it spills out on, or who we hurt with it. We are in deep pain, and sometimes we even *want* people around us to be in pain, also. Seeing happy people around us can even fuel the anger, bitterness and resentment.

We can be angry at someone who directly or indirectly caused the death of our child. We can be angry at ourselves for not seeing or knowing something that could have stopped their death. Not only will being angry not fix anything, but it makes things even worse, especially when we release it on those who had nothing to do with our child dying and may even have their own level of painful grief.

It also makes it worse on ourselves, not just emotionally, but physically. Anger gets pent up in our bodies, causing all kinds of ailments, so we need to release it. If you struggle with anger, find constructive ways to let it out, such as doing something active. Go for a daily brisk walk or find a cardio workout and follow it.

You have a choice to make about all that anger you are feeling. You can either let it take control of you, allowing you to become more and more toxic, or you can find ways to diffuse that anger so that you will not continue to heap more darkness on yourself.

Reflection: The one person who can take that anger and not let it affect their relationship with you and love for you, is God. Most pareavors are angry at God. He could have moved His hand and stopped the death of your child and mine. But He did not do it, for reasons we cannot see or understand, which makes us mad.

It is okay to be mad at Him. He can take it. Yell at Him; have it out with Him. Let Him have it. It will not make Him walk away from you or diminish His love for you one bit. It is okay to be angry, and to work through it. But for your own sake, please don't camp out in this place.

*Shake with anger and do not sin. When you are
on your bed, look into your hearts and be quiet.
Psalm 4:4 (NLV)*

October 23

God in Your Back Pocket

As Christians, without realizing it, we often treat life like we have God in our back pocket to help us control what we want to control. It is like seeing Him as the big brother standing behind us to make all the bullies in life run away.

We can forget that there is more to our time here than just to have a good life. It is also a time for us to grow spiritually, maturing in our relationship with God and grow in intimacy with Him. That does not mean God is only in the good stuff and if something bad happens, He did not do His job as God.

Life is not about all the things in the world I can get. It is about how I am following Him with the twists and turns of this journey. It is about learning how to rest in His love. It is about things like being more compassionate for those around me, or having more wisdom or peace about situations I find myself in.

There is a tension between understanding who God is and what He can do, as we live out our life here on earth. We know that He can do anything, and yet we do not see His constant miraculous provision and protection. If we don't learn how to let God lead and guide us in His ways instead of insisting and begging for ours, we will be crushed and disappointed when we don't get our way.

When something difficult happens to one of our children such as losing a job or a serious health issue, they can begin to question why and what it means. Our heart for them is, "I don't know, but I will be with you as you go through it."

God never causes the bad stuff, but His presence is with us through those times, and it is a chance for us to grow in our relationship with the One who is so great that He created the world, but at the same time wants us to know His heart on an intimate level.

To me, that is the reason to have God in my back pocket. He is with me through anything this life throws my way, no matter how dark. So far, anything I have gone through has, at some point, left me amazed at how good God really is because of what He did for me through it all, and how He stuck with me, making sure something good came out of the darkness that I found myself in.

Reflection: Having God in our back pocket is not so we can manipulate Him, keeping us from having pain and tragedies in our lives. It is so that He can be with us through those times.

So, instead of throwing Him out of your pocket, allow the Holy Spirit to soften your heart to be able to sit with Him and find out what He is doing. Instead of blaming Him, start asking Him, "God, how can I live in you right now? Where are you leading me?" I guarantee He wants to be in that darkness with you, guiding you through it, so you can go forward with your life once again.

For as you know him better, he will give you, through his great power, everything you need for living a truly good life: he even shares his own glory and his own goodness with us!
2 Peter 1:3 (TLB)

October 24

Our Tormenting Fears

It is repeated throughout the Bible that God will never leave you to fend for yourself. So, when it feels like God is far away and you are feeling very alone, God is actually right there with you. He will not leave you to face difficult times on your own, which includes facing the trauma of the death of your child.

Because we are in the darkness of our grief for so long, it can feel like God is not listening or doing anything to help us in our place of horrific pain. However, if you have cried out to Him, I can guarantee that He is at work.

This was the case for Elijah in 1 Kings chapter 18. Elijah had been in hiding because he had been given a word from the Lord that there would be no rain for a few years because of the worship of idols by God's people. King Ahab blamed the messenger and wanted Elijah dead. After three years of famine in Samaria, God had the prophet tell King Ahab to expect an abundance of rain. Elijah sent his servant six times to check for signs that it was coming, and each time there was absolutely no sign of rain.

Even though it looked like nothing was happening, God was working on sending a downpour. When Elijah sent his servant to check for the seventh time, he could see one very tiny cloud, the size of a man's fist out over the sea heading toward them. This tiny cloud was finally a visible sign that God was going to keep His promise to send rain. When God promises to be faithful to us, it does not mean He will make sure that nothing bad will ever happen to us in this life. It means He will be with us when it does. Before the rain came, Elijah called down fire from heaven, but he felt alone and abandoned by God when he had to hide again because now Queen Jezebel wanted him dead. David was a powerful king, but he ended up hiding in a cave to save his life from King Saul. Paul wrote thirteen of the twenty-seven books in the New Testament, but he lived a brutal life, shipwrecked, stoned and left for dead, imprisoned, etc.

When Jesus went into the wilderness after being baptized, God did not send Jesus into that dry and barren place alone but sent Him with the Holy Spirit (Matthew 4:1). While there, Jesus went without food for forty days, putting Him in a very vulnerable place, which is exactly when the enemy made his attack. When that time was over, Jesus came out much stronger than when He went in.

After wandering for forty years in the desert, the Israelites came into possession of their promised land. Believe it or not, our "wilderness" experience can do the same thing for us. We do not have to stay in our dry, painful, vulnerable place for further attacks of the enemy, and can come out the other side stronger, inheriting promises of God that we may not even realize were ours to receive.

Reflection: When Elijah was in hiding, God led him to a brook for water and sent birds to bring him food to sustain him. When David was in the cave, he was surrounded by warriors who protected and took care of him. When the Israelites were wandering around in the desert, God sent a pillar of cloud during the day and a pillar of fire at night to lead them.

God was with them in different ways. We are so very blessed because we have God with us the same way Jesus did. We have the very Spirit of God Himself living inside us. Just like Jesus was not alone as He sat in the wilderness, you are not alone either. And just like Jesus passed through, stronger on the other side, I believe you will, too. Ask the Holy Spirit inside you to show you how He has been there for you, and to help you see the things He is doing to sustain you in the wilderness of grief. I guarantee He is with you, because He promised, and He is faithful to keep His promises.

Don't panic. I'm with you. There's no need to fear for I'm your God. I'll give you strength. I'll help you.

> *I'll hold you steady, keep a firm grip on you.*
> *Isaiah 41:10 (MSG)*

October 25

Our Paralyzing Fears

I want to talk about fear a bit more today. Fear can not only torment us, but it can also paralyze us. I understand it, though. I have had to fight many fears that I did not have before Becca died.

One fear that can keep us from moving forward in a needed way, is to continually be looking back. We can be afraid that we will forget our child, leaving him or her in the past as we move forward with life.

Don't keep looking back, allowing yourself to be paralyzed by the pain of trying to stay in the past which no longer exists. No matter how much you want your child's life back, it is not going to happen. I am so sorry to say that, and I am not trying to be cruel. I want to set you free. I spent time camping out there, and here is what God spoke to me one day.

> *Laura, don't look back! Go forward with everything you've got! Lot's wife looked back, and she was frozen to a place where she died. She could not go anywhere because she looked back. I know that may seem harsh, but it will become a tormenting fear that will paralyze you.*
>
> *Don't look back at the crushing. If you look back to ponder on and relive the death, you won't be able to walk in the power of my resurrection life. LIVE! I speak over you, my daughter, you shall LIVE and not die. I speak life into your soul and into your very being. LIFE!! Receive it! Just receive this new life I am giving you.*
>
> *You will grow stronger in it each day you come up to me to drink. Drink daily. Drink deeply. For it will truly be a wellspring*

of life in you and through you. Cross over from death to life. Cross over from sorrow into joy. Cross over into new depths of my love, and my will and my ways for your life.

(If you do not know about Lot's wife, you can read about what happened in Genesis 19:1-29.)

It does no good to try to hide from your fears or pretend they aren't there, especially from God. I have found that being able to take my needs and my fears to God in prayer makes a huge difference in my life. It keeps me from feeling so helpless in a circumstance that I have no control over. Praying gives me much more control over how I respond to my feelings and my fears. Communication with God may be the *only* thing I feel that I have control over, but that is actually enough.

God wants us to bring all our feelings to Him, even the ones you wish you didn't have. You may be wondering, "He knows these things already. Why should I have to tell Him how I am feeling?" Because you need to admit those things so you can give them to God and let Him work with you at being set free. I have experienced in my life, more now than ever, that there is freedom in surrender. I want you to find that same freedom from any tormenting or paralyzing fears.

Reflection: You already know that fear and anxiety come from the enemy. When you take these tormenting and paralyzing feelings to God, it is a way of affirming your trust in Him, regardless of how you feel. If you do this persistently, your feelings of fear will eventually lose their hold on you, and you will find that your feelings start lining up with faith and trust in His love for you.

What are the fears you are carrying right now? Is it something God wants you to carry? I think you know the answer to that. The question then becomes, are you willing to lay these fears down at the feet of Jesus, who is sitting on His throne as King, and leave them there as many times as needed, so you can move forward in freedom?

Turn your worries over to the Lord. He will keep you going.
Psalm 55:22 (NIRV)

October 26
The King and His Kingdom

"Why bother praying if God is just going to do whatever He wants?"

This is one of the greatest struggles I hear about in conversations with other bereaved parents. We pray for protection for our children, or pray for a healing, and when we do not see God answer those prayers, it is frustrating (or we are outright angry) as it makes no sense, especially when we did everything we were supposed to do on our end.

As I was thinking and praying (yes, talking to God) about this, I believe the Lord gave me an illustration that made so much sense to me. I have since shared it with dozens of other bereaved parents, and it seems to make sense to them as well.

As a king rules his land, his subjects will come to him to petition him for things. A good king will say yes or no, based on his view of the big picture of the entire kingdom. The subject will be happy with the king's answer if he gets what he is asking for. But he can be pretty upset with the king if his request is denied. He may even be angry and slander the king to the other subjects, deciding he isn't a very good king at all for not doing what the subject wanted, forgetting that the king is looking from a completely different viewpoint.

The subject may not always get his request granted, but at least he came before the throne for the king to hear his case. But if that subject did not bother coming to the king with his petition, the king has no obligation whatsoever to move on his behalf.

And *that*, is why we need to keep praying.

I believe this is what "request" prayers are like. I am petitioning the King for what I think I need, or something I desperately want. He answers according to the big picture of eternity that I cannot see, based on information I do not know. Sometimes my request is granted, which makes me feel cared for and loved. Sometimes that request is not granted, and instead of accepting it as a good and right decision from the

King's vantage point and still feeling cared for and loved, I can feel hurt and angry, even believing He is not a good King (or a loving Father).

Things will be easier for us when we can accept the fact that He is a good King who *deeply* loves his people and always makes the best decision based on the Kingdom of eternity, *not just this earthly kingdom*. One day, when we cross over from this earthly Kingdom to the one our children are now part of, I believe we will see why our King made the decisions He did and love Him all the more for being such a wonderful and loving King.

Reflection: Even when I did not get the answer from the King that I wanted for my child, I still need to continue going to Him with my requests. Not getting a huge request answered the way I wanted, which leaves me in so much pain, does not mean that I will get all further requests denied as well. I still need to seek His face and continue to lay my petitions before Him. If I do not bring anything else to Him, believing He no longer cares, then the King has no obligation to move on my behalf.

What is one thing you have been holding back in bringing before your loving King? Lift it up to Him right now, knowing that there are still many times you will get the answer you want. The times that does not happen, give yourself credit for bringing it to Him so that He can at least consider it, and do your best to trust that His answer will make sense on the other side.

> *Do not be anxious or worried about anything, but in everything [every circumstance and situation] by prayer and petition with thanksgiving, continue to make your [specific] requests known to God. And the peace of God [that peace which reassures the heart, that peace] which transcends all understanding, [that peace which] stands guard over your hearts and your minds in Christ Jesus [is yours].*
> *Philippians 4:6,7 (AMP)*

October 27

Sound Familiar?

There are several similarities of Jacob and his son, Joseph, when it comes to grieving the death of our child. You may be thinking that Joseph didn't really die, but the fact is, his father had evidence that he did. It was fabricated by his other sons no less, but it was enough for Jacob to believe it and respond as though Joseph, his son, was dead. (The entire story that I will be referring to can be found in Genesis chapters 37, 39-45.)

Jacob's exact response when given evidence that his son was dead was, "I will continue to mourn until I join my son in the grave," (Genesis 37:35 NIV). That sure sounds familiar, doesn't it? We see the reality of Jacob's pain at the death of his son, even though he had eleven other sons (which were through four different wives). People might tell us, "At least you have other children," thinking that is supposed to comfort us. But we know our children cannot be replaced and when we lose one, we do not ever stop missing them.

Through some very strange circumstances that included being in prison for several years, Joseph ended up being second in command to Pharoah in Egypt. All ten of his half-brothers came to Egypt, begging to get food during a famine, not knowing they were bowing before their own brother whom they had sold off as a slave while faking his death.

Joseph, knowing who they were and that his only full-blooded brother Benjamin was not with them, accused them of being spies. He kept one of the brothers as a prisoner, to make sure when they returned for more food, they would bring Benjamin to prove otherwise.

At first Jacob refused to let Benjamin go when the food got low. He was afraid harm might come to Benjamin and did not think he could live if something happened to this other son from his special wife, Rachel, who had previously died.

We deal with some of those same fears, don't we? With our other children, we're fearful of letting them go anywhere out of our sight. Jacob had to fight the same fears we have.

I am so thankful that God included stories of families like this in His Word. It helps us to see that all throughout history, people dealt with these things and reacted in the same way we do. The story of Joseph is one of my favorites in showing how God can take tragedy, betrayal, heartache, and feeling abandoned by God and turn it into something so unexpectedly, wonderfully redemptive!

Reflection: Here is something that probably is *not* a similarity for you with Jacob at this point. When Jacob finally relented and let Benjamin go to Egypt with his brothers, because they would all die of starvation if he didn't, Jacob had gotten to the point of being able to say, "If I am bereaved, I am bereaved" (Genesis 43:14). After all those years, he was finally able to surrender that fear to God.

This is something so important for us to be able to do with all these new fears we have. We can, and we need to get to the place where we are able to surrender them to God. It takes many years for most of us to be able to believe, "If it happens, it happens, and God will get me through it again." I feel like I was just getting there, around ten years after Becca died. I want to encourage you to ask God to get to that place of surrender and trust way before Jacob did. Maybe even before the ten-year mark...?

When I am afraid, I put my trust in you.
Psalm 56:4 (CJB)

October 28

God Was with Us

Yesterday, I shared an *extremely* shortened version of Jacob losing his son, Joseph, and what really happened behind the scenes that no one in his family knew. You may have noticed that I did not complete the story, stopping when Jacob finally allowed Benjamin to return with his brothers for more food during a severe famine.

When these brothers returned, Joseph revealed himself to them. It took a while for them to get over the shock and believe him, especially since they were the ones who sold him off as a slave and faked his death to their dad. As a matter of fact, they thought they were being punished by God for what they did to Joseph because this Egyptian man, second in command to Pharoah, was giving them such a hard time.

In Genesis chapter 50, we see that Joseph made sure to tell his brothers, "It's not you who sent me here, but God." Joseph did not hate his brothers for what they did to him, as horrible as it was, but saw God's hand in it. That amazes me!

I cannot imagine having your own brothers sell you as a slave to someone in another country. Talk about betrayal and pain! Joseph went from being the son of a wealthy, influential man to becoming a slave in chains and all that came with it. But instead of Joseph being angry and bitter with his brothers, or with God, He acknowledged that God used it for His own plan of good.

Our children may want each of us to know the same thing that Joseph knew; God's hand was in what happened. To our children, it does not matter how they died or who may have caused their death. It matters to us, but not to them because they are in their eternal, forever home. I just picture them letting us know, "It's even better than I could have ever imagined!" I can hear them also telling us, "Don't stay stuck on whose fault it was. Satan may have been behind it, but I'm with God now. I am happy. I am in a place of love and perfection that is beyond what can be described!"

God has the final word on everything. God knows how many days each one of us we will have here on this earth (Job 14:5). I don't know why some of us have children whose days were numbered less than ours. But even when it seems like God has lost control, it isn't true. God's hand was on our children when they crossed over, and God was with *us* when our child died. His plans are always to turn something Satan meant for evil into something good.

Reflection: God really was with you in a way that when you look back, you can see His hand either before, during or shortly after the death of your child. If you have not been able to see that yet, ask the Holy Spirit to show you. But you must want to know and be willing to see these moments the way God shows them to us. Sometimes we are so angry at God, we don't want to admit that He was there for us in ways that maybe we could not see at the time. So, you have to be open to the fact that He was there.

Just take the time to ask God questions like, "Where were you? How were you preparing me? What did you show me or let me see or feel, as I was finding out, or as this was happening, or after I found out my child died?" You may not get an answer right away. Do not be surprised if He shows you where He was at a time when you are not expecting it.

> *The Lord your God will always be at your*
> *side, and he will never abandon you.*
> *Deuteronomy 31:6 (CEV)*

October 29

Do not Compare

After Joseph revealed who he was to his brothers, he sent them to get his father and have them all move to Egypt where he could take care of them. When they returned home and told Jacob that his son Joseph was still alive, he did not believe them at first. When he finally did believe them, the Bible says that Jacob's spirit was revived and he was excited that he would be able to go and see Joseph. (It makes me think about when King David said in 2 Samuel 12:23 that his infant son who died would not come back to David, but David would go to his son.)

You may be reading this thinking, "I wish my child wasn't really dead. Why didn't I get that?" We also think things like, "Why didn't I get the testimony that my child was healed, or my child was spared in an accident?"

Comparisons do not help at all. God is doing something different in each person's life, and I believe that in the lives of those of us who have lost a child from this earth, He is doing a very deep work.

Joseph was seventeen years old when he was sold as an Egyptian slave. Based on the timeline given, he was probably about forty-one years old when the brothers went back to get Jacob to take him to Egypt. That means Jacob thought his son was dead for twenty-four years before he found out that was not true and was able to see and hug his son again.

Some of us are going to have to wait much longer than twenty-four years to see and hug our child again. Barbara Bush, President Bush's wife was twenty-eight when her three-year-old daughter, Robin, died in her arms of leukemia. Barbara did not get to be reunited with her daughter for sixty-five years. Some of us are not even going to have to wait ten years. Once again, comparisons are not helpful.

I just heard a song a couple of days ago that had a line in it that "God is making us into an unshakable mountain." In fact, the song was shared by a mom who lost her son twelve weeks before from an overdose. And just like her, you may feel like you are so far from being an unshakable mountain.

As someone who used to feel the same way and is more than ten years on this journey, it seems we can go through just about anything now, because we've been through the worst of the worst, especially since we have learned in such a deep way that we are *in Him*. That is what makes us unshakable.

Reflection: Death is not the end. It is a door to the next life. We do not know when that door will open for us but while we wait, making any kind of comparisons that frustrate you is not helpful.

Here is something to think about. Even though we don't know how long our separation is going to be, we *do* know that when we get to see our children again, we are not going to have to be separated from them a second time like Jacob and Joseph were, when Jacob died a few years later. And once we are reunited with all of eternity ahead of us, I am convinced it's going to seem like it was just a nanosecond that we were separated, no matter how many years it was here on earth.

*Christ died, and we have been joined with him by dying too.
So we will also be joined with him by rising from the dead as he did.
Romans 6:5 (NCV)*

October 30

God Gives Life

Jairus was a leader in the synagogue who came to Jesus, fell at His feet, and pleaded with Jesus to come to his house and heal his dying daughter. (Accounts of this can be found in both Matthew 9 and Mark 5, which has more details.)

As Jesus was on his way to heal her, He was detained by a woman who had an issue of constant bleeding. When she touched the hem of His garment and was healed. While this was going on, someone told Jairus his daughter had died so there was no reason for Jesus to come now.

We can have that same reaction of not needing Him anymore because our child died. "God, my child's dead. You did not stop it. Don't bother with me now. Leave me alone." But Jesus did not listen to that then, and He is not listening to it now. Jesus told this father not to be afraid, but to believe. What exactly was Jairus supposed to believe? That he would see his daughter again and that she was not really dead, just sleeping.

Jesus raised this girl from the dead on the spot. Obviously, we did not get that miracle. However, we do still get the miracle that our child is not really dead, but just transferred to our eternal home in glory ahead of us. Our children are more full of life than we are!

In this instance with Jairus, we see that Jesus was not bound by earthly time, which is why He could say she was not dead and could bring her spirit back into her body here on earth. When Jesus said that Jairus' daughter was just sleeping, He was calling things that were not, as though they were, like we read in Romans 4:17.

We are used to hearing the part of the verse that says, "calling things that are not as though they are," but did you know that Paul was referring to what God did for Abraham and Sarah? Let's back up a few words and read it. "...whom he (Abraham) believed, who gives life to the dead and calls those things which are not as those that are." (Romans 4:17 GW).

Did you catch that? Giving life to the dead was *exactly* what Jesus did for that girl. I believe that is what He did for our children as well, but gave them life in heaven with Him instead of down here with us like we wanted Him to do. But life is life, no matter where our children are, so I am extremely thankful that He made good on His word, not just to Jairus, but to us as well. How about you?

Reflection: We know that since God's realm is eternity, He is not bound by time, going forward *or going backward*. I believe that means when we pray, laying our requests before Him, those requests are not bound by time as we know it.

We are used to praying for things in our future. But is it possible that we can make a prayer request for something that has happened behind us in time? After all, God already knows every prayer we are ever going to pray. He can answer it before we even pray it because He is not bound by time as we know it, in either hearing the prayer or answering it.

I think it is obvious that we cannot apply that to the actual death of our child. But I do believe we can petition God with a request that our child did not feel alone when they died, or they did not feel pain. We are calling what is not, as though it is, and using the fact that we are bound by time, but God is not. We can pray those kinds of prayers, knowing that God is faithful, and that those are the things that He wants as well.

Abraham believed in God—the God who gives life to the dead and decides that things will happen that have not yet happened.
Romans 4:17 (ICB)

October 31

Wearing a Mask

I understand there are many very strong beliefs among Christians about why we should have nothing to do with Halloween. Whether you feel that way or not, today is a day known for wearing a costume and mask, either pretending to be someone else or hiding who you really are.

Most of us have been wearing a similar mask since a few weeks after our child died. We put on the "I'm fine" mask, pretending we are doing okay and hiding how we are still falling apart behind closed doors.

Sometimes we wear that mask because we don't know how to answer when someone asks, "How are you?" We know it is not a good idea to yell out, "*My child is dead. How do you THINK I am?*" Instead, we have to do an immediate in-depth examination to be able to give an answer.

- Are you asking about this exact moment, or as a whole? This can cause me to have two completely different answers.
- Are you asking because you really want to know, or is it more of a greeting because you don't know what else to say, and you want a quick answer of "fine" so you can move on?
- Is it just the clerk at the store, who is using it more as a greeting, and I really should not unload on her in sarcasm and pain, no matter how I am feeling at the moment?
- Are you a safe person to give a truthful answer to?

At this point, we are exhausted going through all the options in our heads, we put on our mask and say we are "fine." The further we go along, the better we get at wearing the "I'm fine" mask with people around us. But even though we may be able to fool those around us, we cannot fool ourselves. We know that we are not fine.

Reflection: Sometimes we need to wear a mask to protect ourselves from those who want to try to fix us, or those who think we are hanging on to our grief for too long. Sadly, not everyone who asks really wants to know. Not everyone who asks can handle an honest reply, and often we don't want to have the conversation.

However, that does not mean you always have to put on the mask of "I'm fine." May I suggest you think of a couple answers that are truthful, and yet draws a boundary line around your struggle. For instance, "I am doing the best I can, but it is still difficult. Thank you for asking." Or " It's difficult for me to talk about it right now, but thanks for asking." How about, "I am taking it one day at a time. Some days are better than others. Thank you for asking."

If you noticed, all of them ended with a "thank you for asking." That is an easy way to close the door on further conversations that you may not want to have, but also allows you to not have to hide behind a mask, which can feel much better than staying behind it. Take a minute and think of a couple of answers you can have handy, instead of a mask.

Also, remember that God knows the truth of how you are doing, and it is always safe to be real with Him.

> *Come, Lord, and show me your mercy, for*
> *I am helpless, overwhelmed, in deep distress.*
> *Psalm 25:16 (TLB)*

November

November 1

Do not Let Others Pressure You

We all know the end-of-the-year holidays can leave one frazzled, but they can be outright brutal when dealing with deep grief at the same time.

After the death of our child, some of us have become experts at putting the needs of others ahead of our own, allowing ourselves to suffer physically, emotionally and spiritually (with all kinds of excuses and ways of justifying it to ourselves). Most of us put ourselves on autopilot, feeling numb, letting others dictate our holiday schedule. Either way, we often pay a high price at the end of each day and face a big crash at the end of the season.

Let's not do that to ourselves this year. Let's do the smart thing for everyone around us, and "put the oxygen mask on ourselves first," so that we are better equipped to do things for others.

Believe it or not, you *can* cut out some of the traditional activities, even if others are counting on you, are expecting you to step in this year, or think it would be good for you!

Also, believe it or not, there are some things we think we "need" to do, that we really don't. If you are continuing something because you are being pressured (including pressuring yourself out of guilt) or are concerned what people will think if you don't participate, that is the *wrong* reason to keep going.

I mean it!

And that includes things like church services or activities. Yes, I said it. If these things are draining you right now, and you dread going, don't let people guilt you into it.

If you are grieving, you are in recovery. And quite often, recovery means staying home and taking care of yourself or your family. It is okay and I give you full permission. Do not continue doing things for people who are not an intimate part of your life, which take up time and energy you just don't have right now.

Reflection: Unsolicited opinions of others who do not understand deep grief just don't matter at this point. You are heading into the busiest season of the year. You are also heading into several weeks of constant reminders that your child is not here for all the fun and festivities. This is a time to go easy on yourself, not forge ahead and pay for it later with a huge crash.

Take some time right now and ask the Holy Spirit to help you pay extra attention to His guidance for the next few weeks. He knows what you should and should not be doing; the activities that will be okay for you to participate in (and maybe even be good for you) and the ones that you need to avoid. Then ask Him to help you follow His promptings, whether they make sense or not!

> *He lets me rest in fields of green grass*
> *and leads me to quiet pools of fresh water.*
> *Psalm 23:2 (GNT)*

November 2

Feeling Alone

We are often torn, because sometimes we find that while we want to be alone, at the same time, we do not want to be lonely.

It is easy to find ourselves feeling very lonely in a room full of people. Those around us are enjoying conversations, laughing and living a "normal" life, while we are still in a painful fog.

Just being around other people isn't what we are longing for; it is being around people who care, and who will allow us to be whoever we need to be, at any given moment, in our grieving.

Some bereaved parents have a great support system. Others have one or two trusted friends or family members who will allow them to talk and grieve and be whoever they need to be in their painful fog for as long as they are needed.

But I would say most of us just don't have that. The people around us are uncomfortable with our grief if it goes beyond a few months. (Unfortunately, the Body of Christ is much better at rejoicing with those who rejoice than weeping with those who weep.)

We also have little band width for small talk and chattering. The things other people talk about often seem frivolous and we do not have the desire or the energy to be part of those kinds of conversations.

This is why we gravitate to each other as pareavors. It is comforting to be with those who "get it" and we don't have to explain or excuse how we feel, physically, emotionally, or spiritually.

Reflection: Do you feel lonely, even when with other people? You may need to realize there is just no way around it, especially the first couple of years. People will probably have difficulty relating to you, while you also find it hard to relate to them.

Ask God to help you find at least one other bereaved parent that you can share life with. Maybe you can even start a small group in your home like I did, just to talk and share life together.

> *Now, this means that when we come together and are side by side, something wonderful will be released. We can expect to be co-encouraged and co-comforted by each other's faith!*
> *Romans 1:12 (TPT)*

November 3

Falling Apart

There are those who would tell us it is our choice to either lean on God for strength or fall apart, but that was not the case for me. I did both. I leaned on God *as* I fell apart. Those who have lost a child can understand there are times when the intense grief of those first few months and years will emotionally and physically take over, and we really have no choice in the matter. We cannot function, no matter how much we try or how much we might want to.

However, doing things to numb ourselves from the pain will only prolong the grief and even intensify it. At the same time, we need to find ways beyond what is considered "spiritual" to bring ourselves comfort in our time of grief, but it is very easy to do so in unhealthy and even harmful ways.

Obviously, we know the dangers of excessive drugs and alcohol, but there are lots of things we can do excessively that are not good for us like excessive shopping, excessive Internet or TV, and excessive eating or sleeping.

Sometimes we may do some of these things because we just need to shut down for a while, which is okay! But we want to monitor ourselves to make sure it is not a substitute for going to God to help us get through this.

On those days of falling apart, when I felt like I was not going to make it through, I would cry out to God. It was the *only* thing I knew of that would truly help me both in the short and long-term. And in that place of trauma, God has never rejected me.

I still occasionally have times like this, and I can still call out to Him with the tiniest cry at *any* point, and He comes in to give me the strength I need, moment by moment, until I can function again.

Reflection: Is there something you are doing in excess that is not good for you right now? One way to tell is if you get defensive about it. There is no judgment in this. We all do it at some point.

Either ask God to help you work through your grief in a healthier way, or ask for His help so that you don't move into a place of dependence on something that is unhealthy.

My life's strength melts away with grief and sadness; come strengthen me and encourage me with your words.
Psalm 119:28 (TPT)

November 4

Time Does Not Heal All Wounds

No matter what others may think (or even tell us), time itself does not heal our shattered hearts after the death of our children. In the cemetery where Becca is buried, there is a section of babies and infants that were born in the 1970's and 1980's. Almost half of those graves continue to have fresh decorations, forty years later.

But that does not mean those parents are stuck and have never had a measure of healing in their lives that allowed them to function and live life again without their child. It doesn't mean you will be stuck there as well.

It is not time that heals. It's what we do with our time and the decisions we make within the grieving process that impacts how long we are unable to function within the deep grief of missing our child.

Dave and I met a woman whose child had died over ten years earlier, and she said she wasn't any better than when it first happened. I knew that wasn't true, because we were at a grief conference (which means she got out of bed, got cleaned up and came) plus she was talking about her child without being a crying mess. I am pretty sure she wouldn't have

November

been able to function in that same capacity those first few weeks, or even months.

How do you know that you are beginning to deal with the reality of child loss a little bit better?

- When you can make it through an entire day without a meltdown
- When you no longer feel an intense desire to visit the cemetery every day
- When you introduce yourself to someone and don't feel the need to add, "and my child died"
- When you can smile and not feel guilty about it
- When you can find something to be thankful for in your day

These are some of the ways that will let you know you are moving forward in your grief. Of course, you will always miss your child with every ounce of your being, but it's good to know that there can (and will be) moments of joy, too.

Reflection: Look at the above list. Is there anything listed that you have seen happening to you? Quite often, we may have a day or two moving in that direction, and then fall right back into the darkness. But if it happened once, it can happen again.

Quiet yourself and think whether there are signs in your life that show you are starting to have hope that somehow you can live again without your child. It does not mean we don't miss them. It doesn't mean the pain goes away forever, but it does mean it won't always be like this. Hey, that right there is something to be thankful for in your day!

> *Yahweh, you have heard the desires of the humble and seen their hopes. You will hear their cries and encourage their hearts.*
> *Psalm 10:17 (TPT)*

November 5

Lament

I recently discovered the word lament. Well, maybe not the word itself, but the true meaning behind it. I discovered that lament is what I did when Becca died, which is how I was able to come out of the suffocating pit of darkness as quickly as I did. Lament is also why I feel compelled to walk with others through their grief of losing a child. Lament is why you are holding this book.

Let me explain. Lament is a Christian word. People who do not know Christ in a personal way cannot lament. They can grieve. They can sob. But they cannot lament.

Lament is the Christian's unique language for loss and deep pain. It is taking all that suffering and sorrow to God, being raw and real with Him on how we feel about what has happened. It is asking Him the hard questions in our anger and confusion. For those who are angry with God to the point of no longer talking to Him, lament cracks the door open to restore that relationship.

It is a process for our pain and so much more than a Biblical version of the "five stages of grief" (which is actually the stages for someone grieving their own terminal illness, knowing they are going to die). But it isn't just the spewing out of the deep emotions in your soul. Lament keeps our attention on God, preventing us from becoming self-centered with our anger turning into a toxic root of bitterness that poisons everyone around us, including those who are still here whom we still love deeply.

Lament is given to us from God, as a way for us to come to Him with our complaints! Did you know God gave us permission to be upset with Him? As Christians, where there are tears and pain, it is not only normal to lament, but necessary. It is the tension between knowing God can, but that He did not. It is the tension between the pain of deep loss and the truth of God's goodness.

It invites us on a journey. We turn to God, lay out our complaints, ask Him for His help, and get to the point where we choose to trust Him with our pain and the loss. This may sound strange, but lament is something we can learn to embrace as part of this daily, ongoing journey of the deep earthly loss of our child.

How can I possibly say that? Because lament is a path that leads to God's incredible grace. Lament leads to God's faithfulness. Lament leads to God's deep, unfailing love. Lament leads to Him, who will eventually lead us to our children again. Can you see why I said that lament helped me get out of that place of suffocating darkness?

Reflection: Lament is worship! Grief-filled prayers of pain, while talking to God and seeking Him in the dark mess is one of the greatest forms of worship. By doing this, we are acknowledging that we understand He is God - that He is all powerful and holds everything in His hands, including our hearts that are filled with pain and confusion.

Lament changes us, because it lets God in, allowing Him to be at work in us, even if we cannot tell He is doing anything (or it may even seem like He doesn't care). Lament is more than something that just comes out of you. It is the process that is happening inside you, as you grieve. In my pain, I kept coming to God, over and over and over again. I kept throwing my pain at Him, throwing myself at His feet as a crumpled mess. I believe the fact that I kept doing my best to turn toward Him in my pain and confusion, instead of away from Him, was an act of worship which opened the door for my soul to be restored, not to just barely survive, but start to thrive.

This is why I also feel compelled to walk with other pareavors. I know that when we come out the other side of lament, we come out in a good place that we never thought was possible. Being in that place of tension of knowing He could, but for some reason did not, is part of the lament journey. Lament is life-giving. So, keep turning to God. Ask Him the hard questions. Ask the Holy Spirit to help you trust Him and bring you to that place of knowing His incredible grace, amazing faithfulness, and deep love that you did not even know was possible.

Lord, listen to all my tender cries. Read my every tear, like liquid words that plead for your help. I feel all alone at times, like a stranger to you, passing through this life just like all those before me. Don't let me die without restoring joy and gladness to my soul...
Psalm 39:1-2 (TPT)

November 6

Helping Others Remember

When we have to say a final earthly goodbye to our child, it affects everything. For the rest of our lives. Holidays seems to taunt us about our past, present and future, amplifying our painful deep loss in all three timeframes. Celebrations with family traditions are no longer fun and comforting.

You may need to exclude yourself from these traditional family times for the first few years. But if you join them, it may help to know there are some things you can do to make sure that the memory of your child is kept alive at these gatherings in a way that everyone can appreciate.

Here are a few suggestions to help you face events either in the future, or this coming year that you just can't seem to avoid.

1. Set a book on a table, along with your child's photo in a frame, where those attending can write a memory or a note to your child, sharing how much he or she is missed.

2. Ask the group to make a toast, acknowledging by name all the family members who have passed on.

3. Play one of your child's favorite (or a memorable) upbeat song and have everyone dance it up in honor of your child.

4. Have a preplanned silly hat contest, with your child's favorite color featured. Wear the same hats each year or change it up and make new ones, which might make a wonderful yearly tradition.

5. Find photos of your child with the individual attending family members/friends. Make it into a video with music that everyone will enjoy watching.

6. If it is a casual event (like a family holiday gathering) ask some people ahead of time to sit down with you and watch your child's favorite movie that you bring.

November

If none of these suggestions seem like they will make you want to be there, guess what? It's okay! So often we are told in life, "It's not about you." But the truth is, sometimes it is.

Only you know what is right for you, as a bereaved parent, through the difficult events in the coming year. But whatever you do, do it with HOPE, knowing that means:

HOPE - Hold On, Pain Eases!

I will never say the pain ends, but it will eventually ease, as we learn how to carry the pain of our loss in a way that does not consume and devour us. But we will always have moments where it still does, and that is okay.

Reflection: What are your plans for Thanksgiving Day? Some families just leave the area the first two or three years to get away from extended family and the excruciatingly painful reminders. If that is what you need to do, then go for it, even if those you usually spend the day with don't understand.

If you aren't sure yet what the right thing is for you to do this year, maybe you can write down your options, and don't forget about the ideas mentioned that you just read. Then list out the pros and cons of each one and talk to the Lord about it. Others may not understand your decision, but He understands, and so does anyone who has lost a child. Truth be told, we really don't want them to know what this is like, to be able to understand, do we?

> *For no matter where I am, even when I'm far from home, I will cry out to you for a father's help. When I'm feeble and overwhelmed by life, guide me into your glory, where I am safe and sheltered.*
> *Psalm 61:2 (TPT)*

November 7
Our Support System

There are many grieving parents who have a wonderful support system of friends and family after the death of their child. Unfortunately, much of it often only lasts for about six months to a year.

Once a parent hits that one-year mark, many of the people who are in that support system expect us to start "pulling ourselves together" and going back to who we were before, instead of being all gloomy and sad. We might even told we need to see a counselor and get some help to get over it.

Yes, some of us might need counseling, especially those who are dealing with severe PTSD, and there are pareavors who have the blessing of finding a great counselor who is really helping. But many parents I know say they were disappointed with their counselor and dropped out. They felt like the counselor was just going by what he or she learned to say in their schooling. Some pareavors felt like the counselor was relying on their own personal loss of a loved one, not recognizing that child loss is different.

Please note: I am not advising anyone to *not* seek counseling. Find a qualified counselor as soon as possible if you feel it is needed to help you get through some of the worst of the grieving process. Just be aware that not all counselors are equipped to walk with pareavors at a level that is truly helpful.

Not all, but most pareavors find that the most helpful thing they can do is to connect with other pareavors who were dumped onto this same unwanted journey; pareavors who have found hope, are living a life of meaning again, and will walk with others through the dark valleys of deep grief.

When our daughter, Becca, died, I did not want to go to a support group or any kind of gathering for parents who have lost a child. I thought it would be morbid, and I didn't want to sit around with a bunch of people who were a mess like me. I thought I would leave feeling worse than I came. But what I discovered is that it was wonderful being around a group of people who were a mess like me!

November

They "got it!" I did not have to exhaust myself by wearing a mask, making them think I was okay or feel the need to apologize for laughing or crying at any given moment for no apparent reason. It was so very refreshing and healing.

Reflection: Have you met with other bereaved parents? If not, why not? If you don't know any other pareavors in your area, ask God how to find one or lead someone to you. Do you have the same misconception I had? Pray and ask God to help you get past whatever it is that is keeping you away from the very group of people who can be your greatest strength.

If you are meeting with others, pray and ask God to be with those you have come to know and love, and to continue to strengthen your bond and grow these precious friendships.

Now our hope for you is unshakeable, because we know that just as you share in our sufferings you will also share in God's comforting strength.
2 Corinthians 1:7 (TPT)

November 8
Not Wrong, Just Different

Many years ago, God showed me how often I would get upset at my husband, Dave, believing he was doing something wrong. For example, if I drive one way to get to a certain store, taking some back streets to miss a bunch of stop lights, I expected him to take the same route if he was driving and get frustrated with him if he didn't. God made me aware that the way he was taking was not wrong, it was just different.

There have been so many times I have to remind myself that what he is doing isn't wrong, just because I wouldn't do it that way. It is just different.

It is the same with how we grieve over our child. Most of the times it isn't wrong; we are just grieving differently, especially when it comes to our spouse (or ex-spouse). Quite often it is the mom who is crying over photos, going to the cemetery several times a week, sitting on their bed and smelling their clothes. And usually, the husband doesn't want all that stuff to distract him from working through his grief. Neither way is wrong... they are just different.

Great grace is needed within the family during this time. This includes your other children.

The entire family has been shaken to its very core. The siblings are also dealing with a very deep loss, and many of them feel like they have not only lost their sibling but have lost their parents as well. As some of them begin to react in difficult ways (especially the older ones who basically walk out and go live their own life with very little communication, or get caught up in destructive choices), the parents feel like they have lost more than one child.

You would think families would draw close together in the grieving process, realizing how precious life is and how quickly we can lose someone, causing us to treasure each other. But more often than not, everyone either goes to their own corner and isolates themselves, or they turn on each other. The pain is so intense that quite often we just don't think clearly.

This is such a complicated issue, and there is no instant cure. The only things I know to do are to give lots and lots of love and grace through the differences, and hold on to God with everything you have until things start to turn around and relationships begin to mend as these deep wounds begin to heal.

Reflection: We tend to all agree that there is not a wrong way to grieve. It's easy to apply that to ourselves, but much harder when it comes to our spouse, children, parents, close friends, etc., because "if they are not doing it like me, they aren't doing it right."

If you are at odds with someone over grieving the death of your child, ask the Holy Spirit what your part is, to bring peace into that relationship (or at the very least, to yourself within that relationship). It may be setting some needed boundaries. It may be to set your grief aside at times, allowing them to grieve the way they need to which might mean moving toward a place of healing more quickly than you.

Take some time to really listen to what God speaks to your heart, and then ask Him to give you the desire and the strength to act on what He shows you.

So then let us pursue what makes for peace and for mutual upbuilding.
Romans 14:19 (ESV)

November 9

Fear Versus Faith

Fear brings torment, and as parents grieving the earthly loss of our child, it is easy to feel the full weight of that torment.

If we are afraid of something, it means that thing has more power over us than we do over it. So, if we are afraid to face the pain of our grief and work our way through it, our fear will continue to grip us and control us. I don't believe this is what you want for yourself, and I certainly don't want it for you.

There is something much more powerful than our deepest fears: God's love for us! God's perfect love casts out *all* fear (1 John 4:18). If we have fear about our future, it is because we do not believe in His perfect love for us. And that is understandable, because it is hard to reconcile in our minds how we can trust a God who says He loves us and yet allowed this terrible thing to happen to our child and to us.

Once again, it comes down to making choices. I have made the choice to refuse to remain focused on the pain of my loss. I am determined to go forward, focused on who and what I still have. You and I both are blessed with so much that has *not* been taken from us. Most of us know that in our heads and are waiting for our hearts to catch up.

We either believe God is good and Satan is evil, or we don't. We either fear that God is not big enough, or we have faith that He is more than enough. In choosing to believe that He is more than enough, I have given God the shattered pieces of my life and am watching Him make it into something that is actually beautiful. Only a God who specializes in miracles can do that!

I also refuse to live in fear of the "what ifs" of more loss. If that happens, I know, that *I know*, that ***I know*** that God will give me the grace I need to get through it. Why waste my time in the darkness of fearing what will probably never happen? I would much rather live my life full of light and hope of a better tomorrow, both here on earth and in my eternal home with Becca.

Fear and faith have the same root, which is belief in the unknown. We either fear what we don't know is in our future, or we have faith, trusting God that He is already there to meet us in our unknown future and will be with us. Which "unknown" are you going to start believing in and acting on? I recommend faith.

Reflection: What fears are you carrying right now? Are they things God would have you carry? Let me answer that for you. No, they are not.

Spend time picturing yourself taking these fears off your back (like taking off a backpack) and laying them at the feet of Jesus, sitting on His throne as King, so that you can move forward in freedom. Ask God to help you, if it is a struggle to take them off and release them.

> *So here's what I've learned through it all:*
> *Leave all your cares and anxieties at the feet of the*
> *Lord, and measureless grace will strengthen you.*
> *Psalm 55:22 (TPT)*

November 10

The Word "Family"

After the death of our child, the word *family* takes on a whole new meaning. Our family will never be complete again. There are no replacements for child loss...

Ever.

And because of that, phrases with the word family in them can bring on crashing emotions.

- Family photo
- Family reunion
- Family vacation
- Family meal
- Family pack (of tickets, etc.)
- Family holiday
- Family picnic

Even advertisements can be a glaring reminder of how our child is now missing from our family.

At every family gathering or event, we get a front row seat to the meaning of the word *bittersweet*. Graduations, school dances, Mother's Day and Father's Day, birthday parties, weddings, baby showers...all of these and many more events can be overshadowed with a reminder of who is not there, and be bittersweet...

Holidays, like the ones we are approaching, definitely have the same affect on me. Some moments, some days, some years are filled with tears, and others are filled with warm memories that bring smiles and even laughter.

It's okay not to be okay! Let me say that again, a little louder this time.

IT'S OKAY NOT TO BE OKAY!

Well now, this does not sound like a word of hope, does it? At least not to those who have never faced a deep loss like ours. But if you are anything like me, this was a relief when I found out it is not only okay to be like this, but *normal.* No matter how long other pareavors have been on this journey, they still have moments of not being okay with their child being gone from this earth.

If it's okay for them, it is okay for you and me.

Reflection: Allow yourself to feel hope, knowing that there are other bereaved parents out there who were once in the same place you are and yet seem to have figured out how to live without their child.

If you need a good cry, go ahead and have it. Then remind yourself of the family members you still have in your life. Think of each one of them individually, and how much you love and appreciate their good qualities and how thankful you are to have them in your life.

*My prayers for you are full of praise to God
as I give him thanks for you with great joy!
Philippians 1:3 (TPT)*

November 11

I Do Not Feel Very Thankful

Yes, this is the time of year where "thankfulness" abounds. It is everywhere we turn, from store decorations to commercials to social media posts.

But what do we do, when thankfulness is the furthest thing from our minds, and definitely not in our hearts? Do we stay in our house and pull the curtains tight? Do we yell at the TV, telling people who can't hear us to stop it? Do we stay off social media, so we don't have to feel like we are gagging at how happy and thankful everyone else is?

Yes, we might do all of those things and more.

I *know* how hard it is to be thankful or grateful this time of year, especially when those around us who have never lost a child tell us that is what we should do, because it will make us feel better!!! *What would make me feel better is to have my child back, but since you can't do that, don't tell me what to do to make me feel better!* Right?

If this is your first or second year without your child during the holiday season, it might not be possible to feel thankful. But just know that you can eventually become thankful for the memories and the times you had, instead of being swallowed up in the indescribable pain of not having your child with you. It is possible.

From my personal experience, and that of many others who are on the same road, we have learned that finding even the tiniest things to be thankful for can start to make a huge difference on this journey. But it's not because someone told you that is what you should do. It is because you are ready to make a shift out of the darkness and realize that this is one of those steps toward the light.

Reflection: Don't you hate it when someone says, "You woke up today. You can be thankful that you are alive and breathing."? For a long time after our child dies, we don't want to wake up. We don't want to be alive and breathing. We have been begging God to let us die to go be with our child.

It is difficult to hear someone who has never lost a child telling you that finding things to be thankful for will make you feel better. But those of us who have been where you are can gently suggest you move in that direction, knowing from experience that it will help bring a glimmer of light into your darkness. Take a few minutes and ask God to show you at least three things that are good in your life, even if you can't "feel" the goodness of it right now.

*Let all that I am praise the LORD; may I
never forget the good things he does for me.
Psalm 103:2 (NLT)*

November 12

Holiday Memories

It does not seem to matter how many years have gone by since Becca died, Thanksgiving is a holiday I still struggle with, but for a different reason than you might think. You see, my last memory of all of us together for this holiday was at Becca's house.

She was very ill, and wheelchair bound. But in her *love* for hosting and entertaining (it was a God-given gift she was quite good at) she begged to have Thanksgiving at her house instead of the tradition of everyone coming to ours. There were several people who said it would just be too hard; that she couldn't do it. I knew I would still be the one making most of the food, and preferred using my own kitchen, but something in me knew she really needed to do this. So, I rallied around her, and convinced everyone (including her husband who would also need to shoulder much of the load) to let Becca host the family.

This meant she had to be carried up and down the stairs, with her wheelchair following, to be put back in it. It was a lot of extra work for several of us, causing some frazzled nerves, for sure. But she did it and was *so* happy that day as we sat down to eat! My tears are running down my face right now, thinking about it. This is one of those very bittersweet memories for sure.

It is my choice to either dwell on the bitter, or on the sweet. You get to make the choice as well. Not because others (including me) tell you that you should, but because you want your own memories to not only give you pain, but to also bring a smile to your heart within that pain.

As you well know, thinking about the pain of the deep loss, keeps us sucked under the suffocating darkness of grief. But, if we force ourselves to dwell on the sweet (such as how super glad I am that I convinced the rest of the family to let Becca host us, on what became her last Thanksgiving here on earth with us, and the wonderful memories I have because of it) I find myself so very thankful. Oops, there is that word we don't like to hear this time of year.

November

Reflection: When our child first dies, the strongest memories are of the death, and the circumstances surrounding the death which for some of us included a lengthy illness preceding their departure. When the fun and wonderful memories start to return, it is usually with pain, because we know that is all we have left of our precious child.

Eventually, our heart begins to smile at the memories, and it even reaches our face, as we smile at the thought of our child and the joy he or she brought us. And from there, we can eventually find ourselves grateful for the time on earth we had with our child, no matter how short, instead of angry and bitter for the time we lost.

Where are you in this very slow process? Are you still in that place where you lean into the bitter instead of the sweet? Let's try something together. What is a favorite holiday memory of your child? Close your eyes and sit with that for a while, doing your best to let the warmth of it outweigh the pain. If (or when) the tears come, let that liquid love flow, knowing that those tears are also being used to wash over your heart with a measure of healing love.

Peace to the far-off, peace to the near-at-hand,"
says God — "and yes, I will heal them.
Isaiah 57:19 (MSG)

November 13

It Is Only Temporary

The separation from our child seems permanent, doesn't it? In our heads we know we will see them again, but in our hearts, it feels like they have been torn away from us forever. Is there anything we can do to help us reconcile our head with our heart?

Reflections of Hope

Some parents are helped by thinking about it in a different way; that their son or daughter is simply absent. To be absent means "not to be present *for the moment.*" It is not a permanent separation. Our children are simply absent from us while we remain here on this earth. (However, that does not mean their absence isn't extremely painful, especially those first few years.)

The Bible says that for someone who has accepted the gift of salvation, to be absent from the body is to be present with the Lord (2 Corinthians 5:8), which is an interesting thought because that means it really is impossible to be separated from them permanently.

I think about those who traveled west in covered wagons, not knowing what they would face. If your adult child joined a caravan, you had no idea if you would ever see them or hear from them again. You could have grandchildren and never even know it; much less be able to meet them.

What about the pilgrims who came to America on ships? It was the same thing, only there wasn't just an unknown amount of land that separated them, it was also an ocean. Think of those who chose to be a missionary in a tribal nation back when there was no easy form of communication.

Believe me, I know this is not the same thing as knowing your child has left this earth. But it does seem to help give a framework for our children being absent. My daughter, Becca, is absent from my presence for now, but not forever. What a relief!

Reflection: I can either focus on my personal loss that my child is permanently gone from this earth (which sends me in a downward spiral), or I can focus on the fact that my child is absent from my presence for now, but is present with the Lord in glorious joy and perfection. And even though the pain is intense with the temporary separation, I will meet up with my child again in our eternal home, never to be separated again.

Have you thought about the fact that when we get to heaven, we will probably hear stories about our kids who arrived before we did? Can you imagine someone like the apostle Peter walking up to you and saying, "I just have to tell you what (*insert your child's name here*) did that was so funny!" What is something your child might be doing right now that would amuse or bless someone who is with them in heaven?

> *We live with a joyful confidence, yet at the same time we take great delight in the thought of leaving our bodies behind to be at home with the Lord.*
> *2 Corinthians 5:8 (TPT)*

November 14

We Need Each Other

It is impossible for those who have never had one of their children die to know what it is like. They cannot relate to the things we are going through and are dealing with, and we should not expect them to.

We also shouldn't expect them to stop their holiday festivities, and it really isn't even reasonable to think they should be more "sensitive" around us during the excitement of the holidays.

Some of us have a rare friend or two who bless us in those ways. Unfortunately, most of us do not. It can be extremely helpful to spend extra time with other pareavors this time of year, and if you don't believe me, here are six reasons why.

1. We are a safe sounding board. Our grief needs *lots* of grace. The best place to safely share and vent your raw and real emotions is to those who have experienced the same blackness, confusion and turmoil. There is no shame, and no judgment on your thoughts or feelings when it comes to other parents who have been right where you are.

2. We will not only let you talk about your child but are honored to help you keep his or her memory alive, no matter how many years it has been since they left this earth.

3. We understand the turmoil leading up to the sunrise and sunset dates, as well as things like not going to church for holiday celebrations, being unable to get in the "holiday spirit" etc., well beyond just the first year.

4. We have experienced the physical trauma. We know what it is like:
    - to be so forgetful that we think we are losing our minds or are terrified we are getting early dementia
    - to get sick easily because our immune system has been compromised
    - to not be able to handle crowds or noisy places like we used to
    - to have no energy to get out of bed, much less get dressed or take a shower, weeks and months into our grief (including years later for seasons here and there)
    - to not be able to attend certain events for many years because they are grief triggers for us
    - to have "grief fog" for years, and the frustration it brings

5. We understand that the word "family" has a totally different meaning now, and we understand why you don't want to have a family picture taken or go to a holiday family event.

6. You will not get hurtful clichés and inappropriate Bible verses thrown at you to try and fix you or make you feel better.

Sounds good, doesn't it?

Many areas do not have a local support group for bereaved parents, and it is even more difficult to find one that is faith based. Check with your local hospital, hospices and funerals homes, and of course look on an internet search engine for anything close to you.

November

Reflection: It is important that we don't feel alone, especially during the holidays. Even having just one other person in your life who has lost a child that you can spend time with is helpful.

Ask God to lead you to the right person or group of people that might be local or even a group that meets online who understands and can walk with you on this difficult and dark part of the journey. And even if this is somewhat fresh for you, pray about being that person for a pareavor in your area who has just lost a child. (That is how it all started for me. I didn't know what I was doing, but I simply agreed to walk with others so we could figure it out together.)

And while you're at it, ask God to give you grace for those around you who love the holidays and want to pull you into the fun and excitement, not understanding why you can't.

So speak encouraging words to one another. Build up hope so you'll all be together in this, no one left out, no one left behind.
1 Thessalonians 5:11 (MSG)

November 15
They Cannot Possibly Understand

Don't you love it when people become our cheerleaders, telling us we can do this because we are such a strong person? Or that they could never go through what we are going through in losing a child? Or when someone tells us they admire us for how strong we are?

WHAT? News flash: we had no choice in the matter! We are being forced to go through this. Just because you see us in survival mode does not mean we are being strong.

There are also people who mean well, who think we should be at a point in our lives (often within a few months) where we don't fall apart; that we should not continue to miss our child so much verbally or emotionally and something is wrong with us if our continued pain causes us to be unable to function fully like we did before our child died. They don't stop to think that since our love for our child never goes away, neither will the pain of missing them.

Sometimes when we say, "I still miss my child so much!" people respond with, "I know how you feel. I miss her, too." And we know how absolutely absurd it is for them to even think that is possible to know how we feel or to miss our child as much as we do.

And then there is the comparison, "I know how you feel. I lost my _____(fill in the blank)"

These things can make our blood boil to the point of ending relationships. And at times, that may be necessary, if it is constant and becoming toxic to your healing journey.

But a better way is usually grace... we need *lots* of grace and strength.

How can they possibly know or understand what it is like to lose a child? I sure didn't understand until it happened to me, so I probably said hurtful and insensitive things to others in their deep painful loss, trying to fix them or make them feel better.

Our grief is draining enough, without letting things people say and do drain us even more by getting angry and stewing over it. We need to ask God to help us forgive, let it go, and use the little energy we have in better ways.

Reflection: When those things happen, don't be afraid to get encouragement from pareavors around you who know better. We get it, we understand, and we are here for each other.

Once again, ask God to give you the grace needed to let those stupid or hurtful things go, so you are not needlessly drained from things that are not that important when looking at the big picture of learning how to survive and live again. Picture yourself before the throne. Tell Him about your hurts from others and see Him come down, wrapping His arms around you, giving you comfort as a parent would comfort their child. Rest in that powerful love.

So let us come boldly to the throne of our gracious God. There we will receive his mercy, and we will find grace to help us when we need it most.
Hebrews 4:16 (NLT)

November 16

Hopes and Dreams

Everyone has hopes and dreams. Some of our dreams were for our child who is no longer here. When our child leaves this earth ahead of us, not only are our lives are shattered, but so are those dreams for the future because we know, quite painfully, that those are dreams that will never become a reality.

What about the rest of our personal "someday" dreams? Most of us just can't see those ever becoming a reality, either. Our grief leaves us in a suffocating darkness. We now find ourselves struggling in "survival" mode, much less having some sort of inner drive and energy to pursue something bigger than ourselves.

But I am here to tell you that it is possible to dream again. Maybe one or two of those same dreams will eventually resurface, and you will feel a new purpose to fulfill them.

However, many of us pareavors end up with a new set of hopes and dreams that are based on keeping our child alive in the hearts and lives of others, including people who never knew or met our child. That is what happened to me.

Before our oldest daughter died, I had an international children's ministry, and had no idea God was about ready to make a huge shift to totally phase out that ministry and start a completely new one, which was a full-time ministry offering support and providing resources to grieving parents at a national level.

Reflections of Hope

Your dream may become something that was your child's dream, and now you want to keep it alive and make it happen in memory and honor of your child.

Hopes and dreams. They seem to go together, don't they? Even though you may feel like those things were buried with your child, there is something happening deep down that you cannot see or feel. Just like a seed that has been buried, it will come to life when the time is right.

Reflection: Some of you may not believe that you will ever dream again. Some of you are already moving in a direction and doing things you never saw happening in your future. Either way, dream big or dream small. Just start dreaming.

Are you dreaming yet? Or are you still in the "nightmare" stage? Or maybe it's both. Spend some time right now thinking about what you can do that is bigger than you; something that stirs an excitement in you to think about the possibilities. Write it down, and pull it out once in a while, until you feel a stirring that it is time to start moving in the direction of making it a reality.

> *We have become his poetry, a re-created people*
> *that will fulfill the destiny he has given each of us,*
> *for we are joined to Jesus, the Anointed One.*
> *Even before we were born, God planned in advance*
> *our destiny and the good works we would do to fulfill it!*
> *Ephesians 2:10 (TPT)*

November 17

Fight, Flight or Invite

When people around you suggest you might not be handling your grief very well, I want to say please don't feel like you owe them an explanation in the way of excuses, as if you have some kind of disease.

November

I know some of you don't have a problem with this at all, but those of us who are people pleasers, or have a drive to do things right, can struggle when others share with us their thoughts, causing us to question ourselves, as if maybe we *aren't* doing it right or maybe we *should* be further along than we are.

In case you haven't realized it by now, there are going to be things we struggle with for many years (possibly even the rest of our lives) after the death of our child.

You need to know that it's okay to be real and lean into your pain when it grips you unexpectedly.

As I see it, you have three options.

1. Fight it, which is usually obvious and awkward for everyone.
2. Excuse yourself and leave, either for a few moments to compose yourself, or for the rest of the event.
3. Stay put and let those around you know that something triggered your grief, causing you to deeply miss your child. Then ask them to join you for a brief moment, as you think about him or her. Allow them into that scared moment and the sacred space of missing your child.

There is no one right option. Each time will be different, and only you can determine which one is right for you at that moment. Just don't be afraid to go for the third option. It might surprise you how supportive and caring someone might be, and you will have the blessing of having people allow you to share your child with them.

Reflection: Resolving how to handle people telling you things like, "You should be better by now," is something you must do for your own well-being. Not in an angry bitter way, but peacefully, within yourself.

After resolving that within yourself, is there a gracious answer you can have in the back of your mind when someone who means well tries to fix you or tell you what you should or shouldn't be doing? Right now, go through some options in your head and find the one that feels like it will defuse the tension instead of adding to it. (You might want to consider starting it with, "Thank you for being concerned, but...")

And remind them to never tear down anyone with their words or quarrel, but instead be considerate, humble, and courteous to everyone.
Titus 3:2 (TPT)

November 18

Meaningful Gift Ideas for Yourself

When your family and friends start asking for gift ideas, it is okay to let them know that one of the greatest gifts they can give you are things that honor your child or keep his or her memory alive, both for the giver and for you as the recipient.

Here are a few suggestions.

- Have a tree ornament made with your child's name, picture, or something significant.
- Have one of your child's shirts made into a stuffed bear.
- Give a gift in your child's name such as:
    - A donation could be made to a charity associated with something about your child.
    - A group/family could put their money together for something that would be seen by the public, such as a park bench.
    - Donate to an organization like Compassion International, such as purchasing a goat for a needy family in another country.
- Place a memorial brick in a memory garden or memory wall in your community.
- Have a piece of jewelry made that has your child's name engraved on it.
- Have a blanket or a pillow made with a favorite photo of your child.

You can easily do an internet search to find places that will do these things for you, or you could search for more ideas.

Reflection: Go back to the list and decide which of the items is something you would really like to have, or maybe it gives you an idea of something similar. Then think about who you will tell about the gift you would like to receive this year. If you are not comfortable asking friends and family for these kinds of gifts, I give you permission to give a gift to yourself from your child!

He told them to celebrate these days with feasting and gladness and by giving gifts of food to each other and presents to the poor. This would commemorate a time when the Jews gained relief from their enemies, when their sorrow was turned into gladness and their mourning into joy.
Esther 9:22 (NLT)

November 19

Same Path, Different Journeys

Cell phones have come a long way in the camera department! However, we all know when we take pictures of the grandeur and beauty of nature, we cannot capture it fully, even with the best of cameras.

I could show you lots of pictures I took while climbing some mountains in California. I could tell you some of the things God was speaking to me during that time. But it was my personal climb.

Even if we had been together on the same path, we would have seen things through our own personal views. I could point something out to you, but you would be seeing it through your own thoughts and emotions. You would be having your own experience. It would be with me, and yet separate from me. Some of our climb would be the same experience, and some of it would be very different.

In the same way, we are each on our own grief journey. Even as someone who has also lost a child from this earth, there is no way I know how you feel. I know how I felt after my daughter died. I know the suffocating darkness I experienced. I know how I would forget to breathe and have to consciously tell myself to take a breath. I know how I wanted to stop hurting so bad and how the darkness lasted for so much longer than I thought it should.

I know how I did not want to live, which didn't make sense because I knew in my head I still had so much to live for. (I had a loving husband, four other children and two grandchildren at the time – one of those being the nine-year-old daughter of my daughter who had died.) None of that mattered. My heart wanted to be with my daughter who was now gone from this earth, and I knew I could not stay here if the rest of my life was going to be this painful. I was not suicidal, I just didn't want to live anymore and begged God to take me out of here!

You see, we each have many of the same grief experiences, but it is all though our own personal journey of our personal relationship with the one who died. I know how I felt, but that *doesn't* mean I know how you feel, even if you lost a daughter the same way I lost my daughter, through heart damage caused by chemotherapy.

We may be on the same path together, but we are still each on our own journey.

Reflection: My grief journey has been a lot like those mountains I was climbing, and I am guessing yours has been, too. I want to encourage you to keep climbing. If you felt like you started up a mountain and found yourself back down in the valley because the climb was too hard, go again after you are rested.

Where are you right now with your grief? Are you working your way up and the climb is hard? Is the climb easy right now? Are you on a plateau and resting? Are you back in the valley, trying to catch your breath, wondering if it is even possible to try again? Wherever you are, close your eyes and imagine Jesus right next to you. He is not only on the same path, but on the same journey. Let Him give you the needed strength to keep going.

> *God, the Lord, is my strength; he makes my feet like*
> *the deer's; he makes me tread on my high places.*
> *Habakkuk 3:19 (ESV)*

November 20

Making it Through the End of the Year

The end-of-the-year holiday season can amplify everything, especially the questions and the pain. When we face the death of our child, it can feel almost impossible to believe God is for us, or that He is Emmanuel, God with us. So many unanswered questions, many that start with "Why?"

One year, right before Thanksgiving, I was before the Lord and the words, "Emmanuel, God with us," hit my spirit with almost an explosion. I cried out, telling the Lord that I wanted Him to be with me every day of this next month. I wanted to feel Him; I needed to know His peace in a very tangible way.

I suddenly had a picture of our advent wreath. As our children grew up, we had many years where we did the advent wreath to help refocus us from the commercialism and the frazzled busyness of the season, to Jesus. (An advent wreath involves four different colored candles which are lit each night, based on a spiritual reading, the four weeks heading into Christmas Day.)

The thought came to me to have my own advent time with the Lord each night, using the wreath and the candles; to have a time where I specifically focused on who He is as Emmanuel, God with us, within my pain of the loss of my daughter.

I found myself writing something for each night of the advent season, and most evenings went live on Facebook, to light that week's candle and share with anyone who wanted to join me.

This has turned out to be invaluable, to help keep me from spiraling into the darkness because Becca is not here with me to celebrate Christmas. It helps remind me that gift-giving and parties, decorating and shopping really aren't what is important. What's important is to remember that Jesus came as a baby, for the purpose of dying, so that I can be with Him and those I love forever. He came to bring peace, hope love and joy into my life, no matter what trauma and tragedy I face here on this earth.

Reflections of Hope

Reflection: Here is what I found myself writing one day for the week I was meditating on the hope we have in Him.

> *May you be deeply blessed and find a measure of healing as you focus on making this Christmas season one of reflecting on our Savior in the midst of your painful loss. I sincerely pray that in the next few weeks, the Holy Spirit will remind us all that no matter how suffocating the darkness, there is hope for our future, because He truly is Emmanuel, God with us.*

He *is* Emmanuel, God with us. He did not say He is with us to stop all evil in this world, and to make our lives cozy and comfortable while here on this earth. He said He would be with us *through* it. And not only is He with us, He is *in* us, if you have accepted what Jesus did on the cross in paying the price for your sins. Ask God to reveal Himself to you as you connect with Him living inside you, both right now and in the next few weeks.

Note: This turned into an advent book *Hope for the Future,* that many pareavors go through each year during the Christmas season. As of my writing this, I still get on the GPS Hope Facebook page every Sunday evening during the advent season to light a candle and share a word of encouragement with those who want to join me. To find out more, you can go to www.gpshope.org/adventbook.

> *...for you always have God's presence. For hasn't he promised you, "I will never leave you, never! And I will not loosen my grip on your life!"*
> *Hebrews 13:5 (TPT)*

November 21

So Many Different Factors

Any loss takes time to process and work through. The loss of a loved one can take weeks, months, and years. The loss of a child takes a lifetime.

Grief has its own individual journey for each person. We may often hear the words, "There is no right or wrong way to grieve," and yet much of society shouts the exact opposite to those who are in deep mourning. We are asked when we are going to "get over it," or are told we need to let our child go and start moving forward.

What most people do not realize, is that most experts consider the death of one's child traumatic grief, and that up to five years can be considered "fresh" grief. That is important to know. You need to know that it is okay if you are still barely functioning or are unable to go out and "have fun" with friends or attend painful family events that your child should have been part of, years after the loss.

How close you were (or weren't), how he or she died, their age at death and so many other things all play a factor in how *you* grieve and how long it takes to be able to function again, much less actually learn how to live with your child being "amputated" from you.

I will say that for many of us (not all) the second year can be harder than the first. The third year seems to be when some of us move into the "acceptance" phase of, "this really happened and somehow I have to figure out how to learn to live without my child." Year five we can start to feel like life might have meaning and purpose again and be worth living out.

No one can tell you what is right or wrong for you, including another pareavor. Even within this three to five year "acceptance" range, we are all different, including those of us who are "early" or "late." In other words, whether you fit the "pattern" or not, you are in a *normal* place with *your* grief, and the *right one for you*.

Reflection: Year one, two, three, five, ten, or twenty... the rest of this lifetime... and then comes our glorious reunion. And the best part? Each day we remain here on this earth does not mean we are getting further away from our children, but that we are one day closer!

What will that day be like when Jesus looks you in the eye and says, "Welcome home!" Are you like I was for the first few years, more excited to see my daughter than I was to see Jesus? Take a minute to picture your son or daughter wrapped in your arms, giving them the biggest hug that you are saving up, just for them. It's okay if there are tears because it hurts so good!

> *He is given to us like an engagement ring, as the first installment of what's coming! He is our hope-promise of a future inheritance which seals us until we have all of redemption's promises and experience complete freedom—all for the supreme glory and honor of God!*
> *Ephesians 1:14 (TPT)*

November 22

Recovering From a Trauma

You may have already read this or heard it from me, but I think sometimes we need to be reminded of these things. As a parent who has faced the death of their child:

1. The death of one's child is considered by most professionals to be one of the most (if not *the* most) traumatic event a person can deal with in life.
2. The death of our child causes *deep* grief. Deep grief causes physical changes in our bodies, such as our immune system is compromised (we get run down and pick up illnesses easily), chemicals in our brain change (causing things like fogginess and confusion) and there are changes within the heart itself (which can even cause heart-attack like symptoms which need to be

November

checked out). Some of these changes last for years, and we may need help from a doctor or natural health practitioner to get our bodies back in order.

3. Studies have shown that for those who have lost a child, anything under five years is considered *fresh* grief!
4. Someone who has gone through a traumatic experience can often find themselves with PTSD (Post Traumatic Stress Disorder).

I don't think anyone can deny that it is a traumatic experience to walk behind your child's casket and bury them, or to bring your child home as ashes in an urn. And for those parents who found their child's body, or many other possible scenarios, the PTSD can be even worse.

Just like anyone who has faced a deep trauma, it takes a long time to be able to function again, and there are triggers that we will have to be dealt with for the rest of our lives.

I recently had a friend say it is like someone who has been in a horrific accident and almost every bone in their body has been shattered. They will have to relearn how to live again.

We all have to relearn how to live again. Recovery is a process that takes years, but even when we are able to function again, we will never be the same.

Reflection: We already feel like we are going crazy, and having family and friends tell us we "should be getting better by now" may have us locked in a world of deep anger, or wondering if maybe we *are* losing it and need to see someone for help or to be locked up. I am not saying that you might not need to see someone to help you get through the worst of it, but I hope you can see and give yourself grace for why you are still struggling so deeply.

Close your eyes and give yourself permission to be wherever you are in your grieving process. It is *so* important not to beat yourself up (like I did) thinking I should not be such a huge mess for so long. Don't think this is silly or take it lightly. Take as much time as you need, not just to give yourself permission, but to accept that permission. If you can't receive it from yourself, receive it from me. *I give you permission to be wherever you are in your grieving process.*

Please deal gently with me, Yahweh; show me mercy, for I'm sick and frail. I'm fading away with weakness. Heal me, for I'm falling apart.
Psalm 6:2 (TPT)

November 23

Is Everyone Else Forgetting?

I recently met for a couple of hours with a precious friend, Donna, whose son died tragically several years ago. As we were talking, she asked me with tears, "Why doesn't my own family remember the dates? Not a single one of them contacted me this year. I am afraid they are forgetting my son!"

I am pretty sure there are several of you out there who feel the same way, so I thought I would share my answer to Donna with you, as well.

Yes, they may forget dates, but I can guarantee they won't forget your child! He or she was part of their lives as well.

Let me ask you what might seem like some random questions. Do you have high school (or college friends) that you thought would be good friends for the rest of your life, but you haven't seen or heard from them in years? How about people you met on a mission's trip? Was there someone you connected with on a deep level, and you were sure that relationship would continue once you returned home, but it has fallen off? How many coworkers from your last job were you friends with outside of work, whom you barely talk to anymore, after saying you would still hang out together?

We all have good intentions, but most of the time, what is going on right in front of us, is what gets our attention. Does that mean you have

November

forgotten those people from your past? Of course not! It just means you have not made it a priority or made the time to communicate. It is not intentional, it just happens.

I know the sunrise and sunset dates of our child are *extremely* important to *us*. We can't get away from them and we don't want to. But that does not mean those around us are going to remember those dates, or in their own place of grief want to acknowledge those dates. The most important thing is that there are others who remember your son or daughter's *life*, and still share in those memories.

There is just no way our family and friends can know what it means to have others remember those dates with us. Unless you have been where we are, it is impossible for them to know. Like it or not, often it is going to be our effort that keeps them there. That's just the way the busyness of life works.

Reflection: If people know you are already struggling, many of them believe that bringing up our child will make it worse. Or they think we will be upset with them for bringing it up and making us cry if we are having a good day.

The people around us don't know it does just the opposite, *unless we tell them*. We *want* them to talk about our child and remember them! Yes, it may bring tears, but we would rather cry from someone sharing our child with us than cry from feeling like everyone is forgetting him or her.

Write down three to five people who are important to you, that you will commit to having this conversation with. Yes, it will probably be difficult, but once they know and begin to respond, it will be worth it. What if they still don't remember or talk to you about your child? Do your best to give as much grace as possible, both to them and to yourself.

> *Yahweh responds, "But how could a loving mother forget her nursing child and not deeply love the one she bore? Even if there is a mother who forgets her child, I could never, no never, forget you.*
> *Isaiah 49:15 (TPT)*

November 24

A Special Poem

I want to share a poem with you that I read quite often when I speak to a group of pareavors. Most people believe Corrie ten Boom wrote this and attribute it to her. However, it goes back to 1892 when it was printed in two different publications under the name of a woman named Florence May Alt.

Corrie liked to quote the following poem when she spoke because of the depth of suffering she had gone through in her life. Her family was taken to a Nazi concentration camp for hiding Jews during the Holocaust. Her most famous book, *The Hiding Place*, is a biography (made into a movie) that shares the story of her family's efforts and how she found hope in God while she was imprisoned at the concentration camp where her parents and only sibling (a sister she was close to) died.

The Weaving
My life is but a weaving, between my God and me;
I do not chose the colors, He worketh steadily.
Oft times He weaveth sorrow, and I in foolish pride
Forget He sees the upper, and I the under side.
Not til the loom is silent, and shuttles cease to fly
Will God unroll the canvas and explain the reason why
The dark threads are as needful in the skillful Weaver's hand
As threads of gold and silver in the pattern He has planned.
He knows, He loves, He cares; Nothing this truth can dim.
He gives the very best to those who leave the choice to Him.

As Corrie recited this poem, she would show the audience the backside of a weaving, which was nothing but a mess with all of its crisscrossed threads and knots. But when she turned it over, everyone was shocked to see the mess on the backside made a beautiful crown on the front side. The message is a profound truth. What we see is not what the master weaver sees, and that He will make something beautiful out of the pain and messes of our lives if we allow him to.

November

Let's read it again, one thought at a time, maybe even out loud. Stop at each line below and think about what that means to you in a very personal way, wherever you are right now on your grief journey.

My life is but a weaving, between my God and me...

I do not choose the colors...

He worketh steadily...

Oft times He weaveth sorrow and I in foolish pride...

Forget He sees the upper, and I the underside....

Not til the loom is silent, and shuttles cease to fly, will God unroll the canvas and explain the reason why...

The dark threads are as needful in the skillful Weaver's hand as threads of gold and silver in the pattern He has planned...

Reflection: Right now, you are probably overwhelmed with the very dark long thread being woven into the tapestry of your life. First, take a few minutes and think about what some of the gold and silver threads have been. Now, as sincerely as you can, thank God that He has plans to give you more gold and silver threads as you continue to live out your life here on earth.

Finally, remind yourself that you really are seeing the underside, but when you join your child, you will see the upper side that God sees, which was being made into a gorgeous tapestry.

> *"For I know the thoughts and plans that I have for you,"*
> *says the Lord, "thoughts and plans for welfare and peace*
> *and not for evil, to give you hope in your final outcome".*
> *Jeremiah 29:11 (AMPC)*

November 25

Siblings (Or Only Child)

NOTE: Today I want to talk about our child's siblings. **If this does not apply to you, you may want to skip to the Optional Reflection* at the end of today's reading, specifically written for you.**

Imagine a six-year-old as a ring bearer for his sister's wedding. Ten years later, at the age of sixteen, he is a pall bearer for that same sister's funeral. That is exactly what happened to my youngest son. (His two older brothers were also pall bearers for their older sister.)

Siblings are often silent grievers. They are the forgotten mourners. Well-meaning people around the surviving siblings often fail to recognize the depth of *their* loss, making them feel their intense pain is not valid, and they are not supposed to be hurting so deeply.

"How are your parents doing?"

"Remember to be extra good, since your mom is still really missing your brother (or sister)."

"Be strong for your parents. They are really hurting right now."

These are the kind of statements siblings who have lost a brother or sister often hear. What a terrible and unnecessary burden to put on someone who has lost one of the most important people in their lives! This is while many of the siblings are dealing with the fact that they feel like they lost their parents along with their sibling, because their parents are so nonfunctional.

It often causes these precious siblings to stuff their grief away deep inside, which usually catches up with them years later, as they try to figure out why they are dealing with intense emotional issues that are affecting everyone around them.

These siblings, no matter the age, have a lot of things to work through themselves, with a lot of pain. Oftentimes they've lost a best friend, but they believe they can't share their feelings with other family members because they want to protect the others from additional pain.

Sibling grief runs deep. Very deep.

A teenager or young woman might be thinking about how her sister will never be her maid of honor. "Do I even want to have a big wedding now or just have a few family and friends around me who would understand why it would be such a bittersweet day for me?" A brother might have lost his biggest supporter, his most worthy athletic partner, and his greatest confidant, and may want to drop out of a sport that is too painful to continue doing without his sibling.

They watch their parents be unable to function for weeks, months and often years, and can feel responsible to help them. I talked to one woman who said when she lost her brother, subconsciously she took on the responsibility of making up the loss to her mom by doing things like giving her two gifts for Mother's Day.

I can also tell you from my own experience, and from many other bereaved parents, that my other children are what helped me want to live again. But it is not easy, and it can take a long time.

Reflection: Stop and ask yourself some questions. Do I make sure my children know I love them deeply, every bit as much as their brother or sister who died? Do I keep a "shrine" in my house that makes them feel like their life does not matter much anymore? Do I often shut myself away from them in my place of deep grief, or do I include them in missing their sibling so we can share our loss together once in a while?

Ask God to give you a heart to want to see what is really happening, and then the desire and strength to make any changes that might be needed, so that you are not giving your children an extra burden in their own grief.

Love empowers us to fulfill the law of the
Anointed One as we carry each other's troubles.
Galatians 6:2 (TPT)

*Optional Reflection (for those who have lost an only child, or all of your children and do not deal with the sibling issue)

Through this world of pareavors, I now have a dear friend, Sara, who lost her daughter and only child. I know there are struggles, but it constantly amazes me how she has not allowed herself to become a bitter person about not having any children. The grace she has for those of us who have lost a child and still have other children to talk about and live life with, is a work that she has allowed God to do in her.

How about you? Are you struggling with jealousy and anger in that area? I know I would be. I am sure you have let God know how furious you are and how unfair it is. Maybe right now, instead of "letting God have it," you can sit in His presence with all that pain and let Him comfort you.

Cry in His arms. Rest in the fact that He is crying with you. Let go of the "Whys?" for a few minutes, stop demanding answers, and like a child who does not understand what is behind a parent's decision, trust that some glorious day you will see it all through His eyes and understand. But until that day, lean into Him, not away from Him, as He is the One who can bring hope, light, meaning and purpose back into your life again, even if you think you don't want those things right now.

The Lord is close to all whose hearts are crushed by pain...
Psalm 34:18 (TPT)

November 26

Lack of Others Understanding

Unfortunately, there may be people around you who are either ignorant or insensitive, and continually pick at your open wound of grief, who will have to be shut out of your life.

November

Almost every bereaved parent I have met has said their circle of friends made a shift because of the lack of understanding and support when it was needed the most. That is not always an option though, especially when it is someone in our family.

I want to share with you a few things you can do to take care of yourself, to help you deal better with those in your life who think grief is a short event in time, instead of the life-long process that it is.

- Spend time in nature. God's created beauty is a gift from Him that has a way of soothing our soul and feeding our spirits.
- Journaling and/or coloring is highly recommended by grief counselors, and many parents find this to be a big help. (If you have never journaled, and don't know where to start, consider getting *My Grief Journey: A Coloring Book and Journal for Grieving Parents* which can be found in the gpshope.org store or ordered from your favorite book supplier.)
- Spending time closed in with God is one that helped me the most, personally. I know many struggle with this one because of how angry they are with God. But He is the source of peace. Until we are able to turn *to* Him instead of away from Him, even in our anger, the peace we long for is going to elude us. (If it helps any, peace does not always mean the absence of pain. I have learned that peace and pain can live inside of me together because peace is in our spirit while the pain is in our soul.)

The people around you are not going to understand the depth of your loss. I sure did not know this depth of suffocating darkness even existed until Becca died. I hope those around us never have to find out for themselves.

Reflection: There is a way to rise above the conflicts that others create for us about our grief. That does not mean it is easy, and it seems like we are going through enough without having to be the ones to do the work. However, it can be done.

Start by asking yourself what are some of the things that bring you peace? If you are so fresh in your grief that nothing seems to help, what are a couple of things you used to do that would relax you? A candlelight bubble bath? A walk in the woods? Building a puzzle? Knitting? Think of a couple of ways that will help you rise above the painful conflicts, to a place of rest and peace, and write them down somewhere to remind yourself when needed.

> *Let all that I am wait quietly before God, for my hope is in him.*
> *Psalm 62:5 (NLT)*

November 27

He Did Not Change, But I Sure Did

One thing I can say through this whole journey is that His grace has been constant. It is always offered to us. Whether or not we want to accept it and apply it is up to us, but it is *always* there.

A precious friend, Lynn, who lost her five-year-old son from cancer over thirty years ago shared this with me once. Let me say before you continue, that there are some deep truths here that might be hard to accept at the beginning of your grief journey.

> *James 1:17 says "Every good and perfect gift comes from above." It is possible for my faith not to waver just because my circumstances did, because God didn't change. That's the truth. I changed. I'm profoundly different than I was before, but God didn't change. He didn't waver. What was changed, is how much of Him I carry with me now. I carry so much more, because I need Him so much more.*
>
> *I lost my sweet little Joel, but I got so much more of God in the midst of all of that. Not in spite of him and his short life, but because of him. I know that I lost a lot. And losing a child is the most profound thing that any of us could ever experience. I think it's every parent's greatest nightmare.*

But God is good in all of that. And I think that's a powerful thing for us to hang onto. And it is more real when you've walked a mile in the trenches. That's what is hard. I am different today than I was thirty years ago.

But I've learned how to be thankful for the things that I have. And I think that when you're a parent that's lost a child, you see things a little more precious than you did before. When you haven't faced a loss in a profound way, you take things a little more for granted. When you have, you learn to say thank you a little more often for the things you do have, and you don't take those things for granted. And I'm grateful for that. That gratitude that I hang on to is different than it would have been without the loss of Joel.

I couldn't have said it any better myself.

The last sentence, "That gratitude that I hang on to is different than it would have been without the loss of Joel," may make you uncomfortable. You may not have gotten to the place where you feel like there is *anything* to be thankful for, so this makes no sense to you. But if Lynn and I and countless others have gotten there, then please have hope that you can, too.

Reflection: *God didn't change. He didn't waver. What was changed, is how much of Him I carry with me now. I carry so much more, because I need Him so much more.* Wow! What a statement.

And that is what I want you to spend some time thinking about. What do you need to do to allow your heart to carry Him more than you ever have before? Maybe it is to start pulling down some walls you have put up between you and God. Maybe it's letting go of the pride that makes you feel like you are better than God and know more than He does. (If *I* were God...) Maybe it is to stop stiff-arming Him, keeping Him away from your wounded heart, wrongly blaming Him for what happened.

Figure out what that is, so that you can carry as much of Him as you need at all times, especially whenever you are struggling to get through the next minute, or even the next breath.

> *For Jesus doesn't change—yesterday, today, tomorrow, he's always totally himself. Don't be lured away from him by the latest speculations about him. The grace of Christ is the only good ground for life.*
> Hebrews 13:8,9 (MSG)

November 28

The Struggle is Real

Reading the book of Psalms in the Bible can be extremely helpful. Over and over the writer cries out for help from a very dark place of despair. So often he asks God things like, "How long" will this dark and horrible thing be going on in my life? "How long" until You pay attention to me, hear my crying and take this pain from me? "How long" until those who have done wrong to me are judged for their evil?

There are plenty of times when there is no answer from God within that Psalm. It is left hanging, just like we feel like we are left hanging by the One who was supposed to protect our child and who is supposed to never leave us or forsake us.

And yet, there are also many Psalms where David realizes that God is a rock, a refuge, a protective tower to run to and be safe, helping in times of need. He talks about rejoicing in God's faithfulness and everlasting love and mercy.

I spend a lot of time in the book of Psalms when I "relapse" and find myself struggling with the pain and reality that Becca is gone from this earth and I won't see her again until I join her in heaven.

Reflection: With so many relevant Psalms to choose from, it took a while to decide which one to have you read and meditate on today. I believe God led me to Psalm 42 (TLB).

> *As the deer pants for water, so I long for you, O God. I thirst for God, the living God. Where can I find him to come and stand*

November

before him? Day and night I weep for his help, and all the while my enemies taunt me. "Where is this God of yours?" they scoff.

Take courage, my soul! Do you remember those times (but how could you ever forget them!) when you led a great procession to the Temple on festival days, singing with joy, praising the Lord? Why then be downcast? Why be discouraged and sad? Hope in God! I shall yet praise him again. Yes, I shall again praise him for his help.

Yet I am standing here depressed and gloomy, but I will meditate upon your kindness to this lovely land where the Jordan River flows and where Mount Hermon and Mount Mizar stand. All your waves and billows have gone over me, and floods of sorrow pour upon me like a thundering cataract.

Yet day by day the Lord also pours out his steadfast love upon me, and through the night I sing his songs and pray to God who gives me life.

"O God my Rock," I cry, "why have you forsaken me? Why must I suffer these attacks from my enemies?" Their taunts pierce me like a fatal wound; again and again they scoff, "Where is that God of yours?" But, O my soul, don't be discouraged. Don't be upset. <u>Expect God to act! For I know that I shall again have plenty of reason to praise him for all that he will do. He is my help! He is my God!</u>

I love those last four sentences and underlined them. Let's read them out loud together.

> *So I say to my soul, "Don't be discouraged. Don't be disturbed. For I know my God will break through for me." Then I'll have plenty of reasons to praise him all over again. Yes, living before his face is my saving grace!*
> *Psalm 42:11 (TPT)*

November 29

He is the God of Hope

Advent is a time of waiting; waiting for the coming or arrival of something. This is the season when advent is waiting for the arrival of Christmas. For most, it is a time of joyful anticipation, mixed with frazzled busyness.

But for many of us who have faced the death of our child, it is a time of waiting for the season to just... be...over. There are so many painful reminders of who we are missing, and painful reminders of what will never be.

We are also waiting to be reunited with our child, and that cannot seem to come soon enough. I believe God knew from the very beginning of time that we would struggle with feeling so hopeless in our grief, and He did something about it.

1 Peter 1:3-5 tells us that we have an inheritance reserved in heaven; a living hope through the resurrection of Christ from the dead.

Even though the Christmas season is all about Jesus entering the world of the humans He created and becoming one of us, one purpose of His birth was to die, so that we could have life. Not just life after we leave this world, but abundant life here on this earth (John 10:10). And believe it or not, He still wants to make good on that gift, that promise, in your life, after the death of your child.

God tells us that He is near to the broken hearted (Psalm 34:18). I don't think there is anyone more brokenhearted than those of us who have lost a child. But do you know what? No matter how broken you are today, tomorrow always promises new hope.

Reflection: Romans 15:13 has become one of my absolute favorite verses since Becca died. Please see this as a special gift during this advent season for yourself. "Now may the God of hope fill you with all joy and peace in believing, that you may abound in hope by the power of the Holy Spirit" (NKJV).

Right now, let's speak God's hope into our hopelessness together, allowing God to plant His seed of hope right in the middle of your pain. Pause and ask God to give you a glimmer of hope, so that you can open your heart for Him be able to give you the gifts of joy and peace as we enter into the end-of-the-year holidays that can feel so brutal.

> *I pray that God, the source of hope, will fill you completely with joy and peace because you trust in him. Then you will overflow with confident hope through the power of the Holy Spirit.*
> *Romans 15:13 (NLT)*

November 30

Treat Yourself!

Yes, treat yourself. I do not mean to an extra cookie or a glass of eggnog. I mean something that makes you feel pampered and relaxed, like going out for a massage or a pedicure, or going to a professional Christmas concert like The Nutcracker.

Taking some time to treat ourselves triggers a message in our brains that we are valuable and allows us to enjoy ourselves, even if just for an hour or two. This self-care can go a long way in helping us through some of the darker moments of the season.

Tip: If you don't have the finances to treat yourself in this way, when someone asks what you want for Christmas, let them know how much you want an early gift of a massage or a pedicure to help you make it through to December.

One thing that is easy to do and does not cost any money is to take a warm bath. Let me rephrase that: Soak in a hot bath with Epsom salts, burning aromatherapy candles and playing soft music. Much better!

You may tell yourself that you just don't have time to do something like that, or that it isn't worth the time and energy to go to all that trouble. I know, because I have talked myself out of it way too many times. But this is truly something that can be pushed from the luxury column to the necessity column in your life. It affects so many areas when we are over-maxed and over-stressed. And what a way to end your day! Just thinking about it makes me feel more relaxed.

Reflection: This time of year can be wonderful and magical, but for many, it is dreaded and draining, especially those who are in deep grief, like a parent who has lost a child. We just want to sleep through it all and wake up in January.

Start planning for that night of pampering yourself in the tub right now. Look at your calendar and write it in as something you *are* doing. If you don't have a bathtub for this, find someone who will let you use theirs. Do not be horrified by that thought! Think of all the people who said, "Let me know if you need anything," and ask one who really meant it. Let your family know. The anticipation will make it all the more wonderful when you climb in.

Then Jesus said, "Let's go off by
ourselves to a quiet place and rest awhile."
Mark 6:31 (NLT)

December

December 1

We Have Not Lost the Reason

If you are anything like me, Christmas used to be one of my favorite times of year because of the enjoyable time we had together as a family, and how much I liked to make it fun for the children in my life.

That all changed when Becca died.

I have learned to remind myself that while we may all lose our *desire* to celebrate, we never lose the *reason*, which is to **acknowledge the day Jesus came into this world to make a way for us to be together with our children again forever.**

The main reason for Christmas is not to celebrate our children, but to celebrate the One who gave our children life, entrusted us with them for their short time on earth, and then made a way for us to be together for all eternity.

And even though the light of our soul may have gone out, the light of His spirit inside us will never go out. Jesus came for that very reason; so that the same Spirit who lived inside of Him, guiding and comforting Him while on earth, could also live inside us, to guide and comfort us for our time here. Not from some "out there somewhere" place, but directly inside us. He is not just Emmanuel, God with us, He is God *in* us! That boggles my mind when I take time to really think about it.

Reflection: His light and His strength *are* inside you. We each need to draw on these to get us through the darkness and back to a place of hope and light in our lives once again, especially during this holiday season.

Close your eyes and ask God to release His strength inside you in a way that you can feel it. Ask Him to bring light and hope into your darkness and heaviness. And then wait. If you feel something... awesome! If you don't, then do not give up! I believe the work was done so deeply inside that it just hasn't surfaced yet. It will. Maybe not right away, but it will.

I've come into the world as light, so that everyone who

believes in me won't need to stay in the dark.
John 12:46 (NTE)

December 2

I Need to Talk About My Child

As bereaved parents, we have a need to keep our child's memory alive, and one of the ways we do that is to talk about our child.

Eventually, other people don't talk about them, and we don't hear their names come up in conversations anymore. And if the child was young, not very many people had a chance to know our child, so the conversations about them are even fewer. Often, the lack of hearing people acknowledging our child's life intensifies our need to talk about them, which people around us often do not understand.

Following the loss of a child, it is very normal and necessary for a parent to retell the story of the loss of their child. Not all parents will do this, but many want to tell what happened and quite often they are shut off by others who don't want to listen. They change the subject abruptly, or simply say, "You're living too much in the past."

There are also those who are concerned that wanting to talk about our child who has died is a sign that we are not moving on and getting past the grief. The need to talk about our child does not mean we are not moving on...in fact, I would say for most of us it does the opposite. Talking about our child is healing. It helps us to process and reprocess the awful dark truth that we need to learn how to live with the permanent earthly loss of our child.

Child loss is a trauma -- a heartbreaking trauma -- and parents need to be able to talk freely about their child. This is why connecting to other pareavors is so important.

Reflections of Hope

Reflection: This time of year, people are so busy that we can feel almost invisible, which can hurt even more on top of the pain of missing our child so very deeply. If you cannot find a group of parents who meet in your area, make connections on-line. There are many organizations who meet online this time of year for this very reason, including GPS Hope. Ask God to direct you to the one(s) He knows will help you the most right now.

By the way, did you know that each year, on the second Sunday of December, is a Worldwide Candle Lighting Service for those who have lost a child, grandchild, or sibling? Just look online for a group meeting near you or find one online you can join.

> *...the kind things they do will never be forgotten.*
> *Psalm 112:6 (CEV)*

December 3

What Other Pareavors Have Learned from Hindsight

We learn a lot from hindsight, don't we? Looking back to that first year or two, here are some things that I and others have learned that might help you.

1. Try not to stay at home by yourself the entire day when you know there is a difficult date coming up. Plan something that will help you remember some of the good things instead of wallowing in the hard and hurtful things. If you are able to force yourself to focus on and be thankful (even if it is just in your mind and it doesn't quite reach your heart) it lifts some of the heaviness. If you continually focus on what you have lost, it will keep you spiraling downward.

2. Make yourself smile. Smiling releases chemicals in the brain to make you feel better. Even putting a pencil between your lips for

December

a while to make those muscles think you are smiling, can release those needed chemicals to lift some of the heaviness.

3. Realize that it's okay to want your child back and to cry about it. But also force yourself to spend some time with an outward focus, doing a kind deed for someone else who has a need, especially someone who is lonely or struggling with something difficult. You can choose to stay in the darkness of your pit or choose to climb upwards toward the light and help yourself by helping someone else.

4. I know I say this a lot, but join a support group as soon as you can. There are those who *want* to help you and walk with you, who are making themselves available just for this purpose! The enemy wants us to stay isolated so that he can continue to keep us in a place of not being able to function, much less live a life of meaning and purpose again. Community is important. In fact, it is crucial for your well-being to be with others who can help you find your way out.

Reflection: Surviving holidays and special dates after the death of your child may seem impossible. There are *so* many of us who felt the same way those first few years. Some of us want to offer help to those who find themselves in the same place we were in, so the climb isn't quite as steep for you as it was for us, or maybe it will be the encouragement you need to start taking steps out sooner than we did.

If nothing else, let us infuse hope into you that it can be done. Take a look at the four suggestions above and pick one that you will do this week. Then pick which one you will do next and give yourself a deadline. (And if you are really wanting to help yourself, keep going with which one you will do third and fourth, giving yourself deadlines as well. Write them down or put them in your calendar so you don't forget.)

Christ is the one who gives me the strength
I need to do whatever I must do.
Philippians 4:13 (ERV)

December 4

Feeling Lost

When we are going on a trip, sometimes we make plans, knowing exactly where we are going, and get there without any problems. Sometimes we know where we want to go but need a map or GPS to guide us to the right place. And sometimes the road changes and even the GPS has no idea where we are!

That is how we feel after the death of our child. We feel lost and helpless, not knowing where we are going, much less how to get there.

Jesus was born into a world of darkness, unbelief and confusion. He was born as the Light of the World. Even death could not put out that light, because not only was He born to die, but also to be resurrected. He came to bring light into the deepest darkness. He came to bring resurrection life from death.

Not just death that causes our bodies to quit and our spirits to leave them, but the death that happens in our souls after the death of our child.

That is where "Emmanuel, God with us" comes in. He becomes our guide in the darkness. He knows where the path is and will help us navigate to each road we need to be on while traveling this grief journey.

Reflection: Have you ever been lost at night? Everything looks so different when it is dark. But somehow, you were able to find your way out.

After the death of our child, we feel lost. It's so very dark, and everything looks different. But God can see right where we are and can see our path when we cannot. Keep trusting Him to help you find your way out. Right now, picture God's hand being held out to you. Reach out and grab ahold of it. Squeeze tight, just like a frightened child who is needing comforting guidance. Allow His peace to flood through your soul and let yourself feel safe with your hand in His.

> *Hang on tight to God. He will navigate you*
> *through the darkness and back into the light.*
> Matthew 4:16 (TPT)

December 5

Have Yourself ~~a Merry Little Christmas~~

There are some pretty sad Christmas songs out there. I never noticed how many until I was in such a dark place. If you're like me, you could tell me a couple of them right off the top of your head. The worst part is when I am shopping, and one of those painful songs starts playing, such as "I'll Be Home for Christmas", that can quickly reduce me into a puddle of tears.

Even the ones that are supposed to bring cheer usually remind us of our deep loss, keeping us in a place of sadness and darkness. But... I have also noticed those are often songs from the worldly view of Christmas.

The songs about Jesus coming into our world as both God and man are full of hope and reminders that Jesus is the Prince of Peace; that He is Emmanuel, God with us; that He came into the darkness to be the Light of the World. The birth of Jesus really was *good* news to *all* men (and women and children).

God created music to be a pathway to our souls, and at least when I am in my own home, I get to choose if I am letting in reminders that take me to a dark place, or reminders that take me to the promises of why Jesus came as a baby to this earth. Even if they do not make me "feel" happy, they are feeding my weary soul the nourishment it needs. The Christmas songs about Jesus give me strength to keep going, knowing that this is not the end, and I will see my child again, and be able to thank Jesus face-to-face for making that possible.

I have found if my thoughts about Christmas are the decorations, the presents, the baking, the family gatherings and such, I can get into a slump, feeling the pain of Becca not being here and go right on into a depression.

If my thoughts about Christmas are Jesus coming for the purpose of dying to bring peace into my despair, light into my darkness, hope into my hopelessness and eternal restoration to those who are separated from me through an earthly death, then even within my pain, I know I can make it through.

Reflection: Do you have a favorite Christmas song that lifts your soul? Play it right now, as you thank Him for coming to make it possible to have our sins taken from us and be able to spend eternity with Him and our children and other loved ones.

If you haven't found a song that lifts your heaviness a bit, ask God to bring one your way. He knows the right one that will speak directly to your heart, giving you the boost that you need.

> *Then all at once in the night sky, a vast number of glorious angels appeared, the very armies of heaven! And they all praised God, singing: "Glory to God in the highest realms of heaven! For there is peace and a good hope given to the sons of men."*
> Luke 2:13-14 (TPT)

December 6

"How Are You Doing?"

Do you cringe when someone simply asks, "How you are doing?"

Here are three observations I have made about this.

1. In the realness behind the mask, we usually admit the answer given to this question is only a surface answer of the depth we truly feel, which is pointless to try and put words to.

2. Sometimes we can answer with bitterness and sarcasm, not really caring how we come across to the person asking.

3. It is all based on our perspective. Some of us have the view of "how can you even bother asking? You don't really care. And if you did care, you would know and wouldn't have to ask," while others of us have the view of, "Even though I may not be able to give you a full, truthful answer, I appreciate you asking, because it shows me at least you care."

I want to take a minute and look at those last two lines you just read.

Maybe, just maybe some people ask because they really *do* care. Even if they don't want the full-blown truthful answer (and can we really blame them?) at least they are trying to acknowledge the fact that they think you might still be struggling and want to know if that is the case.

So instead of mumbling "fine" and getting away from them as fast as you can, maybe you can thank them for asking, and give an answer they *can* handle like, "It's still a big struggle. I'm just taking it one day at a time."

After all, isn't it better to have someone ask, than to have them painfully ignore and avoid us? Telling someone a simple, "Thank you for asking" helps make them aware that it matters that they at least care enough not to avoid us and have made an attempt at reaching out to us.

Reflection: How about if we work on our answer. If someone you know is asking how you're doing and you can tell they don't really want to know, you can still "educate" them and make them more aware by saying something like, "Since my son/daughter died I have really been struggling. Most days I feel like I am barely holding on. Thank you for asking." By ending with the thank you, it can remove the awkward silence because they can reply with a "You're welcome..."

And if it is someone who genuinely wants to know, after you tell them, you just might want to add, "Thanks for asking," and give them a hug, to show them your appreciation for and caring enough to ask and not just avoiding you.

Do not be angry and frustrated. Do not fret. That only leads to trouble.
Psalm 37:8 (NET)

December 7

So Many Tears

We cry. We can cry hard, and we can cry often. There are so many tears. And when we think there are no tears left, or we think we are finally past all of the crying, something unexpectedly triggers another round of leaking from our eyes. I figure if God keeps my tears in a bottle (Psalm 56:8), I must have one of the biggest bottles in heaven!

The first year of special dates is always difficult for anyone who has lost a loved one, but for a parent who has a child missing it can be almost unbearable. For me personally, Thanksgiving came first and brought with it the memory of how the year before, Becca had insisted on hosting the family, even though she was wheelchair bound. Then came Christmas, Becca's favorite holiday, and then the pain of the first time she was not there to celebrate her birthday, and so on. Eventually it came around to the one-year anniversary of her death.

When this book comes out, it will be my 12th holiday season without Becca. Every year seems to be a roller coaster... I just never know if I will get through it okay, or if I will struggle and have lots of tears.

Jesus knew that when His dear friend Lazarus died, it was only temporary. And yet we know Jesus wept. If you want to cry, go ahead and cry as hard as you need to. Take some time alone and have a good cry, several times if you need to do so. Let your tears be the gift God gave them to be, allowing them to wash away some of the pain.

It will happen for the rest of our lives – the liquid love for our children, spilling from our souls.

Reflection: It has taken me an entire lifetime to learn that tears are a gift from God. Yes, I know some people can't seem to cry, but that is not the case for me. Tears have flowed freely and easily for me all my life. I learned that if I don't allow myself to cry, it means I have allowed my heart to get hard. I did that once and will never do it again, no matter how embarrassing my tears may be.

How about you? What do tears mean to you? Do you see them as a gift or a curse? Take some time and talk to God about your tears and let Him speak to your heart about how *He* sees them. After all, what others think about them really doesn't matter.

> *You have seen me tossing and turning through the night. You have collected all my tears and preserved them in your bottle! You have recorded every one in your book.*
> *Psalm 56:8 (TLB)*

December 8
Because He Lives, My Child Lives

As you are very much aware, this time of year is when we take time to remember the birth of Jesus. But the whole reason He came to earth as a baby was to die, and that made a way for us to be with Him and our loved ones forever. So even though this is the Christmas season, I want to share a thought and verse that is most often heard at Easter.

Luke 24:5-6 gives us a reminder of the truth we so desperately need at times. "Don't seek Him here among the dead, He has risen."

Yes, I know it is something we can't put words to, wanting to be near our son's or daughter's body, even when we know our child isn't really there. We know it is just the part of them that housed their soul and spirit, but it is the part of them that we saw, we heard, and we touched.

But just like the angel told the disciples, I don't need to seek Becca among the dead, because she is ALIVE! In fact, she is more alive, and full of life, than I am. And your child is, too!

So, smack dab in the middle of the pain of this Christmas season, let's remember that even though our children's bodies, that we were so familiar with, are no longer functioning, our children are still very much alive.

Reflection: We know our child is not in their body anymore, but that is hard to comprehend or accept. I remember for months feeling horrible that my daughter was underground. Others are adjusting to their child's body being reduced to ashes in a beautiful urn.

Do not seek your child among the dead. He or she is risen. Jesus told the repentant thief on the cross "Today you will be with me in paradise" (Luke 23:43). Let's take a few minutes to let that sink in, allowing our minds to try and grab ahold of the truth. Ask the Holy Spirit to help you with this.

I speak to you an eternal truth: if you embrace my message and believe in the One who sent me, you will never face condemnation. In me, you have already passed from the realm of death into eternal life! I speak to you an eternal truth: Soon the dead will hear the voice of the Son of God, and those who listen will arise with life! For as the Father is the source of life, so he has given the Son the power to impart life.
John 5:24-26 (TPT)

December 9
The Chain Reaction of Our Thoughts

Some of us are told in this life, "It's not about you." But the truth is, sometimes it is. As a bereaved parent, quite often it *is* about you and what you need, as you live through the painful earthly loss of your child.

Another thing we hear from people around us (who have never lost a child) is that time heals. As a bereaved parent who has been on this journey for over ten years, I do not believe that. And those I have talked to who are much further down the road in child loss than I am, don't believe it either.

December

I believe it is a chain reaction of where we allow and train our thoughts to go, which affects the choices we make, which affects what we *do* with our time, which brings a *measure* of needed healing.

Don't expect people who have never faced a holiday season with the death of their child to understand that it is okay not to be okay for a *long* time. If you are just in survival mode right now, *that's okay.* Do what you need to do to get through it! (Note: If you are thinking of harming yourself, seek help immediately!)

Those of us who are bereaved parents ahead of you on the path know that *it's okay not to be okay*, because we are still not okay without our child.

Reflection: Take apart the statement from above about moving toward a measure of healing and think on each section:

- It is a chain reaction of where we allow and train our thoughts to go
- which affects the choices we make
- which affects what we do with our time
- which brings a measure of needed healing.

It all starts with what we choose to spend time thinking about. We can't stop a thought that pops into our heads, but we *can* control whether or not we dismiss the thought or dwell on it. It is helpful to have a couple of things that you know you can think about when the negative thoughts start coming.

As bereaved parents, we won't say that pain ends, but it can eventually ease, if you continue to do the work of grief. It will take a lot longer than you want it to, or even think it should, but it can and will happen.

> *Finally, believers, whatever is true, whatever is honorable and worthy of respect, whatever is right and confirmed by God's word, whatever is pure and wholesome, whatever is lovely and brings peace, whatever is admirable and of good repute; if there is any excellence, if there is anything worthy of praise, think continually on these things [center your mind on them, and implant them in your heart].*
> *Philippians 4:8 (AMP)*

December 10

A Joyful Heart

How can we possibly smile, or ever be happy again after our child dies? Just the thought of it can make us feel guilty. Not only can we smile and be happy again, but it is exactly what we *need* to do. We need to reintroduce fun and laughter into our lives, because laughter is medicine to the soul.

The goal is not to eliminate the grief. That will never happen. I have friends whose children have been gone for thirty or forty years. (My mind cannot grasp that.) They still get hit with waves of grief at certain times, including unexpected times that take them by surprise.

The goal is to allow God to work in our lives to bring a measure of healing which will allow us to function and live in a way that honors the life of our son or daughter; to have a life that is fulfilling and joyful while we are still here on this earth.

A few months after Becca died, I found myself standing in line at the same funeral home to give a hug to a distant friend whose son died. When this mom and I hugged and I told her how very sorry I was, she began to cry, knowing someone was holding her who could understand the depth of her loss. (It was hard enough just being there, and I will admit, I did not have it in me to stay for the funeral.)

Obviously, that was not a joyful event, but it helped unlock the door to a measure of joy, even though I did not realize it at the time. God began putting other moms in my life who had recently lost a child. I discovered that every time I could strengthen, offer hope, or help someone else in some way, it opened the door wider for more joy to be released. It is God's law of sowing and reaping. Giving is a spiritual act that bears spiritual fruit.

Joy came into the world the night Jesus was born. We cannot deny that.

When there is a joyful event, there is often dancing. As parents who are in deep grief from the earthly loss of our child, I know we don't feel like dancing, nor do we have the energy, even if we felt a twinge of hope in that direction. At least not on the outside.

December

But we can dance on the inside. Why would we want to? Because chances are pretty good that is what our child is doing right now, before the throne in heaven! And anything I can do that makes me feel closer to my child, I want to do.

Reflection: I want you to write your child's name vertically. Then next to each letter, write a word or phrase that starts with that letter as a reason to have joy. What is it about your child that brought joy into your life?

I made myself do it with Becca's name. Here is what I came up with.

Belly laugh

Energy & **E**ntertaining (loved to host and decorate and go all out)

Calling and anointing on her life as a worshipper

Compassion and care for others

Adored her family

God says our grief can turn to joy. "You will be sorrowful, but your sorrow will be turned into joy," (John 16:20 - NIV) is just one of many scriptures with a promise of mourning and sorrow being turned into joy in our lives. I choose to believe His Word, no matter what my feelings tell me at the moment. I choose to plant a seed of hope and watch it grow, being watered by His promises, and become the fruit of joy manifested in my life, however long it takes.

> *Yes, you will be deeply distressed, but your pain will turn into joy. Now you are going through pain, but I shall see you again and your hearts will thrill with joy—the joy that no one can take away from you—and on that day you will not ask me any questions.*
> *John 16:20, 22-23 (PHILLIPS)*

December 11
Christmas Traditions

There are so many memories attached to the holidays, especially based around our own personal and family traditions. These can be triggers over and over again as in-our-face reminders that our child is no longer here on earth and will never again be part of these traditions. Our memories with that child are now all we have, and there will never be another opportunity to create new holiday memories with that child, which is so very wrong, and so very painful.

Things like Christmas shopping can be almost impossible, as we are constantly bombarded with gift ideas that make us think of our child for whom we will never be able to buy another gift.

Some family gatherings will probably be unattended, as it is impossible to watch the other children (young children, teens or adult children) and not to be immersed in the painful emptiness of our child who is missing and who will never again be joining in the laughter, festivities and seeing the growth and changes from year-to-year like everyone else is with their children.

But we are not just thinking of ourselves. We would rather stay home and allow our loved ones to celebrate without the presence of our grief dampening the joyous time for everyone else, as we have learned it is our job to make everyone around us comfortable with our grief (which can be very draining).

Reflection: Since memories are all we have now, anything that helps us remember and honor that memory and life are very precious to us.

Go to the November 6th reading and look at that list. If you haven't picked something from it yet, go ahead and do it now. If you already picked something from it, have you moved toward making it happen? Would you like to pick more than one thing? Go ahead! Do what you need to do to make this Christmas one that helps people remember your child with you in a way that brings you peace and a little bit of joy.

And if family and friends seem to think you are going overboard, tell them that those who have lost a child don't think so. (And maybe consider buying them a book for Christmas that will help them understand, such as *Come Grieve Through Our Eyes*.)

> *The Eternal frees those who are imprisoned*
> *Psalm 146:7 (VOICE)*

December 12

The Gift of Peace

This time of year, especially, we are reminded that Jesus is called the Prince of Peace. Isaiah 9:6 seems to be everywhere, including a main theme for Christmas cards. "For to us a child is born... And he will be called ...Prince of Peace," (NKJV).

Often, especially in Biblical times, a prince was known to lead the battles of a war. He was proving his leadership ability to eventually take over the throne and earning the trust and loyalty of the people of his future kingdom.

In this context, the title, Prince of Peace, means that He is leading the battle for our peace. Every war has many battles. Jesus is the only King who wins every battle He enters, which means He also wins the war. Part of His victory happens by helping us defeat the enemy in our personal battles.

Romans 16:20 promises that the God of peace will crush Satan under our feet. His peace in our lives is part of the battle plan. It is a valuable weapon we need to win the battle of darkness that we have found ourselves thrown into.

Jesus Himself made sure we had access to this powerful weapon of peace, by purchasing it for us at a very high price; the Prince of Peace sacrificed His own life for it.

What an incredible, amazing thought; Jesus left the glory of heaven to come to earth as a baby for the purpose of dying, so that we could have peace in our suffocating darkness! It doesn't make sense, does it? But Jesus made what seems impossible become possible.

Reflection: You may be thinking, "That sounds great, and it works for you, but I don't have that peace. How can I get it?"

You receive it as the gift that it is, just like salvation. We start by laying down the things that cause the darkness in our lives, so we have empty hands to receive. It is an exchange. You might have to let go of anger, guilt or blame. Let it go as best as you can, so you can offer the Prince of Peace room in your heart for the peace He is waiting to give you. And let me acknowledge, it may be simple, but not always easy.

Let's pray this simple prayer together. *Holy Spirit, help me to let go of the things I need to let go of, to be able to receive Your gift of peace. Father God, may the price you paid, the death of Your Son, not be in vain. Prince of Peace, I accept the weapon You battled for me to have, a peace that goes beyond understanding. Amen.*

> *And God, our source of peace, will soon crush Satan under your feet. The grace of our Lord Jesus be with you.*
> *Romans 16:20 (GNT)*

December 13

The Comforter

I do not know of many moms who had the blessing of having a child (whether by birth or adoption), and then losing that child at some point through death, who does not keep a picture of that child in her wallet. My picture of Becca is front and center, so that every time I snap it open, I see her smiling at me. Friends and family might think it would be a painful thing, and it can be, but it is also a comfort in feeling like my child is always with me, will always be a part of me, and will never be forgotten.

Many of us, especially mothers, also have an extra something we wear (which includes getting a tattoo). Oftentimes no one else even knows about it. We don't advertise it; we do not call attention to it. It is just always there with us. Me? I have a pinky ring. My daughter's name, Becca, is engraved on it. On the left side of her name is engraved a little heart, and on the right side of her name is engraved a small butterfly.

Why is something like that so important to us? I don't really know. It just is. Somehow, it keeps them close to us, even though they are now so very far away. It is something tangible we can see and touch that makes us feel like we are still connected to them.

And we are. We are connected to God, His Spirit to our spirit. Our children are connected to God. His Spirit to their spirits. That means we are still connected through Him.

Reflection: Comfort is so important to us, isn't it? I looked up the definition of the word and found "the easing or alleviation of a person's feelings of grief or distress." Having those special mementos of our children do that for us, because it reminds us that they are still with us, in our hearts.

Jesus told us that when He left this earth, the Comforter would come and dwell in us. And I believe the Comforter gives us each our own individual and unique things that make us feel close to our children until we see them again. It is more than just a comfort to our soul; it is spirit to spirit.

Right now, touch that thing that is on you, and allow the Holy Spirit to be your Comforter, as He ministers you both in your soul, and in your spirit.

But I tell you the truth, it is to your advantage that I go away; for if I do not go away, the Helper (Comforter, Advocate, Intercessor—Counselor, Strengthener, Standby) will not come to you; but if I go, I will send Him (the Holy Spirit) to you [to be in close fellowship with you].
John 16:7 (AMP)

December 14

The Lost Link

Sometimes when we share how much we miss our child, people give us a strange look, as if we are weird. Then there are those who let us know they think it is time to move on and get past it. Three years after Becca died, as I was writing my first book, I was accused by someone of trying to drag up the past instead of going forward.

What is my response to people who think that? *It isn't bringing up or living in the past; it is learning how to live in the present and in the future without my daughter, which is the same thing as every other parent who has lost a child from this earth has to figure out how to do.*

Some parents become either withdrawn, or angry and bitter when they are given limits by people around them on missing their children. When others question our grief, at the very least, we have to struggle to keep it from adding to our heaviness. Add to that trying to get through the Christmas season when we have constant reminders of who isn't here with us...

Child loss is an empty ache that never goes away - ever. Child loss is in a category of pain and heartache that is different from any other loss.

As bereaved parents, we will never stop missing our child. It is impossible, because they are a part of our very being. Our children who have died are a lost link to our everyday lives, and to our future.

Reflection: How do you feel when someone indicates that something is wrong with you, because you are still grieving so deeply? Are you one of those who gets angry? Are you able to just let it go, knowing there is no way they can understand the depth of grief from the death of one's child?

The response I gave to someone seen above, is one of hope. We are on a journey to learn how to live both in the present and in the future with our child no longer here with us. In time, it is possible. You *can* do it just like the rest of us have.

And maybe we can all use the reminder that it is just our future here on earth that we will be without them. *Our children are still in our future.* Death did not make that separation permanent!

> *I'm not saying that I have this all together, that I have it made. But I am well on my way, reaching out for Christ, who has so wondrously reached out for me. Friends, don't get me wrong: By no means do I count myself an expert in all of this, but I've got my eye on the goal, where God is beckoning us onward —to Jesus. I'm off and running, and I'm not turning back.*
> *Philippians 3:14 (MSG)*

December 15

Jesus' Mother Did Not Have an Easy Life

In my podcast series of people in the Bible who have lost a child, I looked at Mary, Jesus' mother, who lost her son to capital punishment as a criminal being falsely accused. Since December 25th is the day we celebrate the birth of Jesus, it seems like a good time to visit some of the things I discovered about Mary that I had not realized or thought about, until I had a child who died.

Reflections of Hope

Mary did not have an easy life, and it was all *because* God gave her Jesus as her son! It started as soon as she conceived Jesus through the Holy Spirit.

- Mary found herself as a young pregnant woman with no husband, which left her at the mercy of being stoned to death.

- When she was "heavy with child" (fully pregnant), she was forced by law to travel from Nazareth to Bethlehem which was around an eighty-to-ninety-mile journey of hills. (And transportation at that time was not what it is today!)

- The city was so crowded, that there were not any hotel rooms available. Someone out of kindness offered his barn out back. This is where she gave birth to her very first child. I think I may have been close to being terrified if it were me. (Was Joseph able to find a midwife quick enough in a town he knew nothing about so at least one person knew what to do?)

- If Bethlehem is where Joseph had to go for the census, it means *all* of his family had to go there also. Where were they in all of this? Where did *they* stay? Why didn't his family make sure he and Mary were taken care of? Could it be that the young couple was ostracized because of her becoming pregnant out of wedlock, and instead of Joseph having her stoned, he married her anyway, to raise this illegitimate child as his own?

- It seems that the first visitors were smelly shepherds... not her mom, a sibling, or someone we think of as the normal first visitors, especially when it is our first child.

- Her husband, Joseph, apparently died at some point before Jesus's ministry as he is not included in any scriptures beyond when Jesus was twelve. (The next time we see Jesus with his family, it was only with his mother and siblings at a wedding.)

- Based on Matthew 13:55 and Mark 6:3, Jesus had at least six siblings. Imagine being a widow with seven children!

- Beyond that, John 7:3-5 tells us that His brothers were not believers in who He was. At one point they even went to go drag Jesus away from where He was because they thought He had literally lost His mind (Mark 3:20-21). That must have been **so** hard for Mary, because that means her *own children* didn't believe her story about the angel coming to her and being a virgin when Jesus was conceived in her by the Holy Spirit.

And now, after such a hard life *because* of her first-born son, she is standing at an execution stake, watching that son being torturously executed for a crime he didn't commit. (We need to remind ourselves here that she had no idea that Jesus was going to rise from the dead three days later. When He tried to tell his followers this, *no one* got it.)

Reflection: Have you had a hard life? Maybe, like Mary, much of it was *because* of your child who died. The thing that resonates with me is that God gave Jesus to Mary, *knowing* the heartache she would have, both with His life and with His death.

We each have an appointed time to die; our days on earth are numbered. God knew those days when he placed your child in your womb, but He chose *you* to nurture that child and be his or her parent for those number of days. He knew the sorrow and heartache your child would give you while he or she was alive. He also knew how much joy your child would give you and the deep love you would have for him or her.

Would you rather He chose someone else, and left you never knowing that precious son or daughter? I don't think Mary would have thought that, and I don't think you do either. Take a minute to thank God for giving you the gift of your child's life, even though it meant going through the pain you have had to endure.

> *Everything good comes from God. Every perfect gift is from him. These good gifts come down from the Father who made all the lights in the sky. But God never changes like the shadows from those lights. He is always the same.*
> *James 1:17 (ERV)*

Reflections of Hope

December 16

Memories

Twice in the Bible we are told that Mary pondered something in her heart about Jesus; she thought deeply about it, treasured it and wondered about it. The first (Luke 2:19) was when the shepherds came to worship her Son who had just been born in a smelly barn, was wrapped in strips of cloth and was using an animal feeding trough as His crib.

The second time (Luke 2:51) was when Jesus was twelve and was accidently left in Jerusalem and they did not realize it until they were already a day's journey toward home. That meant it took another day to get back to Jerusalem and it took them three days to find Him! I cannot imagine the sheer panic she must have felt, not knowing for five days where her son was! (Unfortunately, some of you reading this may be able to relate to this, but with a different outcome.)

There is something really important that happened between those two events that we need to look at. When Joseph and Mary went to the temple to have Jesus dedicated to the Lord (according to Jewish law with the first-born son), a prophet named Simeon told Mary that a sword would pierce her heart. It doesn't say Mary pondered that, but I am sure she must have.

It took over thirty years, but when her Son died, Mary felt the pain Simeon told her she would have - the piercing sword of grief that *we* all know too well.

Reflection: After His death, do you think Mary spent time pulling up those memories of Jesus? The ones we were told she pondered and treasured in her heart?

Some of us have very few memories, because our child died as an infant or toddler. We may not have some of the crazy memories that Mary did, but we have ones that are just as precious. At first, those memories can be so very painful! But I want to encourage you that it won't always be that way.

It takes a while, but at some point, those memories will warm your heart and make you smile. Thinking about your child won't be as painful as it is now. Ask God to help you see those memories as the treasure they truly are, allowing that to be a hope that rises in you.

Now then, stand here. I'm going to remind you of all the good things the LORD has done for you and your people. He is a witness.
1 Samuel 12:7 (NIRV)

December 17

Relating to Mary

Honestly, I did not think there would be very much to learn from Mary, the mother of Jesus. But as I started studying this out, I became more and more amazed at how much really is in the Word that we can learn from her, as pareavors.

One of the biggest things is that Mary completely surrendered to the Lord's plans for her life, not knowing what that meant and how painful her future would be. In Luke 1:38 (AMP) we find her telling the angel, Gabriel "Behold, I am the servant of the Lord; may it be done to me according to your word."

As we already noted, I am sure Mary had no idea that her son would die a very brutal death at the age of thirty-three, and she would be there to watch it.

I used to think, "At least Jesus rose from the dead and came back to life here on this earth. I don't have that with Becca!" But as I was studying this out, I realized Mary still lost him permanently from this earth, because He was only here for forty days after he came back from the grave, and then He went to heaven.

The permanent earthly loss of her son here on earth was confirmed at the foot of the cross when Jesus looked down and gave his mom to the apostle John to take care of (John 19:26-27). This is also confirmation

Reflections of Hope

that his brothers still did not believe who Jesus was because the next son in line should have been the one to take care of Jesus's mom.

We may not be able to relate to Mary's exact, unique grief, but she was a mom whose child died and left this earth for her remaining time here, which is something we *can* all relate to.

Reflection: Most of us have made that same declaration. "I am yours, Lord. Take my life and do what you want with it." We have sung and spoken over ourselves that "Jesus is Lord over my life!" Would we have said those things if we knew that making Jesus Lord of our lives trumps our own wants and desires, including our children having a long life and not dying before we do?

Take a minute to thank God that you were like Mary, having a willing heart at one time to say, "I am the Lord's servant and I give you permission to do what you want to do in my life," not knowing the high price you would pay. And if you are struggling, ask Him to help you get back to the place where you can surrender your life to Him again.

One last thing: Remember, our children are alive also! They may not have come back for a few days after they died and then risen up in the clouds in their bodies, but he or she is alive and with Jesus! Thank you, Father that part of Your will for our lives is to reunite us with our children, never to be separated again.

> *I'm desperate, Lord! I throw myself upon you, for you alone are my God! My life, my every moment, my destiny—it's all in your hands.*
> *Psalm 31:14-15 (TPT)*

December 18

Our Hope to See Them Again

Mary watched her son die. Nothing could prevent this mother from standing by her son to the very last, no matter how brutal it was. I can't help but think that some of you have had the same experience of being with your child until he or she took their last breath. You know what that is like to be with them.

I did not have that experience. Becca was in the hospital, with plans of being dismissed the next morning. The night of October 12, 2011, her heart was crashing, and she was fighting everyone, trying to get out of bed, yelling at them to leave her alone. Her husband told her to lie down and let them do what they needed to do and was kicked out of the hospital room so they could work on her. She died surrounded by a bunch of medical staff trying to save her.

I wish I had been with her, sort of... I think it has to be another one of those bittersweet things. Those of us who were not with our child don't have that as another image we have to get out of our heads. On the other hand, we have to fight the guilt that we weren't there with them, feeling like he or she died alone.

Did Mary have thoughts of "If only I had..." or "I should have...."?

Did she think about the last time Jesus gave her a hug? The last time they had a meal together? The last time she heard Him laugh? The last time she was able to say, "I love you?" I can't help but think that she did, because that is what the rest of us do.

The last mention of Mary is in the upper room with the other believers (Acts 1:14). Jesus had risen from the grave, but He had also left this earth permanently. What was that like? There must have been some intense grieving, knowing she had just gotten Him back and now He was gone, never to be here on earth with her again.

I believe knowing that Mary stayed with the group and was in the upper room when the Holy Spirit showed up in such a big way is an example to us that life can be worth living again. Mary knew she would see her son again. She figured out how to keep living, even within the grief.

Reflections of Hope

Reflection: I want to look at a scripture that talks about Jesus' mother, Luke 11:27-28. *As Jesus was saying these things, a woman in the crowd called out, "Blessed is the mother who gave you birth and nursed you." Jesus replied, "Even more blessed are those who hear God's voice and make God's message their way of life."* (VOICE)

So, if we take this scripture to heart, what *is* God's voice to us that we need to hear? I believe it is that we have that exact same hope as Mary. We *will* see our children again, and we *can* fight our way out of the grief. I want to encourage you not to choose to remain stuck in the event of your child's death but learn how to live in a way that honors the life of your child, just like Mary did.

And just like the Holy Spirit showed up in that upper room for those who were waiting for Him, I believe the Holy Spirit will show up for you. He will comfort you, and not only comfort you, but give you the strength to live out your life here with meaning and purpose, until it is time to join your child, and Mary and Jesus in heaven.

Hope in the Lord! For with the Lord there is steadfast love, and with him is great power to redeem.
Psalm 130:7 (NRSV)

December 19

Forms of Comfort

When we first knew we would be living in a motorhome, traveling full time for GPS Hope, I didn't know how I felt about not being around to keep up with decorating Becca's grave site.

I'm not there to take down the fall decorations to make it pretty for Christmas. And we aren't back yet in mid-April to decorated it for her birthday. I now have a pareavor friend I rely on to do this for me. I can't just not have it done, because Becca loved decorating, especially for holidays and special occasions. It feels like a big part of keeping her memory alive because it was a big part of her life. Plus, if nothing is there, I don't want anyone to think no one cares.

I know many parents who agonize over feeling like they are leaving their child behind when they have to move for various reasons, including someone who was even considering having her child pulled up and reburied.

Some of you have been able to avoid those issues because your child was cremated, and their remains stay with you. I know some parents who wear some of their child's ashes in a necklace or a ring. Some take the urn with them on vacation. I know of one mom who took her child everywhere, including putting the urn in her cart when she went shopping. Having your child cremated can present different pain-points that we who buried our child don't have.

My point is not to make us all feel morbid and horrible. I just thought since I need a reminder once-in-a while that brings encouragement in this area, some of you might also.

Yes, I will continue to decorate my daughter's grave when I am home and ask my friend Teresa to do it when I'm not (especially for Christmas). *But I will do so, reminding myself that she is not there, and that I am doing it as a public display of how much I love her, and to show that she will always be in my heart.*

To decorate or not to decorate... buried or cremated... these are things that only matter as a form of comfort in the natural realm. They are temporary. We know our children are not really under the ground or in the urn, but we still need to acknowledge that part of them. After all, we are three-part beings, body, soul and spirt. And their bodies matter to us as much as their soul and spirit do.

Reflection: Becca went all out for Christmas and did lots of decorating. If your child were to decorate their heavenly home for Christmas, what would it look like? Take a minute and use your God-given gift of imagination and picture them decorating and maybe even proudly showing it to you.

I can't wait to wrap my arms around a *perfect* Becca, full of life and glory, and love on her once again. But in the meantime... God, would you please give all our children a huge hug, and tell them how much we love and miss them, especially this time of year?

> *For me to live is Christ [His life in me], and to*
> *die is gain [the gain of the glory of eternity].*
> *Philippians 1:21 (AMPC)*

December 20

Excitedly Waiting for Us

I will honestly say that after several years, I still struggle at times with certain scriptures that talk about trials being a gift, or that we should "count it all joy." But I have accepted the fact that my daughter is not here and have learned how to be happier for her gain, than to live in a place of sorrow for my loss. I have learned how to grow from the painful loss and am learning to live in fulfillment of God's plan that obviously does not include Becca being here.

One of the things that has helped me the most is being aware of my thoughts; how I allow myself to see life now, and my thoughts about Becca.

Please know that I am *not* referring to the beginning time, where grief consumes us as something that is so natural in our deep loss that we cannot stop. I am talking about as time goes on, we get to the point where we can start to choose whether we are going to focus on the pain of our loss or focus on something else.

In other words, I can choose to wallow in my sorrow and pain (which I still do at times), or I can choose to think about something else, including the fact that I have a daughter waiting for me, ready and excited to show me around heaven, who can introduce me to some pretty incredible people she has already been spending time with!

Wow! How many people can say they have that blessing, right?

December

Yes, just like you, I would rather have my child here with me. But that is not going to happen. So, in the meantime, there can be "gifts" that we can receive and unwrap, if we want to find them, while we wait to join our children.

Reflection: Knowing that Becca no longer has to deal with the mess of this world, to feel rejection, to experience physical or emotional pain, and knowing we will be together again *forever* are just some of those gifts I have chosen to receive in my thoughts and unwrap. Picturing her in heaven, and what she might be doing, can truly warm my heart, along with imagining seeing how excited she is to see me when I join her!

This Christmas, I encourage you to take some time and give yourself a gift from your child. Force your mind to think of something that is a gain for him or her, and let it warm your heart, even in the pain. Because another gift that I have discovered is that peace and pain can be inside us at the same time.

> *Overwhelming, never-ending joy will crown their heads with happiness and delight while desperation and depression melt away.*
> *Isaiah 55:11 (VOICE)*

December 21

God's Mercy

Identity. That has drastically changed for us now, hasn't it? Well, the identity we have for ourselves, anyway. God's identity for us has not changed. In order to go forward in God's identity for us, we have to let go of our own identity that we feel has been crushed. How do we do that?

One way I have found, is to do something God told us to do in Psalm 46:10 which is to be still and *know* that He is God. I think some of us hesitate to do that because we are afraid God wants to take us forward without the identity of being the parent of our child, and that He wants to tell us everything we are doing or have done wrong. But God says in James 2:13 that "mercy triumphs over judgment."

Think about this: Out of all the many attributes of God, which one attribute did He choose to be His dwelling place in the tabernacle? He chose mercy. It could have been a judgment seat, but His glory came down and rested on a mercy seat.

When Jesus came to earth, God's dwelling place at that time was behind the veil of the temple in Jerusalem. The original mercy seat started out behind the veil of the tabernacle. Did you know that the word Tabernacle means "dwelling place"?

Before Jesus came, God's glory was limited to behind the veil in the Holy of Holies that was purified by the blood of animal sacrifices. But God did not want His dwelling place to stay behind a curtain, away from the people He created. He longed to be in an intimate relationship with them.

When Jesus died, His blood was sprinkled on the mercy seat in heaven once and for all, on our behalf. God's pureness no longer had to remain behind a curtain, which is why the curtain separating Him from the people was torn in two from top to bottom!

Those who accept the work of the blood of Jesus are seen as righteous (right with God) and God's Spirit can dwell, or tabernacle, *inside us.* That means we don't have to try to reach "out there" somewhere, trying to get ahold of God. *We* are now the temple where God's Spirit rests.

So now, we only have to quiet ourselves and listen to Him from within our own spirit. I can live from a place of rest, knowing He is inside me and will help me with my identity, and have mercy on me as I struggle to figure out who I am without my child.

Reflection: God has so much to say to us – to you, and to me, and much of it has to do with who He is inside us, and how to live from that place of rest and identity in Him. It is not about what I do or what has happened to me; it is all about who I *am*. No matter where my child is, I am still his or her parent, and I am also the dwelling place of the very presence and glory of God!

I truly believe more than anything, God just wants to love on us. But we will not know that for ourselves, until we come to Him in the stillness within our hearts to hear Him speak to us. The more aware we become of His Spirit living fully in us, the less aware we become of our own shattered identity and can grow into His identity for us.

Ask God to help you have moments of stillness to be able to know Him in a greater way; the way you personally need Him to be revealed to you, that gives you peace about your identity.

Surrender your anxiety. Be still and realize that I am God.
Psalm 46:10 (TPT)

December 22

God is a Giver, Not a Taker

Many of us may think that God took our child from us, but that isn't what happened. How can I say this? Because I am discovering more and more just how much God is a giver. In fact, the more I grow in intimacy with Him, the more I am being convinced that it is impossible for God to take.

He is a giver, and He receives. God doesn't take what has not been surrendered to Him. And when we surrender something in our lives to him, He receives it.

If you are like me, I surrendered the life of my children to God. I had them dedicated to Him when they were babies, and I have claimed that Jesus is Lord over their lives. That means when my daughter and your child left this earth, God did not take them. He received them into His glorious presence. They received their full redemption. They received a life with no more pain, sickness or tears.

We think God's job is to set up a bunch of rules, and our job is to live by the rule book. But that only breeds frustration that can lead to anger and bitterness.

Reflections of Hope

Our "job" is to learn how to live loved. To learn how to grow in relationship and intimacy with the Father. To learn how to surrender the parts of our life we are struggling with, and give them to Him, knowing He will restore our souls, He will bind up our wounds, and He will redeem what has been taken from us by the enemy.

God is a giver. A giver of life, not death. He didn't take our children, He received them. Our children are more full of life than we are, and some day He will receive us as well, to join our children forever!

Reflection: How does that make you feel to think that God didn't take your child, but He received your son or daughter into a place of perfection? I know it does not remove the pain of missing them, but it should help us not be so judgmental of the One who loves our child even more than we do.

Pause and thank God for receiving your child into His glorious presence. Even if you don't feel like it and are still angry at Him, you can be thankful that when it happened, your child was received by God Himself.

> *When they arrive at the gates of death,*
> *GOD welcomes those who love him.*
> *Psalm 116:14 (MSG)*

December 23

The Gift of the Holy Spirit

As believers in Christ, we are familiar with who Jesus is and what He did for us. We hear a lot about who God is as well. But how much do we know about the third part of the Trinity, the Holy Spirit? Why do we need the Holy Spirit, and how can He help us in our grief?

December

We can read where Jesus talks about the Holy Spirit in the book of John, chapters fifteen and sixteen. "It's to your advantage that I go away, for if I don't go away the Divine Encourager will not be released to you. But after I depart, I will send him to you." John 16:7 (TPT). I love hearing that the Holy Spirit is our Divine Encourager, don't you?

We often hear the Holy Spirit called our Comforter and Helper. The Amplified version of John 16:7 adds that the Holy Spirit is our:

- Advocate – He is your representative, defending you against the accuser.
- Intercessor – He is before the throne, adding his prayers to yours for help.
- Counselor – He will help you make good and right decisions in the fogginess of grief.
- Strengthener – He will give you His inner strength when you have none of your own.
- Standby – He is standing by, immediately ready to help whenever you call out to Him.

In John 15:26, Jesus also says that the Holy Spirit is the Spirit of Truth and will lead us into truth. Did you know there is one truth that even Jesus had a hard time believing at one point?

Shortly after saying this, Jesus told his disciples that they would be scattered, each one going their own way, leaving Jesus alone, and then stated to them: But I am never really alone, because the Father is with me (John 16:32 ERV). Several hours later He was arrested, badly beaten, and hung on a cross to serve the judgment of a death sentence.

While hanging on that cross, Jesus cried out in complete agony and despair, quoting from King David in Psalm 22:1, "My God! Why have you forsaken me?" (Why have you turned your back on me? Where did you go? Why aren't you here with me!)

But the truth is, God never left Him. The Father never turned His back on His Son. He was WITH Jesus as He hung on that cross, covered in the most hideous sins we can think of, along with all the "little" sins ever done by me, by you, and every person ever to live on this earth. The Holy Spirit was still dwelling inside Jesus because it is not sin that causes God to separate Himself from us. It is our guilt and shame that causes us to pull away from Him. It was so dark for Jesus as He hung there, that God's light could not break through, causing Jesus to feel abandoned and alone in that suffocating darkness.

It may be so dark that you cannot see, hear, or feel God's presence. Jesus knows what that is like! You have not been betrayed, forsaken, or left alone any more than He was. God is right there with you in the horrific darkness because God's incredible gift of His very Spirit lives inside you.

Reflection: Jesus knew there was joy ahead beyond the darkness and pain (Hebrews 12:2), even if He could not see it while in the darkness. There is joy ahead for you as well, but you must lean on His Spirit, living inside you to find it.

A few years ago, I awoke with the words, "Draw from My well of abundance," reverberating in my spirit! I now have that written on a white board (along with some verses and other things I want to remember) that hangs in front of me in my "office" of the passenger seat of the Hope Mobile when we are parked. It is a reminder that God has put in me everything I need to get through this life, because His Spirit is in me. If I need peace, He already has it in me, in abundance. If I need strength, it is there, so I need to draw from that abundance. If there is confusion, drawing from that well of abundance gives me the needed direction.

Pray with me: *Holy Spirit, remind and empower me to draw from Your well of abundance that is inside me, because You are living in me, ready to help in my time of need. Also, please do the work needed to not only see the joy set before me when I join my child, but to live in that joy as I finish out my time here on earth. Amen.*

> *But God now unveils these profound realities to us by the Spirit. Yes, he has revealed to us his inmost heart and deepest mysteries through the Holy Spirit ... His thoughts and secrets are only fully understood by his Spirit, the Spirit of God.*
> *1 Corinthians 2:10-11 (TPT)*

December 24

Changing Our Focus About Christmas

Tomorrow is Christmas day. It is a day most of us used to look forward to with our kids, but now it is a day most of us dread. We just want to skip it.

I used to tell myself that Christmas was to celebrate the birth of Jesus. As our kids grew up, even as non-Catholics, we would read through an advent book as a family, lighting our wreath of advent candles. It was something I could do to remind our kids why we have Christmas.

On Christmas morning I would read the "Christmas story" from the Bible before we opened presents, to remind ourselves once again why we have this holiday. Our traditional Christmas dessert was an ice cream cake that said, "Happy Birthday Jesus" and sometimes we would even sing the Happy Birthday song to Him.

In Children's Church, I would write out lessons about all the symbols of Christmas and how they pointed to Jesus. (When I first studied it all out to be able to teach it, I was sick to my stomach when I found out how much paganism is in our Christmas celebration. But as Christians, we have turned them into meaningful symbols of Christ and the Christmas story, which is what I taught.)

But when Becca died, I realized for me personally, how much of Christmas really *was* about the presents and doing my best to make sure my kids had a fun day and we enjoyed being together as a family. No matter how much I had tried to make it about Jesus, deep in my heart, it really wasn't.

Not only do we *not* want to celebrate Christmas because our child is no longer here with us, but some of us don't want to celebrate because we feel like God really isn't here with us either!

This end-of-the-year holiday can amplify everything, especially the questions and the pain. There are so many unanswered questions, many that start with "Why." Even as I am writing this, I have had to stop and cry, with sobs that I have not had in quite some time. I can barely see

Reflections of Hope

through the tears to continue. But no matter how much pain I am in, somehow, I know that God is the only one who can truly help me.

I have had to learn how to *truly* change my focus about Christmas, and it has not been easy!

Emmanuel - God with us.

Not only is He with us, He is *in* us. He is for us, not against us, even though it may seem like it. I want to feel Him; I want to know His peace in a very tangible way. No, I *need* to feel Him and know His peace in a tangible way. Today and *every* day!

Reflection: There is hope in your future because He *is* Emmanuel, God with us. Not only is He the coming King who will be riding on a white horse in the clouds, but He is here with us now, dwelling inside our very being, comforting us, guiding us, and bringing light back into our darkness.

Pray this prayer out loud with me:

Jesus, on this Christmas Eve, as much as I can (which may not be much at all) I celebrate Your light that pierced the very deepest darkness, including death, when you came to earth. You are truly Emmanuel, God with us - with **me**. *And because Jesus came as a baby, lived here on earth, died and rose again, I know that death is not the end for my child or myself. Thank you for the hope I have in my future, not just when I leave this earth, but while I am still here, as I navigate my purpose without my child here with me.*

Give me strength for tomorrow and be everything I need to make it through the day. But beyond that, help me to not only just get through it, but have moments of joy in watching the happiness of the celebration and may there be some good memories made of those I love who are still here with me.

Amen.

I am the light of the world. If you follow me, you won't have to walk in darkness, because you will have the light that leads to life.
John 8:12 (NLT)

December 25

Before and After

For most of us, Christmas Day is one of those days we cannot get through without tears. It is a day we want our family to be together. We want to experience the fun and laughter of this special holiday with our child. Now all we have are these memories, and we are painfully aware that will not happen anymore.

I read something recently I thought I would pass on to you.

God will not allow the painful things in our lives to be wasted.

Because Jesus came to earth, we can be confident that our stories do not end with suffering. The enemy's plan is to destroy us, but God's plan is using it to set the stage for transforming our sorrow into great rejoicing.

We will not see the end result here, that's for sure. But because Jesus came, making a way for us to be together with Him for all eternity, our children *are* seeing it. And while we are waiting for that final transformation of sorrow into pure joy, let's be determined, within our pain, to lean in, learning how to work with God so that the death of our child is not wasted here on earth.

Before and after – that defines our life right now, doesn't it? That is a dividing line that we never thought we would have. It seems that everything is defined as "before" my child died, or "after" my child died.

Have you stopped to think that there is another dividing line coming in our future? But this "before" and "after" is one we are looking forward to with great anticipation, that will bring us back to a place of great rejoicing! It is "before" I got to heaven and was reunited with my child, and "after" I got here...

This is what Christmas Day is all about. When Jesus entered our world as a baby, it was the beginning of drawing that eternal dividing line of "after" that will be the most wonderful day of our lives!

Reflections of Hope

Reflection: I love to hang on to Romans 8:18. Here are several versions of that wonderful verse. Read each one slowly, allowing its truth to penetrate your soul.

The sufferings we have now are nothing compared to the great glory that will be shown to us. (NCV)

The sufferings we go through in the present time are not worth putting in the scale alongside the glory that is going to be unveiled for us. (NTE)

We have sufferings now, but these are nothing compared to the great glory that will be given to us. (ERV)

What we are suffering now is nothing compared with our future glory. (NIRV)

For I consider that our present sufferings cannot even be compared to the coming glory that will be revealed to us. (NET)

Aren't you thankful that this is not the end, and someday the joy and glory that we will be in will be so fantastic, that it can't even be compared to the depth of our suffering here without our children?

> *Whatever we may have to go through now is less than nothing compared with the magnificent future God has planned for us... And the hope is that in the end the whole of created life will be rescued from the tyranny of change and decay, and have its share in that magnificent liberty which can only belong to the children of God!*
> Romans 8:18, 21 (PHILLIPS)

December 26

'Twas the Night After Christmas

'Twas the night after Christmas and I was still numb;

The holidays felt like they had not really come.

December

It's hard to explain, but it didn't seem fair,

That my child is now gone, and I cannot share

The laughter and joy of this fun holiday

In our wonderful, traditional family way.

She is not nestled all snug in her bed

With memories of another Christmas filling her head.

"Will it ever get better?" I ask in my heart,

Knowing that each year we will remain apart.

As I cry out to God full of heartache and tears,

He reminds me His presence remains very near.

And though I don't feel a desire to celebrate

The reason to do so remains very great.

For Jesus came as a baby on earth

To give life here meaning, value and worth.

And even though I have said goodbye

And I am confused and don't know why,

The truth remains I will see you again

And there will be no more tears and no more pain.

But until that day comes and it's my turn to go

There is one thing that I certainly know,

The love that I have for you is without measure

And you remain in my heart, as a beautiful treasure.

And while dreading to go into a year that is new

I realize each day brings me closer to you.

My Christmas may not have been merry and bright,

But because Jesus came, someday, it will all be made right.

(By Laura Diehl)

Reflection: Tonight, after everyone is in bed, get a hot drink and sit in a place where you can read through this and talk to God about the parts that seem to stand out to you the most. (If you put your tree up this year, maybe you can sit by it with just the tree lights on. Or maybe you can light a few candles and turn out the lights.)

If you need to cry, go ahead. If you need to have it out with Him, go ahead. If you need to put on some worship music and let Him love on you, go ahead. Just *be* with Him and let Him minister to you however you need Him to.

> *Are you weary, carrying a heavy burden? Come to me.*
> *I will refresh your life, for I am your oasis.*
> *Matthew 11:28 (TPT)*

December 27

Bitterness and Resentment

I am guessing other families around you have seemed quite happy with all the festivities, and most are oblivious to your shattered heart and the deep pain you are in.

It can be difficult not to be angry that other happy families have not been destroyed like yours has by the death of a child. "What did I do to deserve having *my* child die? Why my family and not theirs? My child was so sweet and kind, and their child is a horrible person."

These kinds of thoughts and questions can very quickly turn into bitterness, which turns into resentment.

We can resent others who have not had to face a loss as deep as ours. Even worse, we can resent those families much quicker if they are Christians. "Why do *they* get all the good things in life, while I get handed one bad thing after another? They aren't any better of a Christian than I am! If I have to suffer like this, why don't others? Why does God keep doing things like this to *me*? Why even bother being a Christian if this is what He is going to do?"

I want to share something that Job said, keeping His heart in a place of being able to receive what he needed from the Lord in his deep grief and pain of losing his health, his wealth and all ten of his children. *Though he slay me, I will hope in him.* Many translations say, *I'll continue to trust in him.* (Job 13:15 ESV). I love how Job added in the same verse, "At least I'll be able to argue my case to his face!"

One of the last things Job says, after God reveals Himself as the One who sees and knows everything, *I know that You can do everything, and that no purpose of Yours can be withheld from You* (Job 42:2, NKJV).

God's plan or purpose for your child's life (or your life) was not changed by his or her leaving this earth ahead of you. Bitterness and resentment do not change that either. Our painful and negative emotions can wreak total havoc inside us. While we cannot avoid having emotions, how you and I respond to them will determine whether we move forward in a way that pulls us toward light and hope, or whether it keeps us wandering around in the thick darkness.

Reflection: I love Job 42:2,3 in the Message version of the Bible.

> *Job answered GOD: "I'm convinced: You can do anything and everything. Nothing and no one can upset your plans. You asked, 'Who is this muddying the water, ignorantly confusing the issue, second-guessing my purposes?' I admit it. I was the one. I babbled on about things far beyond me, made small talk about wonders way over my head.*

That sounds so much like us, doesn't it? So instead of blaming God about things that are so beyond our comprehension, let's take time to ask Him to remove any bitterness and resentment taking root in our hearts and replace it with trust. I readily admit that is too big for us to do on our own, which is why we need His help.

Do not keep wandering in the darkness. Ask Him to lead you back into a place where you can trust Him again and move toward His light, His love, His peace, His hope and yes, even His joy so that you can live in a way that honors your child (and God).

> *The people who walk in darkness shall see a great Light—a Light that will shine on all those who live in the land of the shadow of death.*
> *Isaiah 9:2 (TLB)*

December 28

Faith Equals Trusting

"Just have faith!" Those are pretty loaded words to us now, aren't they?

I like reading the Complete Jewish Bible at times because it takes the "Christianeze" out of it. For instance, it does not use the word cross, but instead uses "execution-stake." When you read in Matthew 16:24 that Jesus told His disciples to take up their "execution-stake, and keep following me," it takes on a whole new revelation.

Also, this version rarely uses the word faith. Instead, it uses the word trust. Hebrews 11:1 reads, *Trusting is being confident of what we hope for, convinced about things we do not see.*

To me, faith is something I have to strive toward getting enough of. Yes, I know I am told faith comes by hearing the Word. But how much "hearing" is enough? I just never seem to have quite enough to make God do what I need Him to do every time!

Faith is something I have to strive and work for. But trust is something I can rest in. And I can rest in Him because I know Him. We cannot trust someone we don't know, and the more we really truly know Him, the more we trust Him (which means the more faith we have).

If faith comes by hearing the Word, Jesus is the Word, right? So, to spend time in His presence, resting in Him, learning who He is in times of intimacy with Him so I can trust Him to a greater degree means I am "hearing the Word" to be able to have more faith.

It is not my striving to believe more, it is my resting in who He is, knowing He already has everything I need to get through this life!

Picture a young child who is angry at her daddy for a decision he made that she didn't understand. He scoops her up to try and make her feel better, but she is fighting him while in his arms. The child finally becomes exhausted and allows the father to comfort her instead of being angry at him.

I don't see that as something that child had to work at. It is something she finally decided to rest in, which causes trust, as her daddy holds her and hurts with her.

Reflection:

> ...let us grasp the fact that we have peace with God through our Lord Jesus Christ. Through him we have confidently entered into this new relationship of grace, and here we take our stand, in happy certainty of the glorious things he has for us in the future.
>
> This doesn't mean, of course, that we have only a hope of future joys—we can be full of joy here and now even in our trials and troubles. Taken in the right spirit, these very things will give us patient endurance; this in turn will develop a mature character, and a character of this sort produces a steady hope, a hope that will never disappoint us" Romans 5:1-5 (Phillips).

You can not only have hope, but you can still trust God's plans for your future. It is not something you have to work and strive for. Ask God to help you rest in Him, so that you can learn to trust Him once again.

> *So we see that they were unable to enter*
> *(his rest) because of lack of trust.*
> *Hebrews 3:19 (CJB)*

December 29

I Am Not Ready to Go into a New Year!

I remember what it was like heading into the new year, two months after my daughter, Becca, died. I was horrified at the thought of "leaving her behind." It felt like going into a new year without her was another finality of her death that I was not ready to accept.

Who can possibly celebrate the future, when my daughter would not be with us? "Out with the old, and in with the new!" brought heaviness and panic attacks, not excitement.

God knew that. He knew how heavy my heart was. He knew I didn't want to continue with *anything* new. He knew I wasn't ready to let go in a way that would allow me to see hope in a future without Becca. He knew I was *deep* in suffocating grief, and it did not shake His faithfulness to me one little bit.

As I closed myself in with Him day after day, crying buckets of tears, sharing my hurt and pain with Him, He sat with me. He stayed with me in all of my sobbing, ugliness, confusion and depression. And in my moments of brokenness, when I wanted to hear what He had to say that would bring a measure of healing to my completely shattered heart, He was always ready to comfort me and speak to me.

Sometimes it would be through a song that came on my CD player that I kept running 24-7 or on the radio. Sometimes it was a chapter in the Bible, or as little as half of a verse, as I would pick up His Word and search for help. Sometimes it was through an act of kindness from a family member or friend. But many times, it was that still, small voice that spoke to my heart as I sat in my brokenness.

I spent a lot of my time journaling. I wrote my scrambled thoughts and asked Him questions. And quite often, I found myself writing what I heard God speak to me in my heart in answer to those questions.

God has continued to comfort and strengthen me, putting the pieces of my heart back together in a way that I am complete, and yet forever broken. And I'm okay with that, because when we start a new year, it gets me one year closer to being with my Becca forever!

Reflection: Here is one of those scriptures that helped me continue moving forward.

> *We fix our eyes not on what is seen, but on what is unseen. For what is seen is temporary, but what is unseen is eternal* (2 Corinthians 4:18 NIV).

I am *so* very thankful for this, and constantly remind myself this world is only temporary. What a relief! What can you do to help yourself fix your eyes (and your mind) on what is unseen and eternal? Maybe you can do something like write out this verse and put it in a place where you will see often as a reminder.

> *I pray that he will give light to the eyes of your hearts, so that you will understand the hope to which he has called you, what rich glories there are in the inheritance he has promised his people, and how surpassingly great is his power working in us who trust him.*
> Eph. 1:18-19 (CJB)

December 30

Include Your Child

Stop feeling like you owe them an explanation. The people around you are not going to understand. How could they? I know I sure didn't until I was on this side of things.

Know that it's okay to be real and lean into your pain when it grips you, either unexpectedly, or when you know something will be happening that makes you miss your child. Release the guilt of not attending functions that are too difficult, no matter how long ago the loss has been.

There are going to be times when attending a joyful or celebrating event is going to be a slap-in-the-face reminder that your child is not here and will not be part of something they should have been. When I just can't go to events, instead of making my absence about me, I let those attending know it is about them. I don't want to dampen or possibly ruin the celebration for those who are there.

The other option I have found that seems to surprise people, is to ask if there can be a way to include your child. Can a toast be made? Can there be a photo placed somewhere? Can a book be placed on a table where those attending can write a memory or a note to your child, letting him or her know how much they are missed? When I know my child will be acknowledged in some way, it helps bring a healing comfort in the midst of the pain, to know that others miss my daughter too, and have not forgotten her.

Reflection: What are your plans for New Year's Eve? Have you been invited to a celebration, and you just do not have it in you to celebrate the start of a new year? That's okay. If you want to be in bed by seven o'clock and cry yourself to sleep, I get it.

Or maybe there is part of you that wants to go somewhere to be with others who are enjoying the evening. You feel a tug on your heart to let go of the grief for a few hours and have some fun but feel guilty that you are being drawn toward it, because it feels like you are betraying your child. Go! Have fun! Your grief will be waiting for you when you get back.

Either way, it may help to realize that our children are having the best party ever! They are in a place where it is a continual celebration of joy and beauty beyond what we can even imagine. They are beyond celebrating a new year. They are celebrating a new life!

> *None of us are permitted to insist on our own way in these matters. It's God we are answerable to—all the way from life to death and everything in between—not each other. That's why Jesus lived and died and then lived again: so that he could be our Master across the entire range of life and death, and free us from the petty tyrannies of each other.*
> *Romans 14:8-9 (MSG)*

December 31

The Future

Jesus was born into a world of darkness, unbelief and confusion. He was born as the Light of the World. Even death could not put out that light, because not only was He born to die, but also to be resurrected. He came to bring light into the deepest darkness. He came to bring resurrection life from death.

I am sure you have heard the saying that our life here on earth is not a destination, it is a journey that quite often takes us to places we have never been before, such as the death of our child. When we travel to somewhere we have never been, and the path is too dark to see, we need something or someone to guide us.

Not just death that causes our bodies to quit and our spirits to leave them, but the death that happens in our souls after the death of our child.

That is where "Emmanuel, God with us" comes in. He becomes our guide in the darkness. He knows where the path lies, and will help us navigate each road we need to be on while traveling this grief journey, especially as we go into a new year.

Reflection: Just like the GPS that is confused and doesn't even know where we are, that is how we feel after the death of our child. But the good news is, if we keep going, we will eventually either figure out where we are, to be able to get back on our journey, or we can find someone who knows the area who can help us navigate back to the road that we need to be on.

The calendar is changing to a new year whether we want it to or not. And God is already there, waiting for us. He is eternal, which means He is in our past, He is in our right now, and He is in our future. And so is our child. Maybe not our future here on earth, but our eternal future, which I think you can agree is the most important.

*I'm not saying that I have this all together, that I have it made. But I am well on my way, reaching out for Christ, who has so wondrously reached out for me. Friends, don't get me wrong: By no means do I count myself an expert in all of this, but I've got my eye on the goal, where God is beckoning us onward—to Jesus. I'm off and running, and I'm not turning back.
Philippians 3:12 (MSG*

Index of Verses

The dates in *italics* indicate the scripture is within the reading and not the Reflection verse.

Old Testament

Genesis 4:1-8 - *June 29*
Genesis 28:12 - *June 26*
Genesis 37:35 - *October 27*
Genesis 43:14 - *October 27*
Genesis 50:20 - *September 23*
Exodus 12:30 - *September 11*
Exodus 16:2-3 - *October 7*
Exodus 33:13 - October 7
Exodus 33:15 - *October 7*
Exodus 33:14 - September 30
Exodus 33:18-23 - *June 10*
Numbers 6:24-26 - May 2
Deuteronomy 18:9-11 - *June 26*
Deuteronomy 24:16 - *September 25*
Deuteronomy 30:19 - January 31, May 5
Deuteronomy 31:3 - November 2
Deuteronomy 31:6 - October 28
Deuteronomy 31:8 – May 17
Deuteronomy 33:27 – February 20
Ruth 1:20-21 - *October 14*
Ruth 2:20 - *October 14*
1 Samuel 12:7 - December 16
1 Samuel 16:23 - August 3
2 Samuel 12:13-15 - *September 25*
2 Samuel 12:23 - *October 29*
2 Samuel 22:37 - February 29
1 Chronicles 16:11 - May 7
Esther 9:22 - November 18
Job 1:1 - *January 10*
Job 1:21 - *October 9*
Job 1:20-21 - *June 4, October 9*
Job 1:21,22 - *December 27*
Job 3:11,21,25 - *June 4*
Job 5:9-11 - *June 4*
Job 6:1-9 - *June 4*
Job 6:2-3 - August 22

Job 9:33 - *June 2*
Job 10:8 - *June 4*
Job 13:15 - *February 25, June 4, December 27*
Job 14:5 - *July 19, October 28*
Job 14:7 - January 30, July 11
Job 23:10,12 - March 31
Job 23:10, 13-16 - June 4
Job 42:1-3 - June 5
Job 42:1-5 - June 4
Job 42:2 - July 19
Job 42:2-3 - December 27
Psalm 4:4 - October 22
Psalm 6:2 - November 22
Psalm 9:10 - October 6
Psalm 10:17 - November 4, August 9
Psalm 16:11 - July 23
Psalm 18:6 - March 11
Psalm 18:28 - February 8
Psalm 19:14 - March 14, June 16
Psalm 20:4 - July 1
Psalm 22:1 - *December 23*
Psalm 22:11 - September 20
Psalm 23:1-3 - January 23
Psalm 23:2 - November 1
Psalm 23:2-3 - April 15, July 6
Psalm 23:4 - September 10
Psalm 25:4 - September 12
Psalm 25:16 – October 31
Psalm 27:13 – September 2
Psalm 27:14 - June 11
Psalm 30:5 - August 30
Psalm 30:11 - July 16
Psalm 30:11-12 - July 10
Psalm 31:14-15 - December 17
Psalm 31:24 - September 1
Psalm 32:8 - March 22

Psalm 33:22 - January 2, April 5
Psalm 34:8 - March 16, June 12
Psalm 34:18 - May 24, August 1, November 25, November 29
Psalm 34:19 - September 21
Psalm 37:5 - July 15
Psalm 37:7 - February 16
Psalm 37:8 - December 6
Psalm 37:23 - March 31
Psalm 37:23-24 - February 17
Psalm 39:1-2 - November 5
Psalm 40:2 - September 23
Psalm 42:11 - June 9, November 28
Psalm 46:1 - September 22, May 10
Psalm 46:10 - December 21
Psalm 50:15 - August 10
Psalm 50:23 - August 14
Psalm 51:10-12 - May 18
Psalm 51:12 - May 11
Psalm 54:4 - January 8
Psalm 55:22 - November 9
Psalm 56:3 - May 14
Psalm 56:4 - October 27
Psalm 56:8 - February 23, December 7
Psalm 61:1-4 - June 18
Psalm 61:2 - July 7, November 6
Psalm 62:5 - January 18, November 26
Psalm 62:8 - January 13
Psalm 66:12 - September 27
Psalm 66:5 - July 29
Psalm 68:19 - August 11
Psalm 71:20 - February 11
Psalm 73:26 - August 1
Psalm 73:28 - January 28, May 16
Psalm 86:5 - June 13
Psalm 86:15-16 - August 27
Psalm 90:12 - August 24
Psalm 90:14-15 - September 13
Psalm 91:1-2 - May 20

Psalm 91:6 - March 17
Psalm 92:12 October 4
Psalm 94:19 - April 5, June 19
Psalm 103:2 - November 11
Psalm 103:7 - September 12
Psalm 103:10-12 - January 10
Psalm 107:14 - January 27
Psalm 107:20 - February 7
Psalm 112:6 - December 2
Psalm 116:3-5 - October 13
Psalm 116:14 - December 22
Psalm 116:15 - August 16, September 25
Psalm 118:14 - February 3
Psalm 119:25 - May 15
Psalm 119:29-32 - May 15
Psalm 119:28 - November 3
Psalm 119:45-50 - June 7
Psalm 119:68 - June 10
Psalm 119:107 - September 7
Psalm 121:1-2 - June 20
Psalm 130:5 - June 22
Psalm 130:7 - December 18
Psalm 139:7-12 - April 10
Psalm 139:10 - January 19
Psalm 139:13-16 - April 13, Psalm 139:14 - July 18
Psalm 139:16 - July 19, August 16
Psalm 141:2 - April 6
Psalm 142:2 - February 9
Psalm 146:7 - December 11
Psalm 147:1 - May 22
Psalm 147:3 - February 15, April 21
Proverbs 3:5 - June 6, September 19
Proverbs 3:5-6 - March 29, August 5
Proverbs 4:23 - May 28
Proverbs 4:25-26 - March 31
Proverbs 8:17 - January 12
Proverbs 12:25 - October 8
Proverbs 13:12 - July 28

Index

Proverbs 14:10 – August 6
Proverbs 14:27 - June 24
Proverbs 17:22 - March 13
Proverbs 18:10 - September 9
Proverbs 23:18 - May 4
Ecclesiastes 3:1 - October 5
Ecclesiastes 3:11 - May 19
Ecclesiastes 4:9-10 - July 4
Song of Solomon 2:10 - February 24
Song of Solomon 2:10-14 - March 27
Isaiah 9:2 - December 27
Isaiah 9:6 - *December 12*
Isaiah 12:2-3 - August 15
Isaiah 14:24 - January 29
Isaiah 25:8 - May 27
Isaiah 30:18 - July 13
Isaiah 35:10 - October 17
Isaiah 40:29 - February 2, June 28
Isaiah 40:31 - February 27
Isaiah 41:10 - January 11, October 24
Isaiah 41:13 - January 4,
Isaiah 42:16 - *March 31*
Isaiah 43:19 - January 3, March 1, August 2
Isaiah 49:13 - January 25
Isaiah 49:15 - November 23
Isaiah 53:10 – October 17
Isaiah 53:3-5 - March 26
Isaiah 55:8 - June 29
Isaiah 57:1 - June 17
Isaiah 57:19 - November 12
Isaiah 58:10 - August 26
Isaiah 60:20 - September 11
Isaiah 61:3 – *May 25, July 9, July 10, July 11*
Isaiah 62:3 - August 18
Isaiah 65:17 - August 8
Isaiah 66:22 - May 1
Jeremiah 15:16 - September 8
Jeremiah 17:17 - April 5
Jeremiah 29:11 – March 17, *April 25, July 19, August 1*, November 24
Jeremiah 30:17 - July 8
Jeremiah 31:3 - April 3
Lamentations 3:19-23 - April 19
Lamentations 3:19-26 - October 14
Ezekiel 18:20 - September 25
Ezekiel 28:13 - May 22
Daniel 9:3 - July 9
Hosea 6:3 - March 21, June 4
Jonah 2:7 - April 10
Micah 7:8 – October 10
Nahum 1:7 - March 30
Habakkuk 2:3 - January 15
Habakkuk 3:17-18 - February 25
Habakkuk 3:19 - November 19
Zephaniah 3:17 - February 26, August 1
Zechariah 2:5 - June 21
Zechariah 9:11,12 - September 24

New Testament

Matthew 4:1 - October 24
Matthew 4:6 - September 9
Matthew 4:7 - September 10
Matthew 4:16 - December 4
Matthew 5:43-44 - March 24
Matthew 5:45 – *January 10,* September 9, September 11
Matthew 6:9-13 - June 25
Matthew 6:19-21 June 14
Matthew 7:7 - July 17
Matthew 8:20 - April 17
Matthew 9:24 - *February 25*
Matthew 10:29-31 - January 9

Reflections of Hope

Matthew 11:28 - March 8, December 26
Matthew 11:29 - January 22
Matthew 11:28-29 - May 23, March 8
Matthew 11:28-30 - May 23
Matthew 13:55 - December 15
Matthew 14:29 – September 20
Matthew 16:24 - December 28
Matthew 17:1-3 - June 26
Matthew 18:20 - April 17
Matthew 19:26 - August 20
Matthew 25:21 – May 19
Mark 3:20-21 - December 15
Mark 5:23 - May 30
Mark 6:31- February 6, November 30
Mark 6:3 - December 15
Mark 9:24 - April 9
Luke 1:37 - April 22
Luke 1:78-79 - May 6
Luke 1:38 - December 17
Luke 2:13-14 - December 5
Luke 2:19 - December 16
Luke 2:51 - December 16
Luke 11:27-28 - December 18
Luke 16:19-31 - January 10
Luke 18:27 - May 21
Luke 22:31-32 - August 28
Luke 22:42 - June 23
Luke 24:5-6 - December 8
Luke 23:43 - December 8
John 1:5 - January 7
John 4:23-24 - September 14
John 5:24-26 - December 8
John 5:25 - May 30
John 6:68 - February 5, June 6
John 7:3-5 - December 15
John 7:38 - June 21
John 8:12 - December 24
John 8:32 - March 18, May 29
John 8:36 - August 29
John 9:1-3 - January 10

John 10:10 – May 29, June 14, July 19, November 29
John 11:21,32 - January 27
John 11:33,35 - March 19
John 11:35 – February 23
John 12:46 - December 1
John 13:7 –October 1
John 14:1-3 - April 28, October 18
John 14:6 - August 22
John 14:16-17 - September 16
John 14:26 - February 12, September 17
John 14:27 – March 23, July 3
John 15:4-6 - April 24
John 15:26 - *December 23*
John 16:1 - May 9
John 16:7 – September 14, December 13, *December 23*
John 16:20, 22-23 - December 10
John 16:22 - February 13
John 16:32 - *December 23*
John 16:33 – April 11, September 11, September 29
John 19:26-27 - December 17
John 20:30 - January 27
Acts 1:14 - December 18
Acts 20:32 – August 4
Romans 1:12 - November 2
Romans 4:17 - February 25, October 30
Romans 4:18 - April 1
Romans 5:1-5 - December 28
Romans 5:5 - April 5, April 7, June 21
Romans 6:5 - October 29
Romans 8:1 - April 27, June 27
Romans 8:9 - April 2
Romans 8:18 – September 3, September 18, October 9
Romans 8:18,21 - December 25
Romans 8:25 - June 15
Romans 8:26 - April 20
Romans 8:28 - March 30, June 2,

Index

September 9, October 15
Romans 8:31 - January 14
Romans 8:32 - July 30
Romans 8:32, 34 - August 17
Romans 8:38-39 - February 10, March 4, September 28
Romans 12:2 - July 12, July 24, August 14
Romans 12:12 - August 5
Romans 12:15 – April 17
Romans 13:7 - August 21
Romans 13:12 - October 15
Romans 14:8-9 - December 30
Romans 14:19 - November 8
Romans 14:13 - June 1
Romans 15:4 - January 26
Romans 15:13 – January 5, April 18, November 29
Romans 16:20 - December 12
1 Corinthians 2:5,9,12,14 - October 19
1 Corinthians 2:9 - June 30
1 Corinthians 2:10-11 - December 23
1 Corinthians 2:12,14 - October 19
1 Corinthians 2:16 - February 4
1 Corinthians 3:16 - July 26
1 Corinthians 6:19 - September 14
1 Corinthians 10:13 - September 26
1 Corinthians 13:7-8 - February 14
1 Corinthians 13:12 - September 14
1 Corinthians 13:12-13 – October 2
1 Corinthians 15:54 - April 4
1 Corinthians 15:55 - April 4
2 Corinthians 1:3-4 - May 12
2 Corinthians 1:3-4,7 - August 19
2 Corinthians 1:7 – July 5, November 7
2 Corinthians 3:17-18 - August 12
2 Corinthians 3:18 - May 26
2 Corinthians 4:8 - February 19
2 Corinthians 4:16 - July 2
2 Corinthians 4:16-18 - January 26, September 25

2 Corinthians 4:18 – September 18, October 12, December 29
2 Corinthians 5:4-5 - July 21
2 Corinthians 5:6-8 - October 21
2 Corinthians 5:7 - October 21
2 Corinthians 5:8 - September 25, November 13
2 Corinthians 10:4-5 - April 23
2 Corinthians 10:12 - May 31
2 Corinthians 12:10 - April 16
Galatians 5:1 - April 30
Galatians 6:2 – November 25
Ephesians 1:14 - November 21
Ephesians 1:18 - May 26
Ephesians 1:18-19 - December 29
Ephesians 2:4-5 – June 2
Ephesians 2:6 - July 27
Ephesians 2:10 – March 31, November 16
Ephesians 3:16 - February 21
Ephesians 3:16-19 - March 31
Ephesians 3:17 - July 9, September 26
Ephesians 3:18-19 July 22
Ephesians 3:19 - March 4
Ephesians 3:20 - January 20, October 19
Ephesians 4:27 - July 24
Ephesians 4:32 - March 12
Ephesians 6:13-16 – October 20
Ephesians 6:17 - October 16
Philippians 1:3 - November 10
Philippians 1:6 - April 14, July 20
Philippians 1:21- *August 23, September 25*, December 19
Philippians 2:1 September 6
Philippians 2:1-2 - April 26
Philippians 3:10-11 - April 12
Philippians 3:12 - December 31
Philippians 3:13-14 - *June 15*, August 7
Philippians 3:14 - December 14
Philippians 4:4-8 - *March 3*

Philippians 4:6-7 – March 20, October 26
Philippians 4:8 – March 3, December 9
Philippians 4:13 – *February 9,* December 3
Colossians 1:11 – January 21
Colossians 1:11-14 – January 24
Colossians 1:27 – April 25, *June 21,* August 23
Colossians 2:5 – September 4
Colossians 3:2 – June 8
Colossians 3:12-13 – March 28
Colossians 3:13 – March 6
Hebrews 1:3 – July 27
Hebrews 3:19 – December 28
Hebrews 4:11 – May 3
Hebrews 4:12 – April 18
Hebrews 4:16 – February 18, *June 15,* November 15
Hebrews 6:18 – October 9
Hebrews 6:19 – March 7, *April 5*
Hebrews 7:25 – August 28
Hebrews 10:23 – March 9
Hebrews 11:1 – April 5, *December 28*
Hebrews 11:39-40 – *June 5*
Hebrews 12:1 – June 26
Hebrews 12:2 – March 2, *July 27,* August 25, *December 23*
Hebrews 12:11 – *October 6*
Hebrews 12:15 – June 3, August 31
Hebrews 13:5 – *October 9,* November 20
Hebrews 13:8,9 – November 27
Hebrews 13:16 – July 14

James 1:17 – November 27, December 15
James 2:13 – *December 21*
James 4:8 – February 5
James 4:14 – *April 14*
1 Thessalonians 4:13 – March 25, *April 5*
1 Thessalonians 4:13,17-18 – July 31
1 Thessalonians 5:11 – July 25, November 14
1 Thessalonians 5:23 – March 5
2 Thessalonians 2:16-17 – March 15
2 Thessalonians 3:16 – April 11, May 13
2 Timothy 1:7 – January 1, February 4
2 Timothy 2:13 – January 16, September 15
Titus 3:2 – November 17
1 Peter 1:3-5 – *November 29*
1 Peter 5:7 – February 1, April 8
1 Peter 5:8-9 – April 29
1 Peter 5:10 – March 31
1 Peter 5:10-11 – April 16
2 Peter 1:2 – May 8
2 Peter 1:3 – February 28, October 23
2 Peter 3:9 – March 4
1 John 3:20 – September 5
1 John 4:18 – October 3, *October 24,* November 9
3 John 1:2 – February 22
Revelation 12:11 – January 17, *November 5*
Revelation 21:3-5 – *February 23*
Revelation 21:4 – October 11
Revelation 21:5 – January 6
Revelation 22:13 – *January 9*

Acknowledgements

I want to acknowledge the pareavors who helped make this a better book for you. For a full year, as I sent them the daily readings on the corresponding calendar days, every month they gave me such valuable feedback and suggestions.

On an interesting note, when I asked if they saw a theme immerge from the readings each month, *at least two of them* would say they saw hope as one of the themes for every single month.

Thank you, team! You kept me going with the encouragement you gave, along with your suggestions. This book is so much better because of your wonderful input. I love you all!

Carolyn Blackall, mom of Rachel Pilcher, forever 40.

***Rachel** passed away suddenly due to complications to the flu. She was so beautiful and had the most awesome laugh. When she laughed everyone laughed. We love and miss her so very much.*

Amie Boyd, mom of Mason, forever 16

***Mason**, who was unable to wrestle because of an injury due to his rheumatoid arthritis, was driving to support his high school wrestling team for an early Saturday morning tournament when he wrecked and lost his life. He was an avid wrestler with a great future ahead of him with dreams of being an Ohio state champ.*

Mason was highly intelligent and dreamed of being a sports medicine doctor so he could help athletes with diseases and injuries (like his own) to stay on the mat/field/court.

Valerie Breslau, mom of Eric, forever 25

Eric died when he was unknowingly poisoned from a pill cut with fentanyl. He was the third child of my four sons. He loved his family, and really loved being an uncle. He loved skateboarding, the beach, tattoos, and his mom's spicy food.

I miss talking to him every day and making his favorite meals. Eric is forever loved, and his presence will always be missing from our family.

Vickie Hickox, mom of Dominique Cardenas, forever 24

Dominic was a very happy young man. He always had a smile on his face. When Dominic was seventeen, he made an entry in his journal for school that if he could do anything, he would want to cure cancer. He said he would not want any recognition for it; he would want to remain anonymous. The smiles and happiness it would give the families would be thanks enough for him. That was my son! He had a big heart and would help you if he could.

I love and miss you, Dominic. I look forward to the day I will see you again.

Dawn Koeppen, mom of Andrew, forever 33

Andrew loved his family and friends. He loved video games and playing with his niece and nephews. He also loved the Green Bay Packers and playing cards with me. As an adult, Andrew had the mentally of a twelve-year-old, so any challenges he overcame was a big deal to him. Andrew was the light of our family.

Deborah Kuhl, mom of Michael, forever 35

Michael died by suicide. We had no idea or warning that he was feeling so despondent. I spoke to him the week before and he was so happy and excited that Christmas coming soon. It was his favorite holiday.

Michael's personality was sparkling, and he always had a smile on his face! He loved his family and friends fiercely and would do anything for anyone who needed help. He was the life of the party and brought so much joy to so many! Michael is sorely missed. His death has caused such an emptiness in our family that will never be filled.

Melissa Slusher, mom of Jordan, forever 21

I always said *Jordan* was "the greatest gift I never knew I wanted". I grew up with only one sister and had never been around a lot of little boys, so I didn't know if I could handle having a boy. But all of that went away the first moment I held Jordan in my arms...it was definitely love at first sight! Jordan was an avid reader who loved studying the Bible! On his headstone we had written, "A man who sought after God's Own Heart." That sums up Jordan perfectly!

Jordan passed away due to an accidental fall while hiking in Sparta, NC.

Cindy Steinkamp, mom of Jonda Steinkamp, forever 4 1/2 months

Jonda was born with an undetected heart defect that caused her death. She struggled throughout her short life with complications as a result from this. Jonda lives forever in our hearts.

Sara Faith Nelson, mom of Jeanette Marie Nelson Stallcup, forever 36

Jeanette was an amazing teacher, loved by her students for her kindness and caring. She loved cooking and hospitality. She was creative and artistic. She had unknown health issues and died from a sudden massive heart attack.

Yolanda Rory, mom of Sasha, forever 7

Sasha passed away from an irregular heart rhythm. Sacha loved spending time with his family watching movies. His favorite topic was outer space. He loved the planets.

Michele Sulikowski, mom of Matthew Anthony Sulikowski, forever 37 and Melissa Ann Sulikowski Hill, forever 39:

Matthew was the kind of person who would do anything for anyone. He was very outgoing and so very funny He loved his son and loved having family close to him. He found great joy in simple things like repairing cars, watching movies, cooking and travel. Matthew passed from a viral infection due to Myocarditis.

Melissa was a strong yet caring and passionate woman. She was a high school teacher following in her dad's footsteps. She was a phenomenal cook and baker always hosting holiday dinners. She adored her two children more than life. Her other love was her beloved horse Jinx which she fondly referred to as her "Mane Man". Melissa passed from a heart attack brought on by re-occurring sepsis from a previous surgery.

Rhyl Venning, mum of Kari-Lee, forever 25:

*Kari-Lee* was our miracle baby, who grew to be a humble yet inspirational woman, living life to the full, in spite of cystic fibrosis. She danced through this world, spreading sunshine, joy and laughter, traveling to nearly forty countries and blessing the many people she met along the way. Following a double lung transplant, Kari battled a raging infection with courage and determination, accompanied by her trademark humor. When the angels came to carry her home, far sooner than any of us expected, she faced her death with grace and dignity.

About the Author

Laura Diehl is known for extending a light of hope to bereaved parents, especially those whose faith in God has been shattered. Through her writing, speaking (which includes the weekly Grieving Parents Sharing Hope podcast) and singing, she walks with grieving parents in their place of darkness, without judgement or shame, to help them learn how to live a life of meaning and purpose once again.

Laura found herself in a place of suffocating darkness after the death of her daughter, Becca, with no one to turn to for help in navigating out of the deep pit of grief. Today, as a bereaved mom living a life of fulfillment, purpose and destiny, Laura invests her time in helping grieving parents journey from a place of brokenness, to becoming a repurposed vessel in a way that honors the life of their child, instead of living in the shadow of their child's death.

She is the cofounder, along with her husband, of Grieving Parents Sharing Hope (GPS Hope) which serves the "club" no one wants to be in and has no way out - the unique and precious community of bereaved parents. Laura and her husband, Dave, live fulltime in a thirty-eight-foot motor home they lovingly call the Hope Mobile, to provide these resources and face-to-face support around the nation. The Diehl's home base is in Southern Wisconsin, and they have five children (one in heaven and four here on earth) along with a growing legacy of grandchildren.

More about GPS Hope can be found in the resource section, along with information about other books Laura has written.

Other books by Laura Diehl

- *When Tragedy Strikes: Rebuilding Your Life with Hope and Healing After the Death of Your Child*
- Come Grieve Through Our Eyes: How to Give Comfort and Support to Bereaved Parents by Taking A Glimpse Into Our World Of Grief
- My Grief Journey: Coloring Book and Journal for Grieving Parents
- My Grief Journey: Coloring Book and Journal for Kids
- Hope for the Future: An Advent Journey for Bereaved Parents

Laura's books can be found at www.gpshope.org or anywhere books are sold.

Connect with Laura

I would be honored to continue this journey with you on a more personal level. There are several ways to do this through our ministry Grieving Parents Sharing Hope (GPS Hope).

1. Join thousands of pareavors by **signing up for my Weekly Word of Hope email**. Go to **www.gpshope.org/hope**. Your email is safe with us, and you can easily unsubscribe any time you no longer want to receive them.

2. Take a short **Rebuilding Your Life Guidance Course**, based on my award-winning book *When Tragedy Strikes: Rebuilding Your Life with Hope and Healing after the Death of Your Child*.

This course has three options, based on where you are in your journey.

Guidance Course One: How Do I Even Start to Rebuild My Life?

Guidance Course Two: Working Through the Darkness

Guidance Course Three: Looking Toward My Future

To find out more, go to **www.gpshope.org/wtscourse**.

3. Come to a **GPS Hope & Healing retreat**! We host these around the country. Find out more by going to **www.gpshope.org/retreat**.

4. Join us on **The Grief Cruise**! This is a *wonderful* opportunity to spend several days with Dave and myself, along with other pareavors, in a relaxing atmosphere while attending a grief seminar at sea. Check it out at **www.gpshope.org/cruise**.

5. **Meet Dave and me for coffee or a meal as we travel the nation in the Hope Mobile.** This is one of our favorite things to do. If we are within a couple of hours, we do our best to make a meet-up happen. Find out if we will be near you. **Go to www.gpshope.org and click on the calendar under the events tab.**

6. **Have me come and speak and sing at your event or support group.** Email us at **office@gpshope.org** to let us know when and where you would like us to come.

We hope you will take a look at these opportunities and connect to the ones you believe will be the most help to you, as we continue this journey together. Be sure to check the website for any updates or changes on these six ways to connect.

www.gpshope.org

GPS Hope Free Resources

Grieving Parents Sharing Hope (GPS Hope) is here to walk with grieving parents through the suffocating darkness of child loss, navigating them to a place of hope, light and purpose. It is a safe place for the shattered hearts of pareavors to take off their masks and be allowed to grieve as needed.

Below you will find several of the free resources provided, to bring a measure of needed healing, encouragement and strength.

At the GPS Hope website (**www.gpshope.org**) you will find:

- The Grieving Parents Sharing Hope podcast
- Free Members Library with lots of downloadable tools and resources
- A Wall of Remembrance where a parent can have a picture of their child posted along with a paragraph about their child
- Expressions of Hope blog
- GPS Hope store with Laura's books, CD, and "hope" merchandise
- A link to our events page

You can also:

- **Subscribe to the GPS Hope YouTube channel** at **www.youtube.com/gpshope** (Be sure to click the bell icon to receive notifications when a new video is released.)
- Join thousands of other pareavors by **signing up for the Weekly Word of Hope email.** Go to **www.gpshope.org/hope.** Your email is safe with us, and you can easily unsubscribe any time you no longer want to receive them.
- Become part of the GPS Hope community on Facebook.
    - Public page: **www.facebook.com/gpshope**
    - Private page: **www.facebook.com/groups/WhenTragedyStrikesBook**

Do you feel stuck in your grief?

Our unique personalities have a lot to do with how we grieve. However, within that uniqueness, there are a few certain traits we all seem to fall into, and those traits can make us feel like we are spinning our wheels and will never get out of this place of suffocating darkness.

Would you like to find out what that might be for yourself? Take Laura's quiz. Not only will she send you those possible traits, but you will receive some suggestions on how to get unstuck from your specific struggles.

Go to mygriefhope.com to answer a few short questions and get the help you need to start moving forward toward a greater measure of healing for your shattered heart.

mygriefhope.com

www.ingramcontent.com/pod-product-compliance
Lightning Source LLC
Chambersburg PA
CBHW020654060526
44119CB00069B/66